The Pursuit of Power
in Modern Japan,
1825–1995

The Pursuit of Power
in Modern Japan
1825–1995

CHUSHICHI TSUZUKI

OXFORD
UNIVERSITY PRESS

OXFORD

UNIVERSITY PRESS

Great Clarendon Street, Oxford OX2 6DP

Oxford University Press is a department of the University of Oxford.
It furthers the University's objective of excellence in research, scholarship,
and education by publishing worldwide in

Oxford New York

Athens Auckland Bangkok Bogotá Buenos Aires Calcutta
Cape Town Chennai Dar es Salaam Delhi Florence Hong Kong Istanbul
Karachi Kuala Lumpur Madrid Melbourne Mexico City Mumbai
Nairobi Paris São Paulo Singapore Taipei Tokyo Toronto Warsaw
and associated companies in Berlin Ibadan

Oxford is a registered trade mark of Oxford University Press
in the UK and certain other countries

Published in the United States
by Oxford University Press Inc., New York

British Library Cataloguing in Publication Data

Data available

Library of Congress Cataloging in Publication Data

Data available

ISBN 0–19–820589–9

1 3 5 7 9 10 8 6 4 2

Typeset by J&L Composition Ltd, Filey, North Yorkshire
Printed in Great Britain
on acid-free paper by
Biddles Ltd, Guildford and King's Lynn

Preface

It is a commonplace, even a little musty, to say that Japan is a country of consensus and unanimity, not one of differences and debate. Harmonious but essentially conservative human relationships, though remaining mostly on the surface, are sustained by institutional and cultural restraints that have made the people generally refrain from asking questions. As a result they have only recently begun enquiring as a matter of historical know-ledge where their ancestors (and by implication their imperial family) came from and when their settlement on the Japanese Isles took place, issues that had long been relegated to mythology. In this new orientation of interest archaeologists are making valuable contributions, though they still fail to agree on the location of the first identifiable political state.

Japan's modern history is perhaps more controversial than that of her earlier periods, as it involves achievements, failures, and disasters, for which the credit and the blame have been apportioned in the most various ways. Its beginnings, too, are problematic. The Meiji Restoration of 1868 is a convenient starting-point for modernization and a modern Japan, though efforts in that direction had begun earlier under the threat from the West. Domestic reforms undertaken spasmodically by the Edo Bakufu to cope with economic distress and dislocation in the insular country are sometimes regarded as the harbingers of the great reform of Meiji, but their importance is apt to be overestimated.

Probably power is the key concept in understanding the emergence of Japan as a modern state. A modern Japan was born of power struggles both within and without. The pursuit of power, especially on the inter-national scene, became a compelling theme throughout her history.

Japan's modern history can be said to have started in the second quarter of the nineteenth century when her isolationism became strained to the utmost under the threat from western powers to force her open as a junior agent in international trade. In other words, the western 'barbarians' were to exert pressures to make Japan a 'tributory' or dependent country in the new, expanding international relations centred around the European colonial powers. Japan's response to this threat was similar to the one she had shown when threatened by Chinese supremacy: she attempted to learn enough from the West to enable her to become its equal or even its superior. To learn from the 'barbarians' would require a switch from the Confucian to the western system of international order, and this would involve divisions and conflicts in all spheres of the nation's life. Japan's own version of the Middle Kingdom idea was superimposed on her vision of the new Europe-centred world order, and after many vicissitudes in her political stance she chose the road to modernization that would assure her independence, a modernization that later allowed her to take the road of military adventurism. The shock from without which led to all these conflicts and developments was translated and given form in the Expulsion Decree of 1825, an act of xenophobia which epitomized the beginnings of the modern Japan.

The year 1995, the fiftieth anniversary of Japan' defeat in the Asian-Pacific War, is a convenient date at which to end our history because it is nearest to the time of writing this book and also, more importantly, because it was the time when Japan's pursuit of power met with great obstacles as a result of the collapse of a period of untrammelled economic speculation summed up by the expression, the 'bubble economy'. 'The second defeat in war'—in economic war in contrast to the defeat of 1945—is an extreme form of lamentation aired in the press over the impasse into which Japanese politics, finance, and bureaucracy have fallen in these years. It is probably high time to reconsider the traditional stance on power by reviewing the record of Japan's pursuit of it, and of the opposition to this pursuit.

A Japanese history written in English requires some explanation of its idiosyncrasies. The recent style in English of putting a family name or surname before a given name for Japanese names, the style invariably adopted in Japan, is followed in this book. In footnotes, however, the usual western style of putting a given name first will be adhered to, for footnotes are multinational: Japanese and non-Japanese authors are listed side by side. Calendar years present their own problem, for the old lunar calendar was replaced by the Gregorian calendar on 3 December 1872. The general principle adopted here is to follow the old calendar before that date and the new, western calendar after that.

The romanization of Japanese names presents a difficulty arising from the peculiar nature of vowels: long vowels are not always long enough and short vowels are often inaudible. Accent tends to be flat, and this contributes to the equalization of the length of vowels. Place-names like Tokyo, Osaka, Kobe, and Kyoto and people's names such as Ito, Kato, Sato, and Taro can easily be identified without considering the length of vowels. The use of vowel-lengthening marks such as macrons, therefore, is not adopted in this book.

This is a book of synthesis, drawing on many other authors who have written on the topics touched upon in this study. I owe a great deal to these authors who supplied materials for me to work on and sometimes suggested the way of looking at them; but the synthesis is my own, and any faults emerging from the process of putting them together are entirely my own.

My indebtedness to Dr J. M. Roberts is inestimable. He carefully went through all my chapters and his suggestions for correction and improvement were most valuable: often I felt I was working under a very thoughtful and helpful teacher.

This book began as a series of lectures on Modern Japanese History for the students of the International University of Japan at Urasa, Niigata. Students of some twenty different nationalities attended one or other of my lectures, and I was greatly benefited by their keen interest in and searching enquiries on Japan's recent history.

My sincere gratitude is also due to the librarian and her assistants of the International House of Japan, Tokyo, which possesses one of the best collections of books on Japan written in English.

St Antony's College, Oxford, very kindly provided me with the opportunity in May 1997 to give the Richard Storry Memorial Lecture, which was an attempt to draw an outline sketch of the present work. Mrs Dorothie Storry encouraged me in my work, which would have surprised her late husband who knew me only as a student of British history. Earlier in 1986 Sheffield University invited me to give the Jerwood Lecture on Japan. I am grateful to Professor Andrew Gamble, Mr Graham Healey, and the late Mr John Jerwood for their generous help on this and other occasions. I am also grateful to Sir Sydney Giffard of the Japan Society, London, and to Dr Anthony Morris, formerly of the Oxford University Press, for their respective interest in and moral support for my work.

I am also thankful to my Japanese friends who helped me with valuable suggestions and constant support, especially Professor Hosoya Chihiro, Professor Yasumaru Yoshio, and Professor Yoshida Yutaka.

Last but not least, I owe thanks to Ms Ruth Parr, History Editor at the Oxford University Press, Ms Sarah Ridgard, Mr Jeffrey New, and Ms Anne Gelling for their trouble in giving the book its final shape and form.

C.T.

At Hiroo, Tokyo

Contents

PART III. RECONSTRUCTION AND REORGANIZATION,
1945–1995

List of Maps

Introduction:
Land, People, and their
Shaping by History

THE INSULARITY OF JAPAN AND THE JAPANESE

The insular position of Japan off the mainland of Asia has been compared with the similar position of Britain; geography played an important role in the cultural and political formation of the island people subjected to pressures and influences from the continent. Japan, however, was relatively free from the kind of rivalries, both political and cultural, that the British experienced due to the proximity of the neighbouring states, and the greater geographical isolation of Japan caused 'a certain sluggishness' in her effort towards nation-building, as George Sansom wrote.[1] In addition to the hazard of a voyage across the wide expanse of rough waters, the apparent 'sluggishness' was due also to the peculiarities of the tributary system which China had imposed on her 'barbarian' neighbours already in the Han period. This Confucian system of international relations based on the moral and cultural superiority of China allowed Japan to enjoy some of the fruits of Chinese civilization through Korea and also by sending missions of her own to China. But Japan was never sluggish or passive in the China-dominated world order. Indeed, that system worked only intermittently owing partly to Japan's ambition to rival China as the Middle Kingdom, and was allowed to lapse in the ninth century because of the breakdown of Chinese power in the T'ang period: the rise of non-tributary trade at the time hastened its demise.[2] Had there been no Portuguese or European attempts in the sixteenth century to place the country in an international setting of trade and missionary work, Japan, already notorious for her piratical activities, might have established herself as a colonial empire in the western Pacific. Such designs were actually harboured by both her rulers and propagandists then and later. 'It was no failure of the expansive impulse, but only a reluctant recognition of weakness that caused Japan to withdraw into almost complete seclusion in 1640', added Sansom.[3]

---

[1] George B. Sansom, *The Western World and Japan* (London, 1950, Tuttle edn. 1987), 168. Sansom can be counted among the leading authorities on Japanese history. See Appendix II.

[2] W. G. Beasley, *Japan Encounters the Barbarians* (London, 1995), 5–7.

[3] Sansom, op. cit., 169.

True, that seclusion had many holes,[4] but it was substantial enough to guarantee comparative peace in a rigid status-society which lasted for almost two centuries.

The Edict of 1825 issued by the Edo Bakufu to expel all western ships 'without second thought' was a desperate attempt to maintain the policy of national seclusion in an altered international situation: European colonialism, led by Britain and Russia, was about to unleash itself on the Far East. The Edict remained the law of the land under which efforts were made for defence and reform, yet proved itself untenable without modification and was revoked in 1842 in the wake of the Chinese defeat in the Opium War. Both its proclamation and withdrawal indicated weakness and internal divisions, and the history of Japan and the Japanese thereafter was a record of endeavours, sometimes successful and sometimes destructive, to overcome these.

Richard Storry, in his admirable little book on Japan, pointed to several distinctive features of Japanese behaviour and character: the proverbial sense of corporate loyalty; a pattern of obligations between individuals; a preoccupation with wordly values, on the verge of becoming 'materialistic'; expressions of formal politeness (fast vanishing as he wrote); little awareness of ugliness (in spite of an artistic instinct shared by many), or of regimentation for that matter; vanity and lack of sympathy; an excitability capable of 'all degrees of panic or ferocity'; a 'deep concept of impermanence'; and above all, ethnocentrism.[5] This last trait has long been bolstered by *sonno* culture, the culture of emperor worship which survived Japan's defeat in 1945. Moreover, with the end of the Cold War and the collapse of the Soviet Union, ethnicity has replaced or obscured social class as the mainspring both of human emancipation and of conflict. Japan, intensely nationalistic, claims a full share in this worldwide tendency. In the emerging world of globalization, however, the issue of ethnicity takes on a new guise in this country, and an enquiry has begun as to whether the Japanese are really a homogeneous race.

THE FIRST APPEARANCE OF 'NIHON' ('NIPPON')

The appellation 'Nihon' or 'Nippon', 'Nihonjin' or 'Nipponjin' (Japanese), made its appearance in the latter half of the seventh century AD, when Nihon or Nippon was used for the first time as the name of the country in an international setting. Japanese who had studied Chinese had come to dislike the old name *Wa* (which meant a dwarf), and used *Nippon* (which

---

[4] Marius B. Jansen, *China in the Tokugawa World* (Cambridge, Mass., 1992), 35. See also Mikio Sumiya and Koji Taira (eds.), *An Outline of Japanese Economic History, 1603–1940* (Tokyo, 1979), 172–3.   [5] Richard Storry, *Japan* (Oxford, 1965), *passim*.

means the root of the sun) to replace it. In 668, when the Chinese T'ang defeated Koguryo, Japan's enemy for many years in Korea, an embassy was sent from Japan to T'ang (it reached the Chinese court in 670), and the Japanese envoy stated that the new name was chosen because his country was so close to where the sun rises.[6] The ancient state formed around this period, which historians call the 'Ritsuryo Kokka' (the state of penal and civil code), formally replaced the older appellation of *Wa* with *Nihon* or *Nippon*, and began calling its king *Tenno*.

Whether the contemporary Japanese pronounced the two Chinese characters *nichi* (the sun) and *hon* (the root) as 'nihon', 'nippon', or even 'jippon' is not clear. Marco Polo, in his *Voyages*, described Japan as Zipangu or Jipangu, and Japan or Japon, the term widely adopted in Europe, is said to have derived from Chinese pronunciations of *nichi* and *hon*. In 1934 the Ministry of Education sought to unify the pronunciation of *nichi* and *hon* as Nippon, but no law was passed for this purpose. A similar inconclusive attempt was made at the time of a nationalist revival in the 1980s. There is general agreement within government and official circles to use Nippon rather than Nihon, and postage stamps and banknotes reflect their view. Although the matter is largely one of euphony, it also has a political dimension, for those who prefer a small Japan tend to call their country Nihon rather than Nippon.

GEOGRAPHICAL POSITION

Shortly after the end of the Pacific War in 1945 Maruyama Masao, the post-war liberal savant, when he was preparing an article on Kuga Katsunan, one of the ablest journalists in the mid-Meiji period and a liberal nationalist, was impressed by the map of Japan that had provided the background sketch of the title letters of Kuga's newspaper *Nippon* (not *Nihon*). On it were shown Honshu, Kyushu, Shikoku, and Hokkaido, the shape of Japan which had to start again in the new era under the American occupation; Maruyama felt that post-war Japan would need another newspaper like that of Kuga, whose first number had come out on 11 February 1889, the day of the promulgation of the Meiji constitution.[7]

---

[6] From 'New History of the T'ang Dynasty', in Ryusaku Tsunoda, W. T. de Barry, and Donald Keene (eds.), *Sources of Japanese Traditions* (1964), i. 11. It has been suggested that the first official use of the name 'Nippon' was in 702 by an envoy sent to T'ang. Takashi Yoshida, '8-Seiki no Nippon' (Japan in the 8th Century), *Nihon Tsushi* (Complete History of Japan), vol. 4 (Tokyo, 1994), 22.

[7] It is interesting to note that the sketch-map for *Nippon* was expanded so as to include Taiwan in the issue which came out on the emperor's birthday in 1901 (3 November 1901); and after a series of victories in the war with Russia, the last of which was the occupation of Sakhalin, the letters *Nippon* were set against an expansionist map of East Asia from Kamchatka to Luzon following the issue of 6 July 1905. *Nippon* merged with a similar magazine, *Nipponjin* (the Japanese), early in 1907 to become *Nippon and Nipponjin*, which carried on its precarious and increasingly rightist existence until 1945.

Geographically Japan consists of four major islands, Hokkaido, Honshu, Shikoku, and Kyushu from north to south, with adjacent smaller islands. It stretches from the Cape of Soya in northern Hokkaido situated at 45° 31′ N., 42 kilometres from Sakhalin, to the Yaeyama islands which lie between 25° N. and the Tropic of Cancer, of which the westernmost, Yonakunijima, is about 100 kilometres from Taiwan. In fact it numbers over 3,700 islands in the whole archipelago; the length of the chain of the islands is over 3,500 kilometres, and a number of peninsulas and bays make the length of the coastline 28,000 kilometres altogether. The land area of the whole country as it stands in 1995 is about 370,000 square kilometres, approximately the size of the state of California, or roughly equivalent to that of Great Britain and Ireland.

Its great latitudinal range and its location between the Eurasian continent, dry and cold in the north and wet and warm in the south, and the Pacific Ocean, with the warm Black Current from the south and the cold Kurile Current from the north, are among the major factors controlling climate, vegetation, and marine products. Most of the islands are quite mountainous: mountain regions over 300 metres above sea level occupy 61 per cent of the whole area. Mt Fuji, the highest of these, rises from Suruga Bay to a height of 3,776 metres, and there are a dozen peaks and mountains over 3,000 metres high in central Japan. The plains are not very extensive, the largest being the Kanto plain which extends across five prefectures, and where 'spreading industrialization competes with the farmer for use of the precious land'.[8]

The archipelago takes the shape of a series of island arcs which lie on the border areas of the four plates, Eurasian, Pacific, North American, and Philippine. Crust movement, together with volcanic activities (there are seventy-seven active volcanoes), cause frequent and often disastrous earthquakes. To these sources of the terrain's instability should be added another, recently emphasized, the existence of numerous lines of strata dislocation, some right under big cities. One of these, which underwent a sudden jerking readjustment early in the morning of 17 January 1995, destroyed Kobe, one of the most beautiful cities in Japan, and its vicinity.

Climatically Japan is located in the monsoon region of East Asia, and the continental climatic conditions are modified by the seas surrounding the country. The winter monsoon brings about low temperatures and heavy snow on the Japan Sea side of Hokkaido and Honshu. In summer the wind from the south-western north Pacific Ocean brings high humidity and high temperatures to most of the country, except for high mountains and plateaus. With the island chain squeezed between the two waters, heavy snow on the Japan Sea side in winter is contrasted with heavy rain on the Pacific

[8] Storry, op. cit., 6

side, especially in south-west Japan in summer. The latter is also the frequent target of an annual attack of typhoons in late summer and autumn, working havoc with strong wind and floods. Heavy snow and torrential rain have often been blessings in disguise, for they secured good harvests of rice and an abundant supply of water. The violence of nature due to Japan's geographical situations may partially explain some of the characteristics pointed out by foreign observers in her people: communal solidarity oddly combined with callousness and selfishness, a sense of the floating and fleeting nature of the world, and resignation to the inevitable.

THE ORIGINS OF THE JAPANESE, AND PREHISTORIC CULTURE

It has been said that the first appearance in the Japanese archipelago of *Homo sapiens sapiens* was 'culturally' (in terms of the discovered stone knives, scrapers, and gimlets) about 33,000 years ago in the fourth glaciation period, while the earliest human bones found there are only 18,000 years old. We know very little about those who lived in Japan 33,000 years ago when the climate became much colder and a land bridge was formed to connect it with the continent as the sea level went down. Archaeological discoveries, however, have been more informative about the fauna than about the human species.[9] The climate became decidedly warmer from about 15,000 years ago, and humidified from about 13,000 years ago. The ancestors of the Japanese, striding over the closely forested mountain ranges, exploited forest and sea as hunter-gatherers.

Jomon culture associated with the Jomon (which means 'cord pattern') pottery was sustained by these people. The word 'Jomon' came from the description of such pottery by an American scientist, Edward Sylvester Morse, the newly appointed professor of biology at Tokyo Imperial University, who published in 1879 the results of his excavation of the shell mounds at Omori which he had seen while travelling by train from Yokohama to Tokyo. Broadly speaking, the Jomon period lasted from about 10,000 years ago to the third century BC (though its beginning has been updated to 12,000 or 13,000 years ago), and its culture spread from Hokkaido to Okinawa. The separation of the islands from the continent as a result of the rising sea level allowed its culture to mature within the archipelago. The Jomon population increased from about 20,000 to 106,000 in the course of the early period and reached 262,500 during the middle period, probably the highest they attained.[10] They lived in family groups of thirty to fifty people each.

[9] J. Edward Kidder, Jr., 'The Earliest Societies in Japan', in Delmer M. Brown (ed.), *Cambridge History of Japan* (Cambridge, 1993), i. 50 ff., for 'The Pre-Jormon Period'.
[10] Ibid. 63, 68.

On a wider stage, Asian *Homo sapiens sapiens* had begun moving north from south-east Asia at least 30,000 years ago. Some of those who went north along the east coast of the continental shelf or who moved east from China are regarded as the ancestors of the Jomon people. A recent DNA analysis shows that they were akin to the south-east Asian group. Meanwhile, those who reached north-eastern Asia acquired adaptability to the cold climate and could be distinguished as the new Mongoloid or the north-east Asian group from the old Mongoloid or the south-east Asian group.

The next distinguishable cultural period, lasting from the fourth or third century BC to the middle of the third century AD, is termed 'Yayoi', and again takes its name from ceramics, of fine texture and brown-red in colour, discovered in 1884 at Yayoi-cho in Tokyo. The Yayoi people introduced rice cultivation and iron tools and weapons to Japan. They were newcomers from the Korean peninsula, north-eastern China, and eastern Siberia, in other words, the north-east Asian group or the new Mongoloid peoples. Thus the two types of Mongoloid people coexisted. The Kofun (literally meaning an old mound grave) period that followed lasted from the latter part of the third century to the end of the sixth century. During this time the Yamato court gradually emerged. Throughout the Kofun period the number of newcomers further increased; they showed characteristics of the north-east Asians, and lived largely in western Japan, while the people in eastern Japan retained Jomon traits; in western Japan intermarriage between the newcomers and the indigenous Jomon people produced mixed blood, which became common. According to one estimate, the population of the newcomers had reached 70 to 90 per cent of the whole population by the end of the seventh century, the ratio being higher in western Japan. The total number of the immigrants for the period of 1,000 years from the third century BC (the beginning of the Yayoi period) has been estimated at over 1 million.[11]

The peripheral peoples referred to in the eighth-century chronicle *Nihonshoki* as *emishi* or *ezo*, *kumaso*, and *hayato* continued their resistance to the central government. They were little affected by the newcomers and their culture. The Ainu are most typical of such peoples. They are not of Caucasian origin, as is sometimes thought, nor Australoid, but are the descendants of the old south-east Asian group or the old Mongoloid. They originally belonged to the Jomon people, as did the Okinawa people, and E. von Baelz has pointed out strong similarities between the Ainu and the Okinawans. They are both akin to the Jomon people, short and hairy, whereas the Hondo (mainland) people or the majority of the Japanese are

---

[11] Kazuo Hanihara, 'Nihonjin no Keisei' (The Formation of the Japanese), *Nihon Tsushi* (Complete History of Japan), vol. 1 (Tokyo, 1993), 96.

of the north-east Asian group. It is often maintained that the Japanese are ethnically a single nation, but there are two different groups living side by side, and their mixing through intermarriage is still going on. From this we could say that the Japanese are ethnically a 'mixed nation'.[12]

It has been assumed by palaeontologists that in the Old Stone Age, around 20,000 years ago, the population of the Japanese archipelago did not exceed 10,000, and that it even decreased with the rising sea level in the warmer climate. With the beginning of the Jomon period 12,000 years ago, when it became possible to cook or preserve vegetable food in earthen utensils, the population increased to as many as 300,000,[13] but it again declined about 6,000 years ago when the temperature fell. Rice culture, which came to western Japan from the continent in the Yayoi period, contributed to a great increase in the population, which exceeded 1 million by the end of the Yayoi period (AD 300). The population towards the end of the eighth century is assumed by archaeologists to have been 5,600,000. Japan emerged from her prehistoric past with a population large enough and a central government strong enough for her to claim a position that was no longer simply tributary and subservient in the Chinese-centred international order in East Asia.

FROM MYTHOLOGY TO HISTORY

The semi-fascist military regime in 1940 was able to celebrate the 2,600th anniversary of the Japanese empire, basing their calculations on the reign of the legendary first emperor. In this same year Tsuda Sokichi, professor of Waseda University, who had published critical studies of the two official chronicles of the eighth century, *Kojiki* (Records of Ancient Matters; 712) and *Nihongi* or *Nihonshoki* (Chronicles of Japan; 720), and especially of the 'history' of the era of gods, was indicted, charged with *lèse-majesté* and two years later sentenced to three months' imprisonment for having denied the historicity of the first fourteen emperors. Modern Japan, born of the *sonno joi* ('revere the emperor, expel the barbarian foreigners') movement, incorporated mythology into history as it subscribed to the imperial theory derived from these official chronicles.

The two chronicles give an almost identical account of the origins of the country and of the imperial throne, with the Sun Goddess as its divine creator and her grandson as the founder of the Yamato dynasty. A cultural anthropologist suggests that the legend of the emperor's divine descent reflected the removal and replacement of the rulers in Kyushu.[14] Freed from thought control and indoctrination, Japanese historians now agree

[12] Ibid. 104.   [13] 262,500 according to Kidder, op. cit., 68.
[14] Taryo Obayashi, 'Shinwaron' (On Mythology), *Nihon Tsushi*, i. 326.

that historically identified emperorship began with Empress Suiko (554–628) and the real emperorship with Emperor Temmu (?–686), who was anxious to consolidate imperial power and who commissioned the compilation of *Kojiki* and set up a committee to edit *Nihonshoki*. 'The essence of politics is military', Temmu declared, and maintained an armed court with an elaborate military system.[15] Another characteristic of his politics was its religious emphasis; it was Temmu who rewarded the Ise Shrine, which had been no more than a local shrine until the sixth century and which had sided with him in the civil war, by giving it imperial status as enshrining the imperial ancestor, the Sun Goddess. Thus Temmu fortified his state with myth and arms.

It may appear a little far-fetched to compare the civil war of 672 which gave Temmu power with that of 1868, but there is little doubt that modern Japanese society has deep roots in ancient history. Temmu consolidated the earliest foundations of the central government (laid, as we shall see, by his immediate predecessors) by taking the initiative in elevating the myth of the origins of the Yamato dynasty to a state doctrine which was to inspire *sonno* ideology in the nineteenth century. The manner of Meiji leaders adopting western civilization is also reminiscent of the way in which elements of Asian civilization, Buddhism and Confucianism among others, were introduced into Japan in the sixth century and indigenized to meet the needs of society and of the state.

BUDDHISM INTRODUCED

From prehistoric times the Japanese revered animistic spirits, *kamis*, which were supernatural and mysterious and in due course were accepted as clan gods (*uji gami*); it was only late in the sixth century that native *kami* worship became Shinto (the Way of Gods), in order to distinguish itself from the imported worship of Buddhism; and with it the way was cleared for State Shinto. In the course of the fourth and fifth centuries Buddhism had spread from China to the three kingdoms in Korea: Koguryo, Paekche, and Silla, located respectively in the north, south-west, and south-east of the peninsula. Buddhism came to Japan only a few years after Silla's acceptance of it, and Japanese opposition to it was finally overcome in 587, when a chieftain of the Soga clan succeeded in winning over other influential clans. Soga Buddhism was widely accepted, became identified with rites that were thought to provide miraculous benefits here and now, and concerned itself with magic and ceremonies honouring deceased

[15] Kojiro Naoki, 'Kodai Kokka no Seiritsu' (The Emergence of the Ancient State), *Nihon no Rekishi* (History of Japan) (Tokyo, 1973, 1992), ii. 351; Mitsusada Inoue *et al.*, 'Ritsuryo Kokka no Tenkai' (The Evolution of the State of Penal and Civil Code), *Nihon Rekishi Taikei* (Major Currents of Japanese History) (Tokyo, 1995), ii. 38–43, 46.

ancestors.[16] When the Soga family alienated other clan leaders and was destroyed in a *coup d'état* of 645, clan Buddhism began to give way to State Buddhism sponsored by emperors. Buddhism now served as a support of the state whose head remained the chief priest of *kami*, the worship of animistic spirits.

In 607 a Japanese envoy was sent to the Chinese court of Sui to pay respect to the Sui emperor, who promoted Buddhism; but an official message which read: 'The Son of Heaven in the land where the sun rises addresses a letter to the Son of Heaven in the land where the sun sets' displeased the emperor.[17] Sui was about to be replaced by the T'ang empire (formed in 618) and the eastward advance of T'ang into Korea posed a serious threat to Japan. The remedies would be to strengthen imperial rule to meet the challenge of the expanding T'ang empire, and to launch domestic reforms. The outcome was a reform of the state brought about by introducing the continental system of administration.

THE EMERGENCE OF THE CENTRALIZED IMPERIAL STATE AND THE WAR AGAINST THE *HAYATO* AND *EMISHI*

In 645, when the Soga clan was overthrown, Taika, the first era name to be used in Japan, was adopted, and in 646 the Taika Reform Edict was issued under the initiative of the two men who had prepared the new political climate, Kamatari and Prince Nakano Ooe.[18] In this edict the principle of public land and public people was to be guaranteed by house lists, land registers, and an allotment system supplemented by a new tax system. The term 'public people' needs an explanation. Peasants, like land, officially belonged to the emperor and were tied to the land they cultivated in communal labour; serfs in fact (though privately owned land as well as vagrancy began to increase with the cultivation of new lands and the construction of new capitals). Nakatomino (later Fujiwarano) Kamatari and others worked out the Ritsuryo or penal and civil code. The Ritsuryo system created a centralized imperial government and its bureaucracy; along with the establishment of the Shogunate, the Meiji Restoration, and possibly the American occupation, it can be regarded as one of the major political events in Japanese history.

By the eighth century the Ritsuryo state had come to define its boundaries formed by the four outpost regions: Mutsu in the east, Tosa in the south, the Goto Islands in the west, and Sado in the north. At the same time efforts were made to push the boundaries further north and further

[16] Koyu Sonoda, 'Early Buddha Worship', *Cambridge History of Japan*, i. 385, 388.
[17] 'History of the Sui Dynasty' in Tsunoda *et al.* (eds.), op. cit., 10.
[18] Kamatari was the founder of the great Fujiwara familly, and Nakano-Ooe became the emperor Tenji.

south by means both of the forced, systematic migration of people from other areas, and of the pacification and military conquest of the indigenous peoples, the *emishi* and *hayato*. The type of relationships sought by the central state in dealing with the peripheries could be regarded as a miniature version of the tributary system China had set up with her own barbarian neighbours.

A northern campaign was undertaken by the central state in the middle of the eighth century with a view to extending a tributary system and control over the *emishi*. The *emishi*, however, proved even more rebellious than the *hayato* in the south, who had been subdued earlier in the century, and inflicted great losses on the government forces. It was to overcome their stubborn resistance that a 'Generalissimo To Conquer the Barbarians' (*Seii Tai-Shogun*) was appointed. This is the origin of the term 'Shogun' which was to colour Japanese history so deeply for several centuries before Meiji. The military campaign lasted thirty-eight years; further *emishi* outbreaks were gradually pushed northward and the *emishi*, ethnically a mixed people with the Ainu as one of its major components, began to be called *ezo*, a sign of assimilation as well as of new discrimination.

HEIJOKYO AND HEIANKYO

Chinese or T'ang's influence was most vividly felt in the decision taken early in the eighth century to build a new permanent capital city in emulation of the Chinese capital Ch'ang-an. The capital, Nara, or Heijokyo as it was called, dignified with T'ang-style buildings like the Todaiji Temple with its Great Buddha, prospered, its Buddhist culture well protected by the state. It lasted, however, only some seventy years, from 710 to 784. Heijokyo was probably best identified with Emperor Shomu who brought the Buddhist establishment into the government in order to balance court factionalism,[19] though the Buddhist priesthood continued to create difficulties, one monk even threatening the throne itself. Emperor Kammu, in order to be free from Buddhist power in Nara, ordered the removal of the capital, and after trying other places it moved eventually to Heiankyo (Kyoto) in 794. Thereafter, the Fujiwara family responded to the new situation by taking measures that would assure a steady supply of officials from among themselves. The Fujiwara Regency emerged, as the family came virtually to control the imperial family by supplying most of its maternal relations.[20]

By the beginning of the ninth century the new permanent capital in Kyoto had begun to attract people from all walks of life; merchant and

---

[19] John Hall and Jeffrey P. Mass (eds.), *Medieval Japan* (New Haven, 1974; Stanford University Press edn. 1988), 7.   [20] Ibid. 10.

artisan quarters were provided, and aristocratic families were allotted land for residence. The aristocracy, at last prepared to settle down, flowed into the city from their rural estates, making it the political, social, and cultural centre of the country. The aristocracy could now live in the capital as absentee landowners and governors. The system of public land and allotment was abused and neglected, and private ownership in land, like the manorial system in its various forms, was in the ascendency. Aristocratic Heian culture prospered on such a basis. It was a culture confined to an elegant court circle devoted to the formal and the ceremonious, to art and an aesthetic life. *The Tale of Genji* (completed around 1007) by Lady Murasaki, who gracefully narrated a series of exquisite love affairs in this refined society, marked its culmination.

THE BIRTH OF THE SAMURAI AND THE KAMAKURA BAKUFU

The economic and social basis of the Ritsuryo state having been eroded, individual holders of the lands (called *shoen*) sometimes entrusted their holdings to powerful persons on the spot in return for protection from the interference of provincial authorities. A coterie of persons was usually tied to a court noble, including numerous retainers (*samurai*) and personal servants (*toneri*). These *samurai* performed military, police, and guard duties for the household. In the case of a high-ranking household such retainers were often descendants of aristocratic or even imperial families, as was the case with the two great warrior families, the Genji (House of Minamoto) and the Heike (House of Taira). Minamotono Yoshiie, one of the most prominent Genji warriors, who had taken part in the north-eastern war against the *emishi*, organized a samurai corps or Bushidan which extended from north-east to central Japan. Its economic basis was provided by private proprietorship of land, and peasants who cultivated such lands could be mobilized for fighting. Yet a samurai was still a *saburai* (a man in attendance), and even Yoshiie, Japan's greatest warrior in his day, had to serve the Regency family.

The rivalry between the Taira and the Minamoto, linked as it sometimes was with the feud between an emperor and a retired emperor, led to a succession of civil wars in which great warriors were killed or executed and great palaces and temples destroyed. Minamotono Yoritomo, whose father had been defeated and murdered in a civil war of 1159 and who had thereafter been exiled to Izu, succeeded in setting himself up as the leader of the warriors in the east. In the Kanto area numerous Bushidan (warrior corps), large and small, enclosed lands, hills, and forests, reclaimed marshlands, and cultivated vast estates. They ran their properties (*shoryo*) from manor houses which could be used as citadels in war. Their status never being stable, they aspired for protection as well as concerted action under the leadership of the Genji, Yoritomo in particular. Yoritomo entered Kamakura, where in 1180 he built a new residence and celebrated its completion with 311 warriors who followed him. This was the beginning of the Kamakura Bakufu, though the term began to be used much later. *Bakufu* literally means the tented headquarters of a military leader in a field campaign, and Yoritomo's Kamakura residence was called a *bakufu* in this sense. In 1192 Yoritomo was appointed by the court as *Seii Tais-Shogun* (the Generalissimo to Conquer the Barbarians), and this event is sometimes regarded as the real beginning of the Kamakura Bakufu.

After Yoritomo it was his wife, Masako, known sometimes as General Nun, with her brother Hojo Yoshitoki who ran the Bakufu. When a retired emperor sought to challenge Yoshitoki, the massive Bakufu army fought its way to Kyoto and entered it triumphantly, turning the balance between court and Bakufu in favour of the latter. Three former emperors were exiled, the reigning emperor abdicated, and new ones were set up at the discretion of the Bakufu. The Bakufu–court relations now established lasted till the end of the Bakufu itself. The Kamakura Shogunate found its power strengthened rather than weakened by the Mongol's attempts in 1274 and 1281 to invade Japan.

THE MUROMACHI BAKUFU

In the fourteenth century Emperor Godaigo sought not only to destroy the Bakufu but also to create a new system of an absolute monarchy. The defeat of Kamakura and the split of the imperial family into two rival dynasties created a power vacuum. In 1338, having set up a puppet emperor, a prince of the Genji family established a new military government in Kyoto (at Muromachi) with himself as shogun. During the next two centuries fifteen members of the Ashikaga house served in that office, the third shogun Yoshimitsu's years marking the high point of Ashikaga's power and glory. In order to add lustre to his power he sought recognition by the Ming dynasty and resumed in 1401 long-interrupted tribute missions to China. After Yoshimitsu Ashikaga's power and fortune began to decline, and one civil war of the late fifteenth century which devastated Kyoto ushered in the period of a nation at perpetual war, or the period of *Sengoku* as it is called.

THE FIRST CONTACT WITH THE WEST AND THE REUNIFICATION OF THE COUNTRY

The period of uniting the war-torn country coincided with the century when Christians were allowed to carry on missionary work. Francisco Xavier, one of the first Jesuits, who came to Kagoshima in 1549, was one of the first Europeans to report on Japan. He commented on the martial spirit of the country he was to proselytize: 'The Japanese have a high opinion of themselves [as regards] weapon and valour, and so they look down on all foreigners.'[21] The *Sengoku* period may have given the impression, wrongly, that the country had lapsed into anarchy. Though there was much destruction of property and loss of life in the battles, there was also much improvement. The armies had to be fed, and the military class began to pay more attention to the possibility of increasing the yield of their lands by better farming and the promotion of household industry. New families rose to prominence. Indeed, a new governing class was emerging, composed of warriors of modest origin but great enterprise.

Oda Nobunaga, of humble samurai origins in Owari (present Aichi prefecture), came to power through a combination of bravery and cunning reminiscent of Cesare Borgia, the ideal prince of Machiavelli. Having defeated his powerful rival in a surprise attack, he entered Kyoto in 1568 with the brother of a murdered shogun whom he set up as the fifteenth Ashikaga shogun. The shogun began meddling in military politics, and became so insubordinate that Nobunaga deposed him in 1573. This was the ignominious end of the Muromachi Bakufu, which had lasted for 235 years, almost as long as the Tokugawa Bakufu, the end-product of the era of warring lords.

The Christian century in Japan witnessed a military revolution. Guns had originally been brought into the country by Portuguese crews whose ship drifted in a typhoon to Tanegashima, an island south of Kyushu, in 1543. Their use spread rapidly. As many as 3,000 gunners took part on the side of the Oda forces in a battle in 1575. Christian missionaries followed the introduction of firearms. Their early converts were poor peasants in western Japan, but soon the western daimyo, Shimazu, Ouchi, and Otomo were attracted to Christianity by the possibilities it offered of foreign trade. The last Ashikaga shogun gave Luis Frois, the Portuguese Jesuit missionary, licence to preach in Miyako (Kyoto), and Christian missions prospered in the Home Provinces. In 1582, when Nobunaga died, there were 150,000 Christians and 200 churches in Japan.[22]

Toyotomi Hideyoshi, a samurai of the lowest strata of the retainers' group bordering on the peasantry in Owari, in due course proved himself to be a worthy successor to Nobunaga. He treated Osaka as the hub of his universe, where he built a great castle. In order to secure a sound economic basis for his regime Hideyoshi strengthened ties with the great money-lenders of Kyoto, manufacturers of guns and other weapons, and foreign

[21] Michael Cooper (ed.), *They Came to Japan* (Berkeley, 1965), 41.
[22] C. R. Boxer, *The Christian Century in Japan* (Berkeley, 1951), 114; George Sansom, *A History of Japan* (London 1963, Tuttle edn., 1974), ii. 295.

traders in Sakai. He maintained Nobunaga's attitude to the Christians, and the governors of Osaka and Sakai and other of his chief commanders and officers were converted.[23] According to his world strategy, explained to a group of Jesuit visitors to Osaka Castle in 1586 and recorded by Frois, he would entrust home affairs to his brother, while he himself undertook the conquest of Korea and China. Through the Fathers he hoped to obtain two great and well-equipped Portuguese ships. He did not wish to remain in China as the conqueror, but he wanted the Chinese to recognize him as their lord, and he intended to build churches there, commanding all to become Christian.[24] He pressed for tribute from the Philippines and Taiwan. This plan embodied the Middle Kingdom concept for Japan; Portuguese co-operation was sought in order to pursue a continental plan which, strangely enough, would have made Hideyoshi a Christian king.

Suddenly, on his way back from a successful campaign against Shimazu of Satsuma in 1587, to everybody's surprise Hideyoshi issued an edict against Christianity. He had expected to be taken at Hakata to a great Portuguese ship which he had asked to be brought from Hirado for his inspection. The captain of the ship refused to sail into Hakata Bay, which he said was too shallow, and on the following morning Hideyoshi issued his edict. Christian preachers were ordered to leave the country within twenty days, under penalty of death. Christianity without big ships seemed unimportant for his immediate purposes. His intention was not to exterminate Christianity in Japan but to reduce it to the position of a serviceable political tool. He also harboured a suspicion of European plans to gain possession of Japan. The execution of twenty-six Franciscans in 1598 had as much to do with this suspicion on his part as with the enmity between the Jesuits and the Franciscans in Japan.

In 1588 Hideyoshi issued an order for sword hunts, prohibiting peasants and farmers from possessing swords, daggers, bows and arrows, and guns. This was coupled with a land survey—inspection and registration of cultivated lands—which helped separate and fix the status of samurai and of peasants, as the register bore among other items the name of the cultivator who was to pay yearly tribute. Those who could not pay tribute and taxes would become landless people; some of them became artisans and tradesmen; many formed a *buraku* (hamlet or ghetto) of their own, living mostly as casual labourers in construction works or engaged in degrading jobs connected with policing and executions or procuring carcasses for prey-birds. Many joined *ikko-ikki* (*ikko* means 'one direction', referring to a politico-religious body under that name, while *ikki* indicates

---

[23] Otis Cary, *A History of Christianity in Japan* (1st edn. 1909; New York, 1976), i. 98.
[24] Ibid. 100–1.

'solidarity', derivatively 'a riot'), in the hope that the Buddhist deity Amida's Pure Land would bring about their emancipation from drudgery and degradation. The land inspection of 1591 was most extensive, as it covered twenty provinces; this served as proof of the completion of the unification of the country and also as a preparation for the coming invasion of Korea.

The image of the Japanese in Asia at the time was as warlike and belligerent. Wako (Japanese pirates), from their bases at Hirado, Goto, and Satsuma, ravaged the coastal areas of eastern and south-eastern Asia, though the ratio of Japanese in the Wako amounted only to some 10–20 per cent.[25] In 1592 an army of 150,000 men crossed the strait, commanded mainly by Kyushu daimyo. A navy of 9,000 ships was engaged in transport and coastal raids in Korea. The Japanese army made a quick advance from Pusan to Seoul and went on to Pyonyang, where it was attacked by Chinese forces. Konishi Yukinaga, one of Hideyoshi's Christian commanders, hoped for peace and concluded a temporary truce with Ming's special envoy at Pyongyang. Both soldiers and people suffered from famine and plague, and most of the Japanese troops were withdrawn. Nevertheless, a second expedition was attempted in 1596, when the achievements were less spectacular and the sufferings greater. Hideyoshi was seriously ill at this time, and died in 1598. Japanese expansionism had come to an end, but the underlying concept of Japan as the Middle Kingdom remained, in spite of the swing of the pendulum to the other extreme of isolationism contrived by Hideyoshi's successors, the Tokugawa shoguns.

[25] Naohiro Asao, '16 Seiki Kohan no Nihon' (Japan in the latter half of the twentieth century), *Nihon Tsushi*, vol. 11 (Tokyo, 1993), 11.

PART I

From Seclusion to Expansion
1825–1900

I

Japan in 1825: A Crisis in Seclusion

TOKUGAWA HEGEMONY AND THE BAKUHAN SYSTEM

In spite of the civilian nature that the Tokugwa Bakufu later acquired in the years of peace, the whole course of Tokugawa politics was vitiated by the way it was created. The most likely successor to Hideyoshi when he died was Tokugawa Ieyasu, probably the cleverest warlord, originally from Okazaki, Mikawa; but his ambitions were so obvious that a bitter struggle for power ensued among the former warlords, culminating in the Battle of Sekigahara of 1600. In a confused conflict the western army upholding the hegemonic claims of the Toyotomi clan founded by Hideyoshi was out-manoeuvred and thoroughly defeated. Ieyasu at once started redistribution of daimyo fiefs. Most of the pro-Toyotomi daimyo were deprived of a great part of their lands; the domain of Moori Terumoto (who was entrusted with the safety of Hideyoshi's infant son), for instance, was reduced from 1.2 million koku in eight provinces to 360,000 koku in two (Suo and Nagato, soon to be known as Choshu).[1] Confiscated lands were added to Tokugawa's own territory, or awarded to the eastern daimyo who had contributed to the victory, or to Tokugawa's own vassals. These former vassals were now called *fudai* (hereditary) daimyo, and those daimyo who had sided with Toyotomi and survived were called *tozama* daimyo (outer daimyo). It was not before 1602, however, that Shimazu Yoshihiro, who had led his own forces at Sekigahara against Ieyasu, accepted the latter's leadership in lieu of the preservation of his own domain, Satsuma and Osumi. After this Tokugawa Ieyasu was appointed shogun in 1603, and set up his Bakufu in Edo. Satsuma and Choshu, however, remained the two great western han (clan territories) and it was they who were to bring down the Bakufu some 265 years later, when its elaborate system of security proved inadequate to cope with mounting pressures, both domestic and foreign. The marvel is that it lasted so long.

Before the death of Ieyasu in 1616 the Tokugawa had begun eliminating two sources of instability through the annihilation of the Toyotomi family in two perfidious attacks on Osaka Castle in 1614–15, and by the total

[1] One koku is equivalent to about five bushels, or the amount of rice that would enable one person to survive for one year, and was used as the unit to measure the wealth in terms of taxable rice produce of an area.

suppression of Christianity which, it was feared, might help the *tozama* daimyo to build up wealth and power for themselves. The Bakufu officially banned Christianity in 1613, and its decree of 1614 called for the expulsion of all foreign missionaries. The Tokugawa decision to turn against Christianity was distinct from and stricter than that of Hideyoshi (whose edict of 1587 was not fully enforced), while the Catholic daimyo in western Japan continued to present elements of instability. In what was to be known as the Great Martyrdom at Nagasaki in 1622, thirty Christians were beheaded and twenty-five burned at the stake, of whom nine were foreign priests. In the Amakusa–Shimabara revolt of 1637–8 a peasant army of about 37,000, led by Christian samurai held out at Hara Castle against forces of 100,000; only 100 or so among the rebels survived. It marked the end of overt Christianity in Japan before Meiji.

Foreign trade with South-East Asian ports, started by Ieyasu in 1601 granting a special licence (vermillion-stamped) to authorized Japanese ships, had been placed under strict control for fear of greater participation by daimyo. From 1635 all overseas travel by Japanese was banned and the return of overseas Japanese was made punishable by death. In 1639 all foreign residents were ordered to move to Deshima, the man-made island in Nagasaki Bay. The Spaniards and Portuguese having been expelled, it was the Dutch who moved there (in 1641) from Hirado. A Portuguese ship which came to Nagasaki to request trade was burned and all its crew killed. Christianity was outlawed, and foreign influence was reduced to a minimum.

The policy of seclusion was adopted by the early Tokugawa Bakufu, which became far more sensitive than Hideyoshi had been to the risks involved in Christian missions and foreign trade: these, it was felt, might endanger Tokugawa hegemony, still a delicate creature born of forced settlements after the Battle of Sekigahara. Domestic worries as well as foreign pressures, real and imagined, were the factors which brought on the country the two centuries of isolation that were to shape the Japan of 1825, which itself turned out to be most aggressively seclusionist.

In 1622 the rumours of a revolt by some powerful lords led to the wives and children of the *tozama* lords being obliged to stay in Edo virtually as hostages, while fortifications of Edo Castle were strengthened at the cost of these lords. Under the system of *sankin kotai* (alternate attendance) stipulated by the Rules of the Warriors of 1635, the outer daimyo had to reside in Edo in nominal attendance on the shogun during alternate twelve-month periods; and the daimyo's family and a certain number of fief officials had to live permanently in the lord's mansion in Edo. In 1642 this was extended practically to all daimyo, including *fudai*, with certain variations in detail.

Thus emerged a military and political structure of feudal power referred to as the Bakuhan system by historians. It was based on a balance of power between the Bakufu and a motley assemblage of daimyo of varied types. The Bakufu did not tax the daimyo's domains (han) directly, allowing them financial autonomy and responsibility in the expectation that they would voluntarily share in the defence of the country and the preservation of the system itself. Unlike a monarchical power in Europe at the time, the Bakufu did not even attempt to establish judicial rights within the great han.[2] A federal structure of power emerged, consisting of Inners and Outers, *fudai* and *tozama*, with even the Outer, Satsuma and Choshu among others, retaining their autonomy to a remarkable extent.

TOKUGAWA RELIGION AND CONFUCIANISM

Confucianism, especially that of the Sung period or the Neo-Confucianism associated with Chu Hsi, disseminated in the early Tokugawa period, penetrated into the consciousness and customs of the Japanese: such basic concepts as loyalty (*chu*) and filial piety (*ko*) were deeply rooted in Confucian ethics, sublimated almost as a religion.[3] Neo-Confucianism, at the same time, fitted well into Tokugawa feudalism, and was embodied in the Bakuhan system as its moral and ideological support. Thus it enjoyed Ieyasu's special patronage.[4]

In the era of peace, the significance of which was increasingly dawning upon the Tokugawa leaders, the *raison d'être* of the samurai, a parasitic class, had to be clarified. 'There are four orders among men,' asserted Amenomori Hoshu, a Neo-Confucian scholar: 'These are samurai, peasants, artisans, and merchants; and the samurai and those above them labour with heart, while the peasants and those below them labour with muscle. The former are placed above, and the latter below.'[5] Hayashi Razan, the founder of the official Confucian scholar family of twelve generations, himself served the first four shoguns, upholding the hierarchical order of social status derived from eternal 'nature'.

Tokugawa society, however, was too dynamic to be confined in this hierarchical 'natural' order, especially when merchants and commercial capital began to undermine its economic basis and the samurai, detached from the land and gathered into castle towns, led an existence, as Ogyu Sorai would say, 'of living in an inn'.[6] Ogyu Sorai, a Confucian scholar, challenged official Neo-Confucianism and its optimism by introducing

---

[2] Conrad Totman, *The Collapse of the Tokugawa Japan* (Honolulu, 1980), 33.

[3] Robert Bellah, *Tokugawa Religion* (New York, 1985 edn.), 54–5.

[4] Masao Maruyama, *Nihon Seiji Shisoshi Kenkyu* (Studies of the History of Japanese Political Thought) (Tokyo, 1962), 13; English tr. by Mikiso Hane under the title of *Studies in the Intellectual History of Tokugawa Japan* (Tokyo, 1974). Translation in the text is my own.

[5] Quoted in Maruyama, op. cit., 9 (Eng. tr. 9).   [6] Ibid. 220 (219).

'political reasoning' which was to justify institutional changes from above, the periodical 'reforms' combining sumptuary edicts with debasement of the coinage: those of Kyoho under the eighth shogun Yoshimune, of Kansei (1780s and 90s), and of Tenpo (1840s).[7] In fact, 'political thinking' began to help weaken the Tokugawa hegemony by making it appear artificial and temporary, susceptible of change through political action.[8]

TOKUGAWA ECONOMY—THE RISE OF THE MERCHANTS

Under the security provided by the 'Pax Tokugawa' the economy as a whole showed a tendency towards maturity and unification: the creation of a national market for certain commodities, starting with rice, a unified currency; and a banking system. Regional diversities were also reflected in the great variety of goods locally produced. Sea traffic along the coast became the major means of transport. The busiest trade was between Osaka and Edo, and was carried on for most of the Tokugawa period by a regular shipping service which ran vessels of 1,000 koku (*sengokubune*) in spite of strict (and lower) official limitations on their size.[9]

The growth of Edo as a city of consumers was phenomenal. It would soon boast of its '808 streets' and population of 1 million people, making it one of the three or four largest cities in the world. Osaka, after 1615, was transformed from a military into a commercial city, as a centre for converting rice into silver and distributing goods to the rest of the country. Of its population of 450,000, 90 per cent were merchants and their families. Most of the han had financial representatives (lower ranks of samurai) stationed in Osaka, selling the rice of their han for the best price obtainable. Osaka came to be known as 'the kitchen of the nation', and also became the centre of mercantile culture and learning.

The significance of the period of 'the closed country'(1638–1858) may have been overrated, for Nagasaki, the port officially opened to the Dutch and the Chinese, was not the only place available for foreign trade; the islands of Tsushima in the Korean Strait were engaged in trade with Korea, and the Satsuma han with Ryukyu (Okinawa), which had been placed under Satsuma's suzerainty in 1609. The small Matsumae han in Ezo depended for its revenue entirely upon trade with the Ainu. Smuggling too was widespread. In the seventeenth century Japan was the largest silver-

---

[7] Quoted in Maruyama, op. cit., 39 (Eng. tr. 76).

[8] An armed rebellion in Osaka led by Oshio Heihachiro, a former constable, in 1836, demanding relief work at the time of a severe famine, itself a challenge to the Shogunate authority, could be regarded as one such action.

[9] Charles David Sheldon, *The Rise of the Merchant Class in Tokugawa Japan, 1600–1868* (New York, 1958), 59–60. *Sengokubune* was a ship with a capacity for 1,000 koku (roughly 5,000 bushels) of rice.

producing country in Asia, and the export of silver to other Asian countries was an attraction for foreign merchants. Soon gold and copper were added to the list of minerals to be exported from Japan. A vast amount of silver was absorbed into China, either as a tribute from Korea or Ryukyu or as the object of trade. Thus, 'Japanese silver became the means to form the small "Middle Kingdom" that Japan established in the closed country, while at the same time it functioned as an important factor in forming the real Middle Kingdom with China as its core'.[10] Meanwhile, the export of silver caused a shortage of currency at home, which led to a debasement of the coinage, resulting in higher prices. Several han began issuing paper currency (han notes), and they contributed to price inflation.

The money economy grew as an adjunct to and an accretion of the feudal land economy, and it was the function of the merchants to convert tax-rice and salary-rice into money. They soon built up a well-organized credit system, and accounts between Osaka and Edo were settled mostly by bills of exchange. The merchants often became the creditors of their political superiors. Speculative markets developed in goods which were sold in large quantities; in particular, the rice exchange at Dojima, Osaka, became of such great consequence as to influence prices in Edo. Commercial capital, while often transformed into usury capital to take advantage of the daimyo who needed loans, was also used as productive capital in the manufacture of sake, the cultivation of reclaimed lands, and the management of rural industries such as silk, cotton, paper, mats, lantern-making, and so on.

TSUNAYOSHI AND YOSHIMUNE

The Genroku period (1688–1703), which fell within the reign of the fifth shogun Tokugawa Tsunayoshi, has been described as one of peace and prosperity in which the lead was taken by merchant families such as the Mitsui, who opened the first exchange shops, and the Sumitomo, known for silver-mining. The official pleasure-quarter in Edo, the Yoshihara, provided themes for popular literature like the metrical *joruri* romances and for the woodblock prints of *ukiyoe* (*ukiyo* meaning 'the floating and fleeting world'). Ihara Saikaku, known for his novel, *Koshoku-Ichidai-Otoko* (The Life of an Amorous Man, 1682), also wrote *Nippon Eitaigura* (Japan's Family Storehouse, 1688) containing thirty stories about successful businessmen which bore witness to the rise of the merchants, though this rise took place only in the worlds of wealth and literature, never in politics.

[10] Akira Hayami and Matao Miyamoto, 'Gaisetsu 17–18 Seiki' (General View of the 17th and 18th Centuries), *Nihon Keizaishi* (Economic History of Japan) (Tokyo), vol. 1 (1988, 1994), 20. Sumita and Taira (eds.), op. cit., 172–3.

The eighth shogun Tokugawa Yoshimune, formerly the lord of Kii, sought to restore the martial traditions which he felt had been dangerously weakened by the rise in influence and prestige of rich merchants and landowners. He also undertook the census of 1721,[11] and strove to establish better relations with the imperial court in order to enhance the shogun's prestige. Importantly, he also lifted the ban on western books (except for those related to Christianity) in 1720, a new departure which marked the beginning of western studies in Japan. The Yoshimune period witnessed the foundation in Osaka of a merchant academy called the *Kaitokudo*, a school set up 'to reflect deeply into the meaning of virtue'. Miyake Setsuan, a Confucian scholar in Osaka, in his opening lecture given before seventy-six leading merchants, drew from the Confucian *Analects* not the problems of hierarchy and political governance but 'moral philosophy for commoners'.[12] Meanwhile, Yoshimune's policy of retrenchment helped to improve the Bakufu's finances, though fluctuations in the price of rice as well as in the value of metalic currency, coupled with storms and famines, badly diminished its financial strength. By 1745, the year of the retirement of Yoshimune (the greatest of the Tokugawa shoguns after Ieyasu, according to Sansom) the Bakufu 'had entered upon a slow decline'.[13]

TOKUGAWA ECONOMY—RURAL DISCONTENT

The decay and corrosion of Tokugawa society in this period was due largely to changes in the character of rural society caused by the spread of the money economy. The old paternal relationship between the independent farmer and his workers broke down. More serious, however, were risings led by the principal farmers in a number of villages known as *Hyakusho Ikki* (old *Tsuchi Ikki*), involving both rich farmers and poor peasants, and directed against the extortionist fiscal methods of the Bakufu and the daimyo. An agrarian revolt in Shimotsuke and Musashi in 1764, involving 200,000 men, was of the same order as the Amakusa–Shimabara Rebellion of 1637–8.[14] In daily life, villages were 'riven with tensions'.[15] The Tenmei era (1781–8) witnessed one of the worst famines under Tokugawa, accompanied by a series of peasant uprisings and urban unrest, especially rice riots and the destruction of town offices and moneylenders' houses called *uchikowashi* or 'smashing-up'. These

[11] The Bakufu's population census based on temple registers, though having the defect of leaving out the samurai, was 26 million in 1721, the year of its initiation; the number fell to 24,890,000 in 1792 but grew to 27,180,000 in 1828.

[12] Tetsuo Najita, *Visions of Virtue in Tokugawa Japan* (Chicago, 1987), 87.

[13] Sansom, *A History of Japan*, iii. 166, 171.   [14] Ibid., iii. 179.

[15] Anne Walthall (ed. and tr.), *Peasant Uprisings in Japan* (Chicago, 1991), 31.

events characterized 'the politics of anger, which disposed people to seek justice in revenge'.[16]

'A slow decline' of the Bakufu was accompanied not by intellectual inertia, as might be expected, but by the spread of new ideas, the soaring of intellectual curiosity and imagination, and even the appearance of utopias. Ando Shoeki, a medical doctor and agrarian philosopher, was also a utopian. He rejected Confucianism, together with Buddhism and idol-worshipping Shintoism. Expounding a monistic theory of nature, he valued the natural act of direct cultivation of the land and stressed the mutuality of such an act. He refused to accept the dualistic features of East Asian philosophy such as Heaven and Earth or Light and Darkness, and argued for the overcoming of gender and race discriminations. In this he was an advanced thinker, and in his view of nature as life in motion he was also a pioneer ecologist.[17] He conceived of a society based on labour, digging and weaving; it is labour, he believed, that assures natural equality of human beings. Shoeki could be compared to John Ball, the priest of the Peasant Revolt in fourteenth-century England; but Shoeki's Japan lacked a peasant army powerful enough to deal with a king or shogun. Though Shoeki himself was an isolated scholar-doctor living in Akita and his followers were suppressed after his death, late-Tokugawa Japan was rich in men of intellectual calibre in various schools of thought.

NATIONAL LEARNING

The National Learning school had a direct impact on the restoration movement towards the end of the Bakufu's rule through its appeal to the idea of *sonno* (Revere the Emperor). Although *sonno* became a political slogan for imperial restoration, it derived from a historical perception of the correlation that was supposed to have existed between emperors' rule and political stability, ever since the idealized past known as the Era of the Gods. Motoori Norinaga, a practising doctor at Matsuzaka, Ise, who represented National Learning at its height, sought, like Shoeki, to restore natural Shinto or 'the Ancient Way' as it was believed to have existed before it was corrupted by Chinese 'argumentation and cleverness'. But he postulated nature as God's invention, and God to him, unlike Shoeki, was the imperial ancestor, the Sun Goddess; thus he maintained that Japan, the country of the Sun Goddess, should control the barbarians in the west, China and Korea, and advocated that concept of Japan as the Middle Kingdom which underlay Tokugawa nationalism. Hirata Atsutane,

---

[16] Herbert Bix, *Peasant Protest in Japan 1590–1884* (New Haven, 1986), 143.
[17] Shoeki Ando, *Shizen-Shineido* (The Way of Nature and Labour), vol. 1, preface, quoted in E. H. Norman, *Ando Shoeki and the Anatomy of Japanese Feudalism* (Asiatic Society of Japan, 1949, reprint edn., 1979), 194.

Norinaga's follower, turned the mythology of the ancient chronicles into a cosmology centred around Heavenly God and Heavenly Emperor, and sought to strengthen the 'Yamato' (traditional Japanese) spirit of the people. He also wanted to return Shinto to its ancient, purer state, as it was believed to have existed before becoming contaminated and compromised under the domination of Buddhism. His lofty yet eclectic ideas and plebeian style won him the enthusiastic support of the common people, farmers and townspeople.

DUTCH STUDIES

After 1640 and until 1853 the United Provinces was the only European country with which Japan had any direct contact. Deshima in Nagasaki Harbour, where the Dutch merchants stayed, became a tiny window on Europe open to the Japanese, through which a trickle of western learning, medicine, astronomy, and gunnery, infiltrated into the country. These subjects were called *Rangaku* or Dutch Studies. Divorced from their cultural, intellectual, and historical context, however, they remained 'technology without ideology'.[18] Even so, *Rangaku* provided the first step towards Japan's westernization. They created a prototype of an attitude that was to develop into a dominant ideology summed up in the slogan *Wakon Yosai* (Japanese Spirit, Western Arts).

With the lifting in 1720 of the ban on the import of western books in general, great progress was made in *Rangaku*. Sugita Genpaku, the clan doctor for Obama, Wakasa, and Maeno Ryotaku, doctor for the Nakatsu han, both living in Edo, attended the dissection of an executed old woman at Kotsukagahara (literally 'Bonesfield') in 1771, and both had in their bosoms (literally) a copy of a Dutch book on anatomy, in fact a Dutch translation of a German original, Johann Adam Kulmus's *Anatomische Tabellen* (Danzig, 1725), or 'Tafel Anatomy' as rendered into Japanese. Struck by the accuracy of the western diagrams, they began translating the Dutch book which was published as *Kaitai Shinsho* (New Book of Anatomy) in five volumes in 1774. This was the real beginning of Dutch Studies in Japan.

The spread of Dutch Studies in the late Tokugawa period deserves special attention. While a translation bureau was established by the Bakufu in Edo in the early nineteenth century, *Rangaku* or *Yogaku* (western studies) had already begun to be taught at schools in some of the forward-looking han, Mito, Hizen, Choshu, Nakatsu, Sendai, Nagoya, and Fukuoka. Twelve private schools of western medicine were opened between 1786 and 1846, of which Ogata Koan's academy in Osaka was perhaps the most prestigious—Ogata Koan being distinguished for his

---

[18] G. K. Goodman, *Japan: The Dutch Experience* (London, 1986), 118.

public work, notably for vaccination.[19] Another important private institution was a school near Nagasaki taught by Philipp Franz von Siebold, the German physician who served the Dutch at Deshima. Dutch or Western Studies, however, did not necessarily induce scholars to oppose the Bakufu policy of national seclusion.[20] Shizuki Tadao, a distinguished Nagasaki interpreter, was known for his translation (1802) of the *History of Japan* by Engelbert Kaempfer, a German doctor who became a ship's doctor employed by the Dutch East India Company. Shizuki in his translation gave the impression that the author was in favour of the Bakufu's policy of isolation, which was also Shizuki's own position. He used the term *sakoku* (the closure of the country) for the first time to describe this policy. Sugita's student Otsuki Gentaku, known for his own medical and linguistic works, believed that the Japanese, after having mastered Dutch Studies, should have no further traffic with the West. Shizuki and Otsuki shared the view that opening the country would deprive Japan of her free hand in choosing what to borrow from western culture.

VISIONS OF THE WORLD:
HONDA TOSHIAKI AND SATO NOBUHIRO

Honda Toshiaki, a schoolmaster, deserves special attention here because he not only shared the reservations of Shizuki and Otsuki regarding Dutch Studies, but went so far as to advocate national expansion on a grand scale. Born in a samurai-farmer family in northern Echigo, he studied arithmetic, astronomy, and geography in Edo, then went on to open a school teaching these subjects. He travelled widely during the great Tenmei famine of the 1780s; his observation of the many deaths by starvation, and of the practice of infanticide widespread in central and north-eastern Japan, gave him food for serious thought, and he arrived at the idea of 'the Way of Natural Cure' which, he believed, had been discovered in Europe. There, he maintained, national strength depended more on wealth than on arms, and Christian charity provided the main pillar of government rule. Though there were exaggerations in Honda's view of Europe, these nevertheless helped to increase Japanese awareness of the potential western challenge, military or otherwise.

In his *Secret Plan to Manage the Country* (*Keisei Hisaku*, 1798), Honda dwells on money and trade, great emphasis being placed on the amount of metallic currency stored in the hands of the government. Shipping and trade were essential for the welfare of the people and should not be left to the care of merchants, he thought, but rather should be made government

[19] Beasley, *Japan Encounters the Barbarian*, 26.
[20] Donald Keene, *The Japanese Discovery of Europe* (London, 1952), 98–9.

responsibilities, carried out by its officials for the benefit of the nation. 'I discovered', wrote Honda, 'that fifteen-sixteenths of the total income of Japan goes to the merchants, with only one-sixteenth left for the samurai. ' As a proof of this he cites the case of rice priced at 5 or 6 mon (the smallest currency unit, one-thousandth of a kan) per sho (one-hundredth of a koku) at Yonezawa or Akita being shipped to Edo and sold for 100 mon per sho.[21] 'In terms of the production of an individual farmer, out of thirty days a month he works twenty-eight for the merchants and two for the samurai.'[22] Honda proposed the setting-up of trading stations at important sea-ports throughout Japan, so as to control both the transport of rice and its price in such a way as to offset the effects of good harvests against those of bad ones. As for colonization of the northern islands, he felt, in spite of their comparative barrenness for cereal production, that their location in terms of latitude promised a great future.

Honda wrote his second major work, *Tales of the West* (*Seiiki Monogatari*), in 1798 to show the positions occupied respectively by Japan, China, and Europe. He also expounded the Copernican system and the western calendar.[23] He developed a theory of population, starting with its natural tendency to multiplication, and came to the conclusion that Japan, in order to escape from 'industrial deficits' due to overpopulation, would have to expand herself nearly twenty times in the course of thirty-three years. It was a mere coincidence that Honda developed his theory in the same year that Robert Malthus published his *Essay on Population*. His remedy was not moral abstinence (as it was for Malthus), however, but national territorial expansion. Japan should be centred on Kamchatka, to be named Old Japan, extending to America in the east, to Okhotsk, Sakhalin, and Manchuria in the west, and to the twenty-two Ezo islands, the Island of Matsumae (Hokkaido), Japan, and Loochoos to the south; all these would belong to Old Japan-Kamchatka. Moreover, the expansion of Japan should take place not through military conquest but by foreign trade and colonization. His advocacy of expansionism was nòt that of nineteenth-century imperialism but of the earlier mercantilism that placed a great emphasis on metallic currency, government-controlled trade,

---

[21]   Keene, op. cit., 190; *Nihon Shiso Taikei* (Major Works in Japanese Thought), xliv. 33. This reminds us of Charles Fourier's apple. In Paris a friend of his paid 14 sous for an apple, but he knew that in the countryside one could buy 100 apples for 14 sous. Fourier criticized commercial civilization and advocated a co-operative community.

[22]   Ibid. In this connection it is easy to recall some of the Ricardian socialists, such as Charles Hall in his critical essay on the effects of European Civilization, or even Karl Marx himself!

[23]   He had learned Copernican astronomy from Shiba Kokan, a painter and geographer in Edo, but the credit of being the first Japanese to accept it goes to Miura Baien, a doctor and philosopher of Bungo (present Oita) who learned it through an interpreter on his visit to Nagasaki in 1778. Keene, op. cit., 111. Beasley has identified the Nagasaki interpreter as Motoki Ryoei who made the theory known in 1774. Beasley, *Japan Encounters the Barbarian*, 27. Buddhist opposition to it continued until the late nineteenth century.

population-growth, and colonization abroad. He took for granted the need to open the country, though he refrained from meddling with Bakufu rule.

A view of Japan's possible territorial expansion as bold as or even bolder than Honda's was expressed by Sato Shin-en or Nobuhiro, who can be counted among the Dutch scholars, though he came under the influence of Hirata Atsutane at some stage. Shin-en, the son of a country doctor at a Dewa village, was brought up in the family tradition of encyclopaedic learning, especially in medicine, mineralogy, and mining technology. In 1808 he served the Awa-han at Tokushima by giving advice on coastal defence and manufacturing cannons. His lectures resulted in several books, one of which, *Sea Defence*, was a precursor of his later work *The Profound Programme to Unite All the Nations*. Believing that Japan was the most conveniently situated nation for sea voyages and foreign trade and surpassed Britain in her climate and natural products, he urged the nation to prepare herself with armed ships and to develop the sailing skills needed for overseas expeditions. Japan should conclude treaties for peace and trade with China, Annan (Vietnam), and Siam, further develop Ezo, occupy the Russian ports in Kamchatka and Okhotsk, and trade with America through these north-eastern strongholds. As for the south, Japan should develop uninhabited islands in the South Sea, and occupy Luzon, from where she could govern Java and Borneo. This, he believed, would be the best way to prevent Britain from plundering the Far East. He also suggested the development of a ship run by the power generated by explosives.

The major work by which he is remembered today, *Kondo Hisaku* (Secret Policy of Intermixing), came out in 1823. Japan, with its mild weather, fertile soil, and surrounded by oceans, should be able to unite all the nations in the world. It should occupy China, Siam, and India; for this, an imperial capital ought to be built, with a university, a ministry of education, a ministry of religion, and other government offices. Several regional armies of Japan would be sent to the Amur and further into Siberia. Hani Goro, a radical historian, asserts that Sato's utopia showed anticipations of state socialism, and W. G. Beasley summarizes it in a similar way: not content merely to reform feudal society, Sato sought to replace it by 'a terrifyingly modern and totalitarian structure'.[24]

He also advocated a national system of primary education in a later work, an ambitious plan even for a country which had about 40 per cent of its male population (though only 10 per cent of its female) educated in at least reading and writing by the late Tokugawa period.[25] It is difficult to

---

[24] W. G. Beasley, *The Meiji Restoration* (Stanford, 1972), 80.

[25] *Sato Shin-en Kagaku Zenshu* (Works of Family Learning by Sato Shinen) (Tokyo), vol. 2 (1926), 413–43; this book, entitled *Suito Hiroku* (Profound Record of Government), was posthumously published in 1857. R. P. Dore, *Education in Tokugawa Japan* (1st edn. 1965; 1984 edn., London), 254.

evaluate how influential Sato's writings were and what sort of impact they had on the generations that were deeply involved in the turmoil over opening and modernizing the country. It is certain, however, that he represented and even typified that turmoil in a most pronounced, though contradictory form—contradictory because his views were a product of Dutch Studies seasoned with a sprinkling of Hirata theology; in other words, a consummation of the European ideal of national strength accentuated by the Japan-centred 'Imperial Way'. His 'Imperial Way', with all its trappings, was to see the light nearly a century later.

SECLUSION CHALLENGED: RUSSIAN ADVANCE

Such views emerged only at the end of a period during which Japan's isolation had remained undisturbed by the European powers for nearly 150 years. In the West the eighteenth century witnessed the two great revolutions, the American and French, while the mercantilism embodied in the Dutch and British East India Companies failed to awaken Japan out of her complacent 'lethargy', owing partly to their lack of adequate ships and also to their preoccupation with other areas, the British with India, the Dutch with Java. It was the Russians from the north who first gave a serious shock to Japan's seclusion policy.

Russia's eastward movement had gone far enough to cause conflict with China in the Amur region and with Japan in the northern islands, and to threaten by the turn of the century to make the northern Pacific a Russian lake.[26] In fact, Russian adventurers seeking furs, the 'golden fleece', had reached the Sea of Okhotsk by the middle of the seventeenth century, and Russian interest in Japan was encouraged by the mistaken idea of the proximity of the country as well as by the stories of its wealth told by a whole series of castaways, beginning with Gavriil Denbei, the Osaka merchant who ended up as an instructor at a Japanese language school opened in St Petersburg in 1705.[27] In the course of the eighteenth century several Russians explored the Kurile Islands and sailed further south. Baron Moritz Aladar von Benyowsky, a Hungarian adventurer who had engineered a revolt among the convicts in the penal colony in Kamchatka, sailed south in a small vessel in 1771, anchored at a port in Shikoku, from where he was driven away by the menacing attitude of the natives, though given provisions, and dispatched a warning letter to the Japanese via the Dutch factory director at Deshima. This document has been called the 'first piece of national defence literature' in Japan,[28] because it impressed

---

[26] George Alexander Lensen, *The Russian Push Toward Japan* (Princeton, 1959), 15.
[27] Ibid. 26–9.
[28] Donald Keene, *The Japanese Discovery of Europe*, 43; Lensen, op. cit., 71 ff.

on the Bakufu officials the need to take defensive measures against the threat from a powerful empire, possibly for the first time since the Mongol attempts at invasion in the thirteenth century.

Perhaps the most notable victim of shipwreck in the northern Pacific was Daikokuya Kodayu, an Ise merchant whose ship sank on its way to Edo and who drifted north; having spent an arduous period on one of the Aleutian islands and also at Kamchatka, he made an overland journey to Yakutsk and then to Irkutsk, where he came to know Eric Laxman, a Finnish-born professor of natural science at the St Petersburg Academy. Laxman, deeply interested in Japan, thought of sending an expedition under the pretext of repatriating Kodayu and his two compatriots. Catherine the Great encouraged Laxman in elaborating his plan. It was Lieutenant Adam Laxman, the son of the scientist, who actually led the expedition in a government transport ship *Ekaterina*. In September 1792 Laxman Jr. and his men, with Kodayu and two other castaways, set out. They made their way to Matsumae, where it was at length proclaimed that in future Russians should go to Nagasaki if they had castaways to return. They were given a permit for this purpose, the Nagasaki Permit. After nearly a year wasted in time-consuming negotiations, the *Ekaterina* with Laxman and his men on board sailed home again.[29] The Russians for their part failed to make use of the Nagasaki Permit.

Members of the Bakufu's senior council who were interested in coastal defence soon had their fears confirmed by a Russian raid on Japanese outposts in the northern islands. When the Russians resumed their attempt to open up trade with Japan, they were backed by a new organization, the Russian–American Company. An exploration ship left Kronstadt in August 1803, carrying Nikolai Rezanov, a major shareholder of the company, as an envoy to Japan. It sailed round Cape Horn and reached Nagasaki in October 1804, bringing shipwrecked Japanese fishermen as well as a letter from Tsar Alexander I. The letter asking for trade was sent to Edo, while Rezanov was kept waiting at Nagasaki. In April 1805 a reply came from the Bakufu, telling Rezanov that neither his requests nor his presents were acceptable. Nobody could blame Rezanov for losing his temper. He hatched a plan to castigate the rude Japanese officials, and in a report to the Tsar he emphasized the need for determined action 'to force Japan to open trade'.[30] In October 1806 a Russian naval officer in the service of the company and his followers landed at Aniwa Bay, Sakhalin, where there was a small Japanese settlement; the Russians seized Japanese guards of the Matsumae han, carried them aboard their ship, pillaged the warehouses, and set fire to houses and vessels. Then, in May 1807, the Russians

[29] Lensen, op. cit., 96–119.
[30] Ibid. 158–61; Beasley, *Cambridge History of Japan*, v. 165–6.

reached Etorofu Island, a Japanese colony for over a decade with a garri-son of 300 samurai from the Nambu and Tsugaru han, where similar acts of destruction were carried out. Their attack on Kunashiri Island that followed was equally fierce.[31] These military actions were unauthorized by the Russian government, and Rezanov, a sick man, died at Krasnoiark in 1807 before the assault on Etorofu.

Rezanov was mistaken in his belief that he could intimidate the Japanese into surrender, for the raids led only to greater military aware-ness on the Japanese side of the Russian threat to her as-yet unclear northern frontier. Vasili Golovnin, captain of a Russian survey ship, was captured on the island of Kunashiri in 1811 and held until 1813, when the Russians disavowed their military action and admitted that the naval officers who led the assaults on the Japanese garrisons had acted without authorization.[32]

BRITISH AND AMERICAN INTEREST

It was the British who next emerged as a major threat to Japan, this time from the south. In the course of the Napoleonic War, in 1808, a British frigate *Phaeton* entered Nagasaki Bay in an operation against the Dutch ships there, arrested two Dutchmen, and demanded that the Dutch trading house be evacuated: the Nagasaki *bugyo* (officer in charge of the admin-istration of the Bakufu territory Nagasaki) felt himself responsible for allowing this high-handed action to take place, and committed suicide by harakiri.

At about the same time Britain took over the island of Java from the Dutch; Stamford Raffles, the new lieutenant-governor of Java, sought to convert the Dutch trade at Nagasaki into a British trade. In 1813 a British ship came to Nagasaki to take over the Dutch trading house. The Dutch chief of the house, however, was clever enough to dissuade the British representatives from taking further steps by pointing to the danger of serious Japanese reprisals because of the action of the *Phaeton*, which had annoyed the Japanese. Moreover, the British soon came to the con-clusion that the importance of trade with Japan had been overrated. In 1835 the Hudson's Bay Company proposed that the return of three Japanese sailors shipwrecked and rescued from the native peoples on Vancouver Island should be made an excuse for opening trade with Japan, but 'Palmerston would have none of it'.[33] It was not before the aftermath of the Opium War of 1839–42 that Britain appeared in the centre of the drama of opening Japan. But even then Britain was not the main actor, but more or less a shadow partner.

[31] Lensen, op. cit., 170.   [32] Beasley, op. cit., 265–6.   [33] Ibid. 263.

American interest in Japan began as part of the whaling industry in the north Pacific, of which the Americans took a large share. The seclusion law of the Bakufu prevented American ships from entering Japanese ports for water and supplies. Moreover, American trade with China had grown to a substantial size, so much so that Japan loomed large on the strategic horizon. A group of missionaries and merchants sought to gain a foothold in Japan, using the return of Japanese castaways as an excuse for their action, but with no visible success.

THE 1825 EXCLUSION EDICT, AIZAWA SEISHISAI, AND THE MITO SCHOOL

In the second month of 1825 the Bakufu issued the edict to urge the daimyo to expel foreign ships 'without second thought'. In the following month Aizawa Seishisai, the nationalist writer of the Mito school, wrote his *Shinron* (New Thesis), in which he praised the edict highly: 'People in the realm are informed of the decisive measure and are encouraged and stirred. They are all prepared to carry it out.'[34] *Shinron* became 'a virtual bible to activists in the "revere the Emperor, expel the barbarian" movement': its popular versions were widely circulated.[35] Oddly enough, the original proposal, for the 1825 Expulsion Edict came from a scholar of Dutch Studies named Takahashi Kageyasu, who, citing the rules of western diplomacy, advised the Bakufu to repulse ships of the countries with which no trade relations were maintained by firing blank rounds.[36] The earlier edicts of the seventeenth century issued against Christianity and foreign intercourse had been observed without much dissent. It was the changed international situation that made the later edicts appear more serious, potentially controversial, and even provocative.

Tokugawa rule of over 200 years and changes in the outside world had brought about a situation that could be called *Naiyu Gaikan* (worries within, troubles without) for Japan. It was Fujita Yukoku, a patriotic scholar of the Mito school and Aizawa's teacher, who used this Chinese phrase to describe the contemporary Japanese scene. *Naiyu* for Fujita meant the financial difficulties of the domains and the hardship inflicted on the farmers, and *Gaikan* was the threat of Russia from the north, above all. 'Now han finance becomes more strained year by year,' wrote Yukoku, 'morale declines month by month, and people's energy is further

---

[34] Seishisai Aizawa, 'Shinron', *Mitogaku* (Mito Studies), *Nihon Shiso Taikei* (Major Works in Japanese Thought) (1973), liii. 78; Bob Tadashi Wakabayashi, *Anti-Foreignism and Western Learning in Early Modern Japan: The New Thesis of 1825* (Cambridge, Mass., 1986, 1991 edn.), 181. Translation is my own. See also J. Victor Koschmann, *The Mito Ideology* (Berkeley, 1987), 57 ff.   [35] Wakabayashi, op. cit., pp. ix f.

[36] Ibid. 59, 102–3.

trammelled day by day. . . If the wicked foreigners ever took advantage of these weaknesses even an excellent doctor could not cure the patient with medicine, but would only fold his arms and await his death.'[37] Yukoku's treatise, called *Shomeiron* (On Right Status, 1791) became a main pillar of the Mito doctrine as it sought to justify the *sonno* ideology by the Confucian idea of Heaven and Earth, which was applied to the relationship between the shogun, the han lords, and all the officers under the lords.[38]

In the early summer of 1824, when twelve Europeans landed at Otsuhama Beach in Mito territory, Seishisai was appointed as an interpreter and managed to communicate with them by writing (possibly in Dutch). When he discovered that these Europeans were British, he was shocked and wrote: 'To see several foreign ships anchoring and fishing in front of you was hateful enough, but they landed and begged for food. Their contempt for our godly country has gone too far.'[39] He at once set about writing *Shinron*.

Seishisai, like Yukoku, relied heavily on the Confucian *Chronicles of Lu*, especially on the distinctions between the prince and his subjects, and between the Middle Kingdom civilization within and the foreign barbarians without. Again like Yukoku he 'Japanized' Confucianism to such an extent as to equate Heaven with the emperor's eternal rule. His view of *kokutai* derives directly from Yukoku's 'Shomeiron': a divine line of emperors descended from the Sun Goddess rules the country, and affection between the rulers and the ruled prevails.[40] This is how 'our Middle Kingdom' ought to be, whereas the western barbarians use Christianity to annex territories. Some of the scholars in Dutch Studies are dupes who seek to 'transform our Middle Kingdom to barbarian ways'.[41] Barbarians have 'occult religions' as well as 'large ships and cannon' for their weapons. Once 'we took the ocean for granted as a natural barrier. Now the barbarians traverse thousands of miles with whirlwind speed in their huge ships . . . What was once a natural barrier is now a raiders' highway.' The proclamation of the 1825 Edict would mean a declaration of war and Japan has to prepare for it. Firearms must be manufactured and large ships constructed. 'We must now make our islands into a castle and think of the ocean as a moat.' Moreover, the key to defence is attack, so 'we should annex the Ezo islands and absorb the barbarian tribes on the

[37] Yukoku Fujita, 'Teiji Fuji' (An Advice to the Han Lord for the Year 1797), *Mitogaku*, 26.
[38] Yukoku Fujita, 'Shomeiron', *Mitogaku*, 13.
[39] Quoted by Yoshihiko Seya in *Mitogaku*, 482.
[40] Seishisai Aizawa, 'Shinron', *Mitogaku*, 52; Wakabayashi (tr.), 'New Thesis', Wakabayashi, op. cit., 152. See also J. Victor Koschman, *The Mito Ideology* (Berkeley, 1987), 56–80.
[41] For this and the following reference to *Shinron*, see Seishisai Aizawa, 'Shinron', *Mitogaku*, 52, 68–9, 77, 91, 108, 114, 136, 138, 154; Wakabayashi (tr.), 'New Thesis', Wakabayashi, op. cit., 152, 168–9, 180, 196, 215, 222, 248, 250, 273.

continent; we should roll back the tide of barbarism and extend our frontiers ever forward'.

Seishisai thus provided all the essential political vocabulary of the Restoration movement.[42] Fujita Toko, Yukoku's son, was for *kaikoku*, 'opening the country' (and Seishisai too, in his later years, came to accept it), but this policy was to be pursued only after having repelled the foreigners: a strong Japan united under the emperor could deal with foreigners on equal terms.

BANSHA NO GOKU
(SCHOLARS OF WESTERN STUDIES IMPRISONED)

An incident referred to in Japanese history as *Bansha no Gokoku*, with two eminent scholars, Watanabe Kazan and Takano Choei, caught in its trap, illustrates the extent to which the Bakufu would go to suppress views critical of its policy of national seclusion at a time when that policy itself had become doubtful in its efficacy. Kazan, another notable figure in western studies, was born at the Tahara han estate in Edo. The Tahara han, under a typical *fudai* daimyo, had strategic importantance because of its long coastline along the Pacific Ocean in Mikawa, though it was one of the poorest han. Kazan approached Western Studies through painting, at which he excelled; in due course he was asked to help the han administration. He restored the han school, improved han finance and economy, and took charge of a new office created after 1825 for coastal defence. He came to know some of the scholars of Dutch Studies including Takano Choei or Nagahide, the son of a clan doctor who had studied under Siebold at Nagasaki. Siebold on a visit to Edo in 1828, found himself in trouble when he obtained a map of Japan, Ezo, and Sakhalin, together with some travel books, in exchange for a map of Dutch dependencies, some Russian books, and a biography of Napoleon to be deposited with a Bakufu officer in charge of books and astronomy. This exchange of books and maps became known to the Bakufu, Siebold was ordered to leave the country, and his former students were interrogated. It was a great shock to the Dutch scholars, especially to members of a semi-secret society called the Association of the Aged (*Shoshikai*), in which Kazan, Choei, and Sato Shin-en were active participants; the predominant view among them was one of *sonno-kaikoku* (revere the emperor and open the country), and they were consequently critical of the Bakufu for its policy of *joi* (expel the barbarians).[43]

The arrival in 1837 of the American ship *Morrison* coincided with the

[42] Beasley, op. cit., 84.
[43] Choun Takano, *Takano Choei-Den* (Tokyo, 1943, 1971), 259–60.

exploration of the Bonin Islands by the British warship *Raleigh*. It so happened that at Macao at the time there were seven Japanese castaways, all under the protection of Dr Charles Gutzlaff, a German missionary employed as an interpreter by the British trade supervisor in China. Charles King, an American businessman, who was the director of Oliphant & Co., an American trading company at Macao, proposed to send the seven Japanese home on board his ship the *Morrison*. Gutzlaff, who was ordered to guard the castaways and to report back about the ships's expedition, boarded the *Morrison* at Naha, Okinawa, from the *Raleigh*. As soon as the *Morrison* approached Uraga at the entance of Edo Bay, a bombardment began from the shore in accordance with the decree of 1825. The ship was obliged to leave Edo Bay, and another attempt made near Kagoshima fared no better; the *Morrison* returned to Macao. In the following year (1838) a Dutch ship which entered Nagasaki disclosed details about the voyage undertaken by the *Morrison*, but misrepresented the American company as a British firm and the ship as British. The Nagasaki magistrate asked for the Bakufu's view on the treatment of Japanese castaways. Mizuno Tadakuni, who was in charge of sea defence for the Bakufu territories, referred the matter to senior officials and other colleagues, and opinion was divided between those wishing to receive castaways if they were brought back on a Dutch ship and those who opposed reception outright. Mizuno favoured the former view, while ordering the strengthening of coastal defences at Edo Bay. Mizuno's action of consulting the opinion of other officials has been regarded as the beginning of the deliberations to lift the decree of 1825.

Members of the Association for the Aged were alarmed at the intransigent views the Bakufu hawks had shown. Takano Choei wrote *Yume Monogatari* (A Dream Tale) in 1838 and Kazan *Shinkiron* (Cautious Argument) in the same year to express their apprehensions. Both books contained errors and confusions due to rumours and rash judgements such as representing the *Morrison* as a British ship directed by Mr Morrison, a venerable British Sinologist; however, the two works (each a private publication) criticized the blindness of the Bakufu authorities as to the world situation and its recent developments threatening the security of Japan.

Choei's *Dream Tale* takes the form of a dialogue between two scholars, one enquiring about Mr Morrison and his country, Britain, and the other showing an intimate knowledge of Britain and defending her against the allegation made by the Dutch that she is a nation of pirates: Britain is no enemy of Japan, and to bombard her ships for no reason will make Japan appear unreasonable, savage, and unjust.[44] Kazan's *Shinkiron* dealt boldly with the world situation, the advancement of learning in the West, and the

---

[44] Takano, 'Yume Monogatari', Takano, op. cit., 342–52.

conquest of the world nearly achieved by the western powers. He did not say that the opening of Japan was unavoidable, but implied it, and blamed both the blind officials in power and the Confucian time-servers whose obscurantism would invite national disaster. In his other book, *Seiyo-Jijo* (Situations in the West), Kazan criticized the intolerant seclusionist policy by praising western learning for its rational quest for truth.

Now the Edo police jumped on Kazan, Choei, and others under the pretext of investigating their connection with 'Mr Morrison', and in the course of hunting for incriminating evidence they managed to concoct imaginary plots. All this took place in 1839: Kazan, Choei, and several others were arrested. During fresh enquiries Kazan's writings, including those quoted above, were cited as new evidence to prove his subversive intentions. Towards the end of the same year their trial came to an end, with Kazan ordered to live in seclusion at Tahara, and Choei sentenced to imprisonment for life. At Tahara, Kazan, afraid of causing trouble to his han lord, chose to commit suicide by *seppuku* in 1841. Choei, for his part, fled from his prison during a fire. He wandered from Tohoku (north-east Japan) to Kyushu, seeking a possible patron, but in 1850 he committed suicide in order to escape arrest by police officers in Edo.

Bansha no Goku (scholars of Western Studies imprisoned), as this incident was called, marked a climax in the division of opinion on the issue of seclusion or opening of the country in the period when the Edict of 1825 was enforced. The Opium War changed the climate in which this division and the confrontation it fostered were to be carried on. The Edict was unceremoniously withdrawn in 1842 as part of a set of measures combining economic retrenchment and greater efforts for national defence, with a special emphasis placed on gunnery. This has been interpreted (with unjustifiable exaggeration) as a prelude to the Meiji Restoration, but has also been dismissed as a mere feudal reaction. The seas surrounding Japan, in any case, remained turbulent. The 'black ships' were soon to make their dramatic appearance around the island country to bring all the latent interest, ideas, and aspirations to the surface once more, making conflict sharper and compromise less workable.

2

The Opening of the Country

THE ARRIVAL OF COMMODORE PERRY
AND JAPANESE RESPONSE

The Anglo-Chinese Opium War of 1839–42 posed the question of what Japan would do if she became the next target of the West's trade and territorial expansion. The war had created an impression in the minds of western diplomats and traders that 'gunboat diplomacy' worked and could be applied elsewhere, and that 'free trade imperialism', as it was later called, required free access to free ports and should be expanded elsewhere. Even so, the opening of Japan was not to be a carbon copy of that of China.[1]

News of the defeat of the Chinese army in the war, carried by Dutch and Chinese ships to the magistrate of Nagasaki, and relayed through him to the Bakufu, caused a profound shock, but at this point the Bakufu could do nothing but wait and see. Measures for adequate coastal defence, especially the adoption of western gunnery, were urged. In 1844 the Dutch government dispatched a warship to Nagasaki to deliver a royal letter addressed to the 'King of Japan' (the shogun) exhorting him to open the country in order not to bring about a repetition of the disastrous Opium War. The Bakufu in its reply told the Dutch king that Japan would not change her 'ancestral rules'. At about the same time French warships came to Ryukyu demanding a trade agreement, and the British superintendent of trade and governor of Hong Kong prepared secret plans for an expedition to Japan with a formidable naval force, although nothing came of this.

The Americans appeared more involved and committed. With the settlement of the Oregon dispute and the discovery of gold in California, the Pacific coast, and with it the sea route between China and California via Japan, assumed greater importance. Commodore James Biddle was sent to Edo Bay in 1846, only to find his overtures rejected. Commander James Glynn of the USS *Preble*, who had been to Nagasaki in 1849 to secure the release of shipwrecked US sailors, was active in a campaign to send another expedition to Japan, and it was finally decided to send a mission along with a letter from President Millard Fillmore advocating 'friendly commercial intercourse' between the two countries. Britain was content to

---

[1] Beasley in *Cambridge History of Japan*, v. 260 f., 264.

acquiesce when in 1852 the United States announced her intention to do this. The Dutch government too was officially informed at about the same time by the Americans of their intended expedition to Japan, and delivered an official letter to the Bakufu's Nagasaki magistrate urging the need for altering Japan's foreign policy in view of possible armed conflict and the desirability of concluding a trade agreement with the Dutch first of all. The Bakufu ignored these warnings.

Nevertheless, when in July 1853 Commodore Matthew C. Perry of the American East India Squadron with his four warships arrived at the entrance of Edo Bay, it was no surprise operation. Even so, the arrival of four fully armed American warships shook the country profoundly. The death-throes of the Edo Bakufu now began in earnest. Perry refused to move to Nagasaki to receive his reply when the Japanese urged him to do so, and hinted that he would return next year with a much larger force should this be necessary.

Abe Masahiro, the head of the Bakufu's senior council, circulated President Fillmore's letter in translation to all the feudal lords and some officials and scholars, inviting them to express their opinion freely. This was a new departure in the Bakufu's relations with its outer lords and vassals. Of the sixty-one extant replies from daimyo, nineteen were for accepting trade and the opening of ports; nineteen urged rejection of Perry's demands; fourteen stressed the need for avoiding war; seven, though in favour of eventual rejection, advocated the adoption of temporary measures of accommodation; two would obey whatever decision was reached by the Bakufu. Though we are not sure of the 200-odd feudal lords who did not send in replies, it is certain that Abe found no consensus for a policy.[2] He himself, his successors Hotta Masayoshi of Sakura, Shimosa, and Ii Naosuke of Hikone, the great *fudai* lords who usually dominated the Bakufu's council, were in favour of a realistic foreign policy, which meant a compromise arrangement with Perry to be followed by measures to strengthen the country by exploiting the western techniques that would become available under new conditions.[3] This was to become the Meiji policy of *fukoku kyohei* (enrich the nation and strengthen arms), but before it became viable, *joi* (expel the barbarians) stood in its way. The great western daimyo were not in accord even among themselves. Shimazu of Satsuma recommended a delaying tactic to gain time for preparing an adequate defence; Mori of Choshu was interested only in defence now; Yamanouchi Yodo of Tosa suggested turning to the Dutch for help in quick training for self-defence.[4]

Early in the following year (1854) Perry, who had withdrawn to the

---

[2] Beasley, *The Meiji Restoration*, 90.   [3] Ibid. 93.
[4] Marius B. Jansen, *Sakamoto Ryoma and the Meiji Restoration* (Princeton, 1961), 57.

China coast for the winter, returned to Edo Bay accompanied by his full available squadron of eight ships, and obtained the substance of what he had demanded: the opening of Shimoda and Hakodate as ports of call for American ships, just treatment of shipwrecked sailors, and the appointment of a US consul at Shimoda. The delicate issue of trade was dropped. This was a treaty for peace and amity, and similar agreements were made with the British and the Russians in the same year.

Soon a commercial treaty was concluded with the Dutch in 1857, an improvement on the old Deshima arrangements, and a similar treaty was made with the Russians in the same year. The Bakufu negotiators hoped that these would serve as models for a future commercial treaty with Britain, the negotiations for which would be more difficult in view of the Anglo-French attack on China then in progress. Townsend Harris, the US consul at Shimoda, rejected the Dutch model, and lectured Hotta Masayoshi, the head of the Bakufu's council, on the state of the world, the development of modern industry, the threat of Britain, and the advantages of trading with America. In his own words, he tried to teach the Japanese 'the elements of political economy'. In the end Harris got almost all he had wanted: a resident minister in Edo, substantial custom duties for the majority of imports (a regulated tariff), and the right of Americans in Japan to be tried by an American consular court and not to be subject to Japanese law (extraterritoriality). It was the Chinese model treaty with the opium clause left out, likely to 'draw Japan into the network of economic and political relationships the West had established in its dealing with China'.[5] Hotta prepared a memorandum for the benefit of the Bakufu officials, stressing the need for 'friendly alliances', for sending ships to foreign countries to 'copy the foreigners where they are at their best' and strengthen Japan's armaments, and 'gradually to subject the foreigners to our influence until in the end . . . our hegemony is acknowledged throughout the globe'.[6]

Hotta's arguments were couched in the rhetoric of the tradition of the scholars of Dutch Studies such as Honda Toshiaki or Sakuma Shozan, a samurai of the Matsushiro han and a Confucian scholar. Shozan had turned to Dutch Studies, especially gunnery, after the Opium War. In 1842 he wrote a letter addressed to the lord of his han in which he said the British, who had proved their 'violent extravagance and wickedness' in that war, were known for 'their long-cherished desire to conquer Japan'. The urgent task for Japan, therefore, was to manufacture a large number of firearms and procure warships (he recommended the purchase of twenty

---

[5] Beasley, *The Meiji Restoration*, 108; 'Japan was incorporated into the treaty port system' of informal empires, Beasley, *Japanese Imperialism* (Oxford, 1987), 14.
[6] Quoted Beasley, *The Meiji Restoration*, 107.

such ships from the Dutch).[7] In 1858, when the imperial court withheld its sanction for the ratification of the commercial treaty with the United States, Shozan on behalf of his han wrote a letter addressed to the Bakufu, stigmatizing Harris's propositions as 'a plot to hamper the Bakufu, with the trading ports opened and ministers stationed in the vital points in the country, and to make Japan all but a US dependency'. What the American minister had said about 'friendship', he went on, was nothing but deception and threat. Hence, Japan should send an envoy to the American capital to discuss the matter with their officials so as 'to convince them that it would not be wise to make light of us', while strengthening national power and arms with large, powerful ships.[8] Shozan was then under house-arrest for the crime of having encouraged another scholar (Yoshida Shoin) to try to smuggle himself out to America in one of Perry's ships.

Shozan's 'Middle Kingdom' bias inherent in his Confucian background was absorbed into a concept of the struggle of powers for supremacy, an idea particularly congenial to the samurai tradition. He did not associate western civilization with Christianity, but rather with science and technology typified, as he said, in the 'three great discoveries' by Columbus, Copernicus, and Newton.[9] Shozan contributed to the spread of Dutch Studies among the samurai and counted among his disciples Katsu Kaishu, Yoshida Shoin, and Sakamoto Ryoma, all active in *bakumatsu* (end of the Bakufu) Japan, as well as some of the men of the Meiji enlightenment such as Kato Hiroyuki, Tsuda Mamichi, and Nishimura Shigeki. In 1862 Shozan was freed from his life of confinement at Sanada, went up to Kyoto to help the Bakufu, propagating the idea of opening the country for a stronger Japan, and met his death at the hands of a *joi* assassin in 1864.

THE STRUGGLE OVER THE COMMERCIAL TREATIES

Hotta, like Abe in 1853, sounded the views of the lords on the matter of an American commercial treaty: he found their views still critically divided, in spite of a growing recognition among them of the inevitability of foreign trade and diplomatic relations. He proposed a delay in signing the treaty with the United States, then went to Kyoto in the hope of obtaining imperial approval. The reigning Emperor Komei, who is said to have stuck boldly and stubbornly to the policy of *sakoku* and *joi*, ordered seven major shrines and seven large temples to pray for the safety of 'the Gods' Islands'. The politically inexperienced court nobles were prone to traditional xenophobia, and the emperor went so far as to suggest that he

---

[7] *Nihon Shiso Taikei* (Major Works in Japanese Thought), lv. 262–7.   [8] Ibid. 291–6.
[9] Shozan to Yanagawa Seigan, 6 Mar. 1858, ibid. 376–8; Michiari Uete, 'Confucianism, Martial Spirit and Western Studies in Sakuma Shozan', ibid. 670.

would prefer war to the signing of the treaty. A revised draft that would recognize the Bakufu's ultimate responsibility in the matter was rejected at a meeting of about eighty low-ranking *kuge* (court nobles). Hotta, before leaving Kyoto, nevertheless reached an agreement with some of the top court officials that, in the event of a crisis, he would sign the treaty regardless of the imperial order. What the court achieved by its intransigence was not a reappraisal and revision of the Bakufu's policy but the downfall of Hotta, who was replaced in his job as *Tairo* (Great Counsellor) by Ii Naosuke, who had come to the same conclusion but with greater force: 'Better', Ii said, 'to act against the emperor's wishes than to fight a losing war.' State policy, he was convinced, 'is the responsibility of the Bakufu'.[10] The treaty was therefore signed in July 1858, followed by those with Britain, Holland, Russia, and France. These were 'unequal' treaties; the year 1858 marked the beginning of Japan's real struggle with the West and heralded a political conflict at home that, in appearance, had 'many of the hallmarks of revolution'.[11]

THE ANSEI PURGE (1858–1899) AND ITS AFTERMATH

The unequal treaties at once restrained and provoked Japanese politics for years to come. A vague consensus had emerged among the great daimyo who recognized the need for opening the country and learning western technology for the sake of a stronger Japan, as advocated by Sakuma Shozan, and it appeared not too unreasonable to expect that the initiatives taken by the 'reforming lords' might usher in a modern, reformed Japan without a great upheaval. Yet the Tokugawa devices for self-preservation that were built into its system, once centrifugal forces gained momentum, created discord and frictions serious enough to entail the collapse of the system itself. A decade of civil strife had begun.

With a few exceptions, the 'reforming lords' were found largely in western Japan: Shimazu Nariakira of Satsuma, Yamanouchi Yodo of Tosa, Nabeshima Naomasa of Hizen, Moori Yoshichika of Choshu, Matsudaira Shungaku of Echizen, and Tokugawa Nariaki of Mit; the last two, though related to the Tokugawa family, being independent in their approach to Tokugawa politics. They admired western technology, especially in firearms and shipbuilding that might prove useful in maintaining or modifying the bakuhan system in a stronger Japan or a more vigorous han. The number of domain schools teaching 'Western' subjects has been estimated at as many as sixty at the time of the Restoration.[12] Shimazu Nariakira above all was an innovator: he took to photography using an imported camera, had a telegraph service fitted between the gate and the tower in his castle at Kagoshima, and had gaslight installed in its garden. His factory, producing various articles from cannon to agricultural implements, employed as many as 1,200 workers at the time of his death in 1858.

Politically, the 'reforming lords' were groping their way towards some sort of rapprochement between the warriors in power and the imperial court through a regenerated Bakufu leadership and united action of the great daimyo. Shimazu Nariakira shared political visions of this sort with Tokugawa Nariaki of Mito, where a Japanized Confucianism, as we have seen, was inculcated as the Mito ideology. These 'reforming lords' for a while formed an alliance with *fudai* councillors of the Bakufu, especially 'liberals' such as Abe Masahiro and Hotta Masayoshi, but the manner in which the commercial treaties were concluded exacerbated their relationship as it annoyed Sakuma Shozan, and the critical issue of the Shogunate succession put an end to the alliance itself. As to the latter issue, the great lords favoured Hitotsubashi Keiki or Yoshinobu, the seventh son of Nariaki of Mito, reputed to be a young man of excellent qualities, as the possible heir of the ailing and childless thirteenth shogun Iesada. Iesada died in July 1858. But the Bakufu officials, who clung to their own privileged position as much as they valued the blood relations of the Shogunate, had things their own way and the 11-year-old heir of the Kii han succeeded Iesada as the fourteenth shogun, Tokugawa Iemochi.

Ii Naosuke, formerly the *fudai* lord of the Hikone han, now the Bakufu's *Tairo* (Great Counsellor), was criticized for his high-handed action over the Shogunate succession as well as for the signing of the American treaty. Some of the great lords had refused to attend the meeting summoned by the Bakufu to explain the reasons for its acceptance of the treaty. Ii's counter-offensive put Nariaki of Mito under house-arrest. The imperial court for its part issued an edict castigating the Bakufu for signing the treaty without imperial sanction and requesting 'group discussions and decisions' by the lords on this issue, a new development which suggested an alternative method of decision-making to overcome the Bakufu's dictatorial position.

Kyoto had become the centre of opposition to 'the Bakufu dictatorship': the samurai activists had come from various han to exercise pressure on the court nobles and their retainers; the Bakufu's suppression of these activists began in Kyoto and spread to Edo. Altogether sixty-nine people were punished with varying degrees of severity. The victims of the Ansei Purge, as it was called, included twenty court nobles and their retainers; nine Bakufu officials, twenty han samurai, of whom seven (including Yoshida Shoin) were executed; three Confucian scholars; two Shintoist priests; and thirteen farmers and merchants.[13] Ii Naosuke in some way

---

[13] Yoshio Yasumaru, '1860–70 Nendai no Nihon' (Japan in the 1860s and 70s), *Tsushi*, xvi. 14; the number of victims amounted to nearly 100, Shigeki Toyama, *Meiji Ishin* (The Meiji Restoration) (Tokyo, 1st edn. 1951; rev. edn. 1972), 100–1.

personified the political stance of the small vassal lords who controlled Tokugawa policy through the Bakufu council, and he was known as an advocate of the open-door policy; he was in fact in favour of a revival of foreign trade by vessels authorized by the Bakufu and of the creation of a strong Bakufu navy, believing that such a policy would enable Japan to have recourse at will to *sakoku* measures; he remained a xenophobe at heart.[14]

In May 1859 the Bakufu opened three ports, Kanagawa (Yokohama), Nagasaki, and Hokodate, where Russians, British, French, Dutch, and Americans were allowed to engage freely in trade. Han lords and samurai were allowed to purchase weapons at these ports. In January 1860 the first Japanese mission was sent to America in two parties, led respectively by the foreign minister Shinmi Masaoki and by the naval minister Kimura Yoshitake, to complete the procedure for the ratification of the treaty. Shinmi's party, mostly cautious bureaucrats, crossed the Pacific on board an American frigate and was duly received by President Buchanan at the White House in May 1860. The other party, mostly naval trainees, carried across to San Francisco by the *Kanrin-maru*, a training ship built by the Dutch, in a notable symbolic voyage, included among its volunteer members Fukuzawa Yukichi, who was to become a representative figure of the Meiji enlightenment in due course.[15] While the treaty was being ratified, Ii Naosuke, who had been responsible for the treaty, was attacked and cut down outside the Sakuradamon Gate of Edo Castle by loyalist samurais of Mito and Satsuma (24 March 1860). The Mito samurai whose lord had been humiliated by Ii Naosuke had become radicalized, and this act of revenge was also intended to hasten and enliven the *joi* movement.

THE YEAR 1862: AN ATTEMPT AT *KOBU-GATTAI* AND THE EROSION OF THE *BAKUHAN* SYSTEM

Thereafter there was an attempt at reconciliation of the court and the Bakufu. The Princess Kazunomiya, daughter of Emperor Komei, went to Edo and married the shogun Iemochi in February 1862. Iwakura Tomomi, then a chamberlain serving Emperor Komei, was instrumental in preparing the match, which the princess found 'disagreeable' but accepted 'for the sake of peace in the country'. Iwakura had switched his attitude from one of outright opposition to the treaties to a policy of *kobu-gattai* (the union of the imperial court and the Shogunate). He had advised Komei to approve the marriage on condition that the Bakufu should repudiate the treaties, and the Bakufu officials, knowing the impracticability of the

---

[14] Shigeki Toyama, op. cit., 94.   [15] Beasley, *Japan Encounters the Barbarian*, 56–70.

condition attached, promised that they would disown the treaties 'in seven, eight, or ten years' time from now, 'either by negotiation or by force'.[16]

The reaction to this match strengthened the hawks in the court, who urged the Bakufu to put the rhetoric of *joi* into practice. In May 1862 an imperial delegate, Ohara Shigetomi, one of the hawks, escorted by Shimazu Hisamitsu and 800 well-armed Satsuma samurai, went to Edo as an envoy of Komei, with a view ostensibly to promoting the unity of court and Bakufu, but actually to curb Bakufu policies to suit the court preference for *joi*. More importantly, it was under this court–daimyo joint pressure that Matsudaira Shungaku of Fukui was appointed Supreme Political Counsellor and Hitotsubashi Keiki the shogun's guardian, thus putting an end to the control of the Bakufu's policies by the middle-ranking vassal daimyo (like Ii of Hikone), which had constituted the substance of the Bakufu 'dictatorship'. The Bakufu henceforth was to be exposed to outside influence from the court and from the great han. Shungaku, Keiki, and others agreed on the measures of Bakufu reform, and in August it was announced that the Bakufu would introduce the radically modified system of *sankin kotai* (alternative attendance), according to which the daimyo would only spend 100 days in Edo every three years, wives and heirs could go home freely, and they could economize their journey; in other words, the hostage system and forced profligacy virtually came to an end. More warships were to be bought from abroad, and more men were to be sent abroad for naval training and other studies. It was decreed in July that permission to purchase foreign warships would be given freely to all. Under the same pressure, Yamanouchi Yodo of Tosa, an advocate of *kobu-gattai* and a han federation, who had suffered discomfiture in the Ansei Purge, joined Bakufu deliberations in its inner councils. In November Sanjo Sanetomi, the son of a high-ranking court noble by a daughter of the Tosa lord, escorted by 500 Tosa samurai, entered Edo and handed an imperial instruction over to the shogun, telling him to decide on an expulsion policy, consult the daimyo, and name the date for action. Indeed, by the end of 1862 the Bakufu had succumbed to the court pressure for *joi*. The year 1862 has been called a watershed in the history of the Tokugawa Bakufu, for it was now reduced to the position of a regional power, no longer a truly national institution.[17] The *bakuhan* system that had started under the Bakufu hegemony was coming to an end.

[16] Yasumaru, op. cit., 16; Beasley, *The Meiji Restoration*, 175.
[17] Conrad Totman, *The Collapse of the Tokugawa Bakufu* (Honolulu, 1980), p. xxii.

SHISHI LOYALISTS AND TERRORISM

The activists and terrorists in the 1860s called themselves *Shishi*, 'men of high purpose'. According to Marius Jansen, the *Shishi* was a new type of political leader, the 'courageous patriot who gave his all for the Imperial cause'.[18] Most *Shishi* were *ronin* or samurai of a lower order who had left their han for some reason. The reason was often patriotism, and their patriotism often took the form of terrorism.

Their action began to claim victims as soon as foreign trade officially started in the three designated ports in 1859. In July of that year Russian naval officers and sailors were attacked and some killed by *joi* assassins. In February 1860 a Dutch captain was killed at Yokohama. The murder of an American translation officer followed in the same year. In May 1861 the British legation in the Tozenji Temple at Takanawa, Edo, was attacked, and in the following year a new legation under construction at Shinagawa was burned down. It was during a Shimazu journey from Edo in August 1862 that samurai slew an English merchant from Shanghai named C. L. Richardson who, with a Mrs Borradaile of Hong Kong and two English residents of Yokohama, happened to be riding along the Satsuma procession at Namamugi, north of Yokohama. He was the first victim among the foreign mercantile community, whose agitation was calmed only by the persistent cool counsels of the ministers concerned.

Shishi thus acquired positions of some influence and notoriety. As Beasley remarked, the *Shishi*'s commitment to the idea of *osei-fukko* (restoration of imperial rule) lacked a truly revolutionary awareness. They aspired to go beyond the constrictions imposed by their han only in order to devote themselves to 'a righteous and loyal cause'. When *Shishi* among the han samurai became uncontrollable, they were physically eliminated by order of the han lord, like the Satsuma *Shishi* who had planned an uprising in Kyoto in April 1862. Furthermore, there was no peasant support to speak of for the loyalist movement. There were peasants among the Mito loyalists, but they were usually not so firmly committed to the cause as the low-ranking samurai were.[19] It was not solely for the imperial cause that *Shishi* and *ronin* were mobilized. The Bakufu too found them useful in the sense that they could 'use poison to control poison' in order to protect the shogun from unwarranted attacks at a time when his trek to Kyoto was expected.[20] A group of *ronin* organized by the Bakufu and called *Shinsengumi*, under the leadership of Kondo Isami, became legendary for their daring acts against Satsuma-Choshu 'men of high purpose'.

---

[18] Jansen, *Sakamoto Ryoma*, p. x.
[19] Beasley, *The Meiji Restoration*, 152, 155, 171, 224.   [20] Totman, op. cit., 49.

THE YEAR OF *JOI*: 1863

The Bakufu found it increasingly difficult to manoeuvre through the conflicting claims of the *joi* and the *kaikoku*. Its second mission abroad was sent to Europe in 1862 in order to negotiate for a delay in opening two additional ports, Hyogo (Kobe) and Niigata, and two cities, Edo and Osaka, to foreign trade. It was agreed in London with the British that the delay was to be for five years. This was followed by similar agreements with the Dutch and the French.

In March 1863 Shogun Iemochi arrived in Kyoto, the first shogun to do so for 230 years (the last visit by a shogun being in 1634 by the third shogun Iemitsu, accompanied by a vast army of 300,000 men in a great demonstration of the Bakufu's power). Iemochi now found himself in an unenviable position in the imperial capital, the centre of *sonno-joi* politics. Shogunal authority was confirmed in an imperial statement which also contained instructions that the shogun should take steps to expel the barbarian foreigners. The emperor, accompanied by the shogun and the han lords who were in Kyoto, paid a visit to Kamo Shrine, praying for the success of *joi*. On this matter of *joi* the Bakufu naturally prevaricated, but had to name the day for starting *joi*, 25 June (or 10 May in the Japanese lunar calendar), with an important proviso that the measures to be adopted should be of a defensive nature.

Shortly before the shogun's arrival in Kyoto, relations with Britain had grown critical over the issue of the indemnities to be paid over the Namamugi affair. Shimazu Hisamitsu did come to Kyoto in March, but having submitted a statement denouncing the Bakufu for its weakness in accepting *joi*, an act which he regarded as irresponsible, and recommending the abolition of a newly created imperial force, which he felt was useless, he headed for Satsuma to prepare for the confrontation with the British which his seemingly courageous action had done so much to provoke.[21]

The Bakufu leaders who remained in Edo had received a British ultimatum demanding an apology and an indemnity for the Richardson murder, and threatening to start a bombardment if their demands were not met within three days. The indemnity asked for was heavy, amounting to $440,000 (Mexican silver), roughly a third of the Bakufu's regular annual income. It was already 3 May, and the Bakufu found itself in a quagmire of contradictions between the imperial pressure to start *joi*, the expulsion day having been set one week ahead, and the British ultimatum which was soon to expire. On 8 May two British ships approached Edo, ready to start an offshore bombardment. On the following day arrangements were made to

[21] Ibid. 60.

pay the indemnity, with coins that filled over twenty chests and took three days to count and assay. A note was also handed to the British telling them of the court decision to close the ports, but they and other foreigners warned the Bakufu of the possible calamities that would follow if *joi* measures were carried out. The Bakufu did not press the matter further, and this gave rise to rumours about a Bakufu–foreigner collusion against the great han, Choshu above all,[22] but Satsuma as well. The British, incensed at Satsuma's inability to produce the murderers of Richardson, sent a fleet of seven warships to Kagoshima, where, after a brief period of parleys, shots were exchanged on 2 July 1863. Large parts of the city of Kagoshima, including Shimazu Nariakira's industrial establishment, were destroyed, but the British fleet too suffered damage, had to withdraw for repairs, and eventually moved to Yokohama. In November Satsuma paid an indemnity of $100,000, which finally settled the Namamugi dispute.

In fact, Satsuma was ahead of the Bakufu in dealing with the threats from foreigners. Visits made by French and British ships to Ryukyu in 1844–6 had alarmed Shimazu Nariakira, then the heir to the Satsuma lordship, who looked upon their presence as a matter of critical importance not merely to Satsuma but also to the security of Japan as a whole, and who was given wide discretionary power by the Bakufu *Roju* (Chief Counsellor) Abe Masahiro as to the steps to be taken against possible danger. We have already seen how 'reforming' he was as the lord (since 1851) of a great han. He persuaded the Bakufu to revoke the old decree forbidding the construction of large ships (the decree of 1635 against building ships exceeding 500 koku in capacity, 1 koku being about 10 cubic feet), and at once set about the plan of building of fifteen warships and steamboats. Satsuma's plea, in conjunction with this plan, for the use of a *hinomaru* (red disk) flag for their ships was acceded to by the Bakufu, which on its part enforced it on all Japanese ships in 1854; the Meiji government would adopt it as the national flag in 1870.

The Choshu han alone took the *joi* decision seriously and put it into effect. The seat of the han government was moved from Hagi on the Japan Sea coast to Yamaguchi, surrounded by the mountains. Loyalist leaders such as Takasugi Shinsaku returned to Choshu in order to participate in the first action against foreigners (he had been in Shanghai on a secret han mission). On 10 May, the appointed day, a Choshu fort at Shimonoseki bombarded French and Dutch warships and shelled an American merchant ship. A fortnight later a French ship passing the Shimonoseki Strait was attacked. Foreign retaliation was swift: on 1 June a US warship, in answer to a Choshu bombardment, shelled the forts and sank two gunboats which Choshu had just purchased at Nagasaki. A few days later two French

<hr />

[22] Totman, op. cit., 72–3.

warships shelled the forts again and French troops landed and destroyed the remaining forts. The blow Choshu suffered in these encounters, however, failed to convince the Choshu samurai of the unreality of the *joi* policy. Instead, they were determined to carry out a thorough military reform, and as part of such a reform Takasugi proposed a mixed militia of samurai and peasants. Choshu ignored the Bakufu's order to stop attacking foreign ships, and a Bakufu ship was taken over by the *kiheitai* (assault guard), one of the new military units created by Takasugi. Choshu was almost in a state of rebellion. In spite, or rather because of 'a reign of terror' precipitated by Choshu *Shishi* and samurai in Kyoto, however, the Choshu troops were increasingly isolated in the imperial capital.

Meanwhile terrorism spread to Edo: the *ronin* organized by the Bakufu were gathered together as a precautionary measure against possible war with the British, but when the issue was settled by negotiations and the Bakufu succumbed to the inevitable (Shogun Iemochi returned to Edo by sea in June and issued a direction to start negotiations to close Yokohama, which was rebuffed by the foreigners), the number of victims of wanton attacks increased; Edo merchants, Yokohama merchants, an official of a foreign trade administration, and people related to Ii Naosuke were among them. Suspected arson attacks caused fires to rage in Edo in the early winter, destroying great shops.[23]

LEARNING FROM THE BARBARIANS: *JOI* TRANSMUTED

Next to the Bakufu, which was bound to the western powers by the treaties, it was Choshu, committed almost fully to the cause of *joi*, that sent most young samurai to Europe for study. This took place before the powers' bombardment of the Shimonoseki forts, and could be explained by the example of Yoshida Shoin.[24] Interested in western military science, Shoin harboured the idea of studying abroad. An attempt by him to stowaway on board Perry's flagship failed, and he was arrested by Bakufu officials and imprisoned. He was allowed to open a private school at Hagi, the castle town of Choshu, however, to teach the ethics of loyalist devotion, and there he collected a number of future Meiji leaders (such as Inoue Kaoru and Ito Hirobumi) as his students. Shoin was executed in 1859, having been involved in a plot connected with opposition to Ii Naosuke, and became a hero among patriotic Japanese. In his writings, which were surreptitiously circulated, he advocated a new national leadership loyal to the emperor, and like his mentor Shozan, dreamed of Japan's expansion overseas by making use of western science and technology.

[23] Ibid. 94–6.   [24] Beasley, *Japan Encounters the Barbarian*, 130; on Shoin, ibid. 42–3.

It was Inoue Kaoru who took the initiative late in 1862 for undertaking study in Britain with a view to acquiring knowledge and skills for building a modern navy for Choshu; four other men, including Ito Hirobumi, were to go with him in an illegal overseas journey arranged by a representative at Yokohama of the British firm of Jardine Matheson. They arrived in London in November 1863, the year of *joi*, but a series of visits to museums, dockyards, and factories were all Inoue and Ito could manage in the way of learning before they hurried home in the early summer of 1864 in a vain effort to mediate between Choshu and the foreigners.

Satsuma in some way remained more independent than Choshu from the central government of Japan, whether that of the imperial court or the Bakufu. Economically it had benefited from the Ryukyu trade since the early seventeenth century and also from the 'inter-han' trade of selling imported Nagasaki commodities to other han and exporting the latter's specialities. Satsuma's trade policy was in marked contrast with the Bakufu's effort to monopolize foreign trade.[25] Satsuma was more willing than the Bakufu to participate in the Paris Exhibition of 1867 and was allowed to display its exhibits, including products from Ryukyu, separately from those of the Bakufu and Hizen, the only other han that took part.[26]

Satsuma was also prominent in sending students to Europe. The initiative was taken by Godai Tomoatsu, the future head of the Osaka Chamber of Commerce, who had been to Shanghai as a seaman to investigate the prospect of trade, had allowed himself to be taken prisoner at the time of the British bombardment of Kagoshima, and had formed a friendship with Thomas Glover who had set up a trading company at Nagasaki in 1861. He produced a 'report' to the han lord in 1864 in which he proposed to promote trade through Shanghai and to send han students abroad. The latter proposal was at once acted upon. Altogether fifteen students were selected, of whom twelve (including Mori Arinori, a future minister of education) came from the Kaiseisho school, a han school devoted to 'enriching the han and strengthening han arms' by learning from the West; Godai and Terashima Munenori (then known as Matsuki Koan), professor of the han school, who had been to Europe in the Bakufu's diplomatic mission of 1862, were to act as the guardians and mentors of the students. Since overseas travel was illegal until April 1866, great secrecy was enforced.[27] In London the young Satsuma samurai began attending University College as non-matriculated students, while Terajima, through the MP Lawrence Oliphant, a friend of Thomas Glover's and traveller and mystic, made a plea to the British Foreign Office for trade

---

[25] Shinya Sugiyama, *Meiji Ishin to Igirisu Shonin* (The Meiji Restoration and a British Merchant) (Tokyo, 1993), 120.   [26] Beasley, *Japan Encounters the Barbarian*, 114.
[27] For Satsuma students, see Beasley, *Japan Encounters the Barbarian*, 132–5; Sugiyama, op. cit., 123–5; and also consult Ivan Parker Hall, *Mori Arinori* (Cambridge, Mass., 1973).

with the han in spite of the Bakufu's foreign trade monopoly, and this with a view to forming a federation of the great han allied with the imperial court. Godai managed to purchase and send home 2,762 guns and other weapons, as well as machinery, including some for spinning which were to be used at the first modern spinning-mill in Japan, built at Kagoshima in 1867.

Mori, on his visit to Paris, met several Japanese students sent by the Bakufu such as Nishi Amane and Tsuda Mamichi, both on their way home from Holland. The Bakufu had turned to the Dutch for naval training, and sent a party of naval officers and engineers to Holland to learn skills in handling the warships it had ordered through a Dutch trading company. The first party of Bakufu students left Nagasaki towards the end of 1862, consisting mainly of graduates from the Nagasaki Naval School, including Enomoto Takeaki who was to lead the Bakufu navy in the restoration civil war and two members of the *Bansho Shirabesho* (the Bakufu's Institute for the Study of Foreign Books), Nishi and Tsuda, who went to Leiden to study political economy. One of the prominent Bakufu students sent later was Nakamura Masanao, a Confucian scholar who volunteered to go to England to pursue the study of ethics, politics, and law, subjects so far neglected by Japanese students.

After the middle of 1866, when freedom of travel was officially allowed, more han sent students abroad, and the United States became the most favoured place of study because of its cost and accessibility. In spite of the increasing interest in and the expanding contacts with the West, however, the cause of *joi* proved hard to eradicate, with Choshu, formerly the champion of that cause, remaining the centre of discord.

THE CHOSHU WARS (1864–1866)

Choshu, consisting of the two provinces, Nagato and Suwo, forming the western end of Honshu (the mainland), had once (before the Battle of Sekigahara) enjoyed a much larger territory, formerly under the Ouchi family, who patronized Christianity in the sixteenth century, encouraged overseas trade, and were proud of the prosperous Suwo capital Yamaguchi, known as Little Kyoto. The Moori family who replaced Ouchi sought to consolidate the much-reduced (after Sekigahara) yet still large domain and strengthened its ties with Kyoto rather than Edo, especially through marriage bonds with the imperial court.

A palace *coup d'état* in August 1863 placed the *kobu-gattai* nobles in power; Sanjo Sanetomi and six other loyalist nobles fled to Choshu, and the Satsuma and Aizu troops (Matsudaira Katamori, the lord of Aizu, had been in charge of the Kyoto guards) guarded the nine gates to the Imperial Palace to ward off the Choshu troops, who, outmanoeuvred and outnumbered, had to withdraw. When in April 1864 the court for the second time issued an edict entrusting the Bakufu with the affairs of the land, the leaders of Choshu felt it was impossible to regain its former position by peaceful means. Han troops were sent to Kyoto, appealing to the court to acknowledge Choshu's innocence and take necessary steps to expel the foreigners. Their troops were not allowed to enter the city, but their forces had grown in strength, joined by the 'imperial troops' formed by *ronin*. Opinion in other han was divided on the merit of the Choshu action. In desperation the Choshu troops began an attack on the city in July which was repulsed (the skirmish that took place was to be known as *Kinmon no Hem*, the 'Disturbance at the Forbidden Gate'. The damage caused by this act was immense; fires raged for two days, destroying more than 28,000 houses, including several mansions of court nobles and daimyo, temples, and government offices. The court gave Tokugawa Keiki an imperial order to punish Choshu for its assault on the imperial dignity.[28]

Before the punitive action was seriously contemplated, Choshu also found itself in trouble with foreign powers threatening to punish it for its attacks on foreign ships in the year of *joi*. In January 1864 the British minister Sir Rutherford Alcock returned to Yokohama from a visit to England, empowered to take any necessary military action. The United States, Holland, and later France agreed to a joint action against Choshu, which remained the only han firmly committed to *joi* action. As we have already noted, Ito Hirobumi and Inoue Kaoru, who were then in England, hurried home, met Alcock, and asked him to delay action while they would try their best to convince Choshu of the folly of its *joi* policy, but the han government was as zealously committed as ever. The combined fleet of the four western nations, a seventeen-ship armada, began bombarding the Choshu forts on 5 August 1864; by the following day they were completely demolished and the Choshu troops guarding them had been defeated by the landing forces. A peace mission headed by Takasugi Shinsaku was sent, Ito and Inoue acting as interpreters; a peace treaty was signed on 14 August, according to which Choshu would provide necessary provisions for foreign ships, would refrain from building new fortifications along the Shimonoseki strait and would pay an indemnity. This treaty brought the *joi* movement in Choshu to an end. The Choshu samurai had to change the target of their attack from the foreigners to the Bakufu. The *tobaku* (overthrow the Bakufu) movement[29] was given legitimacy as a new stage in the transmutation of nationalism, *sonno*.

The court-sponsored punitive campaign against Choshu was delayed

---

[28] Totman, op. cit., 177.
[29] Albert M. Craig, *Choshu in the Meiji Restoration* (Cambridge, Mass., 1961, 1978), 235.

and then badly carried out. First there was the moral issue of whether such a campaign should be started when Choshu had been bombarded by foreign powers. Then there were the problems of leadership and of funds and provisioning. Saigo Takamori of Satsuma, the adviser to the leadership of the expedition, gradually changed his views as he realized the absurdity of an internal war when Japan was faced with foreign threats.[30] Tokugawa Yoshikatsu of Owari, the chief of the expeditionary forces, only reluctantly moved from Nagoya to Kyoto, and then on to the advance headquarters at Hiroshima, where he implemented 'an unexpectedly lenient policy toward Choshu'.[31] Yet, from a domain civil war that engulfed Choshu after a series of humiliating events, there emerged trimumphant a radical pro-court faction.

This induced the Bakufu, or rather its Edo officials led by *fudai* councillors, to attempt another punitive campaign against Choshu. In May 1865 the 19-year-old shogun Iemochi left Edo to direct the campaign from Osaka. The court was uncooperative and Choshu remained defiant. The foreigners demanding the opening of Hyogo (Kobe) sent a fleet to Osaka Bay. When a court-sponsored meeting of samurai argued in favour of the approval of the treaties, the court at last consented. This was in October 1865. The question of punishing Choshu again came to the fore. In November a Bakufu mission arrived in Hiroshima to meet Choshu representatives, who were questioned about the fighting within Choshu, contacts with foreigners, and the purchase of firearms from them. In December the Bakufu mission returned to Osaka to report that Choshu submission was a mere pretence and that the Bakufu should quickly subjugate the han, which was preparing for war. Yet the vagueness of purpose of the second expedition failed to elicit co-operation from other han. In June 1866 the Bakufu army in this second expedition began an attack on Choshu, which was by this time allied with Satsuma. War against Choshu was fought by the Bakufu troops and the troops of the han allied with it on four fronts, east, south-east, west, and north of the province. A Bakufu senior councillor, however, felt that they could not win the war, because Choshu had the backing of Satsuma and Great Britain.[32] In fact, the Bakufu troops were defeated on all four fronts, and this defeat, at the hands of a single han, 'made clear to all that the Bakufu hegemony was ended.'[33] The scene was now set for the final drama of the collapse of the Tokugawa regime and the beginning of the great political change known as the Meiji Restoration.

[30] Ibid. 239.   [31] Totman, op. cit., 136.   [32] Craig, op. cit., 330.
[33] Ibid. 333.

3

The Meiji 'Restoration'

Modern Japanese history is sometimes said to have begun in 1868, with a civil war and its aftermath which settled the long-drawn-out conflict between the two rival power bases, and with it placed the country squarely on the track of modernization and westernization. What the Satsuma and Choshu samurai and the scheming court nobles achieved in the years 1867–8, however, was nothing more than an imperial restoration. The Five-Article Charter Oath produced in that process, in spite of its democratic content, was adopted and announced in the context of the revival of the 'Imperial Way' or 'Ancient Way'. Moreover, it was not exactly the revival of the Ancient Way that was now accomplished. Those who had looked forward to its restoration felt betrayed. This was well illustrated by the tragic death of a stationmaster at Magome on the Tosando Highway, the hero of a historical novel by Shimazaki Toson, *Before the Dawn*, modelled after his own father, a devoted follower of Hirata Atsutane. With the downfall of the Edo Bakufu, the stationmaster had anticipated the return of the emperor's benevolent rule over the people, but he was driven to despair and insanity when the bureaucracy inherited from the Tokugawa era and strengthened by the new men in power finally quashed his modest hopes of preserving part of a forest for the use of the people. The new men in power were able people; they now launched an overhaul of the ancient regime and introduced a series of reforms, sometimes in the form of a *coup d'état* or *pronunciamiento*, sometimes with revolutionary effect, in order to build up a new state for themselves and for the nation to be united under the emperor. The popular appellation generally used to describe the changes to be expected from the political upheaval was *go-isshin*, which meant 'renovation' along with the honorific *go* that would make it one 'from above'. These Meiji reforms 'from above', together with the preceding imperial restoration, would constitute the Meiji Restoration, though the term itself is a misnomer.

THE PROGRESS OF THE ANTI-BAKUFU MOVEMENT (*TOBAKU*)

The imperial restoration began with the destruction of the Tokugawa Bakufu, a *coup d'état* accomplished by a civil war. An anti-Bakufu movement had gained momentum; a member of a wealthy *goshi* (gentry) merchant family in Tosa, Sakamoto Ryoma, played an important role in this. He excelled in swordmanship, the practice of which he pursued in an Edo fencing school, one of many such schools which became centres of anti-foreigner enthusiasts. When in 1863 the Tosa Loyalist Party was formed 'to reactivate the Japanese Spirit' and to 'go through fire and water to ease the emperor's mind', the name of Sakamoto was found among 192 names signed in blood.[1] The Tosa *Shishi* like Ryoma joined hands with extremists from Choshu and some from Satsuma, while the Lord of Tosa, Yamanouchi Yodo, exerted a moderating influence by suppressing the extreme loyalists.

Ryoma planned to assassinate Katsu Kaishu or Rintaro, who had commanded the *Kanrin-maru* during the Bakufu's first mission to America and was a prominent advocate of opening up the country. He gained access to him in December 1862, but Katsu converted Ryoma to his view that the opening of Japan would help strengthen the country and that the adoption of western techniques would enhance national power and greatness. In 1864 Ryoma moved to Satsuma, where he began a shipping and trading company based in Nagasaki which later developed into the *Kaientai* (Unit for Maritime Aid), a trading company engaged extensively in the purchase and transport of weapons and ammunitions for the anti-Bakufu cause. He managed to bring about co-operation between the two great han, Satsuma and Choshu, and helped Ito Hirobumi and Inoue Kaoru of Choshu to buy 7,000 rifles in Nagasaki from Thomas Glover. Choshu, with the help of Satsuma, also bought a steamship from the same source. The Satsuma–Choshu agreement which Ryoma helped to create was to prevent the Bakufu from crushing Choshu politically, and this contributed to the Bakufu losing national leadership.

Russia, faced by its own problems of reform after the emancipation of serfs, and America, preoccupied with the after-effects of the Civil War, kept aloof from the struggle between the Bakufu and its opponents in the 1860s. It was Britain and France, both with considerable stakes in the Far East, that watched the progress of the anti-Bakufu movement with some concern. Ernest Satow, a young British diplomat, in articles in the *Japan Times* in 1866 showed himself to be in favour of a federation of han under the emperor, which had become the broad aim of the anti-Bakufu movement. In fact, he advocated 'a more comprehensive and satisfactory [treaty than the existing one with the Bakufu]—a fair and equitable Convention with the MIKADO and the Confederate Daimios—the real rulers of Japan'.[2] British policies towards Japan, however, consisted of

---

[1] Jansen, *Sakamoto Ryoma*, 108 f.
[2] *Japan Times*, 19 May 1886, in Grace Fox, *Britain and Japan, 1858–1883* (Oxford, 1969), Appendix II, 575. 'Mikado', literally 'august door to the court', means the emperor of Japan.

two elements: political support for the Bakufu along with criticism of its trade policy; the latter led the British to share common interest with Satsuma and other great han critical of the Bakufu's restrictive policy on trade. In April 1866 the British government decided to take a position of strict neutrality in case of a civil war in Japan, which of course implied a *de facto* recognition of the anti-Bakufu forces. Harry Parkes, who had succeeded Alcock as the British minister in Japan in July 1865, made an official visit to Kagoshima a year later. This had been arranged by Thomas Glover, for whom Satsuma was the largest client for imported ships and who also sold rifles extensively, the Choshu deal under the cloak of Satsuma mentioned above being of great political consequence. His pro-Satsuma stance was now taken over by his government,[3] but not to the extent that Satow, a partisan critic of the shogunate, would have liked to see.[4]

Anglo-French rivalry elsewhere in the world was reproduced in *bakumatsu* Japan. French support for the Bakufu was the result of the four-power attack on Shimonoseki in 1864 in which French contingents played a prominent role. Napoleon III was interested in strengthening the Bakufu against its domestic foes by supplying military aid. Leon Roche, the French minister in Japan since April 1864, helped a pro-French party in the Bakufu; a plan to build a naval shipyard at Yokosuka was launched with French assistance. Roche's own banker in France was instrumental in founding a Far East Import and Export Company to promote Franco-Japanese trade, including the import of Japanese silk and silkworm eggs. Roche's hopes of making Japan for France 'what China is for England',[5] however, were not realized: the Bakufu welcomed aid but not intervention.

Confrontation between the Bakufu and the great han also involved moneyed interests. The Mitsui and other great merchants made cash contributions to the emperor's cause, but they made a practice of contributing to both sides of the conflict. The Mitsui, for instance, 'kept their main stake upon the Bakufu's number until the very end of the Tokugawa regime'.[6] Minomura Rizaemon, the Mitsui's head clerk for many years, was privy to almost all the machinations of both the court and the Bakufu. Through Saigo Takamori, relations between Mitsui and Satsuma were

---

[3] Shinya Sugiyama, *Meiji Ishin to Igirisu Shonin* (The Meiji Restoration and a British Merchant) (Tokyo, 1993), 90, 100, 113–16. For Thomas Glover, see also Alexander McKay, *Scotish Samurai: Thomas Blake Glover 1839–1911* (Edinburgh, 1993).

[4] Gordon Daniels, 'Introduction' to Sir Ernest Satow, *A Diplomat in Japan* (Oxford, 1968), pp. x–xi.

[5] Beasley, *Japan Encounters the Barabrian*, 98. Roche believed that the alternative to the Bakufu was xenophobic feudal anarchy. See Jean-Pierre Lehmann, 'Léon Roche—Diplomat Extraordinary in the Bakumatsu Era', *Modern Asian Studies*, 14: 2 (1980), 303.

[6] John G. Roberts, *Mitsui: Three Centuries of Japanese Business* (New York, 1973; 1991 edn.), 74.

strengthened; Ito Hiurobumi and Inoue Kaoru of Choshu and the court noble Iwakura were among those who frequented Minomura in these years,[7] and Minomura persuaded the Mitsui to support 'the imperial army' in its final showdown with the Bakufu, a crucial decision which earned Mitsui a privileged position as the financial agent of the new government.

A *COUP D'ÉTAT* AND A CIVIL WAR

The *joi* emperor Komei died in 1866 (he is said to have been poisoned by his political opponents).[8] In December of that year Tokugawa Keiki (Yoshinobu) succeeded Shogun Iemochi, who died in Osaka Castle in July 1866. His reform measures seemed to promise a revival of the Bakufu, and he strove to strengthen military resources with the help of the French. Fear now led Satsuma leaders finally to make up their mind to overthrow the Bakufu by force. The death of Komei who had been inclined to *kobu-gattai* (union of the court and the Bakufu) seemed to give Satsuma a free hand. Mutsuhito, the 16-year-old emperor, apparently had no political opinion of his own, and was a weakling who is said to have fainted at the news of the Disturbance at the Forbidden Gate. Iwakura Tomomi, a court noble then closely linked with Satsuma, was a man who embodied the conspiratorial nature of the imperial restoration. In May a secret agreement was reached between the activist samurai of Tosa and those of Satsuma in favour of *tobaku*. There was, however, an important difference between those in Satsuma who sought to overthrow the Bakufu by arms and those who wanted to persuade the shogun to return power peacefully to the emperor. The Tosa-han was the chief promoter of the second alternative, which would have enabled Tokugawa to act as chairman of future daimyo conferences.

On 14 October 1867 Keiki offered to return power to the emperor, the court accepted this, but asked him to remain as shogun until necessary arrangements could be made. This seemed to prove the rightness and success of Tosa tactics.[9] But Satsuma had been preparing a plan to upset the Tosa moves. Satsuma leaders secured the support of Choshu and Aki in

---

[7] Ibid. 74–5.

[8] Ernest Satow wrote on the Mikado's death: 'Rumour attributed his decease to smallpox, but several years afterwards I was assured by a Japanese well acquainted with what went on behind the scenes that he had been poisoned.' Satow, op. cit., 186.

[9] Tosa had a chequered history: defeated at Sekigahara, it was given to Yamanouchi, one of the pro-Tokugawa daimyos, who overcame han opposition through tact, realism, and development policies. Tosa's han government has been described as 'astute and deliberate in its assessment of and participation on the national scene'. Marius B. Jansen, 'Tosa During the Last Century of Tokugawa Rule', in John W. Hall and M. B. Jansen (eds.), *Studies in the Institutional History of Early Modern Japan* (Princeton, 1968, 1970), 345.

a military campaign planned to overthrow the Bakufu, and asked for a secret imperial edict so as to legitimize their action. On the evening of 13 October Satsuma leaders received from Iwakura a secret edict addressed to the Satsuma lord to defeat and overthrow the Bakufu. Probably the prince Nakayama Tadayasu played a role as an intermediary (his daughter Yoshiko, Emperor Komei's favourite concubine, had given birth to a boy, now the emperor, and he had acted as the boy's tutor). The edict itself was neither written by the emperor nor bore the proper signatures or stamps of those who were supposed to have transmitted it. To all appearances it was a dubious document. Yet with this secret decree in hand, Saigo, Okubo, and other Satsuma and Choshu leaders returned to their respective han and prepared for war against the Bakufu. This was indeed 'a veritable *coup d'état*'.[10]

Iwakura Tomomi had conjured up the secret imperial edict, and in December he played a leading role in placing samurai guards at each of the nine gates of the Imperial Palace, inside which was issued the decree for imperial restoration and for a new government to be set up to replace the Bakufu. Later in the same month Saigo Takamori carried out the second stage of the *coup d'état* by inciting trouble in Edo, a fifth-column action which invited an attack on the Satsuma mansion in Edo by Bakufu and pro-Bakufu troops, and provoked the Bakufu leaders in Osaka Castle to move their troops to clear Kyoto of 'the evil subjects of Satsuma'. At the battles at Toba-Fushimi near Kyoto that ensued in January 1868, however, the Satsuma–Choshu troops were victorious, and this enabled the plotters to brand Tokugawa Keiki as guilty of treason.

The end of the Bakufu was soon to come in a civil conflict called the Boshin War (1868–9) that had already begun. Keiki who returned to Edo from Osaka by sea, refused an offer of help from the French, fearing that the confrontation could develop into a full-scale civil war that might invite foreign intervention. In February 1868 he vacated Edo Castle and later in April retired to Mito, his former fief, thus putting an end to the two-and-a-half century rule of the Tokugawa Bakufu. The Aizu samurai, including mere boys, put up a valiant fight against what had by now become an imperial army, but without avail. The last resistance of the Bakufu forces was made by Enomoto Buyo (Takeaki), vice-chief of the Bakufu's navy, but this ended in May 1869 when his Ezo Republic at Hakodate surrendered after a gallant fight.

The Meiji Restoration had thus not been a bloodless revolution. From the battles of Toba-Fushimi to the Hakodate conflict at Goryokaku Castle, where Enomoto held out in a modern fortress, the casualties on the

[10] Shigeki Toyama, *Meiji Ishin* (Meiji Restoration) (Tokyo, 1951, rev. edn. 1972), 191–201; John G. Roberts, op. cit., 75.

government side were estimated at 3,556 dead and 3,804 wounded out of the total strength of 120,000 engaged, while those on the side of the Bakufu and the pro-Bakufu han were 4,707 dead and 1,518 wounded.

It is also difficult to see a revolutionary change in what had happened; it has been pointed out that the change was 'carried out in the name of old values',[11] and the driving power came from feudal elements, especially those of the lower orders, who were awakened by the shock from without. The secret imperial edict, most likely a makeshift document, symbolizes the essence of the restoration, which in the words of a Japanese historian, was a change 'from an old feudal order to a new feudal order',[12] and the creation of 'the emperor system'.[13]

THE CHARTER OATH AND THE IMPERIAL RESTORATION

The Charter Oath, the emperor's oath to his ancestral gods, announced at the height of the civil war against the Bakufu forces, embodied the basic principles of the new government that was to be set up. It was a strange document which at times inspired the nation, and even the imperial family, with rudimentary notions of democracy, yet at other times served as an excuse for aberrations from these same values. Sakamoto Ryoma was one of the small group of people who helped draw it up.

Ryoma had apparently learned something of western political reform from Katsu's friend, an administrator at the Bakufu's Institute for the Study of Western Books, who had once advocated a crude bicameral political system.[14] When he was sailing to Kyoto with Goto Shojiro, a Tosa statesman later active in the Meiji government, Ryoma showed his companion his plan for a new government which contained such items as the establishment of two legislative bodies, an Upper and a Lower House, and the recognition of opinion as the basis of all government measures, a programme which had crucial bearing on the Charter Oath itself.[15] In the event several hands were employed in framing the Oath,[16] of whom the three most directly connected with it, Yuri Kimimasa, Fukuoka Kotei, and Kido Koin, had been associated with Sakamoto Ryoma; Ryoma, though, did not see the completion of the Oath, as he was slain by a *joi* assassin in Kyoto on 15 November 1867.

Yuri Kimimasa, a samurai of the Fukui han who was under the influence of Yokoi Shonan, the reformist adviser to the Fukui lord, was probably the first person who suggested the publication of a statement of the principles of the new government to be set up. His own draft contained all the essential points of the Charter Oath, though it reflected his own predilection

---

[11] Albert M. Craig, *Choshu in the Meiji Restoration* (Cambridge, Mass., 1978), 362.
[12] Toyama, op. cit., 176.   [13] Ibid. 200.   [14] Jansen, *Ryoma*, 168.
[15] Ibid. 295–6.   [16] Beasley, *The Meiji Restoration*, 322–3.

for the common people. He showed his draft to Fukuoka, a samurai of the Tosa han, who revised it to suit the Tosa idea of the federation of han and replaced 'common people' with 'officers, samurai, and common people', and 'samurai and people united' with 'those above and those below united'. Both the Yuri and the Fukuoka drafts assumed that the han lords would make a covenant with the emperor, but the court nobles objected to this idea. Kido Koin (or Takayoshi) of Choshu, agreeing with the court nobles, revised the Fukuoka draft and introduced an idea which would stress the superior power of the imperial regime; Kido's draft resulted in the final version known as the Charter Oath.

On 14 March 1868, one day before the scheduled attack on Edo Castle (which was avoided by an agreement reached between Saigo and Katsu on that very day), the young emperor appeared before the princes, court nobles, daimyo, and other subjects assembled at the Shishinden Hall (the central hall in the court where important ceremonies took place and imperial decrees were read out) in the Kyoto palace: 'he prayed to the gods of Heaven and of the Land and made an oath which was to be widely proclaimed.'[17] It read:

1. An assembly widely convoked shall be established and all matters of state shall be decided by public discussion. 2. All classes high and low shall unite in vigorously promoting the economy and welfare of the nation. 3. All civil and military officials and the common people as well shall be allowed to fulfil their aspirations, so that there may be no discontent among them. 4. Base customs of former times shall be abandoned and all actions shall conform to the principles of international justice. 5. Knowledge shall be sought throughout the world and thus shall be strengthened the foundation of the Imperial polity.[18]

The Charter Oath shows the aspirations of men of high purpose who had gone through the turmoil of the opening of the country. The cause of *sonno* triumphed because nobody had wanted to challenge it when it seemed to provide the only springboard for change. The 'imperial polity' remained as the foundation of all the reforms, of all the efforts towards modernization that had to be made. But the Charter Oath was not a covenant with the people, nor even with the aristocracy, but one between the emperor and the gods. Now the task for the new men in power was to reconcile the old values with the new.

THREE *COUPS D'ÉTAT*

The Meiji 'Restoration', in the sense of an imperial restoration, was only one of three great political changes or *coups d'état* that took place in the

---

[17] Ito Hirobumi Den Hensan Iinkai (ed.), *Ito Hirobumi Den* (Biography of Ito Hirobumi) (Tokyo, 1940), i. 374.   [18] Beasley, *The Meiji Restoration*, 323.

late 1860s and the 1870s,[19] the other two being the replacement of han (clan territories) by ken (prefectures) in 1871; and the virtual expulsion in 1873 of Saigo Takamori of Satsuma from the government, which led to the Seinan (south-western) civil war of 1877 and the downfall of the samurai as a source of power. To these we could add the political change of 1881 which has also been called a *coup d'état*, planned by an inner group of the government, and which paved the way for the Prussian-type constitution 'granted' by the emperor.

Unlike the French Revolution, which was transformed from an aristocratic to a bourgeois and then to a popular revolution before it arrived at its authoritarian stage, the Meiji Restoration constantly upheld *sonno*, even after its linked term, *joi,* had to be dropped, and an authoritarian political structure under the aegis of the emperor was born from the *tobaku* movement led by Satsuma and Choshu samurai. Their movement succeeded in creating on the ruins of the *bakuhan* system a modern state, soon to be called the *hanbatsu* (clan clique) government, dominated by the samurai of the four great han, Satsuma, Choshu, Tosa, and Hizen, and especially of the first two.

THE CREATION OF THE *TENNO* SYSTEM

The *Tennosei* (emperor system) is not an ideological term coined by post-war left-wing historians, though this has been alleged. In fact, emperor worship had been carried on for as long and to such a degree as to justify calling it a system. The substance of what was to be referred to as *Tennosei* can be discerned in the cause of *sonno*, and the resurgence of the mystique of the deified emperor, sometimes referred to as *gyoku* (jewel), which served as justification for the attempt to seize power, began with the imperial restoration of 1867–8. The point to be emphasized in this connection is that the notion of a charismatic emporer emerged in the illusions of the loyalist activists, *shishi*. The *coup d'état* was carried out in order to forestall the possibility of the old system being preserved, with Tokugawa Keiki as the head of a body for public deliberation. After this military coup, 'public deliberation' (a catchword for the reconciliation of the court and the Bakufu) came to be attached to the charismatic authority of the emperor enshrined in the Charter Oath. The young emperor who arrived in Tokyo (the old Edo, renamed in July 1869), spoke of 'the entity of his imperial nation' and expressed his belief in 'honest deliberation'. Iwakura Tomomi maintained that 'public opinion' should be formed through the instrument of the authority of the emperor, who transcended all established beings, and added that 'public deliberation

---

[19] Yoshio Yasumaru in *Nihon Tsushi* (Complete History of Japan), vol. 16 (Tokyo, 1994), 46.

had begun in the age of gods'. In spite of the emphasis placed by the restoration government on 'public deliberation' under the emperor, the process after the imperial restoration was carried out by 'the cabal of the "wicked subjects" of Satsuma–Choshu, especially of Satsuma, and some of the court nobles'.[20]

The Charter Oath, the symbol of the imperial restoration, had a serious defect. It is true, it made allusion in some vague form to democratic ideas, but there was no reference to liberty or freedom, which is by definition in conflict with 'the emperor system'. This is well illustrated by the religious policy of the early Meiji government, and indeed by the *kokutai* ideology to which all governments until 1945 and even beyond tenaciously adhered. Before embarking upon reform measures that would certainly involve closer contact with foreigners, the emperor's government adopted various measures that made Shintoism (shrine Shinto or institutional Shinto) a state religion. Buddhism was divorced from the Shintoist association it had maintained in various forms for many centuries; all the historical links between the imperial family and Buddhism were now severed; and the ban on Christianity was continued. Religious freedom was allowed only to foreigners living in the treaty ports. Even so, the hidden Christians in the Nagasaki area were encouraged by newly arrived Catholic fathers to acknowledge their faith openly, and as a result many of them were arrested and sent to the Takashima coalmines as convicts sentenced to hard labour. This was on the eve of the imperial restoration. In the official gazette of the new government (no. 6), however, a new law against Christianity was found, proclaiming that 'the evil sect called Christian is strictly prohibited'.[21]

The young Okuma Shigenobu, who was then acting as a member of the council of the Governor-general of Kyushu entrusted with the management of foreign affairs there, 'tried all the arts of persuasion to make the converts recant, but with little success'.[22] He was called to attend a conference with foreign ministers at Osaka to explain the government's view that while religious toleration might be feasible in the West, where men's minds were expanding and were not controlled by religion alone, conditions were different in Japan.[23] A mass deportation of Christians took place in 1870. A government mission headed by Iwakura, which was sent to the United States and Europe to prepare for revision of the unequal treaties, was reminded in Washington that it was useless to ask for the desired change in the treaties while the religion believed in by most Americans was treated as it was in Japan. In London, Paris, and Brussels

[20]   Yasumaru, loc. cit., 35.
[21]   Otis Carey, *A History of Christianity in Japan* (1st edn. 1909; 1976 edn.), ii. 26.
[22]   Junesay Idditie, *The Life of Marquis Okuma* (1st edn., 1940; 2nd edn. Tokyo, 1956), 500.
[23]   Otis Carey, op. cit., i. 310–11.

there were movements and agitation to demand the release of the exiled Japanese Christians.[24] One tangible achievement of the Iwakura embassy was to have the Japanese edicts against Christians removed in 1873, and religious freedom was finally incorporated in the Meiji constitution in 1889; but the *kokutai* ideology remained, to restrain and eventually to suppress such freedom.

THE DEMOLITION OF THE OLD REGIME: THE REPLACEMENT OF HAN BY KEN

The second *coup d'état*, of *haihan-chiken* (to abolish han and create ken), was to strengthen the central government by transforming the feudal han into units of a modern local-government system. As early as January 1869 the lords of Satsuma, Choshu, Tosa, and Hizen had offered to return their respective domains to the emperor in the hope, as they stated in a joint memorial, that this would give Japan 'one central body of government'.[25] Most other domains followed suit, though not without misgivings (Lord Shimazu of Satsuma had not been enthusiastic). The decision to abolish the territorial rights of the han lords was announced in an imperial decree issued on 14 July 1871. At the same time all the top offices of the government, which took the form of *dajokansei*, a sort of cabinet system, were occupied by men of the four great western clans (Saigo of Satsuma, Kido Takayoshi of Choshu, Itagaki Taisuke of Tosa, and Okuma Shigenobu of Hizen), and two court nobles, Sanjo Sanetomi and Iwakura Tomomi. The restoration government was now set up as a government of autocracy by high officials (*yushi-sensei seifu*).

The abolition of the old han had been prepared by the Satsuma and Choshu politicians who had staged the first *coup d'état*, with even Saigo, the symbol of samurai solidarity, agreeing to this. Then three fu and 302 ken were created (the three fu were Tokyo, Osaka, and Kyoto, given special title due to historical distinction but equivalent to ken in status); shortly afterwards the number of ken was reduced to seventy-two (Okinawa not included), and in 1888 to forty-three (including Okinawa for the first time), as it is today. Okinawa, the old kingdom of Ryukyu, had maintained a tributary relationship with China even after its conquest by Shimazu early in the seventeenth century. The Meiji government in September 1872 issued an imperial edict to abolish the kingdom and replace it by a Ryukyu han, with its former king as a Japanese peer. It was only in April 1879 that the Ryukyu han was turned into Okinawa ken, a finishing touch in its Japanization to which China duly objected.

---

[24] Ibid. ii. 80–1.
[25] Beasley, 'Meiji Political Institutions', *Cambridge History of Japan*, vol. 5 (1989), 630.

Old han lords, now members of the *kazoku* or aristocracy, and old samurai, now *shizoku*, were assured of state pensions by the new government; han debts, liabilities, and paper notes were also taken care of by the new government. It was not surprising that no serious opposition came from the han to their abolition. After this a new bureaucracy composed especially of those active men from old Satsuma and Choshu came into existence to support the centralized government under the emperor. Decrees were issued in 1871 to ensure freedom of marriage between members of *kazoku*, *shizoku*, and *heimin* (commoners); freedom from traditional customs such as wearing a topknot and carrying two swords; and the abolition of the degrading terms of address *eta* (untouchable) and *hinin* (non-human) applied to the victims of discrimination who were now called *shin-heimin* or new commoners. Early in the 1870s, however, there took place a series of *ikki* (uprisings) protesting against new government policies, involving in one extreme case the setting fire to a discriminated *buraku* (a hamlet, or rather a ghetto) and the massacre of its residents by an excited mob. The adoption of new status names did not alleviate but rather aggravated old prejudices.

THE IWAKURA EMBASSY (1871–1873)

To seek knowledge from all over the world, and especially to learn from the advanced West, one of the major tasks the new government had set itself, became all the more urgent as the deadline for starting negotiations for revision of the unequal treaties (1 July 1872) approached. This would require an effort to reform domestic institutions. Guido Verbeck, a Dutch-American missionary who taught at Nagasaki and counted Okuma Shigenobu, Soejima Taneomi, and Eto Shinpei, all from Hizen, among his students, came to Tokyo to serve the Meiji government as an advisor. He prepared a programme of study for a mission in Europe and America, and Okuma's proposal of himself to lead such a mission was supported by Sanjo Sanetomi, *dajo-daijin* (prime minister), and accepted at a meeting of the ministers; a plan based on Verbeck's programme stated that in order to create a fully independent state agreeable to international law, domestic reform would have to be carried out first, meaning that the negotiations for treaty revision would be delayed for three to five years, and steps would be taken in the meantime to investigate western theories and practices in law, politics, economy, industry, education, social policy, and military matters.

The plan for an Okuma embassy, however, was soon replaced by another as a result of factional opposition led by Okubo and Iwakura, who were anxious to keep the reins of government in the hands of the *Sat-Cho*

(Satsuma–Choshu) group.[26] A large embassy numbering forty-eight people or even more, headed by Iwakura, the minister of the right (vice-prime minister), and supported by four vice-ambassadors including Kido, Okubo, and Ito Hirobumi, left for America on 23 December 1871. Before departure there took place a Shinto ceremony and an audience with the emperor, 'in the manner of envoys going to China many centuries before'.[27] The official party was accompanied by about sixty students who were to remain in various destinations on the way: among them were Tsuda Ume, who was to found the Tsuda Women's College, Kaneko Kentaro who later helped Ito draft the imperial constitution, and Nakae Chomin, later an intellectual leader of the *Jiyu-Minken* (Liberty and People's Right) movement. In the course of the mission's leisurely progress the issue of treaty revision inevitably cropped up, but the Japanese side was not fully prepared and no tangible results ensued. In Britain *The Times* welcomed representatives of the country which it chose to call 'Eastern Britain'.[28] The visitors were impressed by the role that science and technology played in the development of industry and trade, and in the north of Britain they were taken from one industrial city to another and carefully observed cotton- and steel-mills, shipyards, ironworks, potteries, and breweries. Kume Kunitake, Iwakura's secretary and the compiler of a record of the embassy's itinerary, did not fail to point out on his return that European wealth and power only dated from around 1800, implying that progress in Japan should be made at a quicker pace. In Germany the chancellor, Bismarck, personally invited the visitors to dinner and told them that Germany would respect national rights, an attitude which had made a poor Prussia independent and equal to other powers, and that Japan should regard Germany as the most congenial country among her western mentors.[29] The embassy returned to Japan on 13 September 1873 after having visited the United States, Britain, France, Belgium, Holland, Germany, Russia, Denmark, Sweden, Italy, Austria, and Switzerland. Their long sojourn abroad was in fact cut short, the planned visit to Spain and Portugal cancelled, because of a crisis over Korea which had developed in their absence (see below).

LAND TAX REFORM, A MODERN EDUCATION SYSTEM, AND A STANDING ARMY

Shortly before the reurn of the Iwakura embassy the government introduced a land tax reform in July 1873. The peasant was given the freedom

[26] Akira Tanaka, 'Prologue' to Kunitake Kume (ed.), *Tokumei Zenken Taishi Beio-Kairan Jikki* (A Record of the Tour of the Ambassador Plenipotentiary through the United States and Europe), (Iwanami edn. Tokyo, 1977; 1996), i. 399–401.

[27] Beasley, *Japan Encounters the Barbarian*, 165.

[28] *The Times*, 20 Aug. 1972, quoted in ibid. 165.   [29] Kume (ed.), op. cit., iii. 330.

to choose the kind of crops he would cultivate. Privatization of land-ownership was also introduced. The new land tax would depend upon the price of lands, and that would be decided by the government. The land tax reform left the tenancy system untouched. Land-ownership was given to the landlord, not to those tenants who cultivated the land. The government protected the landlord's power to extract rent from his tenants, because the land tax was included in the rent. Roughly speaking, one-third of a tenant's produce went to the government, central and local, as land tax and village charges; another third went to the landlord; and only a third of his own produce remained for the tenant himself.

As for education, already in 1869 the government had set up primary schools for pupils to learn 'national polity, contemporary situations, and the way of loyalty to the emperor and to parents'. The school system introduced by the Education Act of 1872 was modelled after that of centralized French education. The Ministry of Education, which had been set up the previous year, would control universities (eight to be opened in eight university districts) and take charge of the entire school education system, conceived in a hierarchical order down to 53,760 elementary schools planned to cover the whole country. Moreover, education was presented as a system not for the state but for the individual, and accordingly it was the individual who should pay. Even elementary education was not free to begin with. The monthly fees of 50 sen (equivalent to 2 shillings) were hard to bear at a time when an average monthly income was 1 yen 75 sen (or 7 shillings).[30] The first four years in school were compulsory, and the ratio of school attendance was 28 per cent in 1872, 40 per cent in 1878. Early textbooks were often translations from foreign works. Many details stipulated in the Act were so impractical and unpopular that it was replaced in 1879 by a liberal education decree based on an American model, which depended a great deal on initiatives from local government, resulting in a marked decline in the number of pupils attending school. In the following year (1880) radical revision was made to the education decree so as to tighten government control of schools. The spirit of *sonno aikoku* (revere the emporer, love your country) and the myth of the sacred origins of Japan were to be inculcated in history courses. A new education decree of 1886 made primary education obligatory, but it was only in 1899 that state subsidies made primary education free for the first time; six years' free, compulsory primary education was introduced in 1907.

As for the standing army, the major pillar of *fukoku kyohei* (enrich the nation, strengthen arms), there had been differences of opinion between those Choshu leaders such as Omura Masujiro and Kido Koin who were in

---

[30] One pound sterling was five yen 'of our new currency'. Kume (ed.), op. cit., i. 21.

favour of a peasant army and conscription, and those of the Satsuma faction like Okubo Toshimichi who advocated a force composed of picked soldiers from the old Satsuma, Choshu, and Tosa han. Certainly the government would not be satisfied with an army capable only of suppressing domestic disturbances, but wanted one that was strong enough to cope with threats from foreign powers. A *shizoku* army was ruled out. Yamagata Aritomo, formerly the commander-in-chief of the *kiheitai*, the Choshu's revolutionary army, then the army minister, won over to the latter view Saigo Takamori and others who had expressed misgivings about an army of peasants and tradesmen.

In December 1872 an edict for national conscription was issued, stating that ancient Japan had been an armed nation and that the separation of the peasant and the warrior was a mistake. It emphasized that an attempt to prevent national disasters was a defensive act. In the West conscription was often metaphorically called a 'blood tax', an unfortunate term which, transmitted to Japan, caused fears and confusion among those who took it literally. The idea of a conscript army may have derived from the recommendations of Nishi Amane, who had studied the European military system. At any rate, a standing army was created, but it lacked the spirit required for defending a nation-state. All government officers were exempted from the service, as were students studying at a high school; members of the wealthy classes could also be exempted from conscription by substituting a money charge (270 yen), and concessions were made so that a family would not be endangered by paying undue 'blood tax'. In fact, conscription amounted to a sort of *corvée* imposed upon the proletariat.

THE KOREAN ISSUE, THE KANGHWA TREATY, AND THE SEINAN CIVIL WAR

Now a larger issue involving the new national army and the old samurai emerged. The refusal by the Koreans to recognize the new Meiji government annoyed its leaders. The Japanese lord of Tsushima, islands halfway between the two countries, had been instrumental in the exchange of missions and the continuation of a limited trade in the years of *sakoku*. Now Korea frankly admitted that she was a 'dependent country' subservient to China and would call only the Chinese ruler 'emperor', whereas the Japanese ruler would be called 'great king'. It also transpired during the negotiations that Tsushima too, while receiving a stipend of rice and money from Tokugawa, had accepted a dependent-country relationship with Korea which also brought rice and money to the islands.[31] To make

[31] Hilary Conroy, *The Japanese Seizure of Korea: 1868–1910* (Philadelphia, 1960), 24–5.

matters worse, insulting inscriptions appeared on the walls of a small Japanese settlement in Pusan.

Seikanron, an anti-Korean or 'Punishing Korea Proposal', gained the upper hand in the government council at a time when the Iwakura embassy was still touring in Europe. The war party which took this proposal seriously consisted of Itagaki Taisuke and Goto Shojiro of Tosa, and Eto Shinpei and Soejima Taneomi of Hizen. Saigo was 'vigorous yet curiously fatalistic' in his support; he wished to turn the tide of modernization if he could, for he was most sensitive to the grievances of disaffected former samurai over the loss of their erstwhile privileged status and financial security. When forty-four shipwrecked seamen from Ryukyu were killed by Formosan tribesmen in November 1871, Saigo urged a punitive expedition and Soejima, acting as the minister of foreign affairs, agreed. Before this was carried out, *seikanron* itself had become a major issue of national policy.

In the summer of 1873 a conference of the council of state agreed that army marshall Saigo Takamori was to head a mission to Korea, but one which was unarmed. Saigo was prepared to die, and his death might lead to a war of revenge by former samurai, many of them unemployed, but he may simply have intended to seek a solution by diplomatic means before resorting to military action.[32] The return of the Iwakura embassy at about the same time, however, frustrated the strategy of the war party. Okubo, an old childhood friend of Saigo, was opposed to him on the council, and Iwakura as its acting president remained adamant in his opposition to Saigo's plan. The war party, Saigo, and his allies (Itagaki, Eto, Goto, and Soejima) resigned from the council: *seikanron* was defeated.

Okubo, in a document summing up his reasons for opposition, stated that revision of the unequal treaties should come before the Korean business which, given Japan's internal division, might provoke foreign intervention.[33] He strengthened his hand by setting up the Ministry of Home Affairs in November 1873, while Eto, who had returned to Saga (Hizen), formed a 'United *Seikan* Party', hoping for the co-operation of Itagaki and Saigo. Without their help Eto proclaimed an open rebellion in February 1874, which was easily suppressed by Okubo and his government forces. Eto had disapproved of the concentration of government power in the hands of former Satsuma and Choshu samurai and of the corruption resulting from their connections with great merchants, such as the close (possibly scandalous) financial links Inoue Kaoru, vice-minister of the treasury, formed with the Mitsui: destroy the Satcho hegemony, and a people's government would emerge. This was the sort of reasoning Okubo

---

[32] Charles L. Yates, *Saigo Takamori: The Man behind the Myth* (London, 1995), 153–4.
[33] Conroy, op. cit., 47.

had been afraid of. The Satcho hegemony, that had been weakened by the dispatch of the Iwakura embassy, was restored to its former strength. The rebels were to be crushed, and Eto was hunted down as a criminal, arrested in Tosa, and beheaded in April.

In the same month the government took up the dormant issue of a Formosan punitive expedition, which was successfully carried out under the command of Saigo Tsugumichi, Takamori's younger brother, in the summer and autumn of 1874—a limited campaign employing 3,600 soldiers, which, through Okubo's diplomatic activities in Peking, brought in a substantial sum in compensation. The annexation of the Ryukyu kingdom in 1872 had restrospectively made the massacred Ryukyu seamen Japanese citizens and seemingly strengthened the *casus belli*. As the war party was either destroyed or was made to learn hard lessons, and as the Formosan expedition proved successful, so the government oligarchy led by Okubo became all-the-more belligerent. In the summer of 1875 the government sent three ships in great secrecy to Korean waters; they moved up to Inchon, and near the offshore island of Kanghwa there was an exchange of fire between the ships and the Korean shore battery. About thirty Koreans were killed and the battery was silenced. The whole affair (known as the Kanghwa Incident of September 1875) may well be thought justifiable in terms of western international practice. The government, obviously with Perry's 'black ships' in mind, sent a mission headed by Lt.-General Kuroda Kiyotaka of Satsuma and Inoue Kaoru to Korea early in the following year: the outcome was the Kanghwa Treaty concluded on 26 February 1876 for the inauguration of diplomatic relations between Korea and Japan, with three ports opened in Korea; in the English text of the treaty Korea was referred to as an 'independent' nation, though as 'self-governing' in the Chinese text.[34] The Confucian concept of international order still persisted in the minds of East Asian leaders, while Japan had begun asserting herself in more western terms. The *Sat-Cho* government thus restored and made respectable the *seikanron* which it had defeated less than three years before. It was a prescient measure. 'Exit Asia, Enter Europe', a slogan that would later become famous, had been carried into practice a decade before it was first used.

Back in Kagoshima, Saigo had started the *Shigakko* (private school) to teach ethics and military science to the would-be young samurai; the *Shigakko* had twelve branch schools in the castle town, and 124 in other parts of Satsuma where the old tradition of local autonomy and initiative was kept alive in the face of the policies of centralized modernization pursued by the Meiji government, so that Kagoshima (or Satsuma) seemed almost to have become an independent country. In the wake of a succession

[34] Ibid. 65.

of abortive uprisings of disaffected *shizoku* at Kumamoto, Akitsuki, and Hagi in October 1876, the government sought to remove the contents of the arsenals in Kagoshima, a provocation which goaded *Shigakko* pupils into action. In Satsuma it was a case of 'a whole society, a whole way of life . . . fighting desperately for survival', like the Confederate armies in the American Civil War.[35]

In the Satsuma rebellion of 1877 Saigo led an army made up of *Shigakko* pupils and discontented former samurai which numbered 42,000 at its height, and invested the Kumamoto Castle which held out through a fifty-day siege until relieved by government troops from the north. Over 80 per cent of the government force of 58,558 men were conscript soldiers. Saigo and his guards broke through their lines and fortified themselves at Shiroyama, Kagoshima, where Saigo, wounded, committed ritual suicide. The casualties on the government side were 15,801: 6,278 dead and 9,523 wounded. Those on Saigo's side were said to have exceeded 20,000. Those executed or imprisoned after the war amounted to 2,764. The fact that an army of conscripts had defeated the picked forces of Satsuma samurai was an eloquent demonstration of the exit of the samurai from the scene of history. The assassination of Okubo by a group of disaffected former samurai from other parts of the country, which took place at Kioizaka, Tokyo, less than eight months after Saigo's death, could be regarded as one of the final actions of the Seinan civil war. With the defeat of this last challenge from expiring feudalism, with its centrifugal tendencies and moral tone, it could be said that a political revolution had been completed and the country at last united.[36]

GOVERNMENT SPONSORSHIP OF INDUSTRIALIZATION

Plans and measures for *fukoku kyohei* (enrich the nation, strengthen arms) were in full swing. 'Knowledge was sought throughout the world', especially from the West. The Meiji government employed a number of foreign experts and technicians to modernize the bureaucracy and to start railways, a telegraph system, and cotton-spinning. Japan's resident ministers at major world capitals were encouraged to find suitable *oyatoi* (specially hired) experts: the service of Professor David Murry of Rutgers was obtained, because of his deep interest in Japanese education; Gustave Émile Boissonade, vice-rector of the University of Paris, became adviser to the Justice Ministry; Herman Roesler of the University of Rostock served as legal adviser to the Foreign Ministry. The number of *oyatoi gaijin* (hired foreigners) for the period 1868–1912 has been estimated

[35] Charles L. Yates, op. cit., 168.
[36] G. C. Allen, *A Short Economic History of Modern Japan* (4th edn. London, 1981), 33.

roughly at 2,000.[37] In 1875, when the number of foreigners in the service of the central and prefectural governments reached a maximum of 527, 205 of them were technical advisers, 144 teachers, sixty-nine managers and administrators, and thirty-six skilled workmen.[38] The employment of these foreigners were not intended as part of any systematic transfer of technique, but they were mostly engaged in the creation of an infrastructure similar to that in the West. By 1880 they had mostly been replaced by Japanese technicians, some of whom had been sent abroad to study. Of about eighty students sent abroad in the first twenty years or so after the opening of the country, twenty-one studied shipbuilding, seventeen machinery, thirteen construction work, ten mining and smelting, six arsenals, and four chemistry; as for their destinations, twenty-eight were sent to Britain, twenty to the United States, fourteen to France, nine to Germany, and eight to Holland (though none were sent there after the Meiji Restoration). The total number of students sent abroad for study for the early years of Meiji is not known for certain. The number that left Japan in 1870 and 1871 is estimated by one study at 320. As for their subjects, military and naval studies still took first place, followed closely by medicine, science, and technology. Then came law, politics, and economics, subjects appropriate for aspiring bureaucrats. Britain was still the most favoured destination, with ninety-three students, followed by the United States with seventy-five, Germany with forty-six, and France with thirty-seven. Most students stayed at their place of study for a considerable length of time; most extraordinary was the case of Togo Heihachiro, renowned for his victory in the Battle of the Japan Sea in 1905, formerly a low-ranking samurai of Satsuma, who was sent to Britain for naval training in 1871 and spent seven years on one or other training ship, later studying at Cambridge the mathematics useful for navigation skills.[39] The progress of industrialization in Japan owes much to the system of education in engineering which was given a prestigious status with the establishment in 1871 of the College of Technology.

Government assistance, especially in the early stages of industrialization, was of crucial importance. For various reasons which we shall shortly examine, the Meiji government inherited from the Bakufu weak finances and indebtedness. On many occasions during the 1870s the government itself undertook export transactions in order to obtain foreign currency, selling rice, tea, and silk. In establishing factories for cement, glass, and building-materials, it hoped to replace imports by home-made supplies.[40] The first railway, about 30 kilometres in length, was opened between

[37] Beasley, *Japan Encounters the Barbarian*, 145–6.　　[38] Allen, op. cit., 34.
[39] Beasley, op. cit., 151–3; Kiyoshi Ikeda, 'Togo Heihachiro and Britain', in Ian Nish (ed.), *Britain and Japan: Biographical Portraits* (Folkestone, 1994), 106 ff.
[40] Allen, op. cit., 34.

Shinbashi (Tokyo) and Yokohama in 1872 on the proceeds of a government loan raised in England. In the 1870s the government operated western-style cotton-spinning mills in Aichi and Hiroshima. In 1870–2 it set up model silk factories of a French and Italian type at Maebashi and Tomioka. In the late 1860s and early 1870s nine large mines (gold, silver, copper, iron ore, and coal) were operated by the state as model enterprises. In 1874 it bought ocean-going ships from abroad and later transferred these to the Mitsubishi firm which, with government support, operated coastal services and also lines to China and Taiwan. 'There was scarcely any important Japanese industry of the Western type during the later decades of the nineteenth century which did not owe its establishment to State initiative.'[41] Efforts to control economic activity in the interests of the state did not end with the Meiji Restoration, and 'their changing forms have been a central factor in Japan's economic development ever since'.[42] Over 36.4 million yen was invested in government enterprises between 1868 and 1881; non-military enterprises were sold off to private buyers in the course of the 1880s, and this transfer was 'an important factor in the formation of "Meiji capitalism"'.[43]

CURRENCY REFORM AND FOREIGN TRADE

With the opening of the country and the beginning of foreign trade, the Japanese economy was forced to conform to international norms, and the parity in the values of gold and silver had been affected so as to make the domestic ratio of 1 : 5 closer to the international ratio of 1 : 15. The method adopted under pressure from foreign powers was to debase the gold coinage by reducing by two-thirds the quantity of gold it contained. The minting of the new gold coin, the 'Man-en koban' of 1860 as it was called, by nearly trebling the quantity of the gold coinage in circulation due to the exchange between the new and the old coin according to its intrinsic value, led to a sharp rise in the prices of goods and also to a trebling of the price of imported goods by reducing to one-third the purchasing power of the Japanese gold coin abroad. This formed the background of the hyper-inflation of the 1860s and 1870s.

Meanwhile, Meiji paper money came to be accepted as the currency of central government. The new currency unit, the yen, which was to be based on the silver standard (1869), was suddenly made to conform to the gold standard by the new Currency Act of 1871, but the result was a drain or hoarding of gold coins due to an increase in their value relative to silver, and the situation was exacerbated by the outflow of specie caused by

[41] Allen, op. cit., 36.   [42] E. Sydney Crawcour, in *Cambridge History of Japan*, v. 587.
[43] Ibid. 612.

Japan's unfavourable trade balance. After 1874 the Japanese currency system became a controlled system by which the silver standard was accepted externally, while paper money was circulated internally. It was the time when the gold standard was being established in advanced capitalist countries in the West, where the policy to absorb gold and eject silver was pursued. Japan's attempt to adopt the gold standard proved too expensive to maintain.[44] The decline in the value of silver that started in 1873 favoured Japanese exports (such as silk) to the countries that had adopted the gold standard, while restraining imports (such as cotton goods) from these countries and increasing the competing power of competitive goods (such as coal) in overseas market.

Foreign merchants dealt with Japanese merchants for export and import at their settlements or concessions at the open ports or in the open quarters of a city. The major export goods in the years 1868–95 were raw silk (36 per cent), tea, cotton yarn (after 1890 to China and Korea), cotton cloth (same to China and Korea, then other Asian countries), coal and copper (to Asian countries), silk handkerchieves (to United States, Britain, and France), chinaware (to the United States and Britain) and laquerware (to Britain and Europe). Products of traditional small-scale industries were exported to Europe and America, while products of modern industries began to be exported to Asia, thus constituting 'the double structure in export'. European and American merchants were by some means confined to their settlement or concession areas owing to the 'unfair' treaties, and in effect 'settlements' played the role of non-custom trade barriers to protect the domestic market from the penetration of Euro-American capital.

What modern economic historians have in mind when they emphasize the 'continuity' of economic growth in Japan are traditional industries and village industries such as sericulture, the silk yarn and cotton goods industries, and sake breweries. The price of raw silk went up almost four times in ten years after the opening of the ports, and an enormous profit was shared by the merchants and the farmers. The traditional textile industry was able to expand the market for its products by using imported cotton yarn. It was with the introduction and rapid spread of power looms in the early twentieth century that traditional industry began to lose much of its traditionality.

---

[44] It was only after the Sino-Japanese War that Japan adopted the gold standard with the money obtained from China as indemnities. For the brief introduction of the gold standard in the 1870s, see Yuzo Yamamoto, 'Meiji Ishin-ki no Zaisei to Tsuka' (Finance and Currency in the Period of the Meiji Restoration), in Mataji Umemura and Yuzo Yamamoto (eds.), *Nihon Keizaishi* (Economic History of Japan), vol. 3 (Tokyo, 1989; 1994), 139–41. For this section, the author owes much to the studies by Yamamoto and others in the same volume subtitled 'Kaiko to Ishin' (The Opening of the Ports and the Restoration).

From 1873, with Okuma in charge of the Treasury, a period of hectic promotion of industry began. Social capital or infrastructure such as roads, bridges, and harbours had to be provided, and arrangements had to be made for the supply of industrial capital for this purpose. Okuma believed that the money supply was inadequate and that this caused the shrinking of industrial activities and distress all round. The stability of the value of paper money would be assured by industrial growth, to which a greater money supply would contribute. In 1876 the Act of the National Bank was revised so as to make the conditions for national banks to issue paper money much easier. As a result, the number of banks opened by 1879 amounted to 153. Okuma believed in controlled money for domestic purposes, while the unfavourable trade balance would be made up for by the export of specie. (The net export of specie from 1872 to 1881 amounted to over 70 million yen.)

ON THE THRESHOLD OF INDUSTRIALIZATION

The last Tokugawa census was held in 1846, showing a population of 26,910,000. Thereafter there was no census until 1872, when the Meiji government, obliged to scrap the anti-Christian temple registers owing to protests from foreign governments, compiled the *Jinshin Koseki*,[45] which produced a population total of 33,110,000, including Ryukyu (later corrected to 34,800,000). The mid- and late Tokugawa era is known to have been a period of stagnant population growth. There were certainly local variations: the population in southern Kanto and Kinai in which large cities were located decreased, whereas south-western Japan was a fast-developing area with an increasing population, the area that provided the men of innovation and initiative who led the Meiji Restoration and modernization of Japan in the latter half of the century. On the eve of industrialization Japan had a population of about 40 million (39,082,000 in 1889 and 40,500,000 in 1893), the urban population forming about 20 per cent of the whole, with a ratio of annual population increase of 1 per cent and an average life expectancy of forty-five years.

Modern economists are still trying to identify the starting period of Japan's economic growth; the latter half of the 1870s is one possibility and the 1860s is another. There is no doubt, however, that the ground for growth was prepared by the series of reforms, political, economic, and social, carried out, sometimes erratically, by the leaders of the new

---

[45] *Jinshin* refers to the old system of counting years and days, and *koseki* is the Confucian house-status register which lists not only old feudal status but also a new commoner status or *shin-heimin*, discriminated ghetto residents.

Meiji government which still remained under the *Sat-Cho hanbatsu* (clan clique) oligarchy. We have seen some forms of opposition to this regime. Probably the most formidable challenge came from the Liberty and People's Right Movement, which we shall examine in the following chapter.

4

The Decade of Democratic Ferment: Liberty and People's Right

WESTERNIZATION AND ENLIGHTENMENT

The Meiji Restoration (or to be exact, the imperial restoration) had no consistent idea to guide it except for the vague, emotional slogan of *sonno*. New values and ideas that had begun to affect Japanese students and missions sent to Europe and America in the 1860s and the early 1870s suddenly assumed an importance when the ruling oligarchs of the Meiji government tackled the arduous task of creating a new nation-state sufficiently westernized to be admitted into what western nations regarded as the sphere of 'civilization'. The role of the intellectuals (writers, journalists, and educators) in early Meiji was crucially important, as they were not only the harbingers of new ideas but also acted as the advisers or critics of government policies.

The Meiji government in the 1870s and 1880s remained an oligarchy referred to by its critics and opponents as *hanbatsu seifu*, the government by clan clique (of Satsuma and Choshu) or *yushi sensei seifu*, autocracy by government officials. As early as 1868 Fukuchi Genichiro, the pioneer journalist who edited a short-lived newspaper *Kooko Shinbun* in Edo, wrote: 'the Bakufu having been overthrown, Sat-Cho [Satsuma-Choshu] has become a second Bakufu.' Under the new government, however, newspapers mushroomed. They provided space for letters from readers, whose enquiries about institutions and ideas such as the meaning of liberty together with the expositions given on the subject by expert writers formed 'a school of enlightenment, liberty, and people's right'.[1] The *hanbatsu* government led by Okubo Toshimichi, and after his death by Ito Hirobumi and Inoue Kaoru, had to deal with the increasingly vociferous opposition which is known in Japanese history as the movement for *Jiyu Minken* (Liberty and People's Right).

[1] Masahiro Inada, 'Jiyu Minken Undo' (The Movement for Liberty and People's Right), *Nihon Tsushi*, xvii. 90. See also Takaaki Inutsuka, *Mori Arinori* (Tokyo, 1986); there is a study in English of the same subject: Ivan Parker Hall, *Mori Arinori* (Cambridge, Mass., 1973).

JIYU MINKEN

Jiyu (liberty or freedom) and *Minken* (people's right) were new words born in the 1860s. In the *English-Japanese Pocket Dictionary* (1863) edited by Hori Tatsunosuke there was *Jiyu* (liberty) but no *Kenri* (right or rights) yet. *Jiyu*, as understood not in the Chinese sense (action at will, later 'licence') but in the western sense of civil liberty, is said to have been used for the first time by a grandson of Sugita Genpaku in the 1840s. It was, however, not until the translation in 1871 by Nakamura Masanao of J. S. Mill's *On Liberty* that the term gained wide currency in Japan. People began to talk about liberty or rather freedom to move one's domicile after the replacement of han by ken. As for 'people's right', it was Tsuda Mamichi who first used the term in his book *Taisei Kokuho Ron* (On Western Law) in 1868, where it meant the right of the people to partici-pate in national politics. The prime aim of the Liberty and People's Right movement was to break the autocracy of the *hanbatsu* government by demanding a national assembly, a constitution, local autonomy, reduced land tax, and the abolition of unequal treaties, and it could be regarded as the second stage of the Meiji Restoration-Reform, if not 'a bourgeois, democratic, revolutionary movement', as has sometimes been claimed.

Thus the 1870s, a period characterized by the discontented former samurai and their direct actions, was also a decade of intellectual ferment for Liberty and People's Right. Nakamura Masanao, formerly a Bakufu Confucian scholar and professor sent to England to supervise Japanese students studying there, translated *Self Help* by Samuel Smiles in 1871. Among other works of western enlightenment translated in those days were *Representative Government* by J. S. Mill (1875), *De l'esprit des lois* by Montesquieu (1876), *Du contrat social* by J.-J. Rousseau (1877), and *Social Statics* by Herbert Spencer (1877). The rise of a democratic move-ment in this decade certainly owed much to ideas inherent in western political philosophy, but the actual course of events in politics was 'gov-erned not by theory but by the exigencies of a unique domestic situation and by ideas which, though they might at times be given European labels, were native in origin'.[2]

FUKUZAWA YUKICHI ON ENLIGHTENMENT
AND INDEPENDENCE

Fukuzawa Yukichi wrote in his *Autobiography* (1899) that 'the feudal system is my father's mortal enemy which I am honour-bound to destroy'. His antipathy to feudalism was not entirely free from the traditional

---

[2] George Sansom, *The Western World and Japan* (Tuttle edn.), 350.

concept of vengeance, and his writings were sometimes found 'redolent of Confucianism'.[3] His father, a lower samurai of a *fudai* han at Nakatsu, Kyushu, stationed in Osaka to supervise the clan treasury, did not enjoy his job. Fukuzawa, having spent some time studying gunnery and the Dutch language at Nagasaki, was asked in 1858 to go to Edo and open a clan school to organize Dutch Studies for the benefit of the young samurai from his han. Accordingly he opened a school in Edo which later developed into Keio University. Before long a visit to Yokohama convinced him that English rather than Dutch was the language for a business community as well as for studies of European enlightenment.

Fukuzawa was one of the first Japanese intellectuals who had acquired first-hand knowledge of the West before the Restoration. In 1860 he joined Japan's first mission to America in the capacity of personal servant to the 'admiral' Kimura of the *Kanrin-maru*. He made his second foreign visit in 1862 as a 'translator' to the delegation sent to Europe to negotiate for delaying the implementation of the treaties with European powers. In London he carefully observed banking and postal services, but Parliament was 'a perplexing institution', for a debate between government and opposition was beyond his comprehension.[4] In Paris he was interested in the operation of military conscription. The delegation returned home after a visit to Holland and Russia, at a time when the anti-foreigner movement was at its height.

Fukuzawa, however, managed to publish a book entitled *Seiyo-Jijo* (Conditions of the West, first volume, 1866) based on the information he had collected during his two visits overseas and also on the knowledge he had acquired by reading books on political economy. The volume was a succinct account of western institutions such as hospitals, schools, news-papers, taxation, and museums. It sold 150,000 copies, and its success (and that of the second volume, 1870, which dealt with politics and history) made the author famous and testified to the growing interest in the western world among educated people in spite of the mounting crisis threatened by *joi* activists.

After the restoration Fukuzawa emerged as Japan's greatest educator. His second major publication *Gakumon no Susume* (An Encouragement of Learning, 1872–6) proved timely and sold well, sales reaching the astounding figure of 700,000 by 1880. It virtually became 'the textbook of the nation'. 'Men are born of heaven and all men are equal', he wrote, but only those who understand things well through learning would become noble and wealthy, while the ignorant remain poor and humble. Writing,

---

[3] Albert M. Craig, 'Fukuzawa Yukichi: The Philosophical Foundations of Meiji Nationalism', Robert E. Ward (ed.), *Political Development in Modern Japan* (Princeton, 1968), 115.

[4] Fukuzawa, *Autobiography* (English tr., Tokyo, 1981), 134.

bookkeeping, the abacus, geography, philosophy, history, economics, ethics, these are all ordinary human *jitsugaku* (useful learning), which should be acquired by everybody, high and low. Equipped with such learning, men should do their best in their respective callings so that their families could gain independence and the state could enjoy independence too.

Feudal class-distinction would disappear, thought Fukuzawa, for only the marks of enlightenment, virtue and ability, would determine one's position in society. He was against ignorant people because they were unenlightened and therefore ignorant, and would repudiate violent rebellion if it was attempted by ignorant people. Thus he held aloof from the popular People's Right movement. In view of his earlier emphasis placed on the equality of men, he has been taken to task for 'some sort of intellectual deception'.[5] But Fukuzawa's is a typical middle-class attitude; he firmly believed that civilization would arise not from the government nor from the lower people, but from the middle class, 'men like Adam Smith, James Watt, and George Stephenson'. The new middle class, he felt, should be created under the leadership of enlightened former samurai, and recruited from the ranks of the merchants and the artisans who would apply themselves to the study of *jitsugaku*.

Before *Gakumon no Susume*, published as a series of pamphlets, was completed, Fukuzawa had begun preparing another major work, *Bunmeiron no Gairyaku* (An Outline of a Theory of Civilization, 1875) which owes a great deal to two European works: François Guizot's *History of Civilization in Europe* (translated into English in 1837) and Henry Thomas Buckle's *History of Civilization in England* of 1868. From these sources he was able to enlarge on the plurality and progressiveness of European civilization in contrast to the 'solitary dominant principle' of hierarchy and passivity prevalent in non-European, and especially Asian civilization. He felt that Japan must learn the spirit of modern civilization, the spirit of independence and responsibility, before adopting its external forms. He insists that it is the spirit, *mœurs*, custom, intellectual vitality, that count. But the tone of his argument changed when he dealt with the international position of his country. Japan, he argued, was entering a critical period in her efforts to revise the unequal treaties with the western powers. Towards the end of his book he wrote: 'There is no use talking about Japanese civilization if there is no country and no people. This is why I . . . propose . . . that the goal of civilization is simply our country's independence.' Indeed, the year 1875 was 'a transitional point in Fukuzawa's thought' on the road to a fuller nationalism.[6]

[5] Daikichi Irokawa, *The Culture of the Meiji Period* (Princeton, 1970), 64.
[6] Craig, op. cit., 124.

Fukuzawa personified the spirit of Meiji enlightenment as it unfurled itself in the reformist 1870s when, along with the adoption of government measures for westernization of the new Japan, great debates began over popular participation in deciding the fate of the country. Thanks to the local autonomy preserved under the Tokugawa feudal system, the intellectual ferment of the day was seen not only among professional intellectuals who tended to gather in big cities, but also among those high-minded former samurai who remained in local clan centres, anxious to take part in the reformation of their country. It was as though the whole country had become a forum of debate on the issues of liberty and people's right.

THE 1874 MEMORIAL FOR A POPULAR ASSEMBLY

Sparks for such a debate were struck by a memorial presented in January 1874 by eight people including most of the former state councillors, headed by Itagaki Taisuke, who had resigned over the Korean issue, in favour of 'the establishment of a council chamber chosen by the people'. With such an institution, it stated, 'a limit will be placed on the power of the officials, and high and low will obtain peace and prosperity', while 'community of feeling between the government and the people' will be created, and 'they will unite into one body'.[7] In short, the petitioners denounced 'despotic officials' who stood between the emperor and the people, instead of challenging the principle of absolute monarchy.[8] This was a manifesto of the defeated war party aided in its preparation by Yuri Kimimasa, one of the eight signatories and an authority of the day on constitutionalism.

The basic intentions of the Restoration leadership had by now become apparent: the *seitaisho* (constitution) of June 1868, which was to implement the Charter Oath, had asserted the supremacy of the imperial government, and Okubo in his argument against the *Seikanron* (Punishing Korea Proposal) confirmed the need to strengthen 'the foundation of His Majesty's reign'. Kido Takayoshi, while visiting Europe in the Iwakura embassy, had instructed Aoki Shuzo, then a student in Germany, later minister to Germany and then to Britain, to prepare a constitution, probably the first of its kind, which should follow the Prussian model.[9] The quickened pace for centralization and attempts to strengthen the Sat-Cho hegemony after the coup of 1873 seemed to justify the allegation made by opposition leaders about the 'autocracy of the officials'.

---

[7] Ryosuke Tsunoda *et al.* (eds.), *Sources of Japanese Tradition*, ii. 177.

[8] *Cambridge History of Japan*, v. 403.

[9] Joseph Pittau, *Political Thought in Early Meiji Japan 1868–1889* (Cambridge, Mass., 1967), 44.

THE *MEIROKUSHA*, KATO HIROYUKI, MORI ARINORI, AND NISHI AMANE

In 1874–5 Fukuzawa edited the *Meiroku Zasshi* (Journal of Meiroku), the official journal of the *Meirokusha* ('Meiroku' Society, *meiroku* meaning the 6th year of Meiji), the first academic society in Japan, which was founded in 1873 (and named in 1874) under the initiative of Mori Arinori with the support of Fukuzawa, Nakamura Masanao, Nishi Amane, Tsuda Mamichi, Kato Hiroyuki, and others: a galaxy of Meiji intellectuals. They have been referred to as the Japanese encyclopaedists, and their group has been called the first society for enlightenment in Japan.[10]

Mori had just returned from the United States, where he had acted since 1870 as a consul-general at Washington and had made many acquaintances among politicians and literary people. Among his writings published in the United States were *Religious Freedom in Japan* (1872), in which he advocated the introduction of Christianity into Japan in order to create self-reliant individuals, and *Education in Japan* (1873), in which he recommended the replacement of the Japanese language, 'a weak and uncertain medium of communication', by English.[11] In spite of Mori's extreme views, the *Meiroku Zasshi* on the whole supported the moderate, gradualist line of modernization adopted by the government, though its members were divided in their response to Itagaki's plea for an early establishment of a popular parliament. Tsuda, who was critical of the government attempt to create a Peers' Assembly, was in favour of the plea. Mori was opposed to the memorandum because of the obvious political motives behind it, as was Nishi because of its assumption of a social contract as a 'universal principle'. In 1875, when the Libel Act and the Press Act were enacted, the *Meiroku Zasshi* under Fukuzawa's initiative decided to cease publication.

Kato Hiroyuki's position deserves special attention. He considered Itagaki's memorandum premature, but he was the first to elucidate the theory of the natural rights of man. Kato rose from the humble position of assistant professor at the *Bansho Shirabesho* (Institute for the Study of Western Books) to the academic height of president of the Imperial University. He has been called 'the prototype of the bureaucratic scholar at the service of the political master'. From the last years of the Tokugawa era until his death in 1916 he was never out of office. He found himself always on the side of power.[12] As early as 1868 he published a short pamphlet entitled *Rikken Seitai Ryaku* (Outline of

---

[10] William Reynolds Braisted, Introduction to the *Meiroku Zasshi* (Tokyo, 1976), p. xix; Takaaki Inutsuka, *Mori Arinori* (Tokyo, 1986), 163.   [11] Inutsuka, op. cit., 158.
[12] Pittau, op. cit., 55. For a summary of Kato's works see Pittau, op. cit., 57–60, 118–22.

Constitutional Government), in which he defined private and public rights and placed a special emphasis on the latter, on the right of every citizen to elect representatives to public office. In 1870 appeared his *Shinsei Taii* (General Principles of True Politics), in which, true to John Locke, he described the role of government as the defence of the people's rights to life and property. In a country where people were ignorant about civilized life, he added, anticipating Fukuzawa, autocratic government rather than public debate would be suitable, and he praised Friedrich the Great of Prussia for his gradualism in granting rights to the people. Indeed, he was already inclined to follow the Prussian road to a constitution. Unlike England, the countries on the European continent had not achieved political tranquillity, largely because the power of the common people was excessive. But 'Graf Bismarck . . . restored the might of Germany because he resolutely remained in office even though he incurred the deep enmity of the Diet during his early years'.[13] Yet in his *Kokutai Shinron* (New Theory of National Polity), published in 1875, he asserted that 'the emperor and the people are not different in kind; the emperor is a man; the people too are men'.[14] He is said to have been panicked into recantation, however, when his life was threatened by a nationalist scholar of the Mito school who resented the disrespectful manner in which Kato dealt with the imperial throne.[15]

Probably this was one of the causes of his apostasy. The implications of his earlier bold arguments now dismayed him.[16] He repudiated and withdrew his former works. In his new book *Minken Shinsetsu* (New Theory of People's Rights), published in October 1882, he called the Rousseauist idea of natural right 'the greatest chimera in history'and claimed it was in conflict with the law of natural selection, a sort of Social Darwinism to which he now subscribed. In Europe and America natural selection, he said, worked better because it was carried out by the upper middle-class who promoted knowledge and virtue, the arts and property-owning, trade and industry, and created popular liberty and self-rule. The leaders of the socialist and communist parties in Europe might be talented, but their followers were poor and ignorant people, as in the Irish Tenant party. In Japan, meanwhile, former samurai and plebeian youths became radical extremists and seemed to be attempting an overthrow of society by sedition. 'They are not erudite, not wealthy, not skilful in dealing with worldly affairs, not well-mannered and virtuous. Yet they try to mislead the people by plotting.' He urged that the *Minken* advocates should avoid radicalism and try to 'extend the influence of the imperial throne'.[17] Sansom sums up

[13] Braisted (ed. and tr.), *Meiroku Zasshi*, 47–9.   [14] Pittau, op. cit., 58.
[15] Introduction, *Jiyu Minken-Hen* (volume on Liberty and People's Right) in *Meiji Bunka Zenshu*, vol. 2, (1955 edn.), 45.   [16] Daikichi Irokawa, *The Culture of the Meiji Period*, 62.
[17] *Meiji Bunka Zenshu*, ii. 358, 367, 368, 385.

Kato's conversion: 'He had lost his early belief in perfectibility [of man] and now regarded man as a helpless puppet.'[18]

Fukuzawa was the opposite to Kato in his stance towards the power of the day: he contributed to the great Minken debate by drawing attention to the issues of local government. In his writings *Bunkenron* (On Devolution, 1877) and *Tsuzoku-Minkenron* (Popular Theory of People's Right, 1878) he stressed the importance of citizen-participation in local public life and self-governing activities at a time when the establishment of a national assembly in the near future was anticipated. Nishi Amane, who had acted as an official adviser to the Bakufu on European affairs in its last days, accepted the emperor or monarchy on utilitarian grounds, as a convenient system for the welfare of the people.[19] He played a major role in preparing the Conscription Act of 1873, helping Yamagata Aritomo, army minister and the supreme commander of the army staff. His positivism and utilitarianism, derived from his studies of Auguste Comte and J. S. Mill, finally gave way before the authoritarianism and *étatisme* of the Meiji government. Both Fukuzawa and Nishi were in favour of moderate reform in the best tradition of *Meirokusha* enlightenment. Their attitudes to state power, however, showed a striking contrast: Fukuzawa valued independence from the central government, while Nishi identified himself with the Meiji state and helped to promote a new martial spirit among the conscript army by drafting the Imperial Rescript to Soldiers and Sailors of 1882.

THE PROGRESS OF THE MOVEMENT FOR LIBERTY AND PEOPLE'S RIGHT

According to Itagaki, the Meiji Restoration meant the restoration of the people's right as well as that of the imperial right, and the people's right was to be defended by political parties, the first of which was *Aikoku Koto* (the Party of Patriots) formed in January 1874; *Jiyuto* (the Liberal Party), set up in October 1881, was its direct heir.[20] The memorandum 'for the Establishment of a Popular Elective Assembly' which we have examined was in fact a manifesto of the Party of Patriots. Kato Hiroyuki at once objected to it on the very ground the petitioners had feared, the fact that the people were unenlightened and uneducated.[21] To this the Party of Patriots made concessions by saying that 'our proposal to set up an assembly does not mean the universal right for the people to choose their representatives, but allows only that the former samurai and the great

---

[18] Sansom, *The Western World and Japan*, 435.
[19] Thomas Havens, *Nishi Amane and Modern Japanese Thought* (Princeton, 1970), 158.
[20] Itagaki, *Jiyutoshi* (History of the Liberal Party), i. 33.   [21] Ibid. 97–8.

farmers and great merchants should enjoy the above right for the time being'.[22] Democracy was not on the agenda—far from it. Only those classes from which the worthy leaders of the Restoration themselves sprang were to be enfranchised.

Some Japanese historians would call the *Jiyu Minken Undo* (Movement for Liberty and People's Right) 'the first revolutionary movement in Japan for bourgeois democracy',[23] but this is an overstatement. It has also been argued that the initiative for *Jiyu Minken* came from landowning agriculturalists envious of the favoured position of the financial oligarchy, in particular the sake brewers who were opposed to an increase in the tax on brewing sake (*jokouzei*), and who raised the slogan 'Freedom of Enterprise' worthy of 'the purest Manchester Liberal' in nineteenth-century England.[24] Nor was it a question of the brewers alone. Village masters and other big farmers, many of whom were progressive agriculturalists, introducing improvements in sericulture and other rural industries, now found themselves in the ranks of the peasantry in their struggle with the government over the heavy burden of agricultural rent and land tax, and joined the *Jiyu Minken* movement. Prominent leaders of the liberal movement were mostly former samurai, especially of Tosa and Hizen, who no longer shared the fruits of power equally with those from Satsuma and Choshu who formed the leadership of the central government. No wonder the *Jiyu Minken* movement in Japan, the heir to the Party of Patriots, taken as a whole showed a 'deep nationalistic hue', unlike similar democratic movements in western Europe which tended to be individualistic.[25]

In order to spread the movement Itagaki set up its core society called the *Risshisha* (the Society of the Ambitious) at Kochi in April 1874. It was in fact a mutual-aid society of former samurai, but became a breeding ground of *Jiyu Minken* activists. In turn, it organized the *Aikokusha* (the Society of Patriots) as a national body in February 1875, which declared at its foundation: 'We hope to secure safety for ourselves and our families, to maintain the state under the sun, thereby to promote the prosperity of the Emperor and to let our Empire confront and surpass European and American powers.'[26] The *Aikokusha* had its headquarters in Tokyo and planned to set up a branch in each prefecture, but soon lapsed into inactivity.

The *Risshisha* had become radicalized, and Kataoka Kenkichi, a leading member, declared in 1876 that the government should be overthrown if

[22] Itagaki, op. cit., 107.

[23] Takaaki Ikai, 'Jiyu Minken Undo to Senseiseifu' (Liberty and People's Right Movement and the Autocratic Government), in *Koza Nihon Rekishi* (Tokyo, 1985; 1988), vii. 251.

[24] E. H. Norman, *Japan's Emergence as a Modern State* (New York, 1940), 169–70.

[25] Yoshitake Oka in *Minken-ron kara Nationalism e* (From Liberty and People's Right to Nationalism), (Tokyo, 1957), 34.   [26] Itagaki, op. cit., 158–9.

such a subversion was in the interest of the people.[27] The dormant *Aikokusha* was reconstituted in 1878 by Ueki Emori, the Tosa activist, and other democrats, mostly from western Japan, and at its third conference held in November 1879 delegates from eastern Japan, including Kono Hironaka, made their first appearance; Kono, the son of a member of the Mutsu gentry class, had come to know Itagaki at the time of the restoration civil war and now became a leading liberal in Fukushima. It was decided here to start a petition movement for the opening of a national diet. In eastern Japan too, a number of democratic clubs mushroomed, many of them under the leadership of big local farmers.

The *Aikokusha* developed into a national party. At its fourth conference held in Osaka in March–April 1880, 114 delegates from twenty-four affiliated and thirty-five unaffiliated bodies gathered together with petitions, the total number of petitioners having reached 100,000 by this time. It was decided at the conference to transform the *Aikokusha* into the *Kokkai Kisei Domei* (Alliance to Promote a National Diet), which was to decide on the procedure to elect a constituent assembly and to prepare a draft constitution whenever the green light was given by the government. Ueki and Kono Hironaka were among the seven-man committee of the Alliance. The government, however, refused to meet their representatives, and while the conference was still going on an Assembly Act was issued which placed all political meetings under police control; forbidding attendance of military personnel, policemen, students, and teachers at such meetings; and disbanding any meeting judged detrimental to national security. Nevertheless, in December 1880 representatives of all the major Minken groups met and agreed to set up a national *Jiyuto* (Liberal Party) in order to achieve constitutional democracy for the benefit of the people. There was no mention of the imperial glory which earlier memorandums had made so prominent. At least until the government reshuffle or *coup d'état* of October 1881, the leadership of the movement was in the hands of the 'democrats'. Indeed, 1881 was the climactic year of the movement: out of ninety-four private drafts of a Japanese constitution prepared in the period 1867–87, as many as thirty-nine were written in that one year. The Liberal Party was to be launched at a conference to be held in October–November 1881. But now the whole movement was overtaken by the government's own efforts to prepare a constitution.

GOVERNMENT PLANS FOR CONSTITUTIONAL REFORM

The Restoration government still led by Okubo had become visibly weakened by the middle of the 1870s as a result of the resignations of

---

[27] Saburo Ienaga, *Ueki Emori Kenkyu* (A Study of Ueki Emori) (Tokyo, 1960), 125.

many councillors over the *seikanron* dispute (the Korean issue—see the previous chapter); some, too, objected to the Formosan expedition. Ito Hirobumi and Inoue Kaoru took the initiative in arranging a meeting at Osaka early in 1875 to which Itagaki and Kido were invited, and their views were incorporated in a decree to inaugurate constitutional politics consisting of the *Genroin* (senate), the *Daishin-in* (supreme court), and a council of prefectural governors. These, however, failed to mark a new departure in the *hanbatsu* government. The *Genroin*, supposedly a legislative organ, was fettered by imperial orders setting its agenda. In June 1878 the *Genroin* presented a draft constitution which made concessions to democratic ideas, and set out checks and controls on the power of the central government and the emperor. Iwakura Tomomi, then minister of the right (prime minister), was unhappy with the democratic features of the *Genroin* draft, and junior councillors like Yamagata, Kuroda, Inoue, Ito, and Okuma were invited to state their opinions.[28]

They were generally unfavourable to the draft. Iwakura himself was in favour of the Prussian system in which ministers would be responsible to the emperor, not to parliament, and accordingly prepared 'Grand Principles' with the help of Inoue Kowashi, the bureaucrat who had studied in Germany, and who consulted his teacher Hermann Roesler, the German adviser on legal matters for the Meiji government. Yamagata felt the pace of political change had been too fast and feared division, selfishness, and partisanship arising out of party politics. Kuroda Kiyotaka stated that a popular assembly was premature. Inoue was of the opinion that the first step towards constitutional change should be the creation of an Upper House composed of former samurai and nobles to counterbalance and restrain a popularly elected Lower House. Ito was willing to make the emperor the repository of supreme power and felt that the emperor should announce the date of granting a constitution. Only Okuma took a different line, proposing that elections for a parliament should be held by the end of 1882 and that it be convened at the beginning of 1883 with a view to a cabinet emerging, based on a parliamentary majority: in short, he pleaded for the British system of constitutional government.

Okuma submitted his proposals in March 1881. The outcome was a plot to force him out of the government.

THE FOURTH *COUP D'ÉTAT* IN MEIJI

In the winter months of 1880–1 Fukuzawa Yukichi was approached by three state councillors, Okuma, Ito, and Inoue Kaoru, who broached the

---

[28] Pittau, op. cit., 74–7.

project of starting a government newspaper with Fukuzawa as editor to guide public opinion on the issue of a national assembly and constitution.[29] The project came to nothing. Ito was so shocked by the 'unexpected radicalism' revealed in Okuma's memorandum that he became determined to force him to resign. Ito apparently suspected Fukuzawa's influence behind all this, and Okuma's memorandum had indeed been drafted by two able writers and publicists who had studied at Fukuzawa's school.

In July a government scandal was disclosed by the *Yubin-Hochi*, a newspaper close to Fukuzawa and Okuma. The ten-year government development project at Hokkaido was to come to an end in 1881, and government properties were to be sold to a Kansai trading company (owned by Godai Tomoatsu and his partners) for a fraction of their real value with the connivance of Kuroda Kiyotaka, the chief of the development bureau and another Satsuma man. The Hokkaido development had been carried out mainly by scattered units of farmer-soldiers called *tondenhei*; it was about to be pushed forward by making extensive (and inhuman) use of convict labour. Okuma, close to Iwasaki of Mitsubishi, opposed the new government deal (after Iwasaki had been disappointed in an attempt to buy state-owned shipping interests), and Fukuzawa's students were heard speaking against it at Hakodate. The rumour was circulated that Okuma, with the help of Mitsubishi and Fukuzawa, was plotting to take over the government. Kuroda, assured by Ito of the seriousness of the situation, thought of using force (a detachment of farmer-soldiers from Hokkaido) if necessary, and urged Iwakura to expel Okuma and all his followers from the government. On 9 October, while the emperor was touring north-eastern Japan with Okuma accompanying him on the imperial journey, the details of the planned *coup d'état* were decided upon by Iwakura, Sanjo, and other state councillors who had remained in Tokyo. On 11 October, when the emperor returned, a meeting was held in his presence at which it was decided to force Okuma's resignation, to cancel the selling of government properties in Hokkaido, to open a national assembly in 1890, and to prepare a constitution in the meantime. These steps were announced on the following day, and the metropolitan police was mobilized as a precautionary measure against possible counter-coups, either by the Okuma faction or by *Minken* activists. Nothing of the sort happened, though the popular movement for *Jiyu Minken* reached its peak around this time.

Among those who played a distinctive role in this movement were the so-called '*Minken* Trio', Ueki Emori, Nakae Chomin, and Baba Tatsui, all three from Tosa. Ueki Emori, the son of a middle-ranking samurai of Kochi, having been inspired by Itagaki's agitation for the opening of a

---

[29] The following account of the *coup d'état* is based on Daikichi Irokawa, *Kindaikokka no Shuppatsu* (The Beginning of a Modern State), *Nihonno Rekishi*, xxi. 175 ff.

people's assembly, decided to work for the *Jiyuto*. One of the first victims of the Newspaper Act of 1875, he was arrested for a mild allegorical article criticizing the government. When he was released from prison he wrote an article under the title: 'Freedom is worth purchasing with one's own blood.'[30] In August 1881 he published 'A Private Draft of the Japanese Constitution' which endorsed the right of resistance to oppressive government. In this 'Private Draft' suffrage was granted to all taxpayers, including women, and the term *Tenno* or 'heavenly emperor' was replaced by a simple 'emperor' or *Kotei*. Ueki was also an advocate of a small army and a big navy, of local autonomy, and a federation of autonomous regions. Then, in October 1881, came the announcement of the government's own constitutional schedule. The *Jiyuto*, in the same month that it was formed, became destined to fail. A year later, when Itagaki, its president, agreed to visit Europe with money supplied by the government, the party was practically destroyed by internal dissensions, though it formally dissolved itself in October 1884 on the eve of the Chichibu rebellion, a peasant war led by local members of the party, discussed below.

NAKAE CHOMIN, THE 'ROUSSEAU OF THE ORIENT'

Of the '*Minken* Trio', Chomin is perhaps the only one to be compared with Fukuzawa in the originality, broadness, and impact of his ideas. Probably he is more outstanding than his peer as a critic of the *Sat-Cho* oligarchy, but shared with him the common characteristic of the Meiji intellectuals of having traditional values and ideas, but disguised beneath the western forms they had assumed. He was the translator of Rousseau's *Social Contract*, and is sometimes referred to as 'the Rousseau of the Orient'. He accepted the Rousseauist concept of liberty which entailed self-discipline, or internalized moral liberty to be produced by following the 'general will'.

Chomin, born of a samurai family of the lowest standing (*ashigaru*) in Kochi, managed to attend the han school, then studied French at Nagasaki. After this he moved to Edo where he continued his study of French and was employed as an interpreter for Leon Roches, the French ambassador, when

---

[30] Ienaga Saburo, *Ueki Emori Kenkyu* (Tokyo, 1960), 100. Ueki's progress after the dissolution of the *Jiyuto* deserves a brief review. He returned to Kochi and was elected in 1886 to the prefectural assembly. He was much concerned with the conditions of the peasantry and serialized a long essay 'On the Poor' in the *Toyo Shinbun*, a local newspaper, in 1885–7. He discarded his earlier view of suffrage on the basis of a qualification and proposed its extension to the poor. He also advocated trade solidarity, an embryonic trade unionism. When the Meiji constitution was promulgated in February 1889, he switched his major attention from constitutional issues to reforms in the family system, advocating the emancipation of women from the family oppression and the tyranny of husbands. At the first general election for the Diet in 1890 he was elected for a Kochi constituency, but died in 1892 at the age of 36.

Roches visited Kobe (Hyogo) for the opening of the port in 1867. In 1871 he accompanied the Iwakura embassy, but parted company from it at an early stage and arrived in Paris in February 1872. He stayed at Lyons, improving his French, and in 1873 moved to Paris where he met Saionji Kinmochi, the court noble who had seen some of the atrocities committed during the Paris Commune and had described the Communards as 'the violent people' and 'the rebels'. Chomin may have agreed with Saionji, but French political history after the Commune led him to believe that a republican form of government was unavoidable in terms of political evolution. After two and a half year's absence he returned to Japan in May 1874.

Chomin made his first public apperance in 1875 by submitting *Sakuron* (Discourse on a Policy) to the former head of Satsuma, Shimazu Hisamitsu, in which he advocated a *coup d'état* under Saigo's leadership against the government. He was in favour of constitutional politics to be conducted by a legislator who would be assisted in his work by generous, prestigious men. This was a direct borrowing from Rousseau who dwelled on the role of 'an extraordinary man' to act as Legislator in the birth of societies.[31] Chomin was obviously seeking to identify Saigo with the extraordinary man who would work for the creation of a 'common self'. The impact of such Rousseauist ideas applied to the Japanese scene could well be considered calamitous. In the Satsuma rebellion of 1877 one of Chomin's students composed a poem on Rousseau, then went to the battlefield and met his death, prefiguring the pilots of the suicide-planes of 1945.

On 18 March 1881 the first number of the *Toyo Jiyu Shinbun* (Oriental Free Press) appeared, with Saionji as its owner and Chomin as editor. It adopted Rousseau as the Guardian Angel of Liberty and of the Press. In the third number of this paper Chomin developed an argument on the Joint Rule of the Prince and the People. He did not wish to apply a republican solution to Meiji Japan, for he was sceptical of 'those who sought to imitate only form while neglecting spirit'. Less than a month after its foundation, Saionji was compelled by a secret imperial order to withdraw from the paper, and Chomin's *Free Press* was obliged to terminate publication. This imperial pressure enraged Chomin and turned him into a radical democrat.

A year later, in February 1882 appeared the first number of Chomin's *Seiri Sodan* (Review of Political Philosophy), a journal for publishing translated French works on the subject. The most important of these was Rousseau's *Social Contract*, translated by Chomin himself and serialized in twenty-six numbers. The importance of Rousseau for Chomin was

---

[31] *The Political Writings of Jean Jacques Rousseau*, ed. C. E. Vaughan (repr. Oxford, 1962), ii. 51–2.

the way in which he conceived of a civil state as a community of self-disciplined citizens. The central issue was how self-discipline was to be introduced. Chomin emphasized moral liberty in politics in his own way. Rousseau's 'citizen' (*citoyen*) was translated into *shi*, which means samurai or the privileged people above the commoners. According to the Chinese classic of Xun-zi (Junshi), who made much of the idea of propriety, those people of the class of *shi* and above were distinguished by their propriety and self-discipline, while the mass of the people were significant only in terms of their numbers. The masses were excluded; only cultured, enlightened people counted. In his translation of the *Social Contract* Chomin characteristically rendered 'sovereign' into *Kimi* ('prince'). He soon began to wonder whether the constitutional monarchy of England might not be a better form of public rule than the Republican France of his day, and his model of 'joint rule' was indeed drawn from England rather than France. Chomin's evolution as a *Minken* democrat underwent a subtle change at the time of the collapse of the movement.

Chomin portrayed the *Minken* movement as a historical, if not dialectical, process in his masterpiece, *Sansuijin Keirin Mondo* (The Discourse by Three Drunkards on Government, 1887). This was an answer to and a parody of Tokutomi Soho's popular book *Shorai-no-Nihon* (The Future Japan, 1886). Tokutomi Soho, educated at Kumamoto Yogakko (western school) and baptized by Niijima Jo of the Doshisha school of Kyoto, came under the influence of Herbert Spencer, and in the above-mentioned book he placed the Meiji Restoration in the process of evolution as a great turning-point from feudal aristocratic militarism to popular productionism. He felt, however, that modernization of Japan under the leadership of the former samurai was half-hearted and conservative, and would require a 'second restoration' which should bring about a New Japan led by the 'country gentlemen' who had the necessary qualities for independence, self-respect and self-government. Cobdenite pacifism was accepted as concomitant to an industrial society, and his whole argument ended on a note of patriotic nationalism.[32] Chomin was much impressed by Soho's argument and wrote a preface to the second edition of the book; yet he was not quite convinced by Soho's or Spencer's evolutionism, and set down his own view in the form of his *Discourse*. In this, two guests, one a westernized democrat and the other an imperialist expansionist, come to see Nankai-Sensei (Master South Sea, who may be Chomin himself). The contrast between the two corresponds to the distinction Soho made between the industrial and the military type. Nankai-Sensei, having listened to what his

---

[32] Tokutomi Soho, *The Future Japan*, tr. and ed. Vinh Sinh (Edmonton, Alberta, 1989), 182–4; for Tokutomi see also Kenneth B. Pyle, *The New Generation in Meiji Japan* (Stanford, 1969), ch. 2.

guests have to say, expounds his own view on 'the essence of politics', which was an attempt to justify 'granting rights to the people', a concession obviously to the government's effort to frame a constitution by itself. The people's right once granted, though weak and feeble at first, could be made to grow through morality, energy, and learning into the same greatness as a people's right obtained by the people themselves either through force ot by public deliberation.

Chomin was soon to be disillusioned. Under the Public Order Preservation Ordinance of December 1887, 570 undesirable people, including Chomin were expelled from Tokyo. He moved to Osaka and became chief editor of the *Shinonome Shinbun*, the organ of the Movement for People's Right in Osaka, in which, among other topics, he wrote in support of universal suffrage and a militia system. He wanted a popular assembly to check the constitution in the interest of the people. The Meiji constitution was 'granted' in Feburary 1889, and Chomin is known to have read it with marked contempt. An amnesty was also granted, and he again became involved in the resuscitated Liberal Party. At the first general election for the Diet in 1890 Chomin was elected for an Osaka constituency, but he soon resigned, disappointed by the weaknesses of opposition leaders who were willing to accept government bribes.[33]

BABA TATSUI, THE FIRST POLITICAL EXILE

Baba, the last of the *Minken* trio, spent a considerable period of time in the 1870s in England, where in his twenties he was absorbed in the study of western thought, law, and politics.[34] The son of a middle-ranking Tosa samurai, he studied at Fukuzawa's Keio Gijuku school at the time of the Meiji Restoration and was sent to England as a Tosa han student to study naval engineering. When the Iwakura embassy visited England in 1872 he had his status changed to that of a government student and began law studies. In order to contradict Mori Arinori, who had belittled the Japanese language, the young Baba wrote and published a Japanese grammar, the first of its kind.[35] He was aware of the danger that, if English was made the official language as in India, the lower classes

---

[33] His last years were not very dignified as a radical democrat. But towards the very end he published a testament entitled *Ichinen Yuhan* (One Year and a Half), in which he criticized the government, still dominated as it was by clan interests, and reproached the Liberals for their lack of principle. 'People's right is the supreme principle: liberty and equality are the great cause. Imperialisms of the whole world cannot subdue this principle and cause. The Emperor can maintain his elevated position only by paying due respect to this principle.' Thus Chomin remained one of the very few advocates, consistent and dedicated, of People's Right in Meiji Japan.

[34] Shinya Sugiyama, 'America niokeru Baba Tatsui' (Baba Tatsui in America), *Fukuzawa Yukichi Nennkan*, 15 (Oct. 1988), 108.

[35] Tatsui Baba, 'The Life of Tatsui Baba', in Baba, *Zenshu* (Works), iii. 157.

would be shut out of public communication and enlightenment, and the 'common sympathies' between classes would be lost.[36] It is characteristic of the Meiji intellectuals that even Baba concluded his discourse with a nationalistic appeal: 'they [the English people] must come to us on the ground of perfect equality . . . Japan is independent. She has her own empire, and within her realm there is one sovereign, His Gracious Majesty the Mikado of the Japanese empire.'[37]

Having returned to Japan in May 1878, Baba began a series of public speeches and articles; these revealed his views on the 'internal union of liberalism and nationalism' in the tradition of Fukuzawa Yukichi. He joined the *Jiyuto*, but did not trust its president Itagaki for political and personal reasons. He was adopted as an editor of the *Jiyu Shinbun* (Liberal Newspaper), in which he serialized an article on liberty, his major work: freedom of thought, speech, and action was now posited as a prerequisite for the smooth development of the human mind.[38]

The government persecution of *Minken* democrats began, and uprisings by provincial activists were suppressed. Baba himself was deprived of his freedom of speech for six months after he said in a lecture that 'no despotic government exists for long' (citing the French government under Louis XVI). He apparently found himself in an impasse. He was arrested in 1885 for having visited an Englishman in Tokyo who was dealing with explosives, and was detained for six months. He chose the life of an exile, and in the following year left for America where he continued his political campaign in the form of public lectures and occasional newspaper articles criticizing the prison and police system in Japan. He died in Philadelphia at the age of 38. Baba was rare among Japanese intellectuals in choosing an independent life as a political exile.

RADICALIZATION OF THE MOVEMENT AND THE CHICHIBU PEASANT WAR

Among the thirty-nine draft constitutions of 1881 there was one now generally referred to as the Itsukaichi Draft Constitution, prepared by a schoolteacher after a series of study sessions and debates among his friends. This draft constitution was extremely detailed, and in it its author

[36] Tatsui Baba, *An Elementary Grammar of the Japanese Language* (London 1873), Baba, *Zenshu* (Works), i. pp. viii–x. See also Nobutoshi Hagihara, *Baba Tatsui* (Tokyo, 1967), 39.
[37] Tatsui Baba, *The English in Japan* (London, 1875), *Zenshu* (Tokyo 1987), i. 129.
[38] *Jiyu Shinbun*, 1 June–12 Sept. 1882; for a summary see Hellen Ballhatchet, 'Baba Tatsui and Victorian Britain', in *Kindai Nihon Kenkyu*, 11 (1994), 221–60, also in Sir Hugh Cortazzi and Gordon Daniels (eds.), *Britain and Japan 1859–1991* (London 1991), 107 ff. Baba and Ueki were the most outspoken critics of Kato's apostasy: Baba's *Tenpu-Jinkenron* (On Natural Right of Man) and Ueki's *Tenpu Jinken Ben* (On the Natural Right of Man) came out in January 1883.

stated that 'the King may die, but the People never die'.[39] But all such private drafts were now to be set aside, since the government had embarked upon drafting a constitution by itself. This certainly was the direct cause of the radicalization of the People's Right Movement, but there were local variations due to historical accidents.

In fact, a political map of Meiji Japan would show a line of demarcation between the advanced areas in the south-west and the backward north-east; the former had supported the imperial cause, the latter the Bakufu in the Boshin civil war. Powerful politicians from Choshu, military leaders from Satsuma, and business magnates from Kinai and Goshu (Oomi) were representative of the former, while poverty and degradation marked the latter. The Liberal Movement, which began at Tosa as a protest movement within the advanced areas, soon spread east and north-east. As it reached the sericultural districts in Fukushima, Gunma, Chichibu, and Ina, it penetrated down to the common people, small farmers and peasants eking out their living in various trades; these were the people who were hardest hit by the economic policies of retrenchment, deflation, and hard money introduced by the finance minister Matsukata Masayoshi in the 1880s. The difference between the People's Right Movement in the south-west and in the north-east has been presented as one of attitude to the government: the south-west advocates of people's right 'anticipated a compromise . . . with great merchant capital which sustained the Hanbatsu government', while the north-eastern agitators 'aimed at the overthrow of the [*hanbatsu*] government of the south-west'.[40] A series of 'radical incidents' that took place in the early 1880s culminated in the Chichibu Peasant War of November 1884, a major conflict.

In the Fukushima Incident (March–December 1882) the prefectural assembly dominated by *Jiyuto* (led by Kono Hironaka) was forcibly dissolved by the governor, Mishima Tsuyo, a tough Satsuma man, although he met with strong opposition in the form of a tax boycott and an assault on a police station when he set about building roads in Aizu (western Fukushima-ken) with conscript labour and a substitute labour tax. Local *Jiyuto* activists in other areas too were driven to violent action, such as an attack on a police station (in Gunma), a desperate uprising at Mt Kaba, and a planned assault on a prison and armed rebellion in Nagoya. Most of these uprisings were either abortive or on a small scale if carried out; the Chichibu 'incident', though, overshadowed them all, as it amounted to a veritable peasant war .

The Chichibu Incident, an uprising involving over 10,000 people in one

---

[39] Daikichi Irokawa, *The Culture of the Meiji Period*, 104.
[40] Kichinosuke Shoji, *Kindai Chiho Minshu Undoshi* (A History of the Modern Local Popular Movement), vol. 2 (1978), 19.

area, was an expression of the hardship and frustration of the local people. Chichibu is a mountainous region lying to the west of the Kanto plain, and the peasants were not able to live on the cultivation of the land alone. Many of them were engaged in sericulture and various other trades, as dyers, roofingers, blacksmiths, and suchlike. A newly introduced local tax weighed particularly heavily upon the Chichibu area, where the land tax had been relatively light owing to the limited acreage of cultivated land. The peasants were obliged to undertake various trades to pay the tax, but a retail tax and an artisan tax were added to make their life yet more unbearable, forcing them into the hands of moneylenders.

Matsukata's sound-money policy naturally benefited the moneyed interests, the Chichibu usurers among others, at the expense of the borrowers, hard-pressed peasants, artisans, and local traders. The price of raw silk fell drastically. Marui, a local dealer of raw silk, was hard hit; Inoue Denzo, the owner of the house of Marui, began to share the grievances of the local people. He obtained a copy of Rousseau's *Social Contract* translated and annotated by Nakae Chomin, and lent it to his friend, a village blacksmith, who became one of the leaders of the rebellion when it broke out. Yet although the egalitarian sentiments observed among the Chichibu people perhaps may have owed something to Jean-Jacques, they had much more to do with the traditional culture and personal relationships prevalent among the peasant population in the area.

Among those who were arrested after the defeat of the rebellion were many who professed themselves to be believers in the *Misogikyo*, a Shintoist sect, the founder of which was much influenced by Kamo No Mabuchi, the National Learning scholar who, like Ando Shoeki, rejected an artificial social system in favour of the ideal 'life of nature' in ancient Japan. A village master in Chichibu became a *Misogikyo* preacher, and he also joined *Jiyuto*; a mass entry of *Misogikyo* sectarians into the *Jiyuto* ensued. Another traditional feature was gambling. Chichibu was notorious for gambling, and among the gamblers the paternal or blood bonds of the bosses and their followers were all important. Gambling also provided a recreation for the peasants. A Chichibu boss, himself a landowning farmer, would lend money to needy peasants, but was ready to cancel the debts when he decided to support the peasants' uprising. Here was a natural order of the peasant community in opposition to the newly introduced modern system of the prefectural governor (chiefs of *Gun* and *Ko*, smaller units of local administration), dominated at its top by the alien leaders of Satsuma and Choshu who claimed to look after national interests for the moneyed classes.

The Rousseauist village blacksmith prepared, with the aid of Inoue Denzo of Marui, a petition of over 300 names addressed to the *Gun-cho* asking him to persuade the moneylenders to accept deferment of debts, but to no avail. Now petitioners joined the *Jiyuto en masse*, but they were unhappy because the *Jiyuto* convention held in March in Tokyo ignored the demands formulated in their petition. The Chichibu peasants met to form a secret organization, the *Konminto* (the Party of the Sufferers); recruitment to this body now began seriously. The party adopted a programme similar to the petition submitted to the *Gun-cho*, and a series of negotiations with individual moneylenders began. It was a sort of collective bargaining, but the police soon intervened on the moneylenders' behalf. When a new petition, this time to the police, was made and rejected, the Chichibu peasants began to collect guns and swords. Inoue Denzo knew that this was a hopeless fight. Oi Kentaro, the left-wing leader of the party, whom he met in Tokyo told him to wait; the *Jiyuto* having been dissolved, there was no prospect of national support.

The rebellion began on the night of 1 November 1884, when about 3,000 farmers, hunters, small tradesmen, *Jiyuto* members, and schoolteachers armed with rifles, swords, and bamboo spears met at a village shrine. On the following day they entered Omiya, the principal town of Chichibu (now the city of Chichibu) and turned the district government office (Gun-yakusho) into their Headquarters of Revolution. By 3 November the strength of the *Konminto* army had reached 10,000. On the following day the government sent troops and the district of Chichibu was virtually sealed off. The *Konminto* leadership took alarm and defection of leaders followed. The bosses of the gamblers were no match for the government forces. By the morning of 4 November the government troops had recaptured Omiya; what remained of the revolutionary army quickly retreated across the high mountains into Nagano prefecture, where they met their final defeat.

In view of the great number of peasants involved, the government decided to prosecute only the leaders and listed members of the *Konminto* (the latter numbered 103). Seven people, including Inoue Denzo, were sentenced to death; Inoue and another managed to escape, but the remaining five were duly hanged. Altogether 3,618 people (of whom 380 were arrested and 3,238 presented themselves to the police) were tried at several courts of justice; 296 were given heavy penalties, 448 light ones, while 2,642 were fined and 232 were freed. Others in Nagano and Gunma were tried in connection with the Chichibu Peasant War, and the number of those punished for their role in the uprising reached 4,178 in total.[41]

Unlike the national leadership, local branches of the *Jiyuto* were largely concerned with local grievances, and in this they were more democratic and plebeian than the national leaders. Fukuzawa Yukichi, certainly a

---

[41] Koji Inoue, *Chichibu Jiken* (Tokyo, 1968; 1988), 194.

national figure though not of the *Jiyuto*, deplored the local radicals who vilified prefectural governors and who went so far as to call the emperor Mutsuhito by his first name.[42] Communal ties remained strong among the rural population, among the faithful followers of *Misogikyo*, and in the closed world of the gamblers.

THE AFTERMATH OF THE *MINKEN* MOVEMENT: OI KENTARO'S *TOYO JIYUTO* AND FUKUZAWA'S *DATSUARON*

It is noteworthy that *Minken* activists and theorists, after the collapse of their movement, turned to nationalism and expansionism; these had always formed an integral part of their political aspirations. Perhaps the most conspicuous case of 'conversion' was provided by Oi Kentaro, the son of a village master in Buzen, not far from Yukichi's birthplace, who had been steeped in Dutch or rather French studies under Mitsukuri Rinsho, a legal expert and later an associate of the *Meirokusha*. He set himself up as a journalist and lawyer for the *Jiyu Minken* movement and came to be known for his refutation of Kato Hiroyuki's objections to the 1874 memorandum for a popular assembly; he stood by the radical wing of the movement, advocating what virtually amounted to universal suffrage and defending the victims of the Fukushima Incident.[43] Oi's support for the cause of the poor and downtrodden, however, helped to reinforce his championship of national expansion under the plea for Asian independence and reform. Indeed, Japanese liberalism was even more nationalistic than the 'autocratic' Meiji government, which pursued a policy of accommodation towards the West. After the failure of 'the bizarre attempt' to invade Korea in order to help Korean reformers, known as the Osaka Incident of 1885, Oi, the chief conspirator, had to remain in prison till 1890. In 1892 he founded the *Toyo Jiyuto* (Oriental Liberal Party), which has been described as 'the first real attempt at a popular party in Japan'.[44] Its programme, however, reveals the ease with which people's right was identified with national right and national strength: 1. to maintain the dignity and prosperity of the Imperial House, to extend People's Right, and to establish a constitutional government; 2. to adopt a tough, hard-line policy on foreign affairs and thereby to elevate National Right; 3. to adopt a policy of progress on domestic affairs and thereby to enhance National Strength; 4. to tidy up national finance and thereby to sustain People's Strength, especially to protect the poor and the workers; 5. to adopt emergency measures for foreign policy. It is not surprising that a parallel

---

[42] Shinzo Koizumi (ed.), *Fukuzawa Yukichi, Hito to Shokan* (Fukuzawa Yukichi, The Man and His Letters) (Tokyo, 1959), 147.

[43] Marius Jansen, 'Oi Kentaro: Radicalism and Chauvinism', *Far Eastern Quarterly* (May 1952, 305–16).   [44] Ibid.

has been pointed out between Oi and Kita Ikki, the major ideologist for the young officers' attempted *coup d'état* of 1936.[45]

After the political crisis of October 1881 in which he found himself unjustly accused of political plotting, Fukuzawa had started a newspaper of his own, *Jiji-Shinpo* (News of Contemporary Affairs), in 1882 and went on advocating the cause of independence. The shift of emphasis in his plea for independence from individual to national became increasingly pronounced as he discussed the problem of the throne in the articles *Teishitsuron* (On the Imperial Throne, 1882) and *Sonnoron* (On Reverence for the Emperor, 1888). He was convinced that the emperor should be kept above politics. In the West, writes Fukuzawa, religion encourages virtue and a charitable spirit, whereas in Japan, where religion is confined within the precinct of a temple, one should depend on the imperial throne for a virtuous life. Its function was to provide a focus for the people's loyalty which could not be found in mere laws. Loyalty matters most, as in a business firm. 'Rates of pay and hours of work alone could not command the loyalty of an employee towards his employer. He must have some feeling of loyalty. It was the emperor who should be the focus of this emotional side of the people's relations with the government.' He posited the imperial house as 'the non-partisan focal-point at the centre of Japanese society' which would point to 'the harmony and comfort of all the people'.[46] Fukuzawa also began to advocate the idea of harmony between government and people—*Kanmin-chowa*.

Reaction set in after the decade of democratic ferment. The 1880s was characterized not so much by the government-sponsored balls for foreigners held at Rokumeikan Hall, Tokyo, as by the tightening of control over education, including textbook censorship by the Ministry of Education; a Shintoist revival, starting with the establishment in 1879 of the Yasukuni Shrine, a state shrine for all the war dead, to be worshipped as gods for national safety; the suppression of a series of local movements for people's rights; the Public Order Act and Press Law of 1887; and the abolition of the exemption clause for the head of a household in the Conscription Law. A decade of nationalist revival aptly culminated in the promulgation of the emperor's constitution in February 1889. Fukuzawa's nationalist inclinations too became apparent.

He was, however, in two minds about the use of force in giving Korea the benefits of independence and civilization.[47] In 1885, at a time when the abortive uprising of the progressive Koreans at Seoul, inspired partly by Fukuzawa's ideas, and the resulting Sino-Japanese military clash ended in a

---

[45] Ibid.

[46] 'Teishitsuron', *Jiji-Sjinpo* (26 Apr.–11 May 1882); 'Sonnoron', *Jiji-Shinpo* (26 Sept.–6 Oct. 1888); Carmen Blacker, *The Japanese Enlightenment* (Cambridge, 1969), 119–20.

[47] Hilary Conroy, *The Japanese Seizure of Korea: 1868–1910* (Philadelphia, 1960), 128–62.

compromise embodied in the Tientsin Treaty, Fukuzawa published an article entitled *Datsua-ron* (Exit Asia, Enter Europe) in *Jiji-shinpo* (16 March 1885). *Datsua-ron* was a step forward in his scheme for the advancement of civilization in Japan, and was evidently inspired by the Korean situation. He now maintained that in Japan the spirit of the nation had liberated itself from the narrow confines of Asian obstinacy and had moved into the sphere of western civilization. Unfortunately for Japan, her two neighbours Korea and China had failed to alter their Confucianist education and to prepare the way to improvement and civilization. They were fated to be divided up by the civilized countries of the world. Japan, then, should come out of the ranks of Asian countries and throw in her lot with the civilized nations of the West. 'She should treat China and Korea not with special favour as neighbouring countries but in the same way as the western powers would treat them.' Personally Fukuzawa helped Korean students who came to his school in the hope that enlightenment would strike roots in the Korean soil. He was convinced that the Chinese influence on Korea, especially the Confucian code of life, was harmful to the prospect of Korean enlightenment and independence, and regarded Japan's war against China as unavoidable. He supported the war when it broke out in 1894, and personally contributed 10,000 yen to its military expenses.[48]

Fukuzawa advocated the western concepts of individualism (individual independence) and of the nation-state (national independence), and sought to replace the Confucian code of life or feudal values with the utilitarian values of the middle class, a useful body which had yet to be created in Japan. But he soon came to realize that a middle class of the English type could not be conjured up with a stroke of his pen. Therefore he relied on the sentiments of loyalty that would bind the nation as closely as it would hold a business firm together. He was opposed to old tyrannical social relationships, but his opposition to the autocratic Meiji government armed with a Bismarckian constitution was half-hearted, partly because of his belief in *kanmin-chowa* and partly because of his obsession with Asian independence from the West, possibly under Japanese hegemony.

Many streams thus flowed into the current of liberalism that washed Japanese shores in the 1870s and early 1880s. Probably it was befitting to the age of national rivalries that Herbert Spencer and his Social Darwinism attracted more serious attention, in the end, than did utilitarianism or egalitarianism. The contemporary advocates of liberal and radical ideas had one thing in common: a strong concern for national identity almost invariably linked with the *sonno* tradition. The major issue of Japanese liberalism was the building of a nation-state strong enough to cope with the western powers, an interest liberals shared with the ruling oligarchs. It

[48] Kanae Iida, *Fukuzawa Yukichi* (Tokyo, 1984), 206.

is not surprising that almost all the strands of liberal and democratic thought in Meiji Japan had a strong element of nationalism and even expansionism. Even so, the Meiji oligachy became alarmed by the degree to which the movement for Liberty and People's Right had developed, and declared instead for the more congenial alternative of an authoritarian constitutional monarchy. True political liberalism in pre-war Japan was thus doomed. Thereafter its history became entangled with a history of thought control and suppression.

5

The Meiji Constitution

THE SCOPE OF CHANGE

At the centre of the debate about Japan's modernization was the argument that in order to be able to stand on equal terms with European powers, 'the disgrace of extraterritoriality' would have to be eliminated, and that to attain this aim Japan would have to show the achievements of her civilization. It was not enough that the samurai class, with the two swords tucked in the sash, the symbol of their feudal privilege and savagery, should go for good.[1] A modern system of administration, both civil and military, had to be introduced; encouragement was given to trade and industry, and efforts to modernize the system of finance, both public and private, were being made. As a symbolic act of modernization the government commissioned Josiah Conder, the British architect and professor at the Kobu Daigakko (College of Technology), to design the Rokumeikan, a Victorian-Gothic hall at Hibiya, Tokyo, the most elaborate western-style building in Japan at the time, which was opened in December 1883 for the purpose of entertaining foreign residents with lavish balls, concerts, and charity bazaars (it even had a billiard room). Yet to qualify herself as a civilized nation, Japan lacked one important thing: constitutional politics. The *Minken* advocates demanded it, but the *hanbatsu* government feared that parliamentary democracy with popular participation would not be compatible with the eternal rule of the emperor, for the sake of which they had so tactfully carried out the revolutionary changes so far. A Japan-centred world vision lay behind the government's attempt to frame a constitution for itself.

The year 1881 was a turning-point in Japanese politics, because the initiative in preparing a constitution was taken away from the *Minken* movement and was assumed by the government, equipped with the imperial decree of 12 October in which the emperor expressed his hopes for convening a national assembly in 1890. The decree also warned that those who were 'so impatient as to instigate an incident, and endanger the peace of the country' would be 'dealt with by law', implying a strict application of the Press and Assembly Acts.[2] This was the work of Inoue Kowashi, the

---

[1] A decree prohibiting the wearing of swords except by military officers and policemen in uniform was issued in 1876.   [2] A full decree quoted in *Ito Hirobumi-den*, ii. 235–6.

able bureaucrat who had helped Iwakura prepare the 'Grand Principles' on the basis of a Prussian model. Ito Hirobumi was to be sent to Europe to study constitutions there. A counter-offensive by the *hanbatsu* government began, and emperor-centred nationalism, itself the cause of the Meiji Restoration, was to be reaffirmed and given a modern form in a constitution learned from Europe.

ITO HIROBUMI AND CONSTITUTIONAL CHANGE

Ito was the son of a farmer in Choshu, but fortuitous circumstances arising out of his father's adoption into an heirless family called Ito, which had bought the title of samurai from an impecunious samurai, made him both a samurai and a *Shishi* who soon developed into an extreme loyalist activist. He had joined in Choshu's attack on the British legation at Gotenyama, Edo, in December 1862. The Choshu samurai, though, in spite of their intractable xenophobia, had taken a great interest in all things western. They had bought a big steamship from a British firm, and in order to train its crew they sent Ito, Inoue Kaoru, and three others to London. Arriving there, 'the scales were lifted from Ito's eyes'—the magnificent spectacles they saw there represented science, progress, and above all power.[3] In London Ito learned the gross error of Japan's exclusionist policy and (as we have seen) hurried home with Inoue in a futile attempt to restrain Choshu's anti-foreigner actions. Under the new Meiji government he became head of another mission sent to the United States in 1870 to study their taxation and banking systems. Next he was one of the ambassadors in the Iwakura embassy of 1871–3. At Sacramento he said: 'We come to study your strength, so that, by wisely adopting your better ways, we may hereafter become stronger ourselves.'[4]

The imperial decree authorizing preparation for a national assembly changed the nature of the *Minken* movement, which hastened to start forming political parties. Government supporters followed suit. The Liberal Party (*Jiyuto*) that had already been in the process of formation was established late in October 1881. Seven more parties were formed in six months or so, of which *Rikken Kaishinto* (the Constitutional Progressive Party) led by Okuma Shigenobu, and *Rikken Teiseito* (the Constitutional Imperial Politics Party) organized by Fukuchi Genichiro, editor of the pro-government *Tokyo Nichi Nichi* newspaper and his group, were of some account. *Kaishinto*, along with *Jiyuto*, was to have the most direct impact on the emerging constitutional politics in Japan.[5] Yet the

[3] Kengi Hamada, *Prince Ito* (Tokyo, 1936, University Publications of America reprint, 1979), 35–6. [4] Ibid. 66.
[5] Makoto Oishi, *Nihon Kenposhi* (History of the Japanese Constitution) (Tokyo, 1995), 70.

two-year-old Assembly Act was further strengthened in June 1882, empowering the minister of home affairs to forbid public debate on politics if necessary, and even to disband political societies and assemblies deemed in his view 'detrimental to security'. Political activities such as the organization of party branches and correspondence with other bodies were prohibited. As a result, some of the parties decided to dissolve and others were from the start denied recognition, like the Oriental Socialists (*Toyo Shakaito*) of Nagasaki, whose declaration for 'equality' was regarded as harmful to public order.[6]

In January 1882 it was decided at a meeting of the Senate[7] that Ito be sent to Europe to study constitutional principles and practices there. At a farewell party held on his behalf on 6 March Ito declared: 'The people would say that the present government is a *Sat-Cho* government. I know that their allegation is not untrue. This is because since the great political innovation of 1868 the power of *Sat-Cho* has been great in shaping the imperial court as it is now. . . . Yet the reason why I strive to assist the emperor in the court [and the government] is not that I am a member of the *Sat-Cho* government but that I believe in the weightiness of the imperial wishes.' This was indeed the basic stance he took in studying constitutions in Europe.[8]

On 14 March 1882 Ito left for Europe with an able staff of assistants, mostly those well versed in German studies. In July 1882 Inoue Kowshi wrote to Ito criticizing parliamentary politics of the British style advocated by Okuma in the council and more widely by the *Minken* moderates like Fukuzawa. The latter, said Inoue, had become so influential that 'they were as though marching across open fields, leading hundred thousands of picked men'. If the government should decide to adopt the British style, it would be wise for it to assimilate its advocates and turn them into a government party. If the government should decide to reject the British system and to maintain a monarchy of the Prussian type, it would be vitally important to work out 'a constitution of *seifu-shugi* (government-ism)'. Fortunately, he went on, the British-style constitution had not penetrated deep into the popular mind, and a majority of the *shizoku* (former samurai) in the provinces were in favour of maintaining the imperial house. There was no time to waste. 'Two or three years of inaction on the part of the government would allow private constitutions to be triumphant.'[9]

Ito's destination was Berlin. On his arrival there he made a courtesy visit to the chancellor Otto von Bismarck, who was pleased that Ito had chosen Germany as the basis of his constitutional studies. Rudolf von Gneist, law

[6] Oishi, op. cit., 72.
[7] An early legislative body consisting of peers and others appointed by the emperor (1875–90).
[8] *Ito Hirobumi Den*, ii. 256–8.
[9] Inoue Kowashi to Ito Hirobumi, 12 July 1882, ibid. 249–50.

professor of Berlin University and then a member of the Reichstag, agreed to give him a limited number of lectures, and Albert Mosse, his disciple, spent more time instructing him. Gneist was a liberal (he had written a constitutional history of England which became a classic), though turning to conservatism in his later years, and was an advocate of 'self-government', which meant the administration of public affairs by responsible officials appointed by the king. In Vienna Ito attended lectures by Lorenz von Stein, professor of Vienna University, who advocated a theory of social monarchy or a monarchy as protector of the poor and the weak. In a letter to Iwakura from Vienna Ito stated that by learning from Gneist and Stein he was able to grasp the hard core of the state system that would strengthen the basis of the imperial house and would make the imperial prerogative invulnerable. 'I have learned the theories and methods to alter the present situation in Japan, in which the liberal extremists upholding British, American, and French ideas are threatening the safety of the state. . . . If we are to adopt constitutional monarchy, said Gneist and Stein, the monarchical right should be placed above the legislative power. . . . The monarch could not be bound by law, nor be subjected to penalties, but rules the country from a position which is inviolable.'[10] Late in August he was invited to dinner by the German kaiser Wilhelm I, who frankly told him that he, the kaiser, could not congratulate the Japanese emperor on the latter's attempt to open a national assembly and that even if Japan was compelled to set up such an assembly it would be advisable not to have any stipulation that would require the government to obtain the consent of the national assembly in order to raise national revenue, a condition that might lead to civil war.[11] In a letter to Matsukata Masayoshi, minister of finance, sent from Paris, Ito summed up what he had studied so far. 'We may', he wrote, 'have a constitution and a national assembly in 1890, but needless to say, the so-called parliamentary government, in which a prime minister can be deposed by a majority of the assembly, does not suit Japan. Not only is that so, but also this is not a pure monarchical government. There is only one such example, the unique polity of England, which was created by the ups and downs of her politics in the course of several centuries.' The alliance of European monarchies, he continued, defeated Napoleon, but 'the remaining poison' of popular right, liberty, and republicanism affected the European mind in 1848 and resulted in the domination of national assemblies by ignorant, uneducated members and also in the emergence of socialists and nihilists. Ito recounted what Wilhelm I had told him over dinner, and added that this accorded with Gneist's views of a constitution.[12] Ito returned to Vienna from Paris. He was very much devoted to Stein, but the

[10] Ito Hirobumi to Iwakura Tomomi, 11 Aug., 1882, ibid. 296–7.
[11] Ibid. 306–7.   [12] Ito to Matsukata, 6 Sept. 1882, ibid. 311–14.

aged professor declined Ito's invitation to come to Japan as a government adviser. Nevertheless, Ito enjoyed Stein's lectures given in English in the autumn. Back in Berlin he wrote: 'Stein said in his lecture that the law of the imperial household, the government organization, and the legislature are indispensable to constitutional politics. . . . Many of those who argue about the political system take British parliamentary government as a model while claiming to attach due importance to imperial right. However, if you create a parliamentary government, you will have to reduce imperial right. If you attach importance to imperial right, you cannot adopt a parliamentary government.' 'It seems to me', he added, 'that enlightened opinion [in Japan] is biased towards people's right and republicanism and against constitutional monarchy.'[13] Ito referred to the Eastern Question in another letter to Matsukata: Japan was far more civilized, he said, than Bulgaria, Serbia, Montenegro, and Romania, those small countries of 'mountain monkeys' that had been given the status of 'civilization-independence' at the Berlin Congress of 1878 largely because European civilization was only concerned with fellow-Christians: 'they help and love their kith and kin, and seek gradually to exterminate those who are remote and unrelated. Obviously this is the way the Europeans look upon the Orientals. The situation in the East is as fragile as a tower built of eggs placed one on top of another.' 'Therefore', he went on, 'we have to do our utmost to strengthen and enlarge our armament.'[14]

At the request of the Meiji emperor Ito proceeded to St Petersburg as minister plenipotentiary representing Japan at the coronation ceremonies of Tsar Alexander III held in May 1883. Thereafter, by way of Naples, he returned to Japan early in August.

CONSTITUTIONAL FOUNDATIONS

While Ito was away in Europe, in December 1882 Iwakura set up a research bureau to study the system of the imperial house and that of the aristocracy. Iwakura felt a constitution could not be based on any foreign models, though Ito had proposed the system of two Houses as one adopted commonly by European monarchies, as well as emphasizing the importance of the Upper House or House of Peers as a bulwark of the imperial house.[15] Iwakura died on 20 July 1883, two weeks before Ito's return from Europe, but Ito took over his work and in the following year (1884) the Peers' Decree was issued, creating five ranks: prince, marquis, count, viscount, and baron: sixteen counts among the thirty-two 'new

[13] Quoted in Oishi, op. cit., 80.
[14] Ito to Matsukata, 8 Jan. 1883; *Ito Hirobumi Den*, ii. 338–9.
[15] Shinobu Oe, *Nihon Tsushi* (Complete History of Japan), xvii. 6–7.

peers' appointed 'because of their distinguished contributions' comprised eight from Satsuma, five from Choshu, two from Hizen and one from Tosa. In 1887 fifty-one new peers were added, of whom four were counts (one from Hizen, two from Tosa, and one from Bakufu) and twenty-nine viscounts (nine from Satsuma, eight from Choshu, two from Tosa, one from Hizen, three from Bakufu, and six others). Of the eighty-three new peers created by this time, fifty-one were politicians, bureacrats, and military officers from Satsuma and Choshu. These figures show what the primary aim was in creating the House of Peers as a new political force.[16]

Another bulwark for the throne was provided by bureaucratic units placed between it and the people. Ito was also critical of the old system according to which the highest government positions were given to court nobles and great families; and he favoured the principle of 'meritocracy' which would help maintain the supreme position of the Satsuma-Choshu *hanbatsu* (han-clique). In December 1885 he created the modern cabinet system, replacing the old *Dajokan* (chancellor) system introduced soon after the Restoration, and himself became the first prime minister. Most of the ministers appointed were members of the old Council of State (foreign minister, Inoue Kaoru; fnance minister, Matsukata Masayoshi; and home minister, Yamagata Aritomo, for instance), thus ensuring the continuation of a *hanbatsu* government.

In a sense the throne was to be the bulwark for itself in the coming constitution to check and restrain popular democracy, and imperial autonomy was to be assured by providing a solid material foundation for the imperial family. The government transferred to the imperial household part of its holding of shares in the Bank of Japan and the Yokohama Specie Bank to the amount of 3.5 million yen in 1885, and also shares worth 2.6 million yen of the Japan Mail-Boat Company (NYK, Nihon Yusen Kaisha) in 1887. Imperial properties (apart from real estate), which stood at 1.93 million yen in 1883, rose to 7.89 million yen in less than five years, while imperial lands increased in size 160 times in one year following the promulgation of the constitution.[17]

INOUE KAORU AND THE UNEQUAL TREATIES

Inoue Kaoru had been the minister of foreign affairs since 1879, when his predecessor had to resign because of an incident involving the smuggling of opium into Japan, which went unpunished under the pretext that the opium imported was for medical use. After six years of effort Inoue was at last able to announce a draft of the revised treaties in 1886. In the course of a series

[16] Ibid. 10–11. Ito became a count in 1884, a marquis in 1895, and a prince in 1907.
[17] Masayuki Suzuki, *Kindaino Tenno* (Modern Emperor) (Tokyo, 1993), 173.

of meetings with the foreign representatives concerned, the draft underwent revisions, and it was agreed in April 1887 to open the whole of Japan
to foreigners within two years on condition that criminal, civil, and
commercial laws be compiled beforehand and foreign judges form a
majority in a civil court that would involve foreigners. This was approved
by Ito's cabinet, which held a spectacular costume ball on 20 April 1887 at
the prime minister's official residence to congratulate themselves.

Opposition to the new draft jurisdiction treaty at once arose from
several quarters: from Gustave Émile Boissonade, formerly professor at
Sorbonne, then an adviser to the Meiji government on civil and criminal
laws, who generally regarded the new draft treaty as a deterioration rather
than an improvement; from Tani Kanjo, minister of agriculture and trade
who, on his return from a visit to Europe, expressed fears that the draft
would allow foreigners to interfere with domestic administration and
legislation; and from Inoue Kowashi, who sent a memorandum to Ito
pointing out that it would endanger national independence and sovereignty. These criticisms poured oil on the embers of the dying *Minken*
movement. New agitation in turn invited fresh government suppression
that culminated in the Public Order Preservation Ordinance later in 1887.
Inoue Kaoru resigned from his post as foreign minister and was replaced
by Ito himself, and shortly afterwards by Okuma Shigenobu.

MORI AND YAMAGATA

One of the very few cabinet appointments from outside the Council of
State was Mori Arinori, minister of education, who had met Ito in Paris
when Mori was serving as the minister plenipotentiary in London. Both
agreed on the importance of education independent from political parties
and on the need to cultivate a national spirit to serve the state. Before
leaving London for Japan in February 1884 Mori gave an interview to the
Pall Mall Gazette in which he expatiated on 'patriotism'. Referring to
'Japanese progress' from the beginning of the Meiji era, he asserted that
it was 'a return to her historic role, the only difference being that, whereas
we formerly borrowed from the East, we now borrow from the West'. The
passionate love for the state among the Japanese, he argued, arose from
two causes: 'first, the fact that for twenty-five centuries Japan has never
passed beneath the rule of a conquering race—for all that period Japan has
been free and unconquered. . . . The second is that during the same
period—for 2,500 years—we have remained under the same dynasty . . .
No other state can point to such a record.'[18] Mori apparently shared the

---

[18] 'Japanese Progress', *Pall Mall Gazette*, 26 Feb. 1884, quoted in Ivan Parker Hall, *Mori
Arinori* (Cambridge, Mass., 1973), 303, and also in Takaaki Inutsuka, *Mori Arinori*, 245–6.

unsophisticated belief in the mythical uniqueness of the Japanese imperial house disseminated and inculcated all through her history since the time of the empero Tenmu in the seventh century. In spite of his sincere patriotism, however, his views on education, which were at once national and utilitarian, met with a hostile reaction from Motoda Eifu (Nagazane), a scholar from Kumamoto and the tutor to the emperor, an advocate of Confucianist education, who opposed his appointment in 1885. As minister of education Mori was responsible for the reorganization of the school system in 1886. At the 'imperial university' (the former Tokyo University) arts and sciences would be taught in order to satisfy the needs of the state; steps were taken to approach the ideal of compulsory education in primary schools, while some of the middle schools were classified as 'higher' so as to prepare students for elitist education, and a special emphasis was placed upon the normal schools which would train 'the priests of education'.

Yamagata Aritomo, the son of a Choshu samurai vassal of the lowest rank, a disciple of Yoshida Shoin and a commander of the *kiheitai* (Choshu's peasant army), had been responsible as the head of the ministry of the army for the Conscription Act of 1873. In order to suppress the Satsuma rebellion of 1877 he resorted to a strict enforcement of the conscription law while allowing more *shizoku* to enter the prefectural police forces on the government side. In the following year there was a mutiny within the ranks of the imperial guard stationed at Takehashi, Tokyo, caused by lingering *shizoku* discontent combined with the impact of the *Minken* activists critical of the existing government, and fifty-three soldiers were executed by firing-squad. Rumours persisted about political subversion in the army, and in January 1881 the military police (*kempei*) was introduced. At the request of Yamagata, who became the most trusted adviser to the emperor on military matters, 'the Rescript to Soldiers and Sailors' (*Gunjin Chokuyu*) was issued in January 1882 to the army and navy ministers. The Rescript, termed by a foreign scholar 'one of the major documents of the Meiji period', advocated traditional warrior virtues and helped to disseminate the official ideology: loyalty to the emperor, the spirit of self-sacrifice, a mixture of the traditional samurai ethic and imperial nationalism which could be identified as the 'Meiji spirit'.[19]

Yamagata openly distrusted popular parties. He was the head of the Ministry of Home Affairs for two years before he became the cabinet minister in charge of the same in 1885. His efforts to form a new system of local government and to modernize the police force sprang from his

---

[19] Roger G. Hackett, *Yamagata Aritomo in the Rise of Modern Japan* (Cambridge, Mass., 1971), 86–7.

desire to build a strong, unified imperial state. Two German police officers were employed to teach at a newly created training-school for the police. The Public Order Preservation Ordinance of December 1887 (which we have already looked at in connection with its victim Nakae Chomin) was aimed at crippling the liberal opposition at a time when *Minken* democrats from twenty prefectures presented the 'Three Great Propositions' advocating freedom of speech and assembly, cessation of tinkering with the existing treaties, and a reduction of the land tax. The severity of the ordinance disturbed even Mishima Tsuyo, now head of the metropolitan police, for it allowed the police authorities to interfere with political meetings and expelled undesirable persons from within a radius of seven and a half miles of the Imperial Palace.[20] Ozaki Yukio, who had studied at Fukuzawa's Keiogijuku and had taken part in the foundation of Okuma's Progressive Party and who found himself among those expelled from the metropolis, remarked that the ordinance was 'a selective mixture of the Prussian anti-Socialist Law and the Russian law to annihilate the nihilists'.[21] Meanwhile, Albert Mosse, Ito's teacher at Berlin, came to Japan in May 1886 and remained until March 1890. He was involved in drafting the constitution and was also connected with the creation of the local government system which was to embody and ensure patriotic national feeling.

THE CONSTITUITION OF THE EMPIRE OF JAPAN

'In 1889 Meiji Japan was firmly placed under German tutelage', wrote a German historian, or, as some British observers commented mockingly, 'Japan had become virtually infected by the "German measles"'.[22] The German legation in Tokyo tried its best to foster the shift of foreign influence to Germany; Hermann Roesler played a decisive role in shaping modern Japan. A lawyer, he had worked in the Japanese Foreign Ministry as a legal adviser in all matters concerning Japan's relations with the West since 1878. Later he was promoted to the position of Ito Hirobumi's top adviser on constitutional matters. In this capacity he made at least 160 reports on legal and constitutional problems.[23] Moreover, he was the only foreigner allowed to participate in the discussions about the new constitution.

In April 1888 the Privy Council was created and Ito became its president, premiership having been given to Marquis Kuroda of Satsuma. On 18 June the Privy Council began its deliberation on the draft constitution, at the beginning of which Ito gave an address saying that this was the

---

[20] Hackett, op. cit., 105.   [21] Quoted in Oishi, op. cit., 129.
[22] Rolf Harald Wippich, 'Infected with German Measles: Meiji Japan under German Cultural Influence', *The History of European Ideas*, xx. (1996), 399–403 and *passim*.   [23] Ibid.

first time in the East that a people was to be given a constitution, and that compared with the West, which (he said) in its long history of constitutional politics had been helped by Christianity, Japan lacked a viable religion. 'Though Buddhism once flourished and was the bond of union between all classes, high and low, today its influence has declined. Though Shintoism is based on the traditions of our ancestors, as a religion it is not powerful enough to become the centre of union of the country. Thus in our country the one institution which can become the cornerstone of our constitution is the imperial house.'[24]

The Privy Council met frequently to consider two constitutional drafts, one prepared by Inoue Kowashi and the other by Roesler, which provided the basis of deliberations. On two points Roesler's views were rejected. His draft contained an article which stated that the budget, when unable to be agreed upon, was to be decided by the emperor on the responsibility of the cabinet, a Bismarckian stipulation to which Inoue strongly objected, calling it 'an old form of despotism'. Inoue succeeded in having his draft article adopted instead, which proposed that the previous budget be enforced in such a case.[25] Secondly, Roesler objected to the first article of a composite draft prepared at the first stage of deliberations which stated that the empire of Japan was to be reigned over by 'a line of emperors unbroken for ages eternal', for the reason that nobody could predict what would happen to the imperial throne for hundreds years ahead. He sought in vain to replace it with his own, that would declare the Japanese empire to be 'one indivisible constitutional monarchy'.[26] For the rest 'The Empire of Japan' was changed into 'The Great Empire of Japan'; 'male' was added to 'the imperial children and grandchildren'; and 'the consent of the Diet' was replaced by 'the support of the Diet'.[27] Objection to the term 'consent' came from Mori Arinori. Mori argued that the Diet should simply be made 'His Majesty's advisory organ'. He also objected to the section entitled 'The Rights and Duties of Subjects', suggesting 'rights and duties' to be replaced by 'responsibility', because 'subjects' in his view had only 'station' and 'responsibility' vis-à-vis the sovereign. Ito retorted by saying that the essence of making a constitution was 'to limit the power of the ruler and protect the right of the subject'. Mori's historical awareness of the imperial institution had now expanded to a philosophical as well as a political dimension, and he was supported in his arguments by conservative educators like Motoda Eifu.[28] Ito's constitutionalism held sway, however. There were several more alterations and an English translation of the final draft was also prepared.[29]

[24] Pittau, op. cit., 177; *Ito Hirobumi Den*, ii. 618.   [25] Oishi, op. cit., 141.
[26] Pittau, op. cit., 150; Oishi, op. cit., 142.   [27] *Ito Hirobumi Den*, ii. 624.
[28] Ivan Parker Hall, *Mori Arinori*, 400–7.   [29] *Ito Hirobumi Den*, ii. 632.

On 11 February 1889 a ceremony for the promulgation of the constitution was held. At 9 a.m.[30] the emperor, accompanied by the home
minister (Sanjo Sanetomi), the minister of the imperial household, and
the head chamberlain, entered the Sanctuary of the Imperial Palace to
report to the imperial ancestors his adoption of the Imperial Household
Code and the constitution. Then the emperor received Ito Hirobumi and
gave him the highest honour and decoration. At 10 a.m. princes, the high-
ranking court nobles, the prime minister Kuroda, and other government
officials, both civil and military, attended at the main palace hall, with
foreign diplomats, specially invited observers, and journalists standing in
appropriate places. At 10.40 the emperor and the empress appeared and
stood on a platform. The home minister Sanjo reverently handed the
constitution over to the emperor, who gave it to Kuroda. The emperor
delivered a short speech, saying that he gave 'this imperishable great code'
to his subjects of the present and the future 'by virtue of the prerogative he
inherited from his ancestors'.[31] 'No one except those who had been
involved in its drafting knew yet what the document contained.'[32] 'In
ritual fact, the emperor had merely transferred the document from the
hands of one oligarch to another', and it was the same with the way in
which the government was to be conducted. The cabinet would be responsible only to the transcendental emperor, not to the political parties, and
Ito, the author of the constitution, declared that the government must
stand apart from all parties. The American press called this document 'a
German Constitution'.[33]

The constitution was to remain the fundamental law of the state for the
following fifty-six years, which witnessed the grandeur and miseries, the
pride and shame of the nation while it was ruled according to 'the spirit of
the noble achievements bequeathed by the imperial ancestors', as Ito wrote
in his commentaries on the constitution.[34] Article 1, Chapter 1 (The
Emperor) reads: 'The Great Empire of Japan shall be reigned over and
governed by a line of Emperors unbroken for ages eternal.' On this Ito
commented: 'the splendor of the Sacred Throne transmitted through an
unbroken line of one and the same dynasty has always remained as
immutable as that of the heaven and of the earth.'[35] Indeed, this had
been the basis of the Restoration slogan *sonno*, but it was now presented
as the First Principle of the *raison d'être* of the state and the nation, so that
it was easily turned into popular as well as official fetishism and ideology.
Certainly the royal ancestors were considered more important than the

---

[30] With the replacement in December 1972 of the old lunar calendar by the Julian calendar, the
system of 24 hours a day was also adopted.   [31] Ibid. ii. 636.
[32] Carol Gluck, *Japan's Modern Myths* (Princeton, 1985), 49.   [33] Ibid. 43, 44.
[34] Hirobumi Ito, *Commentaries on the Constitution of the Empire of Japan*, tr. Ito Miyoji
(Tokyo, 1906, repr. University Publication of America, 1979), 1.   [35] Ibid. 2.

lives of the people as late as in August 1945. Article 3 says: 'The Emperor is sacred and inviolable.' Article 4 states: 'The Emperor is the head of the Empire, combining in himself the rights of sovereign, and exercises them, according to the provisions of the present Constitution.' Thus Japan was to enjoy a constitutional monarchy. The Emperor rules 'with the support of the Imperial Diet' (Article 5) but he can dissolve the House of Representatives (Article 7). And 'The Emperor has the supreme command of the Army and Navy' (Article 11). Here Ito refers only to domestic issues such as the need for an emperor's army to preserve internal unity and security. 'The great Imperial Ancestor founded this Empire by his divine valor . . . [At the time of the Restoration] His Imperial Majesty issued an Ordinance, proclaiming that He assumed personal military command for the suppression of rebellion.'[36]

The main constitutional bodies under the emperor were the Imperial Diet, the ministers of state, and the Court of Justice. The emperor retained his prerogative power, and ministers of state were responsible to him, not to the Diet. When the Diet and the government clashed, the Diet could make a humble supplication to the emperor, while the government could seek the emperor's decree to coerce the reluctant and recalcitrant Diet. The German kaiser's advice to Ito on the role of the Diet in deciding the budget, however, was not adopted, owing largely to Inoue Kowashi's objection referred to above. This, as Ito predicted, led to friction. As for suffrage, it was limited to those men over 25 years of age who paid more than 15 yen as direct tax, like land tax (the age-limit for those to be elected was over 30 years); Hokkaido, Okinawa, and Ogasawara were excluded from the electoral law (though the revised electoral law of 1900 was applied to Hokkaido and Okinawa); the number of the electors was 450,000 out of the total population of 40 million (1.1 per cent, which increased to 5.55 per cent by 1920 due to a relaxation in the property qualification). In the election of 1895 there was a candidate who was elected with only eleven votes cast for him![37]

On the day of the promulgation of the constitution Yamagata found himself in the Kaiserhof Hotel in Berlin, where he organized a party to celebrate and drank a toast to the emperor. On the morning of the same day Mori Arinori, the minister of education, while waiting at his house for the celebration, was stabbed to death by a young visitor who believed that Mori had desecrated the Ise Shrine. The assassin had been misled by the clever intrigue of the Shintoist priests who, in an attempt to discredit the minister of education, reputedly a westernizer, staged an

[36] Ito, *Commentaries*, 26–7.
[37] Irokawa, *Kindai Kokka no Shuppatsu* (Beginning of a Modern State), *Nihonno Rekishi*, xxi. 486.

act of seeming irreverence on his part when he visited the Ise Shrine in November 1888. The intrigue was so successful that the assassin became a national hero.

The constitution was to be accompanied by the Imperial Rescript on Education issued on 30 October 1890. It read:

I think our Imperial Ancestors established our country on a broad and wide basis and planted virtues very deep, while all our subjects in one mind remained loyal to their emperors and to their parents and produced beautiful results for generation after generation. This is the quintessence of our national polity, and the very source from which derives education. You, subjects, be filially dutiful to your parents, friendly to your brothers, congenially united as man and wife, trust your friends, be economical in supporting yourselves, extend charity to the general public, master learning, acquire skills, cultivate thereby your knowledge and ability, acheive a virtuous existence, further spread public interest, promote public offices, always respect the constitution, obey national laws, in an emergency bravely serve the country so as to help the Imperial destiny. Such are not only my loyal subjects but also the ones who merit the illuminations of the Way of the Imperial Ancestors. This is the Way left by our Imperial Ancestors as a precept to be strictly obeyed by their descendants and subjects. This can be applied no matter when and where you are, ancient or modern, at home or abroad. I wish to share the same virtue with you subjects by receiving it.

30th October, 23rd Year of Meiji

His Royal Highness's Name and Official Stamp.[38]

Prime Minister Yamagata had commissioned Inoue Kowashi to prepare the above rescript, but Inoue saw two difficulties: one constitutional, because this might interfere with 'freedom of religious belief' guaranteed, though conditionally, by the constitution (Article 28); the other political, because the rescript was to show a 'Way' of education which would make the emperor a 'social monarch' rather than a political sovereign. Unlike the constitution, which was signed by the emperor and all the ministers of the cabinet, the Imperial Rescript on Education had no such signatures, and bore only *Gyomei Gyoji*, literally meaning 'his name and his stamp'. Nevertheless, it took the form of an intimate statement by the emperor on education addressed to the nation at large. Yamagata himself had advocated the formulation of a code of national ethics to guide the people. Motoda Eifu (Nagazane), the Confucian tutor to the emperor, was responsible for the wording of the Rescript itself. From the kind of virtues it enumerated and the way these were presented, it could certainly be called a Confucian-Shintoist document, 'a leading text of Japan's state religion'.[39]

---

[38] Translation of the whole text by myself.   [39] Hackett, *Yamagata*, 133.

THE BIRTH OF AN IDEOLOGY

Thought control began as soon as the essence of the state ideology was enunciated. In June 1891 'The Rules on Ceremonies to be Held on Days of Celebration and of Great Festivity at the Primary Schools' was issued. According to the 'Rules', on such days as *Kigensetsu* (National Foundation Day), *Tenchosetsu* (The birthday of the emperor), and similar days of national celebration, it was decided that all the teachers and pupils, led by the headmaster, should assemble in a hall of celebration where 'all those present should make the deepest bow before the photographs of the Emperor and the Empress', 'the headmaster or a teacher should reverently read the Imperial Rescript on Education', 'the headmaster or a teacher should reverently give an admonitory speech on the purpose and intent of this Imperial Rescript so as to cultivate the morale of loyalty to the Emperor and Patriotism', and all should sing together 'a song appropriate to the day'. Furthermore, the song to be sung on such a day ought to be sufficiently patriotic in words and tune to cultivate loyalty to the emperor. As in the Christian Church (which was now to be discouraged in Japan), the emperor was made the object of worship in a primary school, the Imperial Rescript on Education became 'Holy Writ', headmaster and teachers became ministers, and all pupils formed the congregation of the faithful. *Kimiga Yo* (The Emperor's Reign), the song to be sung on such occasions, was a hymn of 'Revere the Emperor, Love the Country', and not a song that would properly be called a national anthem.

Politics, properly speaking, was denied to the people. Several laws adopted in the 1880s forbade teachers and students of public and private schools, apprentices in trade and agriculture, as well as military men and public officers to participate in any political meetings, and a law imposed in 1890 added women as well as minors to the list of the excluded. As for the military, they were instructed by the Imperial Rescript for Soldiers and Sailors (*Gunjin-Chokuyu*) of 1882 'not to be led astray by current opinions nor to meddle in politics'. Civil servants were treated as the emperor's officials, a deeply respected group, especially after the law faculty was created at the Imperial University as the normal preparation for a privileged entry into the higher echelons of the bureaucracy. By the end of the century religion as well as politics was banned from schools— this was largely an anti-Christian move, for Christianity was now regarded as incompatible with loyalty.

The oligarchs, who had once shunned party politics, changed their minds once the Diet came into existence and a period of some termoil began. They co-opted some of the opposition leaders into cabinets, while Marquis Ito went so far as to form a political party of his own, *Rikken Seiyukai*, in 1900. Even so, a clear demarcation existed between the government, which was the emperor's transcendental government or *kan*, and party politics, which was *min*, the people, associated with private interests and liable to inevitable divisions and conflicts. This *min*, too, though, was a privileged *min*, and people as a whole were left out of politics altogether. Under these circumstances journalism played a conspicuous role. In around 1890 *Osaka Asahi* had a daily circulation of 50,000, three Tokyo papers (*Yamato*, *Yubin-Hochi*, and *Tokyo Asahi*) 20,000 each, and there were a number of provincial papers, though with limited circulation. The men the newspapers supported became politicians, Diet members, and their background remained still largely rural.

What counted most in the newly created constitutional government of Japan was not the constitution itself but the monarchy. It became the centre of 'emerging myths' by virtue of the ancestral myths. The emerging ideology already began to claim victims. In January 1891, when the First High School of Tokyo held a special ceremony for the reading of the Imperial Rescript on Education, Uchimura Kanzo, an 'independent' Christian who taught there, made a light courtesy bow instead of the deep bow of worship required. This caused a sensation as it was interpreted as a sign of contempt for the emperor, and was referred to as the '*Lèse Majesté* Incident'. In the prevailing atmosphere of rising nationalism not only Uchimura but also Christianity in general came under attack, and he had to resign from the school. Kume Kunitake, the compiler of the records of the Iwakura embassy (1871–3), who later became professor of Japanese history at the Imperial University, was known for his historiography of ascertaining historical facts and evidence and for his criticism of ideological historical writings like the *History of Great Japan* of the Mito school. When he published an article under the title 'Shintoism as an Ancient Folk Custom to Revere the Heavens' in a history magazine (*Shigaku Zasshi*) in 1891, he too came under attack and had to resign. Nationalism, both modern and atavistic, constitutional and mythical, was well on its way to a position of greater influence.

THE RISE OF MEIJI NATIONALISM

Some of the Meiji youth in the 1880s began to have misgivings about the extent of westernization and its implications. These were voiced by young publicists such as Shiga Shigetaka, Miyake Setsurei, and Kuga Katsunan.[40] In April 1888, in the midst of the popular movement against what were regarded as too great concessions to the western powers on the issue of the revision of the unequal treaties, a handful of young intellectuals, mostly

---

[40] Kenneth B. Pyle, *The New Generation in Meiji Japan, Problems of Cultural Identity, 1885–1895* (Stanford, 1969), 55. The first number of *Nipponjin* came out on 3 April 1888.

graduates of either the Imperial University like Miyake, or of the Sapporo Agricultural School like Shiga, started a society called the *Seikyosha* (Society for Political Education), with a fortnightly magazine, *Nipponjin*. Shiga had visited islands in the South Pacific as far as Australia and New Zealand on board a naval ship, and published a tract in which he advocated a policy to secure 'the foundations of the nation by choosing a task that comports with her geographical position', in other words, 'the building of a New Japan that would be based on commerce'.[41] We can see a revival of the ideas once upheld by Honda Toshiaki and Sato Nobuhiro. Miyake was introduced to western philosophy by his teacher at the Imperial University, Ernest Fenollosa, the young Harvard graduate, and he combined this with his interest in Asiatic studies, such as the Mongol origins of the Japanese people. For a while Miyake was employed by the Ministry of Education, but together with Shiga and others he started a new intellectual movement to look for values and institutions 'compatible with the ideas of the Japanese people and suitable to the environment of Japan'.[42] One of his co-founders of the society declared the need for establishing 'a national ideology', while Shiga searched for Japanese 'uniqueness', something they could be proud of and could identify with. Shiga stressed the cultivation of 'normal patriotism', to be distinguished from the 'abnormal patriotism' derived from isolation. He called *Oshushugi* (Europe-ism) 'mimicry', while *Nipponshugi* (Japanism) was described as 'conservation of energy'.[43] The harmonious Japanese civilization was contrasted with western civilization, which was said to be selfish and commercial. It was a predecessor of the arguments for the uniqueness of Japanese culture that gained wide currency in the 1970s and 1980s at a time of economic success and new nationalism.

Kuga, an able journalist with his newspaper *Tokyo Denpo* (Tokyo Telegraph), appeared as a powerful ally of the *Seikyosha*. He was not against westernization as such. 'To the degree that it does not damage the national character, we can adopt western things', he wrote.[44] But nationalism was 'the basic element in preserving and developing a unique culture'. On the day of the granting of the constitution to the people Kuga launched a daily newspaper, *Nippon*, which stood for the principles of 'Japanism'. He advocated the adoption of the westerners' philosophy and morals, their science, economics, and industry, as long as they would contribute to Japan's welfare. Like the Meiji constitution, his last recourse was to 'an unbroken line of imperial rulers' in Japan. Japanese liberalism was conceived in opposition to foreign interference, and easily became allied with burgeoning nationalism—*sonno joi* had not died out.

---

[41] Quoted ibid. 58. [42] Ibid. 64. [43] *Nipponjin*, 18 June 1888,
[44] Quoted Pyle, op. cit., 75.

OKUMA, MUTSU, AND TREATY REVISION

Ardour for nationalism flared up when the second round of treaty negotiations came to be tackled by Okuma, the foreign minister. The government had prepared a draft of the Amity, Trade, and Navigation Treaty by the end of 1888 which provided for a termination of extraterritoriality after five years, when the interior of the country would be open to foreigners for travel, trade, and residence, and for tariff autonomy after twelve years. On the basis of this draft Okuma proceeded to conclude treaties with the United States, Germany, and Russia, and negotiations with Britain and France seemed promising. The draft, however, was accompanied by a ministerial declaration which would allow for the employment of foreign judges (later naturalized foreign judges) at the Supreme Court and promised the swift compilation of relevant laws. It was an improvement on the previous draft but was not free from the stigma of being an unequal treaty. To the dismay of the foreign minister and those concerned in negotiations, *The Times* of 19 April 1889 published the main points of the Okuma draft, and in May *Nippon* carried its translation. Violent controversy continued for several months. 'We shall be classed with Turkey and Egypt', declared Kuga, who feared that 'mixed residence' might impede the formation of national identity.[45] A majority of commentators were against the proposed revisions, though Taguchi Ukichi, a reformist journalist and a staunch supporter of Okuma, argued in favour of 'mixed residence' on the basis of his belief in the common humanity of all men. Cabinet ministers were increasingly alienated, and Ito resigned from his post as president of the Privy Council. On 18 October Okuma was seriously wounded outside the Foreign Office by an explosive thrown by a right-wing activist, a member of the *Fukuoka Genyosha*. The Kuroda cabinet was forced to resign and the treaties signed with the United States, Germany, and Russia had to be shelved. It took some time for the revision of the treaties to become a diplomatic issue again.

Then a proposal made in 1892 for a revision that would take for granted the 'free residence of foreigners outside the treaty ports' again annoyed xenophobes, both of the right and of the left. The proposal was taken up by Mutsu Munemitsu, the foreign minister in the second Ito cabinet, but Mutsu aimed at an unqualified equal treaty and began negotiations with Britain. A new 'Trade and Navigation Treaty' with Britain, which abolished extraterritorial rights and made rearrangements for custom duties, was signed on 16 July 1894. Similar treaties were concluded with the United States, Italy, Russia, Germany, and France in the following three years. The revised treaties were enforced in 1899, and it was as late as 1911 that tariff autonomy was finally attained.

---

[45] Quoted Pyle, op. cit., 115.

THE CIVIL CODE OF 1890

The controversy over the civil code should be placed in the context of the treaty revisions as well as that of the people's right issues. Efforts to compile a civil code began as early as 1870 and resulted in the adoption in 1890 (after the deliberations of the Privy Council) of one modelled after French law and consisting of sections dealing with property rights, obligations, mortgages, and other related matters (Boissonade, the French legal adviser, was responsible for the section on property law). Before its scheduled enforcement, objections had been raised on the ground that the civil code, based as it was on the natural-right theory, was harmful to society: 'the civil code rises, and loyalty to the emperor and filial duties perish', as Hozumi Yatsuka, professor of constitutional law at the Imperial University, put it. The third Diet in 1892 decided to postpone its enforcement; a Code Investigation Committee was set up; finally, in 1898 a new, revised civil code modelled after German law was enforced. With its stipulations on family relations and succession the new code provided a legal framework for the paternalistic family system. A mercantile law, in the preparation of which Roesler had given a hand, was also put into effect in time for the treaty revision of 1899; Japan had now equipped herself with a modern legal system that would allow her to exploit a position equal to western powers.

CONSTITUTIONAL POLITICS IN PRACTICE

There was 'a certain lack of articulation' in the constitution, however, on the relationship between the power of the government and that of the Lower House; as a result, the Diet's ability to obstruct the passage of a budget proved to be 'a much more potent weapon than Ito had expected', and this he discovered at a time when Japan was about to engage in her first modern war, which made the budget a crucial issue.[46] Indeed, constitutionalism was in the process of formation. The major issue of the first general election held in July 1890, which has been described as 'a complete landlord election',[47] was a reduction in land tax, and members of the popular parties (the resuscitated *Jiyuto* and the *Kaishinto* or progressive party) won a majority (171 out of 300) in the first Diet, which was opened by the emperor in November 1890. The government led by Yamagata Aritomo, however, subscribed to the principle of *chozenshugi* (transcendentalism, or aloofness from political parties), a political stance which well accorded with the aspirations of the emerging bureaucrats.[48]

[46] W. G. Beasley, 'Meiji Political Institutions', *Cambridge History of Japan*, v. 669.
[47] Junji Banno, *Kindai Nihonno Shuppatsu* (Beginning of Modern Japan) (Tokyo, 1989), 157.
[48] Ibid. 160.

Yamagata placed a great emphasis on the need for government unity in the face of party pressures. One of the first measures the government took was to revise the Regulations for Public Meetings and Political Association in order to prohibit collaboration of political parties.[49]

Three days after the opening of the first Diet, one Liberal member, speaking on the problem of treaty revision, asserted that 'I consider it imperative that the ministers of state should first of all listen to the voice of the people and obey it', a declaration of '*de facto* popular sovereignty'[50] which even a *chozenshugi* government could not ignore with impunity. For the budget committee of the Diet, insisting on the preservation of the people's resources (an easement of the tax burden) and an economy of government expenditure, demanded a cut of over 10 per cent from the proposed government budget, and a debate ensued over the interpretation of Article 67 of the constitution which stipulated for a budget due to 'constitutional prerogative'. Ito Hirobumi, anxious to prevent the first Diet from ending in failure, put pressure on the adamant Yamagata, who threatened to dissolve the Diet, while non-*Sat-Cho* ministers like Mutsu Munemitsu (agriculture and trade) and Goto Shojiro (postal service) got in touch with the Liberal opposition. A compromise was reached, and the budget was passed with the help of twenty-nine Liberal members: the amount of the budgetary cut was substantially reduced, while the government promised economy in its expenditure.[51] Already during the first Diet Yamagata's hard-line approach to party opposition stood in marked contrast to the more conciliatory stance taken by Ito.

In May 1891 Yamagata resigned for health reasons and was succeeded as prime minister by Matsukata Masayoshi. Yamagata, however, formed a clique around himself and exerted an influence through his protégés. While he was building the national army he had collected able subordinates, four who would later become generals: Katsura Taro, Kodama Gentaro, Terauchi Masatake, and Tanaka Giichi, all from Choshu. Shinagawa Yajiro, home minister under Matsukata, and his vice-minister, both from Choshu and prominent in the Yamagata clique, became the key figures in government clashes with the opposition parties. At the second Diet (November to December 1891) there was more conflict again over the government budget. Kabayama Sukenori, formerly a Satsuma samurai, now the minister of the navy under Matsukata, spoke eloquently against a proposed reduction of the naval budget, displaying the *banyu* (teremity),

[49] Roger F. Hackett, *Yamagata*, 126–7, 137.
[50] R. H. P. Mason, 'Foreign Affair Debates, 1890–91', in Andrew Fraser, R. H. P. Mason, and Philip Mitchell, *Japan's Early Parliaments, 1890–1905* (London, 1995), 130.
[51] Hackett, *Yamagata*, 139–141; *Ito Hirobumi Den*, ii. 739–40.

as it was called of the *Sat-Cho* government. The Lower House adopted a resolution moved by the opposition parties in favour of a large reduction in the naval budget (for the construction of warships and a steel-mill), and the House was dissolved in retaliation.

During the second general elections, held in February 1892, prime minister Matsukata personally intervened in the contests, trying to manipulate it through bribery and the extensive use of the police forces. Shinagawa, the home minister, and his vice-minister planned and instigated measures for intervention in order to prevent the election of 'disloyal' candidates. Yamagata's biographer concludes that 'the ex-premier gave wholehearted encouragement to crippling the strength of the anti-government parties'.[52] As a result of this ruthless intervention twenty-five people were killed and 388 wounded, but still no more than ninety-three supporters of the government were elected. At the next session the Lower House and the House of Peers clashed over the issue of restoring the rescinded items in the naval budget; the emperor's intervention was solicited, and the House of Peers and the navy won. Deadlocks recurred, and it seemed as if no one could rule Japan without the support of the self-assertive Diet.[53] Ito Hirobumi, who formed his second cabinet in August 1892 after the resignation of Matsukata due to disunity in his cabinet after the electoral intervention, managed to make his hostile Diet toe the line through an imperial rescript which saved the government budget (to build warships) by offering to allocate for this purpose part of the imperial household expenditure and that on salaries for government officials.

The *Kokumin Kyokai* (National Association), a pro-government party, was founded in June 1892, with a platform advocating development of the armed forces, expansion of national power, promotion of industry, and no reduction in taxation. The second Ito government strengthened its ties with the *Jiyuto*. Meanwhile the *Kaishinto*, one of the two major anti-government parties along with the *Jiyuto*, was moving away from its demands for 'tax reduction' to a 'hard anti-foreigner' line. As the *Kokumin Kyokai* began to act as an opposition party vis-à-vis Ito's more conciliatory policy, the *Kaishinto* by allying itself with the *Kokumin Kyokai*, succeeded in obtaining 110 seats as against ninety-four seats held by the *Jiyuto*.[54] Thus Ozaki Yukio of the *Kaishinto*, later to be known as the 'master of constitutionalism', was able in the spring of 1894 to weld together six political groups in the Diet to attack the Ito government for 'compromising and expedient diplomacy'.[55] Ito continued his efforts to

---

[52] Hackett, op. cit., 151.   [53] Beasley, op. cit., 699.
[54] Banno, op. cit., 77; at the general election of March 1894 *Jiyuto* won 119 seats, *Kaishinto* 48, and *Kokumin Kyokai* 26.   [55] Conroy, op. cit., 214.

avoid a full-scale military confrontation with China. When war broke out, the political parties in the Diet were ready to bury the hatchet and enthusiastically supported the war effort. Ito had been the architect of the Meiji constitution; he was to be the civilian conductor of the war with China when it came.

6

The Sino-Japanese War
and its Aftermath

'THE LINE OF ADVANTAGE'

It may have been a natural sequence that the imperial constitution, a landmark of the Meiji 'civilization', preceded the outbreak of the Sino-Japanese War, a hallmark of Japan's 'westernization' in her relations with Asian neighbours. The two facts can be paired as the two ultimate achievements of nineteenth-century Japan in her effort for modernization. Prime minister Yamagata in his first speech to the Diet on 6 December 1890 defined national security as dependent 'first upon the protection of the line of sovereignty [*shukenshugi*] and then [upon] the line of advantage [*riekisen*]', and for that reason emphasized the need 'to make comparatively large appropriations for our army and navy'.[1] Expansionism in terms of securing overseas interests was clearly stated in the premier's speech. As for foreign affairs in general, Yamagata remained uneasy about the 'aggressive imperialism' of France and Britain in East Asia, but his major concern was the threat of Russia expanding into the Far East with the construction of the Trans-Siberian Railway that began in 1891. His answer was to strengthen the army and the navy.[2] Indeed, the fear of Russia's expansion was one of the motives of Japan's war against China, though it was ostensibly fought over the issue of Korean reform.

In May 1891 the Russian crown prince Nikolai Alexandrovitch, later Tsar Nicholas II, on his visit to Japan was attacked and wounded by a policeman at Otsu who believed that the visit marked the beginning of a Russian invasion. The government, thrown into a state of panic, did all it could to mitigate the possible adverse effects the incident might have on Japan's standing as a probationary power. The incident certainly delayed the resumption of negotiations over treaty revisions for a while. By the time that these were taken up and had made some progress, however, Japan was at war with China over the old and new problem of Korean independence, or rather Japanese interest in Korea vis-à-vis China's.

[1] Hilary Conroy, *Japanese Seizure of Korea* (Philadelphia, 1960), 138.
[2] Hackett, *Yamagata*, 157.

FROM THE KANGHWA TREATY (1876) TO
THE TREATY OF TIENTSIN (1885)

We have already examined some of the earlier relations between Japan and Korea in connection with the *Seikanron* (Punishing Korea Proposal) dispute and the subsequent gunboat diplomacy adopted by the government in the Kanghwa Incident of 1875. We have noted the Kanghwa Treaty of 1876, a western-style imperialist treaty for Japan, which was for Korea, nonetheless, a confirmation of the (illusory) Confucian world order. Indeed, Korea was no longer a hermit nation, while China, alarmed at the growing influence of Japan there, intervened in Korean politics, both domestic and international, 'in a manner unwitnessed since the first half of the seventeenth century'.[3]

The soldiers' mutiny of July 1882 in Seoul was partly a Korean reaction to the implementation of the terms of the Kanghwa Treaty, such as the dispatch of Japanese officers to reform the Korean military, and partly a palace revolution in which the seclusionist and anti-foreigner faction of the Taewongun, the father of the king and former regent, overwhelmed the more powerful faction of Queen Min. The Taewongun faction attacked and burned down the Japanese legation in Seoul. Hanabusa Yoshimoto, the minister in Seoul, and other Japanese retreated to Inchon. Hanabusa returned to Seoul in August with a battalion of soldiers as guards. He found Korean politics quite unsettled, but soon discovered that it was the Chinese who were the masters of the situation. China sent her naval and land forces to Korea to restore 'peace' as an act of 'benevolence' towards her dependent nation. The Taewongun was shipped to China, and then the Koreans were instructed to negotiate with the Japanese. The outcome was the Treaty of Chemulpo of August 1882 which provided for an indemnity for the loss of life and the damage incurred by the Japanese and stipulated the punishment of the guilty along with an apology, and which also allowed Japanese soldiers to be stationed around the legation.

There was a premature attempt in 1884–5 by the Independence Party of progressive Koreans, some educated by Fukuzawa, to establish a reformist government in Seoul possibly with Japanese help. Kim Ok-kium, vice-president of the Korean foreign office, and Pak Young-hyo, brother-in-law of the king, the two leaders of the party, had been in touch with Fukuzawa, and Inoue Kakugoro, the Keio graduate, acted as an intermediary. In Seoul there were defections from the progressive ranks, and the whole Min family and the Korean government headed by Queen Min were now definitely turning to China. The Seoul uprising of December 1884, which involved the Independence Party and a number of young

---

[3] C. I. Eugene Kim and Han-kyo Kim, *Korea and the Politics of Imperialism 1976–1910* (Berkeley, 1967), 28 and *passim*.

Koreans trained in a Japanese military school in Tokyo, was doomed to failure through the lack of effective support from the Japanese. In Korea there were 600 Japanese troops facing about 2,000 Chinese, and skirmishes began. Shortly after the failure of the uprising Ito Hirobumi wrote in a letter that although there was a risk in the future of war with China for Korean independence, 'for now we must avoid it'.[4] In order to prevent further hostilities, Ito himself proceeded to Tientsin to negotiate, and the Treaty of Tientsin was signed in April 1885. According to the terms of the treaty both China and Japan were to withdraw their troops from Korea, neither Chinese nor Japanese instructors were to train Korean soldiers, and in case the situation demanded the dispatch of troops from China or Japan, written notice of such an action was to be sent in advance to the other side. Ito bargained hard with Li Hung-chang, the Chinese plenipotentiary, who sought to distinguish between China's relations with Korea based on traditional suzerainty and that of Japan, derived from recent treaties.

At home the Osaka Incident of November 1885, the arrests of Oi Kentaro and other *Minken* activists for amassing weapons to help Korean reformers and their own cause through them, put an end to the Liberals' attempt to act independently for the Korean cause. Speaking at a Diet meeting early in 1891 Inoue Kakugoro, then a Diet member, pleaded for a positive, reformist, and interventionist policy for Korea, and emphasized cabinet ministers' 'duty to consolidate the independent supremacy of Japan in east Asia'.[5]

JAPAN AND CHINA IN KOREA

In the post-Tientsin Treaty period of comparative calm, however, Japanese officials were alarmed by a huge increase in China's share in trade with Korea, a growth which evinced Chinese political ascendancy after 1885. In the total sum of the Korean imports through Inchon, Wonsan, and Pusan, the Chinese share increased from 19 to 45 per cent, while the Japanese share decreased from 81 to 55 per cent in the period 1885–92. Moreover, a very large bulk of the Japanese goods exported to Korea was 'calico' or cotton goods from England processed by Japanese merchants, a business easily transferred to their Chinese rivals.[6]

Yuan Shi-kai, who was to succeed Li Hung-chang as the most powerful statesman in northern China, took charge of Korean affairs such as telegraph, customs, and shipping. 'Yuan', observed Mutsu Munemitsu,

---

[4] Conroy, op. cit., 159.
[5] R. H. P. Mason, 'Foreign Affair Debates' in Fraser, Mason, and Mitchell (eds.), *Japan's Early Parliaments*, 159.   [6] Conroy, op. cit., 193–6.

the foreign minister at the time of the Sino-Japanese War, 'witnessed the gradual decline of Japan's influence in Korea. He also took note of the constant friction between the Japanese government and the Imperial Diet . . . Judging that Japan was now unable to muster sufficient resolve to send troops abroad, Yuan hoped to capitalize on Japan's weakness to extend China's influence in Korea still further.'[7] China also strengthened and modernized her Northern Fleet, which had been formed in 1888. Five cruisers were bought from England and Germany, and Weihaiwei in the Shantung peninsula and Lushun (Port Arthur) in the Liaotung peninsula were fortified as naval ports.[8] Yuan Shi-kai behaved like a Chinese viceroy in Korea, which by 1890 was forced to submit to China, thus substantially abrogating the Confucian relationship that had been weakened by growing concern with security and trade.[9]

The Japanese government too entered upon a programme of new armament. A divisional system was introduced into the army in 1888, and six regular divisions were created, to which were added shortly afterwards the Imperial Guard Division and the Hokkaido Development Corps. The army and navy general staffs were set up in 1889. For the navy, frigates and torpedo boats formed 'the main fleet' to which several cruisers, each of the tonnage of 3,000 to 4,000, were added. Contrary to Yuan's expectations, Japan was preparing for an eventual confrontation.

THE TONGHAK REBELLION AND THE JAPANESE DECISION FOR WAR

In February 1894 the Tonghak Rebellion began in Chollanamdo, the south-western province of the Korean peninsula. Tonghak, a popular religion mixing Confucianism, Buddhism, and Taoism, literally meant 'Eastern Studies' as against Western Studies or Christianity, and the rebellion, with its anti-Japanese, anti-foreigner slogans, developed into a peasant war. The Korean government asked China to send troops to suppress it. When the news reached Tokyo on 2 June, Ito Hirobumi, the prime minister, convened a special cabinet meeting at which it was unanimously decided to send troops 'in order to maintain the balance of power between Japan and China'.[10] The foreign minister Mutsu decided to send nine warships to Korea and at once directed the ambassador to Korea, Otori Keisuke, who had been back in Japan, to return to Seoul with several hundred marines on board *Yaeyama*. On 7 June the Chinese ambassador informed the Japanese government of the dispatch of their troops in

---

[7] Munemitsu Mutsu, *Kenkenroku*, English tr. Gordon Mark Berger (Japan Foundation, 1982), 9.
[8] Tadashi Ootani, 'Nisshin Senso' (The Sino-Japanese War), in Kazuki Iguchi (ed.), *Nisshin-Nichiro Senso* (The Sino-Japanese and the Russo-Japanese Wars) (Tokyo, 1994), 52.
[9] Kim and Kim, op. cit., 64, 65.   [10] *Ito Hirobumi Den*, iii. 54.

accordance with the terms of the Tientsin Treaty, but added that it was to help 'our dependency'. To this Mutsu replied that Japan would never recognize Korea as a Chinese dependency and notified the Chinese government of the dispatch of Japanese troops.[11]

Otori arrived in Inchon on 9 June and proceeded to Seoul with 300 marines, followed by a battalion of soldiers. A 'Mixed Brigade' was soon to come. The Chinese and Korean governments were 'shocked' to find Otori returning to Seoul with such a strong force, wrote Mutsu in his memoirs. Westerners were 'suspicious and apprehensive' about the 7,000 Japanese troops now encamped between Inchon and Seoul.[12] Otori cabled back, saying that it would be unwise to send too many troops since that would invite western criticism. But, added the foreign minister, 'domestic sentiments in Japan have now been aroused to such a fever pitch that there was no possibility of reducing the troop strength already stationed'.[13] Moreover, a truce had been reached by 10 June between the Korean government force and the Tonghak peasant army and the situation around the capital had been peaceful except for the display of Japanese military strength. Prime minister Ito appeared conciliatory in his mood, but Mutsu and the vice-chief of the general staff Lieutenant-General Kawakami Soroku (who was to direct army operations in the war when it broke out) were not: Mutsu believed that a joint withdrawal of Chinese and Japanese forces would be most unlikely. At the cabinet meeting held on 14 June Ito proposed a joint Chinese and Japanese commission for Korea to deal with her domestic discontent and to introduce reform measures, both military and financial, such as 'a Korean peace-keeping force' for domestic purposes and a large government loan for the Korean state. Mutsu added a rider to the effect that, in case China would not accept the proposal, 'the Japanese government will assume sole responsibility for having the Korean government carry out the proposed reforms'. Ito's plan and Mutsu's rider were accepted by the cabinet; Mutsu invited the Korean minister in Tokyo and informed him orally of the cabinet's decision, omitting his own rider,[14] that would mean that Japan might force the Koreans to try to 'civilize' themselves under Japanese protection. On 21 June the Chinese minister Wang replied in writing, saying that it was for the Koreans themselves to reform their country. China formally rejected the Japanese plan, and Japan decided for war. On the following day Mutsu wrote to Wang, telling him that the Japanese government 'finds it impossible to order the retirement of those Japanese troops now in Korea'. This note Mutsu himself regarded as the first declaration of severing ties with the

---

[11] Ibid. 54–5.   [12] Mutsu, *Kenkenroku*, 18–19.   [13] Ibid. 20.
[14] Ibid. 22–3. For other references made here to Mutsu's attitude towards Korea, see *Kekenroku*, 29–30, 36–7.

Chinese government. 'I have never felt that Korea's internal reform was very important in itself,' wrote Mutsu with astonishing frankness, 'nor did I have much confidence that a country like Korea could really carry out satisfactory reforms.' Nevertheless, 'once the situation changed and Japan became solely responsible for Korea's reform, reform itself became a vital issue in our foreign policy'. This argument augured ill for Korea, and was to sustain the Japanese policy of colonialism until the formal annexation of Korea and thereafter.

On friendly advice from the Chinese the Koreans began taking reform measures in order not to give Japan a pretext for fighting. Mutsu was not convinced of their motives and wrote in his memoirs: the Korean actions 'were delaying tactics . . . to avoid the brunt of our pressure'. On 12 July he cabled new instructions, to Otori telling him that 'any pretext for beginning an active movement quickly would be satisfactory, so long as it did not provoke any concerted international criticism'.

THE SINO-JAPANESE WAR: THE CAMPAIGN

On 17 July a decision for war was confirmed at an imperial conference; an ultimatum to expire on 24 July was sent to the Chinese government, and another, expiring two days earlier, to the Koreans. On 23 July Otori allowed the Mixed Brigade to occupy Seoul after fighting with Korean troops. This could be regarded as the beginning of a Japanese war against Korea.[15] Efforts were made, however, to win over the Taewongun, the father of the king, and persuade him to set up a new regime. On 25 July Japanese warships met Chinese men-of-war in an unexpected encounter off the west coast of Korea and sank the *Kowshing*, a transport ship flying the British flag and carrying 1,500 Chinese soldiers. The alleged refusal by Togo Heihachiro, who commanded the Japanese vessels, to rescue survivors except for the British captain and his team brought forth bitter comments in the West.[16] A few days later Japanese forces attacked and drove back Chinese troops in the Asan area south of Seoul. On 1 August the Japanese emperor formally declared war against China.

Referring to the international response to the outbreak of war, Mutsu wrote: 'We saw England as irresolute, and Russia as consumed by boundless ambition . . . While China and Japan were acting out their tragic drama, Russia was also one of the performers, but she remained virtually concealed in one corner of the stage. Britain . . . was . . . an interested spectator with a wealth of comments to make about the performance.' At

---

[15] Takashi Ootani, op. cit., 58.
[16] Stewart Lone, *Japan's First Modern War* (London, 1994), 35. The following account of the development of the war is largely based on Lone, see esp. 42, 54–5, 108–9, 112, 154–5.

any rate, Mutsu, in a style that would be repeated again and again in the future, declared that 'a precipitate Japanese withdrawal might endanger the peace of the Far East, rather than hasten its restoration'.

The Korean government, supposedly bent on domestic reform, was racked by an internal feud as the Taewongun set about seeking vengeance against the queen's relatives in the Min family. Then the Taewongun himself had to be removed because of his continued contacts with the Chinese. Upwards of 20,000 Chinese soldiers poured into north Korea, while China's Peiyang (North Sea) Fleet remained a menace to the movement of Japanese troops. The whole of Korea became a battlefield. Yamagata, now commander of the First Army with the duty of leading three divisions against the Chinese, landed at Inchon on 12 September and immediately approved the decision to strike north made by General Nozu Michitsura, commander of the Fifth Division. On 15 September Nozu ordered a frontal attack on the Chinese army before Pyongyang, and the city was captured after a twenty-four hour battle. Two days later a naval battle was fought in the northern Yellow Sea in which the Chinese lost five warships, and their Peiyang Fleet suffered a death-blow. These victories apparently altered the course of war. 'Henceforth Japan must be reckoned with as a living force in the East', declared *The Times*. The foreign minister took great care to ensure discipline among the soldiers and impress upon them the need to observe the rules of international law. Apparently he persuaded himself that this was a war for civilization. He was elated as he wrote that 'our victories now at last freed them [Europeans] for the first time from the delusion that European-style civilization could survive only in Christian lands. . . . Now that Japan is the recipient of so much praise and commendation from the world, the problem is whether we Japanese will still be able to form a true estimate of ourselves.' For he was not a little disturbed by an excess of patriotism at home: he remembered that Herbert Spencer had regarded patriotism as the legacy of a barbaric age. Nevertheless, he felt, Japan could pursue 'a new foreign policy attuned to the international mood'.

After Pyongyang, Japanese troops advanced northward and captured a large part of the Liaotung peninsula by January 1895. Yamagata's earlier hopes to push onward to Beijing had been abandoned lest this should provoke western intervention. Yet he allowed his troops to occupy a strategic town at the north-western corner of the peninsula. Never robust, he was in direct command only during one engagement at the Yalu River, and after crossing into southern Manchuria he fell seriously ill. For health reasons, and also for a clarification of strategic issues in the front, he was recalled. A Beijing offensive was definitely given up, and instead part of the Japanese forces were landed on the Shantung peninsula, far enough from the Chinese capital, and captured Weihaiwei, the base of the Peiyang Fleet, which surrendered. In March a regiment was sent beyond Taiwan to occupy the Pescadores in the Formosan strait.

These brilliant operations, however, were not without blemishes, notably the atrocities at Port Arthur. Unlike the long-drawn-out bloody battle fought there ten years later, Port Arthur fell on 21 November 1894 in a single day after an intensive bombardment, when an assault of the forces of the Japanese Second Army, about 18,000 strong, led by General Oyama Iwao overwhelmed a feeble opposition from a Chinese force of about 12,000. Japanese casualties were slight, about 280 in total. The Japanese troops entered the city on the same day, and for four days eye-witnesses, mostly Japanese soldiers and sailors, recorded what they had seen. There is little doubt that the Japanese troops indiscriminately killed 'thousands' of Chinese soldiers and civilians. Reports of this in the *New York World* (12 December 1894) attracted wide attention. Mutsu apparently did all he could to counteract its impact by trying to influence some of the European mass media.[17] 'It is my understanding', he wrote, 'that most of those killed were not peaceful civilians, but Chinese soldiers out of uniform', a set excuse for such atrocities, that were sadly to be repeated so often.[18]

The massacre took place at a sensitive moment in Japan's dealings with the United States, for the revised US–Japan treaty was signed in Washington on 22 November and was scheduled to be ratified by the US Senate. As a result of the publicity given by the American press to the atrocities, some senators expressed misgivings as to Japan's qualification as a partner in the 'civilized' world. Probably Mutsu was successful in his attempt to quell such doubts; the treaty was ratified by the Senate on 5 February 1895.

The war 'for civilization' was not a 'civilized' war. It was 'uncivilized' particularly in the absence of proper logistics, the lack of adequate transport and sanitary facilities. According to an army report, the number of Japanese soldiers and army employees who died during the whole period of the war amounted to 13,488, of whom 1,132 were killed in battle, 285 died of wounds received, 11,894 of diseases they had contracted, and 177 from other causes. These figures are grossly underestimated; the number of wounded and sick among Japanese troops from June to December 1894 has been estimated at 285,853, of whom 20,159 died. There were not enough horses, and men had to draw heavy artillery carriages themselves. The number of soldiers and army employees sent to the battlefields during the Sino-Japanese War amounted to 170,000, and the number of army workmen was not much smaller.[19]

The war provided the first occasion for mass contact between the

[17] Tadashi Otani, 'Nisshin Senso', in Iguchi (ed.), op. cit., 68–71.
[18] Mutsu, op. cit., 74.   [19] Otani, op. cit., 61–4.

Japanese and other Asians. Japanese troops tended to show contempt for the Koreans on whose behalf they had come to fight: they regarded their Asian neighbours as 'lazy' and 'having no spirit for progress', but this was the reverse side of the same coin of no support and no collaboration from the Koreans for their bellicose neighbours. Encounters with Chinese troops allowed many Japanese soldiers to form an idea that what mattered in war was martial spirit rather than weapons: in fact, the victories they won were often over Chinese armies of new recruits who showed little spirit.[20]

THE HOME FRONT

It is probably right to say that the gilded image of Meiji the Great was formed with the Sino-Japanese War.[21] The *sonno* nationalism, now almost a half-century old, belonged to the erstwhile samurai class and by definition to the leaders of the *Sat-Cho* government. The Imperial Rescript on Education fostered emperor-worship as a form of conformist nationalism enforced from above. From September 1894 to May 1895 Emperor Mutsuhito (the Meiji emperor's given name) stayed at the headquarters of the Fifth Division in Hiroshima, which became the imperial headquarters. Thus the emperor as soldier reinforced the emperor as god, and made the latter more tangible, while the blending of the imperial myth with martial spirit was reasserted. Moreover, the Diet followed the emperor to Hiroshima, and its emergency session was opened there on 15 October to adopt emergency military spending. Not a single member was absent at its opening (this was unprecedented). The obstructionist Diet of pre-war days had changed into one of unanimity and docility, praising the armed forces and paying special respect to the emperor as the supreme commander. Prefectural, and town and village offices vied with each other in announcing collections and donations from local sources, while large donations came from the aristocracy and businessmen: about 500,000 yen each from the noble houses of Shimazu and Moori, as well as from the *zaibatsu* families of Iwasaki and Mitsui.

Japan was at this time in transition towards a mass-media society catering for an increasingly literate population. Altogether sixty-six newspapers sent a total of 114 correspondents, eleven artists, and four photographers to report on the war. Supplied with information from the government and from the front, with war songs and war stories, the press contributed much to popularizing the war and spreading nationalism and patriotism.

[20] Stewart Lone, op. cit., 60, 66.
[21] Ibid. 78. For a major source of the following argument on 'The Home Front', see Lone, esp. 78, 84, 87, 89, 99.

THE SHIMONOSEKI TREATY AND
THE TRIPLE INTERVENTION

Talks for a peace treaty began at Shimonoseki in the west of Honshu on 20 March: Li Hung-chan, the Chinese plenipotentiary, more than 70 years old, had arrived from Tientsin, while Ito and Mutsu represented the Japanese side. On the 24th Li was shot and seriously wounded by a Japanese ruffian, and this induced Mutsu to accept a ceasefire. Li recovered and the treaty was signed on 17 April. The terms were: 1. China would recognize complete Korean independence; 2. China would cede to Japan the southern portion of the Fengtien province in the Liaotung peninsula, Taiwan, and the Pescadores Islands: 3. a war indemnty of 200 million taels (trade name for liang, about $1\frac{1}{3}$ oz of silver) was to be paid to Japan; 4. four cities and ports were to be opened to Japan (Shashih, Chungking, Suchow, and Hangchow). The exchange of ratified treaties took place on 8 May. Japan now definitely began to partake of the benefits of what has been called 'the treaty port system' or 'informal' and 'economic' imperialism.[22] This was the outcome of an imperialist war, a war between China and Japan over Korea as the sphere of influence for each country, a war which turned out to be a war of conquest for Japan as well. Economic and military imperialism were inevitably tied together. Japan's emergence as an imperialist power was not received by western powers with equanimity, though. Before the exchange of ratified treaties, the ministers of Russia, Germany, and France called at the Foreign Ministry on 23 April stating respectively their governments' stand against the Chinese cession of the Liaotung peninsula to Japan. Mutsu was for rejecting their advice for the time being at least, but Ito thought it would be dangerous to provide Russia, by Japanese defiance, with an excuse for hostility in view of recent Russian actions: at the very moment of Japan's victory at Pyongyang the Russian government had been sending its fleet through the Suez Canal to the Far East for possible intervention. On 24 March the Japanese minister in Washington cabled to Tokyo the gist of the conversation he had had with the American Secretary of State: 'Russian ambitions are currently running very high. . . . Russia wishes to occupy Manchuria and northern China, and is opposed to Japan's occupying any of that territory or serving as Korea's protector. About 30,000 Russian troops have already been stationed in northern China, and their numbers are growing steadily.'[23]

On 4 May it was decided at a meeting of cabinet ministers to accede to the advice of the three intervening powers. The immediate popular reaction to this 'Triple Intervention' was one of political panic, but the acceptance by the Japanese government of their advice and the exchange

---

[22] For 'the Treaty Port System', see W. G. Beasley, *Japanese Imperialism 1894–1945* (Oxford, 1987), 15–18. [23] Mutsu, op. cit., 230.

of the ratified Sino-Japanese peace treaty assured the nation that the crisis was over. But now 'excessive pride' was replaced by a sense of 'intolerable humiliation', wrote Mutsu, who died in August 1897, leaving behind *Kenkenroku* (A Record of Worries and Endeavours), his memoirs of war and diplomacy. In them he stated that 'the origins of the tragic war lay fundamentally in a diplomatic controversy over the suzerain–tributary relationship of China and Korea'.[24] 'Civilization' meant the replacement of this ancient, illusory system with modern international law and international relations. It is small wonder that the Japanese war for 'civilization' degenerated into a colonial war when Japanese rule in Taiwan, one of its achievements, met local resistance. Mutsu would have had to recognize that the Triple Intervention itself formed part of the modern system of international relations and of imperialist rivalries and power politics.

As for local resistance in Taiwan, the Sino-Japanese War did not end with the Shimonoseki Treaty. Japan was dragged into another war to subdue Taiwan, which lasted at least until 1902. Indeed, the number of casualties suffered by the Japanese army in the new military campaigns in this period of 1895–1902, estimated at 8,322, was not much smaller than that in the 1894–5 war. Kabayama Sukenori, who had been a foremost advocate of the occupation of Taiwan, was appointed its first governor-general and introduced military rule there, while the Imperial Guard Division was sent and occupied Taipei without much fighting. The Chinese in Taiwan, who had set up a 'Taiwan Democratic Country' in order to continue fighting against the Japanese, were ordered by Li Hung-chan not to resist, and its leaders fled to China. Resistance to the occupation forces was carried out by the volunteers called *Dohi* (local guerrillas). In August 1895 Prince Kitashirakawa, the division commander, died of illness, officially announced as malaria but more likely deriving from a wound received in an attack made by Taiwanese guerrillas in a village near Tainan; a massacre of the villagers took place as an act of retaliation by the Japanese army. Sporadic fighting continued, while in 1898 Kodama Gentaro, the new governor, with the help of Goto Shinpei, who was in charge of civil administration, began laying the foundations for the development of Taiwan as a colony with a land survey, the construction of a north–south railway and of the Chilung harbour at its northern end, and the opening of the Bank of Taiwan. Government monopoly of opium, salt, and camphor was introduced, while the Taiwan Sugar Company, founded in 1900, grew under state protection. Taiwan finance was put on a sound basis by 1905, though these reforms had been carried out at the cost of the Taiwanese, who lost their land and traditional trade interest.[25]

---

[24] Ibid. 80.
[25] Katsuhiko Murakami, 'Nihon Teikokushugi to Gunbu' (Japanese Imperialism and the Military), in *Koza Nihon Rekishi* (Tokyo, 1985), viii. 172–8. See also Misuzu *Gendaishi Shiryo* (Sources for Modern History), xxi on Taiwan.

KOREA AND THE FAR EASTERN CRISIS
AFTER THE TRIPLE INTERVENTION

Japan had no alternative but to acquiesce in the Triple Intervention by returning the Liaotung peninsula to China: 'unless Japan could challenge a new enemy, she must accept the recommendation.'[26] A Japanese Foreign Office document recording the process of deliberations has been described as 'permeated with realism', a balanced concern for national security.[27] Not only was Japan not able to fight a new enemy, Russia above all, but she was also isolated internationally. When Britain was asked by Japan for support against the three powers, she declined. 'Britain had no wish to become committed to Japan whose expansionist ambitions in China had already been reported by the Tokyo legation.'[28]

The first article of the Shimonoseki Peace Treaty with China began with the Chinese acceptance of Korea as 'a completely independent country', but the treaty failed to clarify Japan's own relationship with Korea. Evidently the Triple Intervention restrained Japanese leaders. Ito, the prime minister, was of the view that although the pretext for the intervention was the Liaotung peninsula, its real motive was 'the Russian fear that Korea might fall into our hands'.[29] Mutsu, the foreign minister, told the British, French, and several other ministers who came to see him that 'the Korean problem' was no longer one between Japan and China but between Japan and Russia; but he thought it strange and suspicious that the Russian minister said nothing about Korea during a long conversation with him.[30]

In another letter to Ito, Mutsu wrote: 'our future Korean policy will have the objective of leaving off interference insofar as possible and causing Korea to stand up by herself.'[31] But how? Inoue Kaoru, then Japanese minister in Seoul, came round to support the king, to the dismay of his erstwhile friends, the reform party. In September 1895 Inoue was replaced as minister by Lt.-General Miura Goro who, in conjunction with the first secretary of the Japanese legation and the Japanese adviser to the Korean army, planned the murder of Queen Min who was known for her sympathy for the Russians. On 8 October, less than a month after Miura had been accredited as the Japanese minister to Korea, the plan was carried out. Korean troops trained by Japanese instructors were used, but the main job was performed by the Japanese garrison in Seoul, the police, and some of the unruly Japanese residents. The queen was brutally murdered, and her body burned in a pinewood. The Japanese government at once recalled

---

[26] Mutsu quoted in Conroy, *Japanese Seizure of Korea*, 291.   [27] Ibid. 286.
[28] Ian Nish, *The Anglo-Japanese Alliance*, 31.   [29] *Ito Hirobumi Den*, iii. 220.
[30] Mutsu to Ito, 23 May 1895; ibid., 232.
[31] Mutsu to Ito, 3 June 1895, in Conroy, op. cit., 299.

Miura, and he and fifty-odd Japanese implicated in the queen's murder were tried at the military tribunal at the Hiroshima district court, but all were acquitted for alleged lack of evidence.[32] Miura, at a preliminary investigation for the trial, stated that the Japanese government had known the impossibility of Korean reforms by ordinary means, and had sought to execute a *coup d'état* under the impression that their action would obtain its tacit approval.[33] After the queen's murder the reformists returned to power for a while, but they were defeated by a pro-Russian *coup d'état* of February 1896 occasioned by the landing at Chemulpo of Russian marines and their successful march to Seoul. The king, who had fled to the Russian legation on this occasion, was assisted by a movement for Korean independence, proceeded to a detached palace, and declared himself as the emperor of the Great Korean Empire in October 1897. Various reforms, such as land and monetary reforms and the laying down of a rudimentary infrastructure, were introduced in order to modernize the Korean economy and to strengthen the court. Although the neutralization of Korea was widely discussed, she remained a pawn in the power-struggle of East Asia.

Japan, in the meantime, had to be content with the Yamagata–Lobanov (the Russian foreign minister was named Lobanov-Rostovskii) protocol of May 1896 which repeated the platitude of Korean independence while agreeing in secret clauses permitting Russia and Japan to keep equal numbers of troops in the peninsula. 'When the statesmen discussed dividing the peninsula into a Russian zone to the north and a Japanese zone to the south, they apparently looked at each other and smiled.'[34] In fact, Japan was doing her best at this stage to make herself strong enough to fight with 'a new enemy'. In 1895 the government decided to double the size of the Japanese army, and in 1896 planned to create a balanced fleet of six modern battlehips and six cruisers. Most of the shipbuilding and procurement of machinary for large vessels was carried out in British yards. By 1900 Japan had come to 'hold the naval balance between the Russo-French and British fleets in the Far East'.[35]

Russia was not so much interested in Korea as she was in Manchuria and northern China. Here her interest came into conflict with that of Germany, who after the Triple Intervention was planning to set up a coaling station in East Asia. In November 1897 the German fleet entered Kiaochow Bay in the Shantung peninsula, using as a pretext the murder of two German missionaries involved in Boxer troubles in the area. China invited Russia to counteract and neutralize the German move, and in December Russia sent a squadron of ships to Port Arthur. The Japanese troops stationed at

---

[32] Ibid. 305–21; Fukuju Unno, *Kankoku Heigo* (The Annexation of Korea) (Tokyo, 1995), 100–2.   [33] Unno, op. cit., 102.

[34] Nish, *The Origins of the Russo-Japanese War*, 33.

[35] Nish, *The Anglo-Japanese Alliance*, 36.

Weihaiwei (entitled to be there until the Chinese indemnities had been fully paid) and the government at home anxiously watched German and Russian manoeuvrings. In March 1898 the Germans secured the lease of Kiaochow for ninety-nine years, and later in the same month Russia obtained a treaty which gave her the lease of Port Arthur (a closed naval port) and Tailenwan (an open commercial port) for twenty-five years and which extended the concession already given to the Chinese Eastern railway (a Russian company) to allow the construction of a branch line connecting it with the leased territory; Russia at last obtained the ice-free port she had long sought. Meanwhile, a British-German loan enabled China to pay the indemnities in full, and this led to the withdrawal of Japanese troops from Weihaiwei, the lease of which was now granted to Britain as it was intended to check the Russians across the northern Yellow Sea and also to pre-empt possible German advances in Shantung.

Evidently Russia could now afford to show a more conciliatory attitude to Japan by offering to withdraw her military and financial advisers stationed in Korea. This appeared to be a chance to end the state of a joint occupation of the country. With cabinet approval, Nishi Tokujiro, the foreign minister, proposed that if Russia entrusted Korea to Japan, Japan would recognize Manchuria as being outside of the sphere of her interest. This is a Japanese formula, called *Mankan-kokan* (exchange of Manchuria with Korea), that was to be adhered to until 1904. The parleys that followed resulted in the Nishi–Rosen Agreement (Roman Rosen was Russian minister to Japan) signed in Tokyo in April 1898, which reaffirmed non-interference with Korean politics, and required mutual consultation in advance of the dispatch of financial and military advisers: the only concession Russia made was her acknowledgement of Japan's large commercial and industrial interest in Korea.[36] In fact, a Japanese sphere of economic interest had gradually been built up in that country.[37] The Dai Ichi Bank, founded by Shibusawa Eiichi, had established a branch in Pusan as early as in 1878. After 1894 it played the role, similar to that of foreign banks in China, of issuing a stable currency as an alternative to the chaotic local one. Dai Ichi almost assumed the function of a central bank in Korea by circulating special yen paper notes from 1901. As for railway rights, those for the Seoul–Inchon line, having been sold to an American, were purchased by a Japanese *zaibatsu* syndicate headed by Shibusawa, and the work on this line was completed in 1901. A larger project to build a Seoul–Pusan line was carried out by another Shibusawa syndicate, helped by the Japanese government under pressure from the army for strategic reasons, and was finished by the end of 1904, though not in time for the

[36] Conroy, op. cit., 327; Nish, *Alliance*, 59–60; Nish, *Origins*, 45–7.
[37] W. G. Beasley, *Japanese Imperialism*, 73–5.

outbreak of the war with Russia. Korea was not closed to investors from other foreign countries, but the situation was such that it did not much attract them.

Taking into account the whole situation in Manchuria and Korea, it has been judged that 'Russia had gained and Japan had lost'.[38] France too, Russia's ally, managed to obtain the lease of Kwangchow Bay in South China in 1899. Meanwhile, there was no co-ordination of policies between Britain and Japan in the so-called 'slicing of the melon', a succession of attempts by the great powers to obtain 'spheres of interest' in China. These two countries, however, were more or less implicitly agreed about the need to restrain Russia. American propositions for an 'open door' policy for China were also aimed at restraining Russia, especially in Manchuria. Then a war scare flared up when Russia obtained the lease of Masanpo, South Korea, in April 1900, but all these menaces were soon overshadowed by the Boxer Rising in China.

CONSTITUTIONAL POLITICS RESUMED

After the Sino-Japanese War the *Jiyuto* (Liberal Party) abandoned its objection to a tax increase as it adopted new policies for greater armament and further extension of the infrastructure. Moreover, the former was to be paid for out of the Chinese indemnities, and the latter through public bonds. Tax increase at the time largely meant the introduction of business tax as a national tax, which met with strong opposition from the chambers of commerce and led to demands for an increase in land tax, which formed 95 per cent of all national tax in 1896. The *Jiyuto*, which more or less represented the landlords' interests, allowed its leader Itagaki Taisuke to join the second Ito government in April 1896 (till September 1896), while the *Shinpoto* (Progressive Party, formerly the *Kaishinto*), though equally dependent upon the support of the landlords, had its leader Okuma Shigenobu enter the second Matsukata government (September 1896–January 1898). Matsukata in due course decided for a land-tax increase. Thereupon the *Shinpoto* terminated its support for the government, which was compelled to dissolve the Diet. As Taguchi Ukichi, the founder of the *Tokyo Keizai Zasshi* (Tokyo Economic Journal) commented, the instability of constitutional politics arose from 'the prejudice of the electoral law in favour of the landlords'.[39] At the fifth general election, held in March 1898, the *Jiyuto* and the *Shinpoto* between them had 189 members elected; the government sought to pass an act to introduce a new assessment of the price of land, but was defeated. The *Shinpoto* withdrew its support from the Matsukata government which was then replaced by Ito's

[38] Nish, *Origins*, 47.   [39] *Tokyo Keizai Zasshi*, Feb. 1898, quoted Banno, op. cit., 217.

third government (January–June 1898) in the middle of the Far Eastern crisis.

A tax increase to meet greater armament expenditure was an urgent necessity. Ito was apparently becoming converted to a more democratic form of constitutionalism than he had envisaged. A government bill was in preparation for a revised electoral law which would reduce the property qualification for suffrage and would increase the electorate from 450,000 to 2 million, but this did not see the light.[40] A government bill to increase land tax was defeated by 247 votes out of 300 and the Diet was dissolved. The two parties merged and formed a new party, the *Kenseito* (Constitutional Politics Party). Ito feared the possibility of a large popular party imposing its narrow party interests to the detriment of the national interest, and sought to form a national party by himself. Yamagata was violently opposed to Ito's plan and convened a *genro* (elders) meeting at which Ito declared that he would form a political party as a private person if he could not do so as a prime minister or a man in public office. Then there would be no need to consult the *genro* meeting. To this Yamagata replied by saying that a party government was against the national polity (the emperor system), detrimental to the spirit of the imperial constitution, and would degenerate into democracy. Ito said that he and Yamagata had basically different views on constitutional politics. All the *genro* were stunned when he proposed to ask the *Kenseito* to form the next government. But no *genro* present dared to try and form a government against the formidable political party in opposition. Shortly afterwards when Ito met Okuma and Itagaki, the leaders of the *Kenseito*, he told them that 'the Sat-Cho factions were no longer beneficial and should not be compared with parties that would strive for legislative purposes in the Diet'.[41] The emperor, though reluctant himself, accepted Ito's advice and ordered the new party to form a government.

The first party government led by Okuma, however, remained in office for only four months (June–October 1898). On the issue of the allocation of ministerial posts the party split into two, the *Kenseito* (former *Jiyuto*) and the *Kensei-Honto* (former *Shinpoto*). Ozaki Yukio, the education minister, had to resign for a so-called 'republican' speech in which he criticized 'Mammonism' which would destroy both 'constitutionalism and republicanism'. 'There is no likelihood in Japan of introducing republican politics', he said; '. . . For the sake of argument, let us assume that we had it in a dream. Perhaps Mitsui or Mitsubishi would stand as a presidential candidate. There is no such possibility in America.'[42]. The second Yamagata government (November 1899–September 1900) was

---

[40] *Ito Hirobumi Den*, iii. 358, 360.　　[41] Ibid. 378–9, 387.
[42] Reference in Banno, op. cit., 230.

formed and passed a government bill for an increase of land tax (to 3.3 per cent) in December 1898. It is noteworthy that the 'transcendentalist' (non-party) governments managed to proceed without a general election for four years (from the sixth general election of August 1898 to the seventh of August 1902).

THE HIGH-TIDE OF NATIONALISM

On 13 September 1894 Tokutomi Soho travelled to Hiroshima in the same train as the emperor. On the same day he declared in his newspaper *Kokumin no Tomo*: 'We must remember that we are fighting before the whole world. Why do some Japanese say we fight in order to reform Korea, or to vanquish Beijing, or to establish a huge indemnity?' He told his readers that they should realize that 'we are fighting to determine once and for all Japan's position in the world'.[43] Soho stayed at Hiroshima till the end of the war, became deeply attached to the emperor, and affirmed his belief in the harmony of *sonno* spirit and populism, for he had altered his views since publishing *The Future Japan* in 1886, which had established his fame as the foremost westernizer and evolutionist. In his study of Yoshida Shoin, published in 1893, he discarded his earlier Spencerian view of the Meiji Restoration and formed an idea that it was a restorationist change caused mainly by internal factors such as the dissolution of feudalism and the rise of *sonno* ideology. Shoin for him was a great pioneer of Japan's expansionism and should be placed in the same pantheon as Honda Toshiaki and Sato Nobuhiro. In his book *Dainippon Bochoron* (On the Expansion of Great Japan), published in December 1894, he suggested that overpopulation in Japan would require overseas expansion, or in more concrete terms an annual acquisition of about 253 square miles, which would make clashes between the Japanese and the Chinese inevitable. It was in this sense that he regarded the war with China as opportune.

Meanwhile, Miyake Setsurei and his *Seikyosha* formed a group called the Oriental Society (*Toho Kyokai*), which sought to divert people's attention from the West to Japan's neighbours in the Pacific and East Asia. The *Seikyokai* and Soho's organization, the *Minyusha* (Association of Friends of the People), were brought into close co-operation. Indeed, Soho admitted that the Sino-Japanese War marked 'the great turning-point' in his life. He later recalled that 'as a result of the Triple Intervention I was baptized to the gospel of power'.[44] He found himself in the mainstream of expansionism now promoted by the government, while the nationalism

---

[43] Quoted in Pyle, *The New Generation in Meiji Japan*, 173; see also Sinh Vinh, *Tokutomi Soho: The Later Career* (Toronto, 1986; Japanese tr., Tokyo, 1994), 64.

[44] Quoted in Pyle, op. cit., 180.

advocated by Miyake, Kuga, and the *Seikyosha* began to be overtaken by the more radical form advocated by Takayama Chogyu, the editor of a popular magazine called *Taiyo* (The Sun), who stood for a forthright type of nationalism which opposed western liberalism and Christianity.[45]

It is interesting to note that the *Nipponjin*, which stood for 'Great Japan' from the beginning, changed its name to *Asia* from the issue of 2 June 1892. In this issue the paper suggested that if Asia proved powerless vis-à-vis the West, Japan would have to 'fight against our common enemies' or else to 'take advantage of Asian weaknesses to advance our own interest'. With the outbreak of the Sino-Japanese War the paper began advocating a 'Great Asian Alliance', though 'Chinese arrogance' had to be defeated.[46] The paper reverted to its old name *Nipponjin* in October 1894, when a Japanese victory in the war was well in sight.

[45] Pyle, op. cit., 195. 'Maruyama, whose father was associated with the Seikyosha, regards Kuga as a proponent of "progressive", "healthy", "liberal" nationalism"', ibid. 185. Maruyama Kanji, the father of Maruyama Masao, later warned against narrow-minded nationalism born of national pride.   [46] *Asia*, 14 July, 21 Oct. 1894.

7

Meiji Industrialization and its Critics

THE ROAD TO *FUKOKU*

Fukoku kyohei (enrich the nation and strengthen arms) was a slogan well on its way to fulfilment by the end of the nineteenth century. A monarchist constitution of the Prussian model had been granted, and a war for 'civilization' successfully fought; it is now time to examine the process of *Fukoku* that provided the sinews of the emerging empire. As the nineteenth century drew to a close with Japan's industrialization proceeding at a fast pace, nationalism, both liberal and illiberal, as well as westernism, such as *Minken* democracy and Christianity, were themselves changing so as to accommodate the demands of new classes that had emerged in the process of industrialization itself.

In the period 1885–1914 GNP in Japan doubled (its average annual growth-rate for the same period is estimated at 2.7 per cent), an achievement which can be favourably compared, says a modern economic historian, with the case of Italy where GNP increased by 30 per cent in the comparable period of her economic growth, 1860–90, or that of Holland, where it took forty years for her GNP to increase 2.2 times from its level in 1860, the year of the beginning of rapid Dutch economic growth.[1] The growth theory of economics, though, tends to emphasize an increase in GNP and other economic units in terms of quantity, volumes, and figures, and pays relatively little attention to structural change and socio-political implications. At a time when economics had no overwhelming claims to human wisdom (at any rate in Japan), there was no need as yet to criticize the dismal science as such, but the process of industrialization brought in its train both the victims and the critics of the process itself, and its effects were very visible.

INDUSTRIALIZATION

In the period of 1885 to 1914 agriculture was the largest industry in Japan; the proportion of those employed in agriculture and forestry in the total employed population fell very slowly from 65.2 per cent in 1885 to

[1] Shunsaku Nishikawa and Abe Takeshi (eds.), *Nihon Keizaishi* (Economic History of Japan), vol. 4, *Sangyokano Jidai I* (The Age of Industrialization I) (Tokyo, 1990), 5, 60.

54 per cent in 1915. Within manufacturing industry, machine engineering was the fastest-growing, with an average growth-rate of 12.2 per cent, but its sustained growth began only in 1894 and remained small in size compared with the textile industry. The proportion of textiles in the total of manufacuring products (in values) was 26 per cent in 1874, 32 per cent in 1887, and 41 per cent in 1897; it then began to decline, but was as high as 32 per cent in 1905.[2] The Osaka Boseki (Cotton Spinning) Company, proud of the first steam-powered mill with over 10,000 spindles, was founded in 1882 with Shibusawa Eiichi as its chief sponsor and with capital from influential merchants and wealthy peers; it proved a great success and was followed by the Kanegafuchi Boseki (established as the Tokyo Cotton Company in 1887, renamed in 1889) and others; the number of spinning mills increased from nineteen in 1887 to thirty-nine in 1890; export of cotton yarn to China began in the middle of the 1890s and the export of the same exceeded its import for the first time in 1897.[3] Domestic cotton had virtually disappeared by the end of the century; in the 1880s the textile industry depended for its raw material largely on Chinese cotton, which was replaced by Indian cotton after 1890, and soon American cotton began to make inroads into the market. A number of smaller textile mills went bankrupt in a period of depression after the Sino-Japanese War, and thereafter the industry developed in a state of oligopoly formed by large mills of a limited number adopting a new market strategy, including dumping in the Korean and Chinese market. In 1906 the Osaka Boseki jointly with two other large spinning companies succeeded in monopolizing the cloth market in Korea, and in 1914 it developed into the Toyo Boseki, the largest of its kind at the time.

It is disputed, however, whether the driving force for industrialization came from the textile industry or from the state's promoting early industrialization with model textile plants and nourishment of heavy industry through army arsenals and naval shipyards.[4] Okuma, the finance minister, in a statement made in 1880 on government-owned industrial enterprises and properties, ennumerated three shipbuilding yards, fifty-one merchant ships, five munition works, fifty-two other factories, ten mines, seventy-five miles of railways, and a telegraph system linking all the major towns. Many of these were to be privatized in due course.

Until the First World War Japan was largely dependent on foreign countries for iron and steel. A great part of her own output was produced by a single government mill, the Yawata Steel-Mill, which began operation in 1901. The idea of starting a government steel mill had been mooted as

---

[2] Nishikawa and Takeshi (eds.), op. cit., vol. 4, 164.   [3] Ibid. 166, 67.
[4] Ibid. 19–20.

early as 1891, and it was decided after the Sino-Japanese War to build it at Yawata near the Chikuho coalfields in Kyushu. The plant depended almost entirely on German technology, and the iron ore was brought in from the Daye mine in Central China. The Yawata Steel-Mill, though, had been preceded by one at Kamaishi, Tohoku, where a western-style blast furnace was built in 1857, and supplied pig iron for agricultural and other tools and implements. Since 1890 heavy demands from the Osaka Arsenal revitalized the then flagging Kamaishi (Tanaka) Steel-Mill. Other private steel-mills made their appearance early in the new century: Sumitomo Steel (1901), Kobe Steel (1905), Kawasaki Shipyard Steel (1906), and Nihon Kokan (1912).[5]

The Meiji government inherited from the Bakufu certain shipyards (Nagasaki, Kobe, Uraga, and others) which were transferred to private ownership in the 1880s. The Nagasaki Shipyard, started in 1857 as an adjunct to the Bakufu's Nagasaki Naval Training School, was given to Mitsubishi in 1884 and remained the largest private shipbuilding yard until 1945. By 1913 there were six yards capable of building vessels of 1,000 tons and over. But according to western standards the shipbuilding output in Japan in 1914 was still unimpressive.[6]

As for railways, until the early 1880s the government undertook almost all railway construction. Then private firms joined in the enterprise. The railway between Ueno (Tokyo) and Aomori (the northern end of Honshu) was built in 1884–91 by the Nihon Railway Company, founded in 1881 with capital supplied mainly by wealthy peers. In 1906, when it was decided to nationalize the major railways, it covered about 6,000 miles, which rose to 7,100 in 1914. In 1906 it was also decided to purchase the railway line connecting Pusan and Seoul in Korea. Urban or inter-urban railways were developed by private capital and some were municipalized.

The creation of the infrastructure needed for sustained economic growth was largely the result of technology transfer, itself part of the worldwide spread of the industrial revolution that originated in Britain in the late eighteenth century. At the request of the British minister Sir Harry Parkes, the construction of lighthouses and telegraph cables began shortly after the Meiji Restoration. We have already seen something of railway construction and shipbuilding. The Mint at Osaka was built as early as 1869 and was placed under the management of an Englishman, T. W. Kinder, who had had experience in this field in Hong Kong.[7] The adoption of the gold standard in 1897, though responsible for a temporary depression, led to a fast development of the deposit market; thus, investment funds were to rely

[5] G. C. Allen, *A Short Economic History of Modern Japan*, 36, 81–2.   [6] Ibid. 84–5.
[7] Hoshimi Uchida on 'Gijutsu Iten' (Technology Transfer), in Nishikawa and Takeshi (eds.), op. cit., 267–71.

heavily on the mobilization of bank deposits of private money rather than on government money or firms' own capital.[8]

Before the Sino-Japanese War, as we have noted, the Diet had resisted the government budget for naval expansion, and nearly succeeded in stopping it. After the war, armament expansion was given priority without much discussion. Matsukata, the minister of finance, known for a sound-money policy, estimated Chinese reparations at 300 million yen, of which 50 million yen was allocated to the army for its expansion and 130 million to the navy for the same purpose. He took the steps that enabled the reparations to be paid in English money in London, an arrangement which allowed the gold standard to be formally adopted. Actually the Chinese reparations, together with other related gains, amounted to £41,907,623 14s. 3.5d. His budgetary plan, however, was deemed by many too conservative, and he resigned. His successor, under pressure from the military, allowed an increase of 50 per cent in the expenses for armament expansion; the amount was further increased in the final execution plan by the decision to issue war bonds.[9]

FOREIGN TRADE

Bare figures relating to export and import, though not adequate by themselves, may help to clarify the nature of industrialization. The top six items among the commodities for export in 1898 were raw silk, cotton yarn, coal, silk cloth, tea, and copper, while the top six imports in the same year were rice, raw cotton, sugar, machinery, iron, and cotton cloth. The top items for export in 1913 were raw silk, cotton yarn, silk cloth, cotton cloth, copper, and coal, and for imports in the same year raw cotton, iron, rice, oilcake, machinery, and sugar. The volume of each item in terms of percentage is given in Table 7.1. A list of major countries with which Japan traded and the volume of each trade is provided by Table 7.2, which shows a breakdown by country of the total value of export which stood at 35.8 million yen (100 per cent) in 1885, and the same of the total value of import in that year of 29.4 million yen, while similar figures are given for the year 1913 when the total volume of export stood at 632.5 million yen, and for the year 1914 when the total import was estimated at 729.4 million yen. Silk remained the most important commodity for export throughout this period, followed by cotton yarn and cloth, and this is reflected in the prominence of China and the United

---

[8] Shigeo Teranishi in S. Nishikawa and Yuzo Yamamoto (eds.), op. cit., vol. 5, *Sangyokano Jidai II* (The Age of Industrialization II) (Tokyo, 1990), 40–1.
[9] Nishikawa and Yamamoto (eds.), op. cit., ii. 14–16.

TABLE 7.1. *Top six items in export and import in 1893 and 1913 (%)*

(a) Export

	Raw silk	Cotton yarn	Coal	Silk cloth	Tea	Copper	Cotton cloth
1893	25.4	12.1	9.2	7.7	5.0	4.5	—
1913	29.8	5.3	3.8	6.2	—	4.5	5.3

(b) Import

	Rice	Raw cotton	Sugar	Machinery	Iron	Cotton cloth	Oilcake
1898	17.4	16.5	10.2	4.9	4.3	3.9	—
1913	6.6	32.0	5.0	5.0	8.0	—	5.4

TABLE 7.2. *Major countries for export and import in 1885 and 1913 (%)*

(a) Export

	USA	China	France	Britain	India	Germany	Australasia
1885	43.6	22.9	18.7	7.0	1.4	1.4	0.8
1913	29.2	29.2	10.5	5.2	4.7	2.1	2.2

(b) Import

	Britain	China	India	USA	Germany	France	Australasia
1885	42.5	21.4	11.6	9.5	5.8	4.4	0.0
1914	16.8	12.6	23.7	16.8	8.7	0.8	2.1

Source: Nishikawa and Yamamoto (eds.), *Sangyoka no Jidai II* (The Age of Industrialization II) (Tokyo, 1990), 100–3.

States in the export trade. It is significant that the compiler of the lists ignores Korea even before Japan's annexation of that country.

ZAIBATSU

The *zaibatsu* emerged at an early stage of industrialization, exerting a great influence on its course. The term *zaibatsu* means 'money clique'. It is applied to an industrial, trading, or financial conglomeration on a gigantic scale, with a core holding company connected with a great family for each group. The four major *zaibatsu* were Mitsui, Mitsubishi, Sumitomo, and Yasuda. They had played a great role in the development of Japanese-style capitalism, and their influence was felt in politics as well. At the time of the Meiji Restoration the new government had to plan ahead in terms of economic viability, and was able to avail itself of the services of a few business families which had for a long time been engaged in banking and commerce on a large scale.

The house of Mitsui, for instance, is said to have employed over a thousand people in its Edo shops at the end of the eighteenth century.[10] Echigoya, Mitsui's main shop in Edo, was probably the world's first department store, and certainly it was already the largest shop in Japan at the beginning of the eighteenth century. In 1691, when its Osaka exchange shop was opened, the Mitsui house became an official money-changer for the Bakufu, along with several others such as Sumitomo and Konoike. At the same time the Konoike as an exchange shop extended its activities to such an extent that it had financial relations with seventy-six han lords, many deeply indebted, at the time of the Restoration, which meant a severe blow to its resources. But the house recovered and set up the thirteenth National Bank in 1877, which developed into the Konoike Bank in 1919 and finally into the Sanwa Bank in 1933. Mitsui and other *zaibatsu* families became agents to execute the government's economic policy and thereby to make themselves partners in political decisions. For instance, Inouye Kaoru, the councillor in charge of foreign affairs and later minister of finance under the Restoration government, and still later the foreign minister in the first Ito government, worked in close contact with Mitsui, and Mitsui in return obtained possession on easy terms of the properties that had belonged to the Shogunate and some of the han lords. Favoured treatment of this type explains the origins of the Mitsui's Miike coalmine concern, which in some ways symbolized the rise and transformation of Japanese capitalism. Meanwhile, the Mitsui Bank was opened in July 1876, with offices in the four largest cities and twenty-four major towns.[11] A group of politicians and bureaucrats connected with the Ministry of Finance, including Inoue Kaoru, founded a company to export rice, which developed into the Mitsui Bussan Kaisha (Trading Company) in 1876. At the time of its founding the most important exports of the Mitsui Bussan were coal from the then still state-owned Miike coalmines and surplus rice; the Bussan imported blankets and woollens for the army.[12] From banking, general trading, and mining the Mitsui developed into the largest *zaibatsu*. By the beginning of the twentieth century it had under its control several leading companies such as Shibaura Seisakusho (later Toshiba), Oji Paper Company, Hokkaido Coalmines and Shipping, and Kanegafuchi Cotton Spinning. Mitsui was so closely involved in twentieth-century politics that Ikeda Shigeaki, the chief director of the Mitsui Bank, after forty-one years in business entered the first cabinet formed by Konoe Fumimaro in 1938.

[10] Allen, op. cit., 21.
[11] John G. Roberts, *Mitsui: Three Centuries of Japanese Business* (2nd edn., New York, 1989), 106.   [12] Ibid. 111.

Mitsubishi was founded by Iwasaki Yataro, the son of a masterless samurai in Tosa. He successfully reorganized the Nagasaki branch of the Tosa Trading Company, the assets of which he acquired early in Meiji together with six steamships. In fact he bought them 'at dirt-cheap prices' and established the Mitsubishi Shokai (Trading Company) in 1873.[13] Iwasaki acted as an agent for the government in carrying supplies at the time of the punitive campaign against Formosa in 1874, when its small fleet was supplemented by thirteen steamers bought by the government for this purpose and was given a substantial subsidy. In the same year Mitsubishi acquired the Takashima coalmine and branched out into the mining industry. More ships were added to the Mitsubishi fleet at the time of the Satsuma rebellion of 1877, and as a national carrier Iwasaki's Mitsubishi was able to loosen the foreign grip on shipping in Japanese waters that had been in the hands of the Pacific Mail Steamship Company of the United States and of the British P&O line. The 1881 *coup d'état* was a blow to Mitsubishi, and the ascendancy of the Choshu clique thereafter brought into existence a rival shipping company, one of the three sponsors of which was the Mitsui. In order to avoid the devastating effects of fierce competition the two shipping companies merged and created the Nihon Yusen Kaisha (NYK) in 1885, which in due course opened regular shipping services to India, Europe, North America, and Australia and which had developed into the world's largest shipping company by the time the Second World War broke out. The land Mitsubishi bought from the government near the Imperial Palace, a wasteland at the time, later developed into model business quarters called Marunouchi. Politically Mitsubishi was associated with Okuma, who was the target of the 1881 *coup d'état*, and with the party which he started. Political alignments formed at about this time had lasting effects. Mitsui allied with the *Seiyukai* party (close to the Choshu clique) and Mitsubishi with the *Minseito* (retaining some of the Tosa tradition) in later constitutional politics which we shall look at in a later chapter.

The Sumitomo family established itself early in the seventeenth century in Osaka as refiners and exporters of copper and developed a number of mines throughout the country. An Osaka exchange shop with branches in Edo and Nagasaki was also started in the seventeenth century, and at the time of the Meiji Restoration the debt of a considerable sum from twenty-six han remained with the Sumitomo shops. The rich copper-mine of Besshi in Shikoku, which the family acquired in 1691, became a springboard for further expansion of Sumitomo interest, especially later in

---

[13] Ibid. 117; Tomohei Chida and Peter N. Davies, *The Japanese Shipping and Shipbuilding Industries* (London, 1990), 6.

Meiji, in many other industrial and financial activities. These included steel, mining (coal, gold, and silver), forestry, the chemical industry, and banking. Sumitomo's links with the military were strengthened from about the time of the Russo-Japanese War; it would have nine companies in munition industries during the Second World War.

The fourth *zaibatsu*, Yasuda, was unique in that it had begun in 1887 as the Yasuda Hozen (Yasuda Preservation) to preserve and develop the family assets of the Yasuda, its founder Yasuda Zenjiro being a self-made man from Toyama, and remained financial rather than industrial with the Yasuda Bank as its main agent. Yasuda, however, gave large financial aid to the smaller Asano industrial *zaibatsu*, the founder of which happened to be another self-made man from Toyama, and which virtually became the industrial sector of the Yasuda, with such affiliated enterprises as Asano Cement, the Joban Coalmines, and Nippon Kokan Steel.

Indeed, all the *zaibatsu* played an important role in financing Japan's foreign wars and her colonial advance. Yet they were regarded as too liberal by the militarists of the 1920s and 1930s. The zenith of their power was reached in around 1929.[14]

INDUSTRIALIZATION AND LABOUR

Turning to economic growth as a whole, we have noted that for the period 1885–1914 GNP doubled or more than doubled (2.2 times); mining and industrial production grew more than four times; and heavy, chemical industries and electricity consumption began to grow. Government intervention also grew. The basic structure of the political economy that was to last until 1945 and even thereafter was established and consolidated around 1900.[15]

The nature of interdependence between the growth of primary production and industrialization is a factor that would determine the type of economic development. In Japan the balance was heavily weighted by the fiscal system against agriculture and in favour of the industrial and commercial classes. It was the peasant population who 'mainly financed the military and development programs of the Meiji state'. A money economy made their tax burden harder to bear; as a result, a great many of them were driven into debt. An increasing number of the farming population had to find employment outside agriculture. Those who remained on the farm had to find part-time jobs in local industries to supplement their income. They were even forced to send their daughters to the textile mills in urban areas. 'Thus labor and income were steadily siphoned off the farm

---

[14] Allen, op. cit., 138.   [15] Nishikawa and Yamamoto (eds.), op. cit., 33–4.

to provide material and human resources for industrial and commercial expansion.'[16] The industrial population in factories and mines, too, were subjected to abuses which were exploitative and inhumane.

The working classes, properly so called, were to be created so that the process of industrialization might gain the momentum of sustainable growth. The population of the country began to increase rapidly after the Meiji Restoration, from 35 million in 1872 to 43 million in 1898. In the same period the number of farm households remained constant, at about 5.5 million, though tenant farmers increased to nearly half that number. An excess farming population, together with craftsmen whose skills became obsolete, along with impoverished samurai, created a labour pool accessible to industrial employers, assisted by the extension of railways and communication systems.

THE CONDITIONS OF THE WORKERS IN THE MID-MEIJI PERIOD

As for the conditions of the workers, we should look at the Osaka Boseki, the model spinning company. Shibusawa, its founder, sought numerous low-wage agricultural workers, and especially farm-girls who were housed in company dormitories while they worked at the firm. As competition among firms intensified, they reduced labour costs by lengthening working hours to eighteen per day in silk-reeling and twelve in cotton-spinning. Workers, mostly young females, earned a wage equivalent to 10 cents a day. Conditions were poor, tuberculosis was rife.

Working conditions in heavy industry, in spite of the subcontracting system widely adopted, were considerably better than in textiles, working hours being from ten to twelve per day. The working conditions of miners, however, have been described as 'nightmarish'.[17] 'Miners worked a twelve-hour shift in 120 degree heat, naked except for a loincloth. They would . . . drag or carry 125 pounds of coal in a bamboo basket several hundred yards to the steam conveyor. . . . The prospect of escape was always on the minds of the miners, but punishment was severe. Workers who disobeyed or tried to escape were often hoisted into the air with their hands tied behind their back and beaten mercilessly.' In the summer of 1884, when cholera broke out at the Takashima mine and killed nearly half the workforce, any workers who showed symptoms of the disease, along with the dead, were tied in bundles of several persons. 'These human bundles were hoisted up on a large iron plate over a huge bonfire. Many miners were

[16] William W. Lockwood, 'Economic Growth in Japan, 1868–1938', in Simon Kuznetz, Wilbert E. Moore, and Joseph J. Spengler (eds.), *Economic Growth: Brazil, India, Japan* (Durham, NC, 1955), 141.
[17] Stephen E. Marsland, *The Birth of the Japanese Labour Movement* (Honolulu, 1989), 27.

burned alive. Word of this got out in 1888, causing a national sensation.'
These atrocities should be attributed to primitive, perverted emotions, and
not solely to the profit motive. The company officials responsible, though
called before a judge, were merely warned not to murder miners again.[18]

Early in the nineteenth century Japan was becoming an advanced mining
country by the standards of the day. The Meiji government inherited the
positive mining policies of the han and the Bakufu. It assumed ownership
and control of the Miike and Takashima collieries with the first Coalmining Law of 1873. State managers of the mines had access to 'a unique
labor pool—the criminal population'. By 1880 40 per cent of the miners
at Miike were prisoners from various jails. In Hokkaido, where the
government took control of the Horonai mines in 1882 as part of its
Hokkaido development plan, 'prison authorities formally supervised some
of the mines'.[19] Occasional convict rebellions were brutally suppressed;
negligible labour costs and improvement in mining methods brought about
exceptionally high profit margins, as much as 50 per cent in 1886–7.

As early as in 1876 the Mitsui Trading Company was granted a monopoly on sales of Miike coal. The Takashima coalmine, which had been sold
to Goto Shojiro, then a *Minken* advocate, fell into the hands of Mitsubishi
in 1881. The wholesale privatization of the coalmines went on throughout
the 1880s, and after public funds had been spent on modernization of the
mines through the introduction of foreign technology, the two remaining
state-run coalmines were sold: the Miike mines to the Mitsui Mining
Company (1888) and the Horonai coalfields to the Hokkaido Coal and
Railway Company (1889). In the late 1880s the three largest mines,
Miike, Takashima, and Horonai, accounted for half of total coal production, a third of which was exported. The mining industry played an
increasingly important role as the supplier of energy in the period of
fast industrialization that followed.

As for work-stoppages or strikes, these at first had the appearance of
peasant uprisings in the Tokugawa period, and were often spontaneous.
No labour organizations emerged in the textiles industry in the period
1868–1900, although about 100 women workers at a silk factory at Kofu
went on strike in 1886 for better treatment, an incident usually referred to
as the first strike in Japan. The high turnover in the workforce in the
industry usually made organizational efforts hopeless. No lasting labour
organizations appeared in mining in the period 1868–1900. Work-
stoppages in coalmining were due to spontaneous riots rather than strikes.
In fact, convict labour became 'the hallmark of coalmining'.[20]

[18] Okochi Kazuo and Matsuo Hiroshi quoted in Marshland, op. cit., 28.
[19] Richard J. Samuels, *The Business of the Japanese State* (Ithaca, NY, 1987), 70.
[20] Marsland, op. cit., 33.

As the century drew to a close the conditions of the workers attracted wider attention. Yokoyama Gennosuke, a journalist associated with the *Mainichi Shinbun*, taking his cue from Charles Booth's studies of the poor in London, made an investigation of the life of tenant farmers, the urban poor, and women and children employed in the textile mills and match factories, the results of which were published in a classic study of the Japanese poor, *Nihon-no Kaso Shakai* (The Low Strata of Society in Japan, 1898). Government bureaucrats, alarmed at the disclosures, started factory surveys of their own, soliciting support not only from Yokoyama but also from social policy experts (professors of the Social Policy Association), medical doctors, and building specialists and issued a substantial report *Shokko Jijo* (Conditions of Mechanics, 1903), pointing to the need for factory legislation which, however, was slow in coming.[21]

THE ASHIO METAL POLLUTION INCIDENT AND THE BEGINNING OF LABOUR ORGANIZATION

The Ashio Copper Mine located about 15 kilometres south-west of Nikko, once owned by the Toshogu Shrine (of Nikko), was privatized in 1871 and fell eventually in 1878 into the hands of Furukawa Ichibei, the son of a Kyoto merchant and the founder of the Furukawa *zaibatsu*. The 'King of Mines', as he was later called, did much to improve the mine by introducing mechanized drainage and ore-carrying methods. Refining techniques remained primitive, however, and consumed a lot of charcoal, which led to the dreary sight of hills stripped of trees and of chained convicts in felling gangs on the steep hillsides, the men being lashed mercilessly when they themselves fell. Furukawa Ichibei encouraged the employment of women in the pits, as he expected that they would then reproduce more miners. New rich veins of ore were discovered and the mine expanded. Technical improvements were carried out, including the adoption of the Bessemer process,[22] and the construction of a hydraulic power plant in 1890, the first of its kind in Japan.

Furukawa also established political connections. The son of the foreign minister at the time of the Sino-Japanese War, Mutsu Munemitsu, was adopted into the Furukawa family, and the minister's secretary, Hara Takashi (the future prime minister), became vice-president of the Furukawa Mining Company. Later, as the minister of home affairs, he sent troops to quell the miners' strike at Ashio in 1907.[23] The Ashio Copper Mine became the largest of its kind in Japan, but it produced, if not the worst,

---

[21] Sheldon Garon, *The State and Labor in Modern Japan* (Berkeley, 1987), 24–7.
[22] A Bessemer converter was introduced at the Yawata steel-mill in 1901.
[23] Yasumasa Murakami (ed.), *Ashio Dozan Rodo Undoshi* (History of the Ashio Copper Mine Labour Movement) (Ashio, 1958), 30.

then certainly the best-known incident of pollution in the pre-1914 industrial history of Japan. The pollution was caused by a copper-sulphate solution which ran into the River Watarase and virtually annihilated local farm production by settling on the fields in the wide areas down river. It began by killing trout and other river fish and depriving local fishermen of their source of income in around 1880. As the mine expanded the pollution spread to the paddy fields and dry fields in several villages. The causes of the pollution were identified by scientific investigation, and in 1891 one thousand people along the river signed a petition asking the authorities to order the mine to be closed. Tanaka Shozo, a member of the Diet from Tochigi, demanded on a number of occasions that the government take the necessary measures to cope with the pollution. Furukawa agreed to install an apparatus to gather powdered copper from the waste, but the effects of the pollution became even worse. The fields were flooded by long, heavy rain in the summer of 1896, and many more fields were affected by the return of the poisonous water, hemmed in by the closure of a flood-control channel. About 3,500 of the affected farmers gathered and planned to march to Tokyo. The government gave in and ordered Furukawa to take preventive measures, such as the construction of a filter and sedimentation reservoir and a desulphuration tower. Furukawa stopped the mining operation for forty days in order to build these facilities. But in spite of all this the pollution still did not stop and, together with the flood which came almost every year, deprived the farmers of their land and work. In February 1900 about 4,000 farmers tried to come to Tokyo to hand in a petition, and clashed with the police en route. Scuffles ensued. In March the government issued a 'Public Order Police Act', thus marking the beginning of the new century with a display of its determination to suppress any protest movement on the part of farmers and workers. In 1901 Tanaka Shozo resigned from the Diet and made a direct petition to the emperor on behalf of the suffering farmers: his 'Petition' had been prepared by Kotoku Shusui, who was later to turn to anarchism.[24]

The issue now turned into one of flood control. A vast reservoir was to be built, and the entire village of Yanakamura had to be demolished. Disputes over the forced evacuation ensued. The Ashio Copper Mine Pollution Incident, followed by the Yanakamura Incident, was perhaps the greatest social problem which Meiji Japan had to tackle. Many novelists, journalists, academics, and students were incensed at the fate of the Yanaka farmers who, they thought, had fallen victims to the Mammon of industrialization.

The adoption of the preventive measures at Ashio was in fact carried out

---

[24] Murakami (ed.), op. cit., 52.

at the expense of the miners. Basic wages were fixed low; fines and other forms of punishment were rigorously enforced; the miners remained at the mercy of the butty system (butty being a middleman-contractor) and of the *hanba* (workmen's temporary dwelling quarters) system run by the butty. The Ashio miners had no trade union at this stage to protect themselves except for the traditional *tomoko* (fellow-son) system, an organization among the miners for mutual help based on the *oyabun-kobun* (boss and his men) relationship. It was the same elsewhere, though sporadic attempts at organization were made from the middle of the 1890s. A 'society of labour and leisure' was set up among the miners in Akita, and a *Nihon Kozan Domeikai* (Japanese Alliance of the Miners) succeeded in abolishing the newly introduced local tax on miners with the help of 'Tanzei Taro' (Single-Tax Taro), a Christian agitator advocating Henry George's social gospel of Single-Tax. A *Dainihon Rodo Shiseikai* (Great Japan Friendly Association of Labour) was formed in 1902, the first stable trade union among the miners, for securing safety measures in the pits and compensation for mining accidents. These activities proved ephemeral in the end, but formed part of a great awakening of the nation to the complexity of the problems caused by the drive towards modernization and industrialization undertaken by the Meiji leaders.

CHRISTIANITY AND PACIFISM: THE CASE OF UCHIMURA KANZO

By the time the ban on Christianity was lifted in 1873, Protestant missionaries, mostly Americans, had entrenched themselves in several outposts in Japan.[25] Three so-called 'Christian Bands' played a decisive role in the development of Japanese Christianity. The Yokohama Band was founded in 1872 by a group of Japanese, mostly students at a school of English conducted by the Revd James H. Ballagh: Ballagh, together with his colleagues Samuel R. Brown and James C. Hepburn, held Bible classes and prayer meetings. These Christian missionaries were all from 'Puritan America'. The Band soon developed into the first Protestant church in Japan.[26] The Kumamoto Band, organized by students taught by Captain Leroy L. Janes at the Kumamoto Western School, migrated to the Doshisha Academy founded in Kyoto by Niijima Jo, the congregationalist minister and educator. The Sapporo Band was founded by students inspired by Dr William S. Clark, president of the Massachusetts Agricultural College, who had been invited to organize and direct a similar school at Sapporo. A

---

[25] John F. Howes, in Marius Jansen (ed.), *Changing Japanese Attitude Toward Modernization*, (Princeton, 1965; 1982), 340.

[26] Caldarola, op. cit., 27; Otis Cary, op. cit., ii. 76–7.

'Covenant of Believers in Jesus', to which Uchimura Kanzo and Nitobe (then Ota) Inazo, among others, put their names had been framed by Dr Clark himself. These covenanters, thirty in all, formed the basis of what was soon to become the Independent Church of Sapporo.

In teaching their young students the missionaries placed great emphasis on moral strength and character. Dr Clark urged: 'Be ambitious not for money or for selfish aggrandizement, not for that evanescent thing which we call fame. Be ambitious for the attainment of all that a man ought to be.'[27] Clark's exhortation, somewhat distorted and shortened into 'Boys, Be Ambitious!', became perhaps the most influential catchword for Japanese youth until 1945. When the Imperial Rescript on Education of 1890 identified the imperial throne with 'heaven and earth', the Meiji Christians stood on the defensive. Yokoi Tokio, the son of Yokoi Shonan (who served the lord of Echizen), formerly of the Kumamoto Band, began to advocate 'Japanese Christianity', a Christianity that would stand on the foundation provided by Buddhism and Confucianism.[28] The outbreak of the war with China afforded the Japanese Christians an opportunity to prove themselves as patriotic as any Japanese. They were equally patriotic during the Russo-Japanese War,[29] though Tolstoyan, pacifist influences were also felt among certain Christians.

One of these was Uchimura Kanzo, the son of a poor *shizoku* and a graduate of the Sapporo College of Agriculture and also of Amherst College in the United States; through contacts he made with the Quakers, he developed into a pacifist and a social reformer.[30] He was not blind to the magnanimity of liberal America, but regretted the inequities in its treatment of American Indians and Negroes. He was now determined not to defend Christianity on the ground that it was the religion of Europe and America.[31] His motto was independence like Fukuzawa's, but with a difference: his was freedom from the patronizing influence of money and sectarian connections, and even from the state. We have already noted the *Lèse-Majesté* Incident which forced him to resign from the First High School.[32] In due course he launched a 'Non-Church' movement for churchless Christianity. In 1898 he founded his own periodical, the *Tokyo Dokuritsu Zasshi* (Tokyo Independence Review), in which he suggested political and social reform such as a reduction in armaments, abolition of the new social distinction of *kazoku*, *shizoku*, and *heimin*, popular election of prefectural governors, local self-government, and expansion of

[27] Caldarola, op. cit., 30.
[28] *Japan Weekly Mail*, 19 July 1890, in Otis Cary, op. cit., ii. 218–19. Uemura Masahisa of the Yokohama Band longed for a 'baptized Bushido'.   [29] Ibid. ii. 322.
[30] Suzuki Norihisa, *Uchimura Kanzo*, 131.
[31] Uchimura Kanzo, *Autobiography*, 119, 133.
[32] See Chap. 5, the section dealing with 'the birth of an ideology'.

education. He became a friend of the common people, the peasant, the fisherman, the small tradesman, and the rickshaw man. He made a tour through the area affected by the pollution from the Ashio Copper Mine and joined in the anti-pollution movement.

Uchimura has been called 'the first Japanese pacifist'.[33] In 1903, when there was a rumour about war with Russia, he wrote on the 'Abolition of War' in *Yorozuchoho* (30 June 1903). Later in the year, when the owner of the newspaper decided to support the war, he resigned, together with two socialist colleagues on the paper, Kotoku Shusui and Sakai Toshihiko, but he did not join with the socialists in opposing the war when it came. His was a pacifism of non-resistance. When the Second World War approached, among the small minority of Christians who refused to succumb to wartime pressure could be found some of Uchimura's followers in the Non-Church movement.

THE BEGINNINGS OF TRADE UNIONISM: TAKANO FUSATARO AND KATAYAMA SEN

The Japanese labour movement was first launched by the efforts of two groups, progressive intellectuals and enlightened workers. Most of them had stayed in the United States either as students or workmen (or both), where they had developed mixed feelings about industrialization. They hoped to avoid the evil aspects of economic growth by setting up trade unions at home. Many were Christians or Christian Socialists. Other foreign influences were also at work. Bismarckian Germany provided a model for the state control of industrial relations under the name of 'Sozialpolitik' or social policy, which attracted professors of Tokyo Imperial University. They made 'scientific studies' of social problems.[34] Germany was also known as the home of Social Democracy; Ferdinand Lassalle and Karl Marx were known to Japanese intellectuals in the 1890s through English translations of their works. We should also take into account a domestic tradition, the 'liberty and people's right' tradition of opposition to the government.

In the last two decades of the nineteenth century there were various attempts at organization among the workers. In 1882 the Tokyo Streetcar Company opened its first line between Shinbashi and Nihonbashi and announced an extension plan. The rickshaw men at once set up an Alliance to Oppose Streetcars and held a mass protest meeting. In 1887 a friendly society was started among metalworkers to promote education and mutual

---

[33] Caldarola, op. cit., 171.

[34] It is no accident that one of the leading spirits of the Social Policy Association (Professor Kanai Noburu) became even more prominent as one of the seven doctors who in a statement pressed the government for a hardline foreign policy against Russia.

assistance in case of illness, but this was short-lived. The years 1889 and 1890 witnessed two such organizational failures in the printing trade. In 1892 shoemakers in Tokyo formed an association of their own in protest against the army's attempt to produce military footwear. In the 1890s various societies for mutual assistance were set up, like that among the railway workers at the Omiya Shunting Yard and Factory. In 1897 the Yokohama ship carpenters formed a union and carried out a well-organized strike. By the end of the nineteenth century labour organizations in Japan had come a long way on the road to modernization.

Takano Fusataro, 'the founder of the Japanese labour movement', born in Nagasaki the son of a poor tailor, moved to Yokohama and studied at the Yokohama Commercial School.[35] He left for America in 1886 to continue his education. It was at this time that a group of Japanese workers in San Francisco formed an organization called the *Shokko Giyukai* (Knights of Labor), apparently a branch of the US Knights of Labor, which Takano joined. The money he was regularly sending to his mother supported the family, including his younger brother Takano Iwasaburo who entered Tokyo Imperial University and later distinguished himself as a social reformer and progressive intellectual. Fusataro in America moved to Massachusetts and came to know Samuel Gompers, president of the American Federation of Labor. He consulted Gompers on the possible form of labour organization in Japan; Gompers always advised him to 'organize by trade' and made him a general organizer for the AFL. As such he returned to Japan.

Takano called together the men who had helped form the *Shokko Giyukai* in San Francisco and who had since returned home. With their assistance he launched a campaign of his own by distributing a pamphlet *Shokko Shokun ni Yosu* (A Summons to the Workers) in 1897. The revision of the unequal treaties, the great aim of the nation through many decades, was practically to come into effect in 1899. This has sometimes been referred to as the second opening of the country. 'The year 1899 will see Japan truly opened up to foreign intercourse', the pamphlet read: 'It will be a time when foreign capitalists will enter our country and attempt to amass millions in profits by exploiting our cheap labour and our skilled workers. . . . In the light of this situation, you workers must quickly begin to prepare yourselves.' He warned the workers against revolutionary arguments like that in favour of equality in property, and proposed that trade unions be organized on 'a nationwide co-operative basis'. The revised treaties would allow foreigners to live in the interior of Japan from 1899; Takano's manifesto took advantage of the workers' fear of exploitation by these foreigners, and of their latent nationalism.

[35] For Takano, see Marsland, op. cit.

In the same year (1897) the Japanese Knights of Labor was set up and held a rally at the YMCA hall in Tokyo; Takano and Katayama Sen, his lieutenant, were among the main speakers. Takano took the opportunity to declare the formation of a *Rodo Kumiai Kiseikai* (Association for Promoting Trade Unions), which was to be a federation of trade unions like the AFL. The *Kiseikai* was duly launched in the same year; Takano and Katayama were invited to speak at meetings of several trade unions. Metalworkers—machinists, boilermakers, casters, forgers, lathe operators, fitters, smiths, etc.—formed the nucleus of the *Kiseikai*.

The *Kiseikai*, although it symbolized the beginning of a new important social movement, was not a success. Its membership reached only 1,346 by 1899. The Public Order Police Act of 1900 proved a fatal blow, and it had practically ceased its activities by 1901. In fact, it took a decade for a proper trade union to be started, and nearly half a century had to pass before trade unions were legally recognized in Japan. But this is to anticipate; Takano, disheartened at the failure of his organization work, moved to China and died in Tsingtau in 1904.

Katayama Sen, who worked with Takano in the early trade union movement, had been brought up as a simple peasant in a small village in Okayama prefecture.[36] He had 'a stubborn and unshakable faith in individual and social perfectibility'.[37] Wanting to improve himself he tried his luck in Tokyo, studying at a private school while working at a printing shop. A wealthy friend whom he had come to know at the school and who was then studying at Yale wrote telling him that poverty was no barrier to higher education in the United States. Having secured minimum funding for the journey, he crossed the Pacific late in 1884 and worked his way through schools and colleges (a BA at Grinnell College, Iowa, in 1892, and graduate studies at the Andover Theological Seminary and the Yale Divinity School). In January 1896, after eleven years' absence, he returned home. Back in Japan he became director of Kingsley Hall at Kanda, Tokyo, the first establishment in Japan by the American Board of the Congregational Church in March 1897. He was now engaged in the work of bringing enlightenment to downtown workers, and the Kingsley Hall Kindergarten, one of the first infant schools in Japan, met with considerable success.

Katayama helped Takano in his work of organizing trade unions. In December 1897, at 'a grand inauguration ceremony' held in the YMCA in Kanda, the *Tekko Kumiai* (Ironworkers' Union) was established. Katayama

---

[36] Kublin, *Asian Revolutionary* (Princeton, 1964), 20. He was originally Yabuki Sugataro, the second son of a family which had former samurai connections, but his mother, in order to evade his future conscription, had her son adopted into a heirless peasant family called Katayama. As his biographer Kublin says, 'Katayama might well have passed his entire life as an obscure peasant in one or another of the many hamlets in the mountains of Okayama'.   [37] Ibid. 42.

edited its organ, the *Rodo Sekai* (Labour World). By the turn of the century about 200,000 workers were organized in several unions, but the defeat of a Factory Act in the Diet in 1898 proved fatal to the trade union movement, as it convinced the workers that the Meiji government was not interested in improving their conditions. (Early attempts at factory legislation were made by government bureaucrats who consulted business associations but never the labour group.)[38] The *Rodo Kumiai Kiseikai* faltered, Takano and other public-minded associates drifted away, and Katayama was left alone in the field.

The founders of the *Shakaishugi Kenkyukai* (Society for the Study of Socialism), which came into existence in October 1898, were all Christians, including Katayama himself. The members met monthly in the library of the Unitarian Church in Tokyo to have discussions and hear lectures on western socialist pioneers. The Public Order Police Act of 1900 augured ill for its future. The Social Democratic Party was formed in 1901, but as it declared its purposes, including the attainment of universal suffrage and a legal status for trade unions, it was declared illegal within a matter of hours. The outbreak of the Russo-Japanese War found Katayama in America. He had been engaged in a semi-Utopian project of sending Japanese immigrants to Texas to set up farming communities. However, he attended the Amsterdam Congress of the Second International in August 1904, where the Russian delegate G. V. Plekhanov took him by the hand and the electrified audience burst into rapturous applause. Yet while he was beaming in the international limelight the situation at home did not appear promising. In February 1906, shortly after his return home, the *Nihon Shakaito* (Japan Socialist Party) was formed with the aim of 'advocating socialism within the limits of the law'. One year later, at its second annual conference, the party dropped all appearance of legality. Kotoku, who had turned to anarchism, demanded an explicit rejection of universal suffrage and parliamentary action. The party, having declared its illegality, was at once suppressed. After the Tokyo Streetcar Strike of January 1912 Katayama was charged with incitement to strike and was sent to the Chiba Prison for five months. He now made a fateful decision to leave Japan for good. His later progress as an international socialist, first in America and then in Russia, belongs to the history of world communism.

KOTOKU SHUSUI AND THE TREASON TRIAL

Kotoku Shusui (Denjiro), whose social background was somewhat obscure, in some ways symbolized Meiji opposition: opposition to the *hanbatsu* government, to the state ideology of emperor worship and eth-

---

[38] Sheldon Garon, *The State and Labor*, 20, 23.

nocentric nationalism and patriotism, to the socio-political defects of industrialization, and to militarism and imperialism. He had very little to offer in place of what he wished to take away, but his brand of anarchist criticism and opposition, widespread throughout civilized nations at around the turn of the century, was anathema to the Meiji state, the guardian and promoter of the mythical national polity and its budding civilization of industrialism. Kotoku had to be got rid of.

Kotoku grew up and was educated in the samurai tradition at Nakamura, Kochi. He became Chomin's disciple and houseboy while the latter was in Osaka, and came to identify himself with the Chomin of later years, a Rousseauist who, however, found the English political model more useful than the French. Industrialization's acceleration in the wake of the war with China in turn drew greater attention to the conditions of the workers. Now Kotoku declared: 'the age of [People's] Rights is over. I am undertaking an investigation of Socialism in order to raise a new standard.'[39] His socialism was an extension of his samurai radicalism, opposition to government by the *hanbatsu* oligarchy. He sought to unite the discontented into a coalition against the central government.[40]

Kotoku's two major works, each only a slender booklet, marked the zenith of radical thought in Meiji Japan as well as the starting-point of new opposition in the new century, an opposition which the Meiji state and its successors had either to suppress or else contain and control. His *Imperialism* (1903), preceding the works with the same title by J. A. Hobson and by Lenin, was a powerful condemnation of contemporary imperialisms: the British in the Transvaal; the United States in Cuba and the Philippines; the French and the Italians in Africa; and the Russians, the Germans, and the Japanese in China. He declared that a great empire was always the result of robbery. The need for overseas immigration should not be accepted as an excuse for expansionism. New markets should not be sought for overseas, but within the nation. 'What they, the capitalists and industrialists, call over-production is not due to lack of demand but to lack of the purchasing power on the part of the people, which should be ascribed to the lack of a fair distribution of wealth and the resulting gap between the rich and the poor.' This is the classic view of under-consumption which J. A. Hobson himself adopted. Kotoku concluded with a warning that 'the imperialist pestilence, contaminating world powers, may destroy our civilization of the twentieth century'.[41] By the time his second major work, *Shaishugi Shinzui* (The Quintessence of Socialism), came out in 1903, socialism had begun to attract intellectuals and workers, though their numbers remained small.

---

[39] F. G. Notehelfer, *Kotoku Shusui* (Cambridge, 1971), 40.   [40] Ibid. 65.
[41] Kotoku, *Teikokushugi* (Tokyo, 1952), 43, 72, 81, 90 f.

In November 1903 Kotoku and Sakai Toshihiko, with the support of the Society for the Study of Socialism, started the weekly *Heimin Shinbun* (People's Newspaper), with 'Democracy, Socialism, and Pacifism' as its slogan. The government did not interfere for some time: an Anglo-Japanese Treaty was to be signed shortly, and it was perhaps thought wise not to appear too autocratic. With the establishment of the *Heimin Shinbun*, though, the main current of socialism shifted from Katayama and other defenders of trade union rights to Kotoku and Sakai, the advocates of political action, because their campaign against war was itself a political action. When war was declared against Russia in February 1904, the *Heimin Shinbun* quickly published an appeal to Russian socialists, stating that there should be 'no barrier of race, territory, or nationality', and that 'we are comrades, brothers and sisters and have no reason to fight each other'. The appeal, however, warned the Russians not to 'be tempted to overthrow the government by force', and it boldly added: 'those who are fighting for humanity must remember that the end does not justify the means.'[42] In its anniversary issue (13 November 1904) the newspaper published the first Japanese translation of the *Communist Manifesto*, and was at once suppressed. In its last number (29 January 1905), printed in red, it was able to report the outbreak of a revolution in Russia with marked satisfaction.

Charged with violating the Press Act, Kotoku was sent to prison where he read Kropotkin and other anarchist works and corresponded with an American anarchist. Shortly after his release, in November 1905, he left for San Francisco where he was introduced to a cosmopolitan community of anarchists, socialists, and industrial unionists. In April 1906 an earthquake and fire destroyed San Francisco, and Kotoku moved to Oakland, where he organized a Socialist Revolutionary Party among Japanese immigrants, then returned to Yokohama in June. The small revolutionary party in California became militant and distributed a leaflet calling for the 'elimination' of the emperor on his birthday in 1907.

Kotoku, on his return, began advocating a general strike in the ranks of the Socialist Party. Katayama being away in America, Kotoku and his supporters exerted great influence on the party organ the daily *Heimin*. An extensive and violent riot which broke out at the Ashio Copper Mine early in 1907 encouraged Kotoku and other direct-actionists, who overwhelmed the parliamentarians at the Second Party Conference; the party was suppressed shortly afterwards. Socialists remained small in number: 3,000 in 1904, reduced to 532 in 1908. Trade unions were all but extinct or at an embryonic stage. In fact, both political action and industrial

---

[42] *Heimin Shinbun*, 13 Mar. 1904.

action were ruled out. What remained was individual action, which meant terrorism.

An incident which was to determine the future course of Kotoku's actions took place in June 1908, when some of his followers were arrested for displaying red flags with the inscriptions 'Anarcho-Communism' at a rally in Tokyo. Kotoku, then away in Kochi, was indignant and left for Tokyo the following month. On his way he visited Oishi Seinosuke, a doctor at Shingu on the southern coast of the Kii peninsula, a graduate of the University of Oregon who had assisted him financially on many occasions. Kotoku also visited Uchiyama Gudo, a Buddhist priest at Hakone, who had a secret printing press at his temple. In October Uchiyama produced a pamphlet on 'Anarchist Communism' which criticized the emperor system and urged the peasants to refuse military service and to boycott the payment of rent and tax. Copies of this pamphlet were sent to several anarchist sympathizers including Miyashita Takichi, an ironworker, who tried to distribute them among the crowd who came to catch a glimpse of the emperor at a nearby railway station (near Nagoya) while the living god was passing it in a special train. Not suprisingly, very few took an interest in the pamphlet. Miyashita now made up his mind to assassinate the emperor in order to show to his superstitious countrymen that the object of their worship was merely an earthly being, capable of bleeding.

Miyashita concentrated on manufacturing a bomb, but the nature of his activities was disclosed to the police through his fellow-workmen. Kotoku was arrested in June 1910 at an inn at Yugawara, where he had been preparing a new book entitled 'Elimination of Christ' (in his mind Christ was equated with the emperor). Under the government led by the veteran clan politician Katsura Taro it was to be expected that the disclosure of a plot involving Kotoku would be used as an excuse for a mass arrest of anarchists, by making it appear part of a subversive nationwide movement. Evidence given at the investigation was naturally twisted and garbled. As a result, the leaders of the three local anarchist groups—Morichika Unpei and his Osaka group; the Kumamoto anarchists whose organ, *Kumamoto Review*, had kept in contact with Kotou; and a Shingu group who gathered around Dr Oishi—were arrested. Altogether twenty-six persons were indicted. Most of them were perhaps anarchists of some kind, but there was no evidence for their having conspired to commit high treason except in four or five cases, namely, Miyashita, Kotoku's common-law wife (Miss Kanno), his two confidants, and possibly Kotoku himself. Their trial began in secret in December, and in January 1911 twenty-four of them were sentenced to death, of whom twelve had their sentences commuted to imprisonment for life. The remaining twelve, headed by Kotoku, were executed in the same month; these included Kanno Suga, Miyashita, Morichika, Oishi, and the priest Uchiyama.

The Treason Trial disclosed the nature of anarchism as well as that of justice in Japan. Abroad there were loud outcries against the judicial murders—because a majority of the condemned had had nothing to do with Miyashita's bomb—and protests were made to the Japanese embassies in capital cities of the major European countries and the United States. The writer Jack London, as 'one of the great army of International soldiers of freedom', sent a letter of protest to the Japanese ambassador in Washington. Local branches of the Independent Labour Party, the Women's Labour League, and the Clarion Scouts sent letters and resolutions to the Japanese embassy in London condemning the action of the Japanese government against Kotoku and his friends. Yet the cases of Katayama and of Takano made it abundantly clear that the Meiji intellectuals themselves had failed in their attempts to get in touch with the masses or the workers. It was the First World War and the economic prosperity created by it at home that was to bring about the conditions for a growth of workers' organizations and for a new awakening of the intellectuals.

PART II

The Road to Catastrophe
1900–1945

8

The Russo-Japanese War and the Annexation of Korea

THE DAWN OF THE TWENTIETH CENTURY

The twentieth century began with hopes and anxieties for Japan, a modern nation-state in the making. Mutsuhito (to be known as the Emperor Meiji) was in his late forties at the turn of the century. He was no longer the weakling he had been when he acceded to the throne, and had proved himself an energetic monarch, probably the most active in modern Japan's history. The last decade of his reign was to accomplish the remaining tasks he and his advisers had set themselves thirty years before in order to build up a modern state, one equal to those which had forced Japan to open up to the world in the middle of the nineteenth century. Foreign policy, which belonged to the imperial prerogatives and remained a matter for the emperor and his advisers to decide, nonetheless began to be commented upon by the press in the name of public opinion, and there was to be an enduring undercurrent of popular aspirations for full citizenship.

The year 1900 began with a petition submitted to the Diet in January for universal suffrage from the *Futsu Senkyo Kisei Domeikai* (Association to Promote Universal Suffrage). In March the Public Order Police Act was enacted so as to place under police control assemblies, speeches, and social protest movements in general, and practically to prohibit strikes; they had threatened to spread when a trade union movement had begun to take root in the late 1890s. These events were symbolic. Twenty-five years later, when universal suffrage at last was obtained, it was paired with a Public Order Preservation Act which was soon to become a ruthless means of thought control.[1] Meanwhile, the Japanese constitutional system, which had taken the first step towards a party government in 1898, remained unstable, not only because of its electoral limitations and the immaturity of the political parties but also because of the obstructive power held by

---

[1] 'Peace Police Law' and 'Peace Preservation Act' are the terms commonly used in English translations. The renderings in the text are preferred here because *chian* means not simply domestic peace but the state of affairs in which subversive elements are effectively controlled to ensure the safety of the state.

the House of Peers and of the influence exerted on the emperor by the top *hanbatsu* politicians already known as the 'elders' or *genro*.

Now the military brought another, potentially more formidable source of instability into the system. From May 1900, the army and navy ministers had to be officers on the active list. The ultimate cause of this could be attributed to the Emperor Meiji, who at the time when Okuma was forming his *kenseito* government, took the trouble to state that 'the Ministry of the Army and that of Navy should be left out of the system', implying that in the case of a party government it was he, the emperor, who would appoint the two ministers in question.[2] Across the sea the Boxer Rebellion, an anti-foreigner, anti-Christian movement that had started in Shangtung the previous year, threatened foreign legations in Beijing; Japan played the role of 'military police' with the other powers, sending the largest contingent among the Allied forces to fight against the Chinese.

In 1901 the beginning of the new century brought events which, in retrospect, seem equally pregnant with foreboding. In February the *Kokuryukai* (Black Dragon or Amur River Society), an aggressively expansionist right-wing body, was launched by Uchida Ryohei and his associates who, incensed at the Triple Intervention of 1895, called for war with Russia to expel her from Asia. In May the Social Democratic Party was formed, advocating the abolition of armaments and public ownership of land and capital. The *Kokuryukai* was allowed to continue, while the SDP was suppressed two days after its formation. Hoshi Toru, son of an Edo artisan, a British-trained barrister and a founding member of the *Jiyuto* who was patronized by Mutsu Munemitsu (foreign minister at the time of the Sino-Japanese War), worked for the rapprochement of that party and the government and contributed to the formation of the *Rikken Seiyukai* (Friends of Constitutional Politics) led by Marquis Ito Hirobumi, itself an amalgamation of former *Jiyuto* members and Ito's followers. Hoshi became the minister of postal services when Ito formed the first *Seiyukai* government in October 1900. He was implicated in a scandal concerning the Tokyo municipal government, resigned his post, and was assassinated by an outraged teacher of swordmanship while in the municipal government office acting as the chairman of its council in June 1901. Political assassinations began to smear and damage constitutional politics.

A growing grass-roots nationalism expressed 'intense contempt for the Asians', as Kotoku had already observed at the time of the war with China. 'It may be', remarks Akira Iriye, 'that in Japan traditional ethno-

---

[2] Junji Banno, *Kindai Nihon no Shuppatsu* (The Beginning of Modern Japan), vol. 13 of *Taikei Nihon no Rekishi* (General History of Japan) (Tokyo, 1989), 222.

centricism had developed into modern patriotism without a substantial metamorphosis.'[3] Ethnocentricism, as we have seen, derived largely from the imperial myth and ideology, the prop of the Japanese version of China's Middle Kingdom world order. Having successfully defeated Chinese claims, Japan inflamed and transformed its own version into a nationalism of a mixed type, modern as well as traditional, with which she was to play a role in international power politics, utilizing the technological achievements of western civilization while simultaneously asserting the supposed superiority of her own culture of loyalty and spirituality.

THE ARMY AND THE NAVY AT THE TURN OF THE CENTURY

One dominant manifestation of this culture was the military. In addition to the Imperial Edict to the Soldiers of 1882 which defined the *raison d'être* of the 'Emperor's Army', a series of revisions were made in the army manuals between 1908 and 1913 which laid less emphasis on European models and stressed principles unique to Japan, 'an extreme cult of martial spirit disregarding scientific rationality, a stubborn belief in taking the offensive, an optimistic belief in the power of assault with bayonets'.[4] This military 'transcendentalism' was also strengthened by the adoption in 1900 of the 'Directives of Imperial Defence' according to which civilian ministers, even the prime minister, were not to have access to knowledge of the actual strength of the armed forces. At about the same time the old hegemony in the army of Yamagata Aritomo and his Choshu followers began to be corroded by the rise of the military technocrats trained in the Military Academy and the Army College. The military in its modern form was now firmly established, and militarism, allied with the ideology of the emperor system, began to spread. (Male members of the imperial household were obliged to become army or navy officers by a decree concerning the status of members of the imperial household of 1910.)

The Japanese navy had started with seven ships confiscated from the Bakufu and eleven donated by the han at the time of the Meiji Restoration. It grew in step with the army and its modernization, with both the army and the navy assuming Russia to be their first enemy. The navy placed a great emphasis on the training of professional officers, and British co-operation proved significant in this as well as in supplying modern vessels: the first Japanese battleships were built by Vickers-Maxim at Barrow-in-Furness.[5] A British naval mission consisting of

---

[3] Akira Iriye, 'Japan's Drive to Great Power Status', in *Cambridge History of Japan*, v. 753.

[4] Yoshida, op. cit., 156. For a more systematic account of the army manuals for this period, see Akira Fujihara, *Gunjishi* (Military History) (Tokyo 1961), 108 ff.

[5] Marie Conte-Helm, 'Armstrong's, Vickers and Japan', in Ian Nish (ed.), *Britain and Japan* (London, 1994), 85–99.

thirty-four teaching personnel headed by Naval Commander Archbold L. Douglas arrived in 1873, and his teaching principles, practised at the Naval Academy at Etajima (moved from Tokyo in 1888), aimed to bring up 'young gentlemen' in the navy. This aim, however, sometimes clashed with the temper of the students themselves, 90 per cent of whom came from the former samurai class.

The navy relied heavily on the volunteer system even after conscription was enforced from 1872, and the bulk of the naval crews who beat the Russian Baltic Fleet in 1905 were volunteers. In contrast with the army, which was 'democratic' in the sense that both officers and men were 'equal before the emperor', the navy was elitist to the degree that Douglas had succeeded in implanting the Royal Navy traditions characterized by preserving the distance between 'aristocratic' officers and 'pauper' sailors.[6] A great majority of the volunteers in the navy came from the social strata whose educational standard was that of a higher primary school. They also formed the bulk of naval petty officers. It was among these classes that the emperor ideology was most effectively disseminated.

The 'military clique' (*gunbatsu*) was also being formed, though the term was a later creation taken from the 'warlords' of Republican China. Marshal Yamagata along with his confidants, General Katsura Taro, prime minister at the time of the Russo-Japanese War, General Kodama Gentaro, vice-chief of the general staff, and General Terauchi Masatake, the army minister, all from Choshu, formed a dominant faction in the army. They were the core of the 'military clique' which was still personal and clannish and which, unlike its more bureaucratic progeny in the inter-war period, retained respect and confidence owing largely to the prestige of Marshal Oyama Iwao of Satsuma, then the chief of the general staff, who resembled Saigo Takamori in his composure and refrained from interfering with politics. Oyama and Yamagata between them kept a balance in the army clique.[7]

THE ANGLO-JAPANESE ALLIANCE

The growing Russian menace in the Far East, especially in Manchuria, during the closing years of the nineteenth century has already been noted. Britain and Japan had more or less agreed on the need to restrain Russia, when the Boxer Rebellion in North China assumed a magnitude that overshadowed foreign interventionist moves, at least for some time. It began as an anti-western, anti-Christian, traditionalist uprising and

---

[6] Kiyoshi Ikeda, *Nihon no Kaigun* (The Japanese Navy) (Tokyo, 1987), i. *passim*. Traditionally the British army was even more 'aristocratic' than the Royal Navy in its officer class.

[7] Masanori Ito, *Gunbatsu Koboshi* (The Rise and Fall of the Military Clique) (Tokyo, 1957), i. 2, 204.

gained government support at a later stage. Among the powers threatened by the Boxers, Russia took an independent line of response and, taking advantage of the turmoil, occupied the three eastern provinces in Manchuria. Britain, whose armies were engaged in the war against the Boers in South Africa at the time, was the first to call on Japan to make a substantial military contribution to the Allied forces in northern China, although Japan was only marginally involved and Russia remained chary of accepting Japanese participation, to say nothing of her prominence in relieving the besieged legations. A new dimension was now added to relations between Britain and Japan, that of practical co-operation.[8]

In March 1898, at the height of the Far Eastern crisis, Joseph Chamberlain, the British colonial secretary, stated at a dinner party given by him to the Japanese minister Kato Takaaki that 'an understanding might be arrived at' with Japan, who would be a useful ally.[9] The statement, however, was not followed up by either side at the time. In the wake of the Nishi–Rosen agreement referred to in Chapter 6, Japanese trade with Korea made great strides, helped by her acquisition of railway rights. Korea remained Japan's predominant concern throughout these years.

In October 1900 an agreement was signed between Britain and Germany for an application of the open-door principle to all Chinese territory 'as far as they can exercise influence', and Kato Takaaki, then foreign minister, sought to make it an Anglo-German-Japanese treaty. Kato was disappointed because Germany was not willing to turn it into a challenge to Russia, the aim shared by Britain and Japan. Kato's hawkish policy towards Russia was in tune with the increasingly vociferous domestic opinion. We have already seen the formation in 1900 of the Amur River Society. In the same year another nationalist body was set up, the *Kokumin Domeikai* (National League), with Toyama Mitsuru, the veteran nationalist, and Prince Konoe Atsumaro, the president of the House of Peers, among its prominent leaders. The League organized speaking tours advocating the need to prevent Russian occupation of Manchuria.[10]

Baron Hayashi Tadasu, a career diplomat and 'an avowed Anglophile', was the Japanese minister in London for the years 1900–6, and did much to prepare the ground for the Anglo-Japanese Alliance. The Beijing peace conference to settle Chinese indemnities for the damages caused by the Boxer Rising ended in September 1901, in the course of which the spectre of the Triple Intervention (exemplified by implicit German support for Russia over Manchuria and by Russia's forcible stance on indemnities) was

---

[8] Nish, *Alliance*, 91.   [9] Ibid. 64.
[10] Ian Nish, *The Origins of the Russo-Japanese War* (London, 1985), 95–6.

revived to frighten Hayashi; but Anglo-Japanese friendship was also cemented there.[11] Sir Claude MacDonald, the British minister in Tokyo, who had previously been in Beijing during the siege of the legations, was back in Britain for a brief visit when he intimated to Hayashi in July 1901 that his government was prepared to enter into an alliance with Japan. On the Japanese side the *genro* met and discussed the British proposal transmitted by Hayashi.

The telegram sent by foreign minister Sone Arasuke, which had been prepared by prime minister Katsura Taro along the lines of advice he had received from Marquis Ito, stated the minimum requirements Japan would expect from an alliance with Britain. It is noteworthy that the central issue for Japan was Korea. 'The policy which Japan must always maintain', it read, 'is to place Korea outside the scope of foreign countries' expansion policies, whatever dangers that may involve, however great the price.'[12] In September 1901 Ito was to leave for the United States in order to receive an honorary degree from Yale University. Inoue Kaoru, the chief advocate of an agreement with Russia, advised Ito to visit Russia after America. Katsura concurred in this by saying that, whether it was acheived by means of an agreement with Britain or with Russia, the main thing was to bring about a satisfactory settlement of the Korean problem.[13] From this it appears that there was no great difference between the so-called pro-Russian group, including Ito and Inoue, and the pro-British group, including Yamagata and Kato, as to their views on East Asia. In Petersburg Ito met the foreign minister Count Lamsdorf and the finance minister De Witte. The gist of the Russian response to Ito was that Russia was to have a completely free hand in Manchuria, whereas Japan could operate in Korea only under severe limitations. He was naturally disappointed. By way of Berlin he travelled to Brussels where he was told by Katsura in a telegram that the preliminary talks for an Anglo-Japanese alliance were far advanced and that there was no need to try further for an agreement with Russia. Ito's last destination was London, where he was welcomed by the prime minister Salisbury. He told a Russian journalist: 'unfortunately the Russians regard us, the Japanese, as a small nation and unworthy of a serious discussion.'[14]

The final text of the Anglo-Japanese Alliance signed by Lansdowne and Hayashi on 30 January 1902 read in part:

Article 1 . . . Having in view . . . their special interests, of which those of Great Britain relate principally to China, while Japan, in addition to the interests which

---

[11] Nish, *Alliance*, 126, 141. For eleven months after the ending of hostilities, the powers 'haggled over the "price" of the Boxer Rebellion'. George Alexander Lensen, *Korea and Manchuria Between Russia and Japan, 1895–1904* (Tokyo, 1966, 1968), 12.

[12] Nish, *Alliance*, 158–9.   [13] *Ito Hirobumi Den*, iii. 523.   [14] Ibid. 546.

she possesses in China is interested in a peculiar degree politically as well as commercially and industrially in Corea, the High Contracting Parties recognise that it will be admissible for either of them to take such measures as may be indispensable in order to safeguard those interests if threatened either by the aggressive action of any other Power, or by disturbances arising in China or Corea . . .

Article 2. [If one of the contracting parties should become involved in war with another Power, the other contracting party] will maintain a strict neutrality, and use its efforts to prevent other Powers from joining in hostilities against its Ally . . .

Article 3. [If the third Power should join in hostilities against the ally, the other contracting party] will come to its assistance and will conduct the war in common.[15]

The treaty would remain in force for five years, and diplomatic notes were exchanged concerning the mutual facilities to be given for the docking and coaling of vessels of war.

Press reactions varied. The liberal newspapers in Britain, such as the *Manchester Guardian* and the *Daily News*, felt that the treaty was unnecessary, while *The Times* welcomed it cordially. Japanese newspapers were almost unanimously in favour of the treaty, though Tokutomi Soho in his *Kokumin Shinbun* maintained that Japan should not rely too much on Britain; she must continue to build up her own strength.

ARMAMENT EXPANSION, RUSSIANS IN MANCHURIA, AND THE RISE OF JAPANESE 'JINGOISM'

The prime concern of all the governments and the parties in this period in Japan, except for a handful of socialists, was the acquirement of larger and more modern armaments. This was acheived mainly with the help of the British. Out of forty-four naval vessels of 194,473 tons in total, launched between the end of the Sino-Japanese War and 1904, as many as twenty-seven (133,367 tons in all, sixty-six per cent of the total) were built in Britain. All six battleships of 13,500 to 15,000 tons were British-made. Four out of six armoured cruisers were also built in Britain. Home-made vessels, mostly small cruisers, destroyers, and communication ships, launched from the Yokosuka and Kure naval yards, formed only 8.5 per cent of the total naval strength. 'As far as major warships were concerned, the Japanese navy was a sub-species of the British navy.' British coal was used to fuel warships in the war with Russia when it came.[16] The alliance also helped stiffen Japanese policy towards Korea,

[15] Nish, *Alliance*, 216–17.
[16] Kazuki Igushi (ed.), *Nisshin-Nichiro Senso* (Wars with China and with Russia) (Tokyo, 1994), 76, 106, 112.

which depended to a great extent on economic penetration. The number of Japanese residents in Korea, mainly at treaty ports like Pusan and Inchon, showed a dramatic increase from 835 in 1880 to 9,354 on the eve of the Sino-Japanese War, 15,829 in 1900, and 171,543 in 1910. Petty treaty-port merchants were 'the shock troops of Japanese economic penetration'.[17] Japan gradually assumed control of mines, postal services, and telegraphs in Korea. Shibusawa Eiichi, chairman of the Daiichi Bank, succeeded in raising a loan in Britain for the construction of the Seoul–Pusan railway.[18]

After the defeat of the Boxer Rebellion by the Allied forces, the Russians refused to withdraw their troops from Manchuria, where they were fighting with the Chinese. Eventually, in April 1902, two months after the conclusion of the Anglo-Japanese Alliance, an agreement was reached between China and Russia according to which the Russians would withdraw their forces from Manchuria within two years in three successive stages. In April 1903, when the time limit for the second evacuation was reached, the Russians not only failed to keep their pledge but also, by making use of lumber concessions granted to a Russian years before, entered upon a new economic and military project in the Yalu River region with a special fund provided personally by the Tsar. Yamagata was in favour of sending two divisions to Seoul to meet the Russian threat, while Oyama remained more cautious.

Meanwhile, the advocates of a bellicose policy grew in number and influence at home. Kuga Katsunan, editor of the newspaper *Nippon*, urged his readers to overcome 'the mental malady of fearing Russia'.[19] Six professors at Tokyo Imperial University and one professor at the Peers' School, the *kaisen shichi hakase* (seven pro-war doctors) as they were called, visited prime minister Katsura to ask him to take a strong policy against Russia, and published a statement that war with Russia was now opportune, whereas one year's delay would make it impossible.[20] Most of the Japanese press which had demanded decisive measures against Russia at the time of Manchurian complications following the Boxer Rebellion, now called for war against Russia as the latter continued to keep troops in Manchuria. Kotoku Shusui, Sakai Toshihiko, and Uchimura Kanzo in the *Yorozo Choho*, and Kinoshita Naoe in the *Mainichi Shinbun* took an anti-war stance, but these socialists and Christians remained a small minority.

---

[17] Peter Duus, *The Abacus and the Sword: The Japanese Penetration of Korea* (Berkeley, 1995), 254.   [18] Nish, *Alliance*, 159.
[19] *Nippon*, 26 June 1903, in Banno, op. cit., 264.
[20] Ibid. 264–5; Shunpei Okamoto, *The Japanese Oligarchy and the Russo-Japanese War* (New York, 1970), 59–67.

THE RUSSO-JAPANESE WAR

It has been pointed out that the argument for *mankan kokan*, the exchange of Manchuria (for Russia) with Korea (for Japan), Japan's basic policy at the time, had two dimensions, one to serve as the means for a Russo-Japanese agreement and possibly co-operation, and the other to provide justification for Japan's war with Russia. Ito took the former position, while the prime minister Katsura and the foreign minister Komura Jutaro took the latter.[21] *Mankan kokan*, however, was an insult to Korea, 'an independent empire' which had never been consulted.[22] Korean complaints were simply ignored. At the imperial council held on 23 June 1903 the *mankan* argument was reaffirmed as the basis of final negotiations with Russia, and immediately after that Ito was kicked upstairs through an intrigue by Katsura and Yamagata, and was appointed as president of the Privy Council.[23] Ito had to cede the chairmanship of the *Seiyukai* party to Prince Saionji, whom Katsura found easier to deal with. General Oyama had just presented a memorandum to the emperor emphasizing the need for an early solution of the Korean problem, for a few years' delay, he believed, would place Russia in a superior position. Oyama, however, had not lost hope for a peaceful solution.[24] From London came news that the Russians had reached an advanced stage in war-preparedness, while the Russo-Japanese talks then going on fell into deadlock.

Negotiations between foreign minister Komura and Baron Rosen, the Russian minister in Tokyo, dragged on from September 1903 to January 1904, when a *genro* meeting adopted a memorandum prepared by Ito to the effect that war with Russia was unavoidable. They were compelled, it said, to make the fatal decision over 'whether to choose a brief respite in view of the insufficiency of our strength, or to take the risk of disrupting Russian strategy by force'.[25] On 6 February the Japanese government informed the Russians of the termination of negotiations and the breaking off of diplomatic relations.[26] Two days later military action started: the Japanese Combined Fleet split into two parts: one squadron covered the landing of an army expeditionary force at Inchon and sank two Russian warships outside the port; the other began an attack on the Russian Pacific Fleet in Port Arthur. The Japanese naval action on 8 February, unlike the surprise attack on Pearl Harbor thirty-seven years later, is considered to have been legal in terms of international law.[27]

---

[21] Banno, op. cit., 270.

[22] Fukuju Unno, *Kankoku Heigo* (The Annexation of Korea) (Tokyo, 1995), 116.

[23] *Ito Hirobumi Den*, iii. 590–9.

[24] Chihiro Hosoya, in James William Morley (ed.), *Japan's Foreign Policy 1868–1941: A Research Guide* (New York, 1974), 365; Masanori Ito, op. cit., 206.

[25] *Ito Hirobumi Den*, iii. 626–7.   [26] Iguchi, op. cit., 80; *Ito Hirobumi Den*, iii, 630–2.

[27] Shinobu Oe, *Nihon Tsushi* (Complete History of Japan), xvii. 62.

On 10 February Japan formally declared war against Russia. The imperial edict issued on this occasion emphasized that the destiny of Korea had direct relevance to the security of Japan, and that the Russian occupation of Manchuria would hamper the preservation of Korea.[28] The Japanese First Army moved north in Korea, crossed the Yalu River in May, and advanced further north into southern Manchuria. The Second Army, which landed on the south coast of the Liaotung peninsula, headed toward Liaoyang. These two armies were engaged in the Battle of Liaoyang in the summer and suffered heavy casualties, but the Third Army, led by General Nogi Maresuke, had the hardest task. In repeated attacks on the modern fortresses at Port Arthur the general lost 16,000 men and officers in the first onslaught, about one-third of his strength, while in the second nearly 1,000 perished. The third attack, made under the command of the chief of Staff Kodama Gentaro, was successful, although Japanese casualties reached 17,000 on this occasion. In February and March the three Japanese armies reinforced by another (the fourth Army) that had landed east of Tailen, 250,000 men in total strength, fought a Russian army of 370,000 near Mukden, the capital of Manchuria, and won the battle, the number of casualties on both sides combined reaching 100,000.

The Anglo-Japanese Alliance had contributed to the strengthening of the Japanese navy. Two cruisers built in Italy for the Argentine government were bought by British brokers on behalf of Japan: renamed the *Kasuga* and *Nisshin* under the Japanese flag, manned by British officers and an Italian crew, they arrived in Japan six days before the declaration of war.[29] In accordance with the terms of the alliance Britain maintained 'a strict neutrality' during the war, while trying to prevent other powers from joining in the hostilities. Yet Britain helped Japan in financial and military matters: loans were arranged with British banks and syndicates. The movement of the Russian Baltic Fleet, which had caused trouble with British seamen in the North Sea, was closely watched by the British. In May 1905, in Tsushima Strait, the Japanese Combined Fleet of forty-one vessels under Admiral Togo Heihachiro intercepted the Russian Baltic Fleet of fifty warships which, after a seven-month voyage halfway around the world, was virtually annihilated in the naval battle that ensued. It has been called 'a victory in an information war', brought about by vessels equipped with wireless.[30]

The Russo-Japanese War was fought mainly in southern Manchuria. Apart from the strategic operations Japan undertook to occupy Sakhalin towards the end of the war, the land fighting all took place outside the two belligerent countries. The logistics of war, the transport of men and

[28] *Ito Hirobumi Den*, iii. 633–4.   [29] Nish, *Alliance*, 273.
[30] Shinobu Oe, op. cit., 64.

resources, became all important. It was the first modern war of the twentieth century. Machine-guns, rapid-firing field guns, and heavy artillery made it difficult to break through the enemy front. Battles took the form of flanking and encirclement, and lasted for long periods. The use of field telephones assisted the mobile operations of great forces. War became a process of attrition. Russian setbacks heightened popular discontent at home, which burst out on Bloody Sunday (22 January 1905) in Petersburg and led to the Russian Revolution of 1905. In Japan the mobilization of men, especially of officers needed for the continuation of land warfare, became increasingly difficult.[31] In the Russo-Japanese War nearly 1,100,000 men were mobilized for land warfare, about 4.5 times as many as the number in the Sino-Japanese War; the number of those who died in battle amounted to 60,000, 42.4 times as many as in the previous war. The Japanese army suffered from a shortage of bullets and shells, which encouraged hand-to-hand fighting with swords and bayonets. Myths of a martial spirit were created, like that of 'the three brave soldiers who formed a human bomb', establishing a tradition which was to glory in the brutality and cruelty of war.[32] The Russo-Japanese War cost Japan a total of 1,730,050,000 yen, an expenditure 8.5 times as great as that for the Sino-Japanese War.[33]

Japanese leaders, both military and civil, knew that the country was incapable of waging a prolonged war, and after victory in the naval battle in Tsushima Strait, the Japanese government conveyed hopes for the termination of hostilities to the US president Theodore Roosevelt. Tsar Nicholas II also agreed to this. A peace conference was held at Portsmouth, New Hampshire, and a peace treaty was signed on 5 September according to which Russia recognized Japan's right to 'guide, protect, and control' Korea, and ceded to Japan her right to the territories around Port Arthur and Tailen and also to the railway between Chanchung and Port Arthur, in addition to southern Sakhalin. Russia refused the Japanese demand for indemnities, but Japan had to acquiesce as she had no strength left to resume the fighting. The failure to obtain indemnities was a disappointment to a nation which had been led, without justification, to believe it had acheived great victories, and this led to a popular protest movement which we shall now examine.

THE 1905 RIOTS

'It looked as if Tokyo had become another Russian capital', commented the *Osaka Asahi Shinbun* (6 September 1905).[34] The terms of the

---

[31] Ibid. 63–5.   [32] Iguchi, op. cit., 81–2.   [33] Quoted in Okamoto, op. cit., 127.
[34] Seizaburo Shinobu, *Taisho Democracy* (Tokyo, 1968), 50; Matsuo, op. cit., 31.

Portsmouth Peace Treaty had been considered 'disgraceful' by the great majority of Japanese newspapers, since these papers had demanded and encouraged their readers to expect ample reparations, the ceding of all of Sakhalin, not just the southern half, and certain rights in the Maritime Province. Some papers urged the outright rejection of the treaty. Mass rallies against it were organized in several towns, and a 'Peace Condolence' national rally was scheduled to be held at Hibiya Park, Tokyo, on 5 September. The government banned the rally and barricaded all the entrances to the park. But a crowd of over 10,000 demonstrators broke through barriers guarded by 700 policemen, and held a meeting inside to pass a resolution against the treaty; scuffles ensued with police stationed near the official residence of the home minister in front of the park's main entrance; many of the demonstrators were wounded by the sabres brandished by the police, and they were finally dispersed by troops in the evening. The police had behaved badly, one police chief encouraging his men to kill the demonstrators, and as a result at least seventeen of them were killed and a great number wounded. That evening the crowd, in several groups, raided almost all the police stations and police boxes in the city and tore or burned them down.[35] On the following day several Christian churches were attacked and some were burned down, because a minister had allegedly delivered a sermon to the effect that Russia had been able to obtain favourable terms because she was a Christian country.

On that same evening attempts were also made to burn a number of streetcars in the Hibiya area, the heart of Tokyo. Martial law was proclaimed, and the turmoil went on until heavy rain on the following evening pretty well extinguished the last embers of the riot. The main force of the rioters consisted of artisans, factory workers, and labourers; shopkeepers, white-collar workers, and students were also prominent among them.[36] The riot shows that the feeling that the spoils of the victory were not adequate surpassed that of rejoicing over the restored peace. Among the rioters 'there was no consciousness of guilt at having set chains on the feet of another nation, the Koreans. The poison of imperialism had already corrupted the mind of the general public.'[37]

It is curious that this popular movement against the Portsmouth Treaty, which demonstrated the strength of feeling for expansionism and ethnocentrism on the part of the masses, should be regarded by some as the starting-point of Taisho democracy because it was against the policies of the *hanbatsu* government. The presence of these two aspects of the movement has led some to describe it as one of 'Constitutional Imperialism',[38] and it is true that the movement for universal suffrage was taken up by the

---

[35] Matsuo, op. cit., 9; Shinobu, op. cit., 40.   [36] Matsuo, op. cit., 10–12.
[37] Ibid. 13.   [38] Ibid. 38.

same people and the same newspapers which agitated against the 'disgraceful' peace. This agitation spread swiftly to all corners of the land: the number of protest meetings, including prefectural and local township rallies which passed resolutions similar to the one at Hibiya Park, reached 237 by 4 October when the treaty was formally approved by the Privy Council. A national rally against the treaty held in Osaka on 11 September, with Kono Hironaka, famous for his *Jiyu Minken* activism, as a speaker (he had also been the main speaker at Hibiya a week before), adopted the declaration: 'The peace terms before us intend to force us to go without the results of our victory, and to lead us into future turmoil. Public indignation rose in anticipation of that future, but was oppressed by unconstitutional violence which has brought about a crisis in our midst. Such violence will destroy imperial glory abroad and will impair the spirit of constitutional politics.'[39] Two months after the acceptance of the treaty by the government, Katsura was replaced by Saionji as premier. Although there was a secret understanding between the two as to the transfer of power, a deal made in exchange for the *Seiyukai*'s tacit support of Katsura over the issue of the peace treaty, it was obvious that the September riot and the popular support for it had finally convinced Katsura of the need for a change of government.

INTERNATIONAL REALIGNMENT AFTER THE WAR

The Anglo-Japanese Alliance did recognize a Japanese sphere of influence in Korea, the preservation of which had been the pretext for Japan to start the war, but the final negotiations between Japan and Russia were made without any reference to the alliance. Even when Japan approached President Roosevelt, asking for his good offices to bring the belligerents together, Britain was not consulted or even informed.[40] Meanwhile, it was expected that a victorious Japan would seek a closer alliance with Britain that would guarantee her a free hand in Korea, while Britain had her own problems along the Indian border. As early as January 1905 Britain admitted that Korea might have to forfeit her independence and that a protectorate under Japan might be preferable to rule by a corrupt court, susceptible to Russian intrigues. In this change in her Asian policy Britain was in agreement with the United States.[41]

The second Anglo-Japanese Alliance, signed on 12 August 1905 by Hayashi and Lansdowne in London, was a new treaty and a defensive and offensive agreement. It stated in Article 2 that if either of the contracting parties should be involved in war in defence of its territorial rights

---

[39] Sakuzo Kasai (ed.), *Ah Kugatsu Itsuka* (Ah! 5th of September), quoted Matsuo, op. cit., 36.
[40] Nish, *Alliance*, 196.   [41] Ibid. 321.

or special interests, the other contracting party 'will at once come to the assistance of its ally'. These interests for Japan were specified in Article 3: 'Japan possessing paramount political, military and economic interests in Corea, Great Britain recognizes the right of Japan to take such measures of guidance, control and protection in Corea as she may deem proper and necessary to safeguard and advance those interests, provided always that such measures are not contrary to the principle of equal opportunities for the commerce and industry of all nations.' British interests were casually mentioned in the preamble, which referred to 'the maintenance of the territorial rights of the High Contracting Parties in the regions of Eastern Asia and of India' as part of the object of the agreement.[42] The new alliance, that would remain in force for ten years, was published on 27 September so as not to influence the Portsmouth Peace Conference that began on 26 August and led to an armistice signed on 1 September.

It is remarkable that a swift rapprochement was made between the two former belligerents after the war. Japan's new policy towards Russia aimed at removing the causes of future trouble by defining the sphere of interest for each country, and at the same time safeguarding their mutual interests against possible encroachment by a third power, especially the United States. Russia too was seeking such an entente so as to devote her attention to the European scene, which showed signs of deterioration. The initiative came from Russia, and the Japanese government, then headed by Saionji responded favourably. After months of negotiations a secret convention with a secret article was signed on 30 July 1907 between A. Izvolsky, Russian foreign minister, and Motono Ichiro, the Japanese minister to Moscow: the 'future development [of] the relations of political solidarity existing between Japan and Corea', a phrase which implied the eventual annexation of Korea by Japan, was recognized, while Japan gave a pledge not to interfere with Russian 'special interests in Outer Mongolia'.[43] It was at about this time that the American threat came to overshadow the Russian menace in the minds of the Japanese. The army still regarded Russia as the most likely enemy, but the navy looked upon the United States as such. In 1910, when P. C. Knox, the US secretary of state, proposed to neutralize the Manchurian railways and form an international syndicate to provide a loan to China, the second Russo-Japanese entente was signed to consolidate the special interests of the two countries, and their sphere of collaboration extended as time went on. It seemed that Japan was shifting her partnership from Britain to Russia.[44]

---

[42] Nish, *Alliance*, 332.
[43] C. I. Eugene Kim and Han-kyo Kim, *Korea and the Politics of Imperialism* (Berkeley, 1967), 141–3.   [44] Hosoya, in Morley (ed.), op. cit., 378.

THE ROAD TO KOREAN ANNEXATION

For a short while around the turn of the century Korea had been a relatively free agent, attempting to balance one powerful neighbour against another. The Anglo-Japanese Alliance had alarmed the Korean government, which feared it might encourage Japan to fight Russia. Korean pleas made to the Japanese and Russian governments to treat Korea as a neutral country in case of war, however, carried no weight. Japan strengthened her military forces stationed in the peninsula under the pretext of giving Korea 'guidance, control, and protection'. With the outbreak of the Russo-Japanese War 'the captive government in Seoul was forced to give up, step by step, its sovereign powers'.[45] A fortnight after the outbreak of war, a protocol was signed in Seoul on 23 February 1904 according to which Korea was obliged to accept Japanese advice and assistance in its administration, to provide full facilities for the Japanese army, and to allow whatever occupation of Korean lands was deemed necessary for war purposes.

At the same time it was decided to send Marquis Ito to Korea as a special minister to 'cheer up the Korean emperor for the sake of the Japanese emperor'. Ito arrived in Seoul in March 1904 and made an important speech before the Korean emperor:

by the promotion of peace in East Asia we mean an effort by Japan, China, and Korea to advance their civilizations respectively in the same way as the western countries have done, and to make each independent. . . . In order to ensure the existence of a state, we should willingly improve or even discard individual manners and customs if these prove to be detrimental. This is the cause to which Japan has adhered for the last thirty years, and which, by laying a sound foundation for her independence, has made her what she is today. If China and Korea adopt the same cause and strive for independence, we can help each other, stand on equal terms with western civilization, strengthen each other, and ensure the survival of the East Asian people. . . . Countries like Russia which have falsified western civilization and carried out selfish acts of aggression, oppression, and injustice ought to be resisted and overcome. . . . It is right to resist those who resort to violence and aggression in the contest for the survival of nations. They are enemies of civilization. They are barbarians, and we should drive out the barbarians.[46]

The argument is a mixture of Fukuzawa Yukichi (on civilization) and Herbert Spencer (his Social Darwinism), and above all an attempt to justify the cause of the Meiji Restoration and extend it to Korea and China. Shortly afterwards Ito returned home. It was obvious that Japan intended to establish a *de facto* protectorate in Korea.[47]

---

[45] Kim and Kim, op. cit., 117. [46] *Ito Hirobumi Den*, iii. 639–42.
[47] Kim and Kim, op. cit., 123.

Thus, the war to most Korean people became a war against the Japanese, for land was appropriated and men and horses were taken away for military purposes and for the construction of railways. Open rebellion and sabotage were not rare. Over about two years from July 1904 to October 1906, thirty-five Koreans were executed, forty-six detained, 100 flogged, and seventy-four fined for alleged offences against Japanese military rule.[48] In April 1905 it was decided at a cabinet meeting (under prime minister Katsura) to make Korea a Japanese protectorate. We have noted that Britain and the United States had been inclined to accept Korea's new status. Clause 2 of the Russo-Japanese peace treaty signed on 5 September 1905 at Portsmouth also stated that the Russian government promised not to disrupt or interfere with measures the Japanese government might deem necessary for 'guidance, protection, and control' in Korea.[49] Even before this, prime minister Katsura and the American secretary of war, William Howard Taft, on the latter's visit to Japan, had signed an agreement according to which Japan would recognize American rule of the Philippines (conquered three years before) while the Americans would do the same for the Japanese right to 'protect' Korea.

In October 1905 the Katsura government decided to change Korea's status from an independent state to a protectorate by transferring her diplomatic right or right to deal with foreign countries to the Japanese government. Once again it was Ito whom the Meiji emperor invited to represent him in Korea so as to 'cheer up' his counterpart there. There is no evidence to show that he felt any compunction at having discarded 'the cause' of independence he had made so much of only a year before. His task was to impose the status of a protectorate upon protesting Koreans and to force them to agree to the loss of their own independence: in short, he had changed suddenly into a bully. In Seoul in November 1905 he explained the new situation to the Korean emperor and answered his queries. The emperor wanted to retain the form, if not the substance, of his country's right to act in diplomatic matters. Ito insisted that there was no distinction between form and substance in diplomatic relations. The emperor, though, lamented being deprived even of the form: 'if there were to be no form such as the delegation of diplomatic rights, the relationship would degrade into something similar to that between Hungary and Austria, or else Korea would be reduced to the position of most inferior countries, say, that of Africa vis-à-vis the European Powers.' 'The matter is so grave', the emperor went on, 'that I have to consult my ministers and know the wishes of the people at large.' Ito replied by saying that his wanting to know the wishes of the people was 'extraodinary', 'because your country has not adopted constitutional politics and remains a mon-

---

[48] Unno, op. cit., 136.   [49] Ibid. 151.

archical autocracy which allows the emperor to decide on all the matters personally. Your intention to refer to the wishes of the people may be a measure to influence the people to resist Japan's propositions.' On the following day Ito invited all the ministers for consultation with him: the foreign minister said he 'would never agree'; the finance minister would 'disown the draft treaty in general'; the minister of law thought the new treaty 'unnecessary'; the minister of education was for compromise, since Korea was 'too weak to reject the proposition', and several other ministers expressed the same view. It was decided, at the strong request of the Korean emperor, to insert a phrase to the effect that the treaty would be valid 'until Korea became wealthy and strong'.[50] The treaty was signed while Japanese troops staged manoeuvres in front of the royal palace and in the main thoroughfare of the capital. Several government officers and a number of private citizens committed suicide in protest. The house of the minister of education was burned down on the night of 17 November when the treaty was signed. Volunteer forces rose against Japanese garrisons and police in the provinces. The emperor later denied that he had ever approved the treaty.

The Korean emperor was never satisfied with the treaty, as he was convinced that it was against international law. He sent two emissaries to the second World Peace Conference held at the Hague in June–October 1907, sponsored by the Russian Tsar Nicholas II and attended by the representatives of forty-four countries. Russia, however, did not accept the mandate issued by the Korean emperor, as she had recognized the Japanese emperor as the authority to issue such mandates for Korea. The response from other countries, too, was cool and inhospitable. The *New York Tribune* commented on the Korean attempt: 'To put it in scientific terms, "the Law of survival of the fittest" prevails among states as well as plants and animals. Corea has been conspicuously unfit.'[51] Ito, then resident-general in Korea, visited the Korean emperor and said to him that 'he should rather declare war on Japan than reject the Japanese right to protection by such sinister means'.[52]

Earlier in March 1906, Ito had arrived in Seoul at the first resident-general who would rule Korea as the representative of the Japanese emperor. Since diplomatic matters in Korea had been transferred to the Foreign Ministry in Tokyo, the Residency-General in Seoul ran a colonial system for the supervision and control of Korean domestic administration. Ito took advantage of the Hague incident so as to extend and strengthen Japanese rule in Korea. In a telegram to foreign minister Hayashi he said

---

[50] *Ito Hirobumi Den*, iii. 683–98.
[51] *New York Tribune*, 20, 26 July 1907, quoted in Conroy, op. cit., 350.
[52] *Ito Hirobumi Den*, iii. 751.

that it was time to take over control of taxation, military service, and jurisdiction. It was under his promptings that, in July 1907, the government decided on the abdication of the Korean emperor who was to be succeeded by the young crown prince. A new treaty signed on 27 July, a few days after his abdication, strengthened the power of the resident-general on all matters related to domestic administration, legislation, and jurisdiction. Again, a few days later, on 31 July, an imperial decree (drafted by Ito himself) to dissolve the Korean army was issued. 'Now Ito was the Korean emperor.'[53] And he was anxious to promote 'wealth and strength' of his new country, as the preamble to the new treaty stated. Many soldiers in the Korean army fought against Japanese garrisons in the provinces when ordered to disband. Many disbanded soldiers joined the Korean rebels known as *uibyong* (the Righteous Army) and dispersed throughout the peninsula to continue their armed resistance.[54] The number of Korean volunteer soldiers who fought against Japanese troops from August 1907 to 1910, the year of the Korean annexation, reached 141,603, of whom 17,688 were killed.[55]

The Hague incident had other repercussions. Toyama Mitsuru, Uchida Ryohei, and other right-wing activists began to advocate the annexation of Korea in some form. These Japanese 'reactionaries' had many Korean friends from the days of the Tonghak Rebellion of 1894, when a Japanese body, *Ten Yu Kyo* (Saving Chivalry under Heaven), including Uchida participated in the uprisings. They appeared to prefer a federation (*gappo*) to annexation (*gappei* or *heigo*, a new word coined by the government). Other groups, such as the *Kensei-Honto* (Okuma's party) and the *Daido Club* (a Yamagata–Katsura group), demanded strong action by the government. Ito at this stage preferred the management of a protectorate by his Residency-General. He was anxious to promote an image of Korea's self-rule as the path towards prosperity under Japanese 'guidance, protection, and control'. He was very much concerned with law reform, the establishment of the Bank of Korea as a central bank, education reform, and economic development, such as the creation of big farms cultivated by tenants and the establishment of credit businesses (through a new national company called *Toyo Takushoku Kaisha*, or the Oriental Development Company). In spite of all this Ito became weary of his position, largely because he failed to control, not to say suppress, the Korean volunteer movement. He could not steal Korean 'heart'.[56]

In April 1909, while in Tokyo, Ito told prime minister Katsura that he had no objection to the annexation of Korea, and in the following month he tendered his resignation as resident-general. It was probably an act of

53 Unno, op. cit., 186.   54 Kim and Kim, op. cit., 156.
55 Unno, op. cit., 188.   56 Ibid. 207.

mercy as well as of revenge when he was shot dead by the Korean patriot An Ju Kon on the platform of Harbin Station on 26 October 1909; Ito was on his farewell trip to Korea and had arrived in Harbin in order to confer with the Russian minister of finance about possible further collaboration between the two countries.

Both Russia and Britain agreed to Japan's proposal to annex Korea. In May 1910 General Terauchi, the army minister, became resident-general there. 'A reign of terror' began in Korea; 'unproclaimed martial law prevailed'.[57] In June the government (prime minister Katsura) adopted 'administrative policies' for Korea after annexation, according to which the Japanese constitution would not be applied to Koreans, who were to be governed by the emperor's prerogative. The right to vote as well as to do military service was denied them. In August 1910 the annexation was enforced in the form of the Korean emperor ceding his right to rule to the Japanese emperor. No objection was raised, no criticism was made among the Japanese.

Terauchi, the first governor-general in Korea, promised honours and monetary aid to various classes of Koreans: from Japanese peerages and stipends for a limited number of elite Koreans, members of the imperial family and officialdom, to a reduction of the land tax for farmers. The Korean emperor and his father were made members of the Japanese imperial family. His last plea to Terauchi was to be allowed to keep his existing number of household servants. It was an ignominious end to the Yi dynasty.[58] Koreans of all classes remained stupefied and powerless. There was a large-scale arrest of Korean nationalists on New Year's Day 1911, but the movement for Korean independence had to wait at least until the cause of national self-determination became widely accepted in the wake of the First World War, and even then the Japanese, who had been taught to regard Korea not as a colony but as their *Gaichi* (Outerland), failed to face the issue squarely.

[57] Kim and Kim, op. cit., 214.   [58] Ibid. 218.

9

Taisho Democracy and
the First World War

AN ERA OF TRANSITION

When the Meiji emperor died on 29 July 1912 an era came to an end, an era of which the Japanese could rightly be proud as one of enormous success in all-round modernization, while the traditional power-structures and equally traditional social and cultural frameworks had been mainly kept intact. Natsume Soseki, the distinguished novelist, bade farewell to Meiji in one of his last works, *Kokoro* (Heart). One of his characters, a university teacher, was made to confess: 'I felt that the spirit of Meiji began with the emperor and ended with the emperor. People like myself who had lived under the strongest impact of Meiji would be anachronisms if we continued to live on. This feeling overwhelmed me.' He was 'to immolate himself on the death of the spirit of Meiji'. General Nogi, who together with his wife committed suicide on the day of the emperor's funeral, is said to have postponed the act of self-immolation for thirty-five years after having disgraced the emperor's army, so he felt, by letting his regimental colours be seized by the insurgents in the Satsuma rebellion. Mori Ogai, a novelist comparable to Soseki and an army doctor by profession, who had known General Nogi personally during the disastrous attack on Port Arthur in 1905, wrote a novel shortly after the Nogis' death dealing with a seventeenth-century samurai who had postponed his own act of self-immolation for over thirty years, a theme which turned the author's attention to the issue of loyalty in history.[1]

Taisho, like Meiji, is an era name, and corresponds to the reign of Yoshihito or the Taisho emperor, the third son of the Meiji emperor by Naruko, the sister of Count Yanagihara Sakimitsu, a court noble and a diplomat. Yoshihito, unlike his father, was never robust. Weak and sickly, he was mentally disturbed in his last years due to the residual effects of meningitis, from which he had suffered when a child, and the crown prince, Hirohito, later the Showa emperor, became regent in 1921.

'Taisho democracy' is the term generally used to describe the democratic

---

[1] Mori Ogai, 'Okitsu Yagoemon no Isho' (The Will and Testament of Okitsu Yagoemon), *Chuo Koron* (Oct. 1912), Ogai, *Works* (Tokyo, 1965), 127 ff.

ferment which took various shapes in the Taisho period (1912–26) and was linked characteristically with nationalism, often with expansionism. Although those two were knitted together from the beginning, the emphasis shifted from democracy to expansionism as time went on. Some Japanese historians, taking their cue from the writings of Yoshino Sakuzo, professor of political history at Tokyo Imperial University at the time, assert that Taisho democracy began in 1905 with the national protest movements against the terms of peace with Russia after a victorious but costly war,[2] and ended in 1925 with the enactment of the Public Order Preservation Act.[3] Some would argue that it ended with the Kanto earthquake of 1923, with its negative impact on the national morale, or else that it came to an end in 1932 with the collapse of the last party government, headed by Inukai Tsuyoshi,[4] but all of these are simply the events which formed a wider background against which Taisho democracy atrophied.

If we pay special attention to the constitutional evolution of Japanese politics, the self-assertions of political parties against traditional rule by the *genro*, which culminated in an event called 'the Taisho Political Change' of 1912–13, could be regarded as the fountainhead of the democratic upsurge that led to other developments. It is reasonable to identify this democratic upsurge rather than the popular demonstrations of 1905 with the beginning of Taisho democracy, for the 1905 crisis, as we saw in Chapter 8, had more to do with expansionism and chauvinism than with the constitutional politics of the day.

THE EVOLUTION OF PARTY POLITICS

One almost perennial problem of constitutional politics in Japan has been the weakness of liberalism. At the outset, the Meiji constitution was scarcely conducive to its growth. The House of Representatives only possessed 'the attribute of a gadfly' in terms of power, hemmed in on all sides as it was by a formidable array of inimical institutions: the Privy Council, the war and navy groups, the peers, the administrative bureaucracy, the top *Sat-Cho* oligarchs, and ultimately the throne, itself open to influence or even control by the oligarchs.[5] This explains why the 'liberal' parties (*minto*), in their quest for governing power, were compelled 'to turn

[2] Sakuzo Yoshino, 'Minshu-Jii-undo o Ronzu' (On the Popular Demonstration), *Chuo Koron* (April 1914), Yoshino Sakuzo, *Select Works*, iii (Tokyo, 1995), 17, 18, 33.
[3] Takayoshi Matsuo, *Taisho Democracy* (Tokyo, 1994), pp. v, vii; Shinobu Seizaburo also sets the period of Taisho democracy in 1905–25. Seizaburo Shinobu, *Taisho Democracy-shi* (History of Taisho Democracy) (2nd edn., Tokyo, 1968).
[4] Yukio Ito, *Taisho Democracy* (Tokyo, 1992), 59–61.
[5] Robert Scalpino, *Democracy and the Party Movement in Pre-war Japan* (Berkeley, 1953), 148–9.

inward to the mechanisms of the bureaucracy rather than outward to seek popular understanding and support'.[6] The Meiji constitution was an attempt to unite two irreconcilable tendencies: imperial absolutism and popular government; and the latter, legally and institutionally handicapped, was obliged to make 'compromises away from democratic ideals' in a variety of ways—one of the lasting effects of this was the general neglect of responsibility.[7] Not only were principles and ideals jettisoned for the sake of immediate party interests, but individual opinions too were sacrificed at the dictate of the totality, or of those who claimed to embody the totality. Although the popular parties made use of their only parliamentary weapon, which allowed them to attack the administrative budget, often at its most delicate points such as the salaries and pensions of officials, their hands were weakened by internal corruption and by the administration's readiness to resort sometimes to outright violence.

The head-on confrontation between the 'transcendentalist' governments, led successively by Kuroda, Yamagata, and Matsukata, and the popular parties like the *Jiyuto* and the *Kaishinto* gave way to a period of 'entente' made possible by the internal peace brought about after the war with China, the first domestic peace since the Restoration. The popular parties had been forced to recognize the limitations of their opposition to the *Sat-Cho* oligarchs, who wielded the powerful weapons of Diet dissolution, interference in elections, and intervention by the emperor. The oligarchs for their part had begun to show signs of a split between the 'civil' faction represented by Ito and Inoue Kaoru, and the 'military' faction including Kuroda, Matsukata, and above all Yamagata, after whom it is often designated as 'the Yamagata faction'.[8]

There followed the phase of the oligarchs' flirtation with the party system, best illustrated by Ito and his new party *Rikken Seiyukai* (commonly referred to as *Seiyukai*), formed in 1900. The Yamagata faction viewed Ito's move with alarm and hostility. After Ito resigned from office as premier during his fourth government in 1901, the older *genro* retired into the position of *eminences grises*. For the next twelve years control of the government went back and forth between Katsura Taro, Yamagata's protégé, and Saionji Kinmochi, Ito's successor as the president of *Seiyukai*; this so-called Katsura–Saionji era was characterized by an uneasy compromise which finally produced 'the Taisho political change'.

The first Saionji government formed in January 1906 announced a liberal policy towards socialism, stating: 'since socialism is one of the

<hr />

[6] Robert Scalpino, op. cit., 149.   [7] Ibid. 150.
[8] Banno Junji, *The Establishment of the Japanese Constitutional System*, tr. A. A. Stockwin (London, 1992), 112. See also Peter Duus, *Party Rivalry and Political Change in Taisho Japan* (Cambridge, Mass., 1968), 10–11.

great currents of thought in the world, it should not be suppressed at will by the power of the police, and its moderate elements ought to be guided in the right direction and made to contribute to the advance of the state'.[9] The Japan Socialist Party, formed in 1906, however, chose to antagonize the government and invite its hostility by coming under the influence of Kotoku and his anti-parliamentary and anti-reformist 'anarcho-syndicalism'. Yet Katayama and his friends continued to work for social and political reform with their journal *Shakai Shinbun* (Socialist Weekly),[10] one of the best and most informative of contemporary socialist newspapers.

In the meantime, the *Toyokeizai Shinpo* (Oriental Economist), founded in 1895, established itself as an influential journal advocating radical liberalism. It is true that the journal supported Japan's advance on the Asian continent on the grounds of overpopulation at home, and thus shared the general liberal stance of constitutionalism at home and imperialism abroad. But the anti-taxation agitation after the Russo-Japanese War led the journal to accept Katayama Sen as its staff member and regular contributor, under whose influence it began to agitate for freedom of combination, especially of trade unions, a factory act, and an extension of suffrage to the workers. It urged disarmament and argued that China, the future great power, should be treated with respect and sympathy. Non-intervention was its policy towards China when the Chinese Revolution of 1911 began its erratic course; it asserted that the Chinese had the right to change their own government, while arguing that the contact of the two cultures, eastern and western, had brought about a great political change both in China and in Japan. The *Tokokeizai Shingo* represented the progressive views of a section of business leaders, and as such bore witness to the spirit of Meiji which was at once liberal and authoritarian.

The end of Meiji came ten months after the collapse of the Manchu dynasty in China, which was overthrown in October 1911, the warlord Yuan Shi-kai soon replacing the revolutionary leader and provisional president Sun Yat-sen. The Japanese military sought to extend its influence in China by assisting forces opposed to Yuan, especially local warlords. At home, Saionji, who had been out of office since July 1908, replaced Katsura as premier in August 1911. At the general election of May 1912 his party, *Seiyukai*, won a clear majority in the Diet: *Seiyukai* 211 seats, *Kokuminto* (former *Kensei-Honto* allied with three small parties) 95, and *Chuo-club* 31. Yamagata and other *genro* were implacably opposed to the growing influence and prestige of the Diet.

[9] Shinobu, op. cit., 89.
[10] *Shakai Shinbun* as *Socialist Weekly* (2 June 1907–26 Apr. 1908) published an English column; then the paper, renamed *Socialist News*, soon ceased to be weekly, though it continued without an English column till 3 Aug. 1911.

THE TAISHO *SEIHEN* (POLITICAL CHANGE)

The erosion of the power of the *hanbatsu* oligarchy was hastened by the political awakening of the urban population especially, to which wars and industrialization had greatly contributed. It was the military, however, that took advantage of the volatile political climate thus created. The army demanded the creation of two new divisions in Korea so as to secure Japanese rule after the annexation of that country in 1910, to prepare for the possible unification of China and to cope with any Russian military buildup which might follow the laying of the second line of the Siberian Railway around the Amur River. Saionji informed the war minister Uehara that his cabinet could not accept the army demand that year; whereupon Uehara tendered his resignation to the emperor, an act that was seen as a case of the army publicly challenging the cabinet. Yamagata refused to recommend a new war minister; Saionji resigned, and Katsura was to form his third cabinet in December 1912. Katsura, then serving as *naidaijin* (minister of the imperial court), a position which, though closest to the emperor, seemed to offer little hope of his returning to the premiership, is said to have instigated Uehara to challenge Saionji and thus start the ball rolling.[11]

In the meantime leading journalists and elite businessmen in the *Kojunsha*, a club founded years before by Fukuzawa Yukichi, launched a powerful movement to defend constitutional politics, in which Ozaki Yukio of the *Seiyukai* and Inukai Tsuyoshi of the *Kokuminto* played prominent roles. A protest meeting they organized at the Kabuki theatre in Tokyo was attended by an audience of 2,000, and the movement spread to provincial towns. Under the circumstances the Council of Elders (*genro*), had had to meet as many as ten times before they were able to decide on the formation of Katsura's cabinet; moreover, Katsura became prime minister by having an imperial prescript issued for him, a seemingly irregular action yet necessary to justify his transferring from the court to the premiership. On 20 January 1913, shortly after he had become premier, however, he announced his plan to form a new party of his own. This is called the 'Conversion of Katsura', and was due to his realization that the influence of elderly statesmen would quickly decline, and also to the cooling of his relations with Yamagata. Those who rallied to him were a motley collection of bureaucrats like Goto Shinpei and Wakatsuki Reijiro, and their strength was less than a quarter of the members of the Diet. When the Diet was convened on 5 February, Ozaki Yukio, former minister of education under Okuma and mayor of Tokyo until one year before, attacked the Katsura cabinet, saying that Katsura had sought to

---

[11] Yukio Ito, op. cit., 14.

overcome his political enemy with an imperial prescript instead of a bullet, and moved a resolution of no confidence in the new cabinet. Hara Takashi, the leader of the *Seiyukai*, brought the full resources of his party behind the Movement for Constitutional Government by assisting provincial rallies held under its own auspices.

On 9 February over 13,000 people attended a rally to defend constitutional politics held at the Ryogoku Sumo Athletic Arena, and on the following day the Diet was besieged by 6,000 people shouting 'Long Live People's Parties', while 2,500 policemen, helped by mounted police and a cycling messenger unit, guarded it. The opposition Diet members, all wearing white roses on their chests and standing on the balcony of the Diet building, responded to the cheers of the crowd.[12] Katsura resigned on the following day. The *genro* had made and unmade governments, but from the beginning of the century its power of control had been on the decline. Katsura's ambition, apostasy, and apparent scheming, reflecting the process of this decline, had called into being a chain of events that produced a massive movement to defend constitutional politics. Now, for the first time in Japanese history, a government resigned because of pressure from the people. This is called the *Taisho Seihen* (Political Change) or the first *Goken* (Defence of the Constitution) movement.

It created, as a by-product, Katsura's new party, the nucleus of which was made up of former government officials. Katsura himself, disappointed and rapidly weakening because of stomach cancer, died in October 1913. After his death, in December, the *Rikken Doshikai* (Constitutional Society of the Like-minded) was formally launched with Kato Takaaki as its first president; he was the son-in-law of Iwasaki Yataro of Mitsubishi, foreign minister under three prime ministers, the last being Katsura, and was himself a future prime minister. The new party contained two more future prime minsters, Wakatsuki Reijiro, minister of finance under Katsura, and Hamaguchi Osachi, another treasury expert, both known later for their bold opposition to attempts at self-aggrandizement by the military in the difficult years of early Showa.

A period of party politics, uncertain and precarious, now began. The new government was led by Admiral Yamamoto Gonbei of Satsuma, appointed by the *genro*, and was supported by the *Seiyukai* with Hara as minister of home affairs and Takahashi Korekiyo, president of the Bank of Japan since 1911, as minister of finance. In the prevailing atmosphere of political reform it carried out relaxations in the qualifications of the army and navy ministers (retired generals and admirals now became eligible) and of other government officials, as well as a curtailment in the number of such officials. A national movement against the government

---

[12] Shinobu, op. cit., 220.

because of unpopular taxes, however, continued, greatly strengthened by a scandal involving naval officers of high rank who were found to have received a rebate on a cruiser and wireless equipment purchased by the Japanese navy from the German firm, Siemens. 'The Siemens Affair' was followed by a similar scandal of greater magnitude, when it was disclosed that Mitsui Bussan had bribed naval officers to make sure that the navy would order a battle-cruiser, *Kongo*, from Vickers of Britain. As the House of Peers decided to cut the government budget for the navy, Admiral Yamamoto resigned, and was succeeded by Okuma as prime minister. This was in the spring of 1914.

JAPAN AND THE FIRST WORLD WAR: THE TWENTY-ONE DEMANDS UPON CHINA

Three days after the British declaration of war against Germany, Britain asked Japan to join the war so as to destroy the German fleet based at Tsingtao. Japan, partly on account of the terms of the Anglo-Japanese Alliance, partly because of her own expansionist ambitions, decided on a military operation including an attack on Tsingtao. Yet Britain prevaricated: for political and economic reasons she was anxious to prevent Japanese troops fighting on land. Japan assured Britain of her intention of limiting land operations, and sent an ultimatum to Germany on 23 August 1914. The former German Caroline, Mariana, and Marshall Islands in the Pacific north of the equator were occupied by the Japanese navy in October. Its primary task had been to guard transport ships carrying Australian soldiers to Europe. Japanese cruisers helped the Royal Navy in searching and pursuing the main strength of the German Oriental Fleet in the southern Pacific. Later, in 1917, the Japanese navy dispatched to the Mediterranean a fleet consisting of two cruisers, one seaplane ship, and twelve destroyers to co-operate with the Allies in dealing with German submarines. This was undertaken after assurances from the Allies that they would support Japanese claims to the former German interests in East Asia and the Pacific at a future peace conference.

Meanwhile, a blockade of the whole coastline of the leased territory of Kiachow in Shantung had been announced on 27 August. A siege of Tsingtao and the fortified hills behind ensued, and the Germans surrendered after a bombardment from Japanese artillery and a final assault in early November in which a British battalion also took part. Both sides used aircraft; the superior Japanese airforce unit was employed not only for reconnaisance but also for bombing, and 'the first aerial combat' was fought over Tsingtao.[13] The battle was an unequal contest of strength:

[13] Charles B. Burdick, *The Japanese Siege of Tsingtau* (Hamden, Conn., 1976), 132.

some 60,000 Japanese men challenged 4,000 Germans; the casuality lists revealed a modest war in its scale: Japanese dead numbered 415, British thirteen, and German 199, while the Japanese had 1,452 wounded, the British sixty-one, and the Germans 294. After the battle the Japanese commander met the former German governor and expressed his sympathy for the country from which he had learned his military art.[14] Tsingtao was placed under military rule, the victorious Japanese taking over the well-organized military administration already in existence in this German-built town. Japanese troops marched through the streets of Tsingtao, heralding the new power relations in the East. Indeed, the First World War was 'a godsend to the new era of Taisho in furthering the development of its national fortunes', as Inoue Kaoru remarked.[15]

Soon friction developed with China over the area of the limited military operation, as well as over control of the railway between Tsinan and Tsingtao. In January 1915 China requested the withdrawal of Japanese forces from the Shantung province because the aims of the operation appeared to have been accomplished. Thereupon the Japanese government handed over the notorious 'twenty-one demands' in five clauses made upon the Chinese which Kato Takaaki, now foreign minister under Okuma, had been preparing in order to promote Japanese interests in China.

Early in 1913 Kato, as Japanese minister in London, had indicated his China programme of placing Japanese interests in Kwantung, South Manchuria, and Eastern Inner Mongolia on a firm foundation in a private talk with Sir Edward Grey, the British foreign secretary. Nor was Kato alone in conceiving a policy of turning the tables in China. Shortly after Okuma took office in April 1914, Sun Yat-sen, the revolutionary leader from South China, then staying in Japan, sent him a plea for help in such suprising terms that Marius Jansen suggests it was ghost-written by Uchida Ryohei of the *Kokuryukai* (Amur River Society), who befriended Sun. Uchida himself was interested in a scheme for the partition of China, the south going to Sun's nationalist republic and the north to Japan, through a revival of the Manchu dynasty. In Sun's plea to Okuma, Japanese help was sought in order to drive out Yuan Shi-kai from office, and a Sino-Japanese alliance was promised, offering various economic benefits which would amount to Japanese commercial domination of China. Sun at this stage sometimes appeared as an apologist for Japanese expansion, and his promises were used as a threat to Yuan Shi-kai prior to the formal presentation of the Demands on 18 January 1915.[16]

The five clauses of the Demands were: 1. China should accept all the

[14] Ibid. 186–7, 194.
[15] Quoted in Seiichi Imai, *Nihon no Rekishi* (History of Japan), xxiii. 58.
[16] Marius Jansen, *The Japanese and Sun Yat-sen* (Cambridge, Mass., 1954), 188–9.

agreements Japan would reach with Germany as to the disposal of German interests in the Shantung province, and should give Japan the right to build a railway connecting Chefoo with the Tsinan–Tsingtao railway (four demands). 2. The period of the lease to Japan of Dairen and Port Arthur and of the Mukden–Antung line should be extended to ninety-nine years; the administration and management of the Kirin–Changchun railway should be entrusted to the Japanese for ninety-nine years; the right to rent, own, or occupy land, and to travel without molestation, engage in business, and develop mines in Southern Manchuria and Eastern Inner Mongolia should be accorded to the Japanese; China should consult Japan on appointing advisers and instructors in political, economic, and military affairs in the same areas (seven demands). 3. *Kanyahyo-Seitetsu-Konsu* (in Chinese, *Han Ye Ping Mei Tie Gong Si*), the greatest iron-manufacturing company in China at the time, consisting of the Kanyo (Hanyan) Iron Works in the Hupeh province, the Daiya (Daye) iron-mine (near Huangshi on the Yangtze) in the same province, and the Hyokyo (Pingxang) coalmine in the Kiangsi province, that had been virtually controlled by Japanese banks and companies and had been supplying a great part of the iron ore used at the Yawata Steel-Mill, should be run as the joint venture of Japan and China (two demands). 4. Ports, harbours, and offshore islands along the coast in Fukien province should not be leased to any other country (one demand). 5. Lastly, influential Japanese should be employed as advisers on political, financial, and military matters for the Chinese central government; local police should either come under a joint Sino-Japanese administration or should employ Japanese in police offices; China should obtain the arms it needed from Japan, or joint arsenals should be set up; the right to preach should be given to Japanese Buddhist priests; the right for the Japanese to build railways from Nanchang should be acknowledged; and the question of admitting foreign investment to railways, mines, and harbours in Fukien province should first be discussed with Japan (seven demands).

These demands naturally caused widespread protest in China, while Chinese students studying in Japan held a great protest meeting in Tokyo in February. When the British and US governments made enquiries about the fifth clause, foreign minister Kato replied that this clause did not make demands but clarified 'expectations'. The bellicose Kato, through threats and minor concessions, sought to have his own way, but there was a degree of conflict between Kato and the *genro* who blamed him for causing an almost certain rupture of negotiations with China and a possible war, and who suggested a compromise solution by eliminating the controversial Clause Five. Sir Edward Grey urged the Japanese not to risk the breakdown of negotiations, and intelligence came in to the effect that the United States was to adopt measures to restrain Japan. The final decision to issue an ultimatum to China with the fifth clause withheld was reached at a conference of the *genro*, cabinet ministers, and military chiefs held in the presence of the emperor on 6 May 1915.

Most Japanese newspapers (with the notable exception of the *Oriental Economist* and the *Yomiuri*) supported these demands and the sending of the ultimatum. Yoshino Sakuzo, who was to become the champion of Taisho democracy, conceded that there was no other way but sending the ultimatum at that stage. In view of Yoshino's attitude towards the Demands, there is a certain justification in using the term 'imperial democracy' instead of 'Taisho democracy' to indicate the tone of the constitutional movement at the time.[17] As early as 10 June 1915, Yoshino, who had once served as a private tutor for the family of Yuan Shi-kai, published a book entitled *Nisshi Kosho-ron* (On the Sino-Japanese Negotiations), a detailed history and analysis of the twenty-one Demands after these had been presented to Yuan Shi-kai. Since the possibilities of China developing into a powerful, independent state were slim and doubtful, argued Yoshino, 'the Japanese empire in competition with other powers should establish her influence and interest in China'. Japan should take into account possible Chinese reaction as well as western interests in China, but what was important was not to miss a favourable opportunity. Yoshino deplored the withdrawal of Clause Five, because he believed that the twenty-one Demands as a whole were the minimum condition 'indispensable for the survival of Japan', and that they would have been accepted by Yuan, whom he knew personally.[18]

In fact, as Yoshino pointed out, Japan had seized an opportune moment. The European powers, preoccupied with the prolonged war in Europe, failed to intervene in China's favour (in spite of their expressed concern about Clause Five), and China had to accept the Japanese ultimatum. The day of its delivery (7 May) and of its acceptance (9 May) respectively became days of national disgrace for the Chinese, and China's government sought to prevent the implementation of the twenty-one Demands as much as it could: leasing land to a foreigner was made punishable by death, and the right of the Japanese to rent land in Southern Manchuria and Eastern Inner Mongolia remained the matter of negotiations between the two countries until 1931.

A NEW DEMOCRATIC CURRENT: *MINPONSHUGI* OR 'PEOPLE-ISM'

One of the awkward issues of Taisho democracy (or 'imperial democracy') was to find a definition of democracy compatible with the monarchical Meiji constitution; the term coined for this purpose was *Minponshugi*,

---

[17] Keiichi Eguchi, *Nihon Tsushi*, xviii. 25.   [18] Yoshino, *Selected Works*, viii. 150, 152–3.

which literally means 'politics based on the people' and was introduced as a concept opposed to the bureaucracy. The first instance of its use in that sense was in an article on the anti-trust campaign published in the *Yorozu-choho* (9 May 1912). This was followed up by Kayahara Kazan, who had spent nearly eight years in Europe and America as foreign correspondent for the same paper, and who now wrote '*Minponshugi* Interpreted' in the *Yorozu-choho* of 27 May 1912. In this article he contrasted *Minponshugi* with militarism. Kayahara, an advocate of such *Minponshugi* and of a Little Japan (i. e. renunciation not only of Manchuria but also of Korea), founded a journal, *Daisan Teikoku* (The Third Empire) in October 1913: this 'third empire' would be the joint rule of the emperor and the people that would follow the first empire of hegemonic power established at the Restoration, and the second empire of the bureaucrats. His journal attracted many prominent writers of the day, liberals and radicals, socialists and anarchists. Uehara Etsujiro, who had studied at the London School of Economics and had become an admirer of the British system of representative government (and who, incidentally, was to become a minister of state under Yoshida Shigeru in 1946), advocated the sovereignty of the people in this jounral (10 December 1913), though he assigned to the emperor the right to rule as stipulated in the Meiji constitution. The *Daisan Teikoku* had readers scattered all over the country, in local towns and villages, and opened its correspondence columns to young men who criticized emperor-worship, patriotism, conscription, and the traditional family system; to coal-miners who advocated trade unions; and to Korean students who condemned oppressive Japanese rule in their country.[19]

Meanwhile Minobe Tatsukichi, professor of the law faculty of Tokyo Imperial University, under the influence of the German legal theorist Georg Jellineck, had developed an 'organ theory' of the emperor in his book *Kenpokowa* (A Discourse on the Constitution, 1912), according to which the state as a corporation possessed the right to rule and the emperor, though supreme, was an organic part of such a state along with other organic parts such as the cabinet, the Diet, and even the people as a whole. In other words, there was a relationship of dependency between the emperor, the cabinet, the Diet, and the people. With a party cabinet and a Diet elected by universal suffrage, he believed it would be possible to attain constitutional monarchy and parliamentary government even under the Meiji constitution. Uesugi Shinkichi, one of his colleagues in the same university and a strong advocate of the absolute sovereignty of the emperor, wrote an article in the *Taiyo* (August 1912) in which he attacked Minobe's organic interpretation of the constitution; this had a great influence among conservative academics and bureaucrats. Now Yoshino Sakuzo, another

[19] Matsuo, *Taisho Democracy*, 121–43.

professor of the Imperial University, published an article entitled 'On The Fundamental Principles of Constitutional Politics and the Way to Carry Them Out' in *Chuo Koron* (January 1916) which attracted much attention. He regarded the masses as volatile and too susceptible to incitement to action; he considered democracy or the sovereignty of the people to be impracticable under the Meiji constitution, and instead advocated *Minponshugi* or a politics that would take the people's wishes seriously; his advocacy of universal suffrage was based on such a limited view of democracy that it would have amounted to a government on behalf of the people. '*Minshushugi* [Democracy] can easily be confused with the dangerous doctrine of popular sovereignty implied in a name like the "Social Democratic Party"', wrote Yoshino. His definition of 'democracy' as popular politics meant 'politics of the people', which could be either 'politics by the people' or 'politics for the people', but not both; and he chose the latter interpretation for the simple reason that the former, which would imply popular sovereignty, was at variance with 'a state like ours which upholds the emperor, who assumes all the national right in his hands'.[20] Meanwhile Yoshino had borrowed the term 'university extension' from the British adult education movement, with which he had apparently become acquainted during his brief stay in England in 1913, and founded a University Extension Society with a magazine of its own, *Kokumin Kodan* (Popular Discourse), in June 1915. In this he had already begun developing his own version of *Minponshugi*. The University Extension Society prepared the ground for a new departure in the midst of excitement caused by a public debate between Yoshino and members of the *Roninkai* (Society of the High-Minded Masterless Men), a right-wing body connected with the *Kokuryukai*, and encouraged the formation of a *Reimei Kai* (Dawn Society) and also contributed to the launching of the *Shinjinkai* (New Men's Society) by the students under his influence in December 1918. The latter became a breeding-ground for the left-wing movements of the 1920s, of which we shall see more later.[21]

WAR PROSPERITY

The economic impact and consequences of the First World War in Japan were important in creating new conditions under which the further development of Taisho democracy took place. The Russo-Japanese War itself had already given a further impetus to the industrialization of Japan. An expansion of Yawata Steel was decided upon in 1906, seventeen private railway companies were nationalized in 1907, and complete autonomy in

[20] Yoshino, *Selected Works*, ii. 23, 25, 43.
[21] Henry Dewitt Smith II, *Japan's First Student Radicals* (Cambridge, Mass., 1972), 35–52.

custom duties obtained at last in 1911, enabling Japan to adopt higher rates, virtually a protective tariff under which industrialization was accelerated. Yet industrialization still greatly depended upon foreign capital, the ratio of which in domestic capital formation began to show a marked increase after the Russo-Japanese war and reached as high as over 40 per cent in the 1902–8 period for long-term loans.[22] Victory over Russia had entailed a direct expenditure of 2 billion yen, and the strains this imposed affected the Japanese economy for a decade, foreign debt increasing from less than 100 million yen in 1903 to 1.4 billion yen in 1907. Between 1909 and 1913 annual deficits in current international payments remained at about 80 million to 90 million yen.

The outbreak of war in Europe in August 1914 changed all this. Indeed, the First World War rescued Japan from the morass of fiscal and balance-of-payments problems.[23] Japan, though an ally against Germany in the war, took comparatively little part in actual hostilities, while she benefited from Allied orders for munitions and other manufactured goods and also from the removal of European competitors in both domestic and Asian markets. International trade and payments showed a striking improvement; the ratio of foreign loans dropped significantly and Japan became a creditor nation for the duration of the war, while a spurt of domestic investment fed an unprecedented boom. Between 1914 and 1918 Japan's real gross national product rose by 40 per cent. Yet a high proportion of output went into profitable exports, and the standard of living remained modest. Distinctions between rich and poor were keenly felt as the distribution of income became more unequal; investors and speculators made large fortunes whereas those living on relatively fixed incomes suffered by inflation. *Narikin* (*nouveau-riche*), as everywhere else, was the term in which admiration was mingled with contempt. But private enterprises as a whole, hitherto dependent upon the government, suddenly became so profitable as to acquire new respectability and political influence. This was most graphically illustrated by the foundation in 1917 of the Industrial Club of Japan in Tokyo by leaders of modern industries, headed by Toyokawa Ryohei of Mitsubishi and Dan Takuma of Mitsui. The Industrial Club was instrumental in the passage in the Diet of a protectionist legislation for the steel industry shortly after its formation, and also in wrecking a draft trade union law later on.

Trade surpluses for the years 1915–19 totalled 3 billion yen. Besides these, there were earnings from shipping services. At a time when freight and charter rates rose to an extraordinary level because of war damages,

---

[22] Takafusa Nakamura and Konosuke Odaka (eds.), *Nihon Keizaishi* (Economic History of Japan), vol. 6 *Nijukozo* (The Double Structure) (Tokyo, 1989, 1994), 16–17.

[23] Crowcour, 'Industrialization and Technological Change', *Cambridge History of Japan*, vol. 6, *The Twentieth Century* (Cambridge, 1988), 436.

Japan's merchant marine expanded its capacity from 1.58 million gross tons in 1914 to 2.8 million in 1919 and increased foreign earnings from 41 million yen in 1914 to a peak of over 450 million yen in 1918. As for heavy industry and machinery, manufacturing output increased by 72 per cent in 1915–19, with an increase in labour employed of 42 per cent. Business was booming to such an extent that the rate of profit for some companies rose to over 50 per cent. Shipbuilding too prospered with a fifteenfold increase in its output in gross tonnage between 1915 and 1918. With the promise of huge profits, even small, ill-equipped yards multiplied to take advantage of war conditions. The output of steam engines, turbines, and internal combustion engines also rapidly increased. Demand for textiles throughout the war remained brisk, and the amount of the dividends of cotton-spinning companies rose from an average of 13 per cent in 1910–13 to 46 per cent in 1919–20 on paid-up capital.[24]

Urbanization continued; the number of cities with a population of over 100,000 rose from nine to eighteen between 1903 and 1920, and the ratio of the urban population increased from 7.9 per cent in 1903 to 13.5 per cent in 1920. Price inflation began, money wages rose, and labour costs increased. The price of rice went up, and led to rice riots (see below).[25] In spite of rapid industrialization, though, Japan still remained predominantly an agricultural nation. A quinquennial census was introduced in 1920, when the population of the home country excluding the dependent territories, stood at 55,963,100. The ratio of those engaged in the primary sector was about 50 per cent of the population employed, and that in the manufacturing sector 12.5 per cent.

THE FACTORY ACT OF 1911 (ENFORCED IN 1916)

The onset of the war boom eased the implementation of the Factory Act of 1911 which had been put in cold storage after successful lobbying by the more vulnerable smaller firms.[26] The harsh conditions of the workers had attracted attention through reports by Yokoyama Gennosuke and through government publication of the results of its own research in this field. In particular, the disclosure of abuses in the working conditions of female labour in textile mills had contributed much to the adoption in 1911 of a minimum set of standards for employment in manufacuring establishments employing fifteen or more workers. This prohibied the employment of persons under the age of 12 and that of minors and women for more than twelve hours a day or for night-work, though the last provision was put into abeyance for fifteen years after objections from the Great Japan

[24] Ibid. 442.   [25] See below Chap. 10. Nakamura and Odaka, op. cit., 23.
[26] Sheldon Garon, *The State and Labor in Modern Japan* (Berkeley, 1987), 29.

Federation of Cotton-Spinning Companies, and the Factory Act itself was enforced only in 1916.[27]

Ishihara Osamu, later professor of Osaka Imperial University, who was then engaged in a survey of factory sanitation, in a speech given in 1913 under the title 'The Female Textile Workers and Tuberculosis', stated that although the percentage of deaths in factories was 0.8, that of workers who had returned to their homes because of ill health was 5.11 per cent for cotton spinning, 1.45 per cent for silk, and 1.94 per cent for weaving, and he pleaded for the enforcement of the Factory Act.[28] An Imperial Ordinance for the Implementation of the Factory Act was obtained in 1916, which elaborated the provisions relating to compensation for industrial accidents, disability, sickness, death, and burial-costs, but it is difficult to judge to what extent the Act actually improved the conditions of the workers. Some employers were already ahead of the Act.[29] The Kurashiki Institute for the Study of Labour Science began in 1920 when Ohara Magosaburo, president of the Kurashiki Cotton-Spinning Company, invited a young graduate of medicine named Teruoka Gito to observe the night-work of his female workers. 'No overseers were around,' wrote Teruoka: 'Only females were at work. One-third of them were asleep. There were workers 9 or 10 years old . . . Their spindles were at eye level. And dense dust filled the air . . . Almost a prison.'[30] Hosoi Wakizo, a textile-worker employed by Kanegafuchi Spinning Company and also by Tokyo Muslin Company, a member of the *Yuaikai* friendly society (see next section), published a detailed study of female textile-workers, *Joko Aishi* (The Sad Story of Female Textile-Workers) in 1925, shortly before his own death, in which he recounted abuses connected with recruiting, housing, working conditions, and punishment of the poor girls. He noted, among other things, the irony of the factory songs adopted by textile mills to educate their workers, one of which ran as follows: 'Weaving and spinning began in the era of gods of the imperial state. We must remember that the great, inspiring achievements of our godly ancestors were the beginnings of our manufacture. . . . The bond of capital and labour will never slacken; the breeze of intimacy carries warmth. Our Chita factory [of the Toyo Spinning Company] gives a hearty pledge to work hard for our godly temple.'[31] Both body and soul were dedicated on the altar of textile-manufacturers and their imperial state.

[27] *Rodo Kagaku Kenkyujjo Rokuju Nenshi* (Sixty Years History of the Institute for the Study of Labour Science) (Tokyo, 1981), 10–11; Koji Taira, *Economic Development and the Labor Market in Japan* (New York, 1970), 138.

[28] *Rodo Kagaku Kenkyujo Rokuju Nenshi*, 12.   [29] Koji Taira, op. cit., 139 ff.

[30] *Rodo Kagaku Kenkyujo Rokuju Nenshi* , 30–1.

[31] Wakizo Hosoi, *Joko Aishi* (Tokyo, 1925), 289.

SUZUKI BUNJI AND THE *YUAIKAI*

In spite of legal and administrative prejudices against organized labour, war prosperity allowed workers to demand improvement in their conditions. In the summer of 1912, on the third day of Taisho, Suzuki Bunji, a graduate of Tokyo Imperial University and a Christian, founded the *Yuaikai* (Friendly Society), though he believed that relief activities on behalf of the workers were not enough and that his organization, when the time came, would develop into a bona-fide trade union.[32] He combined reformism with patriotism as a leading principle of his organization. War prosperity helped strengthen the *Yuaikai*; the circulation of its journal *Rodo oyobi Sangyo* (*Labour and Industry*) reached 3,000 in November 1914, and had increased to 27,000 by April 1917.[33]

Suzuki was assisted in his work for the *Yuaikai* by Abe Isoo, a socialist and Waseda professor; Ozaki Yukio, the minister of justice in the second Okuma government (1914–16); Itagaki Taisuke, the veteran liberal politician; and Shibusawa Eiichi, one of the top business leaders, who had by now retired from *zaikai* and was devoting himself to social work and education. The *Yuaikai* had several departments dealing respectively with legal advice, medical services, physical fitness, savings, recreation, publications, and employment. In 1914 'the Mutual Aid department' was created and placed under its control consumers' co-operatives founded in the Kanto area. The *Yuaikai*'s membership showed a steady increase: starting from a modest beginning of fifteen in August 1912, it rose to 1,295 in June 1913, 4,000 in February 1915, 16,418 in July 1916, and 19,190 in April 1917.[34] Members were predominantly factory workers in the mechanized modern industries. Its reformism appeared so moderate and sound that company directors and city mayors came to give their blessings to the inauguration of local branches.

On a visit to America in 1915 Suzuki met Katayama Sen and learned the tactics of collective bargaining pursued by the American Federation of Labor. Suzuki's major concern was in shifting from co-operation with management to independent trade unionism. On his return he founded a Women's Department of the *Yuaikai*. The number of strikes and of workers involved in industrial disputes steadily increased. Then, in March 1917, the Terauchi government that had succeeded Okuma's took strong action against a dispute at the Japan Steelworks Company at Muroran, Hokkaido, by dispatching an army division to lay siege to the workers on strike. The Muroran branch of the *Yuaikai* was dissolved. Suzuki grew cautious once more, but under the impact of the Russian Revolution and

---

[32] Stephen S. Large, *The Rise of Labour in Japan: The Yuaikai, 1912–1919* (Tokyo, 1973), 14–15.   [33] Ibid. 38.

[34] Ibid. 43.

the Rice Riot his organization developed into a fully fledged trade union, though still unprotected by law, under the name of *Nihon Rodo Sodomei* (General Alliance of Trade Unions in Japan) in 1921, as we shall see later.

As the war ended Taisho democracy seemed to be moving slowly along a path that might lead Japan to the threshold of social democracy and even beyond it, encouraged by the revolutionary events in Europe. Yet traditional politics attuned to imperialist rivalries stood in the way. They were to exacerbate the conflicts and confrontations that characterized the second half of the Taisho era.

10

Taisho Politics and Society: From the Rice Riot to the Public Order Preservation Act

THE SECOND PHASE OF TAISHO DEMOCRACY

The Russian Revolution of 1917, especially the Bolshevik Revolution of October, helped the radicalization of the trade union movement organized in the *Yuaikai* and also the democratic movement among students that had begun under the direct influence of university professors such as Yoshino Sakuzo and Oyama Ikuo (the latter prominent in the Dawn Society). Although the Bolsheviks sought to win outside support by organizing the Communist International in February 1919, it took some time before their influence began to be felt in Japan. No sinister Russian hands were at work in a nationwide 'rice riot' which had begun in a small town on the Japan Sea coast in the summer of 1918.

At that time, across the sea in Siberia, Japanese troops were engaged in a military intervention against the Bolsheviks, whose influence was spreading eastward along the Siberian Railway to Vladivostok. Triumphant Bolshevism certainly had an impact on some sections of the Japanese labour movement as well as on radical intellectuals, while constitutional politics made faltering progress, experimenting with universal suffrage under the unfavourable conditions of the introduction of thought control and the further spread of imperialist endeavours. Wartime prosperity and Japan's emergence as a military power had given a new self-confidence even to the poor whose living standards, however, were hard hit by the inflation that followed. The Japanese, though only a fortunate few of them, became sufficiently well off to indulge in liberalism, especially in literature, and also in women's liberation movements often closely connected with a literary movement.

THE RICE RIOTS

The riots, which began with the housewives of a fishing port in Toyama prefecture, were not a 'failed revolution' as some historians have suggested, but 'a Jacquerie of enormous scale' on the part of people of the lower order in urban areas[1] where *narikin* (*nouveau-riche*) and the poor lived side by side. Wage increases lagged behind the doubling in the prices of food, clothes, and other consumer goods. An Excess Profit Ordinance was rarely used against the hoarders of rice, and the government rice import programme involving major trading companies encouraged popular suspicion about collusion between the Terauchi cabinet and the *narikin*. The price of rice sharply increased in the summer of 1918. The riot started on 23 July at Wuotsu, where some fifty fishermen's wives assembled on the beach and decided to petition the town master and merchants to stop selling local rice elsewhere in search of higher prices; their petition was ignored. Unrest spread to a neighbouring town, where on the evening of 4 August about 600 women started petitioning: one contingent of the protesting women attacked a rice merchant's warehouse. This was only the beginning of a nationwide movement; assaults on rice merchants and other tradesmen spread to larger towns like Nagoya, Kyoto, Osaka, Kobe, and to Kyushu, where coal-miners attacked company property and troops were brought in. Hiroshima, Okayama, Shizuoka, Tokyo, and several towns in Tohoku were also affected. Workers and artisans played a leading part in the riots, and urban elements were very conspicuous.[2] The riots lasted for three months and altogether 700,000 people took part. Socialist leaders remained onlookers, but the government arrested or administratively detained prominent socialists like Osugi Sakae, Arahata Kanson, and Yamakawa Hitoshi. Of 554 designated burakus (or discriminated ghettos) in 1918, disturbances were reported from only thirty-two, but in spite of this relative calmness at burakus, the government made them a scapegoat and arrested a disproportionately large number of buraku people. They accounted for more than 10 per cent of those arrested (887 out of 8,185 prosecuted, about one-third of those arrested or detained), and the two individuals who received the death sentence for rioting were both buraku people. Although no soldiers died in the skirmishes, more than thirty protesters were killed. Throughout the nation over 5,000 people were found guilty, and those arrested in the coalfields accounted for around 25 per cent of this figure. The occupational background of those prosecuted for riot-related crimes shows that they ranged from white-collar workers and minor officials to craftsmen and unskilled workers, students, and journalists, representing a fair cross-section of Japanese society with the exception of the very wealthy.[3]

The Rice Riots, in spite of their outer form resembling the *ikki* or destructionism of the old days, were a spontaneous mass protest movement

---

[1] Michael Lewis, *Rioters and Citizens: Mass Protest in Imperial Japan* (Berkeley, 1990), pp. xxi–xxii.   [2] Ibid. 16–17.
[3] Ibid. 18, 23, 25, 28.

against inequalities amplified by war prosperity, and even involved a degree of protest against Japan's armed intervention in Siberia, which was never popular.[4] The Rice Riots finally led to the replacement of the Terauchi cabinet by the *Seiyukai* government led by Hara Takashi, a 'commoner prime minister'.

One major result of the Rice Riots was the creation of permanent government control for distributing rice, developed in response to numerous petitions demanding self-sufficiency in food supply and the government regulation of rice prices.[5] In view of the scale and intensity of the confrontation with the government, there was little doubt that the riots contributed to the 'mass awakening' and, in an indirect way, to the creation of mass-based organizations defending the rights of factory workers, farmers, women, and buraku people.[6]

THE SIBERIAN INTERVENTION, 1918–1922

Japanese intervention in China since the revolution of 1911 seemed to Marquis Yamagata to have been inconsistent, *saben uko* (looking left and right, unable to decide), as he described it.[7] Japan's policy towards China was to help one or other of the warlords with money and supplies and to set up a pro-Japanese regime. The decision to intervene in Siberia, though, had been reached through a process of careful deliberation as an ally of the Entente Powers in the war. But as an emerging power in East Asia, Japan was also anxious to take some independent action in the peripheries of her expanding empire. This would explain the marked contrast between her preliminary declarations and subsequent actions.[8] In fact, she was seeking to take advantage of the volatile situation that had developed in Russia.

We have already noted how, after the Russo-Japanese War, Japan reversed her policy and sought to strengthen her ties with Tsarist Russia by concluding a series of agreements or ententes for mutual protection of the acquired interests of the two countries in Korea, Manchuria, and Mongolia. In the Russo-Japanese entente of 1907 and another of 1913 a secret understanding had been reached under which Japan would obtain the southern half of Manchuria and the eastern part of Inner Mongolia as her sphere of influence. In February 1915 Yamagata Aritomo, now the most venerable *genro*, addressed a memorandum to prime minister Okuma in which he stated his view of the European war. 'The true cause' of the war, he said, was 'the racial rivalry between the Slavs and the Germans'; he

---

[4] Matsuo, op. cit., 180.   [5] Lewis, op. cit., 244.   [6] Ibid. 248.
[7] Iichiro Tokutomi, *Koshaku Yamagata Den* (The Life of Marquis Yamagata) (Tokyo, 1933), 921.
[8] James William Morley, *The Japanese Thrust into Siberia, 1918* (New York, 1954; repr. 1972), 4.

believed that the future 'rivalry between the Yellow and the White races would be much fiercer than that between the White races themselves', and that in such a conflict White would unite against Yellow. But he could not expect so much solidarity on the part of the Yellow races, and regretted that 'the Japanese empire had not acquired sufficient strength to preserve the Chinese continent single-handed'. Thus he proposed, while emphasizing the need for winning Chinese confidence in Japan, to 'form an alliance with one European power so as to prevent a union of the White in advance' of the coming racial conflict. The European war, he felt, would bring about alterations in the relationships of powers: 'the existing Anglo-Japanese alliance alone would not be adequate to preserve peace in East Asia', and 'it is most opportune now to conclude an alliance with Russia'.[9] Marquis Yamagata was in favour of a defensive and offensive alliance with Russia, which was embodied, together with his proposal for the preservation of China, in the Russo-Japanese entente of July 1916 (the fourth entente), which also rejected the possibility of a unilateral peace with Germany in the war. Motono Ichiro, the Japanese ambassador to Petersburg (now Petrograd), who had negotiated all the ententes with the Russians, returned home in November, having been appointed foreign minister in the newly formed Terauchi government. His successor arrived in the Russian capital in February 1917, only to report the beginnings of the revolution that overthrew the Romanov dynasty in March.

The new provisional Russian government made overtures to the United States for help in the economic development of the country, including Sakhalin and Far Eastern Russia. This was enough to alarm the Terauchi government, and especially its foreign minister Motono, who had committed himself so much to a rapprochement with Tsarist Russia.[10] While the revolution moved eastward to Siberian cities, a new situation developed in the capital—the Bolshevik Revolution of October 1917—which had immediate repercussions on the Far Eastern situation, for the Bolsheviks announced their intention to withdraw from the war, and in response the Allies sought to reconstruct an eastern front against the Central Powers, possibly with Japanese co-operation. Indeed, plans for a Siberian intervention had been prepared and even matured in some quarters of the Japanese government and the military. In Europe, when the Russians began negotiations for a truce with the Germans at Brest-Litovsk in December, Marshal Ferdinand Foch, the chief of the French general staff, proposed sending Japanese or American soldiers to seize the railway between Moscow and Vladivostok, the first plan for a military intervention in

---

[9] Iichiro Tokutomi, *Yamagata Aritomo Den*, 942–6.
[10] Teruyuki Hara, *Shiberia Shuppei—Kakumei to Kansho, 1917–1921* (The Siberian Expedition—Revolution and Intervention, 1917–1921) (Tokyo, 1989), 72–3.

Siberia, although it fell through for lack of support from other delegates at an Allied conference where it was considered.

The spread of Bolshevik activities eastwards presented a menace to Japan's interests in East Asia: Japanese holdings of Russian government bonds had reached an enormous sum, and a lucrative wartime trade had been opened with the Russian ports Vladivostok and Harbin; Japanese companies had established branch offices in northern Manchuria and eastern Siberia, where an increasingly large number of Japanese took up residence. It was also the case that the Trans-Siberian Railway had been all but crippled under wartime conditions and political changes, so that a large amount of goods and munitions destined for the European front had piled up at Vladivostok; this fell into the hands of the Bolsheviks when they took over the port at the end of November.[11] Instability in the region was further increased when General Dimitrii Khorvat, the managing director of the (Russian) Chinese Eastern Railway and governor of the railway zone appointed by the Tsarist regime, came into contact with an aggressively anti-revolutionary Trans-Baikal Cossack, Gregorii Semenov, 'a kind of latter-day Genghis Khan'.[12]

Terauchi's confidant Nishihara Kamezo, formerly a businessman in Korea, had been instrumental in providing the Chinese warlord Tuan Ch'i-jui with a large loan amounting to 145 million yen through the Japan Industrial Bank, the Bank of Korea, and the Bank of Taiwan in an attempt to bolster him in his struggle for power. Nishihara now persuaded his boss Terauchi and vice-chief of staff Tanaka Giichi that the time for a Siberian expedition had come. Tanaka was a leading advocate of army expansion and was known as the founder of the Imperial Reservist Association, formed in 1910. Foreign minister Motono and several of his subordinates in the Foreign Ministry, like the young official Matsuoka Yosuke who later distinguished himself as a pro-Nazi foreign minister, were preoccupied with the German problem. They saw in the Bolshevik spread to eastern Siberia a German penetration into Asia, and argued that help should be given to the anti-Bolshevik elements in the Russian Far East in their attempt to set up an autonomous state which could become a buffer for the Japanese. Nishihara himself prepared 'a timely proposition' in which he warned of the danger of 'a Russo-German thrust into the Japan Sea', and proposed a land blockade against it which would take the form of occupation of the three Siberian provinces, Maritime, Amur, and Zabaikal, by Japanese troops.[13]

[11] Morley, op. cit., 36, 38.   [12] Ibid. 434.

[13] Hara. op. cit., 166–7. Japanese military leaders were either not aware of or indifferent to the difference between the Mensheviks and the Bolsheviks (all forms of socialism were anathema to them), and the Russo-German truce at Brest-Litovsk may have appeared to them to portend a renewal in some form of the Tripartite Intervention.

On 1 January 1918 the British government proposed a joint military intervention in Siberia by Japan, Britain, and the United States. On 13 January 1918 the government announced that warships had been dispatched to Vladivostok in order to protect Japanese residents there; the battleship *Iwami* (the former Russian warship *Aureole*, seized after the Battle of the Japan Sea of 1905) reached Vladivostok on 12 January, two days before the arrival of HMS *Suffolk*, and another Japanese battleship, the *Asahi*, soon joined them. The flagship of the American Asiatic Fleet, the USS *Brooklyn*, was soon to arrive.

Meanwhile the Bolsheviks were successful in winning the cities alongside the Siberian Railway. The Japanese decision to support the Cossacks (or White Russians) was apparently made by Terauchi and Tanaka after consultation with Nishihara.[14] Japan supplied Semenov with a large quantity of munitions, the cost of which was borne by the Kuhara *zaibatsu*, which had special interests in Russia.[15]

As early as December 1917 the army general staff sent intelligence officers to several Siberian cities. One of them, sent to Blagoveshchensk on the Amur to help the Russians, was told personally by prime minister Terauchi to 'build a powerful dyke and set up a moderate self-governing state in the Far East with which Japan can deal by supplying funds and weapons on loan'. A Japanese attempt to dislodge the Blagoveshchensk Soviet from the seat of power failed owing to unpreparedness on the part of a self-defence volunteer corps of resident Japanese and their over-estimation of the Cossacks as an ally.[16]

On 5 April 1918 a force of Japanese marines landed at Vladivostok, an attack on a local Japanese firm having been used as an excuse for intervention.[17] This annoyed and angered Russians of every political persuasion. The Japanese commander, anticipating serious trouble, called for reinforcements: more warships and men arrived. The expedition shook the *genro*, who advised disengagement and urged the replacement of foreign minister Motono. Motono was duly succeeded by Goto Shinpei, a colonial bureaucrat and another expansionist, who formulated a 'policy of aggressive defence' with a Siberian expedition as its core. At about this time the Japanese army was planning to increase aid to Khorvat in Harbin, where Admiral Kolchak, the Arctic explorer and White Russian leader, had recently been entrusted with military matters for the Chinese Eastern Railway, and also to Semenov who was pursuing an erratic campaign in the Trans-Baikal region.

It was not the appointment of Goto nor the movement of either Khorvat or Semenov but that of some 50,000 Czechoslovak troops in Siberia that transformed the scene of the intervention. They had been recruited mainly

---

[14] Morley, op. cit., 78–9.   [15] Ibid. 99.   [16] Hara, op. cit., 177–201.
[17] Ibid. 217.

from disaffected Czech and Slovak soldiers of the Austrian army who had allowed themselves to be captured by the Tsarist army on the eastern front, and now they were to fight for the independence of their own country from the Habsburg monarchy. Tomas Masaryk of the National Czechoslovak Council declared these forces to be part of the Czechoslovak army in France and hoped for their transport to France with Allied support. The Soviet government gave them permission to move eastward along the Siberian Railway provided they took only small arms. This condition being difficult to fulfil, attempts were made to disarm the Czechoslovak troops. A dispute arose between them and liberated Hungarians who had joined the Red Guards. Fighting broke out, and all the cities east of Penza along the Siberian Railway, except Irkutsk, fell into the hands of the Czechoslovak forces assisted by anti-Bolshevik Russians. Indeed, thanks to the Czechoslovaks the moderate socialists and constitutional monarchists were now back in power once more in western Siberia.[18]

The Japanese were not much interested in Soviet allegations of western collusion behind the Czech uprisings nor in the Allies' denial of it. They were still under the impression that 'the Soviet government [was] a puppet of Germany',[19] though they had to revise their insular views of the European situation shortly. The immediate complication was the position of the Czech troops. The commander of the Czech forces at Vladivostok, with British and French approval, started an operation to rescue his compatriots trapped along the Trans-Siberian Railway, and on 29 June he seized the Soviet arms in the city and managed to overthrow the Vladivostok Soviet. This was intended to develop into a *coup d'état* against the Soviet regime and help restore the Autonomous Siberian Provisional Government in this region.[20] The Japanese government rather reluctantly decided to treat the Czechs as an allied army; more arms and ammunition were transported to Vladivostok and to the front as the Czechs were moving westward. The Japanese advisers to General Khorvat did not trust the Czechs, whom they regarded as 'socialist' and therefore useless to restore an imperial government.[21] Khorvat, advancing a few miles inside the Russian Maritime territory, announced a new all-Russian government, anti-Bolshevik and pro-Japanese. General Tanaka, vice-chief of the general staff, now sent instructions to Japanese officers in Manchuria, portraying the Khorvat operation as the vanguard of a Japanese expedition. But the pincer movement of the Czechoslovak forces began, and Irkutsk fell at about this time. The attitude of the Japanese government was also changing: the Czechs, they thought, might be used to promote Japanese ambitions in the Amur basin.

---

[18] Morley, op. cit., 238. [19] Ibid. 241. [20] Hara, op. cit., 346.
[21] Morley, op. cit., 254.

The Americans, too, were changing their attitude and proposed a co-ordinated action with Japan to send the same number of troops to Vladivostok to 'police the area' for the purpose of supporting the Czechoslovak forces. Terauchi's Advisory Council on Foreign Relations met and discussed the American proposal. Hara Takashi, who had been in close touch with Prince Saionji and Baron Makino, said that a small Vladivostok expedition would have to be accepted for the sake of future relations with the United States but a large Siberian expedition was another matter. Viscount Ito Miyoji of the Privy Council gave a finishing touch to the government position in his speech: Japan, as the 'leader of the East', with 'the responsibility of maintaining peace in the Far East', had direct obligations in Korea and the Kwantung leased territory and increasingly in China as well; therefore Japan ought to retain its freedom of action as to the objectives of the expedition, the number of troops to be sent, and the areas of their operation. Hara insisted including in its objectives the rescuing of the Czech forces. After negotiations with the Americans it was decided, in June 1918, that the original figure of 7,000 men requested from Japan could be increased to 10,000 or even 12,000.

In August 1918 a Japanese general (Otani Kikuzo) became the commander of Allied forces, consisting of 14,000 Japanese (increased to 72,000 by November), 9,000 American, 5,800 British/Canadian, 1,400 Italian, 1,200 French, and 2,000 Chinese.[22] Within a fortnight Japan's Twelfth Division chased the retreating 'extremists', as they were called, and occupied Khabarovsk, and early in September made contact at Chita with the Czech troops moving east. This encounter was made possible by the participation of the Seventh Division stationed in Manchuria advancing north in support of the troops led by Semenov. The Third Division was thrown in so as to help rescue the Czech troops that remained in the Trans-Baikal territory. By October 1918 the expedition had achieved its purposes.

Then the British and the French changed their strategy, with the Czech troops also agreeing to their plan to move west instead of east and to help build a Ural front. The situation deteriorated, especially after the Armistice made with the Germans in November 1918, for anti-German fronts and autonomous regimes in Russia and western Siberia now lost their *raison d'être* for being anti-German. They became simply anti-Red, and were soon threatened by the superior forces of the Bolsheviks. Japanese troops who had spread out across wide areas of Siberia suffered from attacks by partisans, as well as from the bitter cold of the Siberian winter. In February 1919 one Japanese battalion and an artillery platoon stationed in a small village in the Amur territory were attacked and, after

[22] Hara, op. cit., 374–7. *Tokyo Asahi Shinbun*, 10 Aug. 1918.

two days' fighting, completely wiped out. A new division was sent in, but both officers and men began to wonder why they had to stay in Siberia and with whom they had to fight at a time when peace was restored. There were no more cheering crowds to send off the soldiers departing for Siberia. In September 1919 the Thirteenth Division had to leave their home town of Takada incognito, to avoid the derision and insults of the otherwise friendly townspeople.[23] The British, French, and Czech troops had already been repatriated. The Americans evacuated in January 1919. 'Vladivostock Painted Red. The Extremists Control the City. The People Cheered the Partisan Chief who Addressed Them. Sympathy With the Americans and Antipathy Towards the Japanese', read a headline in the *Osaka Asahi Shinbun* (4 February 1920).

Disaster struck in March–May 1920, when about 400 Japanese residents at Nikolaevsk, along with the members of the consulate and the garrison of about 300 men, perished in an armed conflict with partisan forces called 'the Nikolaevsk Red Army'. The tragedy began with a surprise attack by the Japanese garrison against the Red Army, but the four Chinese gunboats anchored in the Amur helped the latter and dealt a decisive blow against the Japanese.[24] Hara Takashi, who succeeded Terauchi as prime minister, did almost nothing to improve a worsening situation. Only when Admiral Kato Tomosaburo, naval minister since 1915, became prime minister in June 1922 was a decision taken. The first thing he did was to evacuate the Japanese troops from Siberia, a process that was completed on 25 October 1922.

The Siberian expedition had lasted for four years and two months, while the occupation of northern Sakhalin, which Japan seized as compensation for the losses suffered at Nikolaevsk and which continued till May 1925, made the period of intervention eight years altogether. Six army divisions were thrown in, with casualties of 4,000 men and officers killed or wounded. The continued expedition was looked upon with suspicion by foreigners and with distrust by Japanese citizens. It damaged the morale of the soldiers, while young staff officers who supported Kolchak or Semenov had learned the tricks of political intrigue in a revolutionary situation; an ominous lesson in view of its later implications.

FROM PARIS TO WASHINGTON

The conference to conclude the terms of peace with the Central Powers was by this time long over. It had begun on 18 January 1919 at the Quai d'Orsay, and had been dominated by the 'Big Four', President Wilson,

---

[23] Masanori Ito, *Gunbatsu Koboshi* (The Rise and Fall of the Military Cliques), vol. 2 (Tokyo, 1958), 84–5.   [24] Ibid. 87–9; Teruyuki Hara, op. cit., 518–24.

Georges Clemenceau, Lloyd George, and Orlando of Italy, 'with a Japanese representative hovering in the wings'.[25] This was Marquis Saionji, who in his seventieth year, had come to Paris as though the whole affair was a pleasure trip.[26] The conference allowed punitive measures to be adopted against Germany, while accepting the Wilsonian principle of national self-determination where it was applicable, especially within Europe, and adhering at the same time to the principle of international peace in the form of the League of Nations that would somewhat transcend both the idea of Europe and that of nationalism.[27] The Japanese delegation included another plenipotentiary, Baron Makino, the second son of Okubo Toshimichi, and young diplomats such as Yoshida Shigeru, Shigemitsu Mamoru, and Matsuoka Yosuke. Konoe Fumimaro, 'a new star in politics' who also attended the conference, wrote on his return home that the iron rule of Great Power control had prevailed there, and regretted that the League Covenant had rejected the principle of racial equality proposed by Japan.[28]

The Japanese government had wished to ensure the transfer to Japan of the former German rights and interests in the Shantung province, and also the ceding to Japan of the German islands in the Pacific north of the equator. For the rest, Japan simply sought to adapt herself to the general trend and remained blind to new ferments in the post-war world. Her attitude to the League of Nations was negative on the whole, for fear of its possible infringement of national (imperial) sovereignty. Her proposal for racial equality was in fact an afterthought, derived from an apprehension of possible discrimination on the council of the League.[29] As there was a danger that Japanese delegates might walk out of the conference owing to strong protests from China over the Shantung issues Saionji had to call a special meeting of the delegates and tell them that the League of Nations was far more important to Japan than the Shantung problem.[30]

Both Saionji and Makino were liberal statesmen in Japan. At the peace conference, however, they were apt to remain silent over the issues of the League of Nations and its mandate and waited for directions from the home government before they expressed their views, an attitude that incurred foreign suspicion of selfish intentions on their part. The absence of constructive vision was most striking in the Labour Law Commission: the chairman was Samuel Gompers of the American Federation of Labor, and the British member, George Barnes, was the leader of the Trades Union Congress and a Labour member of the wartime coalition govern-

[25] A. J. P. Taylor, *English History, 1914–1945* (Oxford, 1965), 132.
[26] Yoshitake Oka, *Five Political Leaders of Modern Japan* (Tokyo, 1986), 193.
[27] John Roberts, *The Penguin History of the World* (Harmondsworth, 1995 edn.), 868–9.
[28] Yoshitake Oka, *Konoe Fumimaro* (Tokyo, 1983), 14–15.
[29] Seiichi Imai, op. cit., 196–7.　　[30] Oka, *Five Political Leaders*, 193.

ment. All the Japanese members were bureaucrats who had no real interest in the conditions of the workers, nor any strong desire to advance their status, and who 'depended wholly on government instructions which resembled capitalist demands.'[31] In the end Japan obtained exemptions in the application of the international agreement on labour on such issues as freedom to organize trade unions, an eight-hour working day, and a minimum-wage system. Japan was criticized for her inconsistency in allowing inferior conditions for her workers while asking for racial equality at the same time. The Chinese delegation demanded the preservation of her territories and the restoration of her sovereignty and economic freedom (as regards custom rights), but these were not even discussed at the conference. In other words, the principle of self-determination was not applied to China, to say nothing of Korea, where a movement for national independence culminated in the great popular demonstration of 1 March 1919, which we shall examine in some detail when we deal with Japan's colonial empire.

In the course of the First World War Japan had fished in troubled waters and had attained economic and territorial expansion, but the return of peace and 'normalcy' recoiled upon her wartime gains. The US president Harding called an international conference to discuss limitations on armaments and the issues related to the Pacific and Far Eastern areas. International rivalry in building a big fleet had become an economic burden on every country involved: the military budget for Japan in 1921 amounted to 731 million yen, 49 per cent of the annual expenditure of that year. Japan sent three delegates, Kato Tomosaburo, the navy minister, Tokugawa Iesato, president of the House of Peers, and Shidehara Kijuro, ambassador to Washington, to the conference held in Washington from November 1921 to February 1922. The American proposal to limit the naval strength of the major powers (auxiliary ships excepted) according to the fixed ratio of the United States 5: Britain 5: Japan 3: and France and Italy 1.67 respectively, was accepted, Kato being compliant from the beginning. In the new international situation in which both Russia and Germany had ceased to be an immediate threat, the Anglo-Japanese Alliance was allowed to lapse, while the United States, Britain, France, and Japan signed a Four-Power Agreement in December 1921 to respect each other's territories in the Pacific. A Nine-Power Agreement was concluded in February 1922 by these four countries and Italy, Belgium, Holland, Portugal, and China to respect Chinese sovereignty, independence, and territorial preservation, and also for equality of trade opportunities and an open-door policy in China. The issue of the Shantung province, that had not been settled in Paris, was examined again with the

---

[31] Imai, op. cit., 197.

United States and Britain as intermediaries, and it was decided to return most of the German interests in the province to China.[32] Ambassador Shidehara claimed that the open-door policy had been advocated by Japan ever since the conclusion of the Anglo-Japanese alliance.[33] Under the Washington system, Japan was accepted as one of the three major naval powers in the world, but her economic strength was no match for that of any of the other major powers. After the war Japan once more tumbled into being a debtor nation. Political instability, added to economic difficulties, made Japan's 1920s appear volatile, capable of radical changes (though in fact more to the right than to the left) that gave some justification to the common description of it as a 'liberal decade'.

THE ASSASSINATION OF A PRIME MINISTER

The *genro*, the elder statesmen, though weakened by deaths were still in the saddle of the party politics that continued its precarious existence. Okuma, whose government (April 1914–October 1916) had muddled through because of his foreign minister's strong China policy and his home minister's involvement in a political scandal, resigned and recommended Kato as his successor, but *genro* Yamagata had had enough of Kato, and the *genro* council selected Marshal Terauchi Masatake, governor-general of Korea, who formed a 'transcendental' (non-party) government. The *Seiyukai* led by Hara Takashi was ready to lend its support, while Kato became president of the *Kenseikai*, the powerful opposition party formed at the time out of the *Rikken Doshikai* and two other parties.

After the Rice Riots in the summer of 1918, which forced Terauchi to resign, Hara Takashi formed his government. Though often referred to as 'the commoner prime minister', Hara began his life as a member of the samurai upper class of the Morioka domain, which was on the losing side of the Restoration civil war.[34] He entered a theological school founded by a French Catholic missionary in Tokyo, was baptized, and shortly afterwards changed his social status from *shizoku* to commoner. In the obstinacy and arrogance that characterized his behaviour, however, it is hard to recognize traces of Christian humility. He worked for a while as a journalist for the *Yubin Hochi*, a newspaper owned by Okuma Shigenobu, but after the political crisis of 1881 moved to Osaka where he became chief editor of a pro-government newspaper and established a close tie with the leaders of the *Sat-Cho* clique 'in the hope of gaining sufficient power to

[32] Eguchi, op. cit., 29.
[33] Kijuro Shidehara, *Gaiko Gojunen* (Fifty Years of Japanese Diplomacy) (Tokyo, 1974), 84.
[34] Oka, *Five Political Leaders*, 85.

challenge them in the future'.[35] In 1900 he joined Ito's new party the *Seiyukai*, and served as home minister in Saionji's two governments. He succeeded Saionji as president of the *Seiyukai* in June 1914.

Hara was resourceful as a fund-raiser, while he was capable of bluff. In fact, he was 'a trump card of the ruling classes' in their struggle to maintain themselves in the new situation, while he himself sought to establish a semi-permanent regime of the *Seiyukai* by ingratiating himself and his party with the *genro* and the aristocrats and by excluding radicals.[36]

Seiyukai members occupied all posts in the Hara cabinet except for army, navy, and foreign ministers. Hara was the first prime minister who formed a cabinet as president of a political party and a member of the House of Representatives. Yet he was far from being a commoners' premier. The *Seiyukai* on the whole took a less open stance towards working-class demands than had the *Kenseikai*, which sought to incorporate social reforms such as social insurance in their plan for post-war reconstruction.[37] Again, Hara and the *Seiyukai* were opposed to motions for universal suffrage put forward by the *Kenseikai* and the *Kokuminto*, on the grounds that the proposed bill would jeopardize the social system and therefore be subversive. The government dissolved the Diet while it was still debating a bill for universal suffrage in February 1920. The general election in May was fought under a new electoral system introducing small constituencies, a device intended to secure an absolute majority for the *Seiyukai* at the expense of radical liberals, together with a lower tax qualification reduced from 10 to 3 yen, just low enough to increase voters in rural constituencies for the *Seiyukai*. It is a small wonder that the *Seiyukai* won an overwhelming victory at the election (*Seiyukai* 278 seats, *Kensei* 110, *Kokumin* 29, indepenent 47). A safe majority in the Diet, coupled with the afterglow of a wartime boom, enabled Hara's government to embark on a positive programme, especially an improvement of education (expansion of the institutions for higher professional education), better infrastructure (greater extension of railway lines), adequate national defence (necessary expenditure allocated for the navy's ambitious '8.8' fleet plan so called as it consisted of eight battleships and eight cruisers, resulting in the naval budget taking up 32 per cent of the national budget for 1921), and encouragement of industries.

A string of scandals, however, followed involving *Seiyukai* politicians, the Manchurian Railway Company, and the Tokyo city administration. Inukai Tsuyoshi of the *Kokuminto* attacked the Hara cabinet for its rash

[35] Ibid. 89.
[36] Matsuo, op. cit., 230.   [37] Sheldon Garon, *The State and Labor in Japan* (Berkeley, 1987), 55–72.

attempts to expand *Seiyukai* influence through bribery and intrigue, and asked: 'Were any of the *Sat-Cho* cabinets in the past as corrupt as this one?'[38] Hara himself appeared increasingly culpable as the scandals continued. On 28 September 1921 Yasuda Zenjiro, the founder of the Yasuda *zaibatsu*, was assassinated by a right-wing terrorist who then killed himself, leaving behind a testament attacking evil politicians allied with evil millionaires. On 4 November Hara himself was stabbed to death at Tokyo Station by a young railwayman who had become enraged at what appeared to be the cabinet's spineless diplomacy.

Hara was the first prime minister to be assassinated while in office, but not the last. He is often remembered as a tough politician enforcing party discipline and skilfully managing party administration and strategy, and hence representing a positive, effective leadership. But the negative side of his leadership, the lack of consistent policies or a policy perspective, the chronic defect of Japanese politics, should not be overlooked.[39]

UNIVERSAL MALE SUFFRAGE ADOPTED (1925)

The death of Hara Takashi was followed three months later by that of *genro* Yamagata, who had felt disgraced and remained dispirited after being defeated in an attempt, as the head of the Choshu clique, to foil the arranged marriage of Crown Prince Hirohito with Princess Nagako, the daughter of Prince Kuninomiya and a granddaughter of Shimazu Tadayoshi of the rival Satsuma clique, by alleging the colour-blindness hereditary in the Shimazu family. (His state funeral held on 9 February was attended by fewer people than had been expected.) Deprived of two such powerful personalities, Japanese politics entered a period of instability that might have proved favourable for political reform.

The government led by Takahashi Korekiyo, new president of *Seiyukai*, failed to agree on a retrenchment policy and resigned less than seven months after its formation. Then followed three governments, all 'transcendentalist' (non-party) and dominated by peers and bureaucrats, led respectively by Kato Tomosaburo, Yamamoto Gonbei, and Kiyoura Keigo, two admirals and a bureaucrat. The Yamamoto government resigned when Nanba Daisuke, an anarchist who claimed to assume the mantle of Kotoku Shusui, made an attempt to shoot the crown prince. Within *Seiyukai* Takahashi's followers came round to support universal suffrage. They, together with *Kenseikai* and *Kakushin Club* (former *Kokuminto*), formed 'an alliance to defend the constitution' (referred to as the second *Goken* or Defence of Constitution movement). The Kiyoura government attacked the alliance as 'instigating class struggle', while the three opposition parties

---

[38] Oka, *Five Political Leaders*, 119.   [39] Ibid. 123.

responded by describing the government as 'encouraging class struggle'; thus the government and the opposition had the aim of 'the prevention of class struggle' in common, and only differed in their perception of 'universal suffrage' as a means towards it.[40] At the general election held in May 1924 the alliance won an overwhelming majority (*Kenseikai* 151 seats, *Seiyukai* led by Takahashi 105, *Kakushin Club* 30 against *Seiyuhonto* 109, and independent 69). *Genro* Saionji, with due regard to the election results, nominated Kato Takaaki, president of *Kenseikai*, as prime minister, and Kato formed his government with Takahashi and Inukai among his ministers. The three-party *Goken* government moved a bill for universal suffrage early in 1925, forced the Privy Council to compromise, and passed it through the Diet despite peers' opposition. Now all male adults above 25 years old were given the right to vote, and those above 30 years old the right to be elected; the middle-sized constituency system replaced the small constituency system introduced in 1919. The number of the electorate stood at 12,410,000 in 1928, four times as large as it had been before the change.

It was in December 1924 that an alliance for the promotion of women's suffrage was formed, but all their movement obtained from the government (one led by Hamaguchi in 1930) was a bill to give women civil right (suffrage) on a local level, and even this modest concession was rejected by the House of Peers on the grounds that it endangered the traditional family system. What was more ominous perhaps, was the passage ten days before the (Male) Universal Suffrage Bill of the Public Order Preservation Act, intended to keep Japan free from all subversive activities, which we shall examine shortly.

TAISHO LIBERALISM IN LITERATURE

An emphasis on the individual and his or her emancipation from social trammels was a feature of literary activity in the Taisho period. In May 1912 the Yurakuza Theatre in Tokyo was packed to capacity evening after evening by audiences who came to see Magda, the heroine of a play called *Heimat* (Home) by the German dramatist Herman Sudermann. On the eighth evening of its presentation *Heimat* was banned, on the grounds that deference to parents had been slighted in the play. (In the original play Magda, rejecting her father's demand that she marry the man who has made her pregnant, declares: 'if you grant us freedom, don't be suprised if we make use of it!', whereupon her father collapses with a fatal stroke.) The ban was lifted when the final act was rewritten by the producer, Shimamura Hogetsu, who made Magda repent and say 'It's all my fault'

---

[40] Keiichi Eguchi, *Nihon Tsushi* (Complete History of Japan), xviii. 34.

at the very end. Matsui Sumako, the actress who played the role of Magda, had attracted attention when she acted Nora in Henrik Ibsen's *Doll's House*, and Magda established her fame as the woman of the new age. Sumako, the daughter of a rear-admiral, fell in love with Shimamura, who was a married man with children; the couple organized a new theatre group called *Geijutsuza* (Art Theatre) which presented 'advanced' plays by Oscar Wilde, Ibsen, Chekhov, and Turgenev; their production of Tolstoy's *Resurrection* was a great success.[41]

Both Magda and Nora were given wide attention in the *Seito* (Blue-stocking), a women's literary magazine started by the feminist leader Hiratsuka Raicho, whose poem adorned the first issue when it appeared on 1 September 1911: 'In the beginning, woman was the sun, | An authentic person. | Today, she is the moon, | Living through others.'[42] Raicho, a graduate of Japan Women's University, believed that it was only in the fields of art and literature that women could stand equal to men. Yosano Akiko, known for her anti-war poems and others celebrating the passion of love, came to help the *Seito*, as did other talented 'new women', the anarchist Ito Noe among others. Meanwhile Raicho became increasingly aware of the painful relationship between politics and literature and began working for a new women movement to improve women's status and to strive for women's suffrage. The times, however, were not opportune: with the rise to power of the military, women were made subservient once more to the demands of the family and the state.

Taisho literature, in spite of the political awakening of the masses earlier in the century, remained largely non-political. The literary journal *Shirakaba* (White Birch), founded by Mushanokoji Saneatsu and his friends in April 1910, affirmed the individualistic values of human nature. The writers of this school, mostly sons of peers and graduates of the Peers' School, could afford to ignore traditional values and indulge in a creative individual life, and in this they had much in common with the 'new women'. In 1917 Mushanokoji started an ideal community called Atarashikimura (New Village) in a rural hinterland of Miyazaki prefecture, Kyushu, where people would not only live and let live by their own labour, but would respect one another. Like many other utopian colonies in America and in Britain in the nineteenth century, it failed largely because of its inability to overcome human selfishness. Arishima Takeo of the same school, who inherited a vast amount of farm land in Hokkaido from his father, who had received it gratuitously from the state, allowed sixty-nine tenants to cultivate it without charge in August 1922, a kind of community farm which he called *Kyouseien* (the Garden of Common Life).

---

[41] Seiichi Imai, op. cit., 110–13.
[42] Saron L. Sievers, *Flowers in Salt* (Stanford, 1983), 163.

He anticipated its failure, and less than a year later ended his life at his villa at Karuizawa in a suicide pact with a woman journalist.[43]

OSUGI SAKAE AND THE WHITE TERROR OF 1923

It was Osugi Sakae, rather than Yoshino Sakuzo, the proponent of *Minponshugi*, who respresented a Taisho democracy that could be distinguished from imperial democracy. Unlike the Meiji intellectuals who speculated in terms of the state and national strength, the Taisho men of letters, living in a relatively wealthier society, could afford to speculate on self-fulfilment and self-identity and about the form of society that would allow such self-fulfilment. Osugi Sakae was one of the prominent advocates of the emancipation of the self, which in his case took the form of anarchism.[44]

Osugi, the son of an army officer, entered the Nagoya Cadet School, where he was taught that *Bushido* (the Way of Samurai) was a philosophy of death. A homosexual affair in which he was involved, however, led to his expulsion from the school. In Tokyo he joined the anti-war movement of the *Heiminsha* group, introducing himself as 'the son of a murderer'. He admired Kotoku's vigorous attack on war and emulated him by writing an article entitled 'Shoot Those Who Ordered Us To Shoot', a brief survey of the anti-war movement in France. He frequently found himself in prison, and was sent to the newly built Chiba Prison after the Red Flag Incident of 1908 which we have looked at in connection with Kotoku (see Chapter 7). The two and a half years he spent there saved his life, because, as a prisoner, he was not incriminated in the Treason Incident of 1911. Osugi now turned to syndicalism or syndicalist philosophy, which he expounded in a succession of journals of his own beginning with *Kindai Shiso* (Modern Thought), founded as early as October 1912. He extolled 'an explosion of spirit', soon rephrased as 'the instinctive revolt' of the workers organized in trade unions.[45]

The rapid expansion of industry during the war years led to an increase in the number of trade unions, from the modest six in 1914 to nearly 300 in 1921. The Bolshevik Revolution encouraged a small group of Japanese Marxists, while Osugi gave his support to the Bolsheviks as he waited for the radicalization of trade unions. Syndicalist unions were duly organized among the printers and the newspaper men who sponsored the first Mayday celebration held in Japan in 1920. For a while Osugi toyed with the idea of forming a united front of progressive intellectuals, both pro- and

[43] Ibid. 134–5.

[44] See Thomas A. Stanley, *Osugi Sakae: Anarchist in Taisho Japan* (Cambridge, Mass., 1982).

[45] *Rodo Undo* (Labour Movement), Oct. 1919, June 1920; Sakae Osugi, *Seigi wo motomeru Kokoro* (The Spirit that seeks Justice) (Tokyo 1918), 195.

anti-Bolshevik (anarchist and syndicalist), and made a secret visit to Shanghai to receive funds from Comintern agents. Such an effort only resulted in *ana-boru ronso* (dispute between anarchists and bolshevists), and Osugi had to clarify his position by declaring his opposition to the Bolshevik dictatorship. Some of his followers went further in the direction of terrorism.

White terrors, however, were better organized, and were given an outlet by the Kanto earthquake on 1 September 1923, which wrought havoc over a wide area in and around Tokyo, the number of the dead reaching over 140,000. On 16 September, when the last tremors of the earthquake had died down and the traumatized citizens of Tokyo seemed to be coming to their senses, Osugi, his wife Ito Noe, and his 7-year-old nephew were kidnapped and murdered by Captain Amakasu and his subordinates of the military police. Captain Amakasu was sentenced to ten years' imprisonment, but was released after four years and became a prominent official in the puppet state set up by the Japanese military in Manchuria.

Acts of violence after the Kanto earthquake, commited by the police, soldiery, and the panicked masses, were as frightful as the natural calamity itself: several trade unionists were detained in a police station at Kameido, Tokyo's East End, and handed over to soldiers who stabbed them to death; a large number of Koreans were attacked and murdered in and near Tokyo. Martial law was proclaimed by an imperial order on 2 September for the Tokyo area; the two army divisions, the Imperial Guard and the First, were ordered to take all necessary measures to save the capital from the utter confusion the earthquake had threatened, but it was these very troops who became the instrument of the massacre, mostly of Koreans. Another main agent of the blind violence was the *jikeidan* or 'voluntary guard', vigilante groups which sprang up throughout the area and which, in the words of the home minister, were 'the embodiment of a strong sentiment of neighbourly help and local patriotism'.[46] To Yoshino Sakuzo, for whom it was 'moral responsibility of the Japanese' to make the Koreans 'true Japanese', the massacre was 'an appalling disgrace'.[47] He puts the number of Koreans killed at 2,613, while Korean sources give it as 23,059, nearly ten times as many.[48] Memories of the great protest movement for Korean independence, which we shall examine in due course, still remained fresh, mingled with fear and disdain in the mind of the average Japanese.

[46] Misuzu Shobo (ed.), *Gendaishi Shiryo* (Sources of Modern History), 6 [The Kanto Earthquake and the Koreans], pp. xiv, 2.

[47] Sakuzo Yoshino, *Senshu* (Selected Works), ix. 167, 203.

[48] Ibid., 199–200; Misuzu, op. cit., 362, 345. Yoshino also prepared a detailed record of the whole incident entitled 'The Massacre of the Koreans'. Misuzu, op. cit., 358.

STRIKERS, CO-OPERATORS, AND LEVELLERS

The cause of the common people seemed to make great strides in the early 1920s when the toiling masses began to be organized in trade unions, peasant unions, consumers' and producers' co-operatives, and other similar bodies. Closely associated with many of these organizations was Kagawa Toyohiko, a Protestant missionary known for his work among the poor in a Kobe slum. He turned his attention to the trade union movement, working for the Kobe branch of the *Yuaikai*, the first enduring trade union in Japan, editing its organ *Shin Kobe* (New Kobe), in which he advocated 'a new industrial system based on labor'.[49] In August 1919 the *Yuaikai* developed into a militant union, the *Sodomei*, and at its annual convention held in October 1920 there was a clash of opinions between the Kanto (Tokyo-Yokohama) and the Kansai (Osaka-Kyoto-Kobe) *Sodomei*, the former led by the anarchist Osugi and the communist Arahata, both favouring direct action (a general strike), while the latter, under Kagawa's leadership, was committed to the cause of non-violence. Defeated at the convention, Kagawa began pleading for 'a producers' assembly', and some of the *Sodomei* publications bore his influence, or rather that of British Guild Socialism to which Kagawa had been attracted at the time.[50]

In Kobe two shipyards, Mitsubishi and Kawasaki, vied with one another. A wave of minor strikes culminated in a great strike of the Kawasaki/Mitsubishi workers in the summer of 1921. Ironworkers at Mitsubishi demanded an eight-hour day, which had been obtained by the Kawasaki workers, and a recognition of their union as the bargaining agent. Employees at Kawasaki, though better paid than those at Mitsubishi, had their own cause for complaint: their bonuses had been cut at the very moment when dividends were rising. In the negotiations with the managers Kagawa was asked to represent the Kawasaki workers. A series of mass meetings were organized: one on 10 July 1921 turned out to be the largest ever held in Japan up to that point, attended by a crowd of 30,000 who marched down to the Kawasaki plant with Kagawa at their head. Kagawa in his speech emphasized the right of labour to organize and negotiate, which he said would guarantee industrial peace and non-violence. Nevertheless, troops were called in to help local police. The two companies declared a lockout and skirmishes ensued. After a major clash between the police and 1,600 dockers near the Kawasaki gates on 29 July, Kagawa and other leaders of the strike were arrested and sent to prison; with this the great Kobe strike melted away.

[49] Robert Schildgen, *Toyohiko Kagawa: Apostle of Love and Social Justice* (Berkeley, 1988), 13.
[50] George B. Bikle, Jr, *The New Jerusalem: Aspects of Utopianism in the Thought of Kagawa Toyohiko* (Tuscon, 1976), 123–4.

Kagawa, defeated in the trade union struggle, now switched his attention to the tenant farmer movement; later in 1921 he invited his friends from all over Japan to deliberate on the organization of a peasants' union, and in April the following year the *Nihon Nomin Kumiai* (Japan Peasant Union), *Nichino* for short, a nationwide tenant union, was launched at a meeting held at the Kobe YMCA with, as its first president, Sugiyama Motojiro, a product of the Osaka School of Agriculture and himself a Christian minister. Kagawa was one of the directors. It prospered as a radical tenant union, with its membership reaching 68,000 by 1926 and with rent negotiations successfully carried out on behalf of its members in most cases. In fact, tenant unions mushroomed in the first decades of the twentieth century, from about fifty in 1908, to 173 in 1917, 681 in 1921, 1,530 in 1923, and 4,582 in 1927, when total membership reached 365,332, or 9.6 per cent of all tenant farmers.[51] Kagawa and Sugiyama also played an important role in launching the Labour-Farmer Party in 1926, Sugiyama acting as its first chairman, but later in the year, when the party came under communist influence, the two Christian leaders withdrew. The *Nichino* remained in the party, only to be seriously weakened by the first large-scale round-up of communists and their sympathizers on 15 March 1928, when nearly all of its executives were arrested. The party was dissolved, and the *Nichino* merged with other organizations to form a new National Tenant Union which, after having maintained a precarious existence for ten years, finally succumbed to militarism and wartime control.

In order to pre-empt class organizations among the workers and the peasantry the government had sought to transplant German-type co-operatives under the Industrial Union Act of 1900, which provided for credit-, sales-, purchase-, and productive unions. With government protection and encouragement the industrial unions for small producers rapidly grew in number; there were 14,500 by 1928, with a total membership of 3,300,000. Purchase unions, most prominent among them, however, were not consumers' co-operatives but organizations to purchase raw materials for small industrialists and farmers. Consumers' co-operatives, properly so called, often began as an adjunct of trade unions. The Kobe Co-operative, started by Kagawa in 1920 as a co-operative society for the Kawasaki dockworkers, developed into a model consumers' co-operative based on principles borrowed from the Rochdale Pioneers of nineteenth-century Britain. The number of consumers' co-operatives still remained modest, standing at 129, with a total membership of 119,946, in 1925.[52]

[51] Ann Waswo, 'In Search of Equality: Japanese Tenant Unions in the 1920s', in Tetsuo Najita and J. Victor Koschmann, *Conflict in Modern Japanese History* (Princeton, 1982), 367. See also Ann Waswo, *Japanese Landlords: The Decline of a Rural Elite* (Berkeley, 1977), ch. 5.

[52] Kiyoshi Ogata, *Kyodokumiai Kenkyu* (A Study of Co-operatives) (1st edn., 1935; repr. Tokyo, 1993), *passim*.

Kagawa's Christian belief was blended with Social Darwinism; his sympathy for the discriminated buraku people was lukewarm, as he wrongly believed that they were ethnically different from other Japanese. This was unfortunate at a time when the buraku people began a movement for their own emancipation by setting up the *Suiheisha* (Society of Levellers), demanding human dignity as well as economic and occupational freedom at a conference of 3,000 buraku delegates held in Kyoto in March 1922. 'The masses of 6,000 buraku across the country all rose at once' against acts of discrimination in local administration, schools, and even in the army.[53] The movement led to violent clashes with the police and underwent radicalization, and this apparently further dissuaded Kagawa from taking up their cause. The *Suiheisha*, however, achieved a resounding victory in 1933 through a petition-demonstration carried out by buraku representatives from all over the country against the Takamatsu District Court, which had to rescind its verdict of a prison sentence for a buraku girl, who 'concealing her buraku status', had married a non-buraku man.

Kagawa was essentially a pastor; his evangelical tours extended far and wide and even took him to Manchuria in 1928, while his gospel of communal self-help or village communalism received official sanction in the depressed years of the 1930s. Although he was one of the very few who criticized the military for their aggressive actions at the time of the Manchurian Incident of 1931, he began to explain his co-operatives in terms of the communal spirit of 'the divine land'.[54] His denunciation of the radical left only played into the government's hands. It was small wonder that the labour and peasant unions he had helped to establish, and many of the Christian churches where he had preached peace, were to fall into line with the national effort for war.

THE PUBLIC ORDER PRESERVATION ACT OF 1925

The coupling of the universal suffrage bill, which virtually enfranchised all adult males, with the Public Order Preservation Act was no accident. It was a carrot-and-stick policy, but the latter could be viewed as a culmination of a series of repressive measures against the radicalization of labour, starting with the Public Order Police Act of 1900, Article 17 of which made it virtually impossible to organize trade unions. Suzuki Bunji, the founder of the *Yuaikai*, after a period of cautious leadership, began to advocate its repeal.[55] The *Sodomei* sponsored national rallies against the

[53] Burakumondai Kenkyusho (Institute for the Study of Buraku Problems) (ed.), *Burakuno Rekishi* (History of Buraku), vol. 2 (Kyoto, 1960), 134.

[54] Bikle, op. cit., 200, 202, 230.

[55] Stephen Large, *Yuaikai, 1912–1919: The Rise of Labor in Japan* (Tokyo, 1972), 176.

Act, while calling for universal suffrage, but the Act of 1900 was only replaced by the harsher Public Order Preservation Act of 1925.[56]

The clandestine Japanese Communist Party was founded in July 1922 with a provisional party programme for a two-stage revolutionary strategy that would involve the abolition of the emperor system, a controversial tactical issue on which the party remained undecided, in spite of the 1922 Comintern thesis in favour of it. In 1924 the party finally dissolved itself, preferring the tactic of a united front or infiltration of the *Sodomei*. When it was revived in December 1926 the party was seriously hampered by doctrinaire intransigence, while several waves of mass arrests of party members, beginning with the one in March 1928, decimated and nearly annihilated its strength.

The Public Order Preservation Act, therefore, was aimed directly at the 'dangerous' views that would advocate overthrow of the emperor system and of the capitalist social order. It was in fact 'a long-pending piece of legislation'.[57] Premier Hara had felt the need for more stringent anti-subversive legislation; under his successor premier Takahashi, a bill for the Control of Radical Social Movements was introduced in the Diet in March 1922 by two officials of the ministry of justice, Hiranuma Kiichiro and Suzuki Kisaburo, was passed by the House of Peers, but was then blocked by the House of Representatives, where the *Kenseikai* and *Kokuminto* members attacked the bill. Suzuki Kisaburo became minister of justice under the short-lived Kiyoura government that followed (January to June 1924), and he resurrected the bill from the ashes of the Kanto earthquake. It was, however, Wakatsuki, minister of home affairs, who simplified and implemented the bill, which premier Kato endorsed more because of the risks involved in the resumption of diplomatic relations with the Soviet Union, effected in January 1925, than out of concern about the dangerous views *per se*. Long-term perspectives had been lost sight of, and only a handful of Diet members voted against it in March, when it became the law.[58] Adoption of the Act sounded the death-knell for Taisho democracy by depriving the nation of freedom of thought and speech, especially on the crucial issues of private property and the throne.

KAWAKAMI HAJIME AND JAPANESE MARXISM

Maruyama Masao held the view that Marxism gave a sense of moral commitment to those Japanese intellectuals who lacked the western tradition of

---

[56] Stephen Large, *Organized Workers and Socialist Politics in Interwar Japan* (Cambridge, 1981), 27, 67.

[57] Peter Duus, *Party Rivalry and Political Change in Taisho Japan* (Cambridge, Mass., 1968), 203.

[58] Ibid. 204–6. See also Garon, op. cit., 130–6.

Christian conscience and the experimental spirit of science.[59] Kawakami, the son of a former Choshu samurai family, studied at the law faculty of Tokyo Imperial University and was attracted to Christianity, which appealed to him largely because of its ethic of self-sacrifice that 'echoed the traditional way of the warrior', as his American biographer writes.[60] On graduation he obtained a teaching post as an agricultural economist in his own university, but the dichotomy between economics and ethics always remained with him.

However, the economics accepted at the turn of the century was no longer the *laissez-faire* economics of free trade, but the welfare economics of Alfred Marshall or the state economics of the national, historical school of German economists led by Lujo Brentano. Among British economists it was Arnold Toynbee, the founder of the university settlement movement, who influenced Kawakami more than anybody else. After Toynbee, though, came Tolstoy, under whose influence Kawakami threw economics overboard. He joined a new communal sect known as the Garden of Selfless Love, a splinter-group of Pure Land Buddhism. He did not stay long, but continued searching for remedies that would fill the gap between rich and poor and between economics and ethics, first in social policy and then in the traditional economics of hard work and frugality. In fact, it was as a 'Confucian-tinged nationalist' economist that he was appointed professor of economics at Kyoto Imperial University in 1908.[61]

He spent two years, 1913–14, in Europe as a government scholar, first studying idealist philosophy in Germany. When war broke out he moved to London, but found England generally disappointing. Even George Bernard Shaw, whom he had admired from a distance, turned out to be a great bore. The two and a half months he spent in England, however, were crucial in his development towards Marxist economics. Poverty in the midst of the world's greatest wealth became an overriding issue for him. His *Binbo Monogatari* (Tales of Poverty), which was serialized in the *Asahi Shinbun* in 1916, was an immediate success. Wealth was there defined as 'the means for a man to become truly a man—the aim of human life', truly a Ruskinian idea. The solution would lie in laws forbidding excessive consumption and display, along with measures to ensure equality of income.

Towards the end of his life Kawakami wrote *Jiden* (Autobiography, 1947–8), the bulk of which is devoted to his prison life. In the course of his preliminary interrogation, a prosecutor said to him: 'it is thanks to

---

[59] Masao Maruyama, *Nihon no Shiso* (Tokyo, 1961), 55–61. A Yale study of Kawakami emphasized the moral appeal of an illegal, underground society. Robert Jay Lifton *et al.*, *Six Lives, Six Deaths* (New York, 1973), 160, 177.

[60] Gail Lee Bernstein, *Japanese Marxist: A Portrait of Kawakami Hajime, 1879–1946* (Cambridge, Mass., 1976), 30.   [61] Ibid. 64.

your book *Tales of Poverty* that I became interested in social problems and set myself up as a prosecutor specializing in thought-crimes.'[62] Other people reacted in different ways at the time. One of his former students challenged him, arguing that the cause of poverty lay not in the consumption of luxuries by the wealthy but in the exploitation of the workers by the capitalists. Radicalization of his students, inspired by the Rice Riots and the Russian Revolution, drove him further into the fold of Marxism and Marxist economics. He started his own journal, *Shakaimondai Kenkyu* (Study of Social Problems) in January 1919, in which he devoted himself to the exposition of Marx's historical materialism. But even here he retained his own moral view. Where Marx wrote of self-fulfilment, Kawakami thought of self-sacrifice, which became the focus of his own Marxist morality.[63]

Under his influence, Kyoto University became a breeding-ground for political activists. The police, armed with the Public Order Preservation Act, rounded up radical students, Kyoto campus being the hardest hit, and in 1928 Kawakami himself had to resign. He devoted himself to the task of reviving the Labour-Farmer Party, a front organization of the Communists, which had been suppressed. In 1932 he was asked by the Central Committee of the Communist Party to translate the new Comintern thesis on the Japanese party. His translation, *Nihon no Josei to Nihon Kyosanto no Ninmu* (The Situation in Japan and the Task of the JCP), appeared in the clandestine party organ *Sekki* (Red Flag, 2 July 1932), and he found himself recommended for a membership of the party. In the wake of a new wave of police regression that began in the autumn of 1932, Kawakami was arrested in January 1933. He was tried in August under the Public Order Preservation Act, found guilty, and sentenced to five years' imprisonment. His sentence was commuted to four years on the occasion of the birth of the crown prince. Upon his release in June 1937 he announced that his career as a Marxist had come to an end, and this was accepted as a case of *Juntenko* or 'partial conversion'.

All through his life Kawakami embodied the ethic of absolute unselfishness which was manifested in his work for communism as well as in his declaration of partial conversion. Like Christianity in the sixteenth century, Marxism in the twentieth century touched only a small minority of the population, yet both of these extraneous faiths constituted a serious challenge to traditional values and to the existing social and political structure, or at least they were regarded as doing so. Hence each produced cases of heroic martyrs, as well as a far greater number of apostates.

[62] Kawakami, *Jiden* (Autobiography) (Tokyo, 1947), ii. 397.
[63] Bernstein, op. cit., 119.

11

Economic Crises and Overseas Colonies

'A GENERAL CRISIS OF CAPITALISM'

Yoshihito died of apoplexy complicated with pneumonia on 25 December 1926. Showa, the era name given to the reign of Hirohito, began with a financial crisis. Unlike the beginning of Taisho, marked by a political commotion that heralded a period of democratic agitation, the onset of Showa caused almost no ripples politically, partly because Hirohito had been regent since 1921, and Prince Saionji, the only *genro* now left, went out of his way to tell prime minister Wakatsuki that the period of mourning for the deceased emperor should not preclude his going to the country.[1] Wakatsuki did not act according to the *genro*'s advice, and it was the financial crisis of 1927 that brought down his government.

The 1927 crisis was not the first of its kind: in fact, the inter-war period was rife with financial crises that culminated in the great depression of the early 1930s, and this encouraged the Marxist analysis of a general crisis of capitalism, while stimulating nationalist claims for overseas expansion. In August 1932 General Muto Nobuyoshi, then the new commander-in-chief of the Kwantung Army, sent a secret telegram to the 'hawkish' foreign minister Uchida Kosai, suggesting a solution to the economic crisis: 'To secure Manchuria as a market for our commodities seems to be a way of breaking the [economic] impasse . . . and of removing various causes of unrest at home.'[2] Indeed, factory workers' strikes and tenant farmers' disputes had attracted serious attention since the beginning of the 1920s.

In spite of business bankruptcies and industrial and rural strife, however, the Japanese economy in the period of the chronic depression is said to have been 'growing fast by international standards'[3] by virtue of a great advance in the heavy manufacturing and chemical industries. Though rural areas continued to be depressed, city life enjoyed a period of brash commercial culture represented by 'modern boys' (*mobo*) and 'modern girls' (*moga*), the terms commonly used to describe the young people who frequented western-style bars, cafés, and music-halls. But at the same

[1] Leslie Connors, *The Emperor's Adviser: Saionji Kinmochi and Pre-war Japanese Politics* (London and Oxford, 1987), 101.
[2] Quoted in Masanori Nakamura, *Showa no Kyoko* (Crises of Showa), *Showa no Rekishi* (History of Showa), vol. 2 (Tokyo, 1982), 267.
[3] Takafusa Nakamura, *Economic Growth in Prewar Japan* (New Haven, 1971), 142.

time the urge for imperial expansion was strongly felt and acted upon, while a Japanese-style fascism was growing fast from deep historical roots.

THE POST-WAR FINANCIAL PANIC OF 1920

The First World War had transformed the Japanese economy, as we saw in Chapter 9. Japan for the first time experienced export-led economic growth, and by the end of the war she had, also for the first time, become a creditor nation, though only for a short while. Industrial output quintupled in the war years, and in 1919 overtook agricultural output in value.[4] The termination of war, however, put an end to her economic expansion, and post-war democracy made the working classes more radical than ever in their demands and aspirations.

Early in February 1920 13,000 workers of the Yawata Steelworks went on strike, demanding a wage increase and a shorter working day. Five hundred chimneys stopped smoking and the police and the military police were brought in to 'appease the strikers'.[5] The strike spread, more policemen arrived, and the city of Yawata looked almost like a battlefield. In the end 140 'unruly' workmen were discharged, and work was resumed early in May. Meanwhile, on 15 March, a collapse of share prices at the Tokyo Stock Exchange was reported. The average share price fell by more than 50 per cent in three months; commodity prices also fell, silk yarn by 75 per cent and cotton yarn by 66 per cent. Export of silk yarn to America decreased. Credit unrest spread, and in the three spring months there were runs on 169 banking offices, of which twenty-one were closed. A Yokohama silk-trading company and its main bank went bankrupt; wholesale silk yarn merchants, silk spinning and weaving shops, and finally farmers engaged in sericulture were badly hit. The wartime boom had created a number of unsound businesses supported by second- or third-rate banking houses. The 1920 crisis revealed the weaknesses in the Japanese economy and threatened to sweep away the unsound firms. The government, however, by means of rescue lending and special financing through the Bank of Japan, saved these businesses. As a result, rationalization of industry lagged behind that of other capitalist countries, the competitive strength of firms declined, and Japan's international economic balance deteriorated.[6]

The panic of 1920 wiped out the profits earned in the First World War, and Japan, which had enjoyed a long period of rising prices since the end of the Matsukata deflationary policy, now entered a prolonged period of deflation, part of the worldwide slump in the 1920s.

---

[4] M. Nakamura, op. cit., 30.   [5] *Asahi Newspaper*, 6 Feb. 1920.
[6] M. Nakamura, op. cit., 31–2.

THE EARTHQUAKE BILLS AND THE 1927 FINANCIAL CRISIS

The impact of the Kanto earthquake of 1 September 1923, some of which we have already seen, was far-reaching both in terms of human cost and material damage. The total damage caused by the earthquake was estimated at 4,570 million yen, more than treble the annual budget of the year before. In the city of Tokyo 121 main banking offices and 222 branch offices were destroyed or burned. On 7 September three emergency edicts were issued: one to prohibit excessive profit, one against spreading unfounded rumours, and an emergency edict for a moratorium which permitted deferment for one month of repayment of borrowed money. The prime minister (Admiral Kato Tomosaburo) having died less than a week before the earthquake, the new government headed by Admiral Yamamoto Gonbei was formed on 2 September, with Inoue Junnosuke as the minister of finance. Inoue had been president of the Yokohama Specie Bank and then of the Bank of Japan and was known to be a deflationist. His plan, however, was to allow the Bank of Japan and finally the government to bear the losses caused by a bank's inability under the emergency situation to settle any bill it had discounted before the earthquake. The sum total of the 'Earthquake bills' rediscounted by the Bank of Japan in six months reached as high as 430,810,000 yen, because the figure included 'unsound bills' due to poorly guaranteed lending and loose management.[7]

Smaller banks were in a pitiable state: the net losses of four such banks amounted to three to seven times paid capital, and 40 to 70 per cent of their loans were found to be so unsound that there was no hope for collection. This state of affairs culminated in the financial crisis of April 1927 in which the Bank of Taiwan[8] and Suzuki Shoten were deeply involved. The former held unsettled 'Earthquake bills' to the amount of 100 million yen out of its total of 270 million yen at the end of 1926. The largest debtor who issued such bills was Suzuki Shoten, a merchant house of Kobe that had begun business dealing in camphor and sugar, products of Taiwan, and had set up manufacturing firms such as the Kobe Steel and the *Teikoku Jinken* (Imperial Artificial Silk). Kaneko Naokichi, the top manager of Suzuki Shoten, was a *seisho* (political merchant) who had the Bank of Taiwan serve as his main bank through intermediaries like Goto Shinpei, the first civil governor of Taiwan, and Inoue Junnosuke. During the First World War he had set up a number of overseas branches and

---

[7] Ibid. 32–3.

[8] The naming of Taiwan had nothing to do with the Japanese acquisition of the island in 1895 nor with the establishment of the Bank of Taiwan in 1899. In the Ming period the island was called 'small Ryukyu' and the Portuguese in the 16th century began to call it 'Formosa'. The island came to be designated as 'Taiwan' in 1684 by the Ching government. Taiwan originally meant the areas where the indigenous Taiwanese lived in the southern part of the island.

expanded trading activities which even surpassed those of Mitsui Bussan. The amount of the loans he obtained from the Bank of Taiwan reached 357 million yen, about 70 per cent of the total sum of the loans given by the bank.

Then the Bank of Taiwan decided not to give any more loans to Suzuki Shoten. Other major banks began collecting call loans from the Bank of Taiwan, which in turn sought to obtain loans from the Bank of Japan. Suzuki Shoten went bankrupt, but the government hoped to save the Bank of Taiwan by an emergency edict allowing the Bank of Japan to make loans to it without security. The edict was scrutinized at a meeting of the Privy Council at which Ito Miyoji, a former minister of justice who had close connections with the military, attacked the Wakatsuki *Kenseikai* government not so much for its financial policy as for the diplomacy of foreign minister Shidehara. The emergency edict was disapproved and the Wakatsuki government resigned. The Bank of Taiwan was closed, and several other banks met the same fate. Altogether, twenty-five banks went bankrupt in two months.

It has been pointed out that the main cause of the Showa financial crises was the highly speculative investment boom during the First World War; one can also blame the government's inability to rationalize the financial sector after the 1920 crisis, but the sectional struggles between political parties, *Kenseikai*, *Seiyukai*, and a third party, *Kensei Honto*, made a rational solution almost impossible to adopt.[9] Indeed, when Tanaka Giichi's *Seiyukai* government succeeded the Wakatsuki government, its finance minister Takahashi Korekiyo directed the Bank of Japan to make a special loan to the Bank of Taiwan and proposed an emergency edict for a moratorium which was unanimously approved at the Privy Council. When he saw that the panic had subsided, the 74-year-old minister of finance resigned. Under a new Banking Act the amalgamation of banks gained momentum. The number of banks fell from 1,420 in 1926 to 1,031 in 1928, 782 in 1930, and 538 in 1932. Capital and deposits began to be concentrated in five big banks, Mitsui, Mitsubishi, Sumitomo, Yasuda, and Daiichi, all *zaibatsu* banks which now formed a banking oligopoly.[10] The episode as a whole illustrates the close ties that existed between the government and financial interests, in such features as the government's readiness to undertake rescue operations to save the latter when in trouble; an aspect of Japanese political life that has been maintained to this day.

---

[9] M. Nakamura, op. cit., 73.   [10] Ibid. 83.

BUSINESS AND POLITICS:
THE CASE OF MORI KAKU AND YAMAMOTO JOTARO

The government led by General Tanaka Giichi, now president of the *Seiyukai* party, is remembered for its tough, aggressive policy towards China. The close connections formed between the government, especially a *Seiyukai* government, and a *zaibatsu*, Mitsui in this case, was another historically significant feature of the Tanaka government.

Business leaders, faced by the anti-Japanese movement in China, such as the boycotting of Japanese goods, wanted the government to adopt tougher measures, against the Chinese. Tanaka, himself foreign minister, appointed Mori Kaku, formerly of Mitsui Bussan, as under-secretary of foreign affairs, and Yamamoto Jotaro, a former standing director of the same company, as president of *Mantetsu* (the South Manchurian Railway Company). Mori, born in Osaka, entered Mitsui Bussan after finishing secondary school, and was sent to its Shanghai branch where he distinguished himself by selling weapons in the Hunan province. He helped Sun Yat-sen financially and in other ways in the early phase of the Chinese revolution.[11] In 1920 he retired from Bussan and, as an independent entrepreneur, ran four mines along the Yan'tze river. He joined the *Seiyukai* party and was elected to the Diet. Yamamoto Jotaro came from Fukui, had developed political interest while in Bussan and, like Mori, supported the anti-Manchu and anti-Yuan Shih-kai cause in the Chinese revolution. Implicated in the Siemens affair, he withdrew from Bussan. Elected to the Diet in 1920 for *Seiyukai*, he helped promote the advance of Japanese businesses into the Asian continent.

It is not easy to ascertain exact roles played by Mori and Yamamoto Jotaro in shaping the foreign policy pursued by the Tanaka government. Mori apparently found himself in agreement with a tough China policy such as the consul-general at Mukden had promoted in contrast to Shidehara's gentler policy. The consul-general in question was Yoshida Shigeru, the post-war prime minister. Both Mori and Yoshida attended an Eastern Conference convened in July 1927, consisting of representatives of the foreign, army, and navy ministries and the chiefs of staff of the army and navy, at which Japan's 'strong wishes for the peaceful economic development of China' were discussed, along with her determination to take 'resolute measures in order to protect the [Japanese] empire's rights and interests in China'. It was at around this time that these two formed what came to be known as the 'Mori–Yoshida combination'. 'The hawkish *Seiyukai*', it has been noted, may have been 'promoting Yoshida as a counterfoil to the *Minseito*'s relationship with Shidehara'.[12]

---

[11] Marius Jansen, *The Japanese and Sun Yat-sen* (Cambridge, Mass., 1954), 165, 185.
[12] John Dower, *Empire and Aftermath: Yoshida Shigeru and the Japanese Experiences, 1878–1954* (Cambridge, Mass., 1988), 86–7; *Tokyo Asahi Shinbun*, 8 July 1927.

At a conference held at Dairen in August 1927, sometimes referred to as the Second Eastern Conference,[13] Yoshizawa Kenkichi, Japan's minister to China, conferred with Yoshida, Mori, and representatives of the *Mantetsu*, naturally including its president Yamamoto Jotaro, about Japan's China policy at a time when Nationalist China was translating its newly acquired tariff autonomy into a protectionist policy and Chiang Kai-shek's northern expedition was temporarily halted. As we shall see later, Tanaka's China policy wavered somewhat between an economic and a military imperialism, and in a limited sense the *Seiyukai* influence as illustrated by Mori and Yamamoto contributed to the strengthening of the latter by presenting economic interests in a sharp, uncompromising manner.

Japanese politics had come a long way in the course of fifty years of constitutionalism: prime ministers and their governments, though responsible only to the emperor, had learned to adapt themselves to the growing influence of political parties which, through their members elected to the Diet, had come virtually to control the legislative body. Broadly speaking, political parties, for their part, in spite of their constant and often obscure mutation, presented two major currents: one was in the tradition of the old *Jiyuto* (Liberal Party) of Itagaki Taisuke, absorbed by Ito Hirobumi's *Rikken Seiyukai*, originally allied with landed interest though developing expansionist features through association with Mitsui in particular; and the other linked to Okuma's *Kaishinto* and allied with Mitsubishi, close to 'burgeois' interests and perhaps more liberal than its rival in political orientation, which, after a somewhat baffling process of metamorphoses dominated by Kato Takaaki's *Kenseikai* (Kato was responsible for the introduction of universal suffrage and thought control), had at last settled in *Rikken-Minseito* or *Minseito* for short in June 1927. The attitude of 'transcendentalism' inimical to party politics, once favoured by *genro*, however, was to return in due course in the new guise of military pressures.

Hamaguchi Osachi's *Minseito* government succeeded Tanaka's *Seiyukai* government in July 1929. The new government, which was committed to disarmament (partly for financial reasons), was unpopular among the expansionists and right-wing terrorists. Hamaguchi was shot on a platform at Tokyo Station in November 1930 and died a few months later. The attack on the prime minister coincided with the spread of the world depression to Japan.

THE GOLD STANDARD RESTORED AND ABANDONED

The international economic trend after the end of the First World War was to return to 'normalcy', the *ante bellum* state of affairs in which capitalism

---

[13] *Tokyo Asahi Shinbun*, 21 Aug. 1927.

and the free market economy were supposed to have operated normally with the gold standard (suspended during the war) as guarantor. The United States, which had replaced Britain as the largest creditor nation, took the lead in returning to the gold standard in 1919, followed by Germany in 1924, Britain in 1925, Italy in 1927, and France in 1928. The United States and Britain adopted the old parity, while Germany, Italy, and France, which had all experienced inflation (hyperinflation in the case of Germany), naturally returned to the gold standard with a reduced parity.[14] The restoration with the old parity (100 yen = $49.845) that the Japanese government intended to adopt would mean a huge outflow of gold and deflation, and was bound to be accompanied by the adoption of other measures such as budget cuts, rationalization of industry, and encouragement of savings. Inoue Junnosuke, finance minister under Hamaguchi (in office, July 1929–April 1931), in stubbornly rejecting suggestions for a more realistic reduced parity, may have felt that the old parity would help create a structure which would restrain the expansionist policies of the military.[15]

His predecessor at the time of the Hara government, Takahashi Korekiyo, wanted to preserve specie so as to use it to help China construct railways and build industries (economic imperialism) and thereby curb the pressure from a military which was bent on armed aggression (military imperialism). 'Once Britain and America were to conquer China legally [financially], it would be difficult to undo such action, unlike in the case of military conquest.' This need to preserve specie led him to defer the restoration.[16] Both the *Seiyukai* finance minister and the *Minseito* minister then, wanted to restrain the military, but with a difference: the former by seeking to replace or soften military imperialism by economic expansion; the latter by enforcing budgetary restrictions on military demands. Now in 1929 the finance minister Inoue toured the country pleading for the need to restore the gold standard. He tried to reduce the budget, but his proposal to cut the salaries of government officials was unpopular, and reductions in government subsidies to local government were denounced as a measure to sacrifice the rural population. In January 1930 the gold standard was restored with the old parity, but the country had by now been plunged into the world depression and the shock of the overvalued yen proved disastrous, especially to depressed industries.

The monetary aspect of the blow was that specie to the amount of 220 million yen left the country in the five months following restoration. The suspension of the gold standard by Britain in September 1931 accelerated

[14] T. Nakamura and K. Odaka (eds.), *Nihon Keizaishi* (Economic History of Japan), vi (Tokyo, 1989), *Nijukozo*, 28.   [15] M. Nakamura, op. cit., 186.
[16] Korekiyo Takahashi in *Osaka Asahi Shinbun*, 22 July 1928.

the specie outflow, and by January 1932 the vast amount of specie to the sum of 445 million yen had left the country; and altogether, in two years Japan lost 800 million yen in specie.[17] Share prices collapsed, and commodity prices fell drastically, those of silk yarn, cotton yarn, cotton textiles, and rice among others. In the Diet Mitsuchi Chuzo, formerly a *Seiyukai* minister of finance, attacked the restoration of the gold standard and fulminated against Inoue by saying that 'his views were like those of the people who look at economy in general through the narrow grille of a bank office'.[18] In fact, Mitsuchi had a definite view of the national economy which would emphasize the creation of effective demand, possibly by issuing government bonds—that is, by borrowing. But the government pursued a deflationary policy and managed to introduce a salary cut of government officials. Japanese banks were found to be frantically buying dollars and selling yen. Inoue alone was fighting to save the gold standard, while *zaibatsu* banks now wanted its suspension, largely from speculative motives. Wakatsuki's second *Minseito* government (April–December 1931), which had succeeded Hamaguchi's, now resigned and the new *Seiyukai* government led by Inukai Tsuyoshi (December 1931–May 1932), as soon as it had been formed, announced the suspension of the gold standard.[19]

THE IMPACT OF THE WORLD DEPRESSION

The number of the unemployed swelled to 2.5 million by 1931, with the ratio of unemployment at 9 per cent. Many unemployed workers with no money for train fares trudged back to their homes along railway-lines. Industrial disputes increased in number and intensity, involving transportation, shipbuilding, cotton-spinning, coalmines, and steel-mills. In 1931 the number of trade unions was 818, and of organized workers 368,975, with the ratio of organization at 7.9 per cent, and this marked the highest peak of the trade union movement before the war. Unions were able to support workers in smaller firms, whereas industrial relations in big firms were based on the managerial principle established in the 1920s of identity of interest between capital and labour. Rationalization and mechanization of production processes had been accelerated under the impact of the great depression, with the result that the number of the workers employed was greatly reduced and productivity per employee correspondingly increased. There was little opposition to the rationalization process from the workers, as can be seen with the Mitsui Miike coalmines and many other firms in heavy and chemical industries. In

[17] M. Nakamura, op. cit., 223–34.   [18] Ibid. 232.
[19] Ibid. *passim*.

1924, when the Mitsui mines discharged a large number of miners, the great dispute shook the city of Omuta where the mines were located, but in the course of the 1920s a collaborationist union was created by the company to produce loyal workers. The best-known example of this type of management was the creation of the *Ishikawajima Jikyo* (Self-Emulation) Labour Union of dockyard workers. It was decided in December 1930 by the company, in consultation with the union, to discharge about 550 workers (the number was reduced from the initial 1,000), mostly workers near the age of retirement or who were unmarried. The union made efforts on its own accord to reduce costs and increase productivity. The depression, by making both workers and management defensive, had the paradoxical effect of strengthening the cohesiveness of labour and capital; in fact, workers in large firms began to regard themselves as belonging to the company before anything else.[20] What has been called 'Japanese-style management' in post-war Japan had its origins in the labour policy of large firms in this period, which were economizing on the use of labour through rationalization, while at the same time the lifetime-employment system, long practised in shipbuilding, was adopted by other industries as well. The 'seniority system' of wage differentials and promotion according to years of experience also began to be adopted by large firms in heavy industry. Subcontracting began early in Showa and spread rapidly after 1931.[21]

It has been pointed out that significant wage differentials according to the size of firms first appeared in the 1920s and grew into what might be called 'labour market dualism'. In order to compensate for the lack of 'personal paternalism' which the employees of a small firm enjoyed, the employers of large firms had to provide 'a kind of institutionalized paternalism' in the form of higher wages based on seniority and other forms of benefits. Institutional scrutiny of the personal background of job-applicants sometimes entailed arbitrary discrimination against certain categories of workers (notoriously against the buraku people). It is true that pre-war Japanese paternalism could be regarded as 'a variant of Taylorism', but it went further than Frederick Taylor had imagined, for Japanese management succeeded in controlling employees' 'thinking about how to live'.[22]

The situations in light industries such as cotton-spinning were different. Here too rationalization was introduced; modern machinery replaced the old so as to increase productivity of labour and overcome the effect of the legal abolition of night-work stipulated in the Factory Act amended in

[20] Ibid. 245–8.   [21] Takafusa Nakamura, *Economic Growth in Pre-war Japan*, 220–4.
[22] Taira Koji, 'Economic Development, Labour Markets, and Industrial Relations in Japan, 1905–1955', in *Cambridge History of Japan*, vi. 623–8.

1929. Shorter working hours, however, entailed greater intensity of work due to the high-speed opertion of the new machines. Along with rationalization of this kind went reductions in wages and the mass dismissal of workers (mostly women). A series of strikes broke out in spinning-mills; some of the discharged girls were sent home under pressure from the rural communities from which they had come, their village masters, parents, or village policemen, whom the company had alerted by letter, sometimes sending the price of their tickets home.

The Japanese cotton industry, now armed with cheap labour and a depreciated yen, and also with the new machinery introduced at the time of the depression, drove British cotton goods from the hitherto British-dominated market in South-East Asia, India, South America, and even Africa. The trade friction that resulted became an important factor promoting the formation of block economies, itself a prelude to economic war and eventually to attempts to create a new world order.[23]

The hardest blow of the great depression was felt in the primary industrial sector, in the agricultural and fishing villages where the number of workers was larger than in any other sector (10.3 million people in 1930, 34.1 per cent of the total employed). The drastic fall in the price of silk yarn to be exported to America was an omen of what was to follow, and the 2.22 million farming families who engaged in sericulture as an important means of supplementing their incomes suffered badly.

Next to that of silk, it was the price of rice that badly affected rural communities because of the 'famine due to good harvest' in 1930, when the forecast of an 'excellent harvest' made by the minister of agriculture drove the price of rice down and threw rice markets into confusion. This was followed by the 'famine due to poor harvest' in 1931, following bad weather in Hokkaido and Tohoku. Rural hardship was such that, from a small village called Oguni in Yamagata-ken, thirty-nine girls were sent out as licenced prostitutes, twenty as housemaids, fifteen as barmaids, and eleven as geisha. An old man of about 60 at Shichinohe in Aomori-ken was quoted as saying over a cup of sake: 'my only son is in Manchuria as a soldier. I wrote him a letter the other day telling him to fight bravely for the sake of the country and die in a battle. Then I would get some grant from the government that would enable me and my wife to survive this winter. A father who has a daughter could sell her [into prostitution], but I have only a son and I am thinking of selling him.'[24] Peasant disputes spread throughout the country, especially in Akita, Yamagata, Hokkaido, Niigata, Tochigi, Aomori, and Nagano. Radical ideas, from both right and

---

[23] M. Nakamura, op. cit., 252 ff.
[24] *Tokyo Asahi Shinbun*, 30 Oct. 1931; *Chuo Koron*, Feb. 1932, quoted in Nobuyoshi Tazaki, 'Toshi Bunka to Kokumin Ishiki' (Urban Culture and Popular Consciousness), in *Koza Nihon Rekishi*, vol. 10 (Tokyo, 1985), 168; M. Nakamura, op. cit., 256.

left, spread among young farmers stricken by anxiety and despair for the future.

Another significant impact of the great depression was on heavy and chemical industry. Many firms connected with *zaibatsu* formed cartels and sought to maintain monopoly prices. Nihon Steel and Daioji Paper were the two outstanding examples. As a result, the differences between big firms and middle and small firms became even wider in terms of scale, capital, labour intensity, wages, and available interest rates. The 'double structure' of the Japanese economy became well established at the time of the great depression.

ECONOMIC GROWTH UNDER THE DEPRESSION AND THE NEW *ZAIBATSU*

It has sometimes been asserted that the Japanese economy did not stop growing even in the trough of the 1920s.[25] Takahashi Korekiyo, who served as finance minister under three prime ministers, Inukai Tsuyoshi, Saito Makoto, and Okada Keisuke, in the period 1931–6, was largely responsible for the 'miraculous' recovery of the economy at the time. He pursued a policy of 'reflationary deficit financing', combining financial aid for rural reconstruction and a low interest rate, and seeking to meet the demands both of the military and of business leaders.

In the 1920s, in spite of the depression, the introduction and growth of heavy and chemical industries sustained and led economic development and layed the foundations for the new developments that were to come in the following decade. The construction of hydroelectric power stations and the facilities for high-powered transmission of electricity provided the driving-force for the growth of related industries. New firms made their appearance to produce electric machinery, motors, cables, air-conditioning equipment, elevators, chemical fertilizers, artificial silks, pulps, sodium hydroxide, special steel, and aluminium. Electricity also helped the motorization of small and middle-sized firms in weaving, tea refining, and lumber.

The 1930s witnessed the emergence of new *zaibatsu* such as Nihon Sangyo (Nissan), Nihon Chisso or Nitchitsu (nitrogen), Nihon Soda, Showa Hiryo, later Showa Denko (fertilizer), Riken (everything from piston rings to aircraft), and Nakajima Hikoki (aircraft). The new *zaibatsu* had certain common characteristics: close personal ties with an

---

[25] Chalmers Johnson, in dealing with the Japanese economic 'miracle', cited Professor Arisawa Hiromi as having said as early as 1937 that the increase of 81.5% in industrial output from 1931 to 1934 could be called a 'Japanese miracle'. Chalmers Johnson, *MITI and the Japanese Miracle: The Growth of Industrial Policy 1925–1975* (Stanford, 1982; Tuttle edn., 1986, 1992), 6.

engineering faculty of a college or university; a large share in heavy and chemical industries; dependence not so much on any of the established *zaibatsu* as on the Japan Industrial Bank and other sources of state capital; and strong connections with the military and the reformist (right-wing, expansionist) bureaucrats. Nitchitsu later moved its headquarters to Korea, while Nissan transformed itself into *Manshu Jukogyo* (Manchurian Heavy Industry).[26] Nakajima Aircraft, whose nominal capital was 50 million yen, secured a loan amounting to 2,610 million yen from the Industrial Bank of Japan and an advance of 690 million yen from the government: thus its assets grew from 120 million yen in 1938 to 3,590 million yen in June 1945.[27] Old *zaibatsu*, too, collaborated with the military, but the new *zaibatsu* were geared to the war effort almost without reservation.

JAPAN'S COLONIAL EMPIRE IN THE 1930S

As General Muto suggested in a telegram already quoted, the consolidation of a colonial empire was soon widely accepted as a solution to the economic crisis. It has been suggested, however, that Japanese imperialism was 'more situational than deliberate in design',[28] and this was probably the case before the Versailles system emerged. Japan had established her own colonial empire in the course of the preceding decades of imperialist rivalries, as the spoils of her three successfully fought wars. In the middle of the 1930s it consisted of the homeland of 380,000 square kilometres where a population of 70 million Japanese lived, the 'colonies' of about 300,000 square kilometres with a population of 30 million 'other races', and 'Manchukuo', covering 1.3 million square kilometres and with a population of 40 million Manchus and Chinese.[29] A statistical table for 1937 shows that in primary industry the share of the homeland was 67 per cent and that of all the colonies 33 per cent, while in secondary industry the share of the homeland 87 per cent and that of the colonies 13 per cent. Taiwan was known for sugar, Korea for rice, and Manchuria for beans, maize, and iron-ore. Even so, Japan depended on Asian markets (rather than colonial markets) and also on markets in advanced countries for textile and mineral raw materials. Raw cotton came from India and the United States, and about half of Japanese iron-ore and scrap iron was obtained from America. About 80 per cent of her crude oil also came from

[26] T. Nakamura and K. Odaka (eds.), op. cit., 66–7.
[27] Quoted in Toyama, Imai, and Fujiwara, *Showashi* (History of Showa), 219.
[28] Peattie, in *Cambridge History of Japan*, vi. 223.
[29] Yuzo Yamamoto, 'Shokuminchi Keiei' (Colonial Management), in Nakamura and Odaka (eds.), op. cit., vol. 6, *Niju Kozo* (Double Structure), 237; the accounts and figures in the text are largely based on Yamamoto.

America. Japan depended on her colonies, especially Manchuria, for coal. As a result of a contraction in the export of silk yarn and expansion in the import of raw materials, Japan's trade with America always remained in the red. Her economic dependency on the United States was built into the structure of her 'bloc economy', supposed to be self-supporting.

Karafuto (southern Sakhalin) was regarded in statistical treatment as part of Japan proper and had Japanese yen circulated as the only legal tender. The Bank of Korea and the Bank of Taiwan respectively issued their own banknotes as legal tender, but these were guaranteed free exchange at parity with the yen, and both Korea and Taiwan formed part of the domestic trade area having no customs duties imposed on the movement of commodities. The South Sea Mandate Islands adopted Japanese currencies as their own in 1925, and no customs duties were imposed on the movement of goods.[30] Kwantung province retained its extraneous economic characteristics. Notes issued by the Bank of Korea were treated as legal tender, but Manchu and other Chinese currencies were allowed to circulate. In statistical treatment Kwantung province remained a foreign territory. Manchukuo, when it was set up as a puppet state in 1932, formed a single currency unit with 'gen' banknotes issued by the Manchu Central Bank, and in 1935 the Japan–Manchukuo yen bloc was cemented with the yen–gen parity. Manchukuo became not simply the market for Japanese goods but rather the place for investment of Japanese capital. The 'yen' bloc was to expand so as to form a Japan–Manchukuo–China bloc and finally the East Asia Co-Prosperity Sphere, though the latter largely remained a matter of plans and propaganda.

KOREA

Korea deserves special attention here, as she had been a key factor in Japan's foreign policy and imperialist designs since early Meiji. After the annexation of 1910 Korea had been placed under a military police rule headed by the governor-general, a military officer in charge of the army and naval forces stationed in Korea and directly responsible to the Japanese emperor. The right to free association, speech, and publication was denied to the Koreans, while land surveys initiated in 1912 brought about the transfer of a large amount of land to Japanese businesses and invididuals, with the result that a large number of Korean cultivators had no alternative but to become tenants on their expropriated lands or to drift away, emigrating across the border to Manchuria or to Japan as unskilled labourers. The Japanese military government adopted 'a policy of forced

---

[30] Yuzo Yamamoto, op. cit., 236; the following accounts in the text are largely based on Yamamoto.

assimilation': the teaching of the Korean language and history was forbidden, the Korean press was silenced, and any nationalist who defied the
new regime was jailed or executed.[31] Thus began the dark age known to
Korean historians as the 'period of military rule', which lasted for a
decade.[32] In spite of increased rice production designed for the Japanese
market (partly in response to the Rice Riots in 1918), the consumption of
rice by Koreans after the 1920s actually decreased, and the average Korean
had to eat inferior grains, like millet.[33] As more rice was sent to Japan,
more millet had to be imported from Manchuria to Korea.

The violent protests that had characterized Korean nationalism before
1910 became mute under the military police rule. Resistance, however,
lived on among private educational institutions, religious sects, and overseas Koreans, including students studying in Japan. In Korean private
schools, prayer was suspected as a way of requesting independence, and
even the shedding of tears was regarded as a demonstration of patriotic
sorrow.[34] 'Subversive' songs, 'subversive' history books, and 'subversive'
essay competitions were some of the immediate objects of police prosecution. Secret organizations were formed to try to restore national rights
especially in the northern regions and across the border in Manchuria.
Syngman Rhee, who was to become first president of the Republic of Korea
in 1948, then living in Hawaii, had studied at Princeton when Woodrow
Wilson was president of that university, and was known as an advocate of
the Wilsonian principle of national self-determination for the Koreans.

The number of Korean students studying in Japan was estimated at 682
in June 1920; many of them were imbued with the liberal democracy then
permitted in Taisho Japan, and as many as 600 attended a rally held at
Kanda, Tokyo, on 8 February 1919. A committee selected beforehand
formed an All-Korean Youth Association for Independence, and published
a Declaration for Korean Independence at the rally, deploring the country's
fate as a victim of Japan's imperialist ambitions, 'deceit, and violence', and
pledging 'an eternal war of blood' against Japan if the latter failed to
respond to 'our just demands'.[35] About sixty students were arrested that
day, and this had an impact on the Koreans back home, who were also
grieving over the sudden death in January of their hapless king, Yi
Taewang.

Several versions of the Declaration of Korean Independence were
prepared by various bodies in and outside Korea; appeals were addressed
to the American president and to the Paris Peace Conference, and memorandums were prepared to be sent to the Japanese prime minister and the

[31] Richard H. Mitchell, *The Korean Minority in Japan* (Berkeley, 1967), 12.
[32] Peattie, op. cit., 230-1.   [33] Ibid. 257.
[34] Misuzu Shobo (ed.), *Gendaishi Shiryo* (Sources of Modern History), vol. xxv, pp. xviii, 13,
23.   [35] Ibid., vol. xxvi, pp. xi, 22-6.

governor-general in Korea. The major document was the Declaration of Independence dated 1 March 1919 and signed by the leaders of *Chundokyo* (a religious body derived from the Tonghak sect, whose rebellion had been an immediate cause of the Sino-Japanese War), Christian ministers and priests, and several others, altogether thirty-three names. 'We now announce to all the nations of the world', it read, 'that we shall clarify the cause of humanity and equality and tell our posterity to preserve the just right of national self-determination for ever.'[36] Those who signed the Declaration had decided on a policy of non-violence and non-resistance; on 1 March they celebrated Korean independence among themselves, then telephoned the police department of the government-general and allowed themselves to be arrested. On that same day most of the students in Seoul assembled at Pagoda Park, joining a great crowd of about 200,000 Koreans who had come from the provinces for the state funeral of the deceased king. One student stood on a platform and began reading the Declaration of Independence; the passive resistance of thirty-three people was now transformed into a mass movement. The crowd responded with cheers of 'Long Live Independence', the streets of Seoul were filled with people, and it was feared that a revolutionary situation might develop. But Japanese infantry were at once dispatched to the key positions in the city. For over two months after this the reports of the governor-general and the chief of the police department to the Japanese government presented a record of forceful suppression of the movement, which had inevitably taken the form of an armed rebellion as it spread to the provinces. Japanese sources put the number of Koreans killed at 553, injured at 1,409, and arrested at 26,713 for the period from 1 March to 20 April; while Korean sources for the year following 1 March give the number of those killed at 7,645 and those injured at 45,562.[37] The revolt rallied Christian, Buddhist, indigenous Confucian, and other nationalist movements, and was especially fierce in rural areas where the protest was also directed against Japan's land policy.

The '1 March Movement' fully revealed the extent and serious nature of Korean demands for national independence and eventually brought about a modification in Japanese rule in Korea. A new governor-general, Baron Saito Makoto, who survived a bomb attack on his arrival in Seoul in August 1919, transformed the military rule hitherto pursued into a civil administration. An imperial rescript of August 1919 promised 'a fair and impartial treatment' and 'certain reforms', one of which was the introduction of state Shinto designed as a policy of assimilation with the Chosen Jingu (a Shintoist shrine planned in 1919 and completed six years later) in Seoul enshrining the Sun Goddess and the Meiji emperor, the most

---

[36] Ibid., vol. xxv, 281–2.   [37] Ibid.

privileged among sixty-odd Shintoist shrines established in Korea (though the Koreans boycotted these as long as they could). The new governor-general also permitted the revival of several Korean-language newspapers and promised other reforms. The home government, however, pursued its policy of assimilation,[38] to the extent that in 1940 it was even decided to compel the Koreans to create new personal names based on the Japanese family system of *ie*.

Industrialization of Korea, with its 'cheap electricity, cheap land, and cheap labour', was encouraged. Among those firms which participated in this national project were *zaibatsu*, both new and old: Nitchitsu, Nissan Chemicals, North Korean Petroleum (Mitsui), the spinning-mills of Kanebo and Toyobo, Katakura Fertilizers, and Mitsubishi-Seishin Steel.

During the period of economic depression Korean labourers poured into Japan. In 1914 there were only 3,630 Koreans in Japan; the number increased to 39,000 in 1921, and to 419,000 in 1930. Most of them were employed as labourers, coal-miners, or road repairmen. Laws to restrict Korean immigrants were not strictly enforced. Saito relaxed the restrictions in the interests of Japanese industrialists even during the depression period, eager for cheap Korean labour, and sent agents to Korea for this purpose.[39] The Japanese outcry against restrictions imposed on their own immigration into the United States and Canada probably had some impact on similar attempts made in Japan to impose such restrictions on the Koreans.

As the war against China escalated in the 1930s and skilled Japanese workers were drained from factories and mines, Koreans were taken up as their substitutes. The Japanese government 'first encouraged and then forced' Koreans to come to Japan. The Korean population in Japan increased rapidly: in 1933 there were 456,217 Koreans in Japan; by the end of 1936 the number had increased to 690,503, and by the end of the war there were 2,400,000. Koreans had become permanent residents in Japan.[40]

TAIWAN

The Japanese rule of Taiwan began with a colonial war against the local Chinese and Taiwanese, followed by a policy of carrot-and-stick adopted by the governor Goto Shinpei. Goto employed Nitobe Inazo, an expert on tropical agriculture, to promote the sugar industry, while suppressing anti-Japanese activities with the utmost severity. Again, the Taiwan Jinsha (shrine), established in 1901 at Taipei, which enshrined Prince Kitashirakawa (who had commanded the expeditionary force and died at

[38] Mitchell, op. cit., 23–4.   [39] Ibid. 41–3.   [40] Ibid. 75–6.

Tainan), together with eighty-odd other Shintoist shrines in Taiwan, served as the instruments of an assimilation policy. In 1915, at the time of Japan's Twenty-one Demands upon China, there was concerted action among the Chinese and Taiwanese for independence of Taiwan.[41] The severity of its suppression can be compared with the extraordinary scale of the military operation in 1930 when aircraft were employed against the mountain tribes at Musha in central Taiwan, who had revolted against the policy of *riban* (rationalizing policy, *ri*—or social control by the police—of the 'barbarian' tribes, *ban*) pursued by the governor.[42] In short, Japanese colonial administration was both authoritarian and exploitative, and even measures for modernization adopted in transport and communication were calculated to promote the interests of metropolitan Japan.

THE SOUTH MANCHURIAN RAILWAY (SMR)

The SMR or *Mantetsu* was more than a milestone in the development of the Japanese empire on the Asian continent. General Kodama Gentaro and Goto Shinpei, a pair who had taken charge of the colonial administration of Taiwan at the turn of the century, planned to set up a large-scale railway enterprise in southern Manchuria after the Russo-Japanese War, based on a trunk-line extending from Dairen to Ch'ang-ch'un and Antung, a railway network of strategic importance connecting Kwantung province, central Manchuria, and Korea. Goto wanted an independent administration for this purpose and hoped for research-and-development facilities to be set up so as to exploit the rich natural resources in the region.[43] He was appointed the first president of the SMR in 1906. Soon the SMR obtained more capital from abroad, modernized the entire railway-line, and built warehouses, docks, and 'a spectacular new hotel' in Dairen. In 1907 the SMR ordered 180 locomotives and 2,060 railway cars from American firms, while in London the president of the Industrial Bank of Japan arranged for the issuing of SMR bonds. The company built several subsidiary lines and managed the land on both sides of the railway-lines together with tunnels, bridges, schools, parks, public buildings, hospitals, warehouses, mines, and factories on the attached land.

The SMR prospered, and its total revenue in 1923 reached 185 million yen, favourably compared with the same year's budget for Korea of 101 million yen and that for Formosa of 100 million yen. By the autumn of 1924 the SMR employed a workforce of 37,685, nearly three-quarters of whom were local Chinese. Dairen became China's second-largest port and

---

[41] *Tokyo Asahi Shinbun*, 18 July 1915.   [42] Ibid., 29 Oct. 1930.

[43] See Ramon H. Myers, 'Japanese Imperialism in Manchuria: The South Manchuria Railway Company 1906–1933', in Peter Duus *et. al.* (eds.), *The Japanese Informal Empire in China, 1895–1937* (Princeton, 1989), 101 ff.

was described by a British journalist as 'a sort of Japanese Hong Kong'. An SMR express train could travel from Dairen to Ch'ang-ch'un (a distance of 435.8 miles) in twelve hours. The Research Department started in 1907 carried out a number of research projects to plan ahead for the SMR developing Manchurian resources. In 1915 Japan's lease of the Liaotung and the SMR railway was extended to ninety-nine years. But after 1920 nationalism gained momentum and direction in China, and the Kuomintang government was about to unite the country when actions taken by the Japanese army led to greater confrontation between China and Japan in southern Manchuria. In this, as we shall see, Japanese residents in Kwantung province were to play a significant role.

THE JAPANESE RESIDENTS IN SHANGHAI

Outside her formal empire, Japan partook of the benefits offered in the treaty port system created and developed by Britain in China. An increasing number of Japanese residents came to settle in Shanghai after the Sino-Japanese Friendship Treaty of 1871.[44] The greatest contribution Japan made to the development of the International Settlement there was the clause inserted in the Treaty of Shimonoseki in 1895 which allowed foreigners to set up factories in treaty ports. With this, Shanghai grew in population from half a million in 1895 to 3 million in the 1920s. It became the centre of Japanese investment in the Chinese cotton industry, and the number of Japanese residents in Shanghai showed a rapid increase: by 1915 they formed the largest national group next only to the Chinese in Shanghai. In 1925 their number stood at 18,902 and by 1931 it had reached about 20,000, nearly 70 per cent of the foreign population. It was estimated that out of 1 million residents in the International Settlement in 1932, 25,000 were Japanese while 6,000 were British.

After the settlement of the Canton–Hong Kong general strike of 1925, Japanese trade with China and cotton-mills in Shanghai were in a prosperous state. According to a Mitsui Bussan source, out of 2,100,000 spindles operated in Shanghai, Japanese mills had 1,116,000, the Chinese 699,000, and the British 274,000. The Japanese cotton-mills in China, unlike production facilities in Korea or Manchuria, developed without government assistance and protection. The mill-owners were proud of their independence, but they relied on the Municipal Council for protection and were keen on maintaining good relations with the British. When the Kuomintang forces entered Nanking an incident took place in which

---

[44] The following account is largely based on Harumi Goto-Shibata, *Japan and Britain in Shanghai, 1925–31* (Macmillan, 1995); see also Ian Nish, *Japan's Struggle with Internationalism* (London, 1993), ch. 5 'The Shanghai Crisis'.

foreigners and their properties were attacked and British and American warships bombarded the city in retaliation, resulting in heavy casualties among the Chinese. A Japanese gunboat nearby refrained from taking part, for the Japanese residents in Nanking, remembering what had happened to the Japanese at Nikolaevsk, had expressed a wish not to be involved. The Japanese in Shanghai felt outraged, and demanded strong action over the 'Nanking Incident' and adequate local protection. As the Japanese government sent troops to Shantung in response to the Northern Expedition of the Kuomintang forces, an anti-Japanese boycott movement in Shanghai was further intensified.

By the end of 1928 the Kuomintang forces had achieved unification of the country (except for the three north-eastern provinces) and set up their own government, with Nanking as its capital. The United States recognized the Nanking government early in November, followed by Britain in the middle of December, while Japan delayed her recognition until June 1929. With the onset of the great depression Japan's trade with China showed a marked decline, and badly affected small business merchants in Shanghai who depended on exports from Japan. It was as late as May 1930 that Japan accepted China's tariff autonomy. The protectionist policies pursued by the Nanking government foretold a bleak future for foreigners in China, especially small business people who had survived on a small margin of profit. Unlike Britain and the United States, who sought to achieve rapprochement with the nationalist regime, Japan 'intended to maintain all her prerogatives and privileges, with the result that she could see no way out of the impasse'.[45] Japan's informal as well as formal empire now found itself stretched to breaking-point.

---

[45] Goto-Shibata, op. cit., 113.

12

Fascism, Militarism, and Thought Control

WAS THERE A JAPANESE FASCISM?

Objections have been raised over the use of 'fascism' to describe the 1931–45 period in Japanese history, partly because the term has become a pejorative one, often arbitrarily attached to unpopular ideas or people, and partly because the Japan of this period does not appear to fit in 'the general pattern of European fascism'.[1] Ivan Morris found 'totalitarianism' and 'militarism' equally unsatisfactory as epithets for the period. Robert Butow used a more complicated and comprehensive term, 'a kind of home-brewed ultranationalistic military socialism'.[2] Just as there was no general pattern of socialism in Europe, nor in Asia for that matter, so there was no general pattern of fascism in Europe either, and eastern Europe presented a different pattern from that in Germany or Italy. The volume dealing with the twentieth century in the *Cambridge History of Japan* (1988) paid relatively little attention to the development of the totalitarian or ultra-nationalist regime and movement, and rarely used the term 'fascism'. Even Richard Storry, who had a chapter entitled 'Prelude to Fascism' in his earlier book *The Double Patriots: A Study of Japanese Nationalism* (1957), itself a study of Japanese fascism, altered his perception in the course of the following two decades and wrote that the term 'fascism' would have to be avoided as a political label for Japan's 1930s. There was no powerful dictator like Hitler or Mussolini, the constitution was not set aside, and 'the worst horrors of the Third Reich and of Stalin's Russia had no counterpart in the islands of the Japanese homeland'. Storry conceded, though, that the use of the term is 'at least forgivable in view of the drift of Japanese opinion and the course of Japanese foreign policy'.[3]

When Storry wrote the earlier book his personal memories of Japan in the 1930s were still vivid in his mind. Among Japanese historians such memories lasted longer and their views sometimes supported Storry's. Ouchi Tsutomu, in a volume in one of the earliest series of Japanese

---

[1] Ivan Morris (ed.), *Japan 1931–1945: Militarism, Fascism, Japanism?* (Lexington, Mass., 1963), p. vii.

[2] Robert Butow, *Tojo and the Coming of the War* (Princeton, 1961), 16.

[3] Richard Storry, *Japan and the Decline of the West in Asia, 1894–1943* (London, 1979), 138.

history in the post-war period,[4] wrote on the distinctive nature of Japanese fascism which he summed up as 'emperor-system fascism'. Unlike in Germany or in Italy, wrote Ouchi, fascist power came into existence in Japan not as a result of a fascist movement. All attempts at a *coup d'état* failed. Instead, the established state system, with the army leaders at its head and supported by elder statesmen, the cabinet, and the Diet, adopted a fascist apparatus without any premeditated planning, even without knowing the implications of what they were doing, 'zuruzuruto, taiseini makarete' (dragged along by the general trend). A. J. P. Taylor wrote in a similar vein about Hitler's and Napoleon's plans to conquer Europe.[5] Hitler and the Nazis could be regarded as a product of German society and German ideologies. Japanese fascism or ultra-nationalism essentially arose from similar sources, and its uniqueness was related to the unique *kokutai*, the existence of the sacred and inviolable emperor unilaterally asserted in the constitution: absolute or ultimate power lay with the emperor. Although it is known that Hirohito (the Showa emperor) was personally against the introduction of fascism into Japan, Japanese fascism was promoted under the name of the emperor, who had become a charismatic figure by the 1930s, and was made use of as such by those who would not take responsibility for themselves. In other words, it was a fascism born out of the system of irresponsibility. The 'pluralism of power' that seemed to have existed in this period has been cited against the view of Japanese politics as totalitarian, but such pluralism does not exculpate but only accentuates the system of irresponsibility. Some of the emperor's court advisers, like Makino Nobuaki, advised against his involvement in cabinet or army disputes as inappropriate for a constitutional monarch.[6] In spite of his misgivings about the Japanese army's actions in China, Hirohito let himself be swayed by the views of his advisers, who were cautious and conciliatory towards the military and were inclined to accept the *fait accompli*. The system of irresponsibility was well preserved by Hirohito's simplistic view of himself as a limited monarch, which incidentally was encouraged by his acquaintance with King George V made during his visit to England in 1921 while crown prince. Japanese democracy, even that of Taisho, was handicapped in its scope and depth by the unique *kokutai* and its implications.[7]

---

[4] Tsutomu Ouchi, 'Fashizumu eno Michi' (The Road towards Fascism), *Nihon no Rekishi* (History of Japan), vol. 24 (Tokyo, 1974). See also Sogoro Tanaka, *Nihon no Fashizumu Shi* (History of Japanese Fascism) (Tokyo, 1960).

[5] See A. J. P. Taylor, *The Origins of the Second World War* (London, 1961), 11–12.

[6] Stephen Large, *Emperor Hirohito and Showa Japan* (London, 1992), 37.

[7] Kiyoko Takeda, *The Emperor System in Modern Japan*, The Richard Storry Memorial Lecture No. 3 (St Antony's College, Oxford, 1989), 4–7.

JAPANESE-STYLE FASCISM

Radical ultra-nationalists who were opposed to the faltering liberal capitalist order have been described as 'redolent of European fascism'.[8] All Europe, with the exception of England, Sweden, and Switzerland, was at times controlled by what some call fascist regimes of one sort or another. The common features of fascism in Europe were strong nationalist feeling, anti-socialism (anti-Marxism in many cases), weak parliamentary government, and politicization of the people. In east and central Europe, which remained largely agricultural, however, conservative and reactionary circles dominated, the left never became a real threat, and political power was exercised by traditional types such as landowners, the church, and perhaps the bankers. 'In Hungary and Poland, as in Rumania and Yugoslavia, almost the entire political spectrum was composed of the Right. In such political systems, fascism could make little headway as it lacked the necessary freedom to manoeuvre. . . . Fascism in these countries was a movement from above, an attempt to transform an already existing authoritarian regime into a fascist dictatorship from within.'[9] In Japan too, fascism from above triumphed, but fascism from below was not lacking, and both were inspired by the emperor-worship ideology which proved as effective as the Führer or Duce ideology in its irrational appeal to the national, racial spirit of war and conquest—perhaps even more so.

Japanese fascism was different from its German and Italian counterparts in that it did not create a mass movement, except for the last-minute improvisation of the *Taisei Yokusankai* (the Association to Assist the Emperor's Rule), which was set up in October 1940, replacing the older political parties and preparing the nation for its final confrontation with the West. It was owing largely to the existence of the myth of the emperor that the AAER had the character of a mass movement. Japanese ultra-nationalism, if not fascism, succeeded in spreading 'a many-layered, though invisible, net over the Japanese people, and even today they have not really freed themselves from its hold'.[10]

But why was it that the road to fascism in Japan appeared relatively smooth? The scholar Maruyama Masao paid special attention to the role played by the people whom he called pseudo- or sub-intellectuals, such as village officers, Buddhist and Shinto priests, primary-school teachers, small shopkeepers, small factory-owners, small landowners—in short, the small men who claim to know better. This half-intellectual pettybourgeois strata, he alleged, provided the social foundation of Japanese fascism, whereas the real intellectuals, like himself—professors, lawyers,

---

[8] Large, op. cit., 33.   [9] S. J. Woolf (ed.), *European Fascism* (London, 1968), 6–7.
[10] Masao Maruyama, *Thought and Behaviour in Modern Japanese Politics*, ed. Ivan Morris (1963; pbk edn. 1969, 1979), 1,

and journalists who possessed 'higher knowledge'—remained sceptical and adopted an attitude of passive resistance.[11] But passive resistance often meant connivance in what was taking place; if the real intellectuals knew what fascism was and raised not a finger against it, surely their responsibility for what followed is even greater than that of the pseudo-intellectuals. Moreover, there were intellectuals, university professors, who acted as brains for the military, fascist government. It has been noted that the widespread wartime support among Japanese intellectuals for the notion and projects of the Great East Asia Co-prosperity Sphere and for the war against the West has been 'a besetting problem to postwar Japanese intellectuals'. 'Japan had no Resistance, no stream of exiles, no martyrs except on the Left—and only a few of them, the majority having "recanted" in the early thirties and gone over to patriotism by the time of the Pacific War.'[12] Indeed, Japan's ultra-nationalism was deeply ingrained on all levels, as we shall see when we examine its origins and pedigree, its ramifications and reinforcements.

GREAT ASIANISM

First of all there was an East Asian cultural tie revived early in Meiji. Ho Ju-chang, the first Chinese ambassador who came to Tokyo in 1877, Okubo Toshimichi, then home minister, and some others became interested in the exchange of students, and founded the *Koa Kai* (Rise Asia Society) in 1880. A Chinese school was set up in connection with this and later merged into the official foreign language school. Next came the *Toho Kyokai* (Oriental Co-operation Society), which was sponsored by a motley group of political leaders such as the nationalist peer Prince Konoe Atsumaro, party politicians like Okuma Shigenobu and Inukai Tsuyoshi, and Oi Kentaro and Toyama Mitsuru, leaders of the left and the right respectively.[13] In 1898 Konoe Atsumaro founded the *Toa Dobunkai* (East Asia Common Letters Society) at a time when western imperialist activities in China were most rampant, with a view to preserving the entity of China and promoting reform in China and Korea. The society founded a college, the *Dobun Gakudo*, in Shanghai and schools in Hankow and Tientsin. The Konoe family maintained close ties with these institutions until the end of the Pacific War.[14]

Secondly, an important section of those who advocated 'the Punishing of Korea' early in the 1870s directed the discontent among former samurai

[11] Ibid. 58.
[12] Carol Gluck, 'Introduction', *Showa: The Japan of Hirohito*, ed. Carol Gluck and Stephen R. Graubard (New York, 1992), p. xvi.
[13] Jansen, *The Japanese and Sun Yat-sen* (Cambridge, Mass., 1954), 51–2.
[14] Storry, *The Double Patriots* (London, 1967), 21; Jansen, op. cit., 52.

into the channel of political opposition in the movement of Liberty and People's Right. The *Kyushu Kaishinto* (Reform Party), which was to support Itagaki's Liberal Party, had a strong representation of Fukuoka activists organized in the *Genyosha* (Korean Strait Society), such as Toyama.[15] Toyama Mitsuru, born into a Fukuoka samurai family, became one of the most powerful right-wing political bosses and fixers. In 1881 he, Hiraoka Kotaro, a mine-owner and former samurai who had participated in Saigo's rebellion, and their associates, in response to the movement demanding the opening of a national assembly, reorganized their *shizoku* group into the *Genyosha* with a three-point programme: reverence to the emperor, love of the nation, and defence of people's rights.[16] Their main concern soon shifted to the first two, while the society's conservative as well as expansionist inclinations gained the financial support of Fukuoka mineowners known for their brutal labour practices. The *Genyosha*, however, was to be remembered largely for its patriotic progenies, the most important of which was the *Kokuryukai* (Amur River Socity) organized in 1901 by Uchida Ryohei, a Fukuoka nationalist and nephew of Hiraoka Kotaro, who travelled through Siberia after the Sino-Japanese War and came to advocate war with Russia. The *Genyosha* was committed to the preservation of traditional values by promoting an aggressive foreign policy, while the *Kokuryukai* had a definite aim: the containment of Russia.[17]

Thirdly there was a group of people who might be called advocates of 'Asia for the Asiatics', a great cause shared by many other people in Japan, though in a different context. They were Japanese nationalists who sought to collaborate with Asian nationalists at a time when the penetration of European and American imperialism in Asia brought forth a nationalist reaction, especially in China and the Philippines. This group can be represented by Miyazaki Torazo of Arao, Kyushu, the first Japanese who befriended Sun Yat-sen when the latter came to Japan as an exile in 1897.[18] Torazo wished to identify himself with the cause of the Chinese: 'Once China was restored on the basis of justice', he wrote, 'India would arise, Siam and Annam would stir, the Philippines and Egypt would be saved. America and France, countries that esteem ideals and causes, should not be our enemies. It is in this way that human rights will be restored and a new era will begin.'[19] He introduced Sun to Inukai Tsuyoshi of the reform-progressive party for advice and funding. Sun also gained favour

---

[15] Taisuke Itagaki (ed.), *Jiyuto-shi* (History of the Liberal Party), Iwanami Bunko edn., vol. 2 (Tokyo, 1958), 94–5.

[16] E. H. Norman, 'The Genyosha', *Pacific Affairs*, 17: 3 (Sept. 1944).

[17] Jansen, op. cit., 33–8.

[18] For Torazo and his three brothers see Shinkichi Eto, Postscript, to Miyazaki Toten (Torakichi), *Sanju Sannen no Yume* (Thirty-Three Years' Dream) (Tokyo, 1967), and Hisao Itoya (ed.), Miyazaki Tamizo, *Tochi Kinkyo Jinruino Taiken* (The Prerogative of Equal Enjoyment of Land) (Tokyo, 1948), *passim.*   [19] Miyazaki Toten, *Sanju San Nenno Yume*, 37.

with nationalists like Toyama. Sun and his Japanese friends, Torazo among others, collaborated in an attempt to help Emilio Aguinaldo, who had declared Philippine independence in the wake of the Spanish-American War, though a ship carrying guns and ammunition for him went down in a storm near Shanghai. At the time of the Chinese revolution of 1911 Torazo was instrumental in obtaining a loan for Sun. Though the Miyazaki group remained faithful in their support of Chinese nationalism, it soon became clear that other Japanese nationalists, who were also expansionsists, came to regard Chinese nationalists as enemies.[20]

AGRICULTURAL NATIONALISM:
GONDO SEIKYO AND TACHIBANA KOZABURO

It is to be expected that agrarian interests in a country undergoing rapid industrialization and westernization should hark back to a remote past when natural harmony was supposed to have existed in village communities, and to the bygone days when farming constituted by far the most important occupation in the country. In the recent past there had been a popular agrarianism derived from the moral and practical teachings of Ninomiya Sontoku, who had risen from the desperate poverty of a peasant-farmer in the Ashigara plain north of Odawara to the wealth and fame of a model landowner.[21] His teachings of *kinben* (industry), *kenyaku* (frugality), *suijo* (giving way to others: this was tantamount to saving for one's own future and that of one's descendants, relatives, friends, village, and state), and *bundo* (self-restraint necessary for one's preservation) crystallized into the seminal *Hotoku* (Repaying Virtues) movement, which had a far-reaching effect on national morale in pre-war Japan. Agrarianism in modern Japan was given the name *nohonshugi* (agriculture-as-the-essence-ism).[22] *Nohonshugi*, too, had two currents, one from above and the other from below.

Nohonshugi from above, or 'bureaucratic agrarianism', was responsible for the Credit Association Bill of 1891 inspired by Shinagawa Yajiro, a former Choshu samurai, who had served in Germany as a consul-general and became secretary at the newly created Ministry of Agriculture and Commerce, and by Hirata Tosuke, a protégé of Yamagata, who while in Germany had studied the credit unions advocated by Hermann Schulze-Delitzsch the promoter of a co-operative movement. The Bill failed to become law because of the dissolution of the Diet. Shinagawa and Hirata continued their efforts, which were embodied in the Industrial Union Act

---

[20] Jansen, op. cit., 5.   [21] Tatsuya Naramoto, *Ninomiya Sontoku* (Tokyo, 1993), *passim*.
[22] Thomas R. H. Havens, *Farm and Nation in Modern Japan: Agrarian Nationalism, 1870–1940* (Princeton, 1974), 7.

of 1900, and with this the government was committed to supporting small landowners, a policy which continued until the Second World War. There was a remarkably rapid increase in number of producers' co-operatives in rural areas, and a Central Union of Co-operative Societies was formed. Their activities extended so as to cover co-operative warehousing and banking. Producers' co-operatives were finally merged into the *Nogyokai* (Farm Society) under wartime mobilization.

Output in agriculture continued to increase, though not as quickly as in the manufacturing and commercial sectors, except for a period in the 1920s. Farm prices, however, fluctuated erratically and dropped by 1931 to two-fifths of their 1919 level.[23] Traditional tenant–landlord relations were disrupted. Tenants began to protect themselves through peasants' unions as urban workers did through trade unions. With the government policy to create more owner-farmers on the one hand, and the coercive power exercised by the Public Order Preservation Act of 1925 on the other, their activities were more or less contained.

Nohonshugi from below could be represented by two right-wing ideologists, Gondo Seikyo and Tachibana Kozaburo. Gondo, 'the romantic agrarian nationalist',[24] the son of a Kurume (Kyushu) samurai scholar, part-physician and part-farmer, benefited from his youthful trip to China at the age of 17 and became an active member of the Amur River Society shortly after its foundation. His knowledge of Chinese politics was solicited even by the minister of war. He also became a specialist on Korea and visited Seoul in 1906 to form secret contacts with the annexationist Korean reformers, and helped start a Japanese Foundation to advocate a Korean–Japanese union with local self-government reserved for Korea. The terms of the actual annexation of Korea when it was enforced in 1910 were far from what Gondo had worked for, and Korean aspirations for independence became something beyond his reach. In due course his attention turned to the needs of Japanese farmers, for whom Manchurian development, as he saw it, had become essential, and especially to work out the principle of self-rule among them. In 1920 he set up the *Jichi Gakkai* (Self-Rule Study Society) and in 1927 he published his major work, *Jichi minpan* (People's Guide to Self-Rule). He began giving lectures at an institution called the *Kinkei Gakuin* and also at a private school in Tokyo; among his pupils were Inoue Nissho, subsequently the leader of the *Ketsumeidan* (Blood Pact League), and several young army and navy officers.

Most agrarian nationalists rejected not only parliamentary politics but also the entire political system. Their loyalties were 'to the Japanese as an ethno-nationality group rather than to the state'.[25] Gondo's starting-point was the Japanese people collectively organized into self-governing units

---

[23] Havens, op. cit., 135–6.   [24] Ibid. 164.   [25] Ibid. 188.

under a single ruling authority, the imperial throne. He rejected state-sponsored nationalism of the Prussian type, and vituperated against the bureaucracy, the *zaibatsu*, and the military, the three pillars that upheld the state and supported each other through divisive party politicians and tail-wagging scholars. Gondo denounced the plutocracy for monopolizing the country's basic resources and driving the common people into cold and hunger. His hardest attack was reserved for the military. 'The military officers, men who hold office for life, are guaranteed an adequate living, and so they are usually conspicuously loyal, brave, and noble. And indeed they have to be. But the soldiers who dutifully have to shed their blood are all sons and brothers of the common people. The great majority of these soldiers were born in poverty and hardship; they entered the barracks, and then had to submit to the orders of their superior officers.'[26]

Gondo suggested a colonial policy in which one or more farm villages would create 'a second village' at home or abroad with government assistance.[27] He thus advocated colonial settlement of Japanese farmers on the basis of self-rule rather than on that of state power. It is a tragedy that he failed to see that such a settlement, however voluntary it might be, needed state power for its very existence, and that once state power had gone it was bound to crumble, sacrificing the common people.

Tachibana Kozaburo, the son of a former Mito samurai-turned-dyer, having inherited a fair-sized farm started a community known as *Kyodai Mura* (Fraternal Village), which attracted visitors who heard him speak on the improvement of farmers' livelihood. His intellectual mentors were Tolstoy and Robert Owen.[28] In 1929 Tachibana founded a producers' co-operative association called the *Aikyokai* ('Love One's Home Community' Society) where mutual help was esteemed as much as hard work. At its height the society had nearly thirty branches, mostly lecture clubs, and experimented with joint purchase of seeds and fertilizer, co-operative tilling, and its own insurance and medical care schemes. In 1931 he started a school called *Aikyojuku* (Aikyo Academy) to 'educate proper Japanese workers of the land'.[29] But the school turned out to be a hotbed of rebels and insurgents. Half of the civilians who participated in the acts of rightist terrorism in May 1932 were connected with Tachibana's school. Tachibana not only knew a number of village activists but also some of the young army and airforce officers who came under his influence. He did not take part personally in the terrorist action carried out by the *Ketsumeidan* (Blood Pact League) in 1932, though he had been consulted beforehand. After the failure of the attempted revolutionary coup Tachibana fled to

[26] Seikyo Gondo, *Jichi minpan*, 185–8, in Tsunoda *et al.* (eds.), *Sources of Japanese Tradition*, ii. 264–6.   [27] *Jichi minpan*, quoted in Havens, op. cit., 227.
[28] Ibid. 236.   [29] Ibid. 239.

Manchuria, where he was arrested by the military police. At his trial he was sentenced to imprisonment for an indefinite term, but was freed (together with Inoue, the leader of the plot) as part of the general amnesty in 1940 to celebrate the legendary 2,600-year anniversary of the foundation of Japan. He lived to see not only the defeat of the expansionist war and the collapse of all its related projects, but also the Vietnam War of the 1960s, when he sent a message to the US embassy in Tokyo suggesting village communalism as a solution to the political crisis in that part of the world.[30]

KITA IKKI AND HIS NATIONAL SOCIALISM

Probably the most outstanding exponent of Japanese fascism—outstanding in terms of the impact of his ideas—was Kita Ikki, who, like many European fascists, began as a socialist of a kind, and who provided an intellectual focus for the young army officers who rose against what they took to be a wicked government run by capitalists and bureaucrats. Kita was an autodidact: his hard work under difficult circumstances led him to produce a grandiose plan for the reconstruction of Japan. He accepted Minobe's view of the emperor as an organ of the state, and advocated the creation by *coup d'état* of a national socialist state which was as expansionist as the daydream of Sato Nobuhiro, although he sought to defend it on the ground of Darwinian evolutionism. His intense faith in Japan's mission to regenerate Asia[31] was another feature of his somewhat eclectic 'system' of radical ideas.

Kita Terujiro (later Ikki), son of the mayor of the town of Minato (Ryotsu since 1901) on the island of Sado, shared the passionate commitment natural to Sado culture[32] (the island having been the destination of political exiles for many centuries). As a young man he came under the influence of Miyake Setsurei, editor of *Nipponjin* and an advocate of 'Pure Nationalism'. He was an eager reader of the *Heimin Shinbun*, Japan's first socialist newspaper, though critical of the causes of pacifism and internationalism it upheld. He finally came to live in Tokyo in 1905 at a time when the popular outcry against the Portsmouth Treaty led to mass demonstrations in the metropolis and elsewhere. Kita sympathized with the rioters and came to believe that the emperor system had become a tool in the hands of selfish government leaders. Kita's *Kokutairon oyobi Junsei-Shakaishugi* (National Polity and Pure Socialism), a large volume of 998 pages, came out in 1906, published with money he had obtained from his

[30]   Havens, op. cit., 247.

[31]   George M. Wilson, *Radical Nationalist in Japan: Kita Ikki* (Cambridge, Mass., 1969), 3–4.

[32]   Sogoro Tanaka, *Nihon Fashizumu no Genryu: Kita Ikki no Shiso to Shogai* (The Source of Japanese Fascism: The Ideas and Life of Kita Ikki) (Tokyo, 1949), 2–3.

sympathetic uncle. Ten days later it was banned by the Home Ministry, and Kita decided to sell it instead in the form of a series of separate booklets.

Kita's aim in writing this book was to identify *kokutai* (national polity) with socialism; in other words, he maintained that there was no real conflict between the two because real *kokutai* was social-democratic.[33] Social democracy, with sovereignty in the state, marked an advance in social evolution by creating a *kokutai* which Kita called the *komin kokka*, a citizen or public state. The *komin kokka*, according to him, was 'a state which for its own purposes and interests established state organs by giving privileges to each of its components'.[34] The emperor and the people would act as 'organs' of the sovereign state, each with its separate role to play. He ridiculed the concept of *bansei-ikkei* or the eternal succession of one imperial line, while the idea of Japan as one great family with the emperor at its head, he thought, was absurd. 'The Japanese empire is not a religious body', and had nothing to do with the Shintoist, paternalistic *kokutai*.[35] He criticized the inconsistency of Minobe's theory for making the emperor the highest organ of the state. He was in favour of an 'economic restoration-revolution', which in practical terms meant the nationalization of land and capital. He was against 'economic paternalistic princes who, with their superior power of capital, absorbed other capitalists and peasant farmers', and 'the economic aristocracy who pillaged the state'.[36] He wanted to avoid the bloodshed of civil war and preferred universal (manhood) suffrage, 'the ballot being the bullet of the economic restoration-revolution'.[37] 'There is no socialism', he declared, 'without previous evolution in individualism, no world federation without evolution in imperialism, no communist society without evolution in the private-property system.'[38] Therefore he concluded that Japanese socialists were wrong in opposing the Russo-Japanese War and Japanese imperialism. His book was welcomed by advanced intellectuals of the day such as Katayama Sen, the prominent economist Fukuda Tokuzo, and Kawakami Hajime.

In 1906 Kita joined the *Kakumei Hyoronsha* (Revolutionary Review Society), a semi-socialist group whose main concern was to encourage Chinese revolution. When a revolution began at Wuchang, one of the three Wuhan cities, Kita was sent there by the Amur River Association. He apparently came to know Song Jiao-ren, the revolutionary leader from Honan, who, like Sun Yat-sen, spent some time in Japan. Kita admired his patriotic nationalism and organizational abilities (Song was murdered by an assassin sent by Yuan Shi-kai in 1913), but was at loggerheads with Sun Yat-sen, whom he regarded as a shallow revolutionary who sought to

---

[33] Kita, *Kokutai oyobi Junseishakaishugi* (Misuzu edn., 1959), 360.   [34] Ibid. 345.
[35] Ibid. 253.   [36] Ibid. 234, 377–80.   [37] Ibid. 389.   [38] Ibid. 3.

pursue an American ideal in China. He maintained that the ideal of the Chinese revolution had been inspired by the 'state nationalism' of Japan. Japanese foreign policy, he believed, was based on the preservation of China: Japan fought with Russia for the sake of northern China, and should prepare for war with Britain for the sake of southern China. She ought to occupy eastern Siberia in order to make certain the preservation of China. In other words, 'Japan should fulfil her heavenly task as the protector of the whole Asia'. These thoughts on contemporary China Kita developed in his book *Shina Kakumei Gaishi* (An Unauthorized History of the Chinese Revolution), which he wrote in 1914 and published in 1921. What he advocated, however, was not simply Great Asianism nor an 'Asian Monroe doctrine', but rather Japan's expansionism, as is shown by the special emphasis he placed on Japan's 'heavenly' mission to become the guarantor of a new order in Asia.[39]

The book which established Kita's fame as the foremost advocate of national socialism was *Nihon Kaizo Hoan Taiko* (General Outline of Measures for the Reconstruction of Japan), written in 1919 while he was in Shanghai watching the Chinese masses taking part in anti-Japanese demonstrations, and publisbhed in 1923. This was a programme of action, advocating the creation of a general structure for consolidating the whole of East and South-East Asia under protection of Japanese military and economic power. The domestic policy he advocated was to eliminate the privileged cliques who prevented the true union of emperor and people, that is, the financial, military, bureaucratic, and party-political elite. The method to achieve this aim was *coup d'état*: its agents were to be young officers and a dedicated civilian elite. The military reservist association would supervise local administration for the reorganization. Universal manhood suffrage would be granted, and a parliamentary system would be set up. *Kokutai* was for the emperor, while *seitai* (political form) was for the people. Political reform would be followed by economic reorganization, the first principle of which was to guarantee private property for all the people. Production ministries would operate large firms and enterprises confiscated for exceeding the permitted limit of private wealth. The Ministry of Labour, while protecting the rights of workers, would arbitrate in all labour disputes. He also advocated the worker-shareholder system or profit-sharing, and the division of large landholdings in favour of landless peasants. As for education, English should be replaced by Esperanto as Japan's second language. Women, if they so wished, might be allowed to work, but a woman's proper place was at home. Finally, he sought to vindicate the right of a nation to start a war: in the first instance for self-

---

[39] Kita, 'Shina Kakumei Gaishi' (An Unauthorized History of the Chinese Revolution), *Works*, vol. 2 (Tokyo, 1959), *passim*.

defence; secondly, to help other oppressed nations like China and India; and thirdly, against those who appropriated vast territories and thereby ignored the principle of the coexistence of humanity in regions such as Australia and Western Siberia. 'Japan as an international proletariat should be unconditionally allowed to strengthen her army and navy and start a war in order to rectify the injustice of the present international boundaries', he added.[40] This was Kita's conclusion as an indigenous fascist blending the ideas of *kokutai* and of western socialist thought from which Marx and Kropotkin had been eliminated, leaving only state intervention for 'the proletariat'.

In a society called *Yuzonsha* (the Association of Those Who Still Remain) Kita co-operated for a while with Okawa Shumei, another leading theoretician of the extreme right, but parted company with him in 1923 over the issue of Soviet Russia, Kita being more violently opposed to Russian influence in East Asia. He remained unemployed, but his style of living improved from 1932 to 1936 as he received large sums of money from the *zaibatsu* house of Mitsui—one of the giant economic cliques to be eliminated, according to his own plan.[41]

His name came to sudden prominence in the aftermath of the abortive *coup d'état* by a group of young army officers in February 1936. He had little to do with its preparation; nevertheless, his ideas had influenced a large section of army activists and he himself came to know some of the leaders of the coup.

THE 26 FEBRUARY INCIDENT

The young officers, who were much concerned with the condition of the people in the economic depression (and especially of the hard-pressed Tohoku peasants), responded favourably to Kita's thought, though they were not fully committed to it. Some of them now seriously plotted the destruction of the 'wicked men' around the throne in order to carry out what they called the 'Showa Restoration'. The *Kodoha* (Imperial Way Faction) in the army, headed by General Mazaki Jinzaburo, inspector-general until July 1935, and General Araki Sadao, army minister in the Inukai and Saito governments, favoured and even flattered these young men, 'intoxicated with the sense of great mission'.[42] Araki considered 'a solution of the rural problem' to be 'a prerequisite for the success of army strategy',[43] but in January 1934, when illness forced Araki to withdraw and he was succeeded by General Hayashi Senjuro (known as the 'General

---

[40] Kita, 'Nihon Kaizo Hoan Taiko', *Works*, ii. 342–3.   [41] Wilson, op. cit. 110–11.
[42] Toyama, Imai, and Fujiwara, *Showashi* (History of Showa) (Tokyo, 1959), 90.
[43] Ibid. 105.

Crossing-the-Border' for his unilateral decision to move troops from Korea to Manchuria at the time of the Manchurian Incident), the *Toseiha* (Control Faction), strong in the army bureaucracy and the general staff, began to control the army leadership (as described later in this chapter). The new army minister and Nagata Tetsuzan, chief of the bureau of army affairs, sought to eliminate the *Kodoha* from key posts of the army, and forced the resignation of inspector-general Mazaki in July 1934. Confrontation between the two army factions took on a gruesome form when Nagata, the central figure of the *Toseiha*, who was in favour of legally building up a national structure of war without recourse to right-wing activists, was hacked to death in August by an officer of the *Kodoha*, which now began a counter-offensive. When it was decided in December 1935 that the First Division (Tokyo), the stronghold of the *Kodoha*, was to be sent to Manchuria the following spring, young officers of the division began plotting a *coup d'état*.

On 26 February 1936 officers and men, over 1,400 strong, of the regiments of the First Division began carrying out their plan of killing key cabinet ministers and occupying the central part of Tokyo, under the cover of a white blanket of falling snow. They murdered home minister Saito Makoto, finance minister Takahashi Korekiyo, and inspector-general Watanabe Jotaro, and barely missed killing prime minster Okada Keisuke. The insurgents occupied a large area in central Tokyo for four days. Kita had been apprised of the attempt about ten days before, and had received a copy of the manifesto for the uprising on 24 February. On the morning of the 26th he was informed twice about the project and its progress. He felt the coup would fail, but suggested that a new government be formed headed by General Mazaki. The army ministry was in disarray; incoherent demands from the insurgents were transmitted to the emperor, and the army minister on the afternoon of the 26th issued an announcement stating that the emperor had listened to the justification of their uprising. Martial law was proclaimed, as the young officers had wanted in order to effect a political change. The navy, whose two eminent leaders had been murdered, was critical of the response of the army minister and landed a marine corps to protect the Ministry of the Navy. On the following day it assembled forty ships of the First Fleet in Tokyo Bay ready to bombard the insurgents in the city. The emperor himself, some of whose closest ministers had been killed, had no hesitation in denouncing the insurgents as rebels and called for their total suppression. An order for them to return to their original positions was issued on the morning of the 28th. The diehards among them refused to obey, and their encirclement (with tanks at the forefront) was tightened. By the morning of the 29th it became clear that the *coup d'état* had failed. Explicitly disowned by the emperor, the insurgents chose to surrender. On 28 February Kita was arrested by the military police.

In Kita's scenario of a *coup d'état* the role of the army was not very prominent; he apparently considered it to be the army of the nation. The insurgent troops, however, regarded themselves as the forces of the emperor, ready to execute his wishes, and their action was condemned by the emperor personally. Naturally this marked a turning-point, not only in the fortune of the *coup d'état* but also in the history of Japanese fascism. The success of the first *Sat-Cho coup d'état* at the time of the Meiji Restoration was due largely to the fact that the plotters had got hold of the emperor and kept him on their side. Emperor Hirohito dreaded a civil war, and the price he had to pay for domestic peace was to accept the hegemony of the military that was being consolidated under the leadership of the *Toseiha*, especially after the abortive coup. The two *Kodoha* generals, Araki and Mazaki, the indecisive army minister Kawashima, and the commander of the troops enforcing martial law were all placed on the retired list.

A court-martial tried the young officers in camera. Out of 1,483 personnel involved, only 123 were indicted, of whom seventeen were condemned (thirteen serving officers and four retired). Those condemned were executed in July 1936 except for two who were used as sources of further information until the summer 1937, when they were executed together with two civilians, including Kita.

Five months before the publication of Kita's *Outline*, Mussolini had set up the Italian Fighters' Union or Fascist Union in Milan with a programme comparable to his; six months later Hitler announced his programme for the German Workers' Party which later developed into the National Socialists, a programme combining measures for the protection of the weak, an attack on big capitalists, challenges to the Versailles system, overseas expansion, and anti-parliamentary and anti-Jewish policies. What was lacking in Kita's case was a mass following. Such a following was to be provided by the army with the result that Japanese-style fascism was inseparably linked to militarism, overseas expansionism, and ultra-nationalism.

PROTO-FASCISTS AND FASCIST SOCIETIES BEFORE 1936

Richard Storry, in his book *Double Patriots*, pointed out the three elements of nationalism in Japan as being 'loyalty to the Throne, sense of mission and a belief in the possession of superlative inborn qualities'. These led to an uncritical devotion to the *kokutai*, and 'the grotesque ideology of the *kokutai* was the source of the complex manifestations of Japanese nationalism'.[44]

[44] Storry, *Double Patriots*, 5.

Probably the first nationalist society properly speaking was the *Genyosha* (Korean Strait Society), which we have already described, and which soon developed into 'a terrorist organisation and a school for spies'.[45] In the general election of 1892, for instance, it intimidated anti-government candidates, with considerable bloodshed in the Fukuoka area. It was *Genyosha ronin* who, backed by the Japanese minister in Seoul, carried out the assassination of the queen of Korea after the Sino-Japanese War. Just as the *Genyosha* was in the pay of the government, the *Kokuryukai* (the Amur River Society), its prodigious offspring, received funds from such businesses as Yasuda and Okura. After the Russo-Japanese War Japan emerged as the champion of Asian nationalism, and Chinese, Indian, and Philippino dissidents visiting Tokyo gravitated to the house of Toyama Mitsuru, who was 'the opponent of all established governments in Asia including that of his own country'.[46]

We have already noted Kita's *Yuzonsha*, which he formed on his return from China in 1919 with a programme in line with his *Outline*. Later in 1919 the *Dai Nippon Kokusuikai* (Greater Japan National Essence Society) was founded by Tokonami Takejiro, home minister in the Hara government, with Toyama as an adviser. The society came into existence as a result of Tokonami's intervention in industrial disputes during 1919 with the co-operation of Toyama, who enlisted a body of patriots (or thugs) to help the police maintain public order or suppress the strikers. The *Kokusuikai* at the height of its strength had a membership of 60,000. Branch leaders were usually labour contractors, and the rank-and-file were the workers dependent upon them, while several *Seiyukai* politicians sat on the board of management with Tokonami as President. Suzuki Kisaburo, attorney-general from 1921 and later the leader of the *Seiyukai* party, was closely associated with this society.[47]

Sakai Eizo, a wealthy railway 'magnate', founded the *Dai Nippon Seigi Dan* (Greater Japan Justice Association) in 1925. Sakai had an interview with the Duce in Rome and on his return ordered the society's members to wear black shirts. The association was active in suppressing strikes in labour disputes, a notorious case being that of the Tokyo textile-workers' strike of 1930.[48]

The growth of fascism in Japan was closely related to the politicization of the military. Those elite graduates of the Military Academy who went to Germany for further study and training set up the *Issekikai* (Society of One Evening) at some time in the 1920s for the purpose of preserving the unity of the army against factions within. It continued to exist until the

[45] Storry, *Double Patriots*, 10–11.   [46] Ibid. 12, 14, 18–19.
[47] Ibid. 28–9; O. Tanin and E. Yohan, *Militarism and Fascism in Japan*, (1st edn. 1934, Greenwood reprint, 1973), 75–7.   [48] Storry, *Double Patriots*, 30.

time of the Manchurian Incident, and attracted such notable figures as Itagaki Seishiro, Tojo Hideki, Yamashita Tomoyuki, and Ishihara Kanji. The membership of the *Sakurakai* (Cherry Society), formed in September 1930, contained the hard core of the officers corps; the upper strata of the society joined with the *Issekikai*'s senior officers in constituting the *Toseiha* (Control Faction), while those who were more willing to push forward the idea of reform together with younger officers of lower ranks formed the *Kozakurakai* (Small Cherry Society), which supplied the nucleus of the *Kodoha* (Imperial Way Faction) of the army. The latter, as we have noted, was doomed with the failure of the 1936 *coup d'état*, which marked a culmination of proto-fascism in Japan. In that year there were nearly 750 nationalist societies, many of them formed after the Manchurian Incident of 1931.[49]

We have already examined an agrarian type of nationalism known as *Nohonshugi* and its main advocates. Inoue Nissho, formerly an army spy and adventurist in China and Manchuria and then a Buddhist priest of the Nichiren sect, was the founder of the *Ketsumeidan* (Blood Pact League), which made contacts with politicized agriculturalists. The League grew out of a small group of fanatical nationalists, all from the Mito or Ibaraki area. They were bound together by an oath, sealed with their blood, to eliminate those public figures who were supposed to have betrayed national interests and to have enriched themselves at the cost of the farmers and peasants. The *Gokokudo* (Temple of National Safeguard) in Ibaraki, where Nissho preached social reform to the village youth, can be regarded as a terrorist organization.

The assassination of premier Hara in 1921 and the fatal attack on premier Hamaguchi in 1930 were acts of individual terrorism. In the 1930s terrorism was taken up by the proto-fascist and ultra-nationalist movements. In March 1931 Okawa Shumei and *Sakurakai* officers were actively involved in a plan for a military *coup d'état* which, however, was not carried out. The year 1932 was rife with assassinations. In February Inoue Junnosuke, former minister of finance and the chief of the *Minseito* election committee, and in March Dan Takuma of the Mitsui *zaibatsu* were shot dead by members of the Blood Pact League led by Inoue Nissho, who adopted the deadly tactic of a single assassin killing one target person. On 15 May a group of naval officers shot the premier, Inukai Tsuyoshi, at his official residence. This was part of the organized terrorism planned by the Blood Pact League against party politicians and *genro*.

'Fascism from below', attempted by proto-fascists like those described above, was finally suppressed or contained. The proto-fascist movements were indeed remarkable for their lack of organizational stability and

[49] Ibid. 26.

strength. Constant shifts and rivalries between the numerous groups and societies weakened them. Fragmentation of the movement went further than that of the socialists. All the same, the proto-fascists, because of their impact on public opinion, prepared the mass basis which 'fascism from above' would require when its time came.

THE ROLE OF THE SPECIAL HIGHER POLICE: COMMUNISTS HOUNDED AND ROUNDED UP

Thought control, beginning with the suppression of clandestine communists, was the work of bureaucrats in the Home Ministry and the police; though these were supposed to keep watch over extreme radicals on both the left and the right, their sympathies were not really impartial; it was not rare, indeed, for them to become the means of a 'white terror'. The Public Order Preservation Act of April 1925 ruled Japanese society for twenty years until it was abrogated in October 1945 by a directive from the Americans. The Special Higher Police, known as *Tokko*, had been set up in 1911 in the wake of the Treason Trial and was legally strengthened by the enactment of the Public Order Preservation Act. It was the communists who were singled out as its main target.

Yamamoto Senji, the Diet member who had had the courage to oppose the Public Order Preservation Act, was one of its first victims. Senji, born to a merchant family in Kyoto and converted to Christianity, studied biology at Tokyo Imperial University and taught it at Doshisha University. He was one of the pioneer advocates of birth control, a subject which often provoked hostility. Senji served as interpreter for Margaret Sanger's lecture to doctors in Kyoto in 1923, and from her he learned the connection between the need for birth control and the problem of poverty. He began lecturing workers in Osaka and peasants in nearby villages on birth control and sex education. His speaking tour extended to western and central Japan, and he also gave special lectures for students in Tokyo.

He soon found himself assisting in a peasant dispute in a Kyoto village and a workers' strike at a musical instruments factory at Hamamatsu. He was detained for nearly a month by the Uji police (at his home town) for his participation in the 'Hands Off China' movement at the time of the Shantung expedition in 1927. He was successful when he stood as a *Rodo-Nominto* (Labour-Farmer Party) candidate for Kyoto at the first general election under universal suffrage held in February 1928, becoming one of eight Diet members representing 'proletarian' parties out of the total of 466. A month later, on 15 March, over 1,600 clandestine Communist Party members and sympathizers were arrested, and on 11 April, when the news of the roundup was released, the *Rodo-Nominto*, Senji's party, together with the Japan Labour Council, both condemned as mass organizations of the underground Communist Party, were ordered to dissolve. On 8 February 1929 he spoke in the Imperial Diet, enquiring about 'torture and illegal detention' by the police, who had boasted of being the 'Amakasu of Showa' (referring to Captain Amakasu of the military police who murdered Osugi in 1923). Meanwhile, an amendment to the Public Order Preservation Act making death the maximum penalty for a breach of the Act instead of ten years' imprisonment was adopted by twenty-four to five at the imperial conference of the members of the Privy Council and cabinet ministers held in June 1928, and was brought up for Diet approval in March of the following year. Senji spent several days in February preparing his Diet speech, but was not given time to deliver it. In the Diet a *Minseito* member opposed the amendment, calling it 'anachronistic', while Mizutani Chozaburo, the other Diet member from the disbanded Labour-Farmer Party, spoke against it in the name of the 'proletariat'; but the amendment was passed by 249 votes to 170. On that night a right-wing assassin called on Senji in an inn in the Kanda district of Tokyo and killed him. It was a bloody affair which shocked Diet members as well as the press.[50]

Kobayashi Takiji, the author of 'proletarian novels', was another victim. Born to a poor peasant family in northern Akita and growing up in a working-class district in the city of Otaru, he became a graduate of the Otaru Higher Commercial School then started writing fiction while working in a local bank. In March 1928 the All Japan Proletarian Artists' Federation (abbreviated as NAPF, from its Esperanto name *Nippon Proleta Artista Federacio*) was started, with a journal, *Senki* (Battle Flag), as its organ, in which Takiji's major work, *Kani Kosen* (The Factory Ship) was published in 1929.

As a labour journalist he had come to know life on the crab meat factory ships, often referred to as 'the prison cells on the northern seas'. With intimate touch he depicted the foreman who represented the *zaibatsu* on the boat; the fishermen, mostly peasants who wanted to eke out their hard-pressed living with additional wages; and the factory-hands, mostly boys who often fell victim to the carnal lust of the adults as well as to the savage fury of the foreman. 'All the crab-meat factory ships were old and dilapidated', he wrote; '. . . Moreover, a crab meat factory ship was a factory to which the factory act was not applied.'[51] It has been said that *The Factory Ship* proved successful owing not so much to its socialist message as to 'the vivid, believable details of life aboard the ship'.[52]

Takiji was sacked from his bank for writing another novel dealing

---

[50] *Tokyo Asahi Shinbun*, 6 Mar. 1929; Katsumi Nishiguchi *Yamasen*, (Tokyo, 1959), *passim*.
[51] Takiji Kobayashi, *Kanikosen* (Iwanami Bunko edn., 1951), 29–30. For the English translation, see Takiji Kobayashi, '*The Factory Ship*' and '*The Absentee Landlord*', trans. Frank Motofuji (Tokyo, 1973). [52] Keene, op. cit., 619.

with a bank client. In 1930 he moved to Tokyo and was arrested under the charge of supplying money for the illegal Communist Party while engaged in a speaking tour in Kansai. Released, and back in Tokyo, he was again arrested, this time under the Public Order Preservation Act. Released on bail, he joined the Communist Party and continued writing. On 20 February 1933 he was caught in a trap laid by a police agent in the party, arrested, and tortured to death at the Tsukiji police station in Tokyo.

The clandestine Communist Party, which had dissolved itself, preferring infiltration of mass organizations to an endless debate on party programmes, was revived in 1925–6 under a new leadership which sought to establish an elitist party of the advance guards of revolution. Its sectarianism, while disowned by the Comintern, led to the splitting away of some of the original group (Sakai Toshihiko, Aarahata Kanson, and Yamakawa Hitoshi among others) who favoured permeation of the *Sodomei* and who now rallied to their new organ *Rono* (Worker and Peasant), started in December 1927: hence they were called the *Ronoha* (Rono Faction). They aspired for the overthrow of what they regarded as a fully fledged imperialist capitalism in Japan. After the arrests on 15 March 1928 of over 1,600 Communist Party members and sympathizers, the newspapers published an official announcement of the Ministry of Justice which described the Japanese Communist Party as intending to 'carry out a radical change of our impeccable *kokutai* and to establish a dictatorship of the worker-peasant classes' by means of the 'Bolshevization [*sekka*] of youth and soldiers'; they had to admit that the strength of the party was 'several hundreds' scattered all over the country.[53]

The period between 'the 15 March roundup' and the next 'great simultaneous' arrest of communists four and a half years later witnessed the zenith of Marxist influence in pre-war Japan, especially among students and academics. Some Japanese Marxists had begun to argue that the semi-feudal relationship of production and exploitation was preserved within the modern legal framework of private property, and they advocated a democratic revolution that would soon be turned into a socialist one at its second stage. This was the view of the school soon to be known as the *Kozaha* (*koza* or Lecture Faction). From 1932 these Marxists, with Noro Eitaro, graduate of Keio University, as one of the main theorists, started publishing a series of the *Nihon Shihonshugi Hattatsushi Koza* (Lectures on the History of the Development of Japanese Capitalism). The Comintern thesis on Japan published in July 1932 elaborated the *Kozaha* analysis of the peculiarities of Japanese capitalism in regard to the new developments in international politics, especially in the Far East. It emphasized 'the monarchist state apparatus' as the backbone of the

[53] *Tokyo Asahi Shinbun*, 11 Apr. 1928.

hegemony of the exploiting classes in Japan, and the communists were asked to try their best to overthrow this apparatus. In the event of war with Soviet Russia, they were urged 'to desert to the side of the Red Army . . . without giving up their weapons'.[54]

On 30 October 1932 another 'great roundup' of communists took place and 1,500 leaders and supporters were arrested. In March 1933 the newspapers announced the arrest of Dr Kawakami Hajime and Professor Otsuka Kinnosuke, 'the two giants of the left-wing forum'.[55] The two professors later accepted *tenko* (conversion), Kawakami renouncing a scientific socialism while retaining the ethical attitude that had brought him to it, while Otsuka, when released, wrote little pieces criticizing war and fascism in odd corners of student newspapers and small publishers' journals that were used for advertising books, until 1940. The *Sekki* (Red Flag), the organ of the underground Communist Party, devoted a full page to 'the slaughter of Noro Eitaro', perhaps the most prominent among the *Kozaha* Marxists, who was arrested in November 1933 and tortured to death on 18 February 1934 at the Shinjuku police station where he had been detained.[56] Noro had been appointed chairman of the central committee of the Communist Party after the mass arrest of its members the previous year.

The year 1933 also saw the mass conversion of communists, starting with the two party leaders who had been in prison since 1929, Sano Manabu, formerly of the *Shinjinkai* and a Waseda professor in the post-war years, and Nabeyema Sadachika, an Osaka trade union leader. Sano and Nabeyama in their joint *tenko* (conversion) statement, which was widely publicized in the press, declared that they had parted with the Comintern internationalism that had become an instrument for Soviet Russia, and now stood for 'Socialism in One Country', that is, Japan under its unique monarchy, while pleading for 'solidarity of the advance guard of the proletariat in Japan, Manchuria, Formosa, and Korea'.[57] Within a month 415 of the 1,370 communists and sympathizers who were in detention pending trial, and 133 of the 393 who were already convicted, submitted statements of *tenko*. Sano and Nabeyama, who had been sentenced to life imprisonment, received a reduction in their sentence. This marked a triumph of the Special Higher Police over the communists.[58] The clandestine Communist Party and its trade union organization had been infiltrated by *agents provocateurs*, and internal dissension and

---

[54] George M. Beckman and Okubo Genji, *The Japanese Communist Party, 1922–1945* (Stanford, 1969), 332–51.   [55] *Tokyo Asahi Shinbun*, 18 Jan. 1933.
[56] *Sekki*, 8 Mar. 1934; C. Tsuzuki, 'Tenko or Teiko' (Conversion or Resistance), in Sue Henny and Jean Pierre Lehmann (eds.), *Themes and Theories in Modern Japanese History* (London, 1988), 221.   [57] *Tokyo Asahi Shinbun*, 10 June 1933; Tsuzuki, op. cit., 224.
[58] Shisono Kagaku Kenkyukai (Society for the Study of Science of Thought) (ed.), *Tenko* (Conversion) (Tokyo, 1959), i. 164.

suspicions, in addition to the increasing number of *tenko*, tore the party to pieces. With the cessation of its organ *Sekki* in February 1935, the national propaganda conducted by the communists had come to an end.[59] In fact, *tenko* proved to be a 'positive and offensive' weapon by which the police, the prosecution, and even the judges turned the Public Order Preservation Act into a system of 'brainwashing'. The 'Act to Protect and Observe Thought Criminals' adopted in 1937 was intended to keep watch on the released 'thought criminals' through 'protection' by observation agents, the functions of which were entrusted to the local police and to neighbourhood associations.

In 1935, with a new Manual for the Special Higher Police, its function was enlarged so as to include destructive and subversive activities in general. Thus the *Tokko* became 'a main agent to carry out the measures of coercive homogenization of the nation and its war policies on the ruins of the communist movement'.[60] Professor Kawai Eijiro of Tokyo Imperial University remarked that already in about 1932 the freshmen in his university had ceased to be responsive to Marxist influence and were gradually inclined to nihilistic tendencies, and soon they lost all appetite for a cause.[61] Now the *Tokko* acted as the emperor's police, and as the guardian of *kokutai* it did all it could to spread ultra-nationalist ideology and to foster or impose unquestioning loyalty.

The Public Order Preservation Act was also aimed at suppressing 'pseudo-religions' inimical to *kokutai*, and introducing the system of preventative detention; the chief priest and followers of the Omoto-sect, a reformist Shinto sect suspected of links with right-wing *coup d'état* plans, were prosecuted in 1932 under the Act. The *Tokko* remained an overwhelmingly effective means to suppress deviations from official ideology.[62]

UNIVERSITIES UNDER ATTACK: THOUGHT CONTROL TIGHTENED

The first case to which the Public Order Preservation Act was applied, however, was the judgement given in 1929 at the second trial of the members of the Nihon Student Social Science Association (launched in 1922–4). Twenty-one students from several universities who had been actively involved in the work of this association were sentenced to imprisonment for varying lengths of time (up to seven years) for having sup-

[59] Toyama, Imai, Fujiwara, *Showashi* (History of Showa), 9, 96–7.
[60] Sumio Ohinata, 'Tokko Keisatsu' (The Special Higher Police), in *Nihon Tsushi* (Complete History of Japan), xviii. 310.
[61] Eijiro Kawai, quoted by Shozo Fujita in *Tenko*, vol. 1 (1959), 58–9.
[62] Misuzushobo (ed.), *Gendaishi Shiryo* (Sources for Modern History), vol. 45 (Tokyo, 1975), pp. xiii–xv, 652.

ported the revolutionary ideas of Marxism and Leninism and held meetings of the association with a view to overthrowing the existing system of private property, and in the case of some of them for having joined the illegal Communist Party. Yanaihara Tadao, professor of colonial policy at Tokyo Imperial University and a Christian, wrote about this 'student association incident' (*gakuren jiken*): 'learning is not an amusement: it is difficult to separate one's research, one's convictions, and one's actions from each other. I am sorry for the thirty-odd students who have been caught in a police net and detained without trial for nine months.'[63] In 1928 the Ministry of Education took the initiative in opening a student section in universities as an agent for thought control. In 1931 the ministry set up a committee to investigate the 'thought problem' of students (its chairman was Hatoyama Ichiro of the *Seiyukai* party). In accordance with its report presented to the minister of education, who by that time was Hatoyama, the *Kokumin Seishin-Bunka Kenkyujo* (Institute for the Study of National Spirit and Culture) was opened in 1932 in order to 'clarify our national spirit' and thereby to 'liquiditate Marxism' and other foreign ideas such as individualism, liberalism, and utilitarianism. Members of the Institute were expected to promote 'the Imperial Way' and to pursue their research in a spirit of loyal devotion.[64]

Now it was the turn of liberal academics to be thrown out of their universities. The storm centre was Kyoto Imperial University, where Professor Kawakami had been forced to resign in March 1928 when a faculty meeting of which he was a member failed to defend him. Takigawa Yukitoki, professor of criminal law, had persistently been attacked by officials of the Ministry of Education for his *Criminal Law Reader*, because of its accounts of sedition and adultery: the former in their view, was too lenient to political crimes, the latter too generous to women. In April 1933 minister of education Hatoyama demanded Professor Takigawa's suspension from his post. The president of Kyoto University refused to comply on grounds of freedom of research. The Diet had meanwhile passed a resolution on education reform intended to eliminate radical ideas. In the end the government, in the name of prime minister Saito Makoto, ordered Takigawa's suspension. Thereupon all the members of the law faculty offered their resignation in protest, and students in support of the faculty started a boycott movement. Students in other universities rose to show their solidarity with Kyoto students. The Ministry of Education changed the head of Kyoto University and overcame faculty opposition by accepting the resignations of six determined professors.

The crucial battle for academic freedom had been lost, owing partly to the indifference of other professors in other faculties and other universities.

[63] Ibid. 540 ff., 573.   [64] Ibid. pp. xv–xvii, 32 ff.

A pattern of attack on liberalism and sanity now emerged: a right-wing professor, such as Minoda Muneki of Kokushikan University, would accuse a liberal professor like Professor Takigawa, whose plight we have just noted and who was one of Minoda's prime targets; then some members of the Diet or the House of Peers would take up 'the issues' thus created, and the government would be obliged to put pressure on universities. This pattern is said to have enjoyed strong support from the military.[65]

MINOBE'S 'ORGAN THEORY' ATTACKED

The military began openly intervening in politics by the mid-1930s. In October 1934 the Newspaper Unit of the army issued a pamphlet entitled *Kokubo no Hongi to sono Kyokano Teisho* (The Essence of National Defence and its Strengthening: A Proposal), which began with the words: 'Fighting is the father of creation, the mother of culture', and went on to advocate the rejection of liberal economic ideas and the promotion of economic control for greater equality in distribution of wealth and for the creation of 'a national defence state'. This was a product of the Control Faction of the army in its efforts to assume power from within. Political parties, both *Minseito* and *Seiyukai*, at a Diet session early in 1935 criticized what appeared to them to be army presumption. To this flickering of the embers of party democracy, the army, the peers, and the right-wing bodies launched a concerted offensive in the form of attacking the organ theory of the emperor that had been advanced by Minobe Tatsukichi twelve years before at the time of Taisho democracy, and had since become accepted as a valid and respectable argument.

At a session of the House of Peers held on 19 February 1935 Lt.-General Kikuchi Takeo of the Army Reservists' Association, an obscure baron who had attacked Professor Takigawa, attacked Minobe as 'an academic bandit' and a 'traitor' who advocated a theory which he said was incompatible with *kokutai*. A week later Minobe, himself a peer, gave a speech expounding his theory which was well received. Some of the peers stood up to contradict him, however, and the Reservists' Association and a great many right-wing bodies issued appeals and resolutions denouncing Minobe, while the right-wing Professor Minoda published a pamphlet entitled *Explode the Organ Theory of the Emperor: An Appeal to the Nation*. Members of the two Houses of the Diet connected with the military joined in the general onslaught on Minobe; the *Seiyukai* party was also drawn into the general outcry; in March the two Houses passed a resolution to reject the organ theory. The prime minister, Admiral Okada

---

[65] Misuzushobo (ed.), op. cit., xlii. 170–1; Tsutomu Ouchi, *Nihonno Rekishi* (History of Japan), xxiv. 362–5.

Keisuke, succumbed to general pressure and said he was against the theory. Minobe's books were suppressed, and he himself had to resign from the House of Peers; he was assaulted and wounded by a right-wing thug early the following year. It is notable that no attempt was made to defend Minobe or academic freedom this time. Party democracy died along with Minobe's theory, interred by party politicians themselves. *The Times* correspondent rightly perceived the role played by the military all through the Minobe controversy: his assailants defended the imperial prerogative against encroachment by politicians, but in fact they were 'affirming the Fighting Services' claim to be independent of Cabinet control'. In 1930, when the emperor, acting on the civilian prime minister's advice rather than on the contrary view of the chief of the naval general staff, signed the London Treaty of Naval Disarmament, this was soon decried as an 'infringement of the supreme command'. Now that the organ theory of the emperor seemed to threaten 'the supreme command', 'the ministers of war and marine did not conceal the interest the services took' in suppressing the concept.[66]

LAST VESTIGES OF LIBERALISM

Next on the ultra-nationalist list of forbidden books were those by Kawai Eijiro, professor of social policy at Tokyo Imperial University. He was courageous enough to criticize 'fascism in the 2.26 incident' (as the abortive *coup d'état* of 1936 was called in Japan, referring to the date of the outbreak, 26 February)' and, as a disciple of Thomas Hill Green the English idealist philosopher, asserted that individual personality was an end in itself and should not be made a means for state purposes. In December 1938 five of his books were suppressed, including *Shakaiseisaku Genri* (Principles of Social Policy, 1931) and *Fashizumu Hihan* (A Critique of Fascism, 1937), either for the alleged reason of incitement to socialist action or for their 'propaganda for socialism and anti-militarist thought'. The president of the university sought to untie the knot by trying to persuade Professor Kawai and a right-wing professor and obvious troublemaker to retire. The economics faculty, to which they both belonged, was thrown into confusion, but the president's decision was carried out; moreover, Kawai was prosecuted and fined.[67]

Left-wing writers were watched and arrested: several novelists of the school of proletarian literature and academics of the *Kozaha* were arrested in July 1937, and suppression was extended to claim victims from among the *Ronoha* in the following year. Those who supported *Sekai Bunka*

---

[66] *The Times*, 10 Sept. 1935, in Misuzushobo (ed.), op. cit., xlii. 311–14.
[67] Ibid. 315–49.

(World Culture), a Kyoto journal which reported on contemporary European politics and literature from 1935 to 1937, were suppressed at about the same time on the charge that they sought to organize a popular front in Japan.

NATIONAL SOCIALISM

Left-wing political parties were by now all but extinct. Arrests and suppression drove social democrats into national socialism of an expansionist type. The *Shakai Minshyuto* (Social Popular Party), which came into existence in December 1926, having broken from the *Rodo Nominto* (Labour-Farmer party, disbanded in 1928) when the latter opened its door to left-wing trade unionists, sent a mission to Manchuria and Mongolia shortly after the Manchurian Incident of 1931 and fought the general election of 1932 with the slogan 'Manchurian and Mongol interests for the people'. In the same year the *Nihon Kokka Shakaito* (Japan National Socialist Party) was set up by Akamatsu Katsumaro, a former member of the *Shakai Minshyuto*, who now openly endorsed the imperial system. Again in the same year the *Shakai Minshyuto*, together with another left-wing party, developed into the *Shakai Taishyuto* (Social Mass Party), which regarded the military as allies of the workers. At the general election of April 1937 the *Shakai Taishyuto* managed to have its thirty-seven candidates elected to the Diet.[68] The party had supported the army pamphlet of 1934 and declared its willingness to co-operate in the 'sacred war' when the China incident of July 1937 developed into a full-scale conflict, overriding objections from Abe Isoo, the veteran socialist and party chairman. In February 1940 Saito Takao, the *Minseito* Diet member, criticized the government's China policy, pointing out contradictions beween slogans like 'East Asian New Order' and the actual war situation. Under pressure from the military Saito was expelled from the Diet, and the *Shakai Tishyuto* joined with other parties in 'punishing' him, as well as expelling dissidents like Abe, Katayama Tetsu, Mizutani Chozaburo, and several others from their own party. In July the party dissolved itself in order to throw in its lot with Konoe's new party movement. It was an ignominious but appropriate end to social democracy in pre-war Japan.

THE CASE OF TSUDA SOKICHI

In November 1940 a grand ceremony to celebrate the 2,600th year of the legendary imperial calendar was held in the outer garden of the Imperial

---

[68] Toyama, Imai, and Fujiwara, *Showashi* (History of Showa), 94, 145.

Palace; lantern processions, banner processions, and other marches were held all over the country. A placard put up in the street by the Association to Uphold Imperial Rule was prominently reproduced in the newspapers, which exhorted: 'Celebration is over: Let us work.'[69] It was timely for the imperial calendar that Professor Tsuda Sokichi was indicted under the charge of blasphemy against the imperial house on 8 March in the same year.[70] Tsuda, professor of Waseda University, through a series of bibliographical and comparative studies of the era of the gods, had come to the view that a large part of the contents of the *Kojiki* (Records of Ancient Matters) and *Nihonshoki* (Chronicles of Japan) dealing with that era was not a record of historical events. This appeared treasonable enough in the eyes of a nationalist in those days. Again it was the right-wing agitator Minoda who accused Tsuda of having 'criminal ideas': Tsuda and his publisher, Iwanami Shigeo, were indicted under the Publication Act, and their preliminary investigation was closed in March 1941. Their trial lasted from November 1941 to January 1942, in the course of which most of the issues relating to the early history of Japan were touched upon. The trial itself was a scholarly debate, by and large. In May 1942 Tsuda was sentenced to three months imprisonment and Iwanami to two months, both with a stay of execution for two years.[71] The sentence, much less harsh than might have been expected from the nature of the indictment, in fact reflected Tsuda's compliant attitude during the trial. On the whole, he took the stance that his treatment of the era of gods not as a historical period but as a legend or an expression of ideas would ensure the clarification of *kokutai*. Tsuda was on the side of the imperial throne both before and after the war. As Ienaga Saburo pointed out, his analysis of the ancient chronicles was not meant as destructive criticism of the emperor system, but aimed to 'strengthen it by rational reconstruction of the spiritual pillar of the emperor system'.[72] In July 1941 the instruction board attached to the Ministry of Education issued a booklet, *Shinmin no Michi* (The Way of the Subject), in which 'the construction of a moral world based on the spirit of the foundation of the country' was emphasized. Around May 1943 an elementary schoolboy, looking at a wall picture showing the descent of the heavenly grandson, said to his teacher 'this must be a lie', whereupon he was taken to the teachers' common room and badly beaten with a wooden sword. The nation at large no longer enjoyed the freedom to doubt the historical plausibility of a legend.[73]

[69] *Asahi Shinbun*, 15 Nov. 1940.   [70] Ibid., 9 March 1940.
[71] Misuzushobo (ed.), op. cit., lxii. 353–1089.
[72] Ienaga Saburo, *Tsuda Sokichi no Shisouteki Kenkyu* (Intellectual Studies of Tsuda Sokichi) (Tokyo, 1972), 382–411.   [73] Ibid. 416.

13

The Undeclared War Against China

On 16 January 1938, a month after the bloody occupation of Nanking, prime minister Konoe made 'a historic statement': 'the Imperial Government from now on will not deal with the Nationalist Government and will endeavour to build up a new China, expecting the establishment and development of a new Chinese regime worthy of true collaboration with the [Japanese] Empire and arranging diplomatic relations with this regime,'[1] Japan had been in state of war, not legally but actually, with China since September 1931, when the Kwantung Army had begun a large-scale attack on the Chinese forces in Manchuria. The undeclared war, however, had bogged down in the vast continent, while expanding elsewhere in search of the resources with which to end or 'solve' the war in China itself.

Japan had been bidding for a higher stake in her effort to become a hegemonic power in East Asia. Her victories in three wars in three generations and the progress made in industrialization and greater military preparedness had encouraged the Japanese to enhance their expectations for the future and set their national goal yet higher, aspiring for a great power status which also meant being a great military power. The era of post-imperialism under the Versailles–Washington system witnessed a new American-led diplomacy of imperialism, less particularistic and more attuned to international capitalist co-operation. This too was to collapse owing to the upsurge of nationalism in China and also to the failure of concerted action on the part of the powers of which Japan's unilateral action was one major cause.[2] The distinction between responsible and irresponsible imperialism would give little consolation to the imperialism's victims, but a replacement of the former by the latter took place in inter-war Japan and this process entailed increasingly effective control of politics and the nation's life by the military. Reponsible imperialism represented in Japan by foreign minister Shidehara, was 'responsible' in the sense that it was willing to co-operate with other imperialist powers in the economic exploitation of China (hence the name economic imperialism),

---

[1] *Tokyo Asahi Shinbun*, 17 Jan. 1938.
[2] Akira Iriye, *After Imperialism: The Search for a New Order in the Far East, 1921–1931* (Cambridge, Mass., 1965), 5–22, 57–87.

whereas irresponsible imperialism took the form of aggressive territorial expansion and meant a military challenge to and subversion by force of the existing system.

Even among the advocates of what amounted to economic imperialism there were differences, as we have noted before, between the hawkish *Seiyukai* (and Yoshida Shigeru) and the more cautious *Minseito* (and Shidehara). Similarly, although naked violence was patently part of military imperialism, it was more or less restrained until the Manchurian Incident of 1931, in spite of the foretaste Tanaka Giichi had acquired in the Shantung expedition and the murder of Chang Tso-lin. It was sometimes given an excuse or even a justification under the slogan of 'pan-Asianism', now that Japan had assumed the position of a big brother among the less fortunate Asian brethren. Sun Yat-sen, shortly before his triumphant entry into Beijing towards the end of 1924, visited Japan and gave lectures at Kobe in which he presented a choice between the 'interest- and power-centred culture' of the West and Asian culture of 'the royal way', and urged Japan, 'China's younger brother', to free China from the imperialist yoke in order that the two nations could live as brothers of the same family.[3] The Confucian order of international relations based on familial hierarchy and cultural emulation still lingered on even with the westernized leader of the new China. By then, however, the self-centred Japanese version of the Middle Kingdom had been absorbed into Japan's new ambitions to become a hegemonic world power.

'RESPONSIBLE' IMPERIALISM AND SHIDEHARA DIPLOMACY

The major exponent in Japan of the principles embodied in the so-called Versailles–Washington system was Shidehara Kijuro, Japan's first career diplomat.[4] He was ambassador to Washington from 1919 to 1922, and foreign minister in the three *Kenseikai–Minseito* cabinets led respectively by Kato Takaaki, Wakatsuki, and Hamaguchi, and he developed the liberal diplomatic policy referred to as 'Shidehara diplomacy'. It was based on the principle of international co-operation, which meant non-intervention in China's domestic affairs and collaboration with the United States and Britain. His full support for the open-door principle and for equal opportunity followed the Fukuzawa idea of 'exit Asia, enter Europe', and took for granted the semi-colonial position to which China had been reduced. 'Those who obstruct the just advance of our trade and industry [in China] are breaking the principle of equal opportunity,' he wrote in his memoirs,

---

[3] Ibid. 57.

[4] Shidehara entered the diplomatic service in 1896. After having served in Japanese consulates in several cities in Asia and Europe, he was assigned to the Foreign Office in 1914 and became vice-minister of foreign affairs in 1915.

'and boycotting is one such example.'[5] Referring to the Twenty-One Demands and the subsequent treaty, he wrote: 'China should recognize the sanctity of a treaty. Japan by her own will can freely renounce her own right, but China should submit herself to the sanctity of that treaty.'[6] He could not tolerate 'the openly defiant attitude of the Chinese', which he said 'had poured oil on firewood' at the time of the Manchurian Incident.[7] Marius Jansen takes the view that the differences between Tanaka Giichi, who was foreign minister and prime minister at the time of the murder of Chang Tso-lin in 1928, and Shidehara, foreign minister when the Manchurian Incident took place, were 'neither deep nor principled'. 'Tanaka at least managed, in 1928, to keep things from going further, whereas Shidehara, in 1931, did not.'[8] Shidehara regarded the Chinese action to bring 'the Mukden issue' of 1931 to the attention of the League of Nations as 'an unwise course'.[9]

The second Chinese revolution led by Sun Yat-sen resulted in the establishment of the Kuomintang government in Canton with the support of the Comintern. The Kuomintang launched the northern expedition against local warlords in 1926 and set up the Wuhan government in the following year; by then, however, Chiang Kai-shek had started an anti-communist coup, made Nanking the seat of his government, resumed the northern expedition, and succeeded in unifying China (except for Manchuria) by the end of 1928. In order to protect her own interests along the Yangtze River, especially in Shanghai, Britain sought to carry out a military intervention with the help of the Americans and the Japanese, but Shidehara remained faithful to his non-interventionist principles. The commander of a Japanese gunboat, as we have noted, decided not to join the Anglo-American bombardment of Nanking in March 1927, in view of the strong wishes to the contrary of local Japanese residents, but it was Shidehara who came under attack from the militarists.[10] His China policy was decried as 'weak diplomacy' by the press, and Mori Kaku, the right-wing leader of the *Seiyukai*, along with the hardliners in the army, felt this was an opportunity to unseat the Wakatsuki government of which Shidehara was foreign minister.

TANAKA GIICHI AND THE SHANTUNG EXPEDITIONS

The new government formed in April 1927 was headed by General Tanaka Giichi, the last leader in the direct line of descent from Yamagata in the

[5] Kijuro Shidehara, *Gaiko 50 nen* (Fifty Years of Diplomacy) (Tokyo, 1924), 84.
[6] Ibid. 83.   [7] Ibid. 168.
[8] Marius Jansen, in James William Morley (ed.), *Japan Erupts* (New York, 1984), 125.
[9] Ian Nish, *Japan's Struggle with Internationalism* (London, 1993), 33.
[10] Shidehara, *Gaiko 50 nen*, 108–9.

Choshu army clique. He was minister of war in Hara's *Seiyukai* cabinet, then in Yamamoto Gonbei's 'transcendentalist' government, and pursued the 'positive' China policy of the *Seiyukai* of which he became president in 1925. Tanaka meant to ride two horses, economic (responsible) imperialism and military (irresponsible) imperialism: hence his dilemma. He had once sought to set up an Eastern Colonization Company, combining Japanese capital and technology and Chinese natural resources and labour. It was with a similar aim in mind that he, then vice-chief of the army staff, actively supported the Nishihara loans, mentioned earlier, given to the Beijing regime of Tuan Ch'i-jui in order to promote Sino-Japanese economic co-operation and thereby to reduce China's trade and financial dependence on the West during the First World War. Tuan's army, created by Japanese loans, occupied Mongolia, an anti-Soviet action which invited hostile reaction from other warlords and led eventually to Tuan's downfall.

Tanaka himself attached great importance to economic development in Manchuria and Mongolia, itself a *Seiyukai* policy, which he sought to implement with the aid of Mori Kaku, his parliamentary under-secretary (Tanaka also acted as foreign minister), who was distinguished by his tough interventionist policy towards China. Tanaka began his premiership by sending an army brigade to Shantung under the pretext of protecting local Japanese residents. An expeditionary force of 2,000 was sent from Dairen to Tsingtao in May 1927 and moved to Tsinan in July, but by then the Kuomintang army had begun to withdraw from Shantung. The expedition was meant to be a warning of the cabinet's determination to shield Manchuria from Kuomintang influence and was possibly intended as an aid to Chang Tso-lin, commander-in-chief of the anti-Kuomintang forces controlling Beijing, who might be expected to honour Japanese interests in Manchuria.[11] The Shantung expedition met with strong opposition at home: the *Shakai Minshyuto* (Social Mass Party), which welcomed Chiang Kai-shek's anti-imperialist as well as anti-communist policy, attacked the Tanaka cabinet over the expedition. The *Rodo Nominto* (Labour-Farmer Party) which favoured the left-wing Wuhan government, staged a 'Hands off China' campaign.[12]

In the early summer of 1927 an Eastern Conference consisting of representatives of the government ministries and the army general staff was held in Tokyo to discuss the China problem, and Tanaka made a statement that his government would co-operate with 'moderate elements' in China. It has been alleged that shortly after the conference Tanaka presented to the emperor a memorandum for the conquest of East Asia by crushing the United States first. This apparently spurious document first

---

[11] William Fitch Morton, *Tanaka Giichi and Japan's China Policy* (Folkestone, 1980), 88.
[12] Ibid. 94.

appeared as a pamphlet in Chinese and English in September 1929 a few weeks after Tanaka's death, and attracted attention at the time of the Manchurian Incident when a Shanghai journal republished it. There is no known Japanese original, and Tanaka's cautiously expansionist policy towards China seems to belie its contents.[13] In fact, Tanaka would endorse Shidehara diplomacy to some extent and would avoid antagonizing the great powers; as later events will show, he was afraid of losing the trust of the emperor, who regarded himself as a constitutional monarch and his country as treaty-bound. The trouble with Tanaka was that he was not in control of the army. He agreed with Shidehara on support for Chiang Kai-shek in south and central China, and when Chiang visited Japan in January 1928 a secret agreement was reached with Tanaka whereby Japan would put pressure on Chang Tso-lin to withdraw from Beijing to Mukden provided that he would not be pursued by the Kuomintang army.[14] Nevertheless, plans for intervention cropped up again in the army in face of a renewed northern expedition by Chiang Kai-shek.

In April 1928 Chiang resumed his attack on the northern warlords. The Tanaka government dispatched two army divisions to Shantung and in May there occurred a clash between Japanese and Chinese forces at Tsinan. Chiang's army bypassed Tsinan and pursued Chang Tso-lin's retreating forces, leaving behind in Tsinan a force of about 5,000 to keep order. Then the commander of the Japanese expeditionary forces, 'without conferring with his superiors in Tokyo', sent an ultimatum which was followed by an operation by the Japanese soldiers to clear the entire city of Chinese troops, resulting in the death of some 3,600 Chinese.[15] Until the beginning of 1929 a Japanese military government ruled the Tsinan area, and this military intervention proved disastrous to Japan's reputation. 'Japanese field commanders compiled an unenviable record [of] crudity and mendacity. The death of 13 Japanese opium smugglers, for instance, was reported and accepted in Tokyo as that of 300 Japanese citizens. Anti-Japanese agitation grew steadily, and boycotts hurt Japanese trade.'[16] Chiang's forces entered Beijing on 9 June 1928. The continued presence of Japanese troops (reduced to a few thousand) only hindered solutions to the complex problems of Sino-Japanese relations.

THE MURDER OF CHANG TSO-LIN

The Japanese foreign ministry had been anxious to prevent Chinese civil wars spreading to Manchuria, and Chang Tso-lin was advised in March to return to his stronghold in Mukden before the Kuomintang forces would

---

[13] Morton, op. cit., 109, 205–14.   [14] Ibid. 107.
[15] Ibid. 118.   [16] Jansen, op. cit., 120.

reach Beijing. Some in the Foreign Ministry and the army sought his retirement, especially in view of persistent anti-Japanese movements in Manchuria under his influence. The Kwantung Army wanted to take military action against Chang Tso-lin. Tanaka overruled all such demands, as he believed that Chang could protect Japan's position in Manchuria and Mongolia. Chang was Tanaka's choice for Manchuria, and his safe return to Mukden would vindicate Tanaka's policy.[17] Chang Tso-lin's return journey, however, provided a precious chance for the Kwantung Army officers who wanted to disarm his forces and occupy Mukden. Colonel Komoto Daisaku, a Kwantung Army staff officer, planned Chang Tso-lin's assassination, and under his direction an explosive was set under the railway bridge of the South Manchurian Railway near Mukden at a crossing-point with the Chinese railway from Beijing; this killed Chang, who was travelling in a special train from Beijing, on 4 June 1928. The Kwantung Army blamed the Kuomintang expeditionary forces for Chang Tso-lin's murder, but rumours of a Japanese plot quickly spread, and premier Tanaka decided to court-marshal Komoto and his fellow conspirators. He promised this to the emperor, but then changed his mind under strong pressure from the army, which demanded administrative treatment of the culprits; his own cabinet and *Seiyukai* officials sided with the army. This matter incurred the emperor's displeasure, which caused Tanaka to resign.

Before Chang Tso-lin's murder led to this anti-climax, the Tanaka government had to deal with the problem of treaty revision in China: indeed, treaty revision was an issue which had vexed Japan for many decades and troubled China for a longer period. At the tariff conference held in the autumn of 1925 in Beijing the delegates, among whom British, American, and Japanese were prominent, resolved that tariff autonomy would come into effect from January 1929. Civil war among northern warlords made the conference somewhat inconclusive. Now in 1928 Chang Hsueh-liang, the son of the murdered 'marshal', accepted the authority of the Nanking government which had announced the abrogation of the 1896 Sino-Japanese treaty of commerce and navigation. In the course of 1928 the United States and most European countries agreed to tariff autonomy for China, but Japan continued to refuse to accept it (until May 1930). Tanaka's forceful China policy resulted in a nationwide anti-Japanese boycott in China. This boycott of 1928–9 is estimated to have reduced the volume of Japanese exports to northern China by about 10 per cent and to the rest of the country by 25 per cent.[18]

The emperor Hirohito in his 'Monologue' on these events recorded after the war commented on the incident: 'I heard later that Colonel Komoto had threatened to disclose the whole intrigue of Japan against China if he

[17] Morton, op. cit., 129.   [18] Ibid. 149.

had been tried in a military court, and therefore his trial had to be cancelled . . . I disliked the atmosphere of suspicion thus created, which later brought about the February 26 Incident. This atmosphere led me to decide not to act on my own but to give my sanction to any proposal coming from the cabinet.'[19] The system of irresponsibility was thus further reinforced.

SHIDEHARA DIPLOMACY IN 1930

Tanaka's government fell on 2 July 1929, and a *Minseito* government led by Hamaguchi was formed with Shidehara as foreign minister. Shidehara diplomacy was given a new lease of life, but only briefly. The London Naval Conference of 1930, at which Japan agreed to an inferior ratio of 69.75 per cent—'a de facto overall 70 per cent ratio', 70 per cent being Japan's original demand in tonnage of auxiliary vessels compared to the United States (allocation for Britain being slightly larger than that for America), was naturally unpopular among naval officers, especially those hardliners called 'the fleet faction'. Prime minister Hamaguchi was committed to his cabinet's two basic policies of financial retrenchment and diplomatic co-operation with the western powers. He was supported by the *genro* Prince Saionji and the lord privy seal Makino Nobuaki. Vice-admiral Suetsugu Nobumasa, the vice-chief of the naval general staff, had newspapers publish a statement by the navy flatly repudiating the compromise ratio. The London *Times* commented on this: 'public opinion in Japan is accustomed to see the Army and Navy go to great lengths in advocating their own views, even in opposition to the Government.'[20] Admiral Kato Kanji, the chief of the naval general staff, came to support the compromise plan, as he felt that 'after all, if we concentrate on airplanes, we can maintain our national defense'.[21] Premier Hamaguchi was a man of fortitude and forced Suetsugu to resign from his influential position on the naval general staff. With the support of some of the leading newspapers he compelled the unwilling privy council to ratify the bill for naval disarmament. The ratification of the bill, completed on 2 October 1930, was 'a brilliant record of victory of a party government and a monument of democracy in Japan'.[22] But the monument was at once

---

[19] *Bungei Shunju*, Dec. 1990. The emperor's 'monologue' was a record of an interview given to Matsudaira Yoshitami, Minister of the Imperial Household, and four others, which lasted for four days from the end of March to early April 1946. The record was compiled by Terasaki Hidenari, the emperor's steward. The 'monologue' has been regarded as an attempt to exonerate the emperor from possible indictment for war crimes.

[20] *The Times*, 19 Mar. 1930, quoted by Tetsuo Kobayashi, 'London Naval Treaty', in Morley (ed.), *Japan Erupts*, 39.   [21] Ibid. 43.

[22] Tsutomu Ouchi, *Fashizumu eno Michi* (The Road to Fascism), *Nihonno Rekishi* (History of Japan) (Tokyo, 1974; 1992 edn.), xxiv. 283.

attacked by democracy's opponents. On 14 November Hamaguchi was shot and seriously wounded at Tokyo Station by a young member of the *Aikokusha* (Patriotic Society), a right-wing body formed by a former intelligence officer of the Kwantung Army who had a hand in a series of right-wing actions. A 'reform' movement in the army and to a lesser extent in the navy, and also among right-wing civilians, began to endanger the status quo in Japanese politics. Shidehara diplomacy, itself linked to what Konoe once described as Anglo-American power control, was seriously threatened. Hamaguchi, who was incapacitated by the shot, died in August 1931.

THE MANCHURIAN INCIDENT (SEPTEMBER 1931) AND ISHIHARA KANJI

The Manchurian Incident, which set fire to the inflammable materials already in place, the flame spreading into the fifteen-year Asia-Pacific War, was, by a euphemism common in Japan, also called the '9.18 Incident', as it took place on 18 September 1931. Shidehara Kijuro, foreign minister at the time, later ruminated over the cause of the incident in his memoirs: 'Ill-gotten money will soon be spent.' Wartime prosperity had not lasted, economic depression and financial panic had characterized the 1920s, and finance minister Innoue Junnosuke came to see the need to pursue a policy of financial retrenchment. Both the number of civil officers and their salaries were to be reduced. There was not much complaint from the navy because of the previous measures of rationalization adopted at the time of the Washington Conference. (The 8.8 fleet-building plan for a grand fleet consisting of eight battleships and eight battle-cruisers as the core of the navy had proved financially impossible to implement and was abandoned as a result of the Washington Disarmament Conference.[23]) The army, though, was badly affected: two divisions were disbanded, and several thousand officers discharged. Several generals had to resign. Promotion of officers was stopped at the level of colonel; there was no hope of becoming a general. 'The military as a whole was reduced to a pitiful state. Those who had swaggered about in town simply became ignored; nobody would give up seats to them in trams; parents would hesitate to permit daughters to marry young officers. In short, the pride and self-respect of the military were gone all at once.' The military deplored this state of affairs, and sought to restore the army's honour and prestige that had been built up since Meiji. 'Over-zealous young officers carried their feeling of indignation to an extreme degree . . . and harboured outrageous plans to build a new order by smashing up political

[23] Ikuhiko Hata, in *Cambridge History of Japan*, vi. 276–7.

parties, and even to burn down the Diet building by throwing bombs.'
While General Ugaki remained minister of war (until April 1931), however, control within the army was maintained and no chance was given to
these radical elements. Therefore they 'released their accumulated frustration abroad, in Manchuria.'[24]

Shidehara was confused about the actual reduction in army strength.
The abolition of two divisions he mentioned was only a part of Ugaki's
second plan for army disarmament, and the plan itself miscarried when
prime minister Hamaguchi (who along with Shidehara had backed Ugaki)
was shot; Ugaki himself had to denounce a plot for a *coup d'état* (the
March 1931 Incident) which, if successful, would have asked him to lead a
new government. But Ugaki's first plan for army disarmament in 1925 had
had the effect Shidehara described in his memoirs. Even before him in
1922 Yamanashi Hanzo, the then minister of war, had carried out a
reduction in army strength under pressure of public opinion after the naval
disarmament of a year before. Army personnel was reduced by 59,464 by
decreasing the number of companies in each infantry regiment. Under
heavy pressure for retrenchment after the Kanto Earthquake, Ugaki,
minister of war in Kato Takaaki's *Kenseikai* government, then abolished
four divisions out of the twenty then existing (apart from the Guard
Division). With this he achieved a reduction of army personnel by
33,894, a figure smaller than that of the Yamanashi reform, but the
main feature of his plan was to reduce the number of high-ranking officers
and to use the money thus saved for modernizing the army by such
measures as the introduction of tank battalions, more airforce regiments,
communication and transport schools, and the creation of a system of
national mobilization.[25] Modernization of the army, however, went along
with a confirmation of the traditional martial spirit, such as the 'belief in
inevitable victory' emphasized in the infantry manuals of those days.[26]

The military operation that set off the Manchurian Incident was the
brainchild of Lt.-Colonel Ishihara Kanji, a Kwantung Army staff officer,
and his plan was kept free from meddlesome interference from the home
government by the political skill of Colonel Itagaki Seishiro, a Kwantung
Army senior staff officer who had close ties with some officers (like Nagata
Tetsuzan of the Control Faction) in army central headquarters. Their joint
action was born from the sense of crisis over Japan's interest in Manchuria
and Mongolia.[27] This sense of crisis and the challenge it provoked were
due largely to the Versailles–Washington system or the Anglo-American

[24] Shidehara, op. cit., 167–8.
[25] Shinobu Ooe, *Tenno no Guntai* (The Emperor's Army), *Showa no Rekishi* (History of Showa), iii. 137–8.   [26] Peattie, *Ishihara*, 15.
[27] Hiroharu Seki in *Taiheiyo Senso eno Michi*, i. 359; H. Seki (English tr.) in Morley (ed.), *Japan Erupts*, 145.

power system, which was designed, as Konoe said, to maintain the status quo for the benefit of the old imperialist powers, enabling them to restrain the rise of new imperialist powers. Now the Kwantung Army staff officers sought to break the system through plotting and, above all, by force, and they had their way, thus helping to create the general trend that was to carry the nation into full-scale war and ultimate disaster. In its origins, therefore, the war did not come about by accident, nor was it fought for self-defence; it was a war of violent aggression skilfully and cunningly conducted.

The number of Japanese residents in Manchuria had increased from 68,000 in 1909 to 219,000 in 1930. They comprised employees of the South Manchuria Railway Company, a still relatively small number of farmers, and adventurers of all sorts. A much larger number of Chinese, on the other hand, had drifted to Manchuria, and their number, mostly of farmers, reached 780,000 in 1927. The economic pressure felt by Japanese residents was due more to their inability to compete with these Chinese immigrants, who could put up with a lower standard of living, than to Chiang's anti-Japanese policy, as Colonel Komoto, the arch-plotter, himself admitted.[28] Moreover, as has often been pointed out, Japan could not justify her claims to territorial rights in Manchuria or Mongolia.[29] Yet Ishihara built up his entire plan on the assumption that she had such rights.

It has been pointed out that the Japanese colonists in Manchuria in those days, like the French colonists in Algeria after the Second World War, felt frustrated and threatened by the upsurge of nationalism in the colony.[30] Like the French, they became exceedingly politically minded. In 1928 right-wing activists among the Japanese residents opened a Manchuria Youth Conference at Dairen which announced a policy to 'capture and restore Manchuria and Mongolia'. A Youth League formed at this conference was determined to 'establish a new state in Manchuria-Mongolia' with the emperor as its head, which they called 'the great work of Showa Restoration'.[31]

Their outspoken demands were echoed in the Diet. Matsuoka Yosuke, formerly a director of *Mantetsu*, then a Diet member of the *Seiyukai* party, set them out in January 1931: 'The *Manmo* (Manchuria-Mongolia) problem is one issue which directly concerns the existence of our country. It is the lifeline of our nation. I believe it is so for national defence and also economically. The fact that there are 200,000 Japanese over there and that we have railways over there is not the whole of the problem.'[32] Ishibashi

---

[28] Hata, op. cit., 292.   [29] Ibid.
[30] Mark R. Peattie, *Ishihara Kanji and Japan's Confrontation with the West* (Princeton, 1975), 143.   [31] Hiroharu Seki, op. cit., 362.
[32] Nakamura Naomi *et. al.* (eds.), *Shiryo Nihon Kingendaishi* (Sources of Modern History of Japan), ii. 124.

Tanzan, in the editorial columns of his journal *Toyokeizai Shinpo* (Oriental Economist, 26 September and 10 October 1931) raised a dissenting voice. He compared the young Chinese patriots of his day with the young Japanese men in Meiji busily occupied in building a new, modern state. 'The primary condition to settle the *Manmo* problem', he declared, 'is to recognize the Chinese demand for building a united country for themselves. . . . Our lifeline towards the Asiatic continent is the Japan Sea, and that is sufficient.'[33] Between Matsuoka's speech and the appearance of Ishibashi's editorials there had occurred the '9.18 Incident', the truth about which was to be hidden from the nation till after the defeat of Japan.

The modern currents of Chinese nationalism certainly bred 'insolent' Chinese who annoyed even Shidehara, and who certainly antagonized those who regarded *Manmo* as Japan's lifeline. Also it was in this period that the American presence in Asia became an irritant to many Japanese because of US sympathy with the anti-Japanese stance of the Chinese nationalists; the bad blood between the two nations was further exacerbated by America's Alien Immigration Act. This too formed part of the background of Ishihara's plan for Manchuria.

Ishihara Kanji was 'an imaginative, quixotic, and unconventional officer'.[34] Born in Tsuruoka, Tohoku and a graduate from the Military Academy and the Army Staff College, he studied in Germany in the critical years of 1922–4, taught at the Staff College, and became a staff officer in charge of operations in the Kwantung Army in 1928. In the following year Itagaki Seishiro, another army officer from Tohoku, five years senior to Ishihara at the Military Academy, moved in to become a senior staff officer of the Kwantung Army. These two had met back home at meetings of a group of army officers who did not belong to the traditional Choshu army clique. Its virtual founder, Utsunomiya Taro, on his deathbed in 1922 had assembled his followers, pointed to a world map on the wall of his room, commanded one of them to draw two red lines, one along 60 degrees East and the other along 170 degrees East, and declared that the area in between should be in the hands of the Japanese. The area designated comprised the whole of Siberia, China, India, South-East Asia, Australia, and New Zealand. The aggressive design revealed by Utsunomiya impressed his followers. This is the officers' society already referred to which, in 1929, reorganized itself under the new name of *Issekikai* (Society of One Evening), with 'the solution of the Manchuria-Mongolia problem' as its major task.[35]

Ishihara Kanji, however, was above the factional struggles within the army. His nationalism and knowledge of world strategy were probably

---

[33] Tanzan Ishibashi, *Shonihon shugi* (Small Japanism) (Tokyo, 1984), 104–9.
[34] Peattie, *Ishihara*, 22   [35] Seki, op. cit., 364–5.

more sophisticated than those of the average staff officer. While in Germany he had been introduced to the strategical theories of the military historian Hans Gottlieb Leopold Delbrück, the successor to Heinrich von Treitschke at Berlin University, who wrote on world history as well as on the history of military strategy. The breadth of his interests required an enlargement of the definition of *kokutai* that would transcend national boundaries.[36] Another of Ishihara's intellectual catalysts was Nichiren Buddhism, of which he had been a devoted adherent from his days at the Sendai Cadet School. As George Sansom noted, one source of Japanese nationalism can be traced back to the universalist teachings of the thirteenth-century Buddhist reformer Nichiren on *Rissho Ankoku* (Justice and Security).[37] Under these influences Ishihara began to work out his own ideas about 'the Final War', the conditions of which were the unification of western civilization under American leadership, of Asian civilization under Japan, and the development of aircraft able to circle the earth without landing.[38] China ought to be induced to accept Japanese 'guidance'. In absolute terms, however, Japan must be prepared to fight against the United States, Britain, Russia, and China together. If Japan's enemies were all defeated in 'the Final War', 'the glorious spirit of Japanese *kokutai* will come home to the hearts of the peoples of all nations, and the world will enter an era of peace under the guidance of the imperial throne'.[39] This is the Japanese version of the Middle Kingdom idea brought to its logical conclusion via Delbrück's military strategy of prolonged warfare, with the support of Nichiren's universalism of justice and security.

An ideology had been formulated; action was to follow. Itagaki organized a tour of Manchuria for staff officers in July 1929, in the course of which Ishihara gave a lecture at Changchun under the title of 'Observations on a Modern War'. For Ishihara, the First World War was a European war, and not a world war. The coming 'world war' should be 'the last great war of humanity', and would take the form of 'a war of extermination by aeroplanes' and 'a total war mobilizing the whole nation'. Ishihara called this 'a great war to unite the world as Nichiren himself had predicted'. In a draft solution of the Manchuria-Mongolia problem distributed to the participants of the tour he pleaded for 'war to be started at once so as to capture the political power of *Manmo* if we were to prepare for war with the United States', and added that the capture and development of *Manmo* should ease the unemployment problem at home. At Manchouli he expatiated on a 'Plan to Occupy *Manmo* by the Kwantung Army', in which he referred to 'free competition between the

---

[36] Peattie, *Ishihara*, 37.
[38] Peattie, *Ishihara*, 63.
[37] George Sansom, *History of Japan*, i. 428–9.
[39] Quoted in ibid. 74.

Japanese, the Koreans, and the Chinese under the military regime', but on the whole he preferred a discriminatory division of labour: large-scale industry and brainwork for the Japanese, cultivation of rice fields for the Koreans, and small trades for the Chinese.[40]

In the meantime Colonel Komoto, the assassin of Chang Tso-lin, acted as an intermediary between the Kwantung Army staff officers and some officers in the Ministry of War, such as Nagata Tetsuzan whom Ishihara consulted over the transport of cannons and to whom he even hinted that armed action would begin at Liutiaokou, a suburb of Mukden. In March 1931 foreign minister Shidehara, though, criticized the xenophobia of Japanese residents in Manchuria in a speech delivered in the House of Peers; this incited the Youth League, which launched a campaign to prepare the residents for an armed solution, a form of 'colonial fascism'.[41] Minami Jiro, the new minister of war, was cautious and avoided contact with Colonel Komoto, but succumbed to Nagata's influence and allowed the drafting of an 'Outline of the Solution of the Manchurian Problem' in April 1931, ranging from diplomatic negotiations to curb the anti-Japanese moves among the Chinese, to military action to be conducted by the army general staff. To this the Kwantung Army added an 'Opinion' which stated that 'the essence of our policy' should be a Sino-Japanese war as a preliminary to war with the United States and/or the Soviet Union, and that a pro-Japanese government should be formed in China so that the Chinese would co-operate with Japan in a war with America. Prime minister Wakatsuki, uneasy about new developments in the army, warned Minami who simply prevaricated. Some of the right-wing activists, both civilian and military, planned a *coup d'état* in parallel with the armed solution of *Manmo* (the March 1931 Incident), but internal dissensions prevented its outbreak. Even the emperor became worried about discipline in the army, while *genro* Saionji warned Minami, telling him that the territories of *Manmo* belonged to China and that the matter should be left to the minister of foreign affairs, not to the military. All the same, hardline opinion for armed action gained the upper hand in the *Seiyukai* party, where Mori Kaku was in close touch with the army, and also in the House of Peers. Political feeling at home was quite different now from what it had been three years before when Chang Tso-lin was murdered.

Two incidents took place in the early summer of 1931 which provided an excuse for the army to have its own way in Manchuria, enabling the army minister Minami to go so far as to condemn the government openly for its 'inertia'.[42] Some Korean peasants in Manchuria, suspected of being 'a Trojan horse' for Japanese penetration, had clashed with the Chinese over the issue of irrigation at Wanpaoshan, north of Changchun, in June

---

[40] Seki, op. cit., 367–71.   [41] Ibid. 388.   [42] *Tokyo Asahi Shinbun*, 5 Aug. 1931.

1931, a skirmish that led to an exchange of shots between Chinese security forces and the Japanese consular police.[43] Then, in July 1931, Captain Nakamura Shintaro and his aide were killed by local Chinese while making investigations for some military purpose in north-western Manchuria. Ishihara was determined to settle the matter without intervention from the Ministry of Foreign Affairs. In the same month heavy artillery sent from an arsenal in Tokyo was placed in the barracks of the Railway Garrison at Mukden. This was part of an operation intended to launch a massive attack in Manchuria, but the new commander of the Kwantung Army, Honjo Shigeru, who arrived in August apparently had no knowledge of what was going on among his subordinates. Chang Hsueh-liang, who succeeded his father as warlord in Manchuria, was then in Beijing; he and his Mukden government, alarmed by some knowledge of the plot and the extent of its preparation, did their best not to provoke the Japanese.

On the night of 18 September Lieutenant Kawamoto Suemori and seven or eight subordinates of his in the Railway Garrison managed to detonate explosives placed on the railway-line at Liutiaokou near Mukden. The explosion was designed to overturn an express train that was to come through twenty minutes later, but the damage was comparatively slight so that the train somehow passed the point, helped by acceleration on a downhill slope. Lieutenant Kawamoto started shooting in the direction of the Main North Barracks of Chang Hsueh-liang's Mukden army, which was only a few hundred metres from the site of the explosion, while one of his men reported back that 'the Chinese soldiers from the Main North Barracks blew up the railway line; we are engaged in a shooting battle with them'. The Japanese consul at Mukden, Morishima Morito, hurried to see Itagaki to urge him to settle the matter by peaceful means, but the latter told the consul not to interfere with the military command. The Chinese barracks were bombarded by artillery fire, and the Chinese troops in Mukden were under attack by a Japanese infantry regiment, as scheduled in the plan of action. Chang had advised his troops not to resist. Mukden fell overnight. What was to develop into a fifteen-year war had now began, evidently as designed. Moreover, most Japanese believed the story they were told as to the cause of the 9.18 Incident, that Chang's troops had blown up the railway-line.

Nitobe Inazo, the author of *Bushido: The Soul of Japan* (1900, revised in 1905), a book that aimed to vindicate Japan's martial spirit, formerly one of the five under-secretaries-general of the League of Nations and a member of the House of Peers, was one of those who believed the Kwantung Army's version of the incident. He attended the Shanghai

---

[43] Nish, *Japan's Struggle with Internationalism*, 26; *Tokyo Asahi Shinbun*, 4 July 1931.

conference of the Institute of Pacific Relations held in October 1931, 'a League of Nations meeting of people' as it was called. He blamed the Chinese for the 9.18 Incident, and emphasized the importance of 'a correct mutual understanding between China and Japan'. When a Chinese delegate stood up and criticized Japan for her extraterritorial holdings in Manchuria and for her militaristic and expansionist designs, Nitobe retorted by saying that such insinuations were insulting and would damage the conference; he extorted an apology from the Chinese delegate.[44] Soon he was to be found across the Pacific, lecturing to the Americans and refuting their criticisms of Japanese aggression in China.

Whether the emperor knew the truth behind the 'Incident' is not known. His post-war 'Monologue', however, does refer to 'an incident' in Manchuria: 'Manchuria is provincial and it does not matter if an incident takes place there,' he said, 'whereas an incident in Tientsin or Beijing would invite intervention by Britain and the United States and might lead to a military confrontation with us.' His view of the Incident apparently was not very different from Nitobe's.

FROM THE ESTABLISHMENT OF 'MANCHUKUO' TO THE CHINA INCIDENT OF JULY 1937

In order to occupy all of Manchuria as planned, the Kwantung Army had to move its troops outside the treaty zone along the South Manchurian Railway lines. One of the plots they had concocted was to provoke disturbances in northern Manchuria in which Captain Amakasu, notorious for the murder of Osugi, was involved. It was in this fashion that the plotters finally persuaded Commander Honjo to advance troops to Kirin. Attempts were made to bomb Kirin and Harbin to terrorize Japanese residents as an excuse for moving in troops. Hayashi Senjuro, the commander of the Korean Army, ignoring the general staff, sent an army division across the border into Manchuria. The Wakatsuki government announced its policy of limiting military action, but soon Chinchou in Jehol was bombed and Tsitsihar in northern Manchuria was occupied. Ishihara himself boarded one of the five aircraft captured from the Chinese and personally led the air-raid on Chinchou on 8 October. The bombing of Chinchou, a city in Jehol close to north China, alarmed foreign opinion. Kanaya Norizo, then chief of the general staff, obtained an imperial order commanding Japanese troops to withdraw from Chinchou, which they had occupied. The young officers had become aggressive and self-assertive, but they had to obey the order from the emperor.[45]

---

[44] E. Uchhikawa, *Nitobe Inazo: The Twilight Years*, tr. M. Newton (Tokyo, 1985), 91.
[45] Shidehara, op. cit., 179.

In December 1931 the Wakatsuki cabinet fell, and the new cabinet led by premier Inukai Tsuyoshi of the *Seiyukai* party reversed the policy of Shidehara diplomacy and accepted the occupation of Manchuria as a *fait accompli*. Chinchou fell in January 1932; Harbin in February. Premier Inukai, a member of the Diet from its beginning in 1890 till his death, had had strained relations with the army after the disclosure that he had sent a secret emissary to Chiang Kai-shek to explore the possibilities of a peaceful solution of the Manchurian Incident. On 15 May 1932 nine uniformed army and navy officers came to his official residence and one of them shot him dead.[46]

The Kwantung Army moved quickly to consolidate their newly expanded position. As early as 22 September 1931 the chief of the general staff (General Kanaya) and others agreed on a plan to establish a nominally Chinese administration headed by Henry Pu-yi, the heir of the Manchu dynasty and the last emperor of China, 'a pure puppet government',[47] in which Japan was to control defence, foreign affairs, and transport facilities. Pu-yi allowed himself to be abducted from Tientsin late in November, hoping for the restoration of his Manchu dynasty, and on 1 March 1932 the new state of Manchukuo was set up with Pu-yi as provisional president, later emperor. Manchukuo was placed under army control and became a forward base for Japan's expansion on the Chinese continent.

The anti-Japanese protest movement in China took the form of boycotting Japanese goods, and it was carried out most systematically in Shanghai, the greatest trading city in China. A Japanese officer, an aide to the military attaché in Shanghai, planned an incident to divert western attention from Manchukuo, and staged an assault on Japanese Buddhist priests in Shanghai which was used as a pretext for an attack on a Shanghai factory, the major centre of the anti-Japanese boycott movement. This was in January 1932. The navy took advantage of the situation, and a naval brigade was landed in Shanghai. A stalemate ensued, however. The Ninth, then Eleventh and Fourteenth Divisions were sent from Japan to break the fierce resistance put up by the Chinese Nineteenth Route Army. Finally, with British-American intervention, a truce was agreed upon in May.

In Manchuria a new situation was developing which finally removed Ishihara from positions of responsibility. The new Kwantung Army commander, General Muto, and his chief of staff, Koiso Kuniaki, the future wartime prime minister, were unsympathetic to Ishihara's visions about Manchuria and war and he was ordered to return home. He found himself working temporarily for the Foreign Ministry in the autumn of 1932,

[46] Robert Butow, *Tojo and the Coming of the War* (Princeton, 1961), 55; Yoshitake Oka, 'Inukai Tsuyoshi', in *Five Political Leaders of Modern Japan* (Tokyo, 1986), 172–3.
[47] Iyenaga, *Japan's Last War* (Oxford, 1979), 63.

when he joined the Japanese delegation to the League of Nations and exerted pressure so that Matsuoka Yosuke, the chief representative, would not give in on the issue of Manchuria. Probably Matsuoka did not need such pressure. In February 1933 the League of Nations Assembly adopted by forty-two votes to one a resolution disapproving Japan's control of Manchuria. Matsuoka Yosuke led his delegation out of the assembly hall in protest, and in March Japan formally withdrew from the League. The Lytton Report on Manchuria adopted by the League, however, was a moderate document. It affirmed that the Manchu government was not the result of a Manchu movement for independence but was formed by the Japanese army and Japanese bureaucrats, civil and military. While recommending an autonomous government under Chinese sovereignty, it also recognized Japan's special interest in Manchuria. The League apparently sought to avoid an open breach with Japan.[48] The Soviet Union, too, chose to avoid a clash when Japan advanced her troops into northern Manchuria, the Russian sphere of influence, and sold the Russian-controlled Chinese Eastern Railway to Manchukuo in March 1935, an act construed as Soviet recognition of the puppet state.[49] Thus the Manchurian Incident was a great success for its planners. They now expanded their operations into Mongolia and North China.

As for Ishihara, he was soon involved in the conflict between the Imperial Way Faction and the Control Faction within the army, for he had many ideas in common with the former, while he had friends among the latter, one of these being the murdered Nagata Tetsuzan. He repudiated the use of force by the young officers at the time of the 26 February Incident. Although he was promoted to the rank of major-general in March 1937, he continued to be an irritant in the eyes of the generals of the Control Faction in power. He was finally placed on the retirement list in March 1941.

The old hostility of Konoe to the Versailles system and 'the Anglo-American centred peace' persisted, and he advocated war to destroy the status quo.[50] In 1933 he wrote an article, 'Improving Our World', in which he said that Japan had been placed in the position of a defendant tried before an international court in the name of world peace. The international distribution of land was such that 'we had no choice but to advance into Manchuria and Mongolia'.[51] The time was soon coming when he would lead the nation to the brink of war.

---

[48] Naomi Nakamura, *et. al.* (eds.), op cit., ii. 135–6; Nish, *Japan's Struggle*, 179.

[49] I owe this reference to Mr Chen Shongoin who kindly translated for my use a relevant section in Professor He Hunchao's book, *Forming of New Hotbeds of War* (in Chinese), 1986. See also Nish, *Japan's Struggle*, 88.

[50] Konoe in *Nippon and Nipponjin* (Japan and the Japanese), 15 Dec. 1918.

[51] Oka, *Konoe Fumimaro*, 27–8.

The international status quo was breaking up. At the London Naval Disarmament Conference which began in December 1935 the Japanese delegation, who had insisted upon absolute parity with Britain and the United States, walked out and notified the other parties that Japan would not renew either the Washington or the London Naval Disarmament treaties at their expiration in December 1936, thus initiating an era of uncontrolled naval expansion. The Versailles–Washington system had finally collapsed, obviously to Konoe's satisfaction.

In January 1933 the Kwantung Army had occupied Shankaikan, the gateway to North China, and advanced into the province of Jehol which was soon incorporated into Manchukuo. As early as November 1935 an East Hopei Autonomous Anti-Communist Council was set up at Tungchow, headed by Yin Ju-keng, a puppet of the Japanese army. Political manoeuvring and flagrant disregard of Chinese sovereignty continued. By April 1936 Inner Mongolia had come under the Japanese sphere of influence. Attention was now focused on North China. Simmering conflicts flared into full-scale war on 7 July 1937, the immediate cause of which was a clash between Japanese and Chinese forces at the Marco Polo Bridge (Lukouch'iao). Japanese troops engaged in night manoeuvres that evening, under the pretext that they had been attacked by Chinese garrison troops, demanded to make a search for one allegedly missing soldier, and the Chinese refused the search on the ground that the manoeuvres had not been announced beforehand and were illegal, or at least irregular. After further negotiation the Chinese agreed to a joint investigation, but fighting flared up. A truce was negotiated and the withdrawal of troops on both sides began. A Japanese detachment of about 100 men who remained in the area started firing at midnight of 9 July, apparently for no reason, and within three days the number of men involved had reached 20,000, with air cover and support from 100 aircraft. The Kwantung Army appeared on the scene, and there was the danger of the clash escalating into a full-scale war.[52] Konoe, prime minister since June 1937, unsure of himself, was vacillating, but his cabinet expanded the conflict by sending three more divisions to North China. This was a fresh provocation which only made the situation worse. On 28 July Konoe told the Diet that his government was determined to establish a 'new order' in East Asia. The second Shanghai Incident took place in August, more troops were sent in, and the fighting spread across China without either side declaring war. The Japanese government called it 'the China Incident' (earlier it had been the North China Incident). In November 1937 a supreme war council (*dai honei*) was set up to co-ordinate the army and navy general staffs and to prepare for an expanding war.

[52] Butow, op. cit., 94–5.

THE DEVELOPMENT OF THE WAR
AND THE NANKING MASSACRE

In North China the Japanese army marched southwards and crossed the Yellow River. In Central China Japanese forces drove forward to occupy the capital, Nanking, which fell on 13 December 1937. All through the autumn Japanese forces had been pressing on towards the city. Ishikawa Tatsuzo, the army reporter for the magazine *Chuo Koron*, in his proscribed writing *Ikiteiru Heitai* (Living Soldiers) based on interviews he had conducted with Japanese soldiers shortly after the fall of Nanking, described the state of mind and behaviour of these men before they reached the city. As the troops advanced, he wrote, the number of living soldiers decreased, and the number of those who carried a white box containing the bones of a dead comrade doubled. 'Indeed, this was the march of the soldiers who yet remained alive'. (One recalls the name of the society Kitta Ikki founded, *Yuzonsha*, the Society of Those Who Still Remain.) 'They felt a certain familiarity, a closeness to the bones. . . . They may have been living bones. Thus the dead soldiers and the living solders, hand in hand, closed in upon Nanking.'[53] Nanking fell and atrocities of an unspeakable nature, know as 'the Rape of Nanking', began.

The massacre started immediately after the entry of the Japanese army on 13 December 1937 and went on well into January. Documents and evidence were prepared by an international committee which remained in Nanking even after five American journalists had been ordered to leave the city on 15 December. Twenty-two doctors and missionaries, mostly foreigners (German, American, British), of the two international committees, the Nanking International Safety Zone Committee and the International Red Cross Nanking Committee, did all they could to help refugees under extremely difficult conditions.[54] They, as well as the expelled journalists, told a horrible story of mass murder. Tens of thousands of Chinese were massacred; women were raped; stores and homes were plundered and burned. On Christmas Eve the American director of the Nanking Refugee Committee wrote: '. . . But to have to stand by while . . . thousands of disarmed soldiers who had sought sanctuary with you, together with many hundreds of innocent civilians, are taken out before your eyes to be shot or used for bayonet practice and you have to listen to the sound of the guns that are killing them; and while a thousand women kneel before you crying hysterically, begging you to save them from the beasts who are preying on them . . . this is a hell I had never before envisaged.'[55]

---

[53] The first part, heavily censored, was published in the *Chuo Koron* (Mar. 1938). A complete edition came out in 1945.

[54] Fujiwara Akira, *Nankin Daigyakusatsu* (The Nanking Massacre) (Tokyo, 1988), 10.

[55] Quoted in Meirion and Susie Harries, *Soldiers of the Sun* (New York, 1991), 222–3.

One of the major causes for these atrocities was that the Japanese army had decided not to apply to China the international law on war, including the Geneva Convention on the treatment of prisoners of war of which Japan was a signatory, for the hypocritical reason that war had not been declared against China and therefore all battles were mere 'incidents' in what they still chose to call the China Incident. Partly for economic reasons, moreover, it was decided at the top of the military command at the time of the siege of Nanking not to take prisoners but to 'dispose' of them, which meant killing them all. Not only were the Chinese soldiers who had fled into the city murdered; even civilians whose hair bore the ring of a tight hat or whose hands were calloused were suspected of being soldiers and shot. Tens of thousands of women were raped. One recent study of the subject emphasizes 'a lack of moral sense', an 'insistence on hierarchy', male chauvinism, 'physical brutalization', and 'indiscipline' in the army.[56] Fujiwara Akira criticizes the Japanese army, of which he was once an officer, for the absence of the idea of human rights and self-respect for a soldier, and for the extreme rigour and severity of discipline and punishment. Military discipline was maintained by brute force, the final victims of which were prisoners of war and powerless civilians in the occupied zone. Fujiwara cites 'irrational martial spirit' as the second peculiarity of the Japanese army, which extolled the spirit of the 'human bullet' and regarded being taken prisoner as shameful and worse than death. Insubordination and indiscipline in the army encouraged hardliners, and it was Lt.-Colonel Cho Isamu, staff officer, who gave the order to kill the prisoners *en masse* against the intention of the general commander Matsui Iwane.[57] Fujiwara himself estimates the number of the victims of the Nanking atrocities at 200,000 on the basis of available evidence, which happens to be near the figure reached at the Far Eastern Military Tribunal. In post-war Japan there has been a tendency among 'new nationalists' to belittle the magnitude and significance of the atrocities, but Ishikawa Tatsuzo, on the other hand, has given an account of ordinary Japanese soldiers as capable of diabolical acts of that magnitude in his censored report.

By September 1937 the Japanese navy had imposed a complete blockade of the whole Chinese coast except for Hong Kong and several coastal ports. On 12 December, one day before the fall of Nanking, Japanese shore batteries fired at the British gunboats *Ladybird* and *Bee* on the Yangtze, causing damage to the former. On the same day a flight of Japanese naval aircraft bombed and sank the American gunboat *Panay* and three Standard Oil tankers on the Yangtze not far from Nanking. The

[56] Ibid. 478–84.   [57] Fujiwara, op. cit., 53–5.

Japanese government at once sent apologies, which did little to mitigate the acute tension between Japan and Britain and the United States.[58]

The Nationalist government withdrew to Chungking and continued its resistance. In October 1938 Japanese army units were landed in South China and occupied Canton; other troops seized three Wuhan cities in the same month. The Japanese government began negotiations with Wang Ching-wei, a prominent Kuomintang politician who had defected from Chungking, hoping to set up a neutral zone. Konoe, corresponding with him, issued a statement in which he said that, together with far-sighted Chinese who shared Japan's ideals, his government would strive for the establishment of 'a New Order in East Asia'.[59] This led to the formation of a government headed by Wang in Nanking in March 1940, but Japan's increasingly harsh demands over peace terms made Wang's political future difficult and precarious. In spite of the appearance of a victorious war, the Japanese army was able to control only major cities and railroad-lines, and its authority failed to penetrate the interior.

PRINCE KONOE AS PRIME MINISTER

Prince Konoe was 45 years old in June 1937 when he was recommended to the premiership by Saionji, the only *genro* surviving from Meiji. (Depletion of *genro* had induced Saionji to introduce slight modification in the method of recommending a prime minister to the emperor by asking the Lord Keeper of the Privy Seal to act as an intermediary, and a small circle around the emperor, including the minister of the Imperial Household, also took part in deliberations.) Saionji knew that it had become extremely difficult to find a candidate for the premiership who could restrain military interference in government; although he did not have full confidence in Konoe, he felt that he might be better qualified than others in keeping an effective brake on the military.

Konoe Fumimaro, the direct descendant of Fujiwarano Kamatari, the seventh-century founder of the house of regents and the son of Atsumaro, the very active nationalist peer, had gone through a period of financial difficulties after his father's death, a circumstance which made him suspect the very wealthy. In fact, he came to study under Kawakami Hajime in Kyoto Imperial University and, while in Kyoto, translated Oscar Wilde's *The Soul of Man Under Socialism* into Japanese. His sympathies, however, were closer to the Imperial Way faction in the army and idealistic rightists than to socialists. His objection to the Versailles system, which we have

[58] Arthur J. Marder, *Old Friends, New Enemies: The Royal Navy and the Imperial Navy, Strategic Illusions, 1936–1941* (Oxford 1981), 20.

[59] Oka, *Konoe Fumimaro, A Political Biography*, tr. Shumpei Okamoto and Patricia Murray (Tokyo, 1983), 82.

already noted, provided the keynote of his mature political views. He was not a strong man. His 'diary shows a privately dejected uncertain Konoe', wrote his biographer, 'behind the façade of the firm confident prime minister who had addressed China so uncompromisingly.[60]

Japan's war aims were more or less clearly stated in the peace terms offered to Chiang Kai-shek: the retention of Manchuria and the stationing of troops in China for defensive action against communism or the Soviet Union—in short, the war seemed very much like 'a preemptive strike against communism'.[61] At a meeting attended by Konoe and others close to the emperor, Lt.-Colonel Suzuki Teiichi, later a cabinet member, stated: 'There are absolute enemies and relative enemies. A country like the USSR, which will attempt to destroy our national polity is an absolute enemy.'[62] Chiang, supposedly a relative enemy, however, agreed to form a united front with his former enemy the communists in order to fight Japanese aggression, though he himself secretly harboured a plan to fight against the communists as he had done in 1927–8, apparently with Japanese support.

Britain and America responded to Japan's aggression in China with the same policy of appeasement as they adopted in Europe. They avoided any resolute action, and Britain went so far as to comply with a Japanese request to close, though temporarily, the Burma Road, the supply route for Chungking, in July 1940.

Japan was quickly drawn into the noisy but ineffective Fascist International—the Anti-Comintern Pact between Germany and Japan in November 1936, to which Italy was added in 1937 and Spain in 1939. Then the Nazi–Soviet Pact allowed Germany to attack Poland; England and France went to war with Hitler's Germany in September 1939; after a period of relative inaction called the 'phony war', Germany achieved its blitzkrieg victory over France, driving the British out of the Continent. Bewitched by the German achievements, the Japanese army favoured an alliance with Germany and Italy. The cabinet led by Admiral Yonai Mitsumasa, then in office, was opposed to this and was overthrown.[63] Then, in September 1940, the second Konoe cabinet concluded the Tripartite Alliance, which linked the Japanese army with Hitler's Germany and Mussolini's Italy. This new alignment allowed Japan to move closer to a military showdown with the anti-fascist capitalist democracies and also with Russia. In fact, the German conquest in Europe jeopardized the presence of the colonial powers, France and Holland above all, in South-East Asia (Indochina and Indonesia in particular).

---

[60] Ibid. 61.   [61] Iyenaga, op. cit., 75.

[62] Entry for 18 April 1939, *Kido Koichi Nikki* (Diary), vol. 1 (Tokyo, 1966), 232.

[63] Konoe had been out of office since the beginning of 1939 and was succeeded as prime minister by Hiranuma Kiichiro (Jan.–Aug. 1939), Abe Nobuyuki (Aug. 1939–Jan. 1940), and Yonai (Jan.–July 1940) before returning to power.

A National Mobilization Bill had been passed in April 1938, and state control of electricity and other measures of industrial reorganization were introduced. Under the second Konoe cabinet (July 1940–July 1941) an Association to Assist the Emperor's Rule (*Taisei Yokusan-kai*) was set up in October 1940, but Konoe sought to avoid the pitfall of creating a one-nation, one-party system, which seemed to him 'another Bakufu'.[64] His second cabinet had Tojo Hideki as the minister of the army—Konoe liked Tojo's demanding personality, the opposite of his own—and Matsuoka Yosuke as the minister of foreign affairs, whose appointment was commended by the army. On 1 August 1940 the Konoe cabinet announced the Outline of a Basic National Policy in which the urgency of creating a strong national defence state was stressed, and the ideal of *hakko ichiu* (making the whole world one house) was held up as Japan's basic goal, the first step for which was to build up a 'new order' in Greater East Asia based on the solidarity of Japan, Manchukuo, and China. On the day the Outline was announced, Matsuoka issued a statement emphasizing Japan's mission to proclaim the Imperial Way throughout the world, the immediate aim of Japan's foreign policy being the establishment of a 'Greater East Asia Co-Prosperity Sphere' including both French Indochina and the Dutch East Indies. A new term was coined and began to be widely circulated.

The composition of the second Konoe cabinet gave a foretaste of what was soon to come. It consisted of Konoe's coterie, the 'reformist bureaucrats', and the army group (the Control Faction). The former was represented by Kazami Akira, minister of justice, who led Konoe's semi-fascist movement for *shintaisei* (new system) which ended up in an inflated form as the Association to Assist the Emperor's Rule mentioned above, though originally it had been intended to restrain the army so as to 'settle' the war with China. The army group was headed by Tojo and supported by people like Hoshino Naoki, minister of state and economic planner for Manchukuo and wartime Japan. Matsuoka, the foreign minister, was hovering between the two. He was an uncompromising opportunist, who borrowed many ideas from Hitler's Germany and mixed them with the demands of the army, especially of its Imperial Way Faction. We see some basic similarities between Kita Ikki's *Outline* and Konoe's essay against the Versailles system. Ishihara Kanji and Utsunomiya Taro had similar ideas.

Indeed, these ideas and aspirations hark back to Sato Nobuhiro and his *Kondo Hisaku* of 1823, in which he outlined an expanded Japan. Japan's expansionism seems to have had much to do with the insular nature of the country, both physical and cultural. Isolationism, once officially enforced,

---

[64] Oka, *Konoe Fumimaro*, 95.

did not mean stagnation; it was a protective measure of a proud nation. The avidity and eclecticism with which Japan had absorbed western influences also contributed to maintaining her insularity, reinforcing the Japan-centred view of world order. In fact, expansionism had almost become the second nature of an insular nation: naked aggression and aggressive wars had begun.

14

From Pearl Harbor to Hiroshima

THE 'ABJECT SLIDE' INTO WAR

In emphasizing Japan's effort in the summer of 1941 to come to terms with the Unites States while pursuing her aim of setting up a new order in East Asia, Iriye Akira has stated that her policy was 'more opportunistic than dogmatic, and more ambiguous than systematic'. The indecisiveness which Iriye attributes to 'Japan's continued reliance on external events as a guide to policy as well as its inability to achieve anything through its own initiative'[1] can also be discerned in 'the abject slide' into the war[2] and the more abject way in which the war ended. Takagi Sokichi, naval historian and formerly rear-admiral of the Imperial Navy, wrote: 'What I feel strongly about the Pacific War is the inaction, passivity, and insensibility on the part of the politicians and the military men who assumed the highest responsibility for the war.' 'The conspicuous fact about staff-officers and junior commanders', he declares, 'is the hardening of their spiritual arteries, while the extent of arbitrariness and the lack of objectivity in the judgement of situations made by the imperial headquarters, and the constant changes and absence of flexibility in their plans and systems, seem in retrospect appalling.'[3] Although the Pacific War was fought mainly against the Americans and the British, the shadow of Russia was present at all times; especially before its opening, and at its close, too, the Red Army inflicted heavy blows on Japanese forces in Manchuria. The frontier wars of the 1930s had been more than 'sideshows' to the later Asia-Pacific War; they illustrate the process of the 'abject slide' into the war.

FRONTIER WAR WITH RUSSIA

The Kwantung Army created in 1919 in the midst of the Siberian intervention regarded a Sino-Japanese war as a preliminary to war with the United States and/or the Soviet Union. The staff of this army was more or less convinced that Russia would not intervene in Manchuria, even in

[1] Akira Iriye, *Power and Culture: The Japanese–American War 1941–1945* (Cambridge, Mass., 1981), 13, 14.   [2] Ienaga, *Japan's Last War* (Oxford, 1979), 3.
[3] Sokichi Takagi, *Taiheiyo Kaisenshi* (Naval History of the Pacific War), p. ix.

Manchukuo, as she suffered from diplomatic isolation and internal power struggles. The Soviet Union even allowed Manchukuo to set up a consulate in Moscow.[4] Soviet troops remained north of the Amur River. The Soviet Union, however, was investing heavily in the Far East during the First and Second Five-Year Plans. In 1935, after considerable haggling over the price, the Russian Eastern Chinese Railway which extended 1,732 kilometres from Manchouli to Harbin and further east was sold to Manchukuo. After this the Kwantung Army went ahead with its own plan for general security for the state its leaders had created, notably by constructing road and railway networks connecting various fronts.

In 1933 the Soviet army began building *tochka* (ferro-concrete shelter) positions along the border. The Kwantung Army did the same, while expecting the first fighting to take place within the Russian territory along the border. The strength of the Kwantung Army was increased from 64,900 men in 1931 to 164,100 in 1935 and to 270,000 in 1939, while the strength of the Russian Far Eastern Forces in 1939 stood at 570,000.[5] A series of border incidents began with the clash of two patrols west of Lake Khanka in June 1935. The number of frontier disputes between 1936 and 1938 amounted to 431. In July 1938 a serious incident took place over the obscure but disputed hilltop called Changkufeng (Chokoho) in the Manchurian territory jutting south-east along the border between the Soviet Maritime State and Korea. The retaking of the hilltop that had been occupied by the Russians caused heavy casualties among the Japanese troops, but diplomatic negotiations ended the dispute without threatening intervention by the Kwantung Army.

A much more serious border conflict began in 1939 in West Manchuria, on the sparsely populated plateau south-east of Hilar town. There a 700-kilometre portion of the Manchukuo frontier ran along the eastern edge of the Mongolian People's Republic. The outbreak of the war in China two years before had attracted new attention to Outer Mongolia, which provided the 'Red military route' carrying aid to Nationalist China. Already in November 1934 the Mongolian People's Republic had concluded an agreement with the Soviet Union for reciprocal assistance in case of an attack on either party. The Kwantung Army continued to stir up trouble in an ethnically and religiously mixed district adjoining Inner Mongolia. The Twenty-third Japanese Division created in 1938 was one of the main forces involved in the Nomonhan Incident, which broke out in May 1939 in the disputed border area east of the Halha River. The ensuing battle had a disastrous outcome for the Kwantung Army and especially for the

---

[4] Jiang Niandong *et al. History of Puppet Manchukuo* (in Chinese) (Jilin, 1980), *passim*. I owe this reference to Mr Chan Zhonlin.

[5] Saburo Hayashi, *Taiheiyo-Senso-Rikusen-Gaishi* (An Outline History of the Land Warfare in the Pacific War) (Tokyo, 1951; 1994), 11–13.

Twenty-third Division which was virtually annihilated. The Japanese were not prepared for the enormous Russian offensive which took place in August under G. K. Zhukov. Russian artillery pounded anti-aircraft and machine-gun sites, and more than 150 bombers accompanied by hundreds of fighters attacked the Japanese lines in the first bomber-fighter offensive in Soviet airforce history.[6] Thousands of dead or severely wounded Japanese soldiers were abandoned. By 31 August Zhukov's forces had completed the last phase of their offensive, cleared the Japanese from the disputed zone, and won the undeclared war at Nomonhan.

The following day, on 1 September, the Germans invaded Poland and the Second World War began. The Soviet Union settled the matter of Nomonhan with the Japanese on 15 September, when foreign minister Molotov and ambassador Togo Shigenori signed a ceasefire agreement in Moscow, and then two days later Stalin claimed the spoils promised by the Germans by invading Poland. On 4 September the Japanese government of premier Abe had meekly announced that it had no intention of intervening in the European war but would concentrate on seeking a solution to the Chinese 'incident'. Signs of 'a solution' to the war in China were hard to detect, though, and Japanese committment to the establishment of a new order in East Asia incurred critical American reaction in the form of the abrogation of the US–Japanese commercial treaty which came into effect in January 1940, giving Americans the right to carry out economic sanctions against Japan.

FROM FRENCH INDOCHINA TO PEARL HARBOR

Japan's expansionist war in China was bound to develop into war with the United States, given the US imposition of an embargo on oil going to Japan. Oil had played a decisive role in the course of the war in China. For the years from 1935 to 1937 Japan's dependence on the United States for the supply of petroleum and crude oil amounted respectively to 2,310,000 kl, or 67 per cent of her total supply, and 3,530,000 kl, or 74 per cent. The situation evolved in such way that Japan had to find other sources of oil supply; one of the attractions of the Tripartite Alliance for Japan was to obtain the technology of synthetic oil production that had been developed in Germany, while German occupation of the Netherlands might allow Japan a free access to the Dutch East Indies and its oil. The Dutch and American oil embargo, adopted in the wake of Japan's military occupation of French Indochina, further drove Japan onto the warpath.[7]

---

[6] Alvin Coox, *Nomonhan: Japan Against Russia, 1939* (Stanford, 1985; pbk. edn. 1990), 663.

[7] Misuzushobo (ed.), *Gendaishi Shiryo* (Sources of Modern History), vol. 39 *Taiheiyo-senso* (Pacific War) (Tokyo, 1975). This contains a Japanese translation of the main items in the United States Strategic Bombing Survey, *The War Against Japanese Transportation, 1941–1945* (Transportation Division, May 1947).

The phoney war in Europe came to an end in April–May 1940, when the German army invaded Norway and Denmark and overran western Europe. The Dutch government was exiled to London, while the defeated French set up the collaborationist Vichy regime. The Japanese government at once expressed its concern about the future of the oil-rich Dutch East Indies and intensified its pressure on French Indochina to ensure cessation of aid for Chiang Kai-shek, while watching anxiously for signs of what the victorious Germans would expect from Japan. The Vichy government permitted the stationing of Japanese forces in northern Indochina, and on 23 September 1940 the first Japanese troops were sent there. Two days later the United States arranged a substantial loan to Chiang Kai-shek, and on the following day (26 September) she announced the prohibition of the export of scrap iron and steel to Japan (effective from 16 October). On 27 September the Tripartite Pact was signed in Berlin, binding Japan, Germany, and Italy to co-operate in setting up their respective new orders and to assist one another by using all political, economic, and military means available if one of the signatory nations was attacked by a power not yet involved in the European war or in the Sino-Japanese conflict; while the pact would also seek to preserve the political status quo between each of the signatories and the Soviet Union. The Tripartite Pact was clearly intended to restrain the United States, which had begun taking steps to help Britain, now engaged in an air-battle for survival, and China.

Prince Konoe, back as prime minister since July 1941, was more interested in the possible role of Germany in bringing about a Japanese–Soviet pact and also in mediating in the war with China than in the likelihood of the Tripartite Pact provoking war with the United States. Both the emperor and Saionji were apprehensive, and Konoe later admitted that it was because of pressure from the military that he went ahead with the pact.[8] Matsuoka, the foreign minister under Konoe, visited Berlin and Moscow in March–April 1941, hoping to persuade the Soviet Union to co-operate with the Tripartite Pact nations in the conquest of Britain, although he knew that German operations in the Balkans were causing friction with Moscow. Nevertheless, he concluded the Japanese–Soviet Neutrality Pact while in Moscow in April. The neutrality pact gave some satisfaction to the Russians, who felt threatened by the Germans, while it displeased the Germans, who were to begin the invasion of Russia in June.

In Washington, in April 1941, secretary of state Cordell Hull and ambassador Nomura Kichisaburo started formal negotiations on a Japanese–American draft understanding which included a proposition concerning the possible mediation by the US government in the war with China that would guarantee both the withdrawal of Japanese troops

---

[8] Yoshitake Oka, *Konoe Fumimaro* (Tokyo, 1983), 103–5.

from Chinese territory and the recognition of Manchukuo. Konoe and his cabinet, even the army minister Tojo, welcomed the draft understanding, but Matsuoka on his return from Europe strongly objected to the whole plan. He placed the Tripartite Pact in the centre of his diplomacy and even insisted on the United States having nothing to do with the Chinese issues. He also stressed the need to prevent the Americans joining in the European war against Hitler.[9] The draft understanding was revised and altered by Matsuoka out of all recognition.

The American government had made its own position clear in the draft understanding's emphasis on mutual respect for sovereignty and territorial integrity, which Konoe had himself avowed as his own position. There was no way to reconcile the Matsuoka version and the American position. When the news of the German–Soviet war came, Matsuoka urged that Japan should attack the Soviet Union at once in concert with Germany and should suspend the Indochina operation that had been decided on earlier in June. At an Imperial Headquarters–Cabinet Liaison conference at which the foreign minister made a proposal for an attack on Russia, he was voted down (the anti-Comintern pact was kept intact). At the Imperial Conference on 2 July it was decided not to intervene in the German–Soviet war, though Japan might take advantage of the situation later to settle the northern problem and, more importantly, to risk a war with Britain and the United States in order to advance south. According to the new policy now adopted towards Russia, Imperial Headquarters began reinforcing the Kwantung Army by a secret plan called the 'Kwantung Army Special Manoeuvring', which increased its strength from 400,000 to 700,000 men.

In spite of the enormous strengthening of the military in Manchuria, a greater emphasis was placed on Japan's relationship with the United States. In order to get rid of Matsuoka, who had proved to be a stumbling-block in the negotiations with America, the Konoe cabinet resigned and Konoe himself formed his third cabinet on 18 July with new foreign minister, Admiral Toyoda, who was against war with the United States. On 28 July, shortly after the formation of the new cabinet, however, Japanese forces occupied southern French Indochina (northern Indochina had been under Japanese occupation since September 1940). On the same day the Dutch responded to the Japanese threat by restricting oil exports to Japan. Three days earlier, on 25 July, the US government, having been warned beforehand of the southern advance of the Japanese army, had taken steps to freeze all Japanese assets in the United States, and the British and the Dutch now followed suit. On 1 August the US government imposed an

---

[9] Nihon Kokusai Seiji Gakkai (Japanese Association for the Study of International Politics) (ed.), *Taiheiyo Senso Eno Michi* (The Road to the Pacific War) (Tokyo, 1963), vii. 178.

embargo on oil exports to Japan, who at this time depended on America for more than 80 per cent of imported oil. If economic sanctions continued Japan would soon run out of the war materials, especially oil, needed for 'a solution' in China.

The Imperial Conference held on 6 September adopted an action programme which stated that war preparations should be completed by the latter part of October, with the determination not to avoid war against the United States. Emperor Hirohito, who had been shown the agenda of this conference the day before by Konoe, was greatly disturbed. 'This was unexpected,' he is recorded to have said, 'because war was the main topic and negotiations secondary. I asked Konoe to alter the agenda so as to place the main emphasis on negotiations. Konoe said that was impossible, but he may have had second thoughts for he came to me the following morning and asked me to advise members to proceed with peace in mind. So [at the conference] I read out a song by the Meiji emperor which read: "Why do strong winds blow and heavy seas rage when all the seas around seem to be brothers".'[10] The emperor's pathetic effort to preserve peace did not have the desired effect, and negotiations with the United States came to a deadlock over 'a solution' to the China war. Japan even suggested 'co-operation between Japan and China for the purposes of preventing communistic and other subversive activities'.[11] The Americans demanded that Japan should withdraw her troops from China. On 12 October Konoe called a meeting at his villa in Ogikubo, Tokyo, attended by the army, navy, and foreign ministers (Tojo Hideki, Oikawa Koshiro, and Toyoda Teijiro respectively), and a cabinet planning board president, at which it became clear that the army would not make any concessions. Two days later Konoe directly appealed to Tojo to reconsider the army's stand on troops in China. Konoe felt that, he could not commit Japan to another major war and was inclined to accept the American demands, though temporarily: Japan should 'retreat a little and recoup [her] energy'. 'You are too pessimistic', was Tojo's reply. In view of the army's commitment to war with America and the navy's refusal to come out in opposition to the war (in which it had no confidence), Konoe decided to resign.[12] On 18 October 1941 army minister Tojo Hideki replaced Konoe as premier. The die was cast, as Tojo was in principle opposed to all compromise plans.

Tojo Hideki was born into a family which combined the traditions of Noh drama, Buddhist priesthood, and military service. At the beginning of the turbulent 1930s he was comparatively little known, and it was only

[10] 'Showa Emperor's Monologue', *Bungei Shunju*, Dec. 1990; Hosoya Chihiro (ed.), *Nichibei Kankei Tsushi* (Tokyo, 1995), 145–6.
[11] Joseph C. Grew, *Ten Years in Japan* (New York, 1944), 434.
[12] Oka, *Konoe Fumimaro*, 154–9.

after a number of senior officers of the Imperial Way Faction were placed on the reserve list in the wake of the abortive *coup d'état* of February 1936 that opportunities were open for junior generals like Tojo to move into top positions at the centre of the army.[13] At that time he was in charge of the military police of the Kwantung Army in Manchuria, and took a strict, legalistic attitude towards those who showed sympathy with the attempted coup. He soon became chief of staff of the same army. At the time of the China Incident of July 1937 Tojo led Kwantung Army brigades in a flanking action behind the Chinese. When Lt.-General Itagaki of Manchurian Incident fame became war minister in a reshuffle of the first Konoe cabinet in June 1938, Tojo was recalled from field service to become vice-minister under him. In the second Konoe cabinet, formed in July 1940, Tojo was appointed war minister. His selection, some said, had been due to the 'paucity of suitable candidates at the time'.[14]

The US ambassador Joseph Grew, however, took a benign view of the new government in the hope of avoiding armed conflict between the two countries; he felt it was 'premature' 'to stigmatize the Tojo government as a military dictatorship, and even expected that Tojo, the first prime minister retaining his active rank in the army, would 'exercise a larger degree of control over army extremist groups'.[15] Ambassador Grew was soon disenchanted with the new government, though. The Imperial Headquarters–Cabinet Liaison Conference, which had first come into existence shortly after the outbreak of the China Incident in 1937 and was revived by Konoe in July 1940, now met several times to appraise possible events and situations in case of war in the south. At the Liaison Conference convened on 1 November two programmes prepared by foreign minister Togo Shigenori in the hope of avoiding war with the United States were hotly discussed, but both were bedevilled by the problem of the timing of withdrawing Japanese troops from China (Programme A, in which the period of stationing troops in China was reduced from ninety-nine years to twenty-five after a heated discussion) and from Indochina (Programme B), the latter being linked to a resumption of the American oil supply to Japan and an end to the freezing of Japanese assets. It was decided to continue diplomatic negotiations based on these programmes until 30 November, when a breakdown of negotiations would lead to war. This was a concession foreign minister Togo had exacted from the war party at the conference; 'it was unusual', recalled Togo, 'that Tojo supported me in this'.[16] These conclusions reached at the Liaison Conference were confirmed at the Imperial Con-

---

[13] Butow, *Tojo and the Coming of the War*, 69.   [14] Ibid., 144.
[15] Grew, op. cit., 460, entry for 20 Oct. 1941.
[16] Shigenori Togo, *Jidai no Ichimen* (One Aspect of the Time) (Tokyo, 1985), 224.

ference held on 5 November.[17] Even so, Programme B seemed more practical as it was a temporary draft agreement to gain time for further negotiations. On 26 November the American reply to this, known as the Hull Note, was handed by secretary of state Cordell Hull to the two Japanese negotiators, Admiral Nomura Kichizaburo, then ambassador to Washington, and Kurusu Saburo, a career diplomat.

The Hull Note urged the Japanese government to withdraw all army, navy, air, and police forces from China and Indochina in return for the cancellation of measures to freeze Japanese assets in the United States and the opening of negotiations for a new commercial treaty. At the Imperial Conference held on 1 December war against the United States, Britain, and the Netherlands was formally decided on. 'If I had suppressed the advocates of war at that stage', confessed Hirohito later, 'there would have been a *coup d'état* supported by public opinion as the trained army and navy would not have succumbed to demands from the USA without fighting. At the Imperial Conference held on 1 December . . . I did not utter a word because I knew it was futile to speak against it.'[18]

While last-minute negotiations in Washington were approaching a futile end, the Pearl Harbor strike force consisting of six-aircraft carriers, two battleships, two battle-cruisers, nine destroyers, and three submarines, with 350 aircraft, assembled at Hitokappu Bay on the island of Etorofu in the Kuriles by 22 November. On 26 November, when the news of the Hull Note and its severe American conditions for ending the war in the Far East arrived, the strike force headed for Hawaii. On the same day US President Roosevelt received the startling intelligence that Japan was preparing to start a war within ten days if her demands were not met; but an attack on Hawaii was regarded as unlikely, since the main Japanese attack was expected to be made on the Philippines.

In the early morning of Sunday 7 December 1941 carrier-based planes attacked the US Pacific Fleet at anchor in Pearl Harbor and destroyed most of it; four battleships were sunk and another four seriously damaged. American servicemen to the number of 2,403 were killed—over 1,000 of them lost in the blazing *Arizona*. Invasion of the Malay Peninsula began at the same time. The Imperial Rescript declaring war against the United States, Britain, and the Netherlands was not issued until 11 a.m. on 8 December (Tokyo time), several hours after the raid on Hawaii. The delay in its announcement is now explained as having been caused by negligence on the part of some of the embassy officials engaged in its translation. On

---

[17] Commenting on these programmes the historian Butow wrote: 'The same old jargon was brought into play, as if parrot-like utterances could conjure up a reality which did not in fact exist: . . . military force had been employed in the past out of Japan's love and desire for peace and security; the Japanese nation was sincere, all others were insincere.' Butow, op. cit., 326.

[18] *Bungei Shunju*, Dec. 1990.

9 December the Nationalist government at Chungking declared war against Japan, Germany and Italy. On 11 December Germany and Italy declared war against the United States. Japan's undeclared war against China, the hypocritically named 'China Incident', had by now developed into the Asia-Pacific War, and had dragged her into the European conflict of the Second World War.

How far was Japan prepared in practical terms for such an enormous undertaking? Naval vessels completed in 1941 amounted to 225,159 tons, and the accumulated figure of those added to the naval force in the course of the previous ten years reached 701,929 tons. A comparison of the Japanese and the US/Allied naval forces in the Pacific and East Asia at the time of the opening of the war gives the following figures: aircraft carriers: 9 and 7 respectively: battleships 10 and 19 (including 2 British); heavy cruisers 18 and 19 (including 1 British), light cruisers 20 and 29 (including 7 British and 3 Dutch); destroyers 112 and 228 (including 13 British, 7 Dutch, and 1 Free French); and submarines 64 and 127 (including 13 Dutch).[19] The battleship *Yamato*, 'the trump card of the Japanese navy', having a displacement of 64,000 tons and equipped with seven reconnaissance planes, was launched eight days after Pearl Harbor, though some of its level-firing guns had to be replaced by high-angle guns in 1943 in order to defend her from attack from the air.[20] The figure of tanks and other armoured vehicles produced in 1941 amounted to 2,446, while merchant ships to be used for war purposes came to 6 million tons. Her resources and military preparedness in the autumn of 1941 would allow Japan, as Admiral Yamamoto Isoroku admitted, to 'rage against the USA for at most one or one and a half years'.

JUBILATION SHORT-LIVED

Jubilation over the initial victories in the war against the Allies lasted only six months; then came a series of disasters that continued for more than three years and ended in a final catastrophe. Even the prediction made by Admiral Nagano Osami, chief of the naval staff, to the effect that Japan could fight effectively for two years but no longer, appeared to have been too optimistic.

The British Far East Squadron of two capital ships, *Prince of Wales* and *Repulse*, was destroyed off Malaya on 10 December 1941. Saito Mokichi, the venerable poet wrote: 'More victory news on the radio! I can't sit still, the excitement, the joy, aren't our men superb, divine heroes in action'.[21]

---

[19] Misuzushobo (ed.), op. cit., 804; Junichiro Kisaka, *Taiheiyo Senso* (The Pacific War), *Showano Rekishi* (History of Showa), vol. 7 (Tokyo, 1982), 37.
[20] Kiyoshi Ikeda, *Nihon no Kaigun* (The Japanese Navy), ii. 150.
[21] Quoted in Ienaga, op. cit., 142.

Hong Kong was occupied on 15 December; Manila fell into Japanese hands on 2 January 1942; Rabaul on New Britain was occupied on 23 January and Port Darwin in the Northern Territory of Australia was bombed on 19 February; Sumatra's oilfields were seized by paratroops on 15 February; Singapore fell on the same day, when the British force of nearly 100,000 men surrendered; Batavia (Djakarta) was occupied on 5 March, and the Dutch East Indian force of 93,000 men surrendered; Rangoon was captured on 8 March; American and Philippino resistance at Bataan and Coregidor ended on 27 May. General Douglas MacArthur, commander of the combined American and Philippino forces, having been ordered by President Roosevelt to leave the Philippines for Australia, handed over his command to General Wainwright, saying to him 'I shall return', the words received by his men 'with some skepticism'.[22] The American and Philippino resistance ended in the Bataan Death March, in which nearly 75,000 prisoners suffered exposure, starvation, disease, torture, and aimless killings with the result that almost 11,000 of them died on the road between Mariveles and San Fernando. A series of naval battles were fought around Java in February and March 1942 and resulted in the virtual annihilation of the Allied Fleet in this area. In April the mobile naval fleet attacked Columbo and Trincomalee and dealt a serious blow to British warships in the Indian Ocean by sinking a carrier and three cruisers.

The first stage of the war, which ended in May, was thus a great success: the mastery of air and sea seized by the Japanese navy and army allowed Japan to take full advantage of the initial unpreparedness of the Allies. The whole of the Dutch East Indies with their rich natural resources fell in Japanese hands, and outposts such as Rabaul were seized as bases for further advance. It was time to decide on the strategy for the second stage of the war, and this was the major issue at the Imperial Headquarters–Cabinet Liaison Conference held on 7 March 1942. Here it was decided to extend the victorious war so as to defeat Britain and discourage the United States, and to strengthen military capabilities by exploiting acquired resources for national defence and setting up an economic system of self-sufficiency (autarky).[23] The next plan considered was to secure strategically important spots in the areas outside the territories that had been acquired in the first stage of operations. The navy suggested the occupation of Australia which the army considered was beyond their logistic capacity. The strategic operations on which both the army and the navy agreed were those for eastern New Guinea, especially Port Moresby, Samoa, Fiji, and New Caledonia, and those for the Aleutians.

[22] Marion and Susan Harris, *Soldiers of the Sun* (New York, 1991), 315.
[23] Hayashi, op. cit., 65.

Both operations were of a defensive nature. The one for Samoa, Fiji, and New Caledonia was intended to sever the route that linked the United States and Australia and to prevent their setting up bases for a counter-offensive, but this plan was later given up because the critical strategic situation that emerged in the meantime made the operation impracticable. The one for the Aleutians aimed to limit the possibility of US–Soviet rapprochement in this quarter, and also to prevent the Americans building bases from which to invade the Japanese mainland.

The army command regarded the Pacific War as an extension of the Chinese war, and believed that the aim of the war in the Pacific was to settle the war in China. On 18 April 1942 sixteen US B.25 bombers raided Tokyo; two of these dropped incendiary bombs in Nagoya and one in Kobe. An aircraft-carrier docked at Yokosuka for rigging was also damaged. These bombers came from the aircraft carrier *Hornet* and flew on to air-bases in China. Now Imperial Headquarters determined to attack Chinese air-bases in Chekiang, Kiangsi, and Hunan and launched operations in these areas. It even ordered an operation against Chungking, the Nationalist capital, but this was set aside because of the seriousness of the battle for Guadalcanal.

HOME FRONT: THE *YOKUSAN* MOVEMENT AND WAR FASCISM

The Tojo government, confident of its popularity because of the initial victories in the Pacific war, embarked on a 'General Election to support the Great East Asia War' in April 1942. A special council set up to co-ordinate the election campaign for the government endorsed 466 candidates for the full number of Diet seats, but there were also 613 non-endorsed candidates. The result was the fiercest electoral battle ever fought under the current system of universal suffrage, accompanied by police intervention against opposition candidates, which no doubt helped bring about the high turnout of voters (83.1 per cent). The number of the non-endorsed candidates elected was eighty-five, and their aggregate poll was 34.9 per cent of the total, an index of the comparative unpopularity of Tojo and his government. In the course of the election a *Dainippon Yokusan Sonen-dan* (Greater Japan Adult Association to Assist [the Imperial Rule]) was formed, which succeeded in having over 40 members elected to the Diet. It attracted the middle strata of farmers and peasants as well as owners of small workshops in the towns and won a great victory in local elections, having 32,833 members elected to town and village councils in the same year.

Shortly after the general election the Tojo government set up a *Yokusan-Seijikai* (Political Association to Assist [the Imperial Rule]), which was joined by practically all the Diet members (only eight abstained), for all other political societies were dissolved at the time. The Diet system continued in name only, though one-party dictatorship by the Association itself existed only in name since it had soon split into ten factions, some of which were to challenge the Tojo leadership when the initial victories gave way to a long series of defeats and losses.[24] The Tojo government also allowed the *Taisei Yokusankai* (Association to Assist the Imperial Rule) to amalgamate under its umbrella six leading national *Hokoku* (Grateful Service to the State) organizations, the Industrial, the Agricultural, the Trading, the Shipping, the Youth, and the Women's associations. The neighbourhood associations and hamlet associations were placed under the direction of the *Yokusankai*, Home Ministry bureaucrats, and the police, and entrusted with the vital task of distributing foodstuffs and other essential household goods and of disseminating information and war propaganda. It was in this way that the whole nation was vertically as well as horizontally fastened together. The *Taisei Yokusankai* system, the standardized, coercive structure to control the people, was 'the ideal form of Japanese fascism aimed at carrying out the Great East Asia War'.[25]

The role played by women in this uniform, national system deserves special attention. The *Aikoku Fujinkai* (Patriotic Women's Association) set up in 1901 by upper-class women, maintained close connections with the imperial family. When it widened the scope of its activities as a national body, with the age groups 'maidens', 'girls', and 'women', it came into collision with the newer and more popular rival organization, the *Kokubo Fujinkai* (National Defence Women's Association), founded in 1932 with the support of the Ministry of War. This second organization declared itself devoted to the 'bringing up of sound sons and daughters', the 'safeguarding of the home front', and 'the expulsion of unsound thought', and grew rapidly, its membership reaching over 10 million by 1941. The Ministry of Education sponsored a third women's association, and in 1942 all three were united in the Great Japan Women's Association, with a huge membership of 19,310,000. It emphasized the 'traditional virtues of women in the imperial state to serve the high national defence state system'. Ichikawa Fusae, a pioneer feminist who had started a movement to promote women's suffrage in 1924, decided to join in the general mobilization of the nation under the *Yokusankai*, which she regarded as 'one way for women to participate in administration', and encouraged women to give birth to many children and to join in productive work alongside the men.[26]

[24] Masaomi Yui in *Nihon Tsushi* (Complete History of Japan), vol. 19 (Tokyo, 1995), 16–18.
[25] Yui in ibid. 18.
[26] For women's wartime co-operation, see Sheldon Garon, *Moulding Japanese Minds* (Princeton, 1997), 230 ff.

The Great Japan Industrial *Hokoku* Association had a similar record. It was set up in November 1940 by all the trade unions dissolved to take advantage of the *Yokusankai* movement. It aimed at 'the establishment of a new industrial-labour system as the basis of the high national defence state system', and extolled 'the enterprise as a family' and 'the organic unity of capital, management, and labour services'. It maintained that equality between capital and labour derived from equality before the emperor. A 'military unit system' was introduced in the summer of 1941 into each factory and workshop, with the result that special emphasis was placed upon obedience to superiors, work discipline, and joint responsibility (the workers were grouped into 'five-men units' at the lowest level of organization). The shortage of labour was met by an increase in conscript labourers and unpaid student workers, both male and female. In short, the Industrial *Hokoku* Association was a fascist labour body organizing the workers into a quasi-community of industry and labour, cemented by loyalty to the emperor and maintained by semi-military discipline.[27] The home front was thus tightened and regimented around the imperial rule.

MIDWAY AND GUADALCANAL

The turning of the tide had begun. Already in May 1942 a mobile naval force escorting fourteen troop-ships bound for Port Moresby and other destinations lost one carrier and had another seriously damaged in an engagement with a US mobile force in the Coral Sea; Port Moresby was never reached. Then the tide definitely turned. A Japanese attack on Midway Island blundered from the start. Crucial code messages had been deciphered by the Americans; the aim of the whole operation, whether to occupy the island or to destroy the enemy mobile fleet, remained unclear; and the American reconnaissance planes proved more effective than the Japanese. The main naval force led by Admiral Yamamoto Isoroku, commander-in-chief of the Combined Fleet, for some reason did not take part in the operation, being 555 km (some say 900 km away) from the scene of the naval battle. The First Mobile Fleet, led by Vice-Admiral Nagumo Chuichi, that was to attack Midway Island was an enormous fighting force with 150 ships including four major aircraft-carriers, over 1,000 planes, and nearly 10,000 men. (Nagumo was the commander of the mobile fleet which had brilliantly attacked Pearl Harbor six months before.) The fatal battle for Midway was fought on 5 June 1942, when the debacle of replacing torpedoes with bombs, then bombs with torpedoes for the aircraft only served as one indication of confused leadership. In the end the

---

[27] Yui, in *Nihon Tsushi*, xix. 19–21.

Japanese fleet lost four irreplaceable carriers in one day,[28] but these catastrophic losses were concealed from the public.

It has been argued that Japan was defeated in the second half of 1942 at Guadalcanal, the southernmost island in the chain of the Solomon Islands.[29] Early in March 1942 a force of *Rikusentai* (Marine Corps) landed on the northern tip of Bougainville, the northernmost island in the Solomon archipelago. Early in May another force of *Rikusentai* moved against Tulagi and Gavutu, the former British bases which face the island of Guadalcanal across the Sealark Channel. The garrison there was soon reinforced, and two 1,000-man labour battalions 'composed largely of Korean and Okinawan conscripts' arrived to construct port facilities. On 1 July 2,571 men of the labour battalions and 247 *Rikusentai* landed on the northern coast of Guadalcanal and began constructing an airfield. By 5 August a runway of 800 m in length and 60 m wide was all but completed. General Douglas MacArthur and Admiral Chester Nimitz, the top US army and navy commanders in the Pacific, felt that the time had come for an offensive strategy. The seizure of Guadalcanal before the completion of the airfield was given top priority. On the early morning of 7 August the US First Marine Division began its twin assaults: 11,000 marines landed on Guadalcanal and 6,000 on the island of Tulagi. The landing was supported by a formidable fleet including three aircraft-carriers, one battleship, and eleven heavy cruisers. Most of the Japanese garrison on Tulagi had perished by the following day, and those on Guadalcanal had to retreat behind the airfield. With this landing, the Pacific war entered its second stage, characterized by the Allied counter-offensive and the Japanese retreat.[30]

The staff of the Imperial Headquarters did not take the American landing on Guadalcanal seriously at first, and a force of 916 men on board six destroyers was sent and landed about 30 km east of the Henderson airfield (now so called by the Americans), but it was surrounded by US Marines equipped with tanks near the airfield and virtually annihilated. In the meantime sea battles were going on in the Solomon waters; in six major encounters from August 1942 to January 1943, Japan lost one aircraft-carrier, two battleships, two heavy cruisers, five destroyers, and 161 aircraft and received damage on three carriers, seven heavy cruisers, one light cruiser, and three destroyers, though the Allies also suffered heavy losses.[31] By the end of November 1942 Japan had lost the mastery of both air and sea in the Solomons, although the emperor, when he heard of an exaggerated report of one of the battles issued a statement

---

[28] Kiyoshi Ikeda (ed.), *Taiheiyo Senso* (The Pacific War) (Tokyo, 1995), 60–5; Junichiro Kisaka, *Taiheiyo Senso* (The Pacific War), 110–17.

[29] Eric Hammel, *Guadalcanal: Starvation Island* (New York, 1987), p. xxix.

[30] Junichiro Kisaka, op. cit., 120.   [31] Kisaka, op. cit., 126.

that he was 'glad of it'.[32] He was denied accurate knowledge of what taken place on the island.

Persistent attempts were made to retain it. A fleet of destroyers carrying 6,200 men arrived in Guadalcanal. The men made an assault on the American encampment built on a height south of the airfield, but their desperate bayonet charges were overcome by US heavy artillery with very heavy casualties.[33] They were virtually annihilated in the battle, and the following retreat was as calamitous as the battle itself. Imperial Headquarters then decided to send the picked troops of the Second (Sendai) Division, and moved the Thirty-eighth (Nagoya) Division stationed in Java to Guadalcanal. Early in October these troops landed west of the airfield. Their march through the jungle with heavy arms and ammunition was debilitating, and two assaults on the airfield later in the same month were almost suicidal before the overwhelming power of the American artillery, and they too retreated towards the hills and the jungle behind. By now the Henderson airfield had been reinforced with 100 aircraft, using three runways. The strength of the American soldiers had increased to 34,000 by the end of November. Imperial Headquarters threw in the main force of the Thirty-eighth Division; on paper this comprised 30,000 men, but those able to fight only numbered about 5,000. But Japan's real battle on the island was with starvation; it was a fearful war of attrition. Only on 31 December was the withdrawal from Guadalcanal decided upon at an Imperial Conference. Twenty destroyers were engaged in carrying 15,652 officers and soldiers away from the island early in February 1943. At the same time the Japanese forces in eastern New Guinea were also withdrawn to Lae in the northern region. Only 31 per cent of the original strength of 11,000 men returned. Of the Takasago (native Taiwanese) and the Korean volunteers, each 500 strong, 65 and 15 respectively returned alive. As for the 1,200 Melanesians enlisted and sent from Rabaul to New Guinea, there is no record of any who returned alive.[34]

'TENSHIN' AND THE 'ABSOLUTELY NECESSARY NATIONAL DEFENCE SPHERE'

The withdrawal of the defeated troops was called *Tenshin*, an 'advance in another direction'. In 1943 Japan stood on the defensive under difficult conditions along the northern coast of New Guinea and the Solomon and Bismarck Islands. Two islands in the Aleutians, Attu and Kisca, which Japanese army units had landed on in June 1942 were abandoned a year later. The Americans landed at Attu, and the Japanese garrison on the

---

[32] Kisaka, op. cit., 125.   [33] Ibid. 122; Hammel, op. cit., 228–36.
[34] Kisaka, op. cit., 134–5.

island, over 2,000 strong, fought to the death in May 1943. Those at Kisca returned home in safety. The Americans began their advance by hopping across the chain of Pacific islands from the south. The record of Japanese casualties on these islands is dreadful. In November 1943 3,000 marines and 1,500 non-military employees died on Makin Atholl and Tarawa Island in the Gilbert Islands; in February 1944 4,500 marines and 2,000 employees similarly died on Kwajalein and another island in the Marshall Islands; in the same month Japan's largest naval base in the Pacific, on Truk in the Marshall Islands, was attacked from the air; three cruisers, four destroyers, and thirty-two ships were sunk, and 270 aircraft destroyed.[35] At the Imperial Conference held on 30 September 1943 a contraction of the front was agreed upon in order to ensure the preservation of an 'absolutely necessary national defence sphere' which stretched from the Kurile Islands down to the Bonin Islands, to the western part of the mid-Pacific islands, western New Guinea, the Sunda Islands, then north to Burma. 'The sphere' simply meant the furthest areas Japan was able to hold at that time.

The Japanese navy received a mortal blow in the battle off the Mariana Islands in June 1944, when the First Mobile Fleet suffered heavy damage, and the loss of over 320 aircraft and three aircraft-carriers. Japan had now lost whatever strength in the air she had had in the Pacific. The island of Saipan, the stronghold in the Mariana Islands, fell in July 1944, Japanese civilian residents having been urged or even forced to commit suicide by throwing themselves from a high cliff. The garrison of 30,000 troops and 1,000 Japanese residents fought to the death or killed themselves, with only a small number surviving as prisoners of war. The loss of Saipan gave the Americans airforce bases from which to begin direct bombing of the main Japanese islands.

THE BURMA FRONT

The Burma campaign itself represented the contradictory nature of the Pacific conflict, in trying to cut the supply route to Nationalist China, an operation aimed at finding a 'solution' to the China war, which led to an enormous expansion of the theatre of war. This war to settle the war resulted in a war of aggression on a vast scale, and in which Burmese and Indian nationalist hopes were flattered and encouraged, then finally betrayed.

Japanese infiltration of the Burmese ruling classes had begun well before Pearl Harbor, and Ba Maw and U Saw, two of the three Burmese prime ministers after Burma's separation from India in 1935, made subversive

[35] Kiyoshi Ikeda, *Nihon no Kaigun* (Japanese Navy) (Tokyo, 1987), ii. 345–6.

overtures to the Japanese and were arrested by the British. A *Yomiuri* journalist in Rangoon, Minami Matsuyo, who was in fact Colonel Suzuki Keiji of Imperial General Headquarters assigned to the task of cutting the Burma Road, managed to set up the *Minami Kikan* (Minami Organization) early in 1941 to give young members of the *Thakin* party (*Do Baba Asiayone* or Our Burma League) military training by Japanese officers outside Burma and smuggle them back to the home country. On 31 December 1941 the *Minami Kikan* was dissolved, and the Burma Independence Army was created with *Thakin* (Master) Aung San as major-general.[36]

The Japanese invasion of Burma began in January 1942 across virgin forests and mountain ridges from Thailand. Moulmein, an important port town, fell on 31 January, and Rangoon, the capital, was captured on 8 March. The threat of Chinese troops coming down from the north induced the Japanese to renew their effort to secure Burma; more regiments and divisions arrived and moved north to cut the roads to China. In the battle over Central Burma the Burma National Army fought on the side of the Japanese. Mandalay, the ancient capital, fell on 1 May. Chinese troops were asked to co-operate with the British and Indian forces during their withdrawal into India, while units of the Thai army were found taking part in operations in collaboration with the Japanese.[37] The exodus of civilian refugees, British, Burmese, and Indian followed.

In early 1943 the British made an unsuccessful attempt to reach Akyab overland. Encouraged by the feasibility of an overland campaign, Lt.-General Mutaguchi Yasunari, commander of the Fifteenth Army in the Burma Area Army, conceived the idea of an invasion into India, into the Impahl Plain, an operation which might provide a home base for Subhass Chandra Bose, who had set up a Free India Provisional Government in Singapore in October 1943. Tojo approved of the idea, while Ba Maw, now head of the Burmese Provisional Government, was informed of it.

At the Imperial Headquarters–Cabinet Liaison Conference held on 29 May 1943 an 'Outline Plan for Policy Guidance in Greater East Asia' was adopted according to which Malay and Dutch East India would be made Japanese territories, while Burma and the Phillipines would be given independence. The basic idea behind this was to bind Asian countries closer to Japan to form a defensive ring against the return of the Allied armies. Imperial General Headquarters gave authorization for the Impahl campaign on 7 January 1944. There was political pressure for a victory in South-East Asia in view of the series of disastrous setbacks in the Pacific.[38]

The campaign began in the second week of March 1944 in the Arakan

---

[36] Louis Allen, *Burma: The Longest War 1941–45* (London, 1984), 17–21.
[37] Ibid. 70f.   [38] Ibid. 152–67.

mountains in the south; the decisive factor was use of tanks and aircraft, and British superiority in both had a decisive effect on the whole Burma war.[39] On the northern front of the battle for Impahl the important town of Kohima was captured on 6 April (but held for only a fortnight) by the Japanese Thirty-first Division, which had covered 160 miles over high ridges in twenty days. The Indian National Army co-operated with the Japanese Fifteenth Division which, along with the Thirty-third Division from the south, approached Impahl by the middle of April, but by then the invading forces found themselves in an impasse: the Japanese tactic of encirclement did not work, for the besieged enemies were strengthened by airborne supplies, while the attackers were suffering from their own depletion of ammunition and supplies. Already in early March the British began using gliders towed by transport aircraft and sent in the famous glider unit of 5,000 men who began constructing airstrips in Central Burma in order to cut off the Japanese forces in North Burma and Yunan which were facing US-equipped and trained Chinese divisions.

By June 1944 the failure of the Impahl campaign became obvious. The three division commanders involved were either dismissed for their alleged lack of enthusiasm or resigned, criticizing army commander Mutaguchi for his inept leadership. Between June and October about 30,000 fresh troops arrived to prop up the depleted divisions. By November some of these had to be pulled out because of the development of the war in the Phillipines and tension in French Indochina (Paris was liberated in August 1944 and the Vichy regime was collapsing). In July Mutaguchi, commander of the Fifteenth Army which comprised the three divisions involved in the Impahl campaign, ordered a general retreat. The British and Indian forces chased after the Japanese in what became a rout. The Fifteenth Army had begun the Impahl offensive with 100,000 men: of these about 30,000 were killed in combat, another 20,000 died from illness, and about half of the 50,000 survivors were sick. Those of the wounded and sick who collapsed on the road during the retreat were forced to commit suicide.

LEYTE

The American attempt to recapture the Philippines began with the landing of their troops on Leyte in October 1944 and on Luzon in January 1945. So many aircraft-carriers having been lost, the Japanese thought of turning the Philippines into 'one great air fortress', and a group of airfields were built around Brauen near the east coast of Leyte and a naval airfield at Tagroban on the north-eastern tip of the island. 'Leyte was to be the anvil against which I hoped to hammer the Japanese into submission in the

[39] Ibid. 177, 187.

central Philippines—the springboard from which I could proceed to the conquest of Luzon, for the final assault against Japan itself', recalled MacArthur in his memoirs.[40] A feint operation conducted by Admiral Halsey's mobile fleet against northern Luzon and Taiwan attracted Japanese airforces from Okinawa and southern Kyushu, and these reported a great victory (eleven carriers and two battleships sunk) based on a mirage seen by inexperienced pilots; even when the navy came to know that Halsey's fleet had been little affected, this news was not transmitted to the army. The army, under the false impression that the American mobile fleet had been destroyed, decided to send more divisions to Leyte to prepare for land battles with the Americans, who entered the Gulf of Leyte in the midst of a typhoon and landed on the east coast on 22 October 1944. 'I have returned', MacArthur told the Philippino guerrillas by radio. The Japanese Combined Fleet moved to Leyte, again undecided as to its main task, whether to attack the transport ships in the Gulf of Leyte or to engage in a decisive naval battle with the main American fleet. It sent 80 per cent of its remaining strength to the Leyte waters and was defeated. Four carriers were sunk, and the great battleship *Musashi*, with a displacement of 72,000 tons, which symbolized 'the spirit of the nation' and represented 'our attitude of overtaking and superseding the West',[41] torpedoed and bombed, went down with 1,100 officers and men to the bottom of the Sibuyan Sea. The naval battle off Leyte is also memorable for the *Tokkotai* (special attack units) of suicide *kamikaze* planes, which were now introduced for the first time because it was felt that there were too few experienced pilots. The land war in Leyte turned out to be another war of attrition. The Japanese army of 75,200 was surrounded by American forces three times as strong, and starvation, disease, and group suicide decimated their number. Private (later First Class) Ooka Shohei, a signalman and translator of English at the time of the Leyte battle, later wrote a novel, *Nobi* (Fires on the Plain, 1952), in which he gave an absorbing account of the soldiers making desperate efforts to flee and survive, and being reduced to acts of cannibalism.

On 4 February 1945 the American army entered Manila, and the ensuing street battles devastated the city; it took five more months for MacArthur to announce the official end of the Philippine campaign.

HOME AFFAIRS AND TOJO'S RESIGNATION

The Diet held a secret session on 16 January 1944 at which the chief of the criminal section of the Ministry of Justice gave a survey of 'the conditions

[40] Douglas MacArthur, *Reminiscences* (New York, 1964), 212.
[41] Shohei Ooka, *Leyte Senki* (Leyte War Chronicle) (Tokyo, 1974; pbk. edn. 1995), i. 190.

of thought in Japan'. First, the threat of communism had largely been eliminated. In spite of the formal dissolution of the Comintern, however, attention should be paid to the role of Nosaka Sanji (Sanzo), the former JCP leader, who had appeared at Yenan in May the previous year and had since started a propaganda offensive in conjunction with the Chinese communists to overthrow the military in Japan and to put a quick end to the war.

Secondly, there was the national renovation movement; it had co-operated with the government at first in carrying out the war, but 'the stalemate on the southern front' led some of its activists to attempt another *coup d'état* in September 1943. Nakano Seigo, a right-wing leader, was arrested by the military police for plotting the overthrow of the government: he committed hara-kiri. Thirdly, the Korean Independence movement that had been in the hands of Korean students in Japan had been strengthened by the labourers who had been brought over: they predicted Japan's defeat in the war, which would give them independence.

Finally, the chief of the criminal section admitted that there were signs of defeatism among the people in the form of gossip heard at neighbourhood meetings and graffiti on walls, telephone poles, and in public lavatories. The number of those indicted in relation to such offences increased from 580 in 1942 to 1,400 in 1943. A factory-worker was reported to have said at a meeting of his neighbourhood association that national bonds and savings should be demanded from the rich, not from the poor, and that he would rather die in an air-raid than live a miserable life, and that the war should be ended as quickly as possible no matter whether won or lost. Some said a victory in the war would not make the poor rich. The chief of the criminal section ended his report with a plea for political and administrative guidance to encourage the fighting spirit which had been weakened.[42] There were certainly many signs of war-weariness among ordinary citizens. Their pessimism and cynicism, however, should not be over-generalized, for the nation at large was sufficiently indoctrinated and blinkered not to be led astray from desperate war efforts. It was politics that really reflected the worsening war situation.

In February 1944 Tojo Hideki, the prime minister and army minister, sought to strengthen his position by becoming chief of the army staff; he now became, in effect, a dictator. But he was never a popular figure. His incompetence was criticized, and his attempt to reshuffle his cabinet failed. The loss of Saipan was fatal to him as well as to Japanese cities. He was replaced in July 1944 by Koiso Kuniaki, former chief of staff of the Kwantung Army. There was no sign that the war might end, while American

---

[42] The Diet Office (ed.), *Shorthand Record of the Proceedings of the Secret Sessions of the Imperial Diet* (in Japanese, 1996), ii. 779–84.

bombings of major cities were intensified. Although the production of aircraft increased in the first six months of 1944 from 1,815 in January to a peak of 2,857 in June, the army and navy fought each other for a greater share of the aircraft produced. The loss of shipping due to submarine attacks increased from 880,000 tons in 1942 to 1,600,000 tons in 1943, and newly built ships could make up only half of the loss.

THE BATTLE FOR OKINAWA

The Japanese army which moved to Okinawa, presumably to 'defend the imperial land', was at first warmly welcomed by the Okinawa people, but behaved like an army of occupation.[43] The island began to be bombed from the air in October 1944; the citizens of Naha were ordered to leave the city and hide in the hills; the houses in Naha that remained intact after the air-raid were seized by the soldiers, for whom robbery and rape had become nothing unusual.

The Thirty-second Army, the main Japanese force in Okinawa, consisted of miscellaneous groups, one of which was the Sixty-second Division which had fought with the Eighth Route communist forces in the Shangsi province in China. They were suspicious of the Okinawan people for including a number of repatriates from South America and other foreign countries to which they had emigrated, for retaining Chinese cultural influences, and for not being able to speak good Japanese.[44] The strength of the Thirty-second Army commanded by Lt.-General Ushijima Mitsuru was about 86,400 men and that of the naval units was roughly 8,000.[45] For reasons that have so far not been sufficiently explained, the Thirty-second Army also conscripted about 25,000 male Okinawans who were distributed to various fighting units as auxiliary defence personnel or 'volunteers'. Most of the remaining males were forced to work in labour units. In March 1945 the 1,780 male students of the normal school and the middle school were ordered to form the *Tekketsu Kinno Tai* (Battalion to Serve the Emperor with Iron Blood), and the 581 female students to organize themselves into an auxiliary unit to work as nurses in field hospitals and to do other odd jobs.

The Allied forces, having just won a savage battle at Iwojima in which the attackers suffered heavier losses than the attacked, were now ready to launch a massive assault on Okinawa with twenty battleships, nineteen carriers with 1,160 aircraft, thirteen heavy cruisers: altogether, a force of 1,500 ships and 183,000 men. There was also a British Carrier Force. On

---

[43] Yoshiaki Yoshimi, 'Okinawa-sen Zengo' (Before and After the Okinawa Battle), in *Nihon Tsushi* (Complete History of Japan), xix. 145.   [44] Ibid. 147.

[45] Kisaka, op. cit., 312–13; an American source gives more precise but somewhat smaller figures. See Simon Foster, *Okinawa 1945: Final Assault on the Empire* (London, 1994), 30.

26 March the Kerama archipelago west of Okinawa was seized by the Americans so as to make it a naval repair base. The landing on the main Okinawa island began on 1 April. In the face of desperate resistance making use of defences in caves and hills, it took two months for the Americans to reach Shuri 10 kilometres away.

In the meantime the suicide planes played their deadly role. The *Tokkotai* (Special Attack Units) were under the command of Vice-Admiral Ugaki Matome, former chief of staff of the Combined Fleet, and had been used first in the naval battle off Leyte. The initiator of this bizarre weapon was Vice-Admiral Onishi Takijiro, commander-in-chief of the First Air Fleet, who had a low opinion of the skills of his pilots and came to uphold 'crashing' as the best way to hit a target.[46] A similar special weapon was called *Kaiten* (Round the Heaven), a human torpedo. A naval statistic puts the number of American ships sunk by suicide air attack around Okinawa at twenty-seven, with 164 damaged, while one ship was sunk and seven damaged by human torpedos.[47]

The last great fleet of the Japanese navy, including the battleship *Yamato*, a sister-ship of the *Musashi*, with the fuel just sufficient for a one-way voyage sailed into the Okinawa waters, where the *Yamato* was destroyed by American aircraft on 7 April west of Yakushima. Okinawa fell late in June, with heavy casualties. Lt.-General Ushijima, who had retreated from Shuri on 21 May, continued his resistance at the Mabumi hill overlooking the sea in the south, one garrison after another having been annihilated, with wounded soldiers and civilians killing themselves. On 23 June Ushijima himself committed suicide, and with this the organized resistance of the Japanese forces came to an end.

What accentuated the Okinawa tragedy is the fact that more civilians (94,000 in number) perished than soldiers and military workers (85,136). It has been pointed out that Imperial Headquarters regarded the Okinawa battle as a sideshow, used to gain time for better preparations for the defence of mainland Japan.[48] The chief of the Thirty-second Army emphasized the idea of *gyokusai* (a fight to death) both by the military and by civilians. The massacres of civilians were sometimes carried out by Americans as acts of retaliation or as a way of exterminating those who would not come out of a cave. But many more cases of senseless mass killings by Japanese soldiers took place, on charges of spying or non-obedience, and there were cases of villagers being forced by the military to commit mass suicide. The Showa emperor was deeply interested in the Okinawa battle. He was unhappy about the differences over strategy between the navy, who went out to seek a final battle, and the army,

---

[46] Kisaka, op. cit., 293.   [47] Foster, op. cit., 178 ff.   [48] Kisaka, op. cit., 315.

who sought to preserve their strength, and he called the Okinawa tragedy 'this foolish fighting'.[49]

A DECISIVE BATTLE ON THE MAIN ISLANDS?

The Imperial Conference held on 8 June 1945 in the middle of the battle for Okinawa opted for a decisive battle to be fought on the mainland in order to 'safeguard the national polity and preserve the imperial land', and stressed a strengthening of national solidarity with the national volunteers as its core. This aimed to make the whole nation a *tokko tai* (suicide force). The Suzuki government now sought to organize the National Volunteers, whose formation had been decided upon earlier. The government viewed this as a form of national mobilization, while the army wanted to place it as a fighting force under its control. On 13 June the government dissolved the *Taisei Yokusannai* and its subordinate bodies in order to facilitate the establishment of the National Volunteers and adopted a 'Volunteer [*sic*] Conscription Act' at a special Diet on 13 June. This was to oblige all men between the age of 15 and 60 and all women between 17 and 40 to serve as national volunteers. This was 'the final, extreme form of fascist mobilization in Japan',[50] and provided a glaring example of the strange combination of voluntarism and coercion, the essence of traditional communal consensus. Fortunately, the domestic situation had deteriorated too fast for such a volunteer corps to be started effectively, and the nation was saved from self-destruction by accepting the Potsdam Declaration, though the process of its acceptance was far from smooth and easy.

THE RECKONING OF A LOST WAR

At the time of Pearl Harbor Japan's army and navy airforce jointly possessed 6,980 aircraft of various types, while her aircraft industry was producing 550 aeroplanes a month. For the first nine months in the Pacific War (December 1941–August 1942) average aircraft production was 642 a month, this figure reaching a maximum of 2,552 a month in September 1944. The total wartime (the Pacific War) production was 65,300, while the total losses of army and navy aircraft amounted to 52,000. Command of the air was never maintained except for the initial period of the war, but the American bombing survey alarmingly reports that at the time of her surrender Japan possessed over 9,000 suicide planes, of which 5,000 had

---

[49] Yoshimi, op. cit., 148.
[50] Akira Fujiwara, *Taiheiyo Sensoshi Ron* (On the History of the Pacific War) (Tokyo, 1982), quoted in Masaomi Yui, *Nihon Tsushi*, xix. 42–3.

been given special equipment to attack the Americans on their possible landing.[51]

After Midway and Guadalcanal it became clear that command of the air was all-important, while the serious damage caused by submarine attacks had brought home rather belatedly to the naval command the urgent need of escort vessels rather than big ships. (Of the latter, the battleships had given way to the aircraft-carriers in strategic importance.) Japan entered the Pacific War with merchant shipping of about 6 million tons, but the losses during the war amounted to 8,900,000 tons which far surpassed the total of 4,100,000 tons of ships seized or newly built in the same period. About 17 per cent of army supplies transported by sea were lost along with the ships that carried them in 1943, and the figure went up to 33 per cent in 1944 and to 50 per cent in the first six months of 1945.

Japan's Combined Fleet had by then been virtually wiped out through a series of naval battles. The Pacific War swallowed up 2,530,000 Japanese lives, of whom 420,000 served in the navy. Naval vessels sunk amounted to 754 (1,800,000 tons). The 'navigable' warships that survived three years and eight months' fierce warfare were two aircraft-carriers, three light cruisers, three depot ships, thirty destroyers, and fifty submarines. The former flagship of the Combined Fleet, *Nagato*, was damaged by an air attack while moored at Yokosuka in July 1945, and a year later was used as a target vessel for the atomic bomb experiment at Bikini Atoll, a symbolic end of the Imperial Navy.[52]

Although munition production in Japan reached its highest peak in 1944, even then it was very unfavourable when compared with that in the United States: the number of aircraft bodies assembled was 11.5 per cent of that in America, that of naval ships 11.3 per cent, that of transport ships 17 per cent. The traditional view of a decisive naval battle by the Combined Fleet against an enemy fleet reminiscent of the naval battle of the Japan Sea at the time of the Russo-Japanese War, was slow in being abandoned, and by the time when the need for escort vessels was sufficiently realized a large number of the newly built naval boats turned out to be suicide craft.

The air-raid by over 300 B.29 bombers on downtown Tokyo on the night of 10 March 1945 was almost as disastrous in terms of casualties (the death-toll on that night is estimated at 100,000) as the later atomic bombing of Hiroshima, and was regarded by the Americans as almost 'exemplary' in terms of cost-effectiveness; in the course of the next eight days other great cities of Japan, Nagoya, Osaka, and Kobe, were bombed in an equally thorough fashion. In order to bring the realities of the war

---

[51] This and the following account of Japan's war-preparedness and war damage is largely based on Misuzushobo (ed.), op. cit.   [52] Kiyoshi Ikeda, op. cit., 394, 396,

home to the ordinary Japanese citizen, middle and small cities were bombed too: for two months from the middle of June 54,154 tons of incendiary bombs dropped from B.29 bombers in their 8,014 sallies resulted in the devastation of fifty-two cities and the partial destruction of six others.

For many reasons it is extremely difficult to arrive at accurate figures of the war casualties in the Asia-Pacific War. We have already noted the figure of 2,530,000 as the number of the Japanese who died. According to one Japanese source,[53] the figures of those who died during the whole Fifteen-Year War (1931–45) are 1,536,900 for the army and 446,100 for the navy, totalling 2,010,000. According to another,[54] the number of military personnel (including workers employed by the military) who were killed in battles or died of illness at the front is estimated at 2,300,000; that of civilians who died in fighting in occupied areas at about 300,000; and that of those who died in the US bombing of the homeland at about 500,000. These figures of Japanese war casualties are far surpassed by those of the Chinese, estimated at 11 million.[55] US casualties in the Pacific theatre amounted to 291,543, of which the number of the dead stood at 100,997. The figure for US casualties at Iwojima was 26,000 (including 6,000 dead), whereas that for the Japanese was between 20,000 and 23,000 (practically all died). On Okinawa Japanese military casualties (dead) amounted to ten times as many as those of the American.[56]

The Japanese military leaders sought to avoid a 'humiliating' surrender by any means possible; this was the main reason behind their absurd and futile expectation that the Soviet Union would intervene on their behalf to prevent Japan's surrender to the Anglo-Americans. Then 'the maintenance of national polity [the imperial throne]' became their slogan for avoiding an unconditional surrender. The idea of 'a decisive battle on the mainland with the whole nation fighting as suicide soldiers' was earnestly propagated among the uninformed people. The Supreme War Direction Conference set up in August 1944 consisted a year later of prime minister Suzuki, foreign minister Togo, army minister Anami, navy minister Yonai, chief of army staff Umezu, and chief of naval staff Toyoda; three of the six, namely Anami, Umezu, and Toyoda, insisted on fighting to the bitter end.

TEHERAN, YALTA, POTSDAM, AND HIROSHIMA

At the Teheran Conference of November 1944 Stalin promised that once Germany had been defeated the Soviet Union would enter the Pacific War. In February 1945 the Big Three (Roosevelt, Churchill, and Stalin) met at

---

[53] Misuzushobo (ed.), op. cit., 821.
[54] *Heibonsha Daihyakka* (Heibonsha Encyclopedia), vol. 9 (Tokyo, 1985), 100.
[55] John Dower, *War without Mercy*, 296–7.   [56] Ibid. 299–300.

Yalta, where Stalin demanded the return of all the territories the Tsar had lost to Japan. It was a price the US Joint Chiefs were willing to pay, because an invasion of the Japanese mainland was estimated to be likely to cost the lives of half a million American soldiers; a Russian military operation in Manchuria would be of great help in diverting Japanese forces from the American theatre of war. The Russian demand was secretly agreed to.

The horrible cost of capturing Iwojima and Okinawa led the American leadership to consider the use of the atomic bomb, as they hoped this might shock the Japanese into surrender without fighting. By the time President Truman (replacing Roosevelt, who died in April 1945) arrived at Potsdam he had been informed of the success of the first A-bomb test. The bomb, in fact, became a strong card in the conference held from 17 July to 2 August 1945, and during the conference weeks Truman approved the Joint Chiefs' order to drop the first 'special bomb' after about 3 August on one of four targets: Hiroshima, Kokura, Niigata, and Nagasaki. The Potsdam Declaration adopted at the conference was to restrict Japanese sovereignty to her home islands, to promise stern justice against war criminals, and to force on the Japanese government 'the unconditional surrender of all Japan's armed forces'. The Declaration, which was announced on 26 July, ended with a stern warning: 'The alternative for Japan is prompt and utter destruction.' The premier Suzuki Kantaro pretended to 'ignore' this, and consequently Hiroshima and Nagasaki were to be destroyed.

On the early morning of 6 August the *Enola Gay*, the B.29 bomber carrying the 'Little Boy' atomic bomb, left the Tinian airstrip; weather conditions permitted the dropping of the special bomb over Hiroshima, a city with a population of three-quarters of a million. The city became 'a boiling pot of tar' in which more than 130,000 people perished (Japanese estimates of those who died by the end of the year ranges from 130,000 to 150,000).[57] Two days later Soviet Russia declared war against Japan. On the next day, 9 August, the second of America's nuclear weapons, the 'Fat Boy' (a plutonium bomb, more powerful than the uranium bomb used for Hiroshima), was dropped over Nagasaki (the city of Kokura, the primary target, being shrouded in thick cloud). Though the surrounding hills of Nagasaki saved many lives, at least 35,000 people (60,000 to 80,000 according to Japanese estimates) perished. The devastating effects of the new bombs created a consensus among the majority of Japanese leaders about the need to terminate the war; only a handful of diehards refused to accept it.

[57] Ibid. 591–2.

JAPANESE SURRENDER

The European war had come to an end three months earlier, with the Red Army entering Berlin in April and the German army accepting unconditional surrender in May. The 'new type of bomb' compelled the government to take steps for surrender. Meanwhile, the Russians launched a massive offensive into Manchuria, northern Korea, and Sakhalin. The government, while clinging to a slim possibility of maintaining the *kokutai* or emperor system after surrender, decided to accept peace. On 15 August Hirohito's feeble voice urging the nation to follow him for peace was broadcast by radio throughout Japan.

It is interesting to note Hirohito's own reasoning about the war and the peace, because it was his decision that mattered most at the time of Japan's surrender. According to his 'Monologue', the emperor had lost hope of victory by the end of 1942, when American and Australian forces chased back the Japanese army across the Stanley mountain range in New Guinea. This coincided with the landing of Allied forces in North Africa and the German setback at Stalingrad. 'I wanted to seize a chance for peace by inflicting a blow against the enemy somewhere, but I did not wish to make peace before Germany—this I felt to be an international obligation since we had promised not to make a unilateral peace. I even wished that Germany would be defeated soon.' He seems to have hoped that the Okinawa battle would be such 'a blow against the enemy'.

Russia's entry into the war with Japan fully convinced Hirohito that there was no alternative to unconditional surrender. At the Supreme War Council held on 9 August differences of opinion emerged on the maintenance of the national polity (the *Tenno* system), punishment of war criminals, disarmament of Japanese forces, and the Allies' occupation of the homelands. The debate in the Council dragged on till the following morning when Suzuki, the prime minister, asked the emperor to decide. 'I said, I support the proposal from the foreign minister [Togo] to accept the Potsdam Declaration,' he recalled, 'and it was decided to announce this through Switzerland and Sweden.' Hirohito's acquiescence to unconditional surrender was apparently swayed by his fear of the possible effects of the Allies landing near the Ise and Atsuta shrines, which housed the sacred mirror and the sacred sword respectively, symbols of the continuity of the imperial house. Indeed, at this critical moment he was committed more than ever to the mythical origins of his family. At the conference of members of the imperial families held on 12 August he was asked whether he would continue the war if the national polity was to be endangered by peace, and replied 'of course I would'.[58]

---

[58] Yutaka Yoshida, *Showa Tenno no Shusenshi* (Emperor Showa's History of Ending the War) (Tokyo, 1992), 221.

On the morning of 14 August the emperor convened an emergency conference. Prior to this he had met three marshals, Nagano, Sugiyama, and Hata, but all three insisted on fighting to the end. 'I felt', he said, 'if we accepted the Potsdam Declaration and then refused it, Japan would be discredited internationally.' He signed an announcement to accept the Potsdam Declaration shortly after 9 p.m. that day. The Ministry of War sought to prevent his broadcast and asked the chief commander of the Imperial Guard Division to issue an order to contradict the government decision. The chief commander refused and was murdered; a fake order was issued in his name. Telephone cables in the Ministry of the Imperial Household were cut, and some buildings in the Imperial Palace were besieged by troops. 'Iron doors, which were closed due to air-raids, hid me from the sight of the rebel troops', said the emperor. The chief of naval staff hurried to the palace and managed to placate the excited soldiers.

THE 'GREATER EAST ASIA CO-PROSPERITY SPHERE'—LIBERATION OR EXPLOITATION?

Japan's advance into South-East Asia had the alleged objective of building a 'co-prosperity sphere' and liberating Asians from European domination. In November 1943 the leaders of Manchukuo, the Wang Ching-wei regime of China, Thailand, the Philippines, and Burma were assembled in Tokyo for a Greater East Asia Conference. But were these areas of Asia really liberated from alien domination?

On 20 November 1941 the Imperial Headquarters–Cabinet Liaison Conference adopted 'The Basic Outline for the Administration of the Occupied Areas in the South', which stated: 'To begin with, military rule will be introduced, which will contribute to restoring peace, ensuring quick acquisition of resources important for national defence [of Japan] and to assuring self-support for the [Japanese] troops in operation', and for such purposes the native population 'should be made to bear the heavy burden which is unavoidable'.[59] Policies adopted here were somewhat different from those that had been pursued in China for the preceding two decades.

In China, including 'Manchukuo', the measures adopted after military conquest had been to set up local administration and taxation, and carry out a land survey by organizing the landlords, while establishing a central bank based on the property 'wrested from enemy hands' and assets obtained from Japan, and enforcing a unified currency system linked with the yen. The Manchuria Central Bank set up in June 1932 issued

---

[59] Hideo Kobayashi, *Nihon Gunseikano Ajia* (Asia under Japanese Military Rule) (Tokyo, 1993), 82.

Central Bank notes or National notes which virtually replaced the old currencies that had been issued by a number of provincial central banks. The reason for its success was the seizure by the Kwantung Army of the silver owned by such provincial banks as soon as it occupied the area concerned. Money from Mitsui and Mitsubishi also gave the Bank plentiful reserves.[60] In North China, where the army had hoped to set up a second Manchukuo, however, the situation was quite different: silver owned by Chinese banks had been sealed off by the order of Chiang, and these banks refused to contribute funds to a central bank to be established under Japanese initiative. The Japanese-sponsored China United Reserve Bank (established in March 1938) issued its own notes, which remained weak against the Nationalist tender (legal notes), and the Japanese-sponsored notes were in circulation only in the occupied areas. In Central China the Japanese army intended to use only Japanese yen, as they expected that the war would be of short duration, but soon introduced *gunpyo* or 'military notes' because it was feared that the continued use of yen would affect the Japanese economy. The value of *gunpyo* was sustained by special secret funds appropriated by the Japanese army. Japanese trading companies co-operated with the army in attempts to extend the *gunpyo* areas by using it for trade between Japan and China. As a result, it was only Japanese merchants who used *gunpyo*, while Chinese merchants would sell only for Chinese legal notes, and it was only when Japanese goods were purchased that *gunpyo* was used. It is symbolic of the war in China that the Japanese army not only failed to confront the main Chinese forces but also failed to win the currency war.[61]

As for the southern occupied areas, what mattered there were the acquisition of resources, especially oil, and the self-support of the troops stationed there. The Japanese army soon set the local administrative machinery in motion: in the Philippines and Burma native politicians such as Vargaz, the mayor of Manila, and Ba Maw, the leader of the Burmese independence movement, were prepared to co-operate. Elsewhere direct military rule by the Japanese army was enforced. In Java the old Dutch ruling system was preserved, but Japanese were appointed as governors of the provinces. Officials in junior positions were mostly local people. Singapore was renamed as 'Shonan', which meant Southern Showa. Here too the old ruling structure was kept intact; the only change was the replacement of the British by the Japanese, but daily administrative business was carried out by the local people using English as the official language. Another change was that their salaries were paid in *gunpyo*.

Oil production in southern Sumatra was resumed, and the transport of

---

[60] Kobayashi, op. cit., 31–3.   [61] Ibid. 53, 64

oil to Japan began in March 1942, 167 kl (40 per cent of the total production) in 1942 and 230 kl (29 per cent) in 1943, but thereafter shipping became increasingly hazardous due to Allied attacks on the oil-tankers. The Mankayan Copper Mine in the Philippines, which had been destroyed by the Americans when they retreated, was restored by the Mitsui Mining Company, and a large quantiy of the ore (29,000 tons) was shipped to Japan in 1943. The army and navy were in close co-operation with individual businesses. In the areas controlled by the army in South-East Asia (the Philippines, Malaya, Sumatra, Java, and northern Borneo) as many as 1,290 business units established a foothold or some-thing more substantial. Businesses set up in the areas controlled by the navy (New Guinea, New Britain, Southern Borneo, and Celebes) were 270 in number.[62] As for the currency in the occupied territories in South-East Asia, the basic army policy was to allow local currencies to circulate while *gunpyo* was introduced as a supplement in case of need: hence guilder *gunpyo* in the East Indies, dollar *gunpyo* in Malaya and Borneo, peso *gunpyo* in the Philippines; these were regarded as equivalent to the local currency. *Gunpyo* or no *gunpyo*, the exploiation of resources in South-East Asia was allowed to proceed only for a short time because the Japanese forces soon found themselves on the defensive as they were pushed back along the rim of the Pacific. Moreover, they were not popular among the occupied peoples; they were objects of hatred and fear rather than admiration and respect.

This had much to do with the harsh treatment meted out to the local populations in the form of inhuman exploitation of native workers. As there was a great demand for labourers in Malaya, Sumatra, and Borneo, it was decided to send workers from Java, nominally volunteers but actually bondsmen recruited forcibly from Javanese villages. The number of the *Romusha* from Java, as they were called, amounted to 300,000, of whom 70,000 died of malnutrition and illnesses. The construction of the Thai–Burmese Railway is notorious for its maltreatment of British prisoners of war, but as well as these British soldiers there were Asian workers, *Romusha*, to the number of 250,000, including 100,000 from Malaya,

---

[62] Ibid. 105–7. Of businesses in the army-dominated areas shipping numbered 9, manufactur-ing 525, docks and wharves 43, mining 133, trading 224, fishery 35, shipbuilding 43, cattle-breeding 13, telecommunication 6, agriculture 190, insurance 7, land transport 15, forestry 49; of these, those that were Mitsui or Mitsui-connected numbered 240, Mitsubishi or Mitsubishi-connected 125, Sumito and its connections 13, Yasuda and the same 6, Okura and the same 38, Nissan and the same 57, Furukawa and the same 10, Asano and the same 13, Nomura and the same 48; these *zaibatsu*-dominated businesses formed 42.5% of the total. Of businesses in the navy-controlled areas, trading numbered 102, mining and manufacturing 47, agriculture and fishery 28, cotton cultivation 10, insurance 2, shipbuilding 20, construction 11, transport 30, forestry 20; and those connected with *zaibatsu* were: Mitsui 15, Mitsubishi 33, Simitomo 2, Okura 1, Nissan 9, Nomura 29.

who were treated as badly as the Chinese in Singapore, thousands of whom had been slaughtered earlier in a planned massacre. On the island of Hainan the *Nihon Chisso* (Nitrogen), a Japanese company, began developing iron-mines for which a large number of workers were brought in from Shanghai and Hong Kong, and bad working conditions there caused many deaths.[63]

Atrocities committed by Japanese forces against the Chinese were equally cruel and were carried out on a large scale. At least 41,000 Chinese were sent to Japan as slave-labourers. Of them, 1,000 died on board ship or shortly after arrival, and 6,000 at work sites, mostly from malnutrition, though some were killed when they rioted over bad working conditions. On 1 July 1945, when about 850 Chinese at the Hanaoka Copper Mine (*Akita-ken*), run by the Kajimagumi Construction Company, attempted to riot in protest against inhuman treatment, 420 of them were killed by troops.[64]

The Japanese occupation of South-East Asia does not deserve even the name of neo-colonialism, because under inhuman conditions it failed to develop production in the occupied areas. It damaged the Philippine economy by ordering sugar-fields to be converted to cotton production, a crop more vital to the war effort. Granting nominal independence to a puppet administration there in 1943 did not prevent many Philippinos from joining the resistance. In Burma, premier Ba Maw was treated like a hireling, in spite of the formal independence given to his country in 1943. The Indian National Army, mentioned earlier, was organized by Japanese officers in collaboration with Captain Mohan Singh, its originator, but Indian troops were dispatched to Rabaul and Timor in campaigns having little to do with Indian independence; Mohan Singh left the INA in protest. As for Indonesia, an Imperial Conference held in May 1943 confirmed agreements reached the day before at the Liaison Conference and decided that 'Marai, Sumatra, Java, Borneo, and the Celebes are Japanese territories and a priority effort will be made to develop these as supply areas for major natural resources'.[65] Since this decision was contrary to the idea of co-prosperity, it was kept secret.

It is evident that Japan did not liberate Asia. The Japanese sought and exploited raw materials in South-East Asia to be used in the war against China; 'Greater East Asia Co-Prosperity Sphere', a phrase introduced by foreign minister Matsuoka in 1940, was a typical example of ideology as false consciousness. Later apologists for the Greater East Asia Co-Prosperity Sphere have argued that, given enough time, they could have put into effect

---

[63] Kobayashi, op. cit., 144–52.
[64] Ienaga, op. cit., 168–9; Chikyo Ryu, *Hanaoka Jiken* (Hanaoka Incident) (Tokyo, 1995), *passim*.   [65] Quoted Ienaga, op. cit., 176.

the lofty ideas of coexistence and co-prosperity, and that only military necessity distorted its application. The truth is that military necessity created the 'Greater East Asia Co-Prosperity Sphere' as an ideology, and it was only natural that the ideology went down along with the military. Moreover, ideology, when it is translated into policy, abandons its false appearance and reveals its true colour. A massive report prepared by researchers associated with the Ministry of Health and Welfare entitled 'An Investigation of Global Policy with the Yamato Race as the Nucleus' (1942–3) gives overwhelming proof that the subordination of other Asians in the 'Sphere' was the very essence of the official policy.[66] These researchers of the Ministry of Health and Welfare speculated over a vast area: Japan's *Lebensraum* was to stretch from Australasia to the Middle East. Racism was not a German monopoly. The Japanese, though, equally susceptible to it, evaded the issue by pretending innocence and even benevolence.

[66] See Dower, op. cit. 264.

PART III

Reconstruction and Reorganization
1945–1995

15

The American Occupation:
The New Constitution and the
Tokyo War Crimes Trial

SURRENDER AND OCCUPATION

In a letter to Senator Richard Russell of Georgia dated 9 August 1945, the day when the second atomic bomb was dropped over Nagasaki, President Truman wrote: 'I know that Japan is a terribly cruel and uncivilized nation in warfare but I can't bring myself to believe that, because they are beasts, we should ourselves act in that same manner. For myself I certainly regret the necessity of wiping out whole populations because of the 'pigheadedness' of the leaders of a nation.'[1] Less than five years later the Truman administration had come to treat Japan as the key factor in the balance of power in Asia and as a 'freedom-loving' ally in the new Cold War situation.[2]

'At two o'clock in the afternoon', wrote General MacArthur in his memoirs, 'my C-54, *Bataan* emblazoned on its nose, soared above Kamakura's giant bronze Buddha, past beautiful Mt. Fuji, and swung down toward Atsugi.'[3] It was 30 August 1945, two days after the advance troops of the Allied forces had arrived at the same airport. On 2 September the formal document for Japan's surrender was signed on board the US battleship *Missouri* by the two Japanese plenipotentiaries, foreign minister Shigemitsu Mamoru and chief of the general staff Umezu Yoshijiro, as well as by General MacArthur as the Supreme Commander, Admiral Nimitz for the United States, and a representative each for China, Britain, the Soviet Union, Australia, Canada, France, the Netherlands, and New Zealand. The document stated Japan's acceptance of the Potsdam Declaration, decreed the 'unconditional surrender' of all Japanese troops and all troops under Japanese control, and stressed that the power of the emperor and the Japanese government be placed under the limitations imposed by the Supreme Commander. One of the four pens used in the signing was

---

[1] David McCullough, *Truman* (New York, 1992), 458. But there is a less charitable version of what he said about the bombs at around this time: 'When you have to deal with a beast you have to treat him as a beast.' John Dower, *Japan in War and Peace* (New York, 1993), 155.

[2] Ibid. 157.   [3] MacArthur, *Reminiscences* (pbk. edn., 1985), 270.

given to General Jonathan Wainwright, the hero of the defence of Bataan and Coregidor, and another to General A. E. Percival, the British commander at Singapore in 1942. These two prominent prisoners of war had been held in Mukden, and MacArthur made special arrangements for them to be present at the surrender ceremony on the *Missouri*. MacArthur was appointed Supreme Commander for the Allied Powers (SCAP) on 2 October, and the nominally Allied but effectively American occupation of Japan began. This would come to an end on 28 April 1952 under more prosaic circumstances, when the San Francisco Peace Treaty and a Japan–US Security Treaty concluded several months before came into effect and brought to Japan a qualified, 'subordinate' independence.[4] Equivocation and ambiguity shrouded both the beginning and the end of the occupation, in fact. In spite of an almost revolutionary change at the beginning, there was a virtual restoration of the past at the end; the elements of continuity were at work and remained as strong as the forces of change.

THE 'UNCONDITIONAL' SURRENDER

The 15 August 1945 issue of the *Asahi Shinbun* had on its front page the Imperial Rescript on Ending the War, which took the form of an appeal to the nation and made abundant references to 'our ancestors' and to the *kokutai*. It began with an excuse and justification:

The reason why I declared war against the United States and Britain was to secure the survival of our empire and the safety of East Asia, and it was far from my intention to interfere with the sovereignty of another nation and to invade its territories. After four years of warfare, however . . . the situation has not turned in our favour. In addition, our enemies have used new, atrocious bombs which killed many innocent people and the frightful effects of which are immeasurable in extent. If we continued the state of belligerency, it would result not only in the ruin and annihilation of our people as a race but also in the destruction of human civilization. If this happened, how could I maintain millions of my subjects and report dutifully to the godly spirit of our ancestors? This is the reason why I have made our imperial government comply with the joint declaration. . . . I advise you . . . to unite as one family, believe in the godly islands which are imperishable . . . and do your best to reconstruct our future for the further exhibition of the essence of our national polity and for the progress of the world.

The same issue of the *Asahi Shinbun* also published an exchange of views on the subject of *kokutai* between the Japanese government and the signatories of the Potsdam Declaration, according to which the government on 9 August had informed them that Japan would accept the Declaration with the undersanding that 'no request that might impair the supreme

---

[4] For 'Subordinate Independence', see Dower, op. cit., 130.

power of the emperor as the highest ruler would be implied'. On 13 August the American secretary of state James Byrnes, on behalf of the Potsdam signatories, replied that the ruling power of the emperor and the Japanese government should be placed under the Supreme Commander of the Allied forces until conditions arising from the acceptance of the Declaration would have been fulfilled, and the ultimate political form of the government would be decided by the will of the people freely expressed. The emperor found the conditions acceptable and the government replied to that effect on 14 August. In their view the acceptance of the American note of 13 August would not mean an unconditional surrender, for it seemed that there was a reasonable chance of preserving the emperor system. The full text of the Potsdam Declaration, dated 26 July, was also published at the same time. In it the Japanese public found for the first time a definite statement of the Allied policies towards Japan, such as 'the elimination for ever of the power and influence of militarism', 'punishment of war criminals including those who maltreated prisoners of war', and 'the establishment of basic human rights', as well as the preservation of industries essential for reparation coupled with an assurance of Japan's participation in world trade in future.

Compared to his brother Takamatsu-no Miya, who had made a *volte-face* at a comparatively early stage from a pro-war to a peace-seeking prince, Emperor Hirohito remained formalistic and sometimes appeared blinkered in his attitude to politics and the war, to such an extent that his brother took him to be unfeeling in face of the sufferings of his 'subjects'. There is a contrary view of the emperor's position in August 1945. One Japanese historian has described the initiative he had taken to end the war as 'a momentary, but momentous, restoration of imperial rule', and stressed 'the almost unimaginable pathos it called forth'.[5] It is true that the Imperial Edict of 15 August did mention the war-dead and their families and the emperor's 'heart rent by sorrows and sympathy for them'. The Edict, however, is not a human document but an official statement drafted by the cabinet secretary and revised several times by other hands, mainly from the literary point of view.[6]

When the war ended, the emperor's position was critical: both Takamatsu-no Miya, his own brother, and Higashikuni-no Miya, the first post-war prime minister, privately recommended his abdication. In an American poll of the US public conducted on 29 May 1945, 33 per cent had answered that he should be executed. In a Gallup poll of 29 June 1945, 70 per cent of Americans polled supported either the execution or the

[5] Makoto Iokibe in Ian Nish (ed.), *The Occupation of Japan 1945–1952* (London, 1991), 10–12.

[6] Yoshio Chaen, *Misshitsu no Shusen Shochoku* (The Imperial Edict to End the War Prepared in Camera) (Tokyo, 1989), *passim*.

harsh punishment of the emperor. In Britain too, 67 per cent of Britons questioned replied that Hirohito should be deprived of his throne.[7] Yet influential opinion in both countries moved in a direction favourable to him. General MacArthur writes in his memoirs that at his first interview with the emperor (on 27 September 1945) he was moved by his visitor's 'courageous assumption' of responsibility for the war, though the authenticity of this statement has been questioned by many, including the emperor's own interpreter.[8] In fact, MacArthur had formed a view favourable to the emperor much earlier. As early as July 1944 his intelligence advisers concluded that 'to dethrone, or hang the Emperor would cause a tremendous and violent reaction from all Japanese. Hanging of the Emperor to them would be comparable to the crucifixion of Christ to us. All would fight and die like ants.'[9] Then, on 29 August 1945, while stopping over in Okinawa on his way to Atsugi, MacArthur clearly stated to his top aides that all their policies were to be 'implemented through the Emperor and the machinery of the Imperial government'.[10] In spite of British, Australian, Russian, and Chinese criticisms of his conduct during the war, Hirohito now found a strong protector in the SCAP himself.

It is noteworthy that Japan's surrender was accompanied by greater efforts made by the security authorities, including the police, to maintain domestic order.[11] As soon as the Potsdam Declaration was accepted in principle on 10 August, the Police and Security Bureau of the Home Ministry sent directives to prefectural governors to keep watch on those who might cause civil disturbances, and its special division requested prefectural police chiefs to strengthen the *Tokko* police. The nationwide system of vigilance was further tightened when Japan formally accepted the terms of surrender, and governors and police did their best to guide local opinion so as to comply with the emperor's wishes. As early as 15 August the governor of Tokushima expressed the view that the whole nation should apologize to the emperor for their failings and that the responsibility for the lost war should be attributed to the military, the politicians-bureaucrats, and the people, an attitude soon to be developed by the Higashikuni government into a plea for repentance by the whole nation.[12] This first post-war government set up on 17 August had two principal aims, which were to preserve the national polity and to maintain security measures. Yamazaki Iwao, the home minister, told a foreign reporter that those who advocated the abolition of the emperor system were to be regarded as communists and arrested under the Public Order

---

[7] Dower, op. cit., 342.   [8] MacArthur, *Reminiscences*, 288; Dower, op. cit., 345.
[9] Quoted in Dower, op. cit., 345.
[10] Frazier Hunt, *The Untold Story of Douglas MacArthur* (New York, 1954), 360, quoted in Dower, op. cit., 239.
[11] Masaomi Yui in *Nihon Tsushi* (Complete History of Japan), xvi. 50.   [12] Ibid. 50–1.

Preservation Act. This government decided to double the number of policemen so as to accommodate some of the discharged military personnel, kept security legislations intact, and allowed political prisoners to languish in prison.

The Kwantung Army, the strength of which had reached 700,000 at one stage, had to allow most of its divisions to be dispatched to the Pacific front from the latter half of 1943. It was towards the end of May 1945, after the Battle of Okinawa, that reinforcement came from China and Korea to strengthen the Kwantung Army. A 'mobilization to the last man' was carried out in Manchukuo, and by June 1945 the Kwantung Army had swelled to a vast force of 750,000, consisting of twenty-four divisions and nine independent mixed brigades, including 250,000 civilians newly conscripted on the spot. On 9 August the Russian forces had begun invading Manchuria on several fronts and pushed back the Kwantung Army, of which some fought to death but many negotiated a truce. The staff meeting held on 16 August decided to support the emperor's decision to accept the Potsdam Declaration. On 17 August Prince Takeda-no Miya flew to Changchun and the Kwantung Army received directives from the General Staff to cease hostilities and to start negotiations with the Russians for an armistice and delivery of weapons. On the 19th an agreement was made between Marshal Alexander Vasilevsky, the hero of Stalingrad, now the commander-in-chief of the Soviet Far Eastern Army, and Lt.-General Hata, chief of the general staff of the Kwantung Army, on an orderly disarmament of the Japanese troops in Manchuria, but the Soviet army simply ignored the agreement. Confusion spread as the general command of the Kwantung Army ceased to function and Soviet troops advanced on Harbin, Changchun, and Mukden. In Changchun the families of army personnel were evacuated first, followed by those connected with *Mantetsu*. The Kwantung Army was decried for having deserted ordinary residents and settlers.[13] The number of Japanese civilians in Manchuria at the time was estimated at 1,550,000, of whom 176,000 (including 80,000 from the settlers' villages) perished in utter confusion and privation when the Kwantung Army melted away.[14] Japanese troops disarmed by the Russians in Manchuria began to be sent to Siberia from the end of August, and in the end their number reached 478,200.[15] Including those captured in Sakhalin and the Kuriles, altogether 570,000 Japanese soldiers were detained for hard labour in Siberia and in Central Asia, where 62,000 of them died.

Compared with the tragic situation in Manchuria, the disarmament and

---

[13] Misuzushobo (ed.), *Gendaishi-Shiryo* (Sources of Modern History), vol. 38 (Tokyo, 1972), 444–53   [14] Masaomi Yui, op. cit., 51.
[15] Misuzushobo (ed.), *Gendaishi-Shiryo*, xviii. 464.

repatriation of Japanese soldiers and civilians in China, whose number was estimated at about 2 million, in spite of (or rather because of) the civil war in China was relatively smooth and eventless, except for war criminals whose trials had begun in several cities, and was completed by the end of July 1946.[16] The disarmament and repatriation of the 6.6 million Japanese, both military and civilian, who found themselves overseas at the time of Japan's surrender was not an easy task, but the dispatch of members of the imperial family to several destinations was effective in persuading them to accept the surrender ordered by the emperor.

SOME CHARACTERISTICS OF THE REFORM PERIOD OF THE OCCUPATION

An American official who took part in it called the initial stage of the occupation 'the third turn in Japanese history', after the introduction of Chinese culture in the sixth century and the Meiji Restoration. The occupation authorities disarmed and demilitarized Japan, and created the conditions for a mass consumer society by liberating the peasantry, freeing women, and encouraging labour to organize for self-help.[17]

Officially it was an Allied occupation, and British Commonwealth Forces, mainly New Zealanders and Indians, were stationed in western Honshu (the whole of the Chugoku and Shikoku districts), with their headquarters at Kure, the naval port; but they did not stay long, for economic and other reasons (including Indian Independence), though the British area was officially preserved until the end of the occupation.[18] Possibilities of the Russians occupying Hokkaido and the Chinese the area around Nagoya were mooted but abandoned.

Meanwhile, in September MacArthur set up his headquarters in the Daiichi Life Insurance Building facing the Imperial Palace across the moat, and in the following two months the American occupation forces stationed in various places totalled over 430,000 in number. In December 1945 it was agreed to set up the Far Eastern Commission on which were represented the United States, Britain, the Soviet Union, China, France, the Netherlands, Canada, Australia, New Zealand, India, and the Philippine Commonwealth, which was intended to formulate policies and principles according to the terms of the surrender and to review directives from the SCAP issued in his capacity as the Allied executive in Japan. Its use, however, visibly declined: it approved forty-six policy decisions in the first two years of its existence and only seventeen in the following two, mostly

[16] Misuzu, op. cit., 383.
[17] Theodore Cohen, *Remaking Japan* (New York, 1987), pp. xv, 1–2.
[18] Gordon Daniel and Reinhard Drifte (eds.), *Europe and Japan: Changing Relationship Since 1945* (Ashford, 1986), 106.

endorsing the policies already pursued by the SCAP.[19] This was largely due to the emergence of East–West tensions, to which the Americans were more sensitive than the others on the Commission. In fact, effective control of the occupation was from the beginning in the hands of the Americans, and we may call it the American rather than the Allied occupation.

This was in contrast to the Allied occupation of Germany and Austria where three (later four) victorious nations divided up the territories. Germany had been overrun by the Allied forces, and the Allied authorities (Control Council) carried out measures for denazification which were perhaps easier to define than the purges of ultra-nationalists in Japan, and introduced democratic elections for parliaments in the *Länder* (provinces) and later for a federal government. Divided but direct rule by Allied powers led to the fixation for four decades of a divided Germany. Japan's case was one of unified but indirect rule by the occupation authorities. The Japanese mainland, though badly bombed, had not been invaded, and a Japanese government continued in existence. Though Japan had accepted the Potsdam Declaration in the end, its terms remained ambiguous on some important points: 'unconditional surrender' was only for the armed forces, while the final form of government, according to an attached document, as we have seen, was to be decided by the freely expressed views of the Japanese people. There was a tug of war between the reformist Americans and the conservative Japanese government officials, resulting in occasional sabotage by the latter and dictation by the former.

The American–Japanese, or victor–vanquished relationship has an aspect of mutuality which has been explained as American catharsis and Japanese trauma. This mutuality is due to the nature of the occupation in its early period, that can be viewed as 'a sort of culmination of the era of the New Deal' in America and a continuation on the Japanese side of the tradition of cultural borrowing and assimilation.[20] A victorious, affluent, and liberal America had come to represent the West.

As regards the 'third turn' in Japanese history, there was a continuity of elite liberalism represented by such people as Shidehara Kijuro and Yoshida Shigeru, who were liberals, but liberal imperialists. They had opposed the military assuming absolute power, but had supported Japan's 'peaceful' expansion on the Asian continent, with British and possibly American connivance. After the war they were to become conservative prime ministers. Yoshida has been described as first and foremost a monarchist, and only secondarily a democrat. His devotion to the throne was personalized by his marriage to the daughter of the emperor's close

---

[19] Robert A. Fearey, *The Occupation of Japan* (New York, 1950), 7.
[20] Grant K. Goodman, *The American Occupation of Japan: A Retrospective View* (Lawrence, Ka., 1968), p. vi.

adviser Makino Nobuaki, himself the son of Okubo Toshimichi, one of the founding fathers of the Meiji state. To him, the war brought about by 'military conspirators' was 'an aberration' which had diverted Japan from the laudatory course of building a modern nation. What Japan needed, in his view, was not the introduction of 'reform' but a return to the 'right' track.[21]

There were other more unsavoury cases of continuity. Tsuji Masanobu, the planner of the Nomonhan disaster, a hawk for war with the United States, and the instigator of the atrocities in Singapore, survived the reformist period of the occupation and later was elected to the Diet for Ishikawa-ken. Kishi Nobunsuke, a cabinet minister under Tojo, responsible for the economic management of Manchukuo, was designated as an A-class war criminal but was then released and climbed the political ladder to premiership in post-war Japan. A *Tokko* officer later became minister of justice in an LDP government. The bureaucracy that had sustained the militarist regime was on the whole kept intact and came to play a significant role in post-war politics. The Ministry of Education, the Ministry of Health and Welfare, and the Board of Economic Planning were three outstanding cases of such continuity.

The defeat of Japan meant many things to the Japanese. Certainly there was some real discontinuity, for the defeat meant the collapse of the old value structure. Freed from old taboos and constraints, it was natural that many found themselves capable of trying to reform the institutions and the social environment in which they lived. The reforms imposed by the Americans and those the Japanese adopted for themselves, did in fact alter the framework of society in which post-war reconstruction, hastened by the Cold War, was to be made and carried further.

DEMOCRACY NOT TO BE IMPOSED

Among western intellectuals who knew Japan well, Ruth Benedict, a member of the US Office of War Information and author of a classic work on the cultural anthropology of Japan, *The Chrysanthemum and the Sword* (1946), produced a report on the behaviour patterns of the Japanese prior to Japan's surrender in 1945 based on interviews with prisoners of war. She pointed out that 'faith and confidence in hierarchy' and 'the sanctity of the emperor' lay deep at the root of Japanese culture, and that the Japanese would rely on 'shame' rather than on 'guilt' in their conduct towards others. She made much of cultural differences and argued that a free democratic Japan could not be created by fiat.[22] Sir George

---

[21] Dower, op. cit., 218–25.
[22] Ruth Benedict, *The Chrysanthemum and the Sword* (1946; Tuttle edn. 1954), 314.

Sansom, the pioneer historian of Japan, formerly employed by the British embassy in Tokyo but who had lived in America during the war, also produced a report, entitled 'Postwar Relations with Japan', in 1942 for a conference of the Institute of Pacific Relations, in which he proposed 'non-punitive terms of peace' for Japan so that she could return to the international community of nations at the earliest possible opportunity. He opposed suggestions for the abdication of the emperor, revision of the constitution, and even for the abolition of state Shinto, because he believed that these measures would run counter to 'the natural tendencies of Japanese sentiments'. It would not be possible to produce a change in the 'Japanese spirit' from the outside, he thought. He recommended the Allies to give freedom to all currents of political thought in Japan and to induce the Japanese to change themselves from within. Hugh Borton, the doyen of the experts on Japan at Columbia University, who headed the State Department's advisory committee on post-war foreign policy, took a similar view. He was of the opinion that the unconditional surrender of Japan was not unconditional. Only the armed forces had surrendered unconditionally. Japan as a whole could rightfully attach conditions to her surrender.

The American and British diplomats who had been active in pre-war Japan, the 'old Japan hands' or 'Japan Crowd', Joseph Grew among them, argued in a similar vein. Grew, US ambassador to Tokyo from 1932 to 1941 and under-secretary of state in 1944–5, himself a member of the Harvard-educated elite, held the Japanese liberal elite in high esteem. He idealized the Japan of the Taisho democracy in the 1920s. He allowed himself to be influenced by members of the imperial family. Through his acquaintance with this small coterie of aristocrats and conservative internationalists, Grew formed his view of 'the emperor as the corner stone of a great culture and civilization temporarily derailed by militarists and ultra-nationalists'.[23] He even became sympathetic to the Japanese position in China and clung to the illusion of Japanese elite liberalism to the last. After Pearl Harbor, Grew became a propagandist for a US victory without attacking the emperor and went so far as to declare that Shintoism would be an asset rather than a liability in a reconstructed Japan. He insisted, too, on the inadvisability of demanding 'unconditional' surrender from Japan, and wanted to see the war ended before Russian entry. He failed to persuade the Pentagon but somehow imposed his views on Truman: hence the document of 13 August 1945 that permitted the Japanese government to surrender on condition that the emperor might be retained (depending upon the 'freely expressed' will of the people).

---

[23] Howard B. Schonberger, *Aftermath of War* (Kent, Ohio, 1989), 15.

DEMOCRACY SABOTAGED

A freelance journalist, Mark Gayn, working for the *Chicago Sun*, wrote in 1948 that 'we have fought a costly war for the professed object of converting Japan into the state that would uphold democracy and peace', but in the erroneous 'belief that democratic reform would, or could, be carried out by men who hated it. Before our first Christmas we already knew that the government in Tokyo served as a buffer, to cushion and absorb the Allied pressure.'[24] He had, in December 1945, visited SCAP headquarters where he found occupation personnel engaged in the reshaping of Japan. 'They fought a hard war until they were sick of its foulness. Now they feel as if they are cleansing themselves and the enemy. Headquarters is full of "reformers". Lights burn late in the buildings where these young men work on a blue-print of a new Japanese democracy.' Gayn also visited the Diet building to see what defeat had done to Japan's lawmakers. Dr Joji Matsumoto, the principal drafter of an early version of a new democratic constitution, said he did not believe in the rule of the majority though he was in favour of the government for the people. Premier Shidehara was of the same view: to him democracy was 'a government based on and reflecting public opinion', a government that must be run under the emperor and around the Diet which 'reflects the will of the people'. These are aspects of the political credo of elite liberals in the 1920s or of the Taisho democracy which impressed Ambassador Grew so much. Gayn found the Diet engaged in a debate on the subject of whether the emperor was a god: the premier's answer was: 'He is not a god in the western conception of the word, and yet he is not human.' When MacArthur requested Shidehara to initiate democratic reforms, the latter replied: 'if your democratization means a democratization in the American way, you could not expect it to be easily realized here.' If it meant a respect for the popular will, he continued, it would be realized in the not-too-distant future.[25]

As late as 27 September 1945 newspapers showing a photo of the small, undignified figure of the emperor standing by the grand, domineering personality of Douglas MacArthur were suppressed by the order of the home minister. MacArthur naturally felt outraged, and two days later a directive to abolish all the restrictive laws on newspapers, films, and correspondence was issued,[26] and the photo in question was duly published prominently in the newspapers on 29 September. It was only the widespread shock caused by the death in prison of an eminent philo-

[24] Mark Gayn, *Japan Diary* (New York, 1948), 500–2. This book in translation quickly became the 'bible' of Japanese radical intellectuals.

[25] Quoted in Akira Amakawa, in Nish (ed.), *The Occupation of Japan*, 27.

[26] Daizaburo Yui, *Mikanno Senryo Kaikaku* (Unfinished Occupation Reforms)(Tokyo, 1989), 219–20.

sopher, Miki Kiyoshi, on 26 September that led to the decree of 4 October ordering the government to release all political prisoners and to abolish all thought police, the *Tokko*, and the notorious Public Order Preservation Act of 1925. The political prisoners, 3,000 of them, were all set free within a week. It was these two fiats from the SCAP which put an end to the attempts by the old diehards to keep old institutions intact as long as they could. It was only in this new, liberalized political climate that the two left-wing parties made their appearance: the Japan Socialist Party held its founding conference in November 1945, and the communists, who had maintained their illegal existence throughout the war, held their fourth conference in December.

At about the same time the Government Section was created in the GHQ to deal with Japanese domestic politics. In mid-December General Courtney Whitney was appointed as its chief, and he, with the full support of MacArthur, 'transformed his section into the radical arm to bring about political reform under the occupation'.[27] As Dower noted, the Eurocentrism of the Truman administration, coupled with MacArthur's messianic style, gave his staff in Tokyo 'unusual leeway' for about two years, and 'MacArthur proved to be exceptionally receptive to the recommendations of a small coterie of American liberals and New Dealers'.[28] In spite of genuine ardour for reform among the occupation personnel and among Japanese progressives, sabotage was rampant among the bureaucrats on almost every level. Mark Gayn noticed that thought-control officers became peace-preservation officers, and in spite of the ban they were still prominent among the police. Nevertheless, the government (under Shidehara until May 1946, then led by Yoshida till May 1947), under pressure from the Government Section of the GHQ, had to comply with its requests and began to take an attitude of co-operation, though reluctantly.

Early in January 1946 Gayn received the draft of the emperor's rescript to renounce his divinity which had been prepared in the office of General Ken Dyke, the chief of the Civil Information and Education Section with the help of a *Gakushuin* (Peers' School) professor. In fact, the New Year's Day issue of the *Ashi Shinbun* had this rescript at the top of the front page, written in the old literary style that had been used for his rescripts to start the war and also to end it: 'I remain with you, the people. Your interest is mine; we share joy and sorrow. The bond between myself and you people is mutual trust and respect and has nothing to do with myth and legend. It is not based on the fictitious ideas such as the concept of the emperor as a living god or the view of the Japanese as superior to other races and

---

[27] Amakawa in Nish (ed.), *The Occupation of Japan*, 28; see also Justin William Sr., *Japan's Political Revolution under MacArthur* (Tokyo, 1979).   [28] Dower, op. cit., 165–6.

destined to dominate the world.'[29] The position of the emperor was now being hotly discussed in villages and colleges throughout Japan.

THE NEW CONSTITUTION

'The ultimate intellectual roots' of many of the political changes in post-war Japan under the occupation derived from a paper prepared by Hugh Borton as early as in October 1943. In it he pointed out that constitutional change was desirable, but should not be imposed by the occupation authorities; the Japanese should be encouraged to accomplish this for themselves. He also recommended a curtailment of the authority of the imperial institution, elimination of the privileges enjoyed by the military, a cabinet responsible to the Diet, and introduction of an effective bill of rights with particular attention to freedom of speech, assembly, and worship.[30]

At an early stage of the occupation premier Shidehara appointed his home minister Dr Matsumoto to head a committee of experts to recommend constitutional revision. This encouraged various political parties and private groups to publish proposals for constitutional reform. A draft constitution prepared by the Matsumoto committee and published in the *Mainichi Shinbun* on 1 February 1946 fell far short of the requirements of the Americans, whose interdepartmental State–War–Navy Co-ordinating Committee had adopted its 'Reform of the Japanese Governmental System', known as SWNCC-228, a month before. As for the emperor, this document had stated that 'the Japanese should be encouraged to abolish the emperor institution or to reform it along more democratic lines', although its principal author (again Hugh Borton) was of the view that the imperial institution would continue. MacArthur, while sending a cable to Washington urging against trying the emperor as a war criminal, directed the Government Section to prepare a new draft constitution by providing what has been referred to as the 'MacArthur Notes', which urged abolition of the military and of the remaining aspects of the 'feudal system', such as the peerage. Using the Notes as the basis and with SWNCC-228 for guidance, the twenty-one members of the Government Section headed by General Courtney Whitney 'wrote the Constitution within a week'.[31] The SCAP draft constitution provided that 'the emperor shall be the symbol of the State and of the Unity of the People, deriving his position from the sovereign will of the people' and that 'war as a sovereign right of the nation is abolished. . . . No army, navy, air force, or other war

[29] *Asahi Shinbun*, 1 Jan. 1946.
[30] Ward in Ward and Sakamoto (eds.), *Democratizing Japan* (Honolulu, 1987), 19–21.
[31] Theodore H. McNelly in Ward and Sakamoto (eds.), *Democratizing Japan*, 81.

potential will be authorized'.[32] On 6 March the government published its Japanese version, and MacArthur announced his satisfaction with the decision of the emperor and the Japanese government to submit to the people 'a new and enlightened constitution which has my full approval'. In other words, the emperor became an official sponsor of the democratic constitution written by the Americans.

The venerable Minobe Tatsukichi, then a privy counsellor, objected to the emperor's initiative in constitutional revision for the reason that the Meiji constitution, which stipulated his initiative in its Article 73, had been nullified by the Potsdam Declaration which Japan had accepted; therefore, he said, the appropriate procedure for the enactment of a new constitution would be to hold a representative assembly that would draft a constitution and submit it to a popular referendum. However correct this view was, the pressure for democratization was taken advantage of by the new prime minister Yoshida Shigeru, who supported the proposed constitution so as to facilitate the withdrawal of the occupying troops.[33] Ashida Hitoshi, soon to form the *Minshuto* (Democratic Party), inserted an amendment to Article 9 which now read (with the new insertion underlined): 'Aspiring sincerely to an international peace based on justice and order, the Japanese people forever renounce war as a sovereign right of the nation and the threat or use of force as means of settling international disputes. / In order to accomplish the aim of the preceding paragraph, land, sea, and air forces, as well as other war potential will never be maintained. The right of belligerency of the state will not be recognized.'[34] These underlined additions would make Article 9 allow for rearmament for national defence, because of the qualification made to the second paragraph. Colonel Charles Kades, who was in charge, had no objection as he was impressed by the apparent sincerity and flexibility of the amendment that might permit Japanese participation in a United Nations force.[35] The Chinese delegate to the Far Eastern Commission, however, was shocked by this amendment, which he regarded as a trick by the Japanese militarists. In spite of all this, premier Yoshida and his government held the view that Article 9 forbade even a defensive war. The amended bill was approved on 29 October 1946; the new constitution was promulgated in the form of an amendment of the Meiji constitution on 3 November 1946, the Meiji emperor's birthday, and became effective on 3 May 1947. It is remarkable that even the American-inspired constitution was made to appear to have emanated from the Meiji system of constitutional politics with the result that the forces of continuity were ever anxious to reject discordant elements, Article 9 above all.

[32] Ibid. 81–2.   [33] Ibid. 86, 90.   [34] Ibid. 92.   [35] Ibid. 93.

WAR CRIMES AND THE FAR EASTERN MILITARY TRIBUNAL

At the London conference held in the summer of 1945 to draw up a charter for the Nuremberg Tribunal, the Big Four had decided that the leaders of Nazi Germany should be tried not only for conventional war crimes, but also for two new crimes: against peace and against humanity. Thus, the Nazi leaders in the dock were tried not only for atrocities against foreign military and civilian personnel but also for planning and waging aggressive war and for inhuman treatment of Jews 'before or during the war'. Existing international law for conventional war crimes was clear enough, but as regards individual responsibility for acts of state, such as aggression, the Big Four had to 'codify international law in such a way that German and Japanese acts became criminal and individual enemy leaders became accountable'.[36] Hence 'Victor's Justice' was invoked and condemned by such writers as Minear, the author of the book under that title.

War crimes are a controversial issue. We may recall an extreme view expressed by Justice Pal, the Indian Judge at the Tokyo War Crimes Trial: 'when the conduct of the nations [at the time] is taken into account the law will perhaps be found [*sic*] that only a lost war is a crime.'[37] As late as 1987 one British scholar said he would prefer the appellation 'the Tokyo War Trial' to the official one, 'the Tokyo War Crimes Trial', and would use historical rather than legal criteria.[38] Indeed, individual crimes in international law are difficult to define. Takayanagi Kenzo, the Japanese lawyer for the defence at the Tokyo Trial, argued: 'it is the general principle of the law of nations that duties and responsibilities are placed on states and nations and not on individuals.' Espionage, piracy, and the like are exceptions to the 'general rule of the immunity of the individuals'.[39] To these exceptions we may add individual acts contrary to the agreement in the Geneva Convention of 1929 on proper treatment of prisoners of war.

Occupation policy in Japan, as in Germany, aimed initially at the demilitarization of the country while encouraging moderate elements and inculcating democratic principles. 'From the start American occupation authorities envisaged a war crimes trial as contributing to both these objectives.'[40] The Allied Supreme Commander's special proclamation of 19 January 1946 established the Charter of the International Military Tribunal for the Far East. Article 5 of the Charter empowered the tribunal to try and punish Japanese charged with war crimes, including 'A. Crimes against Peace: namely, the planning, preparation, initiation or waging of a

---

[36] Richard H. Minear, *Victors' Justice: The Tokyo War Crimes Trial* (1st edn. Princeton, 1971; Tuttle edn. 1984), 16.   [37] Quoted ibid. 54.

[38] John Pritchard, *An Overview of the Historical Importance of the Tokyo War Trial* (Nissan Occasional Paper, 1987), 50.   [39] Minear, op. cit., 45.

[40] Philip R. Piccigallo, *The Japanese on Trial* (Austin, Texas, 1979), 7.

declared or undeclared war of aggression, or a war in violation of international law, treaties, agreements or assurances, or participation in a
common plan or conspiracy for the accomplishment of any of the fore-
going'.[41] The IMTFE also exercised jurisdiction over class B and C
offences: conventional war crimes, and crimes against humanity or inhuman acts committed mainly against civilian populations other than
the Japanese.

Sir William Webb of Australia, president of the Tokyo tribunal, opened
the proceedings on 3 May 1946. Joseph B. Keenan of the United States,
chief of counsel by order of President Harry Truman, introduced the
indictment. All the twenty-eight defendants pleaded 'not guilty'. The
indictment consisted of fifty-five counts, divided into three sections under
the headings 'Crimes against Peace', 'Murder', and 'Other Conventional
War Crimes and Crimes against Humanity'.[42] Allied prosecutors excluded
from indictment any representatives of *zaibatsu*, partly because their
possible exoneration might affect the occupation policy of economic
reform. Hirohito too escaped indictment; this was a strictly American
action and caused a furore in Allied circles. Tojo, in his 50,000-word
statement, and also when cross-examined, according to the *New York Times*,
'indicted' the Allied nations for their economic blockade and military
encirclement which, he claimed, had brought Japan in 1941 'to the point
of annihilation' and compelled it to fire the first shot in order to preserve
its 'national existence'. Similar arguments were used by the American
defence counsel, who said that Allied behaviour in the pre-war period
had not differed fundamentally from Japan's. International agreements
such as the Kellogg–Briand Pact (of 1929) became 'worthless', owing to
repeated violations. Takayanagi, for the defence, argued that the Kellogg
Pact recognized the right of sovereign nations to act in self-defence. The
judgement however dismissed these arguments that Japan's had been a war
of self-defence, for the reason that measures taken by the Allied powers to
restrict Japanese trade were intended to induce Japan to abandon a course
of aggression and expansion embarked upon years before.

Justice Pal disagreed, and said: 'Perhaps at the present stage of the
International Society the word aggressors is essentially chameleonic and
may only mean the leaders of the losing party.'[43] He also insisted on the
right to war, because to outlaw war was to freeze the status quo.
'Certainly,' he said, 'dominated nations of the present day status quo
cannot be made to submit to external domination only in the name of
peace. International law must be prepared to face the problem of bringing
within juridical limits the politico-historical evolution of mankind which
up to now has been accomplished chiefly through war.'[44]

[41] Ibid. 11–12.   [42] Ibid. 14.   [43] Minear, op. cit., 59.   [44] Quoted ibid. 60.

Seven men, Tojo and another former prime minister, Hirota, and five generals (Doihara Kenji, chief of the Mukden Special Service Organ; Itagaki Seishiro, responsible for the Manchurian Incident; Kimura Heitaro, vice-war minister at the time of Pearl Harbor; Matsui Iwane, commander-in-chief of the Japanese forces in Central China at the time of the Nanking atrocities; and Muto Akira, chief of staff of the Japanese forces in the Philippines) were condemned to death by hanging. Sixteen defendants received life imprisonment, one (Togo Shigenori) twenty years, and one (Shigemitsu Mamoru) seven years; two (Nagano Osami and Matsuoka Yosuke) died during the trial, and one (Okawa Shumei) was still under psychiatric treatment at the time. The executions were carried out on 23 December 1948. On the following day nineteen other A-class war-crime suspects were released, the list including the future prime minister Kishi Nobusuke and two right-wing fixers later notorious for political scandals, Sasakawa Ryoichi and Kodama Yoshio.

As for the so-called minor war crimes of classes B and C (such as atrocious acts inflicted on prisoners of war and foreign civilian population), the Allied Powers prosecuted no less than 5,700 people and convicted about 4,420, of whom almost 984 were executed.[45]

Justice Pal also condemned the use of the atom bomb, saying that 'if any indiscriminate destruction of civilian life and property is still illegitimate in warfare, then, in the Pacific war, this decision to use the atom bomb is the only near approach to the directives of the German Emperor during the first world war and of the Nazi leaders during the second world war'.[46] Ienaga appreciated what Pal said about the use of the atom bomb, but pointed out that Pal's arguments had been made use of by those Japanese who wanted to justify the Great East Asia War, Japan's war of aggression. Indeed, Pal supported those Japanese who claimed that Japan was fighting against the spread of communism in Asia and had the right to make armed intervention in China for this purpose. In fact, he was one of the earliest Cold War ideologists.

Several problems remain to be addressed. Was the Tokyo Trial valid in international law? Is not international law an empirical, common law which grows with new cases? Was not the so-called 'victors' justice' after 1945 such a case, that fortified international law with new concepts such as crimes against peace and humanity? In short, what was the Tokyo Trial of 1946–8? (The same question can be applied to the Nuremberg Trial of 1945–6.)

---

[45] Fumito Kanda, 'Senryo to Minshushugi' (Occupation and Democracy), *Showa no Rekishi* (History of Showa) (Tokyo, 1983), viii. 173; Rekishigaku-Kenkyukai (Association for the Study of History) (eds.), *Nihonshi Shiryo* (Sources of Japanese History) (Tokyo, 1997), v. 206.
[46] Quoted in Minear, op. cit., 100–1.

Ienaga Saburo, in his book on *Senso Sekinin* (War Responsibility, 1985, 1989), suggests that the Japanese perception of this sensitive issue has become blurred because of the extreme forms it has taken: on the one hand, 'the general repentance of the whole nation of one hundred million people' was advocated shortly after Japan's surrender; and on the other, there were attempts to limit the entire responsibility to the military clique. He also points out that the problems of war responsibility have not been exhausted by the verdict given by the Tokyo Trial. His basic stance is derived from his definition of Japan's Fifteen-Year War as a war of aggression; hence, Japan's international responsibility is first of all for damage of all kinds inflicted on China, Korea, Taiwan, Malaysia, Indonesia, the Philippines, Vietnam, and Burma; secondly for the United States and other western nations whose possessions Japan attacked prior to a declaration of war or even without it; thirdly for neutral countries such as Portugal, whose territories like Timor Japan occupied; and fourthly for Russia, relations with which were more chequered. Internal responsibility of the Japanese state may sound odd, but by this he was drawing attention to sacrifices forced upon the people in terms of life, property, and spiritual freedom. At the same time he raises the question of the Allies' war responsibility, such as for indiscriminate bombing, especially the dropping of atomic bombs. Ienaga argues that both the Japanese state and the Japanese people failed to take war responsibility seriously. War minister Anami, who committed suicide when Japan surrendered, wrote in his will and testament that his death would atone for his 'great crime', which meant a crime against the emperor. Konoe Fumimaro, the prime minister at the time of the opening of the full-scale war against China, and Hashida Kunihiko, education minister at the time of Pearl Harbor, both commited suicide so as to avoid facing trial by the Allies. Shidehara's government, at its cabinet meeting held in November 1945, decided on the general rules on war responsibility: 1. the Great East Asia War was an unavoidable war of self-defence under military and economic pressures from the United States, Britain, and others; 2. the emperor remained a constitutional monarch and followed the rules constitutionally established regarding the declaration of war and carrying out of military campaigns. This government view, which was to be repeated so often by conservative politicians and publicists, is faulty and misleading as it ignores the fatal links between Japan's aggression against China and the Pacific war.

Bert Rölling, a Dutch judge who took part in a symposium held in Tokyo in 1983 on the trial, expressed the view that the Tokyo Trial, like the Nuremberg Trial, in spite of its shortcomings 'did undeniably contribute to a legal development that mankind urgently needed. The United Nations adopted the principles laid down at Nuremberg and Tokyo. The crime against peace has become an accepted component of international law.'[47] 'It is an irony of history', he added 'that the illegal and criminal American atomic bombs probably contributed to the conviction that Japanese aggression had been criminal. War must be brought to an end, and starting a war is illegal, yes, criminal; those opinions were strengthened when, after the capitulation, the atrocities committed were fully exposed.'[48]

Rölling firmly believed that international law was on the move. New concepts were being introduced. 'The common heritage of mankind' was a concept for the future, while national sovereignty was a concept of the past. The great turning-point was the recognition of the universal applicability of human rights, which signified the end of colonialism.[49] As to the Tokyo Trial, Rölling may have been a little optimistic, though he soon realized the grave flaws in the trial resulting from the subjection of legal forms to political content, or rather political dictates. The evidence relating to the atrocities of Unit 731 had been effectively suppressed and remained closed to the trial.[50]

THE REVIVAL OF POLITICAL PARTIES
UNDER THE OCCUPATION

The major concern of the Shidehara government was to put an end to the 'aberration' of wartime military rule and to return to pre-war parliamentary politics or what was known as Taisho democracy. Political parties took advantage of the Potsdam Declaration, especially of its Clause 10 on the restoration and strengthening of democratic tendencies among the Japanese people, which they interpreted simply as the revival of political parties. The socialists were first in the field, the Japan Socialist Party being founded on 2 November 1945, with Katayama Tetsu, the right-wing leader, as its secretary. Among the conservatives the Hatoyama faction of the old *Seiyukai* party took the initiative and started the *Nippon Jiyuto* (Japan Liberal Party) on 9 November, with Hatoyama Ichiro as its president supported by forty-three Diet members who had once formed an opposition group in the wartime Diet. The old *Minseito* party, together with one faction in the *Seiyukai*, founded the *Nippon Shinpoto* (Japan Progressive Party), which was joined by 273 Diet members and had Machida Chuji as its president. The party absorbed most of the main-

---

[47]   C. Hosoya *et. al.* (eds.), *The Tokyo War Crimes Trial: An International Symposium* (Tokyo: Kondansha, 1986), 132; See also Ienaga, op. cit., 363.

[48]   Hosoya *et al.*, (eds.), op. cit., 16, 127–8.

[49]   B. V. A. Rölling and Antonio Cassese, *The Tokyo Trial and Beyond* (Cambridge, 1993), 136.

[50]   See Appendix I for a fuller account of the history of Unit 731.

stream of the wartime 'Greater Japan Political Association', which had developed from the *Yokusan Seijikai* (Political Association to Assist the Imperial Rule). The third conservative party was the *Nippon Kyodoto* (Japan Co-operative Party), formed on 18 December representing rural bosses in the *Sangyo Kumiai* (Industrial Unions) as well as trading and small manufacturing interests in the towns: they were close to Kishi Nobusuke and his right-wing supporters. The Communist Party simply emerged from underground or rather from prison into the open: it regarded the occupation as heralding a democratic revolution, described the occupation forces as an army of emancipation, and called for a people's republican government. It has been said that the communist plea for republicanism awakened the problem of *kokutai* from its state of abeyance because there was no great difference on this issue between the conservatives and the socialists.[51]

The GHQ had a very low opinion of both the Liberals and the Progressives as 'representing reactionary political views',[52] and the prospect of their acheiving a majority in the next Diet led the GHQ to urge the Shidehara government to postpone the scheduled general election and to embark in the meantime on a large-scale purge of war criminals, professional military personnel, members of nationalist bodies, influential members of the *Yokusankai*, directors of colonial businesses, administrators of occupied countries, and other militarists and extreme nationalists. As a result the Progressives lost 260 out of 274 Diet members, the Liberals thirty out of forty-three, and the Co-operatives twenty-one out of twenty-three.[53] By the time the first general election under the new electoral law took place on 10 April 1946, the old party leaders had been swept away. The introduction of women's suffrage and the lowering of the voting age from 25 to 20 swelled the electorate 2.5 times, and 375 new Diet members, amounting to 80.5 per cent of the whole, were elected. The new constitution, the draft of which had just been announced, was to make a prime minister and his (or her) government responsible to the Diet, 'the supreme organ of the state'; unlike under the Meiji constitution, the premier was to be chosen by the Diet out of its members: hence political parties (some party factions as well) had a decisive role to play in forming a government. Now in the new Diet the Liberal Party had 141 members, the Progressives ninety-four, the Co-operatives fourteen, the Socialists ninety-three, the Communists five, and others 119; and thirty-nine women members were elected. Hatoyama himself, though elected, was purged. Yoshida Shigeru, who succeeded Hatoyama as the president of the Liberal

---

[51] Ryuji Miyazaki in Masanori Nakamura *et al.* (eds.), *Senryo to Sengo Kaikaku* (The Occupation and Post-war Reforms) (Tokyo, 1995), 200. [52] Ibid. 201.
[53] Maomi Yui, op. cit., 64; Miyazaki, op. cit., 201.

Party, formed his first government in May 1946. The 'Give Us Rice' movement organized a 'Food May Day' among the starving citizens of Tokyo and began to threaten Yoshida's fragile government. He was, however, saved by MacArthur's appeal to order and by emergency food aid from the GHQ.

All the reform measures carried out by the Yoshida government, such as *zaibatsu* dissolution and land reform, were requested by GHQ directives. Ashida Hitoshi, who was to form the *Minshuto* (Democratic Party) to replace the Progressives, summarized the reforms carried out at the initial stage of the occupation:

The Socialists and the Communists in the radical camp plead for 'Revolution' [*kakumei*], the former for 'bloodless revolution', whereas the conservative camp advocate 'renovative' [*kakushin*] policies. Policy differences between the Socialists and the conservatives are not apparent. In a year and a half after our defeat in the war the two governments that belonged to the conservative camp [led by Shidehara and Yoshida respectively] have accomplished most of the policies that would have been carried out by a revolutionary government in Europe or America.[54]

It is needless to say that these reforms originated in the SCAP and his advisers, who pursued the measures for demilitarization and democratization as 'victor's justice', justice in a political and social sense, to which we now turn.

[54] Quoted in Ryuji Miyazaki in Masanori Nakamura *et al.* (eds.), op. cit., 203.

16

Occupation Reform:
Education, Women, Land, and Labour

REFORM AS AN OCCUPATION POLICY

Ambiguities remained for all the apparent successes of occupation reforms,[1] and the root cause of this could be traced, oddly enough, to the ambiguous position of the Showa emperor. In spite of all the constitutional debates on his new status,[2] the emperor as 'the symbol of the unity of the people' proved a useful tool, as MacArthur had perceived at an early stage, for the Americans to use in carrying out their occupation policies. The emperor, even in his new guise, was a force for the status quo and continuity, which had the effect of blunting the radicalism of the reforms introduced.

Shidehara Kijuro, the pre-war advocate of liberal diplomacy, formed his own government in October 1945. Shortly afterwards he visited MacArthur, who suggested the need for liberal revision of the constitution (which we have already examined) and directed him to introduce 'Five Great Reforms', women's suffrage, encouragement to trade unions, liberalization of education, abolition of the secret police, and democratization of the economic system. In the same month the communist leaders Tokuda Kyuichi and Shiga Yoshio were set free after eighteen years in prison and all other political prisoners were released. Together with the Public Order Preservation Act and the *Tokko* police, the security structure of the emperor's state now crumbled. Militaristic education was prohibited, and government support for state Shintoism was forbidden. The first stage of the American occupation had begun in earnest.

EDUCATION

On 15 September 1945 the Ministry of Education announced a programme of 'New Education' based upon two principles: the maintenance

---

[1] Herbert Passin, 'The Occupation—Some Reflections', in Carol Gluck and Stephen Graubard (eds.), *Showa: The Japan of Hirohito* (New York, 1992), 124–5.

[2] Tsuneo Yasuda, 'Shocho Tennosei to Kokumin Ishiki' (The System of the Emperor as the Symbol and Popular Consciousness', in Masanori Nakamura (ed.), *Senryo to Sengo Kaikaku* (The Occupation and the Post-war Reforms) (Tokyo, 1994), 144.

of the national polity expressed in the Imperial Rescript on Education, and the elimination of militaristic ideas, and in this the education minister Maeda Tamon had support from his old friend Harold Henderson, head of the education department of the CIE (Civil Information and Education Section) set up one week later. 'Japanese-style democracy' was tentatively proposed by the Ministry of Education, which still retained its thought-control section. It therefore naturally became suspect to the Americans, and the SCAP issued a series of directives on education, starting with one on the control of education, especially the elimination of militaristic and super-nationalistic ideology from school textbooks (issued 22 October 1945). The second directive of 30 October led to the screening of teachers, the result of which was the expulsion of 5,211 out of 568,228 screened, besides 115,778 who had resigned voluntarily.[3] The third directive (issued on 15 December 1945) was to ensure the separation of the state and Shintoism and the elimination of Shintoist influences from education. Another directive, issued on 31 December 1945, forbade the teaching of ethics, national history, and geography, the three disciplines that had been pervaded by imperial historiography and emperor worship. Yet the Imperial Rescript itself was left untouched. Abe Yoshishige, the Kantian philosopher, succeeded Maeda as the education minister in January 1946 when the latter was purged from public office. Abe met Kenneth Dyke, head of the CIE, and discussed the rewriting of Japanese history. He insisted that the legendary part of history be retained, whereas Dyke emphasized the need to rewrite Japanese history on a factual basis and succeeded in enforcing necessary revisions and deletions. On the issue of the Imperial Rescript on Education, Abe and Dyke agreed on the need for retaining something of that nature, though on different grounds; Dyke held the view that educational reform could be accelerated by a new imperial edict, which he called an 'emotional springboard' for the re-education of the Japanese, while Abe regarded the existing edict as 'the norm of the everyday moral life of the nation'.[4]

In the meantime an American mission on education arrived in February 1946 and co-operated with a Japanese committee of educationalists which proposed the desirability of a new imperial edict on education, the establishment of local educational committees, and the introduction of a '6-3-3-4 system' (the American system of six years' primary, three years' middle school, three years' high school, and four years' college or

[3] Yoshizo Kubo, 'Senryo to Kyoiku Kaikaku' (The Occupation and Education Reform), in ibid. 162; see also ch. 5, 'The American Occupation of Japan', of Michael D. Stephens, *Japan and Education* (Macmillan, 1991).

[4] Ryoji Okamura, 'Kyoiku Kaikaku to Minshushugi-kan' (Educational Reform and the Views of Democracy), in Masanori Nakamura *et al.* (eds.), *Sengo Minshushugi* (Post-war Democracy) Tokyo, 1995), 38–9.

university education). After three weeks' study the American mission issued a report of great weight, indicating the direction in which educational reform was to be carried out: the recognition of the dignity of the individual as the basic idea of education, an assurance of equality of educational opportunities, freedom of learning and research, and curriculums, textbooks, and teaching methods to be selected freely without government interference; it urged the establishment of elective local education committees, endorsed the '6-3-3-4 school system', and proposed an expansion of universities and the adoption of co-education, while an emphasis was placed on humanities rather than specialization.[5]

The Japanese committee of educationalists developed into an education renovation committee set up in August 1946 under the new prime minister Yoshida Shigeru, which was to prepare the Basic Education Law to be issued and enforced on 31 March 1947, one day before the 6-3 school system (for elementary and middle school) was to start. The Basic Law was very much in line with the recommendations made by the American Mission on Education. As for a new imperial edict, the committee decided not to ask for it. One of its members, Amano Teiyu, the principal of the First Higher School, took the existing edict for granted and feared that a new edict might 'cause embarrassment' to the imperial house. As a result the Basic Law failed to replace the Imperial Rescript on Education, which was still regarded as valid. As late as March 1947 the education minister Takahashi Seiichiro insisted that there was no contradiction between the Basic Law and the Imperial Rescript. It was three years after Japan's surrender, on 24 May 1948, that the education committee of the Diet declared that the Imperial Rescript on Education of 1890 had lost its validity in view of Clause 97 of the new constitution, which stipulated the nullity of decrees and edicts contrary to the constitution. Morito Tatsuo, the minister of education, announced 'the death of the imperial edict' in the summer of 1948. Twenty years later he had come round to denounce democratic influences for disrupting 'the tradition of our motherland', and described 'post-war reform' as 'the brainwashing of the Japanese through education by the occupying country'. He was the chairman of the Central Deliberative Council on Education, which was in fact a successor body of the Education Renovation Committee.[6]

When the new education system began in April 1947, school buildings, teachers, and textbooks were all in short supply. 'The 6-3 system in the barracks' read the caption of a newspaper report. The *shakaika* (Social Studies) were given prominence in the curriculum, as a way of combining ethics, history, and geography stripped of the old patriotic, expansionist values. Amano Teiyu proved himself to be a diehard in opposing the

---

[5] Yoshizo Kubo, op. cit., 167–8.   [6] Ryoji Okamura, op. cit., 48–50, 58.

absorption of his own First Higher School by the new Tokyo University, but new-system universities, and in fact the new education system itself, began to operate in 1949.

Accordingly the American system of 6-3-3-4 (elementary, middle, high, and college) replaced the previous system of 6-5-3-3.[7] The trick was done by creating numerous *Shinsei-Daigaku* (colleges under the new system) by upgrading the middle 3 (junior colleges) and merging some of them with *Daigaku* (the last 3 in the old system). Again, the 5 in the old system (middle school) was inflated and then divided into 3-3 (middle and high). Co-education was widely introduced for the first time under the new system, and this perhaps contributed more to the enhancement of the status of women than did their political emancipation; it also added to the frustration of well-educated women due to the continued discrimination they suffered with respect to job opportunities. Prefectural boards of education, elected bodies, were to certify teachers and administrators and to approve textbooks, and the role of the Ministry of Education was limited to that of providing technical and advisory counsel. It is true that the 228 new-system universities and 264 new junior colleges (the numbers at the beginning of the new system) could be compared favourably with the seven imperial universities, five specialized state universities, and a handful of private universities under the old system. But the variable quality of teaching and facilities at the new institutions added to the prestige of the small number of old, well-established universities, and made competition for entrance to the latter keener than before.[8]

The Japan Teachers' Association founded in 1947 insisted on 'democratic' and 'peace' education, and their annual conferences were harassed by right-wing thugs so much so that it was often difficult for the Association to find a town which would sponsor their conferences by providing a town-hall or similar facilities. By the time of the San Francisco Peace Treaty of 1951 there was a visible reaction in the field of education: Confucian ethics and some of the old subjects were restored, and the Ministry of Education reasserted its power to supervise national education. Elected local boards of education were gradually replaced by appointees; the last elected board, that of Nakano Ward, Tokyo, was voted out at a ward assembly early in 1994. The Ministry of Education resumed censorship of textbooks.

Elitism and professionalism in education were frowned upon. Old higher schools, higher commercial or technology schools, and normal schools were made part of a new university or had themselves upgraded to become the core of a university. As for state universities, their number

---

[7] Mikiso Hane, *Modern Japan: A Historical Survey* (Boulder, Col., 1992), 349.
[8] Takafusa Nakamura, *Showashi* (History of Showa), 502.

increased from twelve in 1945 (excepting Korea and Taiwan) to thirty in 1950. (In 1994 the number of universities, state, prefectural and private, amounted to 552, and that of students to 2,481,800.) Universities became less elitist, increasingly attuned to a mass consumer society. Indeed, mass education, with its obvious defects, was already on its way, but the problems faced by teachers and students at this stage were poverty and deprivation, material rather than spiritual, both within schools and without. And the problems of democratization and anti-militarism, the occupation's primary aims, were nowhere more seriously tackled than in schools and universities.

WOMEN

Women in pre-war Japan had neither political nor civil rights, for married women had no independent right to hold property of their own, like minors; their position in the family was not much above that of servants. It was appropriate for the SCAP to try to make Japan 'a laboratory for one of the world's most radical experiments with women's rights'.[9] A policy alliance was formed between a group of low-ranking American women serving in the occupation and a group of Japanese women leaders, advocates of women's rights in Japan.[10] The latter concentrated their efforts on the attainment of women's suffrage, which was duly gained through the revision of the Electoral Law in December 1945. The thirty-nine women Diet members elected at the first post-war general election in April 1946 formed a women's club in the Diet and began actively supporting the draft constitution, which contained clauses for women's equality.

When the SCAP took over the work of preparing a draft constitution, a small three-member subcommittee to deal with the issues of civil liberties was appointed, one of the members being a woman of exceptional ability and dedication, Beate Sirota. She was born in Vienna in 1923 and brought up in Japan with her father, the head of the piano department of the Imperial Academy of Music in Tokyo. Ms Sirota was a great asset to the subcommittee, from which emanated ideas on the equality of women that were to be embodied in the constitution.

Article 14 of the new constitution, like the American Equal Rights Amendment, was an explicit guarantee of women's equality: 'All people are equal under the law and there shall be no discrimination in political, economic or social relations because of race, creed, sex, social status or family origin.' Likewise, Article 24 dealt with women's status in more precise terms, with regard to marriage and the family: 'Marriage shall be

---

[9] Susan J. Pharr, 'The Politics of Women's Rights', in Ward and Sakamoto (eds.), *Democratizing Japan: The Allied Occupation* (Honolulu, 1987), 222.   [10] Ibid. 223.

based on the mutual consent of both sexes and it shall be maintained through mutual co-operation with the equal rights of husband and wife as a basis. With regard to choice of spouse, property rights, inheritance, choice of domicile, divorce and other matters pertaining to marriage and the family, laws shall be enacted from the standpoint of individual dignity and the essential equality of the sexes.'[11] In February 1946, when the Americans gave their draft constitution to the Japanese for consideration, both Articles 14 and 24 came under attack at once because they threatened the traditional male domination in the family and the family system itself, 'the necessary basis of social order'. When the constitution was debated in the Diet in the summer of 1946, the two articles again met resistance: some Diet members argued that men and women were fundamentally unequal, and some asserted the superiority of the male, quoting from the German philosopher and misogynist, Arthur Schopenhauer. In the end sabotage and resistance failed and the constitution was promulgated with the women's clause kept intact (adopted in November 1946 and enforced in May 1947).

The next battle for the cause of women was fought over the issue of the Women's and Minors' Bureau to be set up in the Ministry of Labour. This new ministry was to be launched in September 1947. There was bureaucratic opposition from the Ministry of Welfare to the splitting away of its labour section. But more fundamentally a serious objection came from the top echelon of the Government Section of the occupation who were determined that 'the encouragement of a feminist movement in Japan must be avoided'.[12] There was, however, a strong group among the SCAP personnel who supported women's-rights policies, including Ethel B. Weed, a Women's Army Corps lieutenant and a former public relations specialist from Cleveland, Ohio. She was assisted by half-a-dozen able Japanese women including Mrs Kato Shizue, a former baroness who had married Kato Kanju, a socialist worker and Diet member. Among the group, which gradually expanded, were Kume Ai, the first woman lawyer in Japan, Tanaka Sumiko, later a socialist Diet member, and Fujita Taki, later president of the Tsuda Women's College. Their persistent efforts to help Lieutenant Weed create the Women's Bureau in the new Ministry of Labour were finally crowned with success. A foothold was gained for the improvement of living and working conditions for working women and working mothers.

Equal rights for women depended much on the reform of the civil code, which under the Meiji constitution had remained the safeguard of the *ie* or 'house system' (otherwise *kazoku seido* or family system). In fact *kokutai*, 'the unique essence of Japanese society', contained two

---

[11] Pharr, op. cit., 224–5.   [12] Ibid. 237.

interrelated elements: the emperor system and the family system: loyalty to the emperor and filial piety had the same roots and complemented each other. The house was considered 'the state in microcosm'; the state was 'the house writ large'.[13] It is true that the power of the head of the house was softened under the impact of industrialization and urbanization, which required the freer movement of house members, but his authority could easily be invoked under critical situations. Indeed, memories of the Takigawa case, and his criticism of the old criminal code which made a wife's adultery punishable but not a husband's, had not faded away. It is of some interest, however, to note that in the revised criminal law enforced in October 1947 clauses related to crimes due to *lèse-majesté* as well as those arising from adultery for both men and women were rescinded.

The new constitution, especially Article 24, gave the direction in which reform of the civil code should be carried out. A government committee was set up to tackle the problem of reforming the civil code, in which young law professors were prominent; they kept in touch with the occupation personnel concerned and proposed the abolition of *ie* in the civil code. The bill to amend the code was passed in November 1947 and became effective on 1 January 1948. Kishi Nobusuke later regretted that the concept of *ie* was absent from the civil code.[14] His advocacy of revision, however, met with strong opposition from women's organizations, and nothing came of it. Later, at the time of high economic growth, the *ie* ideology was revived by the cultural anthropologist Nakane Chie, as 'a concept which penetrates every nook and cranny of Japanese society'.[15] A further attempt was made later to resuscitate the *ie* society 'as the civilization' peculiar to Japan or rather to the Japanese business world.[16] The cult of *ie* which emerged with the rise of the business culture embodied in 'Japanese-style management' is now on the way out, partly because the business culture itself has proved inflexible and costly, and partly for the reason that the traditional family itself has been pushed to the brink of collapse.

LOCAL GOVERNMENT

We have already seen how severe the blow was when the Home Ministry was ordered to dissolve its thought police, the *Tokko* section. It sought to regain some of its lost power by initiating reform itself. By the end of October 1945 the Home Ministry had announced the introduction of an

---

[13] Kurt Steiner, 'The Occupation and the Reform of the Japanese Civil Code', in Ward and Sakamoto (eds.), op. cit., 189.　　[14] Quoted Kurt Steiner, op. cit., 205.

[15] Chie Nakane, *Japanese Society* (Hamondsworth, 1973), 4.

[16] Yasusuke Murakami *et al.* (eds.), *Bunmei toshiteno Ie-shakai* (The Ie Society as Civilization) (Tokyo 1979).

elective system of prefectural governors in an obvious attempt to forestall SCAP intervention on matters related to decentralization, one of the major policies of the democratization of Japan pursued by the Americans. In its first proposal governors were to be elected by the members of a local council. Its hesitant approach was thwarted when in March 1946 the new draft constitution was released and made it clear that all governors and mayors were to be elected by direct popular vote. The Home Ministry, however, made another attempt to retain its power over popularly elected governors by making them government officials, to be controlled by itself. This proposal met with an adverse response from the Diet and from public opinion. The Government Section of the GHQ, too, objected to a fresh attempt at preserving central control. The Local Autonomy Law enforced on 3 May 1947, at the same time as the new constitution, had for its object an assurance of democratic and efficient administration on the local level. It emphasized the power of governors and mayors as the heads of a local community, in other words, they were made local officials contrary to the Ministry's intention. Shortly before this, on 30 April 1947, the Government Section of the GHQ issued a memorandum on the decentralization of the Ministry of Home Affairs. The Home Ministry sought to maintain itself as a body that would be in charge of local government and its finance, and even thought of changing its name to the Ministry of Popular Administration (*Minseisho*), but the Government Section did not allow further prevarication. The GHQ also urged prime minister Katayama to embark upon a radical plan for police decentralization. He directed that the police organization be divided into a small national police and a prefectural police independent of the central government. The Police Law, based on the principles of decentralization and democratization of the police force, was issued on 17 December. On 31 December 1947 the Home Ministry was formally dissolved.

Local government, however, needed a representative in the cabinet in order to protect its own interests, and considerations of this sort led to the establishment of the Ministry of Local Government (*Jichisho*) in 1960. Fortunately, this did not amount to a revival of the Home Ministry. In fact, the principle of local autonomy served as a bulwark against a revival of the pre-war system of central control and supervision.[17]

LAND REFORM

Land reform was truly 'sweeping in its scope': it transferred the ownership of over one-third of cultivated land, and affected 70 per cent of the

---

[17] Akira Amakawa, 'The Making of the Postwar Local Government System', in Ward and Sakamoto (eds.), op. cit., 279.

agricultural, and 30 per cent of the total population. 'It was carried out with a smoothness', said an agrarian economist, 'which perhaps only the presence of a transcendental Occupying Power could ensure.' Its impact on the living standards of farmers, on agricultural productivity, and on the political attitudes and activities of the rural population were far-reaching.[18]

Agriculture still remained Japan's biggest industry; as late as the middle of the 1950s it employed some 41 per cent of the working population and produced 18 per cent of the national income. Cultivation was intensive: the average holding of the country's 6 million farm families was a mere two acres. Yields per man-hour were low, but yields per acre were among the highest in the world.[19] In flat fields ploughing was done with horses or oxen, but 'petrol-driven hand-guided rotor cultivators' had begun to be used, and further mechanization of rice cultivation was on its way.

The Meiji land reforms created unconditional private ownership in land and with it a large number of tenants who tilled lands for landowners. By 1908 the proportion of land cultivated by tenants had reached 45 per cent. In 1946 it was still 46 per cent, though of a considerably larger acreage. Paternalism in traditional Japan put the accent on authority rather than affection, and this was the case with the landlord–tenant relationship. Rent rates generally amounted to something over half of an average crop. Progressive landlords, however, were credited with an active role in developing co-operative organizations at the turn of the century. On the other hand there were 'rapacious landlords' who were concerned only with squeezing the maximum from their tenants. The tenant's position was unprotected by the law, and he was generally in debt. Such was the situation in which tenant farmers found themselves on the eve of land reform.

The exising tenancy system could not go on much longer. The number of tenants' disputes had increased from eighty-five in 1917 to 1,680 in 1921, 3,419 in 1931, and 6,824 in 1935. Even in the year of Pearl Harbor it stood at 3,308. Reform was overdue in the land system when the Allied occupation began. Matsumura Kenzo, the new minister of agriculture in the Shidehara cabinet, was in favour of the creation of independent farmers,[20] and in October the Japanese Ministry of Agriculture drafted a plan which became the government's first Land Reform Bill.

At this stage the US government had not worked out a policy for agriculture. In fact there was a division of opinion in Washington as to the future of Japanese agriculture. Robert A. Fearey, a State Department

---

[18] Seiichi Tobata, Introduction to Ronald Dore, *Land Reform in Japan* (Oxford, 1959), p. xiv.
[19] Ibid. 94–5.
[20] Noriaki Iwamoto, in *Koza Nihonrekishi* (Lectures in History of Japan) (Tokyo, 1985) xi. 84.

official, in conjunction with Wolf I. Ladejinsky of the Department of Agriculture, made sweeping recommendations for reform. The majority opinion of the 'old Japan hands' of the State Department, however, was that to impose a reform on hostile landlords and inarticulate tenants would open the way to disruption and to communism. Then, in October, Fearey was transferred from Washington to Tokyo, to the staff of George Atcheson Jr, the State Department representatives attached to GHQ. Fearey persuaded Atcheson to bring his memo on land reform to MacArthur; Atcheson's covering letter spoke of the 'depressed conditions in agriculture' as having helped the army's rise to power, and of the danger of similar military propaganda if nothing was done to improve conditions.[21] The memo caught MacArthur's imagination, and the decision to press for a land reform was his.[22] MacArthur remembered his own father's connections with Philippine land reform earlier in the century. It was only a few days after this that the Ministry of Agriculture's draft for land reform was presented to the Cabinet. The draft bill made three recommendations: 1. the abolition of produce rents and their replacement by a money equivalent; 2. the compulsory transfer to the cultivators of all lands owned by absentee landlords and all tenanted land of other landlords in excess of 3 cho (1 cho being roughly equivalent to 2.45 acres or 9,917 square meters); 3. the establishment of land committees to administer the scheme in the villages. In the course of cabinet meetings the amount of land permitted to non-absentee landlords was increased from 3 to 5 cho, which meant the number of affected landlords would be reduced from 1 million to 100,000, an attempt apparently to safeguard landlords' interest and to maintain the authoritarian structure of the Japanese state.[23]

In December 1945 the SCAP issued a memorandum to the Japanese government instructing it to 'establish respect for the dignity of man, and destroy the economic bondage which has enslaved the Japanese farmer for centuries of feudal oppressions'. The memo itself was largely a reproduction of Fearey's original. This was enough to frighten the Diet into resigned submission, and the bill, largely in its original form though with a few amendments, passed into law. This law was widely criticized in the Japanese press as a half-hearted attempt to forestall a real reform. The occupation authorities too did not consider it satisfactory. The elections for the land committees, the first step for reform, was postponed indefinitely. Indeed, the government-sponsored first Land Reform Law had many defects, one of which was related to individual holdings, the terms of which made it possible for landlords to escape purchase by distributing land titles among members of their household, including minors.

Meanwhile, in the Allied council, the Russian delegate General

---

[21] Dore, op. cit., 131.   [22] Ibid. 132.   [23] Ibid. 133.

Derevyanko spoke of the connection between the domination of reactionary chauvinistic military cliques and the presence of feudalistic oppression
in the Japanese village. The Russians proposed the expropriation of all
tenanted land, while the proposals of the British Commonwealth were less
sweeping and more detailed. These recommendations were broadly in line
with the SCAP plan, and this was sent to the Japanese government as a
private memorandum in June 1946. The cabinet meekly gave its approval a
month later. The second land reform legislation became law in October
1946.

The land to be purchased was: 1. all the land of absentee landowners; 2.
all tenanted land owned by resident landlords in excess of 43 cho in
Hokkaido and an average of 1 cho in the rest of Japan; 3. all land
cultivated by the owner in excess of 12 cho in Hokkaido and an average
of 3 cho for the rest of Japan; 4. other residential land, buildings, or
grassland, rented by a tenant and necessary to his livelihood as an owner-
farmer. The land was to be purchased directly by prefectural governors
acting on behalf of the state on the basis of plans drawn up by village or
town land committees. Land so purchased was to be sold to those who
were ready to devote their energies to farming as owner-farmers. In the
skyrocketing inflation of the time money was depreciated, and most
tenants paid for their land in cash within a year or two of purchase.
Between 1946 and 1955 (by which time most of the land transfers
occasioned by the reform legislation had been carried out) the ratio of
owner-farmers in the agricultural population increased from 32.6 per cent
to 61.9 per cent, that of part-tenant and tenant farmers decreased from
48.5 per cent to 30.7 per cent, and that of tenants from 28.7 per cent to
5.1 per cent. This reform, asserted a Japanese political scientist, saved
Japanese villages from the infiltration of communism.[24]

The land reform is often praised as the most successful of the measures
undertaken under the American occupation. The enlightened bureaucracy
and public opinion supported the initiative of the occupation authorities.
Land reform was more than an economic matter. Old values of submis-
siveness, self-abnegation, and holism in the context of the family and the
local community were much weakened.[25] As for farmers' unions, having
fulfilled their function to aid land reform they have become an interest
group, and as such the agricultural co-operatives have grown into a gigantic organization ramifying its activities into many channels—banking and
investment, tourism and insurance, and manufacturing of all kinds—
besides providing stable electoral support for the conservatives, the parties
of the status quo, the LDP among others.

[24] Masamichi Royama, *Nihon no Rekishi* (History of Japan), vol. 26 (Tokyo, 1974; 1991), 75.
[25] Ibid. 398.

LABOUR REFORM

The Americans after the war undertook the difficult task of creating a Japanese labour movement almost from scratch; this has been called a 'journey to the unknown'.[26] There was an urgent need to organize trade unions in Japan, because the reconstruction of the war-devastated country deserted by the militarists and the industrialists had to be undertaken by the workers themselves. Takano Minoru, the first general secretary of the *Sohyo* (General Council of Trade Unions), later recalled that soon after the end of the war his small house in West Tokyo had become 'the hub of the resurgent labour movement', iron-founders, engineers, precision machine workers, and printers came to his house and worked all night printing handbills for a new trade union; he visited ruined factories and urged the workers: 'organize your own trade union, repair the roof of your factory, bring in the machines that have been exposed to all weathers, and clean them up.'[27]

By the time that Ted Cohen arrived in Japan to take charge of the SCAP Labour Division, the movement had grown to such an extent as to impress him with its vigour and discipline, even in demonstrations, 'with the placards that, while thanking General MacArthur for democracy, demanded higher wages, special allowances, and more prompt distribution of rations in a strident, threatening tone . . . The marchers . . . represented a new phenomenon—individuals demanding their "right".'[28] The demonstrations, though orderly, were forms of the desperate struggle to survive. Tokyo was still a burnt-out city, with rough wooden huts standing here and there. The great majority of city-dwellers were threatened with starvation, and they joined with trade unionists in a sort of mass action to demand the use of unused factories or large mansions for dwellings, and to call for more equitable and effective distribution of food.[29] The SCAP policy in favour of trade union organization greatly encouraged the workers. The unions mushroomed, and by 1 May 1946, Japan's first post-war May Day, some 2.7 million workers had joined 7,000 unions.[30]

On 10 October 1945 the first labour conference was held in Tokyo, attended by more than 100 'pre-war labour leaders', and this led to the formation of the *Sodomei* (General Federation of Trade Unions), which

---

[26] Cohen, op. cit., 188. Ted Cohen, who was in charge of the SCAP Labor Division during the formative period of the post-war Japanese labour movemen, had been a student of Japanese labour for nearly a decade. He had prepared an MA thesis entitled 'The Japanese Labour Movement 1918–1939' under Hugh Borton at Columbia University in 1939. He was invited to draft the 'Trade Unions' Guide, one of the 22 civil affair guides on Japan prepared shortly before Japan's surrender, and the guide-book he had written was approved by two extra-governmental bodies, the AFL and the CIO.

[27] Minoru Takano, *Nihon no Rodo-Undo* (The Labour Movement in Japan) (Tokyo, 1960), 8–9.   [28] Cohen, op. cit., 191.

[29] Takano, op. cit., 22.   [30] Cohen, op. cit., 191.

adopted three basic principles: the reconstruction of the national economy together with an improvement in wages and other conditions of work; the federation of industrial organizations; and freedom of political affiliation. Meanwhile, the liberated communist leaders set up a rival trade union federation, the *Sanbetsu* or NCIO (National Congress of Industrial Organizations). Takano of the *Sodomei* was horrified when he found that some Americans regarded the Japanese NCIO as equivalent to the American CIO, the Congress of Industrial Organizations, considered to be more radical than the AFL, and hence as more progressive than the rest.[31]

What baffled Cohen at first was not the communist challenge but a tactic called *Seisan-Kanri* or Production Control, first attempted by the Bibai miners in Hokkaido and followed by the workers employed by private railways around Tokyo. This was an attempt to carry on production on the 'self-control' principle, and the management, excluded from the control of production, quickly capitulated. 'To the Occupation authorities', wrote Cohen, this was

bemusing, the kind of labor tactics that could never take place in the United States. The Japanese, with their traditions of class differences and feudal battles, plus the added Marxist conception of class conflict, looked upon strikes as a form of surrogate warfare that could take any shape the fertile imagination could devise. Thus Japan had a long history of go-slow strikes, work-to-rule strikes, strikes where chorus girls kicked half as high or telephone operators cheerfully informed callers that they were on strike but working as usual, and strikes of limited duration, from a few minutes to several days.[32]

These new line, leftist tactics seemed especially appropriate because they would not obstruct production.

In the meantime, the Labour Relations Adjustment Law of 1946 was enacted, in the preparation of which the SCAP Labour Division played a leading role. Labour disputes were now to be treated not as breaches of law and order, which was the traditional Japanese way, but as economic issues. Restriction of strike action was imposed only on those engaged in essential public services such as policemen, firemen, prison guards, and goverment administration employees. Then came the Labour Standards Law of 1947. This was the work of Japanese drafters in the Welfare Ministry Labour Research Section, who made a comparative study of labour legislation of various countries and came out with a law which contained a most comprehensive protection of the workers, guaranteeing adequate working conditions.

When the threatened mass dismissal of workers from the National

---

[31] Unknown to MacArthur, the AFL and the CIO, with the concurrence of the War and Labor Departments, had divided up the occupation labour posts among themselves, Germany to the AFL and Japan to the CIO. Cohen, op. cit., 210.   [32] Ibid. 219.

Railway led to a national strike of railwaymen in September 1946, Cohen expected that General MacArthur would intervene. The 'Old Man', however, would not move. The government had to make concessions to the demands of the railwaymen's union, in which the communists exerted a dominant influence. Japan's organized labour launched an October offensive, to which Yoshida's reply was his New Year broadcast in which he denounced the union leaders as 'a gang of unruly, insolent rebels' (*futei no yakara*). The socialists and the communists joined hands in an effort to overthrow the Yoshida cabinet.

Both the socialists allied with *Sodomei* and the communists with *Sanbetsu* were more or less in agreement on the need for swift economic recovery without 'rationalization', that is without mass dismissals of workers. Railway workers and seamen took the lead in this struggle, and the communist-led *Sanbetsu* organized a series of successful srikes in October 1946 which secured an increase in wages for the workers in the private sector of industry. Then the workers in the public sector, teachers, postal workers, National Railway workers, and central and local government employees followed suit, and formed a Joint Struggle Committee which represented 2.6 million public employees. During the October offensive, 'the labour movement took on an increasingly political hue, combining economic demands with political slogans'.[33] Then the workers in the private sector were roused again, and the communists and socialists, *Sanbetsu* and *Sodomei*, jointly set up an action committee to overthrow the conservative government led by Yoshida. Now 4 million workers were ready to cease work on 1 February 1947. The occupation authorities did not interfere until the very last moment. The immediate issue was a wage increase demanded for low-paid government employees, and the Americans hesitated to take any action that might impair their reputation as an army of liberation.[34] Eleven representatives of the strike committee visited Cohen on 25 January and, after a long parley, were told that a 'general strike cannot be permitted under the occupation'. The Communist Party, which practically took over the leadership of the Joint Action Committee, nevertheless, believed that the Americans would not suppress a strike, even a general strike, which was planned for legitimate purposes, and as late as the morning of 31 January the party headquarters remained excited over the question of who would be the members of a new democratic government of the people to be formed after a successful strike. On the evening of the same day the chairman of the Joint Action Committee, Ii Yashiro, was summoned by the occupation authorities and ordered to make a radio

---

[33] Paul Henriques, 'The Political Development of Japanese Labor and the February 1, 1947 General Strike Movement', unpublished Ph. D. thesis, Claremont Graduate School, 1975, 185.
[34] Ichiro Saito, 2. 1 *Suto Zengo* (Before and After the 2. 1 General Strike) (Tokyo, 1956), 171.

broadcast announcing the cancellation of the impending general strike. 'I was sent by jeep to the broadcast station,' Ii later recalled: 'Tears poured down my cheeks as it suddenly occurred to me that the American pretence that they would help promote trade unionism in Japan and defend workers against oppression was false.'[35]

The massive mobilization of the workers for a general strike, though it misfired in the end, had its effect: government employees won an increase in wages, and the first government led by a Socialist prime minister, Katayama Tetsu, was formed after the general election later in the same year. But February 1947 marked the decisive shift in American policy towards Japan, from that of democratization of the defeated nation to economic rehabilitation of a future ally in the Cold War that had begun.

THE GENERAL ELECTION OF APRIL 1947

In spite of the purge of a large number of Diet members prior to the first general election in post-war Japan (in April 1946) because of their records of war collaboration, the pre-war parties under new names, and the relatives and agents of the purged politicians, as substitute candidates, fared well; in spite of the efforts of the mass media, newspapers, films, and radio (NHK only) for the propagation of democracy, the electorate apparently was content with the continuation of the old forces and interests, as was shown by the 3-to-1 ratio between the conservative Diet members (336) and the radical reformist members (102), (plus twenty-eight independents) at the time of the closing of a special session of the Diet in October 1946. At this stage, 'people ought to have recognized the continuation, without a break, of politics from pre-war to post-war'.[36] One year later, on 25 April 1947, another general election was held, along with elections for prefectural governors and local assembly members, in order to form new deliberative organs to function under the new constitution that was to take effect in May. The Diet, that used to be *gikai* (a deliberative assembly), was to become *kokkai* (a national assembly), and the prime minister, as noted earlier, was to be chosen by ballot from among the members of the Diet. The middle-sized constituency system that had been adopted from the first general election under universal suffrage in 1928 to the last wartime election of 1942 was reverted to.[37]

At this election the Japan Socialist Party (JSP) became the leading party, with 143 members elected (later 144) as against 131 for the Liberal Party, 124 for the Democratic Party, thirty-one for the National Co-operative

---

[35] Quoted Saito, op. cit., 241.
[36] Masumi Ishikawa, *Sengo Seijishi* (Post-war Political History) (Tokyo, 1995), 34-5.
[37] Ibid. 40.

Party, four for the JCP, and thirty-three for independents and others. The socialists won seats in both urban and rural constituencies; their successes were ascribed to the discontent among wage-earners and small tradesmen in cities under the rapidly worsening inflation, and also to the grievances of farmers over land reform, which was still only halfway through its formulation. Trade unions also proved to be strong allies of the Socialist Party. 'Nobody could deny', read the *Asahi* editorial on 27 April, 'that the JSP, through the two post-war elections, has grown into a great national political party.' A setback for the communists had been anticipated in view of the failure of the projected 1 February general strike. The number of women members of the Diet was halved. A coalition government was formed, with Katayhama Tetsu, the chairman of the JSP, as prime minister, Ashida Hitoshi of the Democratic Party as foreign minister, and Miki Takeo of the Co-operative Party as minister of post and telegraph. Although Katayama aspired for a regime that might pave the way for 'the transition from capitalism to socialism', socialists in his government formed a minority, seven out of seventeen. In the Diet too, 'socialist members' (of the JSP and the JCP) numbered 148, whereas those from the four 'capitalist' parties (including the fourth party, the Japan Farmers Party) numbered 300. The so-called 'one and a half' party system that was to remain one of the main features of Japanese politics for nearly half a century was already discernible at this stage.[38] In other words, conservative forces were overwhelmingly powerful, but the opposition remained large enough to prevent a two-thirds majority for them, the condition that would have enabled them to revise the peace constitution to the liking of the militarists and nationalists who were soon to be restored to public life.

Under the circumstances, a socialist measure such as the nationalization of key industries was beyond the reach of the government, which had to put up with a temporary (three-year) legislation for national control of coal-mines adopted in December 1947. Reconstruction of the national economy had to be selective in view of the limited availability of resources, and preferential measures were adopted for the production of coal, such as the allocation of larger rice rations to coal-miners. Steel, another favoured item, was, like coal, sold at less than cost-price, the discrepancy being paid by the government. National control of coalmines was intended to facilitate what was called 'slanting [or priority] production', special favours accorded to the production of coal.

Katayama's coalition government collapsed in February 1948, partly because of a factional struggle between the left and the right of the JSP over the issue of national control of coalmines and the level of wages of government employees, and partly due to Katayama's disagreement with

[38] Ishikawa, op. cit., 41.

the SCAP, as he himself alleged, over the latter's pressure for rearmament.[39] He was succeeded by Ashida of the Democratic Party, who formed another coalition government of the same political complexion. The new government included several socialist ministers, such as Kato Kanju, minister of labour, and Morito Tatsuo, minister of education. The Ashida government, which came into existence in March 1948, however, was compelled to resign seven months later owing to a political scandal connected with financing a major fertilizer-maker in which the minister of finance and several others were implicated. Yoshida Shigeru, now the leader of the Democratic Liberal Party (the enlarged Liberal Party), formed his second government, and after a landslide victory for his party at another general election held in January 1949 he set up a majority government, his third. It appears that the GHQ played some role in the rise and fall of the Japanese governments of these years; in fact, American policy towards Japan had undergone a drastic change as a result of new developments in the international situation.

[39] Ibid. 43–4.

17

Post-war Reconstruction

THE COLD WAR AND 'THE REVERSE COURSE'

The seven years of the American occupation of Japan can be divided into two periods: the period of reform devoted to the adoption of measures for 'demilitarization and democratization'; and the period of reconstruction or restoration, in which the reform ideals became toned down or even in some cases reversed while the quick economic recovery of Japan as America's new ally was given the first priority under the emerging Cold War alignment. The latter period has often been referred to especially among the reformists as 'the reverse course'.

Reflection of US Cold War strategy on occupation policies was unavoidable, but Ted Cohen, the New Dealer, emphasizes that in 1947 and for almost all of 1948 the Washington agencies did not control Japan, while MacArthur and his staff did.[1] Moreover, the US Congressional election of November 1946 had been 'a psychological watershed'. For the first time since 1932 the Republicans and their Southern Democratic political allies decisively defeated the New Dealers. 'Labor was rejected. Business was in the saddle.'[2] The change in American domestic politics had its impact on the Japanese scene. After mid-1947 SCAP officials began to see their practical problems 'through the eyes of Japanese industrialists and banker'.[3]

The year 1947, which began with the SCAP injunction against the 1 February general strike, was indeed a transitional year. MacArthur was in favour of an early peace for Japan (he called for it in March 1947) which was conceived of in the framework of a 'punitive' or a victor's peace. This was in line with State Department planning for a peace treaty, shortly to be drafted by Hugh Borton and his team, which called for international supervision and control over 'sovereign' Japan. All this was appropriate to the political mood of the first period of demilitarization and democratization. Japanese reactions to these moves anticipated the San Francisco settlement made four years later under a drastically altered international situation. The Yoshida governmenment now hinted at a bilateral military agreement with the United States, and in May the emperor, through his personal emissary, conveyed his hopes to GHQ that Americans would

---

[1] Cohen, op. cit., 307–8.   [2] Ibid. 309.   [3] Ibid. 310.

continue the occupation of Okinawa in order to guarantee the security of Japan even after a peace settlement.[4] Although MacArthur's own presidential ambitions were dashed by a shattering defeat in the Republican primary in Wisconsin in April 1948, he did not give up his vision of turning Japan into the 'Switzerland of the Pacific', a reference made as late as March 1949. By then, wrote an American historian, 'time passed him by'.[5]

In fact the Cold War had begun, in the form of the Truman Doctrine expressed in his speech delivered in March 1947 to help 'free peoples who are resisting attempted subjugation by armed minorities or by outside pressures' in Greece and Turkey; in other words, all the peoples threatened by 'totalitarian' communist domination.[6] Dean Acheson, under-secretary of state, in a speech given in May linked the East with the West while separating 'the Cold War from the old war', and declared: Japan and Germany had to be developed as the 'workshops' of Asia and Europe respectively.[7] George F. Kennan, known for his successful containment policy against communism, began his work in May 1947 as head of the Policy Planning Staff to prepare what was soon to be known as the Marshall Plan for the economic recovery of western Europe, especially western Germany. In the early summer of 1947 Kennan and his staff began studying American policy towards Japan: they found Borton's draft peace treaty 'highly dangerous' and totally unacceptable. The rehabilitation of Japan as an industrial-military power in Asia allied with the United States formed an essential part of Kennan's geopolitical view of American security. In a preliminary study issued in October Kennan argued against any peace treaty before Japan could economically and politically be made safe against communist penetration.

It has been argued that the post-war definition of Japan as an engine of the US-dominated world economy was 'hammered out in 1947, co-terminous with (and as a result of) the cold war'. Japan was to remain a junior partner. 'Japan should do well, yes . . . but not so well that it hurt American interests.'[8] In fact, the position of Japan as a US ally in the Cold War, a junior partner, was formed in these years. The year 1947 marked the watershed between reform and a reverse of reform in post-war Japan, beginning with the occupation policy towards Japan's big businesses, the *zaibatsu* above all.

---

[4] Masaomi Yui, *Nihon Tsushi* (Complete History of Japan), xix. 81; Dower, *Japan in War and Peace*, 170–1.   [5] Dower, op. cit., 172.

[6] David McCullough, *Truman* (1992), 546.   [7] Quoted Dower, op. cit., 173.

[8] Bruce Cumings, 'Japan's Position in the World System', in Andrew Gordon (ed.), *Postwar Japan as History* (Berkeley, 1993), 35.

DISSOLUTION OF THE *ZAIBATSU*

An attempt to introduce 'democratic capitalism', of which Japan had no tradition nor experience,[9] proved to be less successful than any other reform measure. Unlike land reform, the initiative for *zaibatsu*-busting came from the SCAP, whose instructions to dissolve large industrial and banking combines led the Japanese government to set up the Holding Company Liquidation Commission (HCLC) in April 1946. The term *zaibatsu* has been defined as 'a political expression referring to the estate of wealth, and by extension, to the source of this wealth, the combines'. But in Japanese usage not all the combines were *zaibatsu*; only family-dominated combines were. When a former HCLC member was asked why the Japan Nitrogeneous Fertilizer Company (Nihon Chisso Hiryo) had not been included, he replied that its founder had died in 1944 and that it was no longer family-dominated.[10] The Japanese government had originally hoped to limit the holding companies to be liquidated to the 'big four—Mitsui, Mitsubishi, Sumitomo, and Yasuda, plus Fuji heavy industries (former Nakajima Aircraft Company). Under SCAP pressure many more were designated, but finally the above five and the five others, Nissan, Asano, Furukawa, Okura, and Nomura, remained to be liquidated, though Nissan was not family-owned. Shibusawa (Daiichi Bank), Matsushita, Kawasaki, and Okochi (for Riken or Physical-Chemical Reseach Institute) were dropped for reasons of size. Top names were Mitsui, Mitsubishi, and Sumitomo, and operations in markets as diverse as banking, insurance, shipping and shipbuilding, coal-mining, electrical equipment, and trading had been integrated through holding companies into 'a private collectivism'.[11] The aim of *zaibatsu*-busting was to broaden the basis of ownership in the modern sector of the economy, and this was regarded as essential to the growth of democracy in Japan.[12]

An American mission to investigate Japanese combines presented proposals for combine dissolution which included not only the liquidation of holding companies but also prohibition of interlocking directorates and dissolution of oversized operating companies. To implement these aims the Anti-Trust Act of April 1947 and the Act to Prevent Excessive Concentration of Economic Power of December 1947 were enacted. By the middle of 1947, however, US policy towards Japan underwent a drastic change; the Act of December 1947 was allowed to pass the Diet by adding 'Excessive' to its title. The number of companies which the act was to deal with was reduced from 325 to eighteen, and these were to be 'chosen on the basis

---

[9] Eleanor M. Hadley, *Antitrust in Japan* (Princeton, 1970), 15.   [10] Ibid. 21 n.
[11] Ibid. 19.
[12] In 1946 the companies of the Big Four controlled 24.5% of the paid-up capital in Japan. Ibid. 47.

that they were interfering with Japanese economic recovery'.[13] The eighteen companies that remained under the act included Nihon Seitetsu (Japan Steel), Tokyo Shibaura Denki (Tokyo-Shibaura Electric or Toshiba), Mitsubishi Jukogyo (Mitsubishi Heavy Industries), and Mitsui Kozan (Mitsui Mining). Of these, eleven companies were broken up into smaller units, four were allowed to continue after disposing of part of their facilities, and three were left untouched except for parting with a portion of shares. In fact, no company was dissolved under the Act. Moreover, the need for rationalization led to voluntary division under the Act or the splitting of as many as thirty-five undesignated businesses. The overall effect of the Act was to eliminate exceedingly large enterprises and thus to make competition among businesses more lively and stimulating.[14] The Anti-Trust Act was also revised in June 1949, allowing mutual share-holding and sharing of directors among businesses and enabling the reassembling of firms which had been separated from the old *zaibatsu* conglomerations. The *keiretsu*, with a main bank as its nucleus, thus effectively replaced the dismembered *zaibatsu*.[15] Attempts at '*zaibatsu*-busting' turned out to be the least enduring of the occupation reforms,[16] and in fact contributed to rationalization of overgrown wartime businesses.

US REFORMISTS REPLACED BY RECONSTRUCTIONISTS

As we have seen, post-war Japanese labour was assigned to the CIO, but the increasing communist influence in the NCIO alarmed American labour leaders, and Mark Starr, educational director of the ILGWU,[17] was sent to Japan in the autumn of 1946 to inspect the situation before the planned general strike. As a result of his visit, coupled with other pressures, MacArthur authorized the hiring of an AFL representative on the staff of the Labor Division in January 1947. Then MacArthur intervened in the general strike, and within GHQ Ted Cohen's supposed radicalism and leniency towards leaders of the strike drew sharp criticism from Japanese and American conservatives and prompted MacArthur to transfer him to a new position in ESS (Economic and Science Section) in March 1947. His successor, James Killen, was selected by the AFL as a labour adviser in Japan. Killen, an organizer in the pulp and paper industry in the United States, was 'constantly amazed at the persistence of feudal patterns of labor–employer relations', and warned the State Department in November

---

[13] Ibid. 166; *Koza Nihonrekishi* (Lectures in Japanese History), xi. 93–4.

[14] Kunio Suzuki in Masanori Nakamura (ed.), *Senryo to Sengo Kaikaku* (The Occupation and Postwar Reform) (Tokyo 1994), 35–6. Takafusa Nakamura, in his *The Postwar Japanese Economy* (2nd edn. 1995), 27, says this 'produced good market mechanisms and was a powerful factor in economic growth'. [15] *Koza Hihonrekishi*, xix. 94–5.

[16] Hane, op. cit., 347. [17] International Ladies' Garment Workers' Union.

1947 that if the United States did not retain 'direct control' of Japan for another four or five years, 'trade unionism would be rapidly supplanted by traditional Japanese labor practices [and] our efforts to bring about a democratic Japan would necessarily fail'.[18]

The Labor Division under Killen often intervened to strengthen the position of moderates over radicals in the unions. He warned the SCAP of the alarming extent of communist infiltration and obtained literature from American unions for distribution among Japanese unions, such as the ICFTU (International Confederation of Free Trade Unions) map of slave-labour camps in Russia. In the meantime, William Draper, under-secretary of the army, on his visit to Japan warned that unsettled labour conditions were one of the most serious obstacles to the granting of American foreign aid, and the view of the Industrial Club of Japan that labour unrest was the most serious impediment to economic recovery was transmitted to Washington. Without consulting Killen, the Civil Service Division of the Government Section recommended the taking away of the right of collective bargaining from public employees (civil servants). Killen could not agree and resigned from the SCAP Labor Division in July 1948.

Surprisingly, the American military and Japanese socialists got along well during Katayama's coalition government (May 1947–February 1948). The nine-month-old Economic Stabilization Bureau was enlarged and strengthened in May 1947; it prepared the First Economic White Paper, a government document which exhorted the people to co-operate in measures for reconstruction, telling them that they should expect 'a temporary period of hardship, of deficiencies [a dearth of food and housing especially], which they should consider as a hardship imposed on them by themselves'.[19] In close co-operation with GHQ, the Bureau carried out its own plan for greater production and for the stablization of prices, with a vigorous execution of a slanting production formula that would give priority in investment to coal and steel and spread its benefits to other industries.[20] This policy stimulated inflationary trends, and only in 1948 did it begin to show some of the expected results. At the same time the reformist hold on occupation policies became increasingly tenuous and unstable.

MacArthur found it more and more difficult to adapt himself to the emerging Cold War situation. Top-level Washington officials decided that someone else was needed in Japan to protect the US Treasury from the Japanese requirements for aid coming through the SCAP.[21] The new

[18] Howard Schonberger, *Aftermath of War: Americans and the Remaking of Japan 1945–1952* (Kent, Ohio, 1989), 120–1.
[19] Shigeto Tsuru, *Japan's Capitalism* (Cambridge, 1993; 1994 edn.), 17.
[20] Takafusa Nakamura in *Nihon Keizaishi* (Economic History of Japan) (1994 edn.), vii. 45.
[21] Cohen, op. cit., 399.

under-secretary of the army, William Draper, was deeply involved in the economic reconstruction of Japan: he declared that the new prime objective of the occupation was to 'reduce the costs to the American taxpayer'.[22] Germany and Japan had been reasonably demilitarized and should be permitted a reasonable economic recovery. While the Marshall Plan for Europe invited Europeans to formulate their recovery projects, Draper was to tell the Japanese what to do. This was the new Republican line.

Draper, a leader in the Wall Street banking community as vice-president of Dillon Read & Company, one of the largest investment banking houses in the world, and a lifelong Republican, served the Truman administration first as an economic adviser for Germany. There he had been critical of American policies for the decartelization of German industry, reparation, denazification, and other reforms. It was not that he feared Russian aggression, but that with him the investment banker's views prevailed. He was convinced that 'the experienced German management' ought to be retained. Truman appointed him under-secretary of the army in August 1947, and shortly afterwards he made a brief visit to Japan, where he found her economic structure tottering. After two years of occupation the industrial production index showed only 45 per cent of its 1930–4 level, and spiraling inflation had pushed up prices ninety times in the two post-war years. To prevent 'disease and unrest' in Japan, the US Congress was providing food and medicine under the GARIOA (Government and Relief in Occupied Areas) programme. A way to 'crank up Japan' had to be found.[23]

After his first visit to Japan Draper was convinced that he would have to scrap the anti-*zaibatsu* programme, terminate the business breakup, and end the economic purge, all in the interest of a quick economic recovery. On his return to Washington Draper launched a campaign for a major revision of the occupation policy, which led to a brief statement of 3 October 1947 entitled 'The Economic Recovery of Japan', 'the first explicit formulation linking economic recovery to a "reverse course" in other Occupation programs'. To encourage Japan to stand on its own feet would certainly relieve American taxpayers of much of the burden of relief aid that Japan would otherwise have required. Kenneth Royall, the army secretary, in a widely quoted speech on 6 January 1948, declared that the destruction of war industries such as shipbuilding and chemical plants would certainly destroy the war potential of Japan but would also 'adversely affect the peace potential', and he suggested a reversal of the original purge plan by saying: 'The men who were the most active in building up and running

[22] Ibid. 401.
[23] For this and the following two paragraphs, see Schonberger, op. cit., 162–4, 166–7, 175–6, 178.

Japan's war machine—militarily and industrially—were often the ablest and most successful business leaders of the country.'

It was in the course of this campaign to replace reform with economic reconstruction that Draper the investment banker came in contact with George Kennan the Cold War strategist. In view of MacArthur's commitment to the deconcentration programme, George Marshall, secretary of state, dispatched Kennan on a mission to reorient SCAP as to the new civil and military strategy due to the developing Cold War. Draper hoped to use Kennan's visit to Japan to weaken MacArthur's resistance and to reassure Congress that economic aid to Japan was still needed. His office had the news leaked, and newspapers carried headlines like 'Drastic Change in Policy of U.S. Envisaged—Kennan Visit Seen as Move to Build Up Japan as Anti-Red Bulwark'. In Tokyo Kennan and MacArthur agreed at least on their slighting of the authority of the Allied Far Eastern Commission, as well as on their appreciation of the Pentagon plan for an arc-shaped series of military bases off mainland Asia. On his return Kennan prepared a report in which he stated that Japan was extremely vulnerable to Soviet-aided communist subversion owing to her weak economy and unstable government, aggravated by SCAP's policy of reforms such as the purge, decentralization of the police, and *zaibatsu* dissolution. He recommended a delay in peace treaty negotiations and a switch of SCAP policy from reform to economic recovery under a stable conservative government.

Draper carefully selected business members for the Economic Mission to be sent to Japan in March 1948. In Tokyo he and Kennan asked MacArthur his view on the controversial issue of rearming Japan; the latter maintained that such a plan would be contrary to the international commitments of the United States. Draper also met Ashida Hitoshi of the Democratic Party, who succeeded Katayama as prime minister and who told him that industrial recovery was dependent upon 'better control over labour'. Draper found MacArthur more pliable on the issue of the curtailment of reparations. In quantitative terms, American proposals to remove industrial and military facilities for reparation purposes diminished from 2,466 million yen (1939 prices) in the Pauley Report of November 1946 to 662 million yen in the Draper Report of April 1948. Actual removal of military and industrial equipment, before these were stopped in 1949, had amounted only to 160 million yen.[24] Draper arranged for the public release of the report of the Economic Mission and gave a major speech on 'Japan's Key Position in the Far East' in May 1948, in which for the first time he stated that the recovery programme of Japan was part of the US military and political strategy against world communism. This was to assure the US Congress of the need for recovery aid for Japan. After certain

[24] Takafusa Nakamura, *Postwar Japanese Economy*, 33; Tsuru, op. cit., 39.

hard negotiations Congress in June approved the foreign aid programme for the fiscal year 1949, according to which the very substantial Marshall Plan was funded as had been planned, while the GARIOA appropriation was slightly less than the sum requested by the administration and included a somewhat reduced sum for an EROA (Economic Rehabilitation of Occupied Areas) programme for Japan, Korea, and Ryukyu (Okinawa). In the end the total US aid to Japan for the fiscal year 1949 amounted to $530 million. At the same time Congress passed the Eastland Bill, which was to provide a substantial revolving fund to finance shipments of raw materials to occupied areas, cotton to Japan among others, thus ensuring Japan as a major market for American raw cotton and also keeping the Japanese textile industry going, textile exports being crucial to Japan's economic recovery. As a Congressman from South Carolina stated, his support for the bill was not out of love for the Japanse but 'to relieve us of the burden of paying the way of our former enemy. . . . Japan should be provided with access to the natural Japanese markets [of Asia] but should not be permitted to compete with and undersell the American producers in the American markets'.[25]

Cotton having been secured for the Japanese textile industry, Draper continued his effort to end the measures for economic deconcentration and kept up pressure on SCAP to de-purge former militarists and ultra-nationalists, while encouraging SCAP to adopt anti-labour policies. In spite of all his efforts, recovery of the Japanese economy remained slow. Draper was little appreciated in Japan, either by the Japanese or by the reform-minded Americans in GHQ, some of whom (like Ted Cohen) had to be kicked upstairs or out altogether because of the shift in occupation policies.

'Draper the banker could not understand MacArthur the populist reformer.'[26] 'American policy was trivialized,' deplored Cohen, 'when what was after all only minor American tax relief was held up as the new ultimate SCAP goal. No one in GHQ talked any more about a "new society". The Occupation as a source of inspiration for a better Japan, a cause that had brought such a sense of liberation to millions of ordinary Japanese in earlier years, just dried up. Their dreams were unsaddled, unbridled, and left for other riders.'[27]

THE DODGE LINE

The Cold War was by now in full swing in Europe. The Russian blockade of Berlin that began in June 1948 was met by the Allied airlift, which proved successful. George Kennan, on his visit to Japan in the autumn of 1947, had warned against 'the socialization of Japan', and on his next visit

---

[25] Schonberger, op. cit., 194.　　[26] Cohen, op. cit., 405.　　[27] Ibid. 408.

he attributed this to communist infiltration in the SCAP staff. A report on American policies towards Japan based on Kennan's recommendations was incorporated in a National Security Council Decision (NSC 13/2) of October 1948, which aimed to reduce the power of GHQ in favour of the Japanese government and to assure economic reconstruction and stability. In order to carry out its propositions Draper recommended Joseph George Merrill Dodge to come over as economic adviser for the SCAP.[28] In February 1949 MacArthur had to receive Dodge, a commercial banker and president of the Detroit Bank, who arrived to implement the Washington directive for a stringent economic policy for Japan, a deflationary (or disinflationary) policy of balancing the budget to curtail the money supply and halt inflation.

Dodge, the son of a poor Quaker artist, never attended college, but he climbed up from a humble position as a bank messenger to gain wide recognition for his abilities as an exceptionally gifted banker, well versed in the vast problems of international economy. He helped General Eisenhower reconstruct the German monetary system when it was in great trouble. Throughout his career Dodge stuck to an orthodox banker's view of the world. 'For him, wealth was created by private accumulation of capital through incentives for profit. An available supply of relatively cheap and mobile labor was an important incentive to capitalists.'[29] He had no use for Keynesian economics. Unlike early US advisers, who supported the creation of a free-market economy of small and medium industries for Japan, he was in favour of 'a capitalism of *zaibatsu* combines operating in an environment of limited government control or regulation'.[30] He made common cause with *zaibatsu* executives in weakening the trade union movement and securing a cheap source of labour, while remaining determined to overcome the mounting inflation which kept big businesses out of competitive export markets.

Dodge arrived in Japan in February 1949 and at once embarked on a stabilization programme. The major objective of the Dodge Mission was to link the Japanese economy on a competitive basis to the US-dominated world economy, a task which required disinflation and increased exports. A strictly balanced budget was enforced and a tight money policy was introduced, especially in the form of suspension of new loans from the Reconstruction Bank, an investment bank which had developed from a department within the Industrial Bank of Japan and which had been a vehicle of fiscal spending policy pursued by the finance minister Ishibashi Tanzan. Tanzan, a Keynesian economist, had expected funds to be channelled in this way into the industrial sector, but this had also proved

---

[28] Takafusa Nakamura in *Nihon Keizaishi*, vii. 49.   [29] Schonberger, op. cit., 199.

[30] Ibid. 100.

a source of inflaton. Under the 'Dodge Line', however, government subsidies were reduced or abolished. The draft budget Dodge had prepared for
the fiscal year 1949 showed a surplus of 150 million yen. Finally, a single
exchange rate of 360 yen to 1 dollar (an undervaluation of the yen which
necessitated greater rationalization in export industries) was introduced
from 25 April, after which Dodge returned home.

There is a sceptical view about the effects of the Dodge Line, because
inflation had already become less severe as production had begun to
increase in the latter half of 1948, and such draconian measures were
probably unnecessary.[31] It has also been pointed out that the Dodge Line
in many ways resembled Japan's own wartime programme. Like the
Japanese planners of the 1930s, Dodge sought to prop up large business
because of advantages due to scale. By promoting production for export he
hoped to make prices attractive to the large South-East Asia market. The
creation of the MITI (Ministry of International Trade and Industry) in
1949 was intended to cement the government–business partnership.[32]

A large-scale reduction of the number of government employees was an
essential part of the Dodge budget. The discharge of some 126,000 railway workers, about 20 per cent of the total workforce, in the spring of
1949 precipitated a wave of violent strikes.[33] In the midst of great and
intense labour disputes three mysterious incidents took place: Shimoyama
Sadanori, the president of the Japan National Railway, disappeared, and
his mangled body was found on the railway tracks in a suburb of Tokyo;
an unmanned electric carriage suddenly started up, driving into a small
square near Mitaka Station, Tokyo, and killing several people; a goods
train was derailed near Matsukawa Station on the Tohoku line, killing
three people, including the driver. All three incidents were ascribed to
sabotage or acts of homicide on the part of local communists. After so
much bad blood has been shed, and such brilliant writers as Matsumoto
Seicho and Hirotsu Kazuo have indulged in investigation and speculation,
it is now generally agreed that Shimoyama committed suicide, while the
two other incidents (partly in view of the absence of evidence from the
American side) are widely accepted as having been staged by American
agents provocateurs seeking to discredit communist trade unionists and
communism in general.[34]

---

[31] Takafusa Nakamura, *Postwar Japanese Economy*, 35–6, 41.
[32] Michael Schaller, *The American Occupation of Japan*, 145.
[33] Schonberger, op. cit., 208; according to Nakamura (*Postwar Japanese Economy*, 43), no
fewer than 100,000 railway workers were fired, while 220,000 were discharged from the postal
and telephone and telegram services.
[34] Yoshio Asai in Masanori Nakamura (ed.), *Senryo to Sengo Kaikaku*, 94. Chalmer Johnson
presented a speculative account of one of these cases to suggest that Russian agents, either JCP or
the repatriates from Siberia, were to blame. See his book, *Conspiracy at Matsukawa* (Berkeley,
1972).

CONSOLIDATION OF THE CONSERVATIVES,
THE RED PURGE, AND THE KOREAN WAR

At the general election of January 1949 the Democratic Liberal Party, of which Yoshida Shigeru was president, won a clear majority in the Diet (Democratic Liberal 264, Democrat 69, Socialist 48, Communist 35). One outstanding feature of this election was that as many as sixty-two former bureaucrats were elected, most of whom joined the Democratic Liberals, including Sato Eisaku and Ikeda Hayato, the future prime ministers. They were the people who occupied key positions to connect the conservative party with the top echelons of the bureaucracy and big business. Thus came into existence a stable conservative regime which was to carry into effect new American directives after the shift in occupation policy. The Administration Personnel Act which passed the Diet in May 1949 was to cut the number of employees in government departments, national railways, and public corporations by 280,000 and that of local government employees by 130,000; the three mysterious incidents looked as though they resulted from plots of some sort to frustrate and foil workers' opposition to these measures.

In May 1950, over a month before the outbreak of the Korean War, MacArthur accused the Communist Party of being 'the agent of international aggression', and directed a purge of communist leaders, forbidding them to pursue political activities. Their newspapers were suppressed, and 336 radical journalists in other media were also discharged. The Red Purge involved many more journalists and also led to the dismissal of 11,000 employees in the private sector of the economy and of 12,000 public employees. While this Japanese version of McCarthyism raged throughout the country, the Yoshida government decided to de-purge as many as 10,090 people who had played prominent roles during the war. Young officers of the former army and navy, to the number of 3,250, were also de-purged so as to provide the core officers of the Police Reserve Forces that had been created in July 1950.

The Dodge deflationary policy brought considerable hardship on several hundred thousand discharged workers. A succession of small business bankruptcies ensued. Under the exchange rate, in which yen was undervalued, the export drive caused a wage cut all round in order to keep costs down. But rescue was at hand: it was the outbreak of the Korean War and the subsequent special procurement boom that saved the country from a crisis threatened by Dodge's policy for retrenchment and stabilization.

The Korean War can be seen as resulting directly from Kim Il Song's moves to unite Korea, and also in a larger Cold War context as a North Korean and Chinese attempt to stop the American strategy of 'rollback of Soviet control' before it began with the unpredictable Singman Rhee as a cat's-paw, helped by America's junior partner Japan.[35] In fact, the Korean War helped Japan to regain its strength as a world power. World trade became buoyant overnight. Japanese exports rose 2.7 times from 1949 to 1951, and production increased by 70 per cent.[36] The Japanese economy was enlivened by 'special procurements', that is, American purchase of Japanese goods for war purposes as well as a rapid expansion of exports. The former consisted of cotton cloth, automobile parts, trucks, coal, and linen sacks, the total amount for five years till June 1955 reaching $1,620 million. By 1951 the Japanese economy was restored to the pre-war level. Indeed, the Korean procurements have been called 'Japan's Marshall Plan'. A war in which 3 million Koreans died was described by Yoshida as 'a gift of the Gods'.[37]

STABILIZATION

It is true that the Red Purge left a nasty taste in the mouth of Japanese radicals, and the *Sohyo* (General Council of Trade Unions) and the socialists, undaunted, carried on campaigns for peace. Yet by the early 1950s some kind of stabilization had been achieved even for Japanese labour. Trade unions as a whole entered a period of stablization, with the notable exception of the unions in declining industries such as coal-mining.

This settlement or stabilization was a result of combined historical factors, practices established in pre-war factories, practices developed during the war, and those imposed by the aggressive, often radical labour movement after the war.[38] In the 1920s, when heavy industry such as machine industry and shipbuilding began to expand, a new attractive pattern of long-term or career employment with a seniority system and company welfare facilities began to take shape and replaced the old pattern of 'travelling' skilled workers.[39] In 1938 bureaucrats, politicians, some managers, and a few workers had started the *Sangyo Hokoku Renmei* or *Sanpo* (Industrial Patriotic Association), with the slogan of the 'enterprise as one family' (it was later renamed *Sangyo Hokokukai* with more patriotic aims). But in spite of company-wide discussion councils set up in many factories, workers' participation remained a matter of half-measures.

In the post-war period of production control and rapid organizational gains, Japanese workers very nearly achieved their aims: guaranteed job security, a need-based seniority wage ('living' wages were obtained first by the electric power industry workers in 1946), and a voice in the manage-

[35] Peter Lowe, *The Origins of the Korean War* (London, 1986; 1995), 156 ff.
[36] Takafusa Nakamura, *Postwar Japanese Economy*, 43.   [37] Cumings, op. cit., 50.
[38] Gordon (ed.), op. cit., 329.   [39] Ibid. 133, 138.

ment of factory affairs. Then the 'reverse course' encouraged managers in their effort to recover managerial authority. They began to link productivity and wages. The emergence and persistence of moderate company unions in large part resulted from intense government and business pressure on unions. But these unions were allowed to retain the gains already made in wages and job security, as well as the benefit of 'citizenship' in the firm and in society. Under the austere deflationary policy of the Dodge Line the union movement lost major battles in 1949–50, but in the recovery that followed, they continued to place job security high on their list of priorities, and managers began to prefer industrial peace to dismissals. The road to comparative stability seemed to have been well mapped out.

THE SAN FRANCISCO SYSTEM AND THE '55 SYSTEM'

At the peace conference held at San Francisco in September 1951 the Japanese delegation, headed by premier Yoshida, signed a Peace Treaty with forty-eight nations and a military agreement with the United States. The Peace Treaty was generous and non-punitive, while the Security Pact was an unequal treaty.[40] It was not an all-round peace, which the left had demanded, but a separate peace. Yugoslavia, Burma, and India, though invited, were absent: Burma was dissatisfied with the level of reparations stipulated, and India was unhappy over the continued occupation of Okinawa by the Amerians, with the US–Japanese Security Treaty, and also with the fact that China had not been invited. (Britain favoured the two-year-old People's Republic of China, while the United States supported the Kuomintang government which had been driven out to Taiwan in December 1949. Japan was to conclude a peace treaty with the latter in April 1952 when the American occupation came to an end.) The Soviet Union, Czechoslovakia, and Poland refused to sign the treaty. On 28 April 1952 both the Peace Treaty and the Security Treaty took effect.

With the Security Treaty, however, Japan was incorporated into the Pax Americana, and this prevented her from pursuing an independent foreign policy. The main point of the Security Treaty was a Japanese request to the United States for stationing 'land, air and sea forces in and about Japan'. The primary purpose of these forces would be for defence against external attack, but there was no specfic commitment of that kind. Moreover, if requested by the Japanese government, US forces could suppress internal disturbances.[41] The possibility of Japan rearming herself as an ally of the Americans caused such fear among her neighbours that they had to be placated by a trilateral security treaty, ANZUS, between the United States,

---

[40] John Dower, *Empire and Aftermath* (1979, 1988), 370.
[41] Schonberger, op. cit., 259.

Australia, and New Zealand and a bilateral US–Philippine Security Treaty. Probably most vexatious to the Japanese was the Administration Agreement which stipulated the extent of the extraterritoriality of the US forces in Japan. Special facilities and areas were to be selected by a joint committee for use by American forces; the United States would have the right to garrison and control these places and alter the infrastructure and facilities there. The Agreement gave the Americans the right to arrest and try all US personnel for all crimes committed in Japan. In other words, American courts would have sole jurisdiction even when crimes were committed outside military bases by off-duty Americans against Japanese. In some ways Japan was reduced to the same state of subordinate independence she had endured one hundred years before in the 1850s, with the 'black ships' in Edo Bay and unequal treaties forced upon her.

Under heavy pressure from America for rearmament, Article 9 of the constitution served as a restraining factor in the San Francisco system. Prior to the San Francisco Conference, the Socialist Party had adopted three principles of peace: an all-round peace treaty, opposition to bilateral military pacts, and neutrality in the Cold War; to these was added in 1951 opposition to Japanese rearmament. Over the San Francisco settlement the socialists wrangled among themselves, providing a left–right split in October 1952: the left was against both the Peace Treaty and the Security Treaty, and the right was for the former but against the latter.

The demand for or concern about peace, however, was often associated with 'victim consciousness' (*higaisha ishiki*)—cost of the war to the Japanese—which cut across the political spectrum and which was beyond the comprehension of Japan's neighbouring countries. The issues of peace and independence sometimes became messily entangled. Yoshida, a passionately anti-Soviet politician, did not regard Russia as a direct threat to Japan and reluctantly accepted the continued presence of US troops and bases 'as an unavoidable price for obtaining sovereignty along with assurances of US protection'.[42]

In one of many visits Dodge made to Japan he had a talk with Ikeda, the finance minister in Yoshida's government, about the 1952 budget which had to incorporate new obligations under the peace and security treaties. He was astonished to find that the largest item was 'reserves'. Japanese reparations estimates, too, were a puzzle. The proposed budget included only 35 billion yen for reparations in 1952 to nations occupied and ravaged by the Japanese, while providing 30 billion yen for injured Japanese and for the families of Japanese war dead. 'This is ridiculous . . . [it] would infuriate Indonesians, Filipinos, and others', said Dodge.[43] Certain rectifications were made, but the spirit of the budget remained. As

[42] Dower, op. cit., 11.   [43] Schonberger op. cit., 231–2.

for reparations, these were made to serve the interest of Japan as much as of the receiving countries, and the Americans—Dodge again—lent a hand in this. He, along with John Foster Dulles, secretary of state, energetically promoted Japanese trade with South-East Asia by using reparations as an instrument to open up markets and using US aid funds to develop sources of supply for Japan.[44] The Peace Treaty itself, in Dulles's, view should have protected Japan against further demands for reparations or restrictions on industries or raw-material supplies.[45] As for reparations, the Allies in general were satisfied with taking the assets held by the Japanese in their respective countries. Those countries occupied by Japan, such as Burma, Indonesia, (South) Vietnam, Laos, and Cambodia (India and Chiang Kai-shek's China relinquished their claims) were to deal separately with her, and negotiations continued until 1958, by which time the aggregate amount of Japanese obligations reached US$1,012 million, which in the form of annual instalments meant 0.4 per cent of Japan's national income in each relevant year.[46]

Meanwhile, the '55 System' (so called as it was established in 1955) assured the conservative hegemony in domestic politics. The general elections of October 1952 had allowed the return to national politics of hundreds of formerly purged politicians, including Kishi Nobusuke. Yoshida's fortunes were in decline, and at the general election of April 1953 his party, the Liberals, lost forty-one seats, while the two socialist parties won twenty-seven more seats between them. Yoshida's party and government were incriminated in a large-scale shipping scandal early in 1954, while his high-handed manner was disliked by moderate Dietmen. Hatoyama, with Kishi and Ishibashi, launched a new anti-Yoshida conservative party, absorbing Shigemitsu's Progressive Party (*Kaishinto*), and set up the Japan Democratic Party in November 1954. In December Yoshida resigned and Hatoyama's Democratic government was formed. Hatoyama had two distinct policies for his government: normalization of diplomatic relationship with the Soviet Union, and revision of the constitution, especially of Article 9. The latter became the major issue at the general election of February 1955, at which the Democrats increased their seats from 124 to 185 while the Liberals had theirs reduced from 180 to 112. Socialist parties also increased their strength: the right-wing socialists from 61 to 67 and the left-wing socialists from 74 to 89; and between them the socialists obtained a little over one-third of all the seats (467). There were four seats obtained by *Ronoto* (the Worker-Farmer Party), and two by communists. The total of 162 was enough to prevent an attempt to revise the constitution. Moreover, the two socialist parties were in the process of uniting themselves, and the united Socialist Party came into

[44] Schonberger, op. cit., 234.   [45] Ibid. 245.   [46] Tsuru, op. cit., 39.

existence in October 1955. This gave another incentive for the two conservative parties to unite. Already in the summer of the same year John Foster Dulles, at a meeting in Washington with Shigemitsu, the foreign minister, conveyed his expectation that the conservative forces in Japan would unite to Kishi, who accompanied Shigemitsu. The Americans wanted a strong conservative party for a strong Japan as an effective barrier against the spread of communism in Asia.

The *Sohyo* (General Council of Trade Unions), which had been set up as an anti-communist labour federation in July 1950, had come round to support the socialist principles of international peace. In January 1955 it mobilized some 800,000 workers in the first concerted wage demonstration, which was to be institutionalized as *shunto* (Spring Wage Offensive). It became a vehicle for enterprise unions to act industrially in wage negotiations and also induced the two rival socialist parties to act together. As the *Sohyo* played a role in achieving socialist unity, so the *Zaikai* (organized business world) such as *Nikkeiren* (Japan Federation of Employers), *Keidanren* (Federation of Economic Organizations), *Keizai Doyukai* (Economic Fellowship Association), and *Nissho* (Japan Chamber of Commerce) urged a conservative merger. A chain of action and reaction ensued. The prospect of conservative unity worried the two socialist parties, which at a unity conference held on 13 October 1955 decided to form the Japan Socialist Party with the left-winger Suzuki Mosaburo as chairman and the right-winger Asanuma Inajiro as secretary. A month later, at a combined conservative conference (held on 15 November), the Democrats and the Liberals merged into the Liberal Democratic Party (LDP), with Hatoyama as its first president. The strength of the two united parties was 155 Socialists in the House of Representatives and 69 in the House of Councillors, and 298 LDP seats in the former and 115 in the latter, the relative strength being roughly two to one in favour of the LDP. The so-called '55 System' thus created was to provide the basic political structure for nearly forty years.

'THE POST-WAR RECONSTRUCTION IS OVER'

The 55 System also embodied the existing alignment of social forces, labour, and capital at the time of incipient economic growth. It was in 1955 that GNP passed the pre-war peak for the first time, symbolically marking the attainment of economic recovery. In 1955 too, Japan was admitted to the General Agreement on Tariffs and Trade (GATT). At the election for the House of Councillors held in July 1956 the Hatoyama government failed to deprive the socialists of their 'one-third' trump card that could safeguard Article 9 of the constitution. As a result Hatoyama decided to concentrate on a restoration of diplomatic relations with the

Soviet Union. Shigemitsu, the foreign minister, was warned by Dulles not to give up Japan's claims to the southern Kuriles. In view of the stubborn objection on the part of the Russians, Hatoyama decided to visit Moscow, with the issue of the northern territories kept in cold storage. In the Japan–Soviet Joint Declaration signed on 19 October 1956 it was agreed that the state of war between the two countries be terminated: the Soviet Union would renounce its right to reparations and would support Japan's application to join the United Nations (to which Russia had been opposed), and the two countries would continue negotiations to conclude a peace treaty which might stipulate the return of the two offshore islands east of Hokkaido. But no peace treaty has been concluded, and the issue of the southern Kuriles has remained unresolved.

Post-war Japan had started again from scratch. Occupation reforms amounted to what one economic historian called 'a revolution'.[47] It was from the middle of 1946 that measures began to be taken for the reconstruction of the economy. We have examined the 'slanting' or priority production policy which encouraged the production of steel and coal, and through them the development of other related industries; the Dodge Line, which introduced deflationary measures as a preliminary for a free-market economy; and the 'special procurement' for the American army at the time of the Korean War, which brought about an economic boom and enabled economic recovery to proceed with added momentum. Greater exports remained the target of recovery. Rationalization or rather technological modernization, also began. Shipbuilding, which had adopted electric welding techniques was able to boast the largest exports in the world in terms of tonnage by the middle of the 1950s. Toyo Rayon and Teijin, which produced synthetic fibres, made rapid progress. From 1951 to 1955 gross national expenditure increased by 38 per cent which meant an annual growth of 8.6 per cent. It has been suggested that the high-growth economy of Japan started at this period although the economy retained many features of a transitional stage: consumer's consumption played a great role, while capital investment remained relatively low. Those employed in the primary sector of the economy still formed 41 per cent of all the employed. The number of self-employed in the secondary and tertiary sectors (traditional shops and workshops) recovered to the pre-war level by 1950 and surpassed it by 1955. It was only in the period of high economic growth in the 1960s and 1970s that the primary sector and traditional industries would shrink and give place to a new structure geared to high technology.

The advent of a mass consumer society also began in the mid-1950s.

[47] Takafusa Nakamura, *Keikakuka to Minshuka* (Planning and Democratization), *Nihon Keizaishi*, vii. 41.

The MITI announced a 'citizen's car project', and housewives were eager to obtain three 'divine' electrical appliances: an electric washing machine, a refrigerator, and a television set. Consumption of these and other durable consumer goods might be called 'luxury' in a sense. 'Luxury', that had once been frowned upon as inimical to the Tokugawa social order and that had since been suppressed as 'unpatriotic' by the wartime regimes, now for the first time became a small privilege, if not a virtue, of common people as well as a symbol of economic recovery and growth.

The White Paper on National Economy for 1956 prepared by the Economic Planning Board stated that 'the post-war reconstruction' was over now that real national income, industrial and agricultural production, consumption, and population all exceeded the levels of 1934–5; the Japanese economy had entered the period of 'normalization', which did not mean a return to the pre-war conditions but a modernization of technology and the market system aimed at high efficiency, high wages, and a high standard of living.[48] The post-war hardship seemed over now, but post-war democratic reforms had just begun to take effect, in a tortuous way. On 18 December 1956 Japan was formally admitted as a member of the United Nations. Shegimitsu Mamoru, who had signed the document for Japan's surrender in 1945 and had been condemned as a class A war criminal (he was released after two years' imprisonment and de-purged in 1952), was now the Japanese representative at the UN. He gave a speech at the General Assembly lasting eighteen minutes, faltering at first, but soon regaining composure and conveying his country's message that Japan would become a bridge between East and West.[49] While he was in New York, Hatoyama's government, of which he was foreign minister, resigned, and Shigemitsu himself died of a heart attack a month later at his villa at Yugawara. He had been foreign minister under Tojo (from April 1943 to July 1944) and personified Japan's transformation from the war period to the end of the post-war reconstruction. He was one of those diplomats who believed in 'the victory of surrender'.[50]

[48] *Asahi Shinbun*, 17 Jan. 1956.   [49] Ibid. 19 Feb. 1956.
[50] Mamoru Shigemitsu, *Shuki* (Records) (Tokyo, 1988), 399.

18

From Political Conflict to Economic Growth, 1950–1965

The '55 System' gave the LDP a monopoly of the government for thirty-eight years. At its beginning, however, it did not appear to be long-enduring. First of all, this delicate political balance (rather than a 'system') had to stand the extra-parliamentary challenge of 1960, better known as the Anpo (Security Treaty) Struggle. The Anpo protest itself was aimed against the revision and extension of the US–Japanese Security Treaty, especially against the undemocratic way in which the ratification of the new Security Treaty was forced through the Diet by the Kishi government. Post-war pacifism and faith in democracy, the legacy of the initial stage of the American occupation, were pitched against the growing US–Japanese consensus on security in the Far East under the Cold War situation. Creeping rearmament provoked protest actions by those for whom memories of war atrocities and misery remained vivid and overwhelming. Economically, however, the year 1955 was the beginning of rapid growth which resulted in the emergence of Japan as a world economic power. Ikeda, Kishi's successor as prime minister, shifted the government posture away from political confrontation towards economic accommodation starting with his pledge for 'the doubling of income' with which very few would demur except those employed in the declining industries.

REARMAMENT

The rearmament of Japan, albeit on a limited scale, began in earnest in 1950 shortly after the outbreak of the Korean War. MacArthur, in a letter to prime minister Yoshida on 8 July stated that Japan's police force should be strengthened by the creation of a 'national police reserve of 75,000' and that her maritime safety force should be expanded by 8,000 men. He said nothing about the Korean War, but it is obvious that MacArthur, the sponsor of the new constitution, who had fought a costly war against the Imperial Army and had since resisted pressures from Washington to revive Japanese military capabilities even under Cold War conditions, decided, though reluctantly, to part with his pet idea of creating a pacific Japan. He had been appointed commander of the United Nations Forces in

Korea one day before. Yoshida, whose proposals to strengthen the decentralized police force had once been cold-shouldered by the SCAP, was
delighted, and was 'naturally most grateful' for MacArthur's letter, and
added in his remark to the British ambassador that he would like to 'model
this new force upon the London Metropolitan Police'. It took some time
before he realized that what the Americans demanded was not simply a
strong police force but an 'embryonic army'.[1]

It was not simply the American side, Kennan and Dulles, Royall and
Draper, who wanted a revival of the old military Japan as an ally of the
United States in the Cold War. Those wartime Japanese leaders who had
been purged and de-purged under the occupation were anticipating the day
of resurrection. Yoshida was not in the mainstream of these conservative
forces, and as we shall see, he had to be ousted from power by Hatoyama
and Kishi, who were intent on demolishing the pacifist and democratic
post-war structure which MacArthur, with Yoshida's passive co-operation,
had built up.

In fact, when Japan surrendered in 1945 there had been futile attempts
to ensure the continued existence of military forces under the guise of a
police force. There was a rescue operation for the Guard Division to
transform its picked men and officers into a 'Guard Force' to defend the
Imperial Palace. This, too, was doomed, as GHQ directed in January 1946
that any such guard be abolished and that all the weapons they held be
surrendered.[2] Four years later, when the Cold War erupted into a hot war
in Korea, the 'reverse' course that had been pushed for some time was
given a finishing touch.

The 'Police Reserve Force' to be created was defined as a security police
strong enough to cope with military confrontation, riotings, and large-
scale political strikes. The first president of its headquarters (the civilian
head of the PRF), Masuhara Keikichi, later recalled: 'our task was to
create four divisions, if we may use the old expression, and to allocate
the total strength of 75,000 men to each of these. The Americans gave us
carbines and light machine-guns, followed by heavy machine-guns and
bazookas. "This is Rearmament of Japan", commented the newspapers
and other media: "The military forces are being established once more." I
instinctively felt that this was a correct perception.'[3] The creation of the
new armed forces was not debated in the Diet but was carried out by a

---

[1] Richard B. Finn, *Winners in Peace: MacArthur, Yoshida and Postwar Japan* (Berkeley, 1992),
263.
[2] Tetsuo Maeda, *Nihonno Guntai* (The Japanese Military Forces) (Tokyo, 1994), ii. 21; Akira
Fujiwara, *Gunjishi* (The Military History) (Tokyo, 1961), 226; Frank Kowalsky, Jr, 'The Rearmament of Japan' (unpublished MS), Japanese tr. by Kinjiro Katsuyama, *Nihon Saigunbi*
(Japan's Rearmament) (Tokyo, 1969; 2nd edn. 1984), 36–8.   [3] Maeda, op. cit., 35.

government decree of 10 August 1950. Its relevance to the constitution was kept blurred from the beginning.

It was obvious that the four divisions of the Police Reserve Force were to fill the gap created by the dispatch of the four US divisions from Japan to Korea. Major Frank Kowalsky of the Government Section of GHQ was entrusted with the task of creating the nucleus of the Japanese army, which he knew he could not tell the Japanese about because of Article 9 of the constitution. 'This noble aspiration of the human race is about to be smashed. Now begins the "Great Lie" in which America and myself as an individual are to participate . . . The Constitution of one country, which can be said to be the greatest achievement in the political history of humanity is about to be violated and stamped down by the USA and Japan.'[4] On 13 August all the police stations throughout the country began collecting applications to join the PRF. Men beween 20 and 35 years of age were qualified to apply. The monthly stipend of about 5,000 yen was much higher than the initial salary of a policeman, which was 3,730 yen, and the length of service was two years, at the end of which 60,000 yen would be paid as retirement money. In three days 382,003 men applied, from whom 75,000 were selected after physical and intelligence tests. About 40 per cent of them were from an agricultural background, and most of them had been soldiers in the Imperial Army.[5]

Hattori Takushiro, a former major and secretary to Tojo when the latter was war minister, was invited by General Charles Willoughby of the G-2 Section in charge of security in GHQ to work with him in preparing a war history. Willoughby, one of MacArthur's Bataan boys, had great sympathy with the Spanish dictator General Franco, and MacArthur used to call him 'my dear fascist'. Hattori was prompted by Willoughby to work out a new plan for the four divisions, with 400 former officers of the Imperial Army as its nucleus. Opposed to this retrogressive step were Yoshida and Masuhara Keikichi, who managed to defeat the plan with the help of the Government Section of GHQ and of MacArthur himself. Masuhara, president of the PRF, was a former Home Ministry bureaucrat, and his was a victory of the bureaucracy in the old Home Ministry police and of the anti-Tojo (and anti-Hattori) men in the former military, some of whom insinuated that those who had failed as professional soldiers ought not to assume the leadership of an armed force again.[6] Moreover, personnel, budgetary, and operational matters were entrusted to the bureaucrats in the name of 'Civilian Control', which has remained as a safeguard against possible military dictatorship.

In April 1951 MacArthur, who had disagreed with Truman over the

---

[4] Kowalsky, op. cit., 64.   [5] Maeda, op. cit., 42.
[6] Takashi Ara in *Nihon Tsushi* (Complete History of Japan), xx. 154.

military strategy in Korea, was dismissed by the latter from his position as commander-in-chief of the forces in the Far East and was replaced by Lt.-General Matthew B. Ridgeway, who at once embarked on the restoration of former army and navy officers; by the end of the year altogether 63,805 names had been struck off the list of purged officers. The former regular army officers began to pour into the PRF. Most of them were anxious to keep up the tradition of the old army.[7]

As for the Japanese navy, it had never ceased to exist. The task of minesweeping in the seas around Japan, in addition to the transportation of repatriates from overseas, kept the navy men constantly employed in spite of the formal dissolution of the Navy Ministry in November 1945 (the Army Ministry was dissolved a month before). The Maritime Security Board looked almost like 'a small navy in the ministry of transport'.[8] When the Korean War broke out the Japanese minesweeping units were ordered to clear mines from around Wonsan on the east coast where the Americans were to land their troops. The 'Special Minesweepers' were sent to other Korean ports as well. Admiral Arleigh Burke, deputy chief of staff to Admiral Joy, Commander Naval Forces Far East during the Korean War, on a visit to Washington stressed the need for an eventual Japanese navy, though the Japanese should start with minesweepers and patrol craft.[9]

In July 1952 it was decided to create a Security Bureau combining the PRF and the Maritime Patrol Force with an augmented strength: the former with 110,000 men and the latter 7,590. The budget, too, increased to 170 billion yen, 20 per cent of general government expenditure, and 2.78 per cent of GNP.[10] Yoshida had to explain to the sceptical nation that the Security Force was not an armed force, while the Americans exerted greater pressure for further steps for rearmament.

Japanese business leaders organized in the Defence Production Committee of *Keidanren*, looking for new opportunities for expansion after the Korean War, found them in Japanese rearmament and prepared their plan in conjunction with a group of former military officers. The government, too, worked in the same direction. In October 1953 Ikeda Hayato, Yoshida's emissary, visited Washington and had a talk with Walter Robertson of the State Department on the strengthening of Japan's defence capabilities, and suggested a plan which put the land force at 10 divisions and 180,000 men, with the naval and air forces equally strengthened. Ikeda apparently had his way. Now the way was opened for a US–Japan joint defence of the Far East.

When Kishi became prime minister in February 1957, he determined to

---

[7] Maeda, op. cit., 51.   [8] Ibid. 56.
[9] James E. Auer, *The Postwar Rearmament of Japanese Maritime Forces, 1945–71* (New York, 1973), 76.   [10] Maeda, op. cit., 70.

achieve revisions of the Japan–US Security Treaty. In 1958 the Kishi government decided on a three-year plan for defence, with 180,000 men in the Land Self-Defence Force, vessels of 124,000 tonnage for the Naval Self-Defence force, and 1,300 aircraft for the Air Self-Defence Force. This was partly aimed at enabling partial withdrawal of US forces stationed in Japan, and it gave a fillip to the former munition industry such as the Mitsubishi Jukogyo (Heavy Industries) in Nagoya, famous for its Zero fighters during the Pacific War. Furthermore, the establishment of the Self-Defence Force allowed its armed forces to be used against large-scale demonstrations: in fact 20,000 men with fifty tanks were kept reserve in April 1960 at the time of the anti-Security Treaty struggle. Kishi asked Akagi Munenori, the head of the Defence Bureau to move his men against the demonstrators. Akagi opposed this, for he feared that such a move on the part of the SDF might lead to a revolution.[11] Indeed, a revolution was precluded, though revolutionary situations developed because of Kishi's intransigence.

POLITICAL DEVELOPMENT[12]

It must be emphasized that the Red Purges, the Japanese version of McCarthyism, ushered in the 'reverse course' pursued by successive conservative governments. In 1952 a Subversive Activities Act, aimed largely against communists, was passed, though there were repeated protests and strikes against it, causing bloodshed in Palace Square on May Day of that year. In 1954 the Yoshida government successfully introduced a new Police Law in order to recentralize the police system. In 1956 the Hatoyama government introduced legislation to recentralize education, including the new Education Committee Law to replace elective committees with appointed ones (this caused a mêlée in the Diet and was forced through the House of Councillors guarded by 500 policemen), and an act to empower the Ministry of Education to authorize textbooks which had to be withdrawn, owing to vehement protest; screening of textbooks was strengthened, however, by a new system of authorization introduced by the Ministry.

With the fanfare celebrating Japan's entry into the UN in December 1956 Hatoyama resigned, and was succeeded by Ishibashi Tanzan, the old liberal and Keynesian. Ishibashi set himself two targets: a restoration of diplomatic relations with China, and a positive economic policy. Assisted by his finance minister Ikeda Hayato he was ready to proceed with a budget

---

[11]   *This is Yomiuri*, May 1990, quoted in Maeda, op. cit., 107.

[12]   Arthur Stockwin's 'Political Chronicle', in his *Japan: Divided Politics in a Growing Economy* (1982 edn.), provides a succinct account of what happened on the Japanese political scene in this period.

embodying income tax reduction and the construction of roads and housing aimed at the attainment of full employment. This was to become a model of government finance in the period of high economic growth.[13] Early in the following year, however, he became seriously ill and resigned in February 1957.

Ishibashi was succeeded by Kishi, whose government implemented some of the economic policies initiated by his predecessor such as the National Pension Act. It was also under his government that the Minimum Wage Act was passed (February 1959). In spite of a temporary relapse the Japanese economy continued to grow: GNP doubled in five years, from 5.5 billion yen in 1955 to 10.9 billion yen in 1960, and exports, which had been slow to recover, reached their pre-war level in 1959. On economic matters the Kishi government appeared successful, but politically his attempt to create a strong, independent Japan allied with the United States, and the overbearing manner in which he pursued his ends led to his undoing.

KISHI NOBUSUKE: FROM A CLASS A WAR CRIMINAL TO PRIME MINISTER

On 24 December 1948, the day after the execution of Tojo and six other army generals condemned to death in the Tokyo War Crimes Trial, Kishi and several other class A war criminals were released. The fact that he was not a member of the Cabinet–General Staff Liaison Meetings obviously favoured him. About eight years after his release Kishi became prime minister of Japan. Some called him a monster, 'a bogey of Showa'.[14]

Kishi Nobusuke connects the Japan which fought a war of aggression and the Japan which became America's loyal ally. Born at Yamaguchi as the son of a prefectural official, Kishi spent his youth as a student of the law faculty of Tokyo Imperial University and an admirer of Kita Ikki. His acquaintance with Okawa Shumei, another advocate of Greater Asianism, led him to seek his future career in Manchukuo. In October 1936 he moved to Manchuria and soon found himself practically in charge of the Department of Industry of Manchukuo as its deputy director. He at once set up the Five Year Plan for Industrial Development of Manchukuo, and was instrumental in the birth of a great concern, 'Mangyo' (former Nissan). While in Manchuria he established close personal relationships with the successive chiefs of staff of the Kwantung Army and even with young officers, but his relationship with Tojo was closest of all: they were united through a huge political fund derived from the opium trade carried out secretly by some of the Manchukuo officials.[15]

[13] Masanori Nakamura, *Nihon Tsushi* (Complete History of Japan), xx. 20.
[14] Takao Iwami, *Showa no Yokai* [the Monster of Showa], Kishi Nobusuke (Tokyo, 1994).
[15] Yoshihisa Hara, *Kishi Nobusuke* (Tokyo, 1995), 69–76.

In October 1939 Kishi returned to Tokyo to become under-secretary of the Ministry of trade and industry. When Tojo became prime minister in October 1941, Kishi accepted the position of Minister of Trade and Industry under him. His policies were to strengthen government control of industries for greater production, which involved control of storage, distribution, and management, and to achieve the autarky of the Greater East Asia Co-prosperity Sphere as a whole. In November 1943 when a new Ministry of Munitions was created to speed up the production of airplanes, Tojo became minister and Kishi vice-minister; the fall of Saipan, however, broke up the Tojo–Kishi partnership: Kishi felt that it had become impossible to continue the war, since the munition factories would be destroyed by bombers from Saipan. Tojo sought to reshuffle his cabinet so as to replace Kishi, but Kishi refused to be elbowed out. Yonai Mitsumasa, former minister of the navy, also refused to succumb to Tojo's 'dictatorship', and this led to the resignation of the latter. It was to be expected that Kishi made much of his opposition to Tojo later when he was arrested. His detention and imprisonment lasted three years and three months, and his diary tells how his mind wavered restlessly between 'execution' and 'release'. In November 1948, shortly before his release, he noted in his diary that America should organize a Japanese volunteer corps to fight against Mao Tse-tung. The development of the Cold War, he later recalled, was 'our only hope at Sugamo [prison]'.[16]

On 24 December 1948 Kishi was released, but had to wait for the resumption of his political career until April 1952 when the San Francisco Peace Treaty of the previous year came into force and he was de-purged. He joined the Liberal Party in due course and was elected to the Diet at the general election of April 1953. He was one of the architects of the second conservative party, the Japan Democratic Party, the programme of which announced its intention 'to rectify the institutions introduced since the beginning of the occupation and to complete independence and self-defence'. It marked a clear departure from the occupation system, the post-war politics led by Yoshida.[17] It was Kishi who was to transform Japanese politics under the occupation into the politics of an independent Japan, and to achieve the unity of conservative forces based largely on the strength of wartime bureaucrats.

In November 1955 the Liberal Democratic Party was born, and conservative unity was achieved. Kishi became deputy prime minister in January 1957 and prime minister the following month. He concentrated on 'the rationalization of US–Japanese relations'. In order to make Japan an equal partner with the United States, he felt, Japan should assume a position as 'the leader of Asia'. His post-war interest in Asia was a

[16] Hara, op. cit., 129–30.   [17] Ibid. 164.

continuation of his former 'Great Asianism' and of his experiences in Manchuria. It was not surprising that his first political act as prime minister was to prepare the Police Duties Law Amendment Bill which his government introduced in 1958 to enhance police power to control demonstrations. But Japan of the 1950s was not the same as Japan of the 1930s and early 1940s. The Bill met with fierce opposition within and without the Diet, and had to be allowed to lapse.

In fact, anti-militarism and democratic sentiments had taken root in Japanese soil. Campaigning against American military bases in Japan had begun in earnest. A US attempt to expand the Tachikawa military airbase at Sunagawa, a suburb of Tokyo, in 1955 called forth fierce opposition from local people and radical students which lasted for several years. A movement against nuclear weapons started with a housewives' petition in Suginami ward, Tokyo, at the time of the American hydrogen bomb test at Bikini Atoll in 1954. The bikini test affected a Japanese fishing boat, one of whose crew died from the effects of radiation. Kishi's political future did not appear very promising. Moreover, the seemingly prosperous Japanese economy had to strangle a dying industry.

THE MIIKE COAL-MINERS' STRUGGLE

Coal-mining was once a great industry in Japan, and in 1936 Japan became one of the important coal producers in the world with an output of more than 40 million tons.[18] Dramatic increases in wartime coal production were due not to technological innovation but to a huge influx of new miners, including forced labourers from Korea and China. All the foreign miners who had survived hardship and torture were repatriated after the war, and coal production became largely a matter of labour policy to obtain a sufficient number of miners. The Slanting or Priority Production System introduced in 1946 boosted the production of coal and steel. The number of organized miners reached half a million in 1948, more than the wartime maximum of 420,000 in 1944. The deflationary policy (the Dodge Line) and the rationalization programmes badly affected the coal industry. Assisted by war demands during the Korean War, the number of miners, which had dwindled for some time, again increased to 370,000 in 1951, a figure never reached again. Meanwhile, in 1950 the SCAP allowed the reopening of Japan's Pacific coast oil refineries which had been closed under the occupation.

Confronted with competition from this cheaper source of energy, the coal industry had to fight for its survival. At the same time management began to prepare for the eventual withdrawal from coal. Profit-taking or

[18] Richard J. Samuels, *The Business of the Japanese State* (Ithaca, NY, 1987), 87.

the greatest possible exploitation under existing conditions, rather than investment either for safety or for development, became important to the industry, which began accumulating capital for other enterprises.[19] It was under these circumstances that the miners, organized in an industrial union, the Japan Coal-miners' Union or *Tanro* (membership: 270,000 in 1953) and also on the basis of each mining company, reacted critically against the notice of dismissal of a substantial number of miners; those employed by the Mitsui Mining Company began a strike which lasted 113 days in 1953. In August of that year the company announced a rationalization plan, according to which the number of redundant miners would be 5,738; the plan listed those liable for dismissals, which included not only the elderly and physically weak but also those who were not 'cooperative', whose character and behaviour were 'undesirable', and so on. The National Federation of Mitsui Miners' Unions, whose total membership stood at 48,000 at the time, declared that the types of miners mentioned in the company list would amount to 20,000. In November the strike came to an end, as the union and the company had reached an agreement which led to the reinstatement of a certain number of dismissed miners.

The second post-war boom at the time of the Suez Crisis of 1956 was of short duration, and when Mitsui Mining announced a workforce rationalization in January 1959, it led to the longest and largest strike in the history of Japanese labour. This began sporadically at the Miike mines in October 1959 after a series of unsuccessful negotiations. The company's second proposal for rationalization announced in August would involve 4,580 miners being designated as redundant. In December the company sent a dismissal notice to 1,297 union members. *Tanro* supported the Mitsui Miike Miners' Union, and *Sohyo* decided to back up *Tanro*. In January 1960, at the time of the Anti-Security Treaty Struggle in Tokyo, the company declared a lockout at all Miike mines, while the Miike Miners' Union went on strike for an unlimited period. In March a new Miike Miners' Union was formed with an initial membership of about 3,100, claiming to be against the class-war tactics adopted by the old union. In the same month *Tanro* declared an unlimited strike for all the major miners' unions, though there were several unions which refused to comply with the strike directive. Late in March the company removed its lockout ban from the members of the new union and ordered them to start work from 28 March. *Tanro* (temporarily as it turned out) changed its tactics and ordered the Miike Union (now Old Union) members to stop the strike and start working in spite of the lockout ban against them. On 28 March there were violent clashes between the members of the two unions,

---

[19] Samuels, op. cit., 105.

old and new, as they entered the mines at the same time, and this resulted in a mêlée with considerable casualties on both sides. On the following day a member of the old union was stabbed to death by one of the *yakuza* armed with swords and revolvers who had assisted the new union and the company. In June the old union started picketing at sea: on 7 July, when the company sought to bring in materials for the mines by using eleven boats, these were met by thirteen picketing boats, and a 'great naval battle' took place during which forty policemen, eighty company officials or members of the new union, and eighty members of the old union were injured. A few days later *Sohyo* managed to organize a rally of 40,000 supporters of the old union near the mine. Later in July the Central Conciliation Board, headed by two academics, announced the terms of peace, the third of its kind, which proposed the replacement of designated dismissals by voluntary retirement and an increase in retirement allowances. Both the union and the company accepted the terms and the Miike strike and lockout came to an end on 1 November 1960 after nearly 200 days.

It was in the wake of the Miike struggle that *Nikkeiren* advocated 'the establishment of a new order [in industrial relations] by revitalizing Japan's good old tradition' based on solidarity and co-operation of labour–management, supported by welfare arrangements within a business and social security measures by the government. A long-term stable wage system, traditional company unions (placed in harmonious relations with modern national industrial unions), life-time employment, and a seniority system were factors essential to such management. The special report in which these points were made summed up its remarks by saying: 'Let us make full use of Japanese flavour.'[20] It was obvious that labour had been defeated at Miike. As a result of the defeat, and faced with oil import liberalization coming in 1963, *Tanro* drastically changed its tactics, and in co-operation with management began lobbying the government for protectionist measures, and later for measures to facilitate labour mobility in face of unemployment due to the increasing number of mine closures.

The tragedy of the Miike miners did not end with the adoption of 'Japanese-style management'. Owing in part at least to increasing negligence on the part of the company over the introduction of modern safety measures, and perhaps also to the deterioration of general morale, on 9 November, three months after the appearance of the *Nikkeiren* report, a coal-dust explosion accompanied by the filling of the pits with coal gas killed 450 miners and incapacitated over 300 men at the Mitsui mine. This was a sad epitaph to the Japanese coal industry which was about to die. It was not long afterwards that we heard of 'Joban Hawaian Land' in

[20] *Nikkeiren Times*, 2 May 1963.

the Joban coalfield in the north-east of mainland Japan, where all the mines had been closed and a hot-spring pleasure resort was opened. The Chikuho coalfield in nothern Kyushu, once known for its association with right-wing politicians like Toyama Mitsuru, which had boasted the largest coal output in the country at one time, was practically extinct by the 1980s.[21] Between 1961 and 1971 the share of coal in primary energy supply in Japan declined from 31.3 per cent to 6.1 per cent. Production decreased from 55 million to 31 million tons; 579 mines had been reduced to sixty-eight, and the number of the miners declined from 210,000 to 40,000. By 1975 only thirty-five mines, employing 20,000 miners, remained open in Japan. The great mine at Takashima was closed in 1987. The great Yubari Collieries in Hokkaido were wound up in 1990. Mitsui–Miike, one of the three coal mines still operating in Japan at the beginning of 1997, discharged 1,200 miners and was closed on 30 March of that year.

THE ANTI-SECURITY TREATY STRUGGLE OF 1960

Kishi, as soon as he was de-purged, resumed his political activities, forming a League to Reconstruct Japan with the double purposes of attaining both a revision of the new constitution that would allow rearmament and a revision of the Security Treaty to make it an agreement between equals. If Kishi were to have his own way, a great many people feared, Japan would re-emerge as a military power like the one they had seen before. As prime minister he went so far as to state in his reply in the House of Councillors that Japan should be permitted to use nuclear weapons within the limits of the right of self-defence. Since revision of the constitution was unthinkable under the conditions in which the socialists and their allies controlled one-third of the Diet seats, Kishi concentrated on the revision of the Security Treaty. The new treaty prepared between Kishi and his foreign minister Fujiyama Aiichiro would allow a degree of independence by stipulating for preliminary consultation beween the two governments, deleting a clause on US participation in suppressing civil strife in Japan, and adding a clause concerning the termination of the treaty in the future. On the other hand, the new treaty would assign to the US forces in Japan a new task of defending 'Far East' areas, and this caused alarm as to the possibility of involving Japan deeper in an American world strategy that would increase tensions in Asia.[22]

[21] See also Matthew Allen, *Undermining the Japanese Miracle: Work and Conflict in a Coal Mining Community* (Cambridge, 1994), 68 ff.
[22] Masumi Ishikawa, *Sengo Seijishi* (Post-war History of Japanese Politics) (Tokyo, 1995), 88–9.

Early in 1959 the JSP proclaimed a foreign policy based on 'positive neutralism' and a new emphasis was placed on nuclear disarmament.[23] Neutralism originated in the foreign policy of the Indian prime minister Nehru and other non-western statesmen in the international context of emerging Cold War confrontations, and its stance was sometimes referred to as the 'third force' or 'third bloc', as put forward by the Praja Socialist Party of India. In March 1959 the JSP general secretary Asanuma Inajiro on his visit to Beijing made a remark to the effect that 'American imperialism is the common enemy of the peoples of Japan and China'. *Sohyo*, under the new leadership of Ota Kaoru, who had replaced Takano, was more interested in industrial action and organization than a mass campaign for political purposes, but its success in thwarting Kishi's Police Duties Bill of 1958 demonstrated how effective a mass movement could be. The right-wing faction, called the Nishio faction, led by Nishio Suehiro, 'a tough and rather unintellectual ex-trade unionist',[24] did not like the leftward swing of the party, began to spread its own ideas about a 'people's' party or rather a national party, split the JSP, and set up the Democratic Socialist Party (DSP) early in 1960. Numerically much weaker, the DSP did not affect the mounting tide of the national movement against Kishi's attempt to revise the security treaty.

The 'reluctance to become involved in the East–West confrontation after the war', it has been said, 'gave neutralism a powerful appeal'.[25] Neutralism was also regarded by many as the best way for Japan to resume its role as an important power in Asia, while there was a broad consensus that Japan should not get involved in a war to be fought for Chiang Kai-shek or Syngman Rhee. The leftist opposition to Kishi and the proposed revision of the Security Treaty reflected 'the basic anxieties of the whole nation'.[26]

The important day was 26 April 1960, because this was the day when the LDP could push the treaty through the Lower House so that it might be ratified automatically by the Upper House before the regular session ended on 26 May. Tactics pursued by Kishi's opponents were varied. Shimizu Ikutaro and Uehara Senroku, two well-known left-wing professors, led a group of 300 teachers from nine universities in Tokyo to petition the Diet on 19 April, and many other scholars' groups followed their example. The National Council, a co-ordinating body, was torn apart over the question of tactics for 26 April. *Zengakuren* (the National Student Union) urged a massive assault on the Diet. The JSP representatives urged that the demonstrations be held in the Diet vicinity. The

[23] Arthur Stockwin, in his book, *The Japanese Socialist Party and Neutralism*, (Melbourne, 1968), distinguished 'neutrality', which means an effort of a nation to avoid involvement in war, from 'neutralism' or a neutralist nation which 'seeks (probably in concert with other like-minded powers) to make a positive contribution to world peace'. [24] Ibid. 94.
[25] George Packard, *Protest in Tokyo* (Princeton, 1966), 12. [26] Ibid. 32.

JCP 'observer' (a party representative attended the council as observer) stood alone in counselling against action near the Diet. Finally it was decided that the demonstrations on 26 April, though they would take place near the Diet, should be calm and orderly. The demonstrations turned out to be larger than ever before in this crisis. The vast majority of demonstrators were from *Sohyo*, with a record number of students—about 13,000—added to the crowd. The crowd under the National Council marched by the west side of the Diet building in an orderly fashion, presenting petitions to the waiting JSP Dietmen who applauded in return. On the opposite side of the Diet building, however, the mainstream (anti-communist) *Zengakuren* factions, consisting of some 4,000 students, charged the main gate and were met by a reinforced police force who had raised barricades of armoured cars.

Between 26 April, when no vote was taken in the Lower House, and 19 May the leftists continued to put pressure on the government. But on 19 May 1960, soon to be compared to the day of the surprise attack on Pearl Harbor, Kishi 'delivered a surprise political attack against the nation and against democracy'.[27] The LDP members of the steering committee that had been appointed, now meeting by themselves, quoting the motion for an extension of the session, announced that a plenary session would begin at 5 p.m. Socialist Diet members staged a mass sit-down outside speaker Kiyose's office to prevent him from reaching the rostrum. At this point they were still unaware of Kishi's plan to vote on the treaty as well, and sought only to block the extension vote. At 11.00 p.m. Kiyose, still 'incarcerated', ordered 500 policemen to break up the blockade. During the next forty-five minutes each and every socialist was carried away bodily by three or four policemen. Then Kiyose, flanked by a squad of Diet guards, made his way to his seat on the dais; a minute later he opened the plenary session in the presence of LDP members only. The fifty-day extension was quickly approved, and Kiyose announced that a new session would be convened 'tomorrow'—just after midnight. The session ended at 11.51 p.m. and fifteen minutes later, at six minutes past midnight, the plenary session opened. The chairman of the Special Committee made his report and Kiyose called for a rising vote on the treaty and related bills. The proceedings recorded that 'all present rose'. After the traditional 'Banzais' the stormy session adjourned at 12.19 a.m. This meant that, without any action by the House of Councillors, the new treaty would automatically receive the Diet's approval exactly thirty days later, on 19 June 1960.

The newspapers attacked Kishi, who retorted by saying that it was presumptuous of the press to assume that they alone represented public

---

[27] Rokuro Hidaka (ed.), *Gogatsu Jukunichi* (The 19th of May) (Tokyo, 1960).

opinion. The National Council mobilized tens of thousands of demon-strators around the Diet; this time moderates, non-communists, Christians, Buddhists, office clerks, and artists found themselves in demonstrations, many of them for the first time. Some called themselves members of the Society of the Voices of the Voiceless People.

On 10 June James Hagerty, President Eisenhower's press secretary, was sent to Japan to make final preparations for his visit. Communist-led anti-mainstream *Zengakuren* students appeared at Haneda airport in large numbers. Hagerty, surrounded and mobbed, had to be rescued by a US marine helicopter. Kishi was still determined to greet the president on 19 June, the day when the treaty was to be formalized, although police officials told him that after the Hagerty incident they could not guarantee the president's safety.

On the afternoon of 15 June, with *Sohyo*'s strike and a demonstration by some 70,000 people already proceeding, students began to gather near the main gate of the Diet building. The police brought in 5,000 men and blockaded the entrances with rows of trucks. At 5.15 p.m. on the opposite side of the compound a scuffle broke out between a demonstrating Modern Drama Group and 200 rightists, when the latter drove their truck into the midst of the marchers. By 6 p.m. the students had smashed the South Gate, and by 7 p.m. about 1,500 students swarmed through the gate into the compound. During the following half-hour the police counter-attacked. In this mêlée Kamba Michiko, a 20-year old student from Tokyo University, was crushed to death.

The treaty struggle was 'anti-climatic' after 15 June. Kishi met his advisers at midnight and told at a news conference on the afternoon of 16 June that this was not an appropriate time to welcome a state guest. Eisenhower's visit was cancelled. On 20 June the treaty passed its last parliamentary hurdle. On the morning of 23 June the necessary procedures for ratification were carried out, and on the same morning Kishi announced his decision to resign.

A disturbing after-effect of the struggle was the resurgence of right-wing terrorism. On 12 October the JSP chairman Asanuma was stabbed to death by a rightist youth while speaking on the platform of the Hibiya Public Hall; the ghastly scene was televised, to the horror of viewers. In February 1961 the home of the president of the Chuo Koron publishing company was attacked; he was absent, but his wife was wounded, his maid killed.

A new nationalism was emerging. Nakasone Yasuhiro, the future prime minister, expressed a typically conservative nationalist thought in the midst of the crisis: it was absurd, he said, for Japan to be divided between pro-American and pro-Soviet camps at a time when the Japanese ought to be pro-Japanese. But positive neutralism and pacifism were to be maintained by the leftists, and their views were shared by citizens' movements especially at the time of the Vietnam War. Perhaps the most disturbing element was the view expressed by Hayashi Fusao, formerly an advocate of the popular front, now a rightist writer, who argued that the Second World War was a culmination of the 100-year war which began when the United States made its first attempt to 'colonize' Japan in the 1850s. During these 100 years, according to Hayashi, Japan had accomplished her historic mission of checking the Western colonization of Asia and of proving to the world that the white and coloured races were equal.[28] His was not a lonely voice.

ECONOMIC GROWTH

The political confrontation of 1960 soon gave way to the rising tide of economism all round, for Japan had gone through the hardships of reconstruction and had entered a period of high economic growth. In spite of American bombing of Japanese cities, a great number of plants and factories built in the 1930s and during the war years had survived war damage, and these provided the starting-point for economic reconstruction after the war. The GNP for 1955 surpassed the pre-war level, and the rate of yearly increase of GNP was 9.1 (1955), 8.0 (1956), 8.0 (1957), 5.4 (1958), 9. 2 (1959), 14.1 (1960), 15.6 (1961), 6.4 (1962), 10.6 (1963), and 13.3 (1964).[29]

The recovery and growth of foreign trade, however, was delayed. General principles of reparations were laid down in the peace treaty, but individual settlements with South-East Asian countries had to be made before normalization of relations with these countries would take effect: 7,200 million yen annually for Burma, (1955–65); 9,000 million (later 10,800 million) yen annually for the Philippines, (1956–76); 7,200 million yen annually for Indonesia, (1958–69); and 3,600 million (later 1,620 million) yen annually for Vietnam (1960–5). The largest annual sum for reparations (reached in 1960) was $75 million (27,000 million yen). As Japan suffered from a shortage of foreign currency in those days, reparations took the form of 'service reparation'. Moreover, when the total amount of reparations was reduced to $1,700 million, an economic loan was incorporated in the system and amounted to 70 per cent of reparations; as a sort of economic development aid it consisted of building hydro-power plants, factories, and bridges and providing materials and machinery, using these as opportunities for exporting capital goods from Japan.[30] As for western Europe and other areas of the world, the admis-

[28] See Fusao Hayashi, 'Daitoa Senso Koteiron' (An Affirmative View of the Great East Asia War), *Chuo Koron*, Sept.–Dec., 1963.

[29] 'Kodo Seicho', ('High Economic Growth') *Nihon Keizaishi* (Economic History of Japan), viii. 11. This and the following paragraphs in this section depend mainly on this source.

[30] Ibid. 70.

sion of Japan into GATT in 1955 did not prevent as many as fourteen countries, including Britain, France, Australia, and India, afraid of the influx of cheap-labour goods from Japan, from refusing to extend most-favoured-country treatment to Japan; this type of discrimination continued well into the 1960s.

The Cold War continued to breed international crises and tragedies—the Hungarian Revolution and the Suez Crisis of 1956 and the Cuban Revolution of 1958–9—but the latter half of the 1950s witnessed a thaw or *détente* characterized by deStalinization and the introduction, though modest, of pluralism into socialism. On the other hand, military confrontation across the Taiwan Strait vitiated US–Chinese relations and Japanese trade with China was strictly restrained: a Japanese delegate at the Bandung Conference of Afro-Asian countries in April 1955 had to confess that 'Japan had not obtained complete independence both on political and economic matters, and cannot act on her own will, but China–Japanese relations ought to be normalized as quickly as possible'.[31] Furthermore, Japan was allowed to adopt 'neo-mercantilist' measures in a world in which the laissez-faire free-market economy was the exception rather than the rule. It was possible to shut out foreign competition in the domestic market of new industries by selective import restriction through foreign currency control. Tax relief and low-interest capital supply were resorted to as part of the policy to promote new industries.[32]

Although the GNP increase was about 8 per cent from 1955–9 and rose to 12 per cent in 1960–4, the rate of yearly increase of plant investment by businesses was nearly 40 per cent in 1956–60. The (Second) Steel Rationalization Plan (1956–60), the Electricity Development Plan (1951–60), and the (First) Petrochemical Industry Plan (1958–9) had stimulating effects on related industries. The Steel Plan in this period centred around the construction of strip-mills to produce thin steel plates for automobile bodies, the outer structure of home electric appliances, and engineering machines, and made the steel industry the third largest in the world next to those in the United States and West Germany. New industrial sites were developed in coastal areas like Yokkaichi and Kawasaki, later Chiba and Kashima, for the petrochemical conglomerates or combines to produce ethylene. Large hydroelectric plants were built, like the one at Sakuma, but as early as 1956 the shift from hydro-power as well as from coal to oil as the source of electricity generation was seriously planned. The supply of cheap oil was to become one of the mainsprings of the high economic growth in the 1960s.

Prime minister Ikeda Hayato who succeeded Kishi in July 1960, announced the National Income Doubling Plan. An average growth rate

---

[31] Quoted, ibid. 74.   [32] Ibid. 89–90.

of 7.2 per cent was to be maintained annually for ten years (1961–70) and the national income in real terms was to be doubled. In order to achieve this aim, public investment should be planned so as to improve infrastructure such as roads, harbours, and urban facilities; spontaneous growth of private businesses was to be encouraged by relying on private initiatives and devices rather than government control; the agricultural population be reduced so as to supply workers and technicians for the growing industrial sector. Measures for modernization and mechanization adopted around 1960 in agriculture and also in small and medium businesses were expected to overcome the shortage of labour at the time. As a result, the occupational distribution of the population underwent a drastic change. The percentage of those employed in the primary industry, which had gone up over 50 per cent after the war, declined rapidly in the 1950s and the trend was accelerated in the 1960s. The ratio of those employed in the primary industry in 1955 was 41 per cent and that of those in the secondary and tertiary industries in the same year 59 per cent, whereas twenty years later, in 1975, the respective figures were 13.9 and 86.1 per cent.[33] A breakdown of employed persons by industries on the basis of population census is as shown in Table 18.1.

After the years of economic boom sustained largely by heavy capital investment came a reaction, a severe recession in 1964–5, which was overcome by the issue of national bonds as a stimulus for recovery. Government financial policies had been adapted to the cyclical changes in the balance of trade, with alternate measures of stimulation and tightening which were called the stop-and-go policy. This type of cyclical growth came to an end in 1969 when the balance of trade settled in a constant surplus.[34]

The Japanese economy had achieved full employment by 1960. Under such conditions high saving and high investment would assure high economic growth. High household saving became almost proverbial, and various reasons have been cited for it, such as the bonus system, insufficient social security, expensive housing and education, and cultural factors like the habit of parsimony. As for investment, the share in Gross National Expenditure of private plant investment which constituted the largest component in capital formation, rose from 7 per cent in 1955 to 20 per cent in 1970. Throughout the boom years of 1965–70 it maintained the high share of over 15 per cent. The motivating factor in the development of the Japanese economy in the period of high economic growth can be said to lie in private plant investment.[35]

---

[33] 'Kodo Seicho', op. cit., 17–18.   [34] Ibid. 20–1.   [35] Ibid. 23.

TABLE 18.1. *Employment of persons, by industry* (%)

	1950	1960	1970	1980	1990	1993
Primary	48.3	32.6	19.4	10.9	7.1	5.9
Secondary	21.9	29.2	34.0	33.5	33.3	33.7
Tertiary	29.7	38.2	46.6	55.3	59.0	59.9
Others	0.1	0.0	0.0	0.3	0.6	0.5

Source: 53rd edition of *Nihon Kokusei Zue* (The Chart of Japan's National Strength), (1995/6), 96.

The automobile industry began to expand in the 1950s with protective tariffs, import restrictions, and technological transfer from advanced foreign firms (such as Nissan from Austin, Isuzu from Rootes, and Hino from Renault), and the number of passenger cars produced went up to 165,000 in 1960 and 3,179,000 in 1970 (9,948,000 in 1990, the highest so far). The expansion of the automobile industry had a stimulating effect on industrial linkage and helped establish 'nucleus' firms in machine engineering and special steel manufacturing. Similar effects were observed around the expanding electrical appliances industry. In short, the rapid expansion of heavy industries was greatly helped by the protective policy of the government, beginning with the strict control of foreign exchange and also by the technological transfer from advanced industrial countries. Financially, Japanese firms in those days relied heavily on borrowing from banks or a main bank, the practice which regrouped the firms in various industries into *keiretsu*. Firms in the same industry competed with each other for a margin of superiority both in quality and cost of the goods produced, and this encouraged the growth of a subcontract system and the creation of parts-makers, mostly small businesses which could produce quality goods at low cost.

EDUCATION GROWTH AND THE EMERGENCE OF A MASS CONSUMER SOCIETY

In such a high-growth economy, with a double structure, the conditions of labour are liable to escape due attention. Productivity of labour is appreciated, but not always the needs of the workers as men and women. Moreover, the change in the nature or function of education, from education of better men to training for better jobs, along with the 'doubling' of personal income, brought about a drastic reduction in the number of those who began working immediately after secondary school, and an equally great increase in the number of university or college graduates. The former decreased from 630,000 in 1955 to 550,000 in 1965, to 60,000 in 1975, while the latter increased from 90,000 in 1955 to 170,000 in 1965, to

TABLE 18.2. *Numbers of students at levels of education*

	1960	1970	1980	1990	1992	1993
Primary	12,591,000	9,493,000	11,827,000	9,373,000	8,947,000	8,769,000
Junior High	5,900,000	4,717,000	5,094,000	5,369,000	5,037,000	4,850,000
Senior High	3,239,000	4,232,000	4,622,000	5,623,000	5,219,000	5,010,000
Junior College	83,000	263,000	371,000	479,000	525,000	530,000
University	626,000	1,407,000	1,835,000	2,133,000	2,293,000	2,390,000

Source: Ministry of Education Survey, March 1993, from *Charted Survey of Japan 1994–95*.

350,000 in 1975.[36] Businesses, however, adopted their own training systems and new recruits had to undergo a period of firm training which was intended to foster firm loyalty as well as to impart necessary skills. In view of the long period required for mastering skills and techniques it is said that those who sustained high productivity in the period of high economic growth were the recruits from secondary and high schools (who joined the firms in large numbers at an early stage of economic growth), rather than university graduates employed (whose number increased at its later stage).[37] The numbers of students enrolled at various stages of education are shown in Table 18.2.

As for modern infrastructure, the bullet train began its regular service between Tokyo and Shin-Osaka in October 1964, the year of the Tokyo Olympics; communications technology also made rapid progress and the number of telephones increased from 3.6 million in 1960 to 7.4 million in 1965 and to 31.7 million in 1975 (the number of telephone subscribers in 1992 is 57,650,000).[38] Urbanization was accelerated, while depopulation of rural villages progressed, leaving old people and women behind as full-time farmers, with men, in many cases, as part-timers. A mass consumer society emerged with durable consumer goods like TV sets and electric washers and cookers mass-produced at a price which the less-well-off could afford. 'Leisure' became a Japanese word, but what characterized the consumer society most was its uniformity and standardization. Commoditization of moral and artistic values permeated national life. Education was no exception. Conformity, which bore authoritarian features and characteristics, was accentuated at the same time. Thus the national economy was by and large regimented into what might, with some exaggeration, be called 'Japan Incorporated', while the business firms became the centres of loyalty of those employed. These developments provide the themes for the following chapter, in which the Sato administration that followed Ikeda's will be examined.

[36] 'Kodo Seicho', op. cit., 30.   [37] Ibid. 31.
[38] Asahi Shinbun, *Japan Almanac* (1995), 177.

19
'Japan Incorporated' and
Radical Challenges, 1965–1973

The latter half of the period of high economic growth fell roughly with the whole span (1964–72) of the Sato Eisaku government, which is the longest in the constitutional history of Japan. High economic growth, the legacy he inherited from his predecessor Ikeda, continued all through this period, yet the appearance of economic success and prosperity failed to conceal the undercurrent of political instability, which was exacerbated partly by Japan's involvement in the Vietnam War and partly by the government's attempt to revive the old institutions that had been suppressed by the initial occupation policies of demilitarization and democratization. It is noteworthy that the radical student movement became increasingly militant and erupted into a series of direct actions exactly at a time when the Vietnam War was at its fiercest and rapid economic growth reached a zenith. Sato received the Nobel Peace Prize in October 1974, an honour which puzzled many, for his success in manoeuvring through the negotiations for the restitution of Okinawa was not universally appreciated. The stability of his government depended largely on continuing high economic growth, an analysis of which will be our first theme in this chapter.

RAPID ECONOMIC GROWTH AND ITS PROBLEMS

It has been pointed out by an economic historian that until the oil crisis of 1973 the Japanese economy, in spite of occasional trade cycles, booms, and recessions, showed 'a straight line of economic growth' (an average annual growth rate of 10 per cent).[1] Increases in investment in plant and equipment were most conspicuous, presenting a growth rate of 22 per cent from 1951 to 1973. The rise in prices was also very much noticeable and it would be justified to call it an inflationary trend, for the impression was widely shared in those days that prices would go up and would never come down. The economic growth in the 1950s and 1960s was accompanied by a series of short-term business cycles caused by a shortage of foreign currency: the limits of the ability to import were soon reached under a

[1] Takafusa Nakamura, *The Postwar Japanese Economy* (2nd edn., Tokyo, 1995), 53–5.

growth economy, and a reverse of the trend became unavoidable. After 1967 the deficit in international payments was checked before causing a recession; the foreign currency reserve steadily increased; Japan's international competitiveness was strengthened; exports grew, while imports stagnated. This led to the upward revaluation of the yen which, together with the rising price of oil in the 1970s 'tolled the death knell for the era of rapid growth'.[2]

A closer examination will reveal what happened to various factors that bore on the national economy in the period of rapid economic growth. First of all there was a deterioration of the American balance of payments aggravated by the Vietnam War, until President Nixon put an end to the dollar's convertibility into gold in August 1971. The western nations responded by switching to the floating exchange rate system, while the Smithsonian Agreement of December 1971 introduced a real devaluation of the dollar and established a new rate of 308 yen to the US $1 for Japan. With the old exchange rate of 360 yen introduced as part of the Dodge Line in 1949, Japan had strengthened international competitiveness and had very much depended on the US market for exports and imports. Hence the Japanese economy remained sensitive to American business cycles. It was after she had attained a sustained surplus in her balance of payments that she was able to pursue a more independent line of monetary policy. Yet Nixon's new economic policy came to her as a 'shock'. In 1973 a general switch to the floating exchange rate system was introduced, and the yen–dollar exchange rate was pegged at around 260 yen, but it fell to 300 yen after the first oil crisis. Obviously the Japanese economy was in trouble.

Japan's economic growth was heavily export-oriented, starting with the export of textile products, the weight of which however declined from about 50 per cent in all exports in 1950 to 37 per cent in 1955 and down to 5 per cent in 1975, while the share of steel in exports rose to 34 per cent by 1960 though it fell to 10 per cent subsequently. Machinery, ships, and automobiles replaced steel as the leading export goods, and this reflected the structural shift of domestic industries to the production of high-value-added goods which depended on the level of technology as well as on the import of low-cost materials such as cheap crude oil.[3]

Another factor worthy of special attention was the rise of new managers, the old-time owner-managers had either been purged or else had lost control of their firms due to post-war inflation, thus promoting the tendency of the separation of management from ownership and producing an aggressive new type of manager in a business world which became fiercely competitive. They were younger than their predecessors by ten years, on

---

[2] Takafusa Nakamura, op. cit., 58.   [3] Ibid. 65–8.

average. They were mostly those who had climbed the ladder of promotion within firms, and were experienced specialists.[4] Their aggressiveness, as distinct from 'soundness', in business management would explain the decline of firms' ratio of equity (or own) capital to gross capital from the pre-war level of over 60 per cent to 25 per cent.[5] As the proportion of borrowed funds together with interest payments increased, aggressive new managers strove for bold business expansion to increase profits, for which they depended more on borrowed capital, in a kind of vicious circle which enhanced the role of banks and encouraged the regrouping of businesses in *keiretsu*. When times were bad a helping hand would come from the government in the form of recession cartels and tax reduction or exemption. In the great age of technological innovation Japanese managers were able to combine imported technologies so as to create low-cost mass-production systems. Managers would prefer high growth and larger shares in the output to high profit rates.

They were helped by the stable labour–management relationship preserved in 'Japanese-style management'. Each of its three distinctive features—company unions, lifetime employment, and a seniority wage system—had its origins in pre-war management, but it was consciously and substantially adopted after the war, especially after the fierce confrontation of capital and labour in the years of economic reconstruction. Economic growth and technological progress were not carried out without costs and sacrifices. The 'energy revolution' from coal to oil led to the downfall of the great coal industry. Technological progress in heavy and chemical industries caused pollution of air and water: the 1950s and the early 1960s saw the spread of the 'Minamata disease' due to eating poisoned fish from Minamata Bay in western Kyushu polluted by waste water from Nippon Chisso (Nitrogeneous Fertilizer), and the 'Yokkaichi asthma' due to air pollution caused by waste gas from petrochemical factories set up along the north-eastern coast of Ise Bay. Criticism of industrial pollution became increasingly vociferous, and the principle of compensation by the firms responsible was worked out and established with the passage of the Environmental Pollution Prevention Act of 1970. Nevertheless, it took nearly forty years before the neglected groups among the victims of the Minamata pollution were given compensation through a conciliation judgement in court.

One controversial factor is the role of the government in promoting economic growth by providing administrative guidance or even industrial planning. 'Japan Incorporated', a cliché coined by the US State Department, may be an exaggeration. There was industrial planning of a sort in

---

[4] Hideo Kobayashi, *et al.*, *Nihon Kabushikigaisha no Showa-shi* (Showa History of Japan Incorporated) (Osaka, 1995), 203.　　[5] Takafusa Nakamura, op. cit., 70.

Manchukuo, Japan's puppet state, but wartime Japan experienced a 'control economy' which is said to have revived in the post-war sytem under the different paradigm of economic efficiency.[6] A close government–business co-operative relationship is not unique to Japan, as has been pointed out: defence industries in the United States provide another case tending in the same direction; but what is thought by Americans to be exceptional was the norm for Japan's industrial sectors during the period of rapid economic growth.[7] But 'a Japanese model' can be discovered in which an elite bureaucracy is given 'sufficient scope to take initiative and operate effectively', 'market-conforming methods of state intervention' are brought to perfection in the form of 'administrative guidance', and there exists 'a pilot organization like MITI' which controls industrial policy without being doctrinaire.[8] The model appeared to work well for the period of rapid economic growth.

Equalization of income distribution was more or less achieved in the 1960s.[9] Wage levels obtained by trade unions through their annual *shunto* (Spring Wage Offensive) provided a target income level for the whole working class, farmers, the self-employed, and family workers. The *shunto* itself rapidly expanded in size and raised its targets yet higher. The number of union members who joined a *shunto* increased from 700,000 in 1955 to 4 million in 1960, and 6.35 million in 1965; the rate of wage increase in major firms went up from 6.3 per cent in 1955 to over 10 per cent in the late 1960s. Trade unionism itself formed part of the high-growth economy.[10] This equalization of income at a comparatively high level brought about a sense of belonging to the middle class among the people.[11] Indeed, the era of high economic growth was marked by changes in class consciousness. According to the surveys made by the Japanese Sociological Association, the ratio of those who identified themselves with the middle class rapidly increased from 41.9 per cent in 1955 to 54.8 per cent in 1965, and to 76.4 per cent in 1975. This middle-class consciousness, fostered as it was by the reappearance of the 'salaried man' (*sarariiman*) (which had made its debut in the 1910s) as the term applied to almost all working men, permeated through the people. With it the status consciousness as *shain* (members of a company) was strengthened by the privileges assured by Japanese-style management. The amount of one's salary, the degree of celebrity of one's firm, its welfare facilities, its pension system, and one's ambition as a *sei-shain* (a formal or regular member of the company, as dintinguished from irregular members or part-timers) all became important. Such new terms as *kaisha ningen* (company man)

---

[6] Hideo Kobayashi *et al.*, op. cit., 200. [7] Chalmers Johnson, *MITI*, 312.
[8] Ibid. 314–21. [9] Takafusa Nakamura, op. cit., 117.
[10] Masanori Nakamura, in *Nihon Tsushi* (Complete History of Japan), xx. 38.
[11] Takafusa Nakamura, op. cit., 118.

and *kigyo senshi* (enterprise fighter) were created without much effort. Thus, a company became the centre of loyalty of its members, 'almost equal to the state and the army in by-gone days'.[12] This tendency, fashioned in the heyday of rapid economic growth, continued well into the 1980s.

High economic growth, while enabling 'high welfare, high income burden', had a built-in pattern of 'the dual structure' in employment, characterized by the existence of the under-employed or the half-employed, especially women part-timers. In large firms there was a permanent labour force enjoying the benefits of Japanese-style management, but in both large and small firms there were considerable numbers of temporary workers whose wages were about half those of permanent staff, and who suffered inferior working conditions. The number of temporary workers could be reduced at will according to business fluctuations. The dual structure can also be detected in the existence of small businesses employing workers for low wages under inferior working conditions. They are the first to go when business deteriorates.

High economic growth lost its momentum. The 'Nixon Shock' came when the Japanese economy was in a recession, and the Bank of Japan boldly increased the money supply in order to stimulate domestic demand, for recovery through an export drive seemed difficult. The new exchange rate, however, did not weaken Japan's international competitiveness, and idle funds that accumulated in businesses were used primarily to buy land for speculative purposes. This trend, helped by Tanaka Kakuei's grand plan of spreading the benefits of a growth economy (the details of which will be examined later), intensified land speculation, which pushed up land prices, and rises in general commodity prices followed. The tight money policies then introduced failed to curb inflation. The shock of the oil crisis of October 1973 caused panic buying and brought about a 'crazed prices' inflation. Japan's inflation in 1973–4 was second only to that of Britain, but it subsided shortly afterwards. With sharp rises in raw material and fuel prices, profit margins were greatly reduced. Mining and manufacturing production declined by 19 per cent from the last quarter of 1973 to the first of 1975, the severest decline in production in post-war Japan.[13] Only a few of the strongly competitive export industries like automobiles and the food industry directly related to daily life escaped a decline in production. Employment restructuring became a serious issue. These were the signs of the end of the high economic growth that had continued for almost twenty-years.

---

[12] Masanao Kano in *Nihon Tsushi*, xxi. 26.   [13] Takafusa Nakamura, op. cit., 217.

SATO EISAKU AND HIS GOVERNMENT

Sato Eisaku, the younger brother of Kishi Nobusuke (Nobusuke was adopted back into the Kishi family), born in Yamaguchi prefecture and a graduate of the law faculty of Tokyo Imperial University, spent over ten years as a local railway officer. Promoted to the head of the Railway Section of the Ministry of Transport in 1946, he was elected as a Liberal to the Diet in January 1949 and remained loyal to the party leader Yoshida. In November 1964 he became prime minister, with a strong backing from *zaikai* (top leaders of the business world), succeeding Ikeda, who had been seriously ill. He accepted most of the former ministers into his government as well as Ikeda's policy of the 'doubling of income', was in favour of a revision of the constitution, and would work for the restitution of the Southern Kuriles and Okinawa.

With the Japan–Korea Basic Treaty or Korea–Japan Normalization Treaty signed in June 1965, diplomatic relations were established between the two countries, the old annexation treaty was formally annulled, Japan recognized the (South) Korean government as 'the only lawful government in Korea', and stipulations were made for the status of Koreans in Japan and for the revival of trade relations that was to encourage Japanese investment in Korea. It is noteworthy, however, that the draft treaty had incurred bitter criticism both in Japan and Korea, and had to be carried forcibly by the LDP in the two Diet houses, while in Korea it came into force thanks largely to the dictatorial regime of General Park Chung-hee.

Early in 1966 the government moved a bill in the Diet to revive the anniversary of the legendary Emperor Jimmu's accession; in view of strong objections to this revivalist step among opposition members the Sato government decided to call it the Day to Commemorate the Founding of the State (DCFS), and to insert it in the government proclamation of the Amended National Holidays together with the Day of Respecting the Aged and the Day of Physical Exercise. The controversial DCFS was adopted by a government decree issued in December, when Sato emphasized 'community consciousness as a race', and the first DCFS was celebrated on 11 February 1967: ever since it has become the day not to unite but to divide the nation. Sato began to show his true colour, a hawkish one, on a new labour issue, which he handled as though engaged in the suppression of a political strike. The ILO Treaty 87 adopted in 1948 was an international treaty to guarantee the right of combination of workers; the Japanese government had consistently refused to ratify this under the pretext that restrictions had been imposed on public employees since 1948 in accordance with a directive from SCAP of that year. The *Sohyo* (General Council of Trade Unions), which had started a movement to restore the right to strike for public employees, appealed to the ILO. The ILO sent an investigation committee, and the government was obliged to have Treaty 87 ratified. Ratification would require revisions of some of the existing laws related to public employees, the implementation of which governments have delayed even to this day, while new labour practices such as arbitration and recommendation by the Central Labour Conciliation Commission gradually became accepted.

The Sato government was reconstituted in February 1967, putting an emphasis on the establishment of political morale. A Council to Promote Price Stabilization was set up in July with the catchphrase: 'the introduction of a tax system that would link spending on 3C to that on H', '3C' standing for cars, colour TV sets, and coolers (or air-conditioners), and 'H' for housing. In July an Anti-Pollution Measures Basic Law was enacted, a sure sign of the spread to an alarming extent of pollution caused by rapid growth in the manufacturing and chemical industries. The Basic Law introduced the concept of regional environmental standards for effective regulation, and clarified the principle that the costs of pollution and preventive measures were to be borne by the relevant businesses. 'In harmony with the sound development of the economy', a phrase inserted in the law, however, had to be eliminated when the law was revised in 1970 in view of the further spread of pollution and of the appearance of new types, especially air pollution due to exhaust gases, and pollution of the evironment caused by the dumping of industrial waste.

After another reconstruction of the government in January 1970 the year of the World Exposition at Senri, Osaka, with the main theme of 'Progress and Harmony'—the Sato government tackled its last job. The Centre for Measures against Pollution set up in July 1970 in response to the Expo's slogan was reorganized one year later into the *Kankyocho* (Board, or rather Ministry, of Environment). Oishi Buichi, the first environment minister, stopped and then cancelled construction work on the Oze–Tadami 'international tourist highway' that had been planned. Oze and its highland marshes have been preserved as a national park, carefully shielded from effects of modern tourism.

SATO AND THE SECURITY TREATY

In the equally delicate field of international relations, Sato managed to secure an automatic extension of the Japan–US Security Treaty in June 1970. The current treaty, revised in 1960, had a fixed period of ten years' duration, and the LDP and the government preferred its automatic extension (under which the treaty would continue unless either of the treaty powers gives notice of its annulment one year in advance) to another ten years' extension that might invoke another national movement against the treaty. Meanwhile, the government encouraged the view that the Security

Treaty had saved Japan a considerable amount of military expenditure and thus ensured peace and economic prosperity.

Moreover, the new Security Treaty marked a new departure in US–Japanese relations as it formed an essential part of the new American world strategy. This new treaty for mutual co-operation and security was more than a treaty for mutual defence, for it stipulated political and economic co-operation. Pax Americana had a theoretical support in Walt W. Rostow's thesis of the 'taking off' of a developing economy. Traditional society, with its mass poverty, induced many Asian nations to look to Russia and China for quick economic growth. However, an economy at the stage of 'take-off' will need foreign aid to introduce new technology and also to develop hitherto-unused natural resources. It should be America and her allies, Japan above all, who would supply this aid and thereby protect the 'free world' based on capitalist businesses. As early as in 1955 the Japan Centre of Productivity was opened to provide new technology for Japan and to help the adoption of an employer–employed collaboration system in each firm, and this also marked the beginning of efforts to set up a closer relationship with East Asian countries to promote economic development. Dictatorial regimes committed to development came into existence one after another in East and South-East Asia in the 1960s: the Park regime in Korea, the Lee Kuan Yew government in Singapore, the Marcos regime in the Philippines, and the military regime founded by General Haji Mohamed Suharto in Indonesia. The Sato government supported the Park regime with $500 million of aid in 1965, gave the Suharto regime an emergency aid of $30 million in 1966, the beginning of a succession of economic aid to that country, and also assisted the South Vietnamese government with economic aid. It was in this way that 'the "triangle of United States, Japan, and South-East Asia", which had remained on the level of plans and ideas, came into being'.[14]

THE VIETNAM WAR AND JAPAN

American nuclear submarines used Naha, Okinawa, as a base, adding Sasebo a little later. A powder-magazine ripe for explosion in this region was Vietnam, where the French surrender at Dien Bien Phu in 1954 had led to the establishment of the People's Republic under the veteran communist leader Ho-Chi Minh in the north, while an anti-communist regime was set up in Saigon in the same year, obviously with American support. The National Liberation Front was formed in South Vietnam in 1960 and by the beginning of 1964 it had succeeded in 'liberating' over two-thirds of

[14] Masanori Nakamura, op. cit., 56–7

the whole south. The Kennedy administration had decided to intervene in South Vietnam. Under his successor, Lyndon Johnson, the United States began bombing North Vietnam in February 1965 and threw in regular American forces to fight the Vietnamese, or Vietcong as they were called, in the south. In spite of the presence of a token force of Asian troops on their side, it was all but a war of genocide on the part of the Americans, involving indiscriminate bombing that destroyed schools and hospitals, and the use of Napalm bombs, poison gas, defoliants, and other chemical weapons. For all the legends of brave actions (that sometimes verged on atrocities), the Americans failed to subdue the Vietnamese, who fought for their survival, independence, and national freedom. For the first time in history a developing nation had defeated the military might of the most powerful nation in the world.

In this war, the Japanese mainland (to say nothing of Okinawa, that was still under American military rule) provided bases at Yokota and Iwakuni for American fighter planes, fighter-bombers, and other facilities for their forces in Vietnam. While America suffered from the worst inflation since the Civil War, American war needs helped to sustain prosperity in Japan: the balance of US trade with Japan showed a deficit for the first time in 1965, and this minus figure went on increasing as the war escalated. The Vietnam War also stimulated pacifist and neutralist opinion in Japan. A loose federation of radical groups came into existence in the form of the *Betonamu-ni-Heiwa-wo Shimin Rengo* (Citizens' Federation for Peace in Vietnam), soon to be known as the *Beheiren*. This was set up in April 1965, and its founder, Oda Makoto, drafted a 'Citizens Pact Between Japan and America For Peace and Against War', in which he urged 'international disobedience' and some form of direct democracy and direct action by citizens. The *Beheiren* attracted attention by its clandestine acts of aiding American soldiers who deserted while on leave in Japan.

THE REVERSION OF OKINAWA

Sato was the first prime minister to visit Okinawa after the war. In August 1965 he declared that, 'until the restitution of Okinawa is realized, our "post-war" will continue'. At a US–Japan top meeting held in November 1967 the return of Okinawa as well as the Bonin Islands was promised, while Japan affirmed her total support of the American policy in Vietnam and gave a pledge to maintain the Security Treaty and to strengthen economic aid to those South-East Asian countries that were striving for the containment of Chinese communism. The Japanese side acknowledged that the American bases in Okinawa were playing an important role in ensuring security, not only for Japan but also for 'free countries' in East Asia. In November 1968 the Sato government decided on the basic policy of 'the Integration of Hondo [Mainlands] and Okinawa'. In Okinawa radical forces were gaining in strength. Yara Chobyo, the radical candidate, won in the first public election of Governor of the Ryukyu government held in June 1968, and another radical candidate was elected as the mayor of the city of Naha. The radicals, who pleaded for an 'instant, unconditional, total restitution' of Okinawa, planned a general strike which was averted by pressure from premier Sato, though 55,000 teachers and workers took part in a demonstration at Kadena in February 1969. Three months later Sato stated in his speech at the Diet that he would negotiate with the United States for the restitution 'without nuclear bombs, on conditions equal to those obtained in mainland Japan'. At a US–Japan top meeting held in November 1969 a secret agreement was reached according to which Japan, in an emergency situation, would accept US proposals for bringing nuclear weapons to Okinawa and was to keep designated storage ready for the use of such weapons. Actual negotiations for the restitution of Okinawa began in January 1970. Many Okinawans were critical of the fact that the return 'without nuclear weapons' was not explicitly stated and that the vast US military bases were allowed to continue. Governor Yara did not attend the ceremony for signing the Agreement for the Restitution of Okinawa held in June 1971.

Sato, having fulfilled his own pledge of the restitution of Okinawa, resigned the premiership one year later in June 1972. In spite of his success in repairing the damage done by his brother to Japan–US relations, he failed to catch up with new developments in America's Asian policy. China's Cultural Revolution was coming to an end; Lin Piao was killed in an air accident; President Nixon was to visit Beijing; and with American blessing the Chinese People's Republic was admitted to the United Nations. It was Sato's successor, Tanaka Kakuei, who was to restore Japan's relations with communist China.

Sato made his exit from the political scene at a time when radical forces achieved remarkable successes in local elections: after the radical governor Yara came Ninagawa Torazo, who was elected with socialist and communist support for the sixth time as governor of Kyoto in April 1970. One year later both Tokyo and Osaka elected a radical governor: Minobe Ryokichi was re-elected with an overwhelming majority in Tokyo and Kuroda Ryozo, a socialist-communist candidate, won Osaka with a small majority. By the end of 1973 each of the six largest cities of Japan had a radical mayor. The number of radical mayors reached over 100 at one time. In 1975, when Kanagawa prefecture elected a radical governor, nearly 40 per cent of the whole population of Japan was living under a radical local government which was generally more energetic and active in carrying out pollution-prevention projects and promoting measures for social security.[15] 'Student Power', which formed one feature of the Sato era, was only part of the radicalization of society.

STUDENT POWER

The post-war student movement in Japan consolidated itself in 1948 when the *Zengakuren* (*Zen Nihon Gakusei Jichikai-Sorengo* or All-Japan General Federation of Student Unions) was set up. It had a militant tendency acquired in the course of struggles against an increase in tuition fees and against those in SCAP-GHQ, the government, and the university whom they regarded as inimical to the cause of peace and democracy. Its members belonged to the generations who had heartily welcomed and remained committed to the initial reform measures introduced by the SCAP. Their relations with the JCP were tenuous from the start, though their militancy was encouraged for a while by the communists when the JCP adopted tactics of promoting token 'guerrilla warfare' during the Korean War.

It was not until 1956, when the revelation of Stalinist atrocities stirred world opinion, that radical forces outside the JCP found strength enough to stand on their own feet. Radical students, many of them, now declared themselves to be anti-Stalinist or anti-communist, and some were openly Trotskyist. In this same year the *Zengakuren* held its 'second founding congress' at which it was decided that the main purpose of the student movement was to promote the struggle for peace. Disappointment with the JCP led to the rise of an 'Independent Marxist' group which formed a Japanese Trotskyist Federation in January 1957, soon to be renamed as the *Kakukyodo* (*Kakumei-Kyosanshugisha Domei*) or Revolutionary communist League. To them the communists appeared too nationalistic and conservative. In fact, the communists were now suffering from new fetters, a revised *Kozaha* doctrine of two-stage revolution: first, a people's democratic revolution through the establishment of a 'national democratic united front' which would allow an alliance with 'national' capitalists; then a socialist revolution as the second step. The major enemy for Japanese communists was American imperialism, which had replaced, in their minds, the old semi-feudal Japanese capitalism with the emperor at its top. This communist programme was a reflection to some extent of the worsening relationship between China and the United States, but it has to be acknowledged that the JCP was only a pawn in the global game of Cold War.

There was a lull after the storm of 1960. High economic growth in the

[15] Akira Fujiwara *et al.*, *Nihon Gendaishi* (Modern History of Japan) (Tokyo, 1955), 195–202, 209.

1960s seemed to confirm the LDP hegemony, while the opposition parties consoled themselves with the modest achievement of retaining one-third of the Diet seats to safeguard the peace clause of the constitution. Though the radical students in the *Zengakuren* busied themselves with almost endless debates over the abstract theories of a revolution that never came, and such fruitless exercises only divided and subdivided their forces into warring sects, their movement as a whole nevertheless embodied criticisms of the human costs involved in high economic growth.

In 1967 militant students, with the aid of activist workers, started a series of direct actions against the American war in Vietnam: a sit-in demonstration at the American airbase at Tachikawa in May, and the 'Haneda Incident' in October when, in an attempt to prevent premier Sato's visit to South Vietnam, about 2,500 students and their working-class supporters clashed with riot police. The students and their allies, although armed with wooden staves and helmets painted with the colours and names of the sects to which they belonged, were no match for the well-equipped police.

By this time the *Zengakuren* had recovered from its lethargy after the 1960 struggle, and sects flourished. In the following year 1968, the students' extra-campus struggles escalated: a massive demonstration in January against the visit to Sasebo of the American nuclear submarine *Enterprise*; support for the stubborn resistance of the peasants who refused to let their land be used as a site for the new international airport at Narita in the spring (this was to last for another twenty-eight years); and above all, the riotous demonstration in Shinjuku on 'International Anti-War Day', 21 October, when Shinjuku Station was virtually occupied by demonstrators and a riot act was read. It was from this Shinjuku riot that Mishima Yukio, the novelist and a cultural fascist, expected a final confrontation of opposing forces, the Reds or militant leftists and the Army of the Emperor, although this army only existed in his imagination. Mishima apparently aspired to and even braced himself to play the role of a fascist poet-leader like Gabriele D'Annunzio in Italy.

Student power in Japan coincided with the May Revolution in Paris and other similar events in America and Europe. It was widely felt that university education was degrading into a process of mass production, as in factories, and resistance to this tendency was the main cause of the students' revolt in those years. The immediate issue was redress of such grievances as an increase in fees, the internship system for medical students, the reluctance on the part of university authorities to give full autonomy to students in the management of their hostels and union buildings, and more generally the inevitable defects of mass education: enormous classes and overworked professors, and hence 'alienation' in classrooms. When the students felt that they had discovered the causes of 'alienation' by reading Marx and Marcuse (e.g. the latter's *Reason and Revolution*), and had linked these with theoretical 'situations' such as Japanese 'Monopoly Capitalism', 'American Imperialism', and 'Russian Stalinism', it required little intellectual exercise for them to conclude that they should strive for revolution, even world revolution, with the total negation and extermination of all their enemies. This rather simplistic mental process wrought havoc in many Japanese universities, as elsewhere. At the height of the campus disputes it was estimated that 110 out of the 489 universities in Japan were in serious trouble, nearly half of them occupied by students.[16] But many students had real anxieties. Yamamoto Yoshichika, a 27-year-old graduate student studying physics at Todai (Tokyo University), the leader of the *Todai Zenkyoto* (University Joint Struggle Committee), who played an important role in co-ordinating the warring sects of the 'New Left', had this much to say: campus occupation with barricades signified 'negation of the university which produces men to serve capital as if in a factory, and also negation of the existence of students whose only future is to be cogs in the power machine'.[17]

One of the strongholds of student power was Nichidai or Nihon University, the largest 'private enterprise' in education, where irregularities in university finance incurred the wrath of a good many of its 86,000 students, who repudiated the spirit of 'money-making' in a 'mass-production university'. Another, more symbolic battlefield was Todai—Tokyo University at Hongo—where a dispute over the status of graduate students in the notoriously autocratic faculty of medicine, and an allegedly erroneous judgement passed by the governing board on one of the militant students, led to the devastation of the Todai campus symbolized by the battle over the student-occupied Yasuda auditorium in January 1969. The University Emergency Measures Act was rushed through the Diet in August 1969, and the government threat to close troubled universities had its effect: student power began to crumble.

A frightening sequel to student power was terrorism. The *Sekigunha* (Red Army, or rather Revolutionary Army Group) was born from a sect of socialist students, some of whom hijacked a JAL plane which was forced to land at Pyonyang in April 1970. Dreadful, senseless killings were to follow, both among themselves and among innocent people, including the slaughter of passengers waiting at a lobby in Tel-Aviv (Lod) airport in May 1972. (A quarter of a century after these atrocities the surviving hijackers are reported to be still living in North Korea; two leaders of a sectarian fratricidal carnage, sentenced to death more than twenty years later in 1993, have published their memoirs and confessions; and the sole surviving

[16] *Asahi Shinbun*, 4 Aug. 1969.
[17] Yoshichika Yamamoto, *Chisei no Hanran* (Revolt of Intellect) (Tokyo, 1969).

terrorist from the attack on Lod Airport, sentenced to life imprisonment in Israel, was traded off with Israeli hostages and disappeared into the international terrorist world of the Middle East.)

When the storm was over, most of the non-committed radical students found themselves apathetic and apolitical, and increasingly absorbed in the world of private comforts and material gains that the high-growth economy had provided for them. It has been pointed out that the Japanese New Left, unlike their equivalents in West Germany and France, failed to forge and create an enduring political force, and unlike those in America, did not lend a hand in bringing about a civil-rights movement for minorities. Nevertheless, it provided active participants for the citizens' movements that had been going on since 1960.[18]

CITIZENS' PROTEST

The citizens' movement can be traced to the Anpo struggle of 1960, when a group called the Voice of the Voiceless People's Association put in its appearance to support the rioting students. This was a spontaneous act on the part of unorganized citizens to show their sympathy with the students' protest. They were private citizens, locally oriented, less ideological and political than other activists.[19] The citizens' movement ramified into various activities: consumers' interests were looked after by *Shufuren* (Association of Housewives), and *Seikyo* (Consumers' Co-operatives) participated in local government on matters of housing and public work. The two most prominent activities were the anti-nuclear movement and the anti-pollution movement. The latter is almost invariably a local movement of the people directly affected by a nuclear plant or by water pollution (at Minamata) or air pollution (at Kawasaki and Yokkaichi). The former is known for its national protest movements, such as the annual Hiroshima demonstration against nuclear weapons, but it has also suffered from ideological splits: the Consumers' Co-operatives, for instance, are well represented at such demonstrations, but they are not prepared for ideological battles nor for presenting an alternative plan or policy. Environmenalists, for their part, have failed to create a stable political organization like the Green Party in Germany. Radicalism has been internalized and has become cynical. Herein lies one cause of the weakness of the Japanese opposition.

[18] Fujiwara *et al.*, op. cit., 206.
[19] See Ellis S. Krauss, *et al.* (eds.), *Conflict in Japan* (Honolulu, 1984), chs. 8 and 9.

20

The Heyday of the LDP:
From Tanaka to Nakasone

Tanaka was closely associated with LDP politics during most of the period of high economic growth as minister of the Treasury (1962–5) in the LDP government led by Ikeda and then by Sato and as minister of trade and industry (1971–2) under Sato. Ikeda had succeeded in altering the political climate from that of confrontation over security and defence to the pursuit of an economic target. High economic growth allowed greater government expenditure in public works, budgetary transfer to local government, and other forms of financial aid. To look after local interests became the proper job for a politician. Cynics would say that politics had come to mean the exchange of aid money for votes.[1] Tanaka, as a professional politician, excelled in such politics, though his concern with local interests developed into a grand vision for a fairer distribution of the benefits of high economic growth throughout Japan, a solution of 'the north–south problem' within Japan.

Tanaka personified both the attractive and the lamentable features of the LDP in power, a regime for the nation. His downfall was followed by a period of warring lords of the party tinkering one after another with an economy, overgrown perhaps but never solid and sound. Nakasone came in to provide a new confidence, a new identify for the nation, but the evolution of the national and international economy belied his nationalist ambitions, which proved flashy but entirely out of date.

A JAPANESE ARCHIPELAGO RECONSTRUCTION
PLAN BY TANAKA

Sato, Tanaka's predecessor as prime minister, is said to have obtained *nawa* (rope) [Oki*nawa*] by making concessions on *ito* (yarn or textiles), for he had succeeded in securing the reversion of Okinawa while conceding to American demands for restraints in textile exports from Japan.[2] The end of his government was marked by a fierce struggle between Tanaka

---

[1] Jun-ichi Kyogoku, *Nihonjin to Seiji* (The Japanese and Politics), 90–1, in Takafusa Nakamura, *Showashi* (History of Showa), (Tokyo, 1993), 513.

[2] Masumi Ishikawa, *Sengo Seijishi* (Postwar Political History of Japan), 121.

Kakuei and Fukuda Takeo, minister of foreign affairs under Sato at the time, whom Sato favoured. Tanaka won the election for party chairman; it is said that a large amount of money was distributed in the course of the campaign, which was called the 'Kaku–Fuku war'—'this dirty election', according to Fukuda.[3] Fukuda, a graduate of the Law faculty of Todai and a model bureaucrat of the Treasury, rather patronizingly called Tanaka, who had only an elementary education, 'Tokichiro [Hideyoshi] of Showa'.[4]

The publication in June 1972 of Tanaka's book *On the Reconstruction of the Japanese Archipelago* was well timed for the above election. The book (helped in its compilation by government experts) was indeed 'a signal gun' for launching the Tanaka government and sold 1 million copies.[5] The attraction of the book lay not so much in the grand, bright vision of a new industrial Japan as in what Tanaka called 'contradictions in prosperity'.[6] It is true, he said, that Japan had achieved a remarkable economic growth with an annual increase of over 10 per cent in GNP for the period 1954–70. He depicted post-war Japan accomplishing a three-step jump from the stage of mere survival to high economic growth, then to internationalization of her economy, bringing about a nationwide urbanization that was accompanied by inflation, pollution, overcrowded big cities, and depopulation in the countryside.[7] His plan was an amplification of an 'Urban Policy Programme' which he had prepared as the minister of trade and industry in 1968 and which consisted of four items: the setting up of a public corporation for building bridges between the main island and Shikoku; a special legislation for a Shinkansen network; a new car tax (to be used for road and railway construction); and reallocation of industries or removal of factories from large cities to less developed areas. Tanaka was the minister of the Treasury in 1964 when government control of foreign exchange was lifted according to the recommendation of the IMF, and was acutely conscious of the internationalization of Japanese economy.

In international politics Tanaka was a politician of detente, owing largely to external circumstances. The Soviet leader Brezhnev, who came to power in the autumn of 1964, sought to come to terms with the United States over the limitation of strategic armaments and nuclear tests. By 1972–3 American participation in the Vietnam War had come to an end. Tanaka was now able to declare that 'the basic structure of the Cold War is collapsing, and the world is heading towards a period of peace and co-existence, while the North–South problem is getting increasingly serious',

---

[3] Takeo Fukuda, *Kaiko 90 nen* (90 Years in Retrospect) (Tokyo, 1995), 202.

[4] Ibid. 203.

[5] Motoo Goto, Kenzo Uchida, and Masumi Ishikawa, *Sengo Hoshu Seiji no Kiseki* (A Study of Post-war Conservative Political History) (Tokyo, 1994), ii. 181.

[6] Kakuei Tanaka, *Nippon Retto Kaizoron* (Tokyo, 1972), 17.   [7] Ibid. 18.

and from this perception he arrived at the slogan, 'peace and welfare', the continuation of 'the post-war Japanese way of life as a peace state' with a special emphasis on the attainment of 'welfare' or the standard of social security achieved by advanced countries. Hence his insistence on the growth of the national economy through the construction of social capital stock for national well-being rather than through export-led economic expansion.[8] The North–South problem replacing that of East and West would become the most important international issue for the rest of the twentieth century, and 'new development of Japan would depend upon how far we could contribute to the economic independence of the South and to the advancement of the life of the people there'; he added that 'Japan, *vis-à-vis* Asian countries, should review and repent of its record of the days when it pursued its own interests at the cost of theirs, and should sincerely carry out aid programmes that are really useful to them'.[9] Towards the end of his premiership in January 1974, when he visited five countries in South-East Asia, he was met by hostile demonstrations in Bangkok and Jakarta largely because Japan's economic advance in Thailand and Indonesia (apparently in other areas as well) was not of the nature that he had advocated in his book.

A major part of his book, however, was devoted to what he called 'redrawing the industrial map' by moving industries from the industrial-belt zones along the Pacific coast to the remote areas of backward Japan with the help of Shinkansen and express-road networks: proposals for a solution of Japan's own north–south problem. He advocated the setting up of heavy industrial plants for steel, petrol refining, and for the petro-chemical and electricity industries in remote areas such as Mutsu-Ogawahara (the area including Rokkasho-mura) in northern Honshu, Tomakomai East in Hokkaido, and Shibushi Bay in southern Kyushu and the development of high-tech industries (computers, office-automation machines, precision instruments, cameras and automobiles) in rural areas inland. The government policy of *gentan* (a forced cut in the area of cultivated land used for rice due to a great increase in productivity made possible by mechanization and other scientific advances in agriculture, as well as to changes in Japanese eating habits) had produced a redundancy in the rural labour force which had to be met through the creation of job opportunities by industrialization of rural Japan; for this purpose a series of pivotal cities were to be developed in the provinces, and Sanjo-Nagaoka in Niigataken (Echigo) appeared prominently in his redrawn industrial map.[10] He dwelt on the prospect of 'pollution-free industrial sites', of a 'welfare-type nuclear power station' that would supply hot water and snow-melting systems locally, and on an 'information-based archipelago'.

---

[8] Ibid. 23–4.   [9] Ibid. 75–6.   [10] Ibid. 83–5, 89–92.

When he expatiated on the need for and feasibility of the industrialization of heavy snow areas and cold and chilly regions, it is obvious that he had in his mind his own village in wintry Echigo.[11]

TANAKA AND ECHIGO: THE EMERGENCE OF A DEVELOPER

Tanaka, born in a small hamlet on the outskirts of the Echigo plain, owing to strained pecuniary circumstances had to give up hopes of entering a middle school, a five-year course that would lead to higher education, and instead chose the two-year course of the 'higher primary school'.[12] Then in Tokyo he studied at night school and obtained a certificate as a first-class building engineer. In due course he opened the Tanaka Kakuei Office of Construction and got to know Okochi Masatoshi, the founder of Riken (Rikagaku Kenkyusho or the Institute for the Study of Physics and Chemistry), a new *zaibatsu*. Tanaka's small office began to tackle big projects coming from Riken, such as the construction of rotary kilns for an alminium plant at Nasu or the building of various Riken factories in Niigata-ken. In March 1939 we find him among the new recruits in the Third Brigade of Cavalry grouped at Hiroshima and soon to be sent to Eastern Manchuria, where border skirmishes had threatened to develop into a major war. He was stationed on the front facing Vladivostok, roughly 30 miles away, running a canteen for the men and securing forage for horses. He fell ill, suffering from pneumonia, was sent home early in 1941, and was discharged from military service in October, two months before Pearl Harbor. In 1944, when the American bombing of major cities on the Japanese mainland began, Riken was ordered to move its plants from the Tokyo area to Korea and Manchuria. Tanaka undertook the removal of a piston-ring plant at Oji, Tokyo, to Taejon, Korea. Tanaka himself, accompanied by half a dozen staff members, crossed to Korea and set about the task of constructing a new plant on a large scale. While they were collecting building materials for the plant, news came of the Russian declaration of war against Japan. The Koreans stopped speaking Japanese. At Taejon, Tanaka announced to his workers that he would give all his personal property and building materials gratis to New Korea. His speech was well received. On 18 August he left Taejon.

Back in Japan he was comparatively well off, in possession of houses to let in Echigo besides his own house in Tokyo, which had survived the devastation of the city. His own company, Tanaka Construction, had developed political contacts and he was persuaded to contest the first

---

[11] Tanaka, op. cit., 92–4.

[12] This and the following biographical account of Tanaka are largely based on Isao Togawa, *Tanaka Kakuei Den—sono Dochakusei to Taishusei no Kiseki* (The Life of Tanaka Kakuei: The Evolution of his Indigenous Nature and his Appeal to the Masses) (Tokyo, 1972).

post-war general election of April 1946 for the third district of Niigata-ken. (The election was fought on the basis of a large constituency system for the last time.) Tanaka was among those defeated, though he was eleventh (among thirty-seven candidates) with a respectable poll of 34,060 votes. At the following general election held in April 1947 Tanaka was the third among five successful candidates in the Niigata third district, polling 39,043 votes. Tanaka was now a Diet member for the *Minshuto* or Democratic Party (the former *Shinpoto* or Progressives), which joined with the Socialists in Katayama's coalition government.

In June 1947 the coalition government prepared a bill for state control of coal, a controversial issue in the reconstruction of the Japanese economy, to which a section of the Democrats led by Shidehara Kijuro was opposed. In the Diet Tanaka led the opposition to the bill, which nevertheless with some alterations, passed the two Houses by the end of the year; Tanaka, together with other Shidehara Democrats, was expelled from the mainstream Democratic Party and joined the Liberals. He was also arrested by the Board of Prosecution under pressure from GHQ, which suspected that his opposition to the bill had been conducted with the aid of money from mine-owners. For once his innocence was proved on this issue. In 1958 he became minister of postal affairs under Kishi; while Kishi was preoccupied with the Security Treaty, Tanaka was busy developing his own interests in Echigo.

TANAKA AND ECHIGO:
LOCAL GRIEVANCES AND THE *ETSUZANKAI*

At the time of the general election of May 1958 Tanaka stated in his election bulletin that he would be glad to become 'a Diet member for the navvy' because he was so much involved in building roads and bridges and improving riverbanks, harbours, and agricultural land, and that although he approved of the anti-A bomb movement and of the world federation movement, he felt he should start from his own immediate surroundings.[13] At this election he came top in his constituency, polling 86,131 votes. Later, when he became prime minister in 1972, he polled twice as many votes at the general election of that year. The size of his poll was an expression of a tremendous increase in his popularity. In the mountains and fields of Echigo peasant disputes had been rampant in the pre-war days, tenant farmers protesting against oppression from large landlowners, and in the post-war years *Nichino* (the Japan Farmers Union), which acted as the parent body of the Socialist Party in rural areas, had succeeded in

---

[13] Asahi Shinbun Niigata Branch, *Tanaka Kakuei to Echizankai: Shinso no Kozo* (Tanaka Kakuei and the Echizankai: The Structure of Deep Layers) (Tokyo, 1982), 24.

building political strongholds for the common people. 'Why and how did the *Etsuzankai* [the local support body (*Koenkai*) for Tanaka] set up its own citadels and outposts on the soil rich in the spirit of resistance?', asked the *Asahi* newspapermen in Niigata.[14]

Shinanogawa, the longest river in Japan and one of the wildest, had often changed its course and brought flooding to the lands along its banks. These natural conditions, together with the centuries-old tradition of periodical redivision of landholding, itself a product of frequent flooding, formed the background of Tanaka's popularity and strength in the Kamagashima hamlet on the left bank of the river south of Nagaoka. In the Edo period the hamlet had been on the right bank, but in 1868, the first year of Meiji, the Echigo plain was flooded, and vast areas between Nagaoka and Niigata lay under water for a month. After one of the worst floodings the Echigo people had ever suffered, the peasants of Kamagashima found themselves on the left bank of the river. On their left the old river had shrunk to a rivulet called Yakitagawa; in other words, this hamlet of about 100 houses and their farmlands now formed an island in the great river Shinanogawa, and a ferryboat across Yakitagawa provided the only transport that connected the hamlet with the rest of the world. Again in 1944 and 1945, the last two years of militarist Japan, Shinanogawa flooded and washed away a considerable portion of Kamagashima's lands. The choice before the villagers was either to have a sound concrete riverbank constructed and remain on the island, or to move to a safer area west of the Yakitagawa river, as recommended by the officials of Niigata-ken. The village master was in favour of building a sound riverbank, as he believed that poorer peasants could not make both ends meet if they had to be removed from their farmlands. 'Let us all remain on the island.'

It was at about this time that Tanaka put in his appearance. The *Etsuzankai*, his support organization, was founded, and the petitioning for a sound riverbank carried on by the village master was continued after his death in 1952 by the secretary of the local *Etsuzankai*, who frequented Tanaka's house in Tokyo to negotiate over the construction details. The new Kamagashima riverbank of 4.5 kilometres in length, and all the other work for land improvement within it were completed by 1967. But there was still a problem for the villagers of Kamagashima. All their land used to be common property, that was periodically reallocated according to the number of shares held by each farmer grouped into subunits. This system was suitable given the changing size of the total land available due to the recurring floods, and had been in use in a number of villages in the Echigo plain, but it was only at Kamagashima that it survived the land reforms in early Meiji and again under the US occupation. In February 1968 the

[14] Asahi Shinbun Niigata Branch, op. cit., 25.

office of Kamagashima hamlet witnessed the last drawing of lots, for the construction of a permanent riverbank and freedom from frequent floods now made it possible for the villagers to do away with the old system of land division, coupled with the equally old landlord–tenant relationship. Land reform had come to Kamagashima at last, many villagers felt, thanks to Tanaka and the new riverbank he had helped to construct.[15]

The *Etsuzankai*, Tanaka's support group in his constituency, had links with socialist elements in the rural areas. It was customary in the heavy snow country for men to spend five winter months working in the breweries away in Gunma, Saitama, or Tochigi, and for women to work as factory girls in the spinning-mills in Aichi and Osaka for the same period. In those days the Socialist Party seemed to offer a bright future for the peasants by upholding land reform under the occupation. Ironically, the success of land reform alienated the peasants from the Socialist Party as they obtained their own land to cultivate, and gradually they began to identify the Socialists with urban interests which were sometimes opposed to theirs. One local communist persuaded his friends in *Nichino* (the Japan Farmers' Union) to support Tanaka's *Etsuzankai*, as he believed that both *Nichino* and the *Etsuzankai* were local associations 'from below' and that, *Nichino* having accomplished its aim of land reform, it was natural for them to support the *Etsuzankai* so as to improve their living conditions. There was a difference between the tactics of the two organizations: *Nichino* was for resistance, the *Etsuzankai* for petitioning; but this was due largely to the different nature of politics as they saw it, either as a system of oppression or as a form of governance, and also to the degree of popular democratic participation.

A certain Matsuzaki was elected village master for Yamakoshi-mura in 1947. Wearing a western suit which he had obtained from an acquaintance and a pair of wooden Japanese shoes, he visited a local prefectural office. Asked what his greatest concern was, he suggested that aid money be given to his village in order to complete a tunnel that was under construction. The villagers of his hamlet used to walk across the Nakayama Pass to visit Koide, a neighbouring town, for shopping. The 7-kilometre mountain road, buried under deep snow and almost impassible in winter, was the only route connecting the village with the outer world. It was in November 1933 that the then-youthful Matsuzaki and several other volunteers began digging the tunnel with picks and shovels. In ten years they dug 320 metres, and the work was temporarily stopped in 1943 because of the shortage of men and materials due to the war. Matsuzaki obtained subsidy from the prefecture after the war, but digging had to be carried out by the

---

[15] For Kamagashima, see Asahi Shinbun Niigata Branch, op. cit., ch. 2, pp. 27–39.

volunteers. The 1 kilometre-long Nakayama Tunnel completed in 1949, however, was primitive and remained unsafe.

In 1976 Matsuzaki, accompanied by the chairman of a local *Etsuzankai*, visited Tanaka in Mejiro, Tokyo, and handed over to him a booklet entitled 'A Record of the Nakayama Tunnel' which he had written. Shortly afterwards Tanaka was arrested under suspicion of involvement in the Lockheed scandal. He is said to have read the booklet in prison and been moved by it. Five years later, when prefectural roads of 5,500 kilometres in total length were promoted to the status of national roads, National Road 291 was extended from Koide through the Nakayama Tunnel, obviously a detour, on to Kashiwazaki. Apparently the upgrading of the status of the section of the road that includes the tunnel was decided upon through Tanaka's intervention; the construction of a proper tunnel began.

It was a personal political decision. Matsuzaki, when he visited Tanaka in Tokyo, used to bring as souvenirs wild edible plants and colourful carp, the latter being the only valuable products of his hamlet, and Tanaka received them saying that these would make a good advertisement for his village. It is difficult to call this bribery, though the carp in the pond of Tanaka's house at Mejiro later became famous in that light.

There were many other cases of Tanaka building up his support group by identifying himself with local interests of the periphery. In rural Echigo there were clandestine strongholds here and there of radical peasants, socialist and communist. Land reform, however, brought about relative affluence, and resistance and confrontation gave way to concession and consensus. Tanaka, too, was moving from the periphery to the centre, to his establishment in local politics as well as in the national power struggle.

Nagaoka, the capital city of the third district of Niigata, had a tradition of opposition to or distrust in political power. At the time of the civil war in 1868 the Nagaoka-han fought against government forces and the city was burned down; it met a similar fate when incendiary bombs fell on built-up areas on 1 August 1945. Tanaka had little influence in the city when he began his political campaign, for Nagaoka, as the old castle town, was too proud to accept an upstart of humble origin. Tanaka's power, as we have seen, was initially limited to the rural areas. He presented himself in Nagaoka first as a businessman rather than a politician,[16] and soon found himself in control of the transport network in the Nagaoka area. His connection with Nagaoka remained that of business ever since. Tanaka, when he visited the city in 1974, said in a speech that the mayor was putting into effect his plan for the reconstruction of the Japanese Archipelago. The mayor had set to work creating a new town west of

---

[16] Asahi Shinbun Niigata Branch, op. cit., 218.

Shinanogawa; a National Nagaoka Technical College was to be opened in the same area, and a new industrial centre was also to be started there.

It is obvious that the *Etsuzankai* had ceased to be a political group to assist common people suffering from various disadvantages, and had transformed itself into an organ to consolidate or distribute, for its own sake, benefits arising from Tanaka's political connections.[17] The desire to become affluent and respectable was perhaps the strongest national propensity in post-war Japan. Tanaka and his *Etsuzankai* remained successful as long as they embodied such a propensity, shared by so many people. Its two components, affluence and decency, however, were not always compatible, and the discrepancy between the two became wider as the economy ceased to grow rapidly and money politics became warped and degraded to such an extent as to become equated with corruption.

TANAKA AND HIS CABINET

The 'Kaku–Fuku war' of July 1972 was in fact a factional struggle to decide Sato's successor. Tanaka had inherited a large part of the former Sato faction, while Fukuda took over most of the faction once led by Kishi with whom he had worked closely. The Ohira and Miki factions came round to support Tanaka, while the Nakasone faction had supported him from the beginning. Ohira Masayoshi was appointed foreign minister, Miki Takeo minister of state without portfolio and vice-premier, and Nakasone Yasuhiro minister of trade and industry. Moreover, it seemed, under Tanaka, that the conservative government structure in post-war Japan had completed itself with three pillars of the LDP, the bureaucrats, and big-business leaders supporting each other and encroaching not only on the agricultural votes but also on those of the organized workers in big businesses.

The first achievement the Tanaka government made was to 'normalize' the China–Japan relationship by recognizing the People's Republic as the sole government of China, but this seemingly daring act had nothing remarkable about it in the wake of the American initiative, though Tanaka's rival Fukuda, like Kishi before him, was firmly committed to the nationalist government in Taiwan. In September Tanaka visited Beijing, where a joint statement was made in which the 'normalization' of the relationship between the two countries was announced and the Japanese side officially admitted and regretted that 'Japan is responsible for the grave damage inflicted on the Chinese people through the last war'.

The general election held in December 1972 belied Tanaka's hopes of securing a stable majority for his government: the LDP was reduced to 271

[17] Ibid. 233.

seats from 300 before the election, while the Socialists increased their strength to 118 (from 90) and the Communists to 38 (from 14), now becoming the second opposition party. The changes in the political map reflected urban discontent over inflationary tendencies in the high-growth economy. Nevertheless, the first budget prepared by his government for the year 1973 faithfully reproduced the main proposals of his plan for the rebuilding of the whole country. This further stimulated land speculation and price inflation, which was exacerbated by commodity speculation by major trading companies.

From about the time of the publication (June 1972) of Tanaka's book about the reconstruction of Japanese Archipelago, the price of land began to show a sharp rise. The rate of increase for the year 1971 was 12.8 per cent, whereas *for the six months* from April to September 1972 it was 8.4 per cent (10.3 per cent for the six largest cities). It was not only the estate companies but also private railways, construction, textile, banking, insurance, and non-ferrous metals companies that joined in competition to buy up lands and pushed up land prices. Trading companies were most active in this land speculation and one well-established trading company was sometimes referred to as 'Itochu of Real Estate'.[18] Businesses believed at the time and later that the price of land would rise forever.

They also felt that share prices would go up likewise, and indulged in speculation from which some earned huge profits: Sanko Kisen (Sanko Steamer) gained 5.5 billion yen and Marubeni 3.7 billion yen in 1972 (first half of fiscal year) by buying and selling shares.[19] The publication of Tanaka's book was indeed timely; it became 'the bible for land speculation in the Japanese Archipelago',[20] and this speculation had repercussions on that in shares. There was also criticism, nevertheless, that Tanaka's idea of moving industries to depopulated or underdeveloped areas would spread pollution and scatter and reproduce industries, with their 'inherent' contradictions of a double structure consisting of protected and unprotected human resources. It is true that Tanaka expected local welfare services to derive from a nuclear power plant, but he was not aware of the 'inherent' danger of nuclear energy to human lives. His plan for rebuilding and reallocating resources on a national level had already brought adverse criticisms of a serious nature.

Worse was to come. In the course of the fourth Middle East war that began early in October 1973 the oil-exporting Arab countries announced an increase in the price of oil by 21 per cent (later twice as high as before) and a cut in oil production for pro-Israeli countries by 5 to 30 per cent.

---

[18] Giichi Miyazaki, *Kokumin Keizai no Tasogare* (The Twilight of the National Economy) (Tokyo, 1995), 70–1.   [19] Ibid. 74.
[20] Ibid. 82.

Taken aback by the Arab oil strategy, the Tanaka government at its meeting of 22 November 1973 decided on a general policy-change to 'opposition to Israel' and 'support for the Arabs', and 'humbled itself' so low as to send Miki to the eight Arab countries to beg for oil.[21]

'Frenzied' price inflation accelerated by the 'oil crisis', forced Tanaka to reverse his economic policy and postpone his archipelago plan. Fukuda, Tanaka's political enemy, was now chosen as minister of finance, an appointment which marked the beginning of the policy of low economic growth.

Another setback, however, was more immediate and personal. An article entitled 'Tanaka Kakuei Kenkyu—sono Kinmyaku to Jinmyaku' (A Study of Tanaka Kakuei: His Gold Seam and Human Seam), published in the November 1974 issue of Bungei Shunju, began with a sensational declaration: 'There is probably no need to dwell on Tanaka's money politics. It is rumoured that he spent 3 to 5 billion yen to become elected as the party chairman [a reference to the first Kaku–Fuku war], 5 to 10 billion yen for election to the House of Councillors, and 1 to 1.5 billion yen as summer gifts to consolidate his supporters in the second Kaku–Fuku war after the election of the House of Councillors.' As we have seen, Fukuda had criticized 'the dirty election' at the time of the election of the party chairman, and after the election of the House of Councillors he, like Miki before him, resigned from the Tanaka government, criticizing its money politics. Tachibana Takashi, the author of the article, now implied that Tanaka extorted money from the business world[22] and that he bought the seat of prime minister with money collected through his support organization.[23] He now took up and examined the 'Muromachi Industry', one of Tanaka's paper companies, which earned a vast amount of money through land transactions.[24]

Tanaka's money politics, as disclosed by Tachibana, first attracted the attention of foreign journalists who questioned him at a meeting of their club; this provoked the Japanese press and the resulting uproar finally led to his resignation. Tachibana's view of Tanaka's money politics was widely accepted as a warning against political corruption, and as such it aimed to uphold the normal functioning of party politics advocated by Fukuda and Miki. But it failed to reach the local roots of Tanaka's politics, the hopes and grievances of the common people in the snow country for whom Tanaka remained 'a hero'.

---

[21] Fujiwara et al., Nihon Gendaishi (Modern Japanese History), 249.
[22] Takashi Tachibana, Tanaka Kakuei Kenkyu Zenkiroku (The Whole Record of the Study of Tanaka Kakuei), vol. 1 (Tokyo, 1976), 26.   [23] Ibid. 27 ff.
[24] Ibid. 69.

AFTER TANAKA: FACTION GOVERNMENTS (MIKI, FUKUDA, OHIRA, AND SUZUKI) AND THE LOCKHEED SCANDAL

Tanaka resigned in December 1974 in the midst of outcries against his money politics, and was succeeded by Miki Takeo, 'clean Miki' as he was called. Miki's government was in fact a coalition of four LDP factions, led respectively by Ohira, Fukuda, Nakasone, and Miki himself, the largest faction, that of Tanaka, staying outside. Miki was 'clean' but weak and had to make concessions to the LDP hawks. Measures to control monetary contributions, especially those from businesses, to the funds of political parties were debated and some were passed into law, but these were not effective enough to prevent further scandals. In the mounting inflation of 1973–5 the workers' offensive for a wage increase regained its former vigour, and a co-ordinating body of the public employees' unions, led by the National Union of Railway Workers and the All-Japan Postal and Telecommunication Workers' Union, staged a ten-day national strike in November 1975 for the explicit purpose of restoring the right to strike that had been denied them since 1948. All train services on the National Railway lines were stopped for eight days, 192 hours, the longest record of a railway strike.[25] Public opinion after the demise of Tanaka's money politics and the political climate in which the LDP was divided and dispirited favoured the claims of the workers, but the hawks in the party got the upper hand, pushing Miki to declare that he would not deal with an illegal strike, and the strike failed. The defeat marked a turning-point in the Japanese labour movement, for the last bastion of orthodox trade unionism based on collective bargaining, including strikes, now crumbled. It was submerged under the hegemony of collaborationist company unions nestling in big industries, which helped businesses weather the shocks of the oil crisis by assisting restructuring to achieve 'lightweight management'.[26]

Miki is also remembered as the first prime minister who prayed for the dead soldiers enshrined in the Yasukuni Shrine on 15 August, 'the Day To Commemorate the End of the War'. He was further carried away by the LDP hawks and committed himself to a new alignment for defence and security. 'The Korean clause' in defence argument arose in 1969 when a joint statement by Sato and US President Nixon referred to 'the security of Korea as indispensable to the security of Japan'. In August 1975 Miki paid a visit to Washington and he and President Ford issued a joint statement which emphasized that 'the security of Korea [South Korea] is indispensable to the maintenance of peace in the Korean peninsula, and the maintenance of peace in the Korean peninsula is necessary for peace and security in East Asia including Japan'. This was three months after the

---

[25] Ishikawa, op. cit., 135.   [26] Fujiwara *et al.*, op. cit., 257.

withdrawal of the last American soldiers from Vietnam, and the need was felt to reaffirm the maintenance of the US–Japan–Korea defence co-operation. The statement led to further strengthening of a US–Japan joint operation system. At a cabinet meeting held in November 1975 it was decided to keep the total sum of defence expenditure within 1 per cent of GNP, the utmost Miki could do in the way of resisting the requests from LDP hawks and the Americans.

Miki's fragile government was shaken to the ground by the repercussion of the Lockheed scandal. Early in February 1976 it was disclosed at a public hearing of the US Senate Subcommittee on Multinational Businesses that money from the Lockheed Corporation had been given as a bribe to Japanese government officials of high rank through the Marubeni Trading Company and Kodama Yoshio, the right-wing activist. Kodama, known for the Kodama *kikan* (machine) he set up in China during the war to obtain supplies for the Navy Air Force, had exerted influence among conservative politicians for anti-leftist causes in the post-war years and was now revealed as a 'secret agent' for Lockheed. It was at once rumoured that the scandal was part of Tanaka's 'Gold Seam'. Tachibana Takashi, prompted by the editors of the *Weekly Bunshun*, published an open letter in that journal (19 February 1976), suggesting that the decision to purchase the Tristar aircraft from Lockheed had been made by Tanaka for Zen-Nikku (ANA), a deal leaving mysterious receipts behind.[27] Tachibana later sought to contradict an allegation that he had written the open letter under the instigation of Fukuda's faction.[28] He may be right, but Tachibana, an activist at the time of the campus struggle of 1968–70, had always been soft on Fukuda, a close follower of Kishi, the old-style nationalist in his writings. Tanaka was arrested in July on the charge that he had received 500 million yen as a reward for complying with the request of Marubeni to exert his influence in favour of Lockheed. On the very day of his arrest Fukuda, then the head of the Board of Economic Planning, urged Miki to take the responsibility for this and resign for the sake of unity and a new departure for the LDP. Fukuda felt that 'Miki became completely self-righteous, and took a wrong road'.[29]

There is little doubt that Tanaka was made use of in the bribery operation by Marubeni, and it is obvious that behind Marubeni the Lockheed Corporation had played a major role in the whole operation. The Marubeni people involved were indicted for perjury as well, because they had made false statements in order to defend the name of their company, while Mr Corchan, a Lockheed vice-president and the agent for the deal, disclosed all his underhanded transactions quite blatantly,

[27] Takashi Tachibana, *Tanaka Kakuei Kenkyu: Zenkiroku*, vol. 2 (Tokyo, 1976), 10–17.
[28] Ibid. p. 382.   [29] Fukuda, op. cit., p. 221.

having been exempted from legal prosecution. Three years later, when the Americans sought to sell reconnaisance aircraft to the Japanese Self-Defence Force, a similar scandal took place involving Kishi, Fukuda, and Nakasone on the one hand and the Nissho-Iwai Trading company on the other. A managing director who had worked under the vice-president of the company involved committed suicide by throwing himself from his office building: he left behind a short note: 'The life of the company is eternal. We should serve that eternity.'[30]

As for the Lockheed scandal, the arrest of the former prime minister, a former minister of transport, and a former parliamentary secretary of the Ministry of Transport and the possibility of implicating several other politicians was a severe blow to the LDP. 'Clean Miki' was criticized for his 'cheerfulness' and a move was made to 'pull him down'. Tanaka, who had been released on 200 million yen bail, and his supporters began to exert considerable influence in LDP politics. Fukuda Takeo and Ohira Masatoshi, both aspiring for premiership, co-operated in attempts to remove Miki. At the general election of December 1976 the LDP lost over twenty seats, over thirty if an increase in the number of Diet members from 491 to 511 was taken into account (the numbers elected were: LDP 249, Socialists 123, Komei or Clean Politics 55, Democratic Socialists 29, Communists 19), and Miki resigned.

In 1976 the Japanese economy was pulling out of a long recession that had continued from the time of the oil crisis of 1973. The recovery was due largely to a remarkable increase in the export of automobiles to the United States because of the more economic fuel consumption of Japanese cars. 'Lightweight management', or a reduction in labour cost in which labour co-operated with management, was another factor which made the Japanese recovery so much easier and quicker than in other countries. Meanwhile, opposition parties, while strengthening their position vis-à-vis the LDP, began to demonstrate ideological incompatibilities and disunity and to realign themselves in terms of left, right, and centre. This led to the collapse of progressive local governments one after another. In fact, the centre parties such as the *Komei* (Clean Politics), based on the *Sokaa Gakkai* or Institute to Create Values, a mass Buddhist organization, and the *Minsha* (Democratic Socialists) chose to ally themselves with the LDP rather than with the *Shakai* (Socialists) and the *Kyosan* (Communists), as was the case with the election of the governor of Tokyo in April 1979, at which an elite bureaucrat from the Ministry of Local Government defeated a veteran trade unionist.

Fukuda, who suceeded Miki as prime minister in December 1976, regarded himself as an expert on economic matters. At a time when the

---

[30] Giichi Miyazaki, op. cit., p. 103.

yen appreciated from 292 yen per dollar at the beginning of 1977 to 175 yen in October 1978 (though down to 203 yen in December 1978), he managed to keep down the rate of price increase at 8.1 per cent in 1977 and 3.8 per cent in 1978, but the recession became more serious and the number of bankruptcies increased. In his foreign policy Fukuda was equally conservative, though he called his diplomatic idea *Zenhoi-Heiwagaiko* (peace diplomacy in all directions).[31] It was certainly a smiling diplomacy in all directions. Like Kishi he felt a special attachment to Nationalist China at Taiwan, led by Chiang Kai-shek. 'His [Chiang's] kindness shown in his laudable attitude towards the Japanese stranded in China and in his generous stance on the issue of reparation is beyond description', wrote Fukuda: 'We owe him a great deal for the recovery of Japan, for the fact that Japan unlike Germany, was not divided, and our imperial house was allowed to continue.'[32] In spite of his sympathy with Taiwan, though, he had to take into account changes in the international situation, especially the American approach to Communist China, and through his foreign minister Sonoda was able to conclude a Japan–China Peace and Friendship Treaty in August 1978. Opposition to 'hegemony' (i.e. the Soviet Union) was inserted in the treaty in such a way as not to bind the signatories in their respective realtions with a third country. Fukuda had come to an agreement with Russia on the fisheries in northern waters, leaving aside the issue of northern territories.[33] He succeeded Kishi as president of the Japan–Philippine Friendship Society which had germinated from Kishi's close relationship with J. P. Laurel, president of the Republic of Philippines under Japanese occupation, who had attended the wartime Great East Asia conference led by Tojo.[34] Fukuda was an old-fashioned nationalist, and on 15 August 1978 paid a formal visit as prime minister to the Yasukuni Shrine in which, as it soon became known, fourteen class A war criminals, headed by Tojo, had been enshrined (as gods, like those fallen in battle). He was also in favour of a study of the dispatch of the SDF overseas at a time of crisis, which, he declared, was a state duty.

Fukuda now appeared in his true colours. At a cabinet meeting held in October 1978 it was decided to continue an era name by law rather than by government decree. This was the culmination of a nationwide movement to obtain legal sanction for an era name associated with the reign of an emperor. Under the pressure from the LDP and right-wing bodies all the forty-six prefectural assemblies, with the single exception of Okinawa, and 1,170 town and village councils adopted a resolution to support such a move. The centre parties endorsed it too. A national council consisting of the central office of Shintoist shrines, the association of the war-bereaved,

---

[31] Fukuda, op. cit., 271.   [32] Ibid. 177.   [33] Ibid. 240.
[34] Ibid. 281.

former military officers and right-wing intellectuals exerted pressure on the government. Those who opposed such a measure, like liberal and Christian university professors and radical journalists, did their best. Backed by nationwide agitation, however, Fukuda was happy to proceed with this restorationist and royalist measure, which was to keep Japan provincial, self-centred, and emperor-oriented not only in counting calendar years but also in recording her history. Officially an era name was to be preferred to the international calendar year. The Japanese version of the Middle Kingdom idea, which seemed to have been doomed as fatally as the Great Japanese Empire, was thus kept alive in a surreptitious way.

In November 1978 the LDP tried a new method, suggested by Miki, of selecting its president; 1.5 million party members and 170,000 friends of the party were registered for this purpose and they were the people mobilized by the factions through *koenkai* or supporting businesses. Four candidates were in the contest: Fukuda, Ohira, Nakasone, and Komoto. Fukuda, the most likely winner, was as hawkish as ever, and was surpassed in this special trait only by Nakasone who advocated constitutional revision and armament expansion. Ohira and Komoto advocated moderate, liberal lines of policy. In the end Ohira, with the support of Tanaka with whom he had been on friendly terms, won the contest. The new government led by Ohira, a Christian and a philosopher prime minister, was able to put an end to the hawkish trend left by his predecessor, but had to allow the controversial dynastic era name to be legitimized in order to placate the right wing of the party. It weathered the second oil crisis caused by the OPEC decision in December 1978 for a fresh rise in oil prices. This was an after-effect of the Iranian revolution of 1978 to 1979 which caused a temporary suspension of oil production in that country, and the price of crude oil more than doubled in the course of 1979. Government campaigns to save energy were sometimes pathetic or even comic, but the government policy of tightening the money supply succeeded in keeping the inflationary trend at a minimum. The Japanese economy did not suffer as much as those of the other advanced economies, for the campaigns to save oil were effective, transfer to other energy sources had made much progress, and the storage of oil increased even in 1979. Recovery of the Japanese economy was noticeable: the growth rate of GNP had fallen to −0.2 per cent in 1974 (after the first oil crisis), but began to increase after that: 1.4 per cent in 1975, 5.3 per cent in 1976, 5.3 per cent in 1977, 5.1 per cent in 1978, and 5.2 per cent in 1979. In spite of appreciation of the yen exports kept on growing, and the number of Japanese automobiles produced in 1980 reached 11.04 million, surpassing that of America, while the output of steel in the same year equally outnumbered that in America with 111.41 million tons. Japan now became the top export country in both automobiles and steel.

The major economic problem was an increase in the national debt in the form of government bonds issued in order to balance the annual budget, and Ohira was determined to introduce a general consumer tax to remedy budgetary deficiencies. Having successfully hosted the Summit Conference of G7 held in Tokyo for the first time, Ohira dissolved the Diet in November 1979, hoping to secure a stable government based on a sound majority. At the general elections that followed the LDP fared badly, largely owing to Ohira's proposal for a consumer tax, which was unpopular. The party managed to maintain a bare majority, but factional struggles flared up again; Fukuda, Miki, and Nakasone all demanded Ohira's resignation. The squabbles went on for forty days, until Ohira narrowly defeated Fukuda at the Diet vote for the premiership. Ohira formed his second government, but in May 1980 a Socialist motion of no confidence in the government was carried in the Diet, with LDP members of the Fukuda and Miki factions abstaining. The Diet was again dissolved, and in June elections took place for the two houses of the Diet on the same day. In the course of his election campaign, however, Ohira died of a heart attack. Popular sympathy with him now helped the LDP, which won a great victory in the elections, gaining an increase of thirty-six seats in the House of Representatives.

Suzuki Zenko, a rather colourless figure of the Ohira faction, was unanimously selected as the party president and succeeded Ohira as prime minister. He was in favour of 'administrative reform' or a small government, and by implication all that that would entail under that name as advocated by business leaders, such as a reduction in government expenditure on welfare and education, and 'restraint' on public works and on the salaries of government employees. His was the first government which attempted 'collective worship' at the Yasukuni Shrine. When he visited President Reagan in Washington, he signed a joint statement on the 'US–Japan Alliance' implying military co-operation, which he disowned when he returned home. In the government budget for 1982 defence expenditure was given a 7.754 per cent increase while all other ministries were allowed no increase in their respective budgets. In government-censored history textbooks Japanese 'aggression' was changed into 'advance', while mention of the Nanking massacre and the bloody suppression of the Korean independence movement were minimized; this naturally brought criticism from the Chinese and Korean governments. Suzuki had manifestly lost control of both domestic and exernal politics, and he knew that he had not the personal capacity needed to be a prime minister. He was ready to retire, and the LDP elected Nakasone as the party president and successor to Suzuki as prime minister. Nakasone gained overwhelming support in the party election with the help of Tanaka, who now appeared as a kingmaker.

Tanaka for his part was sentenced to four years' imprisonment and a fine of 500 million yen in October 1983, though he at once appealed to the higher court. But in February 1985 he became bedridden due to cerebral arteriosclerosis, and he died on 16 February 1993. His sentence was confirmed at the highest court two years later.

With or without Tanaka, Japan was under strong pressure from America to provide military capabilities that would match her new status as a world economic power.

BUSINESS CULTURE AND NEW NATIONALISM

It is now possible to look back on the rise and decline of 'business culture' as a historical process. It was a set of business practices supposed to be unique to Japanese management, forming part of the national culture. It was at the same time an ideology, which explained this uniqueness by making use of some of the concepts of behavioural sociology and social anthropology. It was above all a reflection of high economic growth, 'the Japanese Miracle' as it was once described,[35] of the emerging sense of national identity as an economic power (and a great one at that), encouraged by the flattering observations of Japanologists, both Japanese and non-Japanese. As an ideology, even as a practice, however, business culture was closely entwined with the rise of the new nationalism in the 1970s and the 1980s.

We have already seen how prime ministers after Tanaka moved to the right in the political spectrum: at the crest of the wave of new nationalism stood Nakasone, who formed his own government in December 1982. In his first speech as premier in the Diet he emphasized the creation of Japan with 'a robust culture and welfare' as one of the aims of his politics.[36] Perhaps there is nothing wrong with this slogan, but many wondered if it was not the Nakasone style to 'show bits of his suit of armour under the robe he wears'.[37] His armour began to shine through when defence expenditure in his first budget for the year 1983 emerged with an increase of 6.8 per cent compared with a general increase of 1.4 per cent. In January 1983 he visited Korea and promised economic aid of $400 million. In the same month he flew to Washington and, in a talk with President Reagan, expressed his view that the United States and Japan formed 'a community of destiny'. In an interview for the *Washington Post* he stated that he was ready to 'make the Japanese Archipelago an unsinkable aircraft carrier' and to 'seal off the four straits' (later altered to three

---

[35] Ezra Vogel, *Japan As Number One* (Cambridge, Mass., 1979), 9.

[36] Kenichi Takemura (ed.), *Nakasone Yasuhiro, Boei [to] Kenpo wo kataru* (Nakasone Yasuhiro speaks of Defence and the Constitution) (Tokyo, 1984), 246.

[37] Nakamura, op. cit., 648.

straits) if the Soviet Union were to attack Japan. Later in the same month he addressed the Diet, saying that Japan was 'at the great turning-point of her post-war history' and that he would 'reconsider the accepted institutions and frameworks by ignoring taboos'. The mainstream of the *zaikai* (the circles of business leaders) and the major conservative political forces inflated their self-confidence by ruminating over Japan's achievements in having weathered two oil crises without serious damage and set herself up as an economic power equal to the United States, and now set out on the road to becoming a military power by further strengthening the US–Japan military alliance. 'Nakasone was entrusted with the task of a helmsman as he had an excellent qualification for such a role.'[38]

Nakasone has sometimes been compared to Ronald Reagan and Margaret Thatcher as a champion of new nationalism. But Japan's new nationalism has its own roots: its immediate cause was Japan's economic success, which was given a cultural and scientific (sociological and anthropological) veneer that seemed to point to her uniqueness as a great power. It also harked back to the pre-war tradition of nationalist culture in the days of imperial expansion; it still bore the imprints of the now moth-eaten concept of the Middle Kingdom.

NIHONJINRON AND NIHONSHIKI-KEIEIHO AS PART OF THE NEW NATIONALIST IDEOLOGY

Two ideological pillars which support the new nationalistic business culture are *Nihonjinron* (views on the uniqueness of the Japanese) and *Nihonshiki-keieiho* (Japanese-style management). The former culminated in the establishment of the International Centre for the Study of Japanese Culture set up in 1987 in Kyoto, with an able staff at its core (known as the 'Kyoto school'), and above all with powerful support from prime minister Nakasone. Its task appears to be to link the global trend of internationalization with the national identity of the Japanese and of Japan. Umehara Takeshi, its first director, has emphasized three distinctive aspects of Japanese culture: 1. an irrationality which is bound up with its origins, as he claims, in the distant past of the Jomon era, in which appeared the belief in revengeful or vindictive spirits and the practice of pacification of such spirits; 2. an intuitive thinking which combines sensitivity and wilfulness; and 3. an emotionality which manifests itself in emotional conformity. The European culture of modernization, Umehara urged, had come to an impasse and should be superseded by a 'superior' Japanese culture, especially by its basic layer of Jomon culture. Meanwhile, Ueyama Shunpei, a leading member of the institute, stressed continuity

---

[38] Fujiwara *et al.*, op. cit., 300.

between the Meiji constitution and the new constitution, for in his view there had been no change in the national polity or the emperor system, and a community of destiny of the Nippon race, with the emperor as its core, has continued unbroken.[39] Without the success of Japan as an economic power at the same time, these academic exercises of the Kyoto school would have appeared simply atavistic.

In fact, *Nihonjinron* made its first appearance as an attempt to account for Japan's economic success; a large number of works were published during the 1970s starting with Nakane Chie's influential book in English, *Japanese Society* (1970), which we have already noted.[40] To her, Japan was 'a homogeneous society built on a vertical principle' like that of *ie* (the traditional family). She emphasizes group consciousness which is expressed and symbolized in *kaisha*, and regards communal sentiment or consensus as the essence of Japanese democracy as well as the key to her economic success.

The origins of *Nihonjinron* can be traced to the theories of national culture in the 1930s, characterized as it then was by militant chauvinism and the denigration of the West. The superiority of the Japanese and uniqueness of Japanese culture were clearly discernible in Watsuji Tetsuro's *Fudo* or climatological analysis of Japan published in 1935.[41]

The *Nihonjinron* of the 1980s could be summarized as 'the comercialized expression of modern Japanese nationalism'.[42] A disturbing element in *Nihonjinron* is an increase in the number of anti-Semitic books published in Japan, a fact closely related to economic *Nihonjinron*. About eighty of such books had appeared before June 1987. 'It can hardly be coincidental that these works flooded the market precisely in the two years when Japanese finance managed to capture 31.6 per cent of the international banking system.'[43] *Nihonjinron* inevitably has links with emperor ideology, 'devoid of its original human symbolic focus, where instead the Japanese and their nation take on the centrality previously accorded [to] the emperor'.[44]

As for Japanese-style management, it was not an ideology to start with. James C. Abegglen interviewed the managers of manufacturing firms in the 1950s and was struck by the peculiarities of Japanese management, lifetime employment above all, and by traditional arrangements such as consultation on various levels in decision-making. He appreciated the role

---

[39] Summaries in Hiroshi Minami, *Nihonjinron* (Tokyo, 1994), 268–9.

[40] See the section on women in Ch. 16.

[41] Mour and Sugimoto, *Images of Japanese Society* (London, 1986), 41–2.

[42] Peter Dale, *The Myth of Japanese Uniqueness* (London, 1986), 14. For a sociological study of *Nihonjinron*, see Kosaku Yoshino, *Cultural Nationalism in Contemporary Japan* (London, 1992).

[43] Peter Dale, *The Myth of Japanese Uniqueness Revisited* (Oxford: Nissan Institute, 1988), 7.

[44] Ibid. 25–6.

that pre-modern human relations played in the industrialization of Japan.[45] In the 1960s the characteristic features of Japanese-style management began to be emphasized as important factors to explain the secret of Japan's rapid economic growth. Attempts were made to trace its origins to the familial management system widely introduced at the time of the First World War and after.[46] Family traditions, with their seniority relationships and lifelong connections, were superimposed on businesses. Paternalistic social security allowances were adopted as counter-measures against the spread of socialism and militant trade unionism. After the war the American system of management and control based on individual efficiency was introduced, but this did not alter the traditional system. Lifetime employment and the seniority system came to be taken for granted. Strong human ties between managers and workers, characteristic of Japanese labour relations, sustained the *esprit de corps* of Japanese firms in spite of relatively inferior conditions of work.

Japanese-style management has its own *tatemae* (appearance) and *honne* (realities), and the merits of its *tatemae* have been made the most of, owing largely to its appeal to the psychology or mental habits of the average Japanese. But its *honne* has been ignored, despite the extensive use of overtime work and especially the existence of a large section of underprivileged workers due to a contract system (the double structure of employment), and consequently dissatisfaction has been accumulated. As the Japanese economy has entered a period of slow growth, the *tatemae* itself, both lifetime employment and the seniority system, looks increasingly worm-eaten and is in danger of being dismantled.[47]

SLOW ECONOMIC GROWTH

A marked downturn in the rate of GNP growth began after the oil crisis of October 1973. The government responded to the crisis by cutting oil and electricity supplies to major industries by 10 per cent; GNP in real terms (adjusted for price fluctuation) for 1974 recorded a decrease for the first time in the post-war years, while prices, both wholesale and retail, showed a yearly increse of over 20 per cent. The official rate of interest was raised from 4.25 per cent in 1972 to 9 per cent in 1974, but 'stagflation' (economic stagnation under inflation) continued for some time.

Compared with other advanced countries, the Japanese economy fared well: the rate of inflation was less than that in the these other countries and the rate of GNP growth was among the highest in the 1970s and the first

---

[45] See James C. Abegglen, *The Japanese Factory: Aspects of its Social Organization* (Glencoe, Ill., 1958).

[46] Hiroshi Hazama, *Nihonteki keiei no Keifu* (*The Pedigree of Japanese-style Management*) (Tokyo, 1963).   [47] Summary in Minami, op. cit., 363–4.

half of the 1980s. The rate of unemployment began to increase after 1973 and, accelerated by the second oil crisis of 1978–9 it reached over 3 per cent in 1987, which was still low, however, compared with the rate in other countries. The relatively well-managed adaptation to the oil crisis in the 1970s and the early 1980s, due mainly to the 'elasticity' of the labour market, attracted almost as much attention among foreign observers as the achievement of high economic growth in the 1960s had done.

The prevailing mood of Japanese society tends to be volatile; when it is cheerful it is usually very cheerful, on the verge of arrogance; when it is depressed it tends to be very depressed, and depression calls forth self-discipline as well as self-protection. This is what took place at the time of the first energy crisis of 1973. From 1973 to 1975 industrial production fell by almost 20 per cent, and the rate of profit for companies declined from 6 per cent to almost 1 per cent.[48] It appears that Japan was the most successful among the OECD countries in adjusting to the economic challenges of the time—swallowing the rise in oil-prices, holding down inflation at a low figure, and altering her industrial structure, with its weight moving away from declining to competitive industries.[49] How did the Japanese achieve this? It was made possible by: 1. the 'monsoon-like' swelling of exports; 2. the great increase in government expenditure by means of floating a large amount of National Debt for public investment to counteract deflationary tendencies; and 3. the introduction of a 'lightweight' management.[50] It was in this period of an export-drive on a massive scale that floods of cars, TVs, and audio appliances went abroad to the United States, Europe, and to other Asian countries, and a surplus trade balance was rapidly accumulated, while overseas investment increased by leaps and bounds. By 1985 Japan became the largest creditor country in the world, while the United States tumbled to the status of a debtor nation. The term 'lightweight management' needs an explanation. It is a euphemism for rationalization, an effort to cut down drastically the number of workers employed by sending them out to other firms that are less depressed, by reducing the number of new recruits, and by introducing automation and robotization. Lifetime employment became an empty slogan; restraint on wages was taken for granted, and the threat of mass dismissal compelled the workers to accept it. Elite workers were separated from other, nondescript employees, and promotion was arranged accordingly. The Spring Offensive of trade unions became a controlled offensive, and throughout the 1970s wage increases always lagged behind price increases.

---

[48] Masanao Ito, *Kodo Keizai-Seicho kara 'Keizaitaikoku' e* (From High Economic Growth to 'an Economic Power') (Tokyo, 1988), 46.
[49] Ron Dore, *Flexible Rigidities*, (London, 1986), 6.   [50] Ito, op. cit., 46.

Thus came into existence an enterprise society in which the values of entrepreneurship, such as competitiveness, efficiency, and conformism, began to influence communities, schools, and families. Within a firm an employee found it extremely difficult to refuse to change to another job, to do enforced overtime work, or take part in social activities sponsored by his or her company or union. A similar state of affairs can be observed at schools, where competition and conformism stunted the minds of both teachers and pupils. Thus, it was largely at the expense of the workers and ordinary people that Japan achieved an economic miracle.

The same miracle can be viewed from a different, more optimistic angle: one where flexibility is seen to have overcome the difficulties presented by rigidity in the economy.[51] Investment to control environmental pollution increased, and an emphasis was placed on the role to be played by know-ledge-intensive branches of production, computers, robotics, fine ceramics, business machines, electronics, high-quality printing, and so on. The high-technology and information-led sectors of the economy are making up for a decline in some of the old industries such as textiles, aluminium, machine tools, shipbuilding, and iron-smelting. Interlocking relationship of firms within the same group, as we have noted elsewhere, brought about a special management culture which values market share rather than profits. Trimming of the labour force—the 'lightweight management' again—was made possible by substituting part-timers for full-time employees, especially in the case of women, and by moving redundant skilled workers to other jobs such as external sales or even 'weeding the flowerbeds beside the factory gates'. This was carried out despite lifetime gurarantees, because 'occupational consciousness is low' among the Japanese workers. Finally came *shimei kaiko*, or 'designated dismissals' of recalcitrants, as illustrated by the dispute at Oki Electric and the unfair treatment of members of the National Union of Railway Workers. But all in all, there is a consensus shared by government officials, business interests, and union leaders as to the need for restructuring the national economy. 'Japan Incorporated' may be an overstatement, but this was and still largely is a society permeated with 'business culture' as its ideology.

The Japanese economy entered a period of slow growth after 1973, and the rate of GNP growth each year remained roughly between 3 and 5 per cent (in real terms) until the bubble years (1988–91), after which it dropped even further. Probably the most remarkable change that took place in this period of slow growth was the shifting of employees from primary industry to the secondary and especially to the tertiary industries. From 1970 to 1980, those employed in tertiary industry increased by 6 million and those in secondary by 1.5 million, while those in primary

---

[51] Ron Dore, op. cit., *passim*.

industry decreased by 3 million. In terms of expenditure, this change meant greater household expenditure on education, leisure, medical care, and transport, and equally greater business expenditure on information services, market research, and advertising. Public expenditure, too, was on the increase because of the costs of combating pollution, expenditure due to natural disasters, and the expenses of an ageing population. Direct overseas investment and transferring of plants also increased with the appreciation of yen and the relative cheapness of labour abroad. By the mid-1980s business culture was preparing to support a spending-spree and money game called the 'bubble economy', that was soon to come.

NAKASONE AND THE NEW NATIONALISM

It was at the general election of April 1947 that Nakasone Yasuhiro was elected for the first time to the Diet: he had toured his constituency, the third district of Gunmma, riding on a bicycle painted white, speaking against communism. On the matter of faction dynamics he depended on Tanaka, who was elected at the same general election for the same party, the then Democratic Party. He aspired to put an end to the old conservative tradition of the mainstream LDP started by Yoshida. His was a 'New Conservatism'[52] which was to continue or restore pre-war national culture and develop it in the context of the Cold War. It was in this respect that his new conservatism resembled that of Ronald Reagan and Margaret Thatcher who both dominated the 1980s, the last and most critical stage of the Cold War.

Nakasone had two faces, one that of a hawkish nationalist and the other that of a weathercock (*kazamidori*).[53] A graduate of the law faculty of Tokyo Imperial University, a naval officer during the war, and an elite bureaucrat in the Home Ministry after it, he gave up this position and joined in a crusade against communism in 1946. At and around Takasaki, his native city, he collected around him the young people who shared his anti-communist views. They formed the Blue Cloud School, one of the earliest *koenkai* (support clubs), which contributed to his election to the Diet in April 1947. Young men in his support club were 'inducted into the army', or rather received a few days' training from a unit of the Self-Defence Force for the sake of experience. Serious discussions were also held on defence, foreign affairs, the national economy, and agriculture.[54] In the Diet he wore a black tie to express his sorrow at the occupation of his country. He stressed the need for the setting up of a Self-Defence Force

[52] Masumi Ishikawa, op. cit., 156.
[53] Osamu Watanabe, *Nakasone Yasuhiro and Post-war Conservative Politics: An Historical Interpretation*, (Oxford: Nissan Institute, 1993), 3–4.
[54] Nathaniel Thayer, *How the Conservative Rule?*, (Princeton, 1969), 93–7.

after amending Article 9 of 'the so-called MacArthur Constitution'. He even wrote a 'Song for the Revision of the Constitution'.[55]

He once thought of amending Article 1 of the new constitution on the status of the emperor from 'the symbol of the state' to 'the head of the state', but soon changed his view so as to comply with public opinion. He once advocated abdication of the Showa emperor in favour of the crown prince: he believed that this would 'console the feelings of the war-bereaved families and others who suffered from the war, consolidate the moral foundation of the Emperor system, rejuvenate it, and enable it to be firmly and indomitably maintained'.[56] In the 1960s, when the politics of confrontation gave way to that of consensus, Nakasone also changed. He perceived that the constitution was supported by the people, and now suggested that its revision should be gradual. He was, however, critical of a welfare state and preferred a middle-class state based on privatization of all industries and a free-market economy.[57]

Nakasone's political stance in this period is most clearly seen in his attitude to the Yasukuni Shrine Bill. Yasukuni Shrine, a state Shintoist shrine honouring the war dead (founded in 1879) was disestablished after the Second World War. When the occupation came to an end, a movement supported by the Head Office of Shintoist Shrines and the War Bereaved Society began to request the re-establishment of the shrine as a state institution. A private member's bill to this effect was introduced into the Diet in the mid-1960s, and a heated controversy followed within the LDP. In 1969 Tanaka Kakuei, then the secretary-general of the LDP, allowed a government Yasukuni Bill to be shelved and traded off for a revision in the law on the Self-Defence Forces and the University Control Act, which seemed more urgent at the time. In 1972 Nakasone, chairman of the General Council of the LDP, suggested that Japan should have a war memorial to replace the Yasukuni Shrine Bill. Finally the Bill was abandoned in 1975.

When he took office for the second time in 1984 Nakasone emphasized a new departure by insisting on 'settling accounts with the post-war period'. Japan should cease to be a mere economic animal and should become a political state. Japan, he said: 'must advance rapidly as an international state and from this standpoint, it is extremely important to re-evaluate and re-establish Japanese "identity".'[58] The 1980s thus became a decade in which a number of Japanese intellectuals and non-Japanese writers responded to the call from Nakasone wittingly or

---

[55] Watanabe, op. cit., 7–8; Takemura, ed., op. cit., 84–6.
[56] Nakasone's parliamentary speech on 31 January 1952, Watanabe Osamu, op. cit., 9.
[57] Nakasone, *Nippon no furontia* (Frontier of Japan), Bungei Shunjusha, 1965, quoted Watanabe Osamu, op. cit., 16.   [58] Quoted in ibid. 24.

unwittingly, and produced works on the identify of the Japanese or *Nihonjinron* which we have already examined.

Nakasone's new nationalism also took the form of a strong yen, which meant as much to him as a strong dollar did to Reagan. In the first half of the 1980s the yen remained relatively weak at about 260–30 yen = 1 dollar, while the strong dollar proved disastrous to American exports. Nakasone sought to alter the relative strength of major currencies and was one of the sponsors of the Plaza Agreement reached in September 1985, when ministers of finance from the United States, Britain, France, Germany, and Japan met at the Plaza Hotel, New York, and agreed to intervene in financial markets so as to remedy the too strong dollar. For him it was 'an emancipation of the weak yen from the yoke of the strong dollar',[59] but rectification went too far and the yen appreciated so high as to reach 120 yen per dollar by the end of 1987. This entailed the change of trade policy from export-oriented to a stance of 'international co-operation' which meant further 'internationalization' of the Japanese economy.

The Nakasone government managed to lift the 1 per cent GNP limit on the defence budget, a breakthrough achieved in the budget for 1987. At the same time *gyosei kaikaku* (administrative reform), acclaimed by business leaders, began to take effect. This meant the curtailment of government expenditure, especially on agricultural subsidies, social security, and education. Above all it meant the privatization of nationalized industries, which was given another euphemism, *minkatsu* (people and energy). In April 1985 NTT (Nippon Telephone and Telegram) and JT (Japan Tobacco Industry) were set up. The giant National Railway was to be divided into six private regional companies, and six JRs (Japanese Railway Companies) began operation in April 1987, leaving the National Railway Workers Union in the lurch. Resort development was also encouraged, and Nakasone advised the Treasury to sell and privatize government-owned lands, some located in the best part of great cities: the price of land began to rise sharply again.

Nakasone was also interested in *kyoiku kaikaku* (education reform), and an education deliberation committee inspired and initiated by Nakasone produced a final report in 1987 in which it was stated that 'a good Japanese' was to be brought up so as to develop into 'a tough international man'. The old national anthem and the old national flag were imposed by the Ministry of Education upon schools, teachers, and pupils, though some remained reluctant to comply, and the teaching course 'Social Studies', inspired by the reformist ideas of the early days of the

---

[59] Masanao Kano, *Nihon Tsushi*, xxi. 35.

occupation, was practically abolished. An 'economic giant' ought to be a 'political giant', free from the memories of past humiliation.

The movement for the Yasukuni Bill was now replaced by a movement to request the prime minister's official worship at the Yasukuni Shrine. Nakasone responded, and became the first prime minister to attend the New Year ceremonies of worship there in 1984. On 15 August 1985 Nakasone and all members of his cabinet (except for two who were abroad) made official visits to the Yasukuni Shrine to pray. The Chinese government expressed its concern at this official Yasukuni worship, which would 'hurt the heart of Asia'. Nakasone the weathercock decided not to attend the autumn ceremony of the Yasukuni Shrine.

At a meeting of the House of Representatives Budgetary Committee held in September 1983, Nakasone expressed his views on the distinction between a defensive and an offensive war. It was recognized by the whole world, he said, that the Russo-Japanese War was a defensive war for Japan. As for the Japan–China War, the international perception is that it was Japan who invaded a foreign country. 'The Pacific War has many causes: Hitlerite illusion, the attraction of the theory of Haves and Have-nots, the rise of militarism at home, but to a great many soldiers and officers on the front it was the war for the emancipation of Asia. Many fought and died, believing that it was a sacred war.' There is a criticism, he conceded, that Japan gave independence to some Asian countries only when she began to lose the war.[60] Nakasone's was in fact a tortuous argument for 'peace in Asia', the very phrase reminiscent of the ideological slogan, 'the Great East Asian Co-Prosperity Sphere'.

The JSP challenged the Nakasone regime by coming one step closer to it, announcing 'the (New) Road to Socialism in Japan', differentiating itself from Russian-style socialism or from 'the poverty stricken revolution', and declaring the Self Defence Forces to be 'not illegal' though 'unconstitutional'. This ambiguity and obscurity surrounding its position was to cost the party dear.

Trade unions, too, were in the process of transformation. The four national central bodies, the *Sohyo* (General Council of Trade Unions), *Domei* (All-Japan Labour General Alliance), *Churitsu-Roren* (Neutral Trade Unions Communication Congress), and *Shin-Sanbetsu* (All-Japan Industrial Unions Federation) that had sprung up in the 1950s and 1960s were now groping their way for unification in view of greater difficulty in obtaining wage increases and of a rapidly declining ratio of organized workers. The latter three bodies, catering mainly for the workers in private industries, were amalgamated into *Rengo* in 1987, which absorbed *Sohyo* in November 1989 and became the largest labour organization (All-Japan

---

[60] Takemura (ed.), op. cit., 77–8.

Trade Unions General Federation) in Japanese history, with seventy-eight organizations and a membership of 798 million workers.

At the general election of July 1986 the LDP gained a great victory with 304 seats in the House of Representatives (JSP 85, Komei 56, DSP 25, CP 26, NLC 6, SDL 4). In August Nakasone boasted of the strength of his party which he hoped would extend its influence over parties on its left such as the New Liberal Club, the Democratic Socialists, and the right wing of the Socialist Party. In September Fujio Masayuki, his minister of education, wrote in *Bungei Shunju* that Korea was partly responsible for Japan's annexation of that country in 1910, and the Korean government strongly protested. Nakasone was obliged to remove him from the post at once. Later in September Nakasone himself made a careless speech which would reveal his real way of thinking. At an LDP study seminar at Karuizawa he said: 'in America there are a considerable number of blacks, Puerto Ricans, or Mexicans, and this makes the average level of intelligence [of the Americans] very low.' The US House of Representatives took strong exception to his speech, and he publicly apologized.[61]

THE RECRUIT SCANDAL AND THE END OF THE LDP HEGEMONY

Nakasone's term of office was to end in October 1987; he nominated as his successor Takeshita Noboru, the leader of the largest LDP faction, formerly led by Tanaka. A few months after the formation of the Takeshita government, however, another scandal involving Nakasone and several other LDP leaders was disclosed. Shares of the Recruit-Cosmos Company which were to be listed shortly were distributed by its president among several influential LDP politicians. Nakasone or his secretary received 19,000 unlisted Recruit shares, which would give a profit of 43 million yen by selling them when listed. To this should be added a Recruit contribution of 45 million yen to his political fund. The prosecution, however, decided not to pursue the former prime minister any further.

The Recruit Company was set up in 1960 as a business selling advertising in university newspapers. The company became widely known for its 'Recruit Book' for students looking for jobs, in which businesses advertised. In fact, the president of Recruit distributed unlisted shares of his own company in exchange for political power, such as several posts in the Ministry of Education which would enhance the value of his media. The scandal marked the beginning of the end of the LDP hegemony which had manifested itself in Nakasone's new nationalism and his aspirations (shared by many LDP members) to make Japan 'a political giant' equal

[61] Masumi Ishikawa, op. cit., 168–9.

to its economic strength. The latter too, however, began to burst in the 'bubble economy' that coincided with the death of Hirohito. The end to the timeworn illusions was soon to come.

Political corruption such as the Recruit-Cosmos scandal meant more than unsavoury relationships between business leaders and politicians, for the LDP government was now facing a stronger opposition which would certainly take advantage of government weaknesses, including the forcible introduction of the unpopular consumer tax in November 1988. Doi Takako, the first woman party leader in Japan, who had become chairman of the JSP in September 1986, now emerged as a rallying-point of opposition to the LDP hegemony, and in the election for the House of Councillors in July 1989 the LDP was thoroughly defeated by the JSP and its allies (JSP 46, LDP 36, Rengo 11, Komei 10, JCP 5, DSP 3). Apparently Japanese politics had entered a period of fluidity soon to be marked by the appearance of new parties and the formation of new alliances. The emperor's death coincided with, and symbolized, the acceleration of such changes.

21

The End of Showa and the End of the Bubble Economy

THE END OF SHOWA

On 7 January 1989 the emperor Hirohito (soon to be known as Emperor Showa) died of cancer of the duodenum after being in intensive care from September of the previous year. His death was an event which not only stirred public opinion in Japan but also caused more than a ripple in world opinion which his long reign had disturbed, shocked, alarmed, and astounded on so many different occasions. This was foreshadowed, for instance, by the different ways that Europe and America had received him when he visited the two continents in the 1970s.

The emperor and empress, with a large retinue of palace officials and media representatives, alighted at Copenhagen airport on 28 September 1971, and their European tour of just over two weeks began. The issue of the war inevitably cropped up in the course of his tour. In Denmark, noted Stephen Large, demonstrators critical of Japan's role in the Second World War 'threw faeces at him and distributed handbills condemning him as a war criminal'. In the Netherlands, where anti-Japanese sentiments were naturally much stronger, he was 'greeted by placards which read, "Hirohito Go Home!", "Murderer!", and the like'. Similarly, in England, a symbolic tree of Anglo-Japanese friendship he had planted in Kew Gardens on his first visit in 1921 was chopped down as a protest against Japanese brutality towards British prisoners of war. He and the empress, on their arrival in London, were 'received with a gorgeous show befitting the age of colour TV', reported the *Asahi Shinbun*, though it added in small print that Lord Mountbatten, former supreme commander of the Allied forces in South-East Asia, stayed away from London while Hirohito was there. In Germany he was met by people with placards declaring of him, 'Hitler killed six million Jews while he killed fifty million Asians'.[1] It was widely noted that Hirohito did not apologize for the war; he was simply an emotionless marionette whose movements and utterances were determined by the Imperial Houshold Agency and the Foreign Ministry. The visit to the

---

[1] Stephen Large, *Emperor Hirohito and Showa Japan* (London, 1992), 184; *Asahi Shinbun*, 6 Oct., 1971.

United States in 1975 was a different affair. President and Mrs Ford came to greet the emperor and his wife at Hawaii, their first landing-place. The highlight of the tour was Hirohito's speech at a banquet in Washington. He expressed 'my gratitude to the people of the United States for the friendly hand of goodwill and assistance their great country afforded us for our postwar reconstruction immediately following that most unfortunate war, which I deeply deplore'.[2] The wording of his speech, especially its last part, had been carefully worked out by Japanese embassy officials in consultation with the Foreign Ministry in order to make sure that the emperor would not say anything that might be construed as admitting his war guilt. The American media reported his tour sympathetically. He immensely enjoyed his visit to Disneyland and always treasured a Micky Mouse watch given him (it was buried with him when he died).

Hundreds of memoirs and articles, books and magazines were published at his death, about the emporer himself and about the end of Showa. The era Showa (December 1926—January 1989), lasting into its sixty-fourth year, was the longest in Japanese history, surpassing Meiji by twenty years, and almost as long as the reign of Queen Victoria (June 1837—January 1901). The era was divided between the first twenty years, when the emperor was a god and Japan braced herself for 'enriching the nation and strengthening arms', its legacy from Meiji, and ended up in military fascism and a disastrous war; and the remaining forty-four years. These lasted as long as the Meiji era, but the emperor was now seen as a man and Japan started from scratch to build a nation again. There were Meiji endeavours, but less encumbered by military build-up or intransigence, and all the time attached and subjected to the United States as a junior partner in a military alliance. The dividing-line was the 'unconditional' surrender which overwhelmed every effort in the hot August of 1945, in the land of near ruins in the midst of war-wasted Asia. Hopes ended and hopes began; emotion was stirred but reconciliation had to be made; more than the lingering on of the archaic little man as a reformed emperor, a benign but firm American occupation precluded the possibility of a civil war. Memories of Showa and records of Showa were highly charged with passions due to the conflicts and contradictions, sorrows and resentments embodied in the era itself, in spite of all the soothing words of dispensers of consensus and harmony.

It is also true that forty-odd years after the 'termination' of the war, a great majority of the population had no personal recollections either of the war itself or of Hirohito, flaunting a military uniform, mounted on a white horse; those who were born in the last thirty years knew only the prosperous

---

[2] Large, op. cit., 188.

Japan and the amiable old man who took as much pride in Japan's economic success as they did. The older generations, who were now in the forefront of national life in the fields of politics, business, journalism, and academism, as well as a critical minority among the young, were profoundly disturbed by the end of an era, and their reactions were naturally diverse.

On 24 February 1989, the day of the state funeral of the Showa emperor, *Yoroku* ('Additional Notes') in the *Mainichi* newspaper lamented the death of Nasu Ryosuke the cartoonist, who had passed away a few days before. Nasu was born in southern Kyushu where some of the descendants of the Nasu clan had been living a secluded life as *ochimusha* or dispersed warriors. The Nasu had been one of the leading warrior families in the Kanto region, being at one time allied with the Minamoto in their war with the Taira. (Nasuno Yoichi, the Japanese William Tell, was a skilful archer and one of the most celebrated warriors in Japanese history. He had shot a fan off the top of a pole in a rocking boat, when signalled to do so by a beautiful Taira lady standing by the pole during the battle of Yashima in 1185.) Nasu Ryosuke, the cartoonist, had spent eight years as a conscripted soldier during the war with China; he and thirteen lucky men in his platoon survived the war. 'I was able to survive because I had got used to eating roots of various plants since childhood. As for salt, I licked my own skin. The common soldiers all suffered. But look at things now. The officers from the old days appear on TV to brag, to say something pompous and seemingly important about themselves. These are the people who, being served personally by the common soldiers on duty, said to them: "Can't you obey the order of the Emperor!" . . . We once made a grave mistake. We should not repeat it. Yet things have grown odd recently.' The funeral of Mr Nasu was solemnly announced in *Yoroku*, which ignored the other, State Funeral, as an act of defiance and protest against the excessive prominance given by the mass media to the terminal illness of the emporer and all its implications.

In November 1988 the Meiji-Gakuin Daigaku, a Christian university in Tokyo, held a special 'week to think about the problems of the emperor', when over sixty staff from the university gave or joined in special lectures and symposiums and talked freely with students, as they all felt that 'we should not make the emperor a taboo again'. A month before the president of the university had issued a statement to 'oppose attempts to turn the emperor system into a system of absolutism'.[3] It was very brave indeed of him to take such initiative at that moment, when sensational reporting of the emperor's illness in the newspapers helped the extraordinary spread of reverence mixed with sympathy for the man who was now presented as a

---

[3] *Asahi Shinbun*, 3 Dec. 1988.

fatherly figure, and in consequence the nation suddenly became patriotic as well as patriarchal. Menacing letters and threatening telephone calls came pouring in upon him and his staff from right-wing activists. The same treatment from rightists was meted out to the mayor of Nagasaki, Motojima Hitoshi, who had stated that the emperor had been responsible for the war and its disastrous effects. A year later, on 19 January 1990, Mayor Motojima was shot and seriously wounded in front of the city hall.

It was the sombre and restrained atmosphere of this period, artificially created by the government, especially by the Ministry of the Imperial Household, and supported by the mass media that made some people really anxious about the future of the nation as a democratic free society. The daily announcements of the sick emperor's condition, his temperature and pulse, resembled a weather-chart showing atmospheric temperature and pressure, so much so that the emperor system appeared almost as a natural phenomenon. The government and the press between them encouraged the people to come and pray for the emperor's health. Festivities were deprived of their colour and joy, or cancelled altogether.

It seems that the ruling party, the LDP, felt a strong sense of crisis over the approaching death of Hirohito. Indeed, the late emperor had once embodied national identity as well as national polity by virtue of his exalted position as the demigod of a culturally tribal nation, as it were, that was to have a lion's share in the would-be geopolitical redistribution of world resources in the first half of the twentieth century. In the post-war years national identity and national purpose had become blurred and obscure owing to the introduction of individualism and democracy through the American-sponsored reforms; so national purpose had to be rediscovered and reaccentuated, and national cultural continuity had to be reasserted; and this was all the more urgent because Japan began to take an active part again in the redistribution of world resources as an 'international state'. Reassertion of national identity of a traditional type became a vital issue when firms were becoming multinational as fast as they could, while well-protected domestic markets were under pressure to be thrown open to foreigners, and trade frictions occurred over market share and technology transfer. Nakasone was probably the most anxious among leading politicians to restore self-confidence to the nation. The *zaikai*, too, were committed to the clarification of national purpose. A suggestion was made by a business leader to set up a Memorial House to commemorate the emperor's virtues.[4] It seemed as though Showa had been an era of peace, progress, and prosperity, and that the late emperor had ensured all these blessings.

---

[4] Ibid. 14 Mar. 1989.

THE IDEA OF SHOWA

It was pointed out that Showa, unlike Meiji, did not begin as a self-conscious age, and a decade later when it became conscious of itself it was the right-wing intellectuals who used the term 'Showa Restoration' which implied that there remained unfulfilled missions of the restoration of 1868.[5] By 1940, when the wartime calendar heralded the 2,600th anniversary of the beginning of Japan's imperial history, the idea of Showa submerged. Whether Japan's post-war has ended or is still continuing is an issue that is still debated. It has been suggested that the 'long post-war' is peculiar to Japan and that the insistence on a seemingly perpetual *sengo* might be expected to affirm that 'Japan had . . . been born again, however imperfect the transformation'. But exactly this imperfect nature of the transformation would explain why the debate has to go on.

Thus the pro-and-con debate on the new constitution is still continuing in spite of the fact that the nation at large has come to identify it with the peace and prosperity it enjoys. In Germany, which has accepted a similarly imposed constitution, there is no sign of such debate, and one might be tempted to ask how such a marked difference can be accounted for. The Shintoist version of the modernization of Japan which was reasserted in the state funeral of the deceased emperor may provide one clue. In cultural terms, the old Japanese version of the Middle Kingdom idea dies hard.

There is a tendency among the Japanese to blur the distinction between nature and human agency. Thus, the China War 'occurred', and Pearl Harbor 'was attacked'. In a similar vein, the Ministry of Education sought to substitute the neutral term 'advance' for the more accurate 'invasion' of China in school textbooks, making it sound as though Japan felt that she had a right to invade China. Here too, traces of Japan's traditional Asian policy can be discerned. Showa remains as enigmatic as before, and the circumstances surrounding the death of Hirohito only confirm that Japan's post-war did not end with Showa.

THE EMPEROR AND THE WAR

The *Mainichi* newspaper[6] published the emperor's views on the war as they had been reported in various documents such as the Kido Diary, the Sugiyama memorandum, the Konoe manuscripts, and the like. These, arranged as they were, give the impression that Hirohito was dragged into the war by the military even though he had not fully agreed with the arguments presented by them, headed by General Sugiyama, the chief

---

[5] Carol Gluck, in Carol Gluck and Stephen R. Graubard (eds.), *Showa: The Japan of Hirohito* (New York, 1992), *passim*, for this and the following references.
[6] *Mainichi Shinbun*, 9 Jan. 1989.

of staff of the army. He wanted to act constitutionally, and this was his last defence, paraded whenever the need arose for it. The military became a real power like the Bakufu of the old days; or rather, there was no real power but only a system of irresponsibility due to efforts, often futile, to achieve a balance of power. Yet the emperor was not a shadow or a robot; he lent authority and legitimacy to the arbitrary decisions made by the military which controlled the system of irresponsibility before and during the war.

The period between the death of Hirohito and his state funeral on 24 February was crowded with further debates and reminiscences, showing intense passion and highly strung emotion over what the Showa emperor meant to the nation. Mizukami Tsutomu, a novelist, remembered what a sergeant had said to him in a transport battalion to which he belonged during the war: 'all the horses should be treated as the emperor's horses'; the men were intimidated, dispirited, and became selfish and unkind. 'The war was not glorious but dehumanizing, and I curse the war', he wrote.[7] The hard fact, however, was that the war was fought 'for the sake of the emperor' and an overwhelming majority of the nation believed it.

THE EMPEROR'S FUNERAL

The state funeral took place at the Shinjuku Gyoen, an extensive park in Tokyo, once an imperial garden, on 24 February 1989, attended by 9,800 people altogether, 'the largest funeral in history', wrote the *Asahi Shinbun*.[8] It consisted of two parts, the Shintoist rite *Sojoden no Gi* (The Rite at the Funeral House) and the *Taimo no Rei* (The Ceremony of Great Mourning). The communist members of the Diet abstained from attending because they felt the government failed to observe the constitutional stipulation of the separation of the state and religion, and most of the socialist members attended only the latter part of the ceremony for the same reason. The Shintoist rite was conducted in the presence of the imperial family, behind a black curtain and an improvised *torii* (shrine gate) into which the hearse of the deceased emperor had been carried in a *mikoshi* (moving shrine). The black curtain and the *torii* having been removed, the civil part of the funeral began. Britain's Prince Philip, the eleventh among the foreign mourners, 'bowed only slightly, as if not to bow at all'.[9] The *Asahi Shinbun* quoted the diary of Natsume Soseki, who had witnessed the state funeral of Queen Victoria in 1901: 'the new century has just begun in an inauspicious way', said the attendant of the shop where Soseki bought a pair of black gloves for the occasion.[10] The

---

[7] *Asahi Shinbun*, 13 Jan. 1989.   [8] Ibid. 24 Feb. 1989.   [9] Large, op. cit., 201.
[10] *Asahi Shinbun*, 24 Feb. 1989.

new era, to be called Heisei, now began in the midst of a bubble economy which was to expose all the frailties of the nation.

THE BUBBLE ECONOMY

There is certainly no direct connection between the end of Showa in 1989 and the bubble economy that took the form of an 'abnormal' rise in share- and land prices in the period 1987–90. Yet these two incidents can be presented as the two sides of the same coin. In the 1980s the government 'stepped up its efforts to mould him [the emperor] as a new-nationalist symbol', and in 1988 Takeshita, Nakasone's successor as prime minister, allowed defence expenditure to pass the 1 per cent barrier and reach the equivalent of $41 billion, the world's third highest according to one estimate.[11] A 'great power' consciousness seized the government and the people as Japan's economic success seemed everlasting. When all Japan awaited 'X-day', the emperor's death, practically all Japan, the people and the businesses, anticipated huge material gains by joining in the money games which seemed to point to never-ending rises in share- and land prices, though in fact this was a temporary situation brought about by abnormal lending.[12]

The 'high yen recession' of 1986–7 had affected business profits badly. The employment situation deteriorated. The government sought to revive the economy by allowing the Bank of Japan to reduce the discount rate successively from 5 per cent at the beginning of 1986 to 'a record low of 2. 5 per cent' in February 1987.[13] Industries other than those engaged in exports, however, 'enjoyed something of a boom'. Government spending also began to increase, and the construction industry that had remained depressed since the first oil crisis, regained its vigour. Corporate equipment investment caught up and there was a rush to install new plant equipment. 'In any case,' wrote an economic historian, 'the mid-1980s brought to a close the long period of adjustment, characterized by a search for stability, that had continued since the oil crisis, and ushered in an entirely new period.'[14] What was this new period going to be?

The low interest rate persisted; the record 2.5 per cent remained steady for over two years. The worldwide stock-market crash starting with a near panic at Wall Street in October 1987 contributed to this. When the economy was not really depressed, but on the contrary was actually booming, the government's expansionist financial policy led directly to 'abnormal monetary relaxation' and a great increase in the money supply.

---

[11] Large, op. cit., 195; Reinhard Drifte, *Japan's Foreign Policy* (London, 1990), 35.

[12] For an analysis of this abnormal lending, see Hiroyuki Itami, 'Price Distortion and Industry: Japan in the 1980s', *Ikkyo Ronso*, 115: 5 (May 1996).

[13] Takafusa Nakamura, *The Postwar Japanese Economy*, 256.   [14] Ibid. 261.

Excess liquidity was directed to financing investment in stocks and lands, the prices of which began to soar. To be precise, 83 per cent of the increase in bank lending from 1985 onwards was accounted for by four major areas, finance and insurance; real estate; the service industries; and individuals (housing loans and estate speculation). The Nikkei stock price average began rising steadily in 1988 and 1989 and reached a peak at 38,915 yen in December 1989. The rise in land prices was even more startling. Taking 1970 values as the basis, the nationwide urban land prices had increased 4.8 times by 1991, while land prices in the six largest cities had increased tenfold and those in business areas of cities by as much as twelve times. Soaring land prices brought about a number of cases of residents being driven out by land speculators and residential areas converted to new office blocks. Evictions were sometimes carried out with the help of *yakuza*.

The abundant money supply, along with a decrease in the prices of imports due to yen appreciation, allowed for 'conspicuous consumption', best illustrated by the purchase by a major insurance company of Van Gogh's *Sunflowers* for 58 billion yen.[15] The 'abnormal' rise in land and stock prices is said to have contributed to an increase in consumer spending which was also stimulated by cheaper imported goods. This, together with renewed equipment investment, led to a relative high economic growth of 4.49 per cent in the period 1985–90 (compared to 3.72 per cent in 1979–85).[16]

The bubble, however, was bound to burst. The official discount rate was at last raised to 3.25 per cent in May 1989, and went further up in stages to 6 per cent in August 1990. In March 1990 the Ministry of Finance introduced real-estate loan restrictions which compelled financial institutions to check reckless operations. Prices, first of stocks and then of lands, tumbled. In the midst of the subsequent recession, Japan was told that she had become the world's second largest exporter after Germany, ranked at the top in terms of net foreign claims, and also emerged as the world's leading donor of aid to developing countries and of contributions to international organizations.[17] Stock prices went on falling for thirty-three consecutive months until August 1992, with a rate of decline of 63.1 per cent, while land prices in business areas in Tokyo (as shown in the official list of estate prices) were more than halved in 1990–4. The collapse of the bubble economy disclosed a succession of financial scandals, bad credits, and fictitious deposits. The final settlement of an enormous amount of bad

---

[15] There is a possibility of this being a forgery. See *Daily Telegraph*, 4 July 1997; *Sunday Times*, 26 Oct. 1997; *Asahi Shinbun*, 27 Oct. 1997.

[16] Juro Hashimoto, *Sengono Nihon Keizai* (Post-war Japanese Economy) (Tokyo, 1995), 220–1.

[17] Takafusa Nakamura, op. cit., 273.

credit would entail further disclosures of scandals and even criminal acts on the part of those who went 'mad' in the bubble boom.

The prospect of the Japanese economy is ambiguous. Yen appreciation in 1994–5 is said to have been 'abnormal', as the exchange rate dropped below 80 yen per dollar in April 1995, though it has since been restored to 120–30 yen.[18] On the other hand, the official discount rate has been kept at a 'super-low' rate of less than 1 per cent to enable banks to cross out bad credits. Automobile and electronics industries are moving not only parts production but also main plant equipment to South-East Asia in search of cheap labour costs; 'the 'hollowing out' of industries accompanied by increasing unemployment has become a serious issue. Moreover, the bubble economy weakened banking institutions and dealt a blow to their reputation and credibility; we still do not know the extent of the damage wrought on them by the money games they engaged in during the bubble economy.

THE COLLAPSE OF THE LDP HEGEMONY

When Emperor Hirohito was dying, the Recruit scandal caught in its web of bribes most of the members of the Takeshita LDP government, including Takeshita himself, and Uno Sosuke, the foreign minister, who was not implicated, succeeded him as prime minister. Sixty-eight days later he too resigned, partly over a sexual scandal involving a former geisha and partly over the setback to the LDP at the election for the House of Councillors in July 1989.

It is ironic that Uno's successor Kaifu Toshiki, the favourite of 'clean Miki', riding on the crest of the bubble economy, managed to maintain a stable majority at the general election of February 1990, but stumbled over American demands for Japan's greater contribution to the Gulf War of 1990–1. Kaifu, though unable at first to decide his government's attitude to the war, had to concede to American requests by expending $13 billion in support of the multinational forces and for other related purposes. Pressures, both domestic and external, on him to dispatch the SDF to the war area mounted, and Kaifu, though unwilling at first to comply, wavered and gave in. The government introduced a UN Peace-Keeping Co-operation Bill to the Diet in October 1990, but owing to criticisms from opposition parties and also from some LDP members who pleaded for caution, the bill fell through. Kaifu placed a great weight on 'political reform', which meant change from the middle-sized constituency system to a supposedly less costly small constituency system, but faction leaders refused to co-operate and the related bills all miscarried. His government

---

[18] In May–December 1997.

was forced to resign, and he was succeeded by Miyazawa Kiichi in November 1991.

Miyazawa, who 'inherited' the former Ohira faction as an electoral asset, though often brilliant in his arguments had seemed to lack forcefulness as a political leader. Once in power, however, he changed and forced a Peace-Keeping Co-operation Bill through the Diet despite strenuous opposition from the Socialists. The new law allowed SDF units to leave for Cambodia in September 1992, the first overseas dispatch of the SDF. Moreover, the bubble economy was collapsing and the recession helped to uncover another political scandal which shook the whole LDP. In order to placate public opinion Miyazawa, like Kaifu before him, tackled 'political reform', that is, the adoption of a small constituency system. The opposition parties which preferred a combined system of small constituencies and proportional representation brought in a motion of no confidence in the government. This, with the support of LDP dissidents like Ozawa Ichiro and Hata Tsutomu, was carried, and the government dissolved the Diet.

The end of the unified LDP had come. Hata, Ozawa, and their faction formed a New Life Party (*Shinseito*); another former LDP group set up a new party, the Pioneers (*Sakigake*), with Takemura Masayoshi, the former governor of Shiga prefecture, as its leader; while Hosokawa Morihiro, the former governor of Kumamoto prefecture, started a Japan New Party (*Nihon Shinto*). At the general election of July 1993, which recorded the lowest polling rate in post-war history, the Socialist Party suffered a drastically reduced electoral strength (from 137 seats to 77), a great setback that itself reflected the collapse of the 1955 political system. (Results were: LDP 228, *Shinsei* 60, *Komei* 52, *Nihon Sinto* & *Sakigake* 52, *Minsha* or Democratic Socialists 19, Communists 15.)

It was Ozawa's tactic to form a two-party system consisting of two conservative parties, the LDP and his own *Shinseito*. The latter being still weak, he attempted a non-LDP coalition (excluding the Communists) with Hosokawa as candidate for premiership. It was Yamagishi Akira of *Rengo* (the Trade Union Federation) who supported Ozawa and drew the Socialists into Ozawa's coalition.[19] Hosokawa was elected as prime minister, and after twists and turns he managed to carry through 'political reform', a compromise system consisting of 300 small constituencies and 200 for proportional representation. He also managed to introduce 'partial liberalization' of rice imports, helped by the bad harvest due to the cold, wet summer, and to help bring the Uruguay Round of GATT to a successful conclusion. His third major policy was to introduce a 7 per cent consumer tax under the more palatable name of 'welfare tax'. Because of

---

[19] Fujiwara *et al.*, *Nihon Gendaishi*, 378

the unpopularity of this tax proposal, coupled with his own involvement in yet another financial scandal, he was obliged to resign in April 1994. At a press conference shortly after he had become prime minister, Hosokawa had stated that 'the last war was a war of aggression', and this had been well received abroad, but under the pressure from the domestic hawks he had gradually retreated from this position.

He had increasingly been made to serve Ozawa's strategy for strengthening the *Shinseito* as one of the two major conservative parties. His own party, the *Nihon Shinto*, severed its ties with Takemura's *Sakigake* party and formed an alliance with the *Shinseito* and the *Komeito*, and Hata of the *Shinseito* was designated as their candidate for premiership. The Socialists too were persuaded to join in this supposedly anti-LDP alliance, and Hata was elected in the Diet as prime minister, defeating the LDP candidate Kono Yohei. Thereupon the *Shinseito*, the *Minshato*, and the *Nihon Sinto*, together with some of the dissident LDP members, formed a new coalition party without having consulted the Socialists. The JSP, considering they had been cheated into supporting Hata, angrily withdrew from the alliance of *Shinsei*, *Komei*, *Minsha*, and *Nihon Shinto* that were the forces behind Hata's minority government. But Hata proved unable to control even his own ministers. Nagano Shigeto, the minister of law, true to the tradition of the *Shinseito* hawks, stated in a press interview that 'the Nanking massacre was a frame-up', the last war was 'a war to emancipate Asia', and 'the comfort women in the war were public prostitutes'. He was a graduate of the pre-war Military Academy, had gone through the post-war Police Reserve Force, the Security Force, and the SDF, and was a military man to the bone. Asian neighbours protested and he resigned.[20] The Hata government, having failed to come to terms with the Socialists when faced by the LDP's no-confidence motion, resigned in June 1994 after two months in office.

A reshuffle of the political pack was attempted, Ozawa hoping to split the JSP as well as the LDP. The JSP allied itself with the *Sakigake* party, and the LDP, from which Kaifu and several others had been snatched away to Ozawa's party, decided to join in this new alliance. At the subsequent Diet vote for the premiership Murayama Tomiichi, the Socialist chairman, was elected. Kono Yohei, the LDP president, became foreign minister, and Takemura of the *Sakigake* party finance minister. 'It is simply stunning, many would say, to see the LDP and the JSP, the two parties that had fought each other for so many years, forming a coalition government', commented the *Tensei Jingo* ('Vox Populi, Vox Dei') column of the *Asahi* newspaper.[21]

The election of Murayama as prime minister of the coalition govern-

---

[20] Fujiwara *et al.*, op. cit., 385.   [21] *Asahi Shinbun*, 1 July 1994.

ment meant a drastic change in the time-honoured socialist policy of neutralism and anti-militarism, which had perhaps become a little musty in the post-Cold War world. The LDP–JSP–*Sakigake* coalition, before the election of Murayama as prime minister, had ageed on the basic policy of maintaining the SDF and the US–Japan Security Treaty. In a Diet debate held on 20 July Murayama declared that 'we shall adhere to the policy of "defence only" [*senshu boei*] and ensure that the SDF, which is the minimum organization necessary for self-defence, is constitutional'.[22] The Socialist Party, at its conference held on 3 September 1994, approved of Murayama's stance on the security issue by 222 votes to 152.[23] Ten days later the Murayama government decided to send the SDF to Goma, Zaire, where disorderly elements in the camps of Rwanda refugees had become a serious threat after the withdrawal of US and Israeli troops. This policy was apparently pushed by the Foreign Ministry, which aspired to show off Japan's readiness to join the UN Security Council as a standing member.

In the meantime, the opposition parties, *Shinsei*, *Komei*, *Minsha*, and *Nihon Shinto*, closed ranks in order to prepare for the next election that would be fought largely on the new basis of a single-member small constituency. They formed a new party, *Shinshinto* (New Frontier Party), in December 1994 with Kaifu as president and Ozawa as secretary. This was unity for the sake not of political principle but of electoral convenience. At the same time the JSP was in danger of a serious split, as a former party chairman from the right wing had started forming a party within the party to launch another new party together with some of the former Democratic Socialists now in the *Shinseito*. Socialist discord, however, was swept away by a natural disaster, the greatest since the Kanto earthquake of 1923, that heralded the fiftieth anniversary year of post-war Japan.

JAPAN IN 1995 IN DISARRAY

The *Asahi Shinbun* on its New Year's Day issue of 1995 published the result of an opinion poll about the causes of the fifty years' peace: 25 per cent of the respondents atrributed it to 'the peace constitution', 24 per cent to 'the wretched war experiences', and 22 per cent to 'the efforts of the people'. These causes do not exclude each other, but the peace constitution was given the top priority for the first time since 1978 when this particular question was added to the survey. As to the issue of the general acceptance of democracy in Japan, 54 per cent of respondents, compared to 42 per cent in 1971, felt that it was widely accepted. Thus the year 1995, the fiftieth anniversary of the 'termination' of the war, began with national life in a state of apparent stability.

[22] Ibid. 21 July 1994.   [23] Ibid. 4 Sept. 1994.

The new year, however, was rudely shocked by the Kobe earthquake of 17 January, the number of the dead reaching 6,308. Kobe, the vanguard city of Japan's modernization and Europeanization, suddenly became the victim of an enormous destructive power. The government, both central and local, failed to respond to the needs of the suffering in Kobe. Karel Van Wolfren, a Dutch journalist who knows Japan well, complained: 'There is nobody who would take responsibility for the life of the people. Nowhere could be found those who would consider priority and make decisions for the people.'[24] Two months later, on the morning of 20 March, a poisonous (sarin) gas attack was made on commuters travelling in four underground trains in the heart of Tokyo, killing eleven people in a pretended 'war' staged by the cultists of Aum Shinrikyo. These young men and women, many of them university graduates, who were under the hypnotizing influence of a guru, Asahara Shoko, had been led to believe in an approaching Armageddon in which they could survive by fighting with modern (chemical) weapons.

On 3 May, the anniversary day of the promulgation of the new constitution, premier Murayama was in Beijing, expressing 'deep regrets over Japan's aggressive acts and colonial rule which brought unbearable sufferings and pains to the people of China and other Asian countries'. Both (state) chairman Jiang Ze-min and Premier Li Peng, who received him, while criticizing the hawks in the Japanese Diet, confirmed a closer relationship between China and Japan in the future.[25] On his return his coalition government was to adopt a joint No War resolution in the Diet. The JSP would naturally support him. But the LDP and the *Shinshinto*, altogether unhappy about such a resolution, organized their Diet members to the number of 286, insisting that an 'apology' for the last war would 'trample on the endeavour and honour of our predecessors'.[26]

A compromise was reached, and 'No War' was rescinded from the resolution which now read: 'This House in this fiftieth post-war year conveys its sincere condolence to all the war-dead and victims of wars of the whole world. Also it contemplates many a case of aggressive action and colonial rule in the modern history of the world, takes cognizance of such acts our country performed in the past and the painful suffering these inflicted on other nations, especially on Asian nations, and expresses deep regrets. We should overcome differences in historical views of war in the past, be humble enough to learn lessons from history, and build a peaceful international society. . .' The wording shows traces of clever adjustment by bureaucrats which made 'learning from history' almost meaningless by relegating Japan's acts of aggression and colonialism to a relatively obscure

[24] *Asahi Shinbun*, 16 Feb. 1995.   [25] Ibid. 4 May 1995.
[26] Ibid. 24 Feb. 1995.

place alongside many such acts by other countries in modern history and by emphasizing the existence of different views of history, including patriotic historiography, in an attempt to make the latter respectable.[27]

Prime minister Murayama in his discourse on the fiftieth post-war year given on 15 August 'apologized' for Japan's 'colonial rule and aggression'. He also sent a letter to the British prime minister John Major, expressing 'profound remorse and apology' for what the Japanese army did to the British in the last war. In an interview, however, Murayama stated that reparation issues had been legally settled and he had no intention of passing state compensation to individual claimants. In July a 'National Fund for Asian Peace for Women', a voluntary association under government sponsorship, was set up to collect a fund to provide compensation money to former 'sex-slaves' of the Japanese army. The UN Committee on Human Rights at its meeting held on 19 April 1996 adopted a resolution on violence to women in which it welcomed, but formally only took note of, a special committee report in favour of 'recommending' state compensation for former sex-slaves. There had been strong pressure on the UN committee from the Japanese government which refused to accept the 'recommendation'.[28] It is largely due to legalistic and bureaucratic considerations that the Japanese government has remained adamant on the issue of state compensation.

Then came the Okinawa issue, which had reached almost breaking point. Ota Masahide, the governor of Okinawa prefecture since 1990, had been calling for a 'reduction' of US military bases in Okinawa. The Japanese government offered no help and even welcomed the Pentagon report of February 1995 on East Asian Strategy which stressed the stationing in Okinawa of about 75 per cent of the 100,000-strong American forces in Japan as well as the maintenance of the US–Japan Security Treaty as vital to regional stability. Then an incident took place that profoundly upset the Okinawa people: the rape of a 12-year-old schoolgirl by three American servicemen. On 28 September Govenor Ota announced his decision not to sign public documents necessary for the Japanese government to keep American forces in the expropriated lands of Okinawa. His action was aimed at bringing the issue of the military bases to court in order to force the Tokyo government to clarify its position. Almost all the Okinawa people were behind him. Governor Ota, however, was defeated in his legal action, but the Tokyo government had to explore the possibilities of moving some of the American bases from Okinawa to other prefectures in Japan. After almost two years' shilly-shallying the new LDP government under Hashimoto Ryutaro, with the support of all other parties except the SDP (former JSP) and the JCP, had the Diet pass special legislation to

[27] Ibid. 10 June 1995.   [28] Ibid. 20 Apr. 1996.

enforce state appropriation of the lands designated for US military bases in Okinawa. The new law in fact further alienated Okinawa from the Tokyo government. The anti-Security Treaty struggle of 1960 faded into the remote past.

'Japan has long been in the grip of a collapse in asset prices, which now threatens to spill over into a deflationary decline in the general price level and to destabilize the financial system', commented the *Financial Times* in the summer of 1995.[29] Since the bursting of the bubble in May 1991, the Japanese economy had rolled down a steep hill; an enormous amount of bad credit was accumulated in banks and loan companies. The government decided to allocate 685 billion yen to save the *jusen* (housing loan companies) in its budget for the fiscal year 1996–7. The writer Sawachi Hisae, recalled the destruction of an old, humble residential area in Tokyo and its transformation into office blocks.

The huge amount of money circulated through the *jusen* . . . altered the face of Japan, and brought about environmental destruction. The nightmarish times when people ran amok after money and yet more money had to be ended, and the false, inverted sense of success which produced the pleasure of being an economic animal had to be stopped. . . . This is not limited to the *jusen* issue, but is deeply related to the quality of the state and of the nation. . . . Our country is generous to the strong and cruel to the weak . . . Why is it necessary to save by our taxes those who should be penalized for having indulged in money-games?[30]

Murayama's coalition government lasted for 555 days; the lingering economic depression brought about political apathy which characterized the era of transition. On 9 April Tokyo and Osaka each elected a comedian as prefectural governor by rejecting candidates supported by the existing political parties. At the first and only regular election under Murayama, that of the House of Councillors held on 23 July, the polling rate was 44 per cent, the lowest for a national election; the Socialists were the main losers and the *Shinshin* the major winner thanks to the organizational strength of the old *Komeito*, one of its components. The *Shinshinto* went ahead and elected party secretary Ozawa Ichiro as party president in December. He was a believer in Japan as 'a normal country', a term by which political power commensurable to its economic strength was implied. The *Shinshinto*, however, was a hotchpotch of a variety of political forces: the LDP dissidents scheming for a greater conservative party, the religious populists in the old *Komeito*, and the collaborationists, both industrial and political, in the former DSP. The party sought to take issue with the coalition government on the *jusen* problem, but having no viable policy on the issue its 'resistance' melted away.

[29] *Financial Times*, 10 July 1995, also in *Japan Times*, 11 July 1995.
[30] *Asahi Shinbun*, 8 Mar. 1996.

The Socialist Party at its conference held on 19 January 1995 had changed its name to the *Nihon Shakai Minshuto*, identical to the party's official English name the 'Social Democratic Party of Japan', and declared itself to be an 'open party of citizens'.[31] Under the new electoral system, however, its future seems bleak and unpromising.

On 5 January 1996 Murayama 'abruptly' announced his resignation from the premiership and opened the way for Hashimoto Ryutaro, the LDP leader, to succeed him. The Hashimoto coalition government was formed on 11 January 1996, with Kan Naoto of *Sakigake* as health and welfare minister, who was to investigate his own officials so as to unearth buried truths regarding HIV (AIDS) infection among haemophiliacs and apparent collusion between the ministry, pharmaceutical corporations, and specialist doctors in the early 1980s. In September 1996 Kan Naoto and Hatoyama Yukio (of *Sakigake*, and the grandson of Hatoyama Ichiro) started the *Minshuto* (Democratic Party) drawing on the moderates of the SDP and some sections of the *Sakigake* party, and at the general election later in that year emerged as the third party in the Diet (LDP 239, *Shinshin* 156, Democrats 52, Communists 26, SDP 15). The new LDP in power has not proved itself sufficiently competent to deal with Japan's economic difficulties.

The year 1995 was a time for reconciliation, partly because the coalition government led by Murayama provided mechanisms as well as initiatives working in that direction. A national body of the victims of the Minamata lead pollution and their defence lawyers, at a meeting held at Minamata on 28 October, decided to accept the government proposal for a final settlement: the government would make clear its responsibility by giving financial assistance to enable the Nihon Chisso (Nitrate Fertilizer Company) to pay consolation money of over 20 billion yen to about 8,000 people. 'Time is harsh on the weak', a 'political settlement that was too late', commented the newspapers.[32] It has been forty-two years since the first victim was identified, and forty years since the Minamata disease was officially acknowledged.

Intellectual sanity is not the strongest characteristic of the Japanese: the year 1995 began with an article denying the existence in Nazi Germany of the gas chambers, published in the magazine *Marco Polo* of the Bungeishunju-sha, a prestigious publishing house. In view of protests from German and American firms as well as from the Israeli embassy, the journal was obliged to close. Economically it was a dismal year, the growth rate of GDP hovering at around 0.6 per cent. The rate of unemployment hit a 'record high' of 3.4 per cent.[33] It was reported in December

[31] Ibid. 19, 20 Jan. 1956; *Japan Times*, 20 Jan. 1995   [32] *Asahi Shinbun*, 29 Oct. 1995.
[33] *Japan Times*, 27 Dec. 1995.

that the prototype fast-breeder nuclear reactor *Monju* on the Fukui coast had leaked three tons of liquid sodium. This was to be followed by further disasters of a similar kind.

The rate of increase of population was 0.27 per cent, the lowest ever, and the total population as it stood on 31 March 1995 was 124,655,498.[34] The ageing of the population became a social problem, threatening the level so far achieved of pensions and social-security benefits. No doubt 1995 was a year of transition marked by signs of uncertainty and ambiguity. Meanwhile, scandals and corruptions involving top bureaucrats and business leaders were uncovered one after another. Japan and the Japanese now found themselves in disarray, faced with the stark realities underlying their inflated image of themselves.

CONCLUDING REMARKS

In 1995 the *Asahi* newspaper already showed scepticism, if not pessimism: 'a standard of living which a half-century ago was beyond anyone's imagination has come about, but why is it', it asked, 'that the bottom of our heart is encrusted with uneasiness and irritation?'[35] The uneasiness is related to the loss of self-respect which is the reverse side of the inflated self-image of the Japanese. By virtue of the high economic growth that was once called 'a miracle', they assume that they deserve respect from other nations, but at the same time they feel that they are not sufficiently respected and suspect that this is because they are too self-centred. This is part of the identity crisis which has repeatedly been revealed, and is due to the absence of a common historical perception of the major issues and events in the nation's past. Sir Sydney Giffard, quoting the Anglican Bishop of South Tokyo from around the turn of the century, wrote: 'in Japan patriotism was "so nearly universal as scarcely to be counted a virtue".'[36] This may still be the case now. People simply do not speak of it, except on the lunatic fringe on the right. It is possible, however, that *aikokushin* (patriotism) has become a rare species. In some way patriotism is narcissism writ large, and the case of Mishima Yukio, who embodied it in his life and work, would testify to the truth of this; but Mishima has been studied more by foreigners than by his compatriots, for whom he has become a taboo or an irrelevance.

The present loss of national identify or something approaching to it can be explained by the deadlock reached in Japan's pursuit of power. Japan

---

[34] *Mainichi Shinbun*, 12 Aug. 1995. Average life-expectancy for men in 1995 was 76.36 years and that for women 82.84: this had grown by 5 years for men and 6 years for women over the preceding ten years. Office of Statistics, Government Bureau of General Affairs, *Japanese Statistics* (1997), 25.   [35] *Asahi Shinbun*, 1 Jan. 1995.
[36] Sydney Giffard, *Japan Among the Powers, 1890–1990* (New Haven, 1994), 23.

was an industrial and military power before the war, and re-emerged as an economic power after the war. A long recession after the collapse of the bubble economy, however, has exposed the weaknesses of Japanese finance capitalism. People are beginning to wonder whether the decline of Japan as an economic power has started. The decision made by Ozawa in December 1997 to dismantle his *Shinshinto* and replace it with a new nationalist party, which assumed the name of *Jiyuro* (Liberal Party), may be a vain struggle against the process of decay that has already gone too far.

Japan was remade by the Americans after 1945 and established as a junior partner on security matters after 1951. It is as though the Pax Americana, as far as Japan is concerned, had taken the place of the old Confucian international order of the Middle Kingdom in which Japan had rarely felt comfortable. The United States is the big brother. Japan, the little brother, feels as uncomfortable as ever. It seems that Japan has not found her proper place in the community of nations; hence her uneasiness and identity-crisis.

The transformation of post-war Japan has not altered the quality of man. Her status as a junior but grumbling partner in the Pax Americana is something not unfamiliar to the Japanese. Is Japan 'independent' or 'self-governing'? This is the old Korean dilemma. This dilemma has made Japanese politicians and businessmen sometimes arrogant and sometimes obsequious. The important thing, however, is to put an end to their pursuit of power and to their traditional perception of the power relationship, including Mr Ozawa's aspiration for a 'normal country' status, and for Japan to learn to live as a member of the community of nations.

According to an opinion poll conducted by the *Asahi* newspaper (26 April 1997), 46 per cent of respondents were in favour of altering the post-war constitution, whereas 39 per cent felt that there was no need for its revision. The revisionists had increased from 29 per cent in 1983, while the non-revisionists fell from 41 per cent of that year. The demands of the revisionists, however, varied: some wanted to make clear Japan's 'military contribution in international disputes' and 'right to self defence', while others asked for 'the introduction of the public election of a prime minister and a national referendum'. As for Article 9 (no war provision), 69 per cent supported it. These figures are still not decisive enough to give clear direction. In order to find some meaning or a meaningful direction in the course of Japan's tortuous history, the Japanese have to try hard to learn from history itself. Indeed, the identity-crisis itself is rooted deep in Japanese history.

Epilogue

History cannot be confined within the time limits required for a written history. This is especially true of its closing period. The year 1995 is significant not only for it being the fiftieth anniversary of Japan's defeat in the late war but also because it provided enough signs of an identity crisis of the modern Japanese to make them halt and reflect. Japan's decline as an economic power has been the topic of serious debate. The transitory nature of many of the newly formed political parties only confirms the end of the political balance that once existed between the LDP and the Socialists.

During the two or three years since 1995 the Japanese economy has gone from bad to worse and has carried her trading partners in the Asia Pacific region down with her to financial disaster and economic depression. These are the countries where the 'East Asian Miracle' had only recently been trumpeted (like the Japanese miracle a decade or two ago). In Japan business confidence has been seriously impaired. According to a survey published in the *Asahi Shinbun* (27 September 1998) of 200 leading businesses (100 manufacturing and 100 non-manufacturing companies), 123 believe that the economy is deteriorating, forty-nine that it is slowly declining, and twenty-seven feel that it is standing still. Their pessimistic judgements are based first on the trends in personal consumption, secondly on the size of business profits, and thirdly on the shaky state of banks and other financial organizations. As for personal consumption, an average consumer spends much less now in view of the uncertain future of the economy, and more directly in view of the precariousness of his or her employment, coupled with the increased costs the consumer will have to pay for health and other social welfare services. The number of un-employed has reached 293 million, with an unemployment rate of 4.3 per cent, a record high, in October 1998. (Thereafter the rate steadily increased and stood at 4.8 per cent (5 per cent for men) in April 1999). All department stores and supermarkets have seen their earnings visibly declining. For the reasons cited above, consumers will not touch savings desposited in the banks as long as they can afford not to; this in spite of the notoriously low bank interest rate, which now stands at 0.2 per cent (this is the rate applied to a 10 million yen deposit for three months in the last week of October 1989). On the other hand, the banks, preoccupied with the mounting pressure of bad credits and with regulations on the ratio of backup funds, are reluctant to give new loans. It even appears that interest has ceased to be a factor in the market economy, or that capitalism has stopped functioning in Japan. In fact, under the newly enforced Finance Restoration Law a failed bank will be nationalized, though temporarily.

At the height of the bubble economy a character in a film called *Marusano Onna* or (Lady Tax Inspector), a land-broker of the *yakuza* type, was made to confess: 'We are engaged in pushing up land prices by threats and intimidation in order to make Tokyo the financial centre of the world. We are doing this for the sake of Japan.' The bubble economy swelled then collapsed. Tokyo failed to qualify as a world financial centre. The land speculation that had once overflowed even to America and Europe (as if to flaunt Japanese money before the whole world) retreated, causing considerable losses. The Daiichi and Kangyo Bank sold a Ritz-Carlton hotel in Hawaii, the Mitsubishi Estate the Rockefeller Center in New York, and Nikko Securities and its group the Watergate Hotel in Washington, DC, for about half the purchase prices. These major evacuations took place in 1995–6. It was as though the imperial army at Guadalcanal had had to make *tenshin* (an 'advance in other directions').

Depreciation of the yen, which reached 146 yen per dollar in June 1998 and 145 yen in August, seemed to favour not only such a retreat (by making losses lighter) but also export industries, such as automobiles. Here too, reduced domestic consumption proved to be a more powerful factor than the value of yen, which appeared volatile enough to go up again to 120 yen one year later.

Meanwhile, some of the banks and other credit institutions, the very source of the speculative funds that had sustained the bubble economy, began to founder under the heavy load of bad credits. The Hanwa Bank of Wakayama went bankrupt in November 1996, with bad credit amounting to 19 billion yen, the first case of bank failure in post-war Japan. A year later in December 1997 the Hokkaido Development Bank was closed with bad credit reaching over 900 billion yen. Some of the major banks have closed all or part of their overseas branches, Daiwa, Fuji, and Sakura among others.

At the same time, one illegal but largely tolerated business practice became the object of prosecution. This is the use by company chiefs of *sokaiya*, *yakuza* groups specializing in the job of intimidating and silencing shareholders at their general meetings. In order to placate the general public who (like Sawachi Hisae over the *jusen* matter) were uneasy about the government policy of infusing public funds (i.e. their tax money) into needy banks, sound or unsound, it was obviously imperative to show Japanese businesses to be pure and uncorrupted, or if corrupted, to be ready for correction. In March 1997 it was disclosed that Nomura

Securities had provided *sokaiya* with a large amount of profit gained through insider dealings. Shortly afterwards a director of Ajinomoto Foods was arrested on the charge of giving money (much less than that given by Nomura) to another *sokaiya*. The 'Nomura Incident' soon revealed large-scale *sokaiya* operations which implicated other major financial firms such as Daiichi Kangyo Bank, Yamaichi Securities, Daiwa Securities, and Nikko Securities. Close, underhand contacts between the chiefs of the financial giants and Treasury bureaucrats were also disclosed in the course of the investigation. It has become apparent that 'Japanese-style management' had another important feature which could be described as a system of irresponsibility and illegality born of timidness and avidity on the part of management.

The downfall of one of the giants was soon to come. In November 1997 Yamaichi Securities decided to terminate business because it had been disclosed that its unaccounted debt amounted to 264 billion yen and that Yamaichi had for several years been engaged in the illegal practice of transferring and rotating losses to and among several paper companies, some in Japan, some abroad. 'It was we, the management, who were in the wrong', wept Nozawa Shohei, president of the company for only the last few months: 'Not our employees!' There is good reason to suspect that Yamaichi's illicit transactions had been carried out with the connivance of a Treasury bureaucrat responsible for the section dealing with securities.

Then came what the *Mainichi Shinbun* chose to call 'the Disposal of the Chogin' (Long-Term Credit Bank). In October 1998 Chogin, taking advantage of the Finance Restoration Law, applied for 'special public control' (temporary nationalization). It was announced that Chogin's bad credit amounted to 4,620 billion yen, losses arising from the reduced share and estate prices to 500 billion yen, and Chogin's own capital to 160 billion yen. It has been suggested that the LDP government abandoned its earlier attempt to save Chogin by the infusion of public funds in order to appease the opposition parties who were much stronger in the House of Councillors than the LDP. Politics reflects economy and vice versa.

It was the issue of confidence or no confidence in the Hashimoto regime at a time of economic 'crisis' that induced the non-committed electorate to go and vote (against the government), commented the *Nihon Keizai Shinbun* of 13 July 1998. The voting rate of 58.84 per cent at the election for the House of Councillors of the Diet held in July 1998 showed an increase of fourteen points over that of the previous election three years before. The results showed a disastrous defeat for the LDP and a great advance for the Democrats and the Communists. The LDP won 44 seats (16 losses), the Democrats 27 (9 gains), the Communists 15 (9 gains), *Komei* (Clean Politics) 9 (2 gains), *Jiyuto* (formed by Ozawa shortly before) 6 (1 gain), and the SDP 5 (7 losses). The LDP failed to win a single seat in all the large urban electoral districts (Tokyo, Osaka, Aichi, Kanagawa, Saitama, Hyogo, and Kyoto), where the effects of economic failures and irregularities were felt much more seriously than elsewhere. The SDP suffered from its past alliance with the LDP. Many of its former supporters switched their allegiance to the Communists, whose leaders appeared much more amenable than before in their attitude to other opposition parties or to the Democrats, whose leader Kan Naoto emerged as a politician who could deal squarely with the entrenched interests of the bureaucracy. According to an opinion poll conducted by the *Nihon Keizai Shinbun* (4 August 1998), 28.6 per cent of respondents would like to see Kan as prime minister compared with 10.4 per cent, who preferred Obuchi Keizo, who had been chosen by the LDP (still the largest party in the Diet) as the successor to Hashimoto who had resigned after the election. Obuchi, a conciliator who lacks leadership, has been advised by his aides-de-camp to accommodate demands from the opposition. Accomodation can easily be turned into manoeuvring to split the opposition.

The closing years of the twentieth century saw the termination of the Ienaga lawsuit against the screening of school textbooks by the Ministry of Education. Professor Ienaga had started his lawsuit in 1965, believing that the screening of textbooks would amount to a violation of the freedom in expression, learning, and teaching guaranteed by the new constitution. The issues contested were some specific points in modern Japanese history such as the Battle of Okinawa, atrocities committed by the Japanese army in northern China, the Nanking Massacre, and Unit 731. Over 20,000 people gave their support to his courageous but long-drawn out struggle. This time it was his third lawsuit started in 1984 that was examined by the guardians of law. In August 1997 the Supreme Court gave its verdict, ruling against the demand by the Ministry of Education to rescind discussion of 'Unit 731' from his textbook (in addition to another demand made on the Nanking Massacre which had been found unwarranted at a lower court, and two other similar issues) but deciding that the screening was not censorship and therefore not unconstitutional. It is true that, thanks to Professor Ienaga's persistent efforts, some progress has been made in the understanding of modern history on the part of those who practised screening, but the distinction between 'safe' and 'unsafe' history which remains in the mind of government officials is not conducive to fostering an enquiring spirit and will strengthen conformism, one of the root causes of Japan's trouble in her *fin-de-siècle*.

It now seems as though Japan has been frustrated in her bid to become a world economic power. When the bubble speculation subsided and the reaction came, the corrupt and irrational features of her economy at once became apparent. Bad credit accumulated and threatened first *jusen*, then the banks themselves. The banks, protected as they are by the super-low interest rate on the one hand and by government assurances of the infusion of public money on the other, seem mindful only of their own existence. The securities and estate companies, the very agents of the bubble economy, have been lying low.

Throughout the post-war years business leaders were concerned more with market share than with profit (for the shareholders), and became expansionist like the pre-war military leaders. Reckless operations are the feature common to both. Fukuzawa Yukichi taught the Meiji Japanese to learn from the West not only its industrial and institutional skills but, more imporantly, the spirit behind its material achievements. The emphasis he placed on the independence of an individual, however, did not last long, even with Fulazawa himself. The military (and many others, including politicians, educationalists, and business leaders) combined western skills with the Japanese spirit true to the tradition of many of the *Bakumatsu* loyalists who came round to accepting *kaikoku* while upholding the cause of *sonno*. Post-war business leaders marched along a similar path. They, along with their hard-working employees, achieved high economic growth and a better-off society emerged. *Sonno* is probably outdated now. It has been replaced by a pride in a 'unique' national communal culture which is now regarded by some as a liability rather than an asset in maintaining economic soundness. American Cold War strategy gave Japan footholds for economic expansions in South-East Asia; globalization of the world economy provided opportunities for Japan's business leaders to advance in America, Europe, and elsewhere. But like the military leaders of half a century ago, they failed to make a correct estimate of themselves, their rivals, and of the world situation. They became as arrogant as many of the army officers in the late war. The age-old and shadowy concept of the Middle Kingdom, though forgotten as such, hovered over the glory of economic conquests.

Then came the time for evacuation and withdrawal. The economy at home was practically shattered by the accumulated effects of greed and acts of irresponsibility on the part of business leaders and bureaucrats. The Economic Planning Board has announced the estimated rate of economic growth for 1998 to be −1.8 per cent. The rate of economic growth for 1997 was −0.7 per cent; two years of consecutive economic decline is something new in the post-war economic history of Japan. Japan's pursuit of economic power is coming to an end with dismal results. It has left some achievements (superior infrastructure and a higher standard of living, for instance) and calamities (industrial pollution, destruction of the natural environment, social maladjustment of young people, and so on). Clearly Japan will have to start again, perhaps not from scratch but certainly with a new concept to sustain its national identity, and perhaps its global identity too.

APPENDIX I:

Unit 731 and the Human Logs

Modern Japanese history has many dark spots, and probably the darkest of all could be found in northern Manchuria under Japanese rule, where a laboratory for medical research was built for the secret purpose of experimenting on biological weapons for mass killing.

Unit 731 was a bacteriological warfare research unit stationed at Ping Fan, a suburb of Harbin, Manchuria, which perpetrated infernal acts which, though much smaller in scale, can be compared to the gas chambers at Auschwitz. Ishii Shiro, the mastermind and directing officer of its laboratory, was born in 1892 in Chiba prefecture, had studied at the Medical School of Kyoto Imperial University, and soon found himself engaged in researches on epidemic prevention and water filtration at the First Army Hospital in Tokyo. Curiously he became interested in the possibilities of chemical and biological warfare when the Geneva Disarmament Convention of 1925 outlawed such warfare.[1] His patron was Koizumi Chikahiko, then the president of the Army Medical School at which Ishii became professor of immunology. Koizumi is known as the founder of the *Koseisho* (Ministry of Public Health) in 1938, where he himself served as its minister (1941–4): he committed suicide shortly after the defeat of Japan in the war. Koizumi allowed Ishii to carry on his research in a compound in the Army Medical School which became Ishii's Tokyo centre until 1945.

A few months after the Japanese occupation of Harbin in February 1932, Major Ishii Shiro and his associates arrived there and were given a free hand by the army to begin their work. The original research laboratory in the city was soon found too small to carry out a large-scale experiment, and a site was obtained at Beiyinhe outside the city, where a huge compound containing some 100 brick buildings was duly built. The Zhong Ma Prison Camp, as it was called locally, held 500 to 600 prisoners, a mixed lot consisting of 'bandits' (Kuomintang followers), communist rebels, and common criminals, and Ishii and his disciples pursued 'research' connected with three principal contagions: anthrax, glanders, and plague. He is said to have performed pioneering work on the problem of frostbite. 'Select body organs' were obtained. Beiyinhe continued to use prisoners for deadly experiments until the autumn of 1934, when a rebellion disrupted the camp routine and endangered the security of the camp. 'All the prisoners fled, except ten persons who were too weak from the blood-taking experiments to run away. Burdened by the shackles that hobbled their legs, many of the prisoners were soon recaptured and were subjected to sadistic treatment as reprisal. However, some sixteen prisoners made good their escape.' Word soon spread throughout the area.[2] There was also an explosion in the camp. Ishii, now surgeon lieutenant-colonel, abandoned the

---

[1] Sheldon H. Harris, *Factories of Death: Japanese Biological Warfare, 1932–45, and the American Cover-up* (London, 1994), 18. [2] Ibid. 29.

Beiyinhe facilities in 1937 and moved to an enormous new complex completed in 1939 at Ping Fan, about 20 km from Harbin. The camp comprised barracks, an arms magazine, barns for test animals, an autopsy/dissecting building, a laboratory for frostbite experiments usable all the year round, two special prison buildings that housed human test subjects, a private airfield, and a special railway line to Harbin. The place 'rivalled Auschwitz-Birkenau in size'.[3] Japanese officials told local people that the area was being developed for a lumber mill. The *maruta* (logs), as the prisoners were cynically called, destined for the Ping Fan lumber-mill were largely from Harbin, and consisted of Chinese immigrants, White Russians including Harbin Jews, Soviet prisoners captured in border skirmishes, Mongolians, Koreans, and Europeans of various nationalities accused of a variety of crimes; the total number commonly accepted by authorities of those who perished as *maruta* amounts to at least 3,000.[4] Harris considers this figure too low.[5] This figure, says Harris, does not take into account those killed before 1941 and also 5,000–6,000 humans annihilated in similar death factories at Mukden, Nanking, and Changchun which were not directly under Ishii's control. In addition, epidemics occurred each autumn for several years around Ping Fan which claimed the lives of several tens of thousands more.

Ishii's unit, which formally began its operation in 1936, rapidly grew and in 1940 had about 3,000 personnel (5,000 if satellite units are counted), including 600 to 800 doctors and scientists who came from various universities and research institutes at home, among them Naito Ryoichi, a 'fugu toxin' expert, 'one of Ishii's brightest disciples'[6] and the founder of the now enormously successful medical firm *Midori-juji* (Green Cross),[7] whose close and sometimes scandalous connections with the *Koseisho* has recently been brought to light. Dean Koizumi continued to provide Ishii with the men and materials he wanted. Here they experimented and produced bombs for biological warfare. The most eerie part of their experiment was research on human reactions to typhoid, cholera, glanders, gangrene, venereal diseases, smallpox, and countless other diseases. They succeeded in manufacturing a defoliation bacilli bomb that could blight an area of 50 square kilometres. When the Russian army advanced into Manchuria towards the end of the war, those unfortunate *maruta* prisoners who were still alive were massacred in an attempt to destroy all traces of the bestial laboratory.

Morimura Seiichi, a popular novelist, shocked the nation in the 1980s with his book *Akuma no Hoshoku* (Devil's Gluttony, 3 vols., 1983–5), describing the army's experiments on humans for biological warfare. John R. Pritchard also described the Unit in *Secret of Secrets: The File on Unit 731* (1987). His other book on the Tokyo War Trial also devotes nearly half of its pages to this criminal deed. Professor Harris of California State University has produced a more detailed study on the subject, *Factories of Death* (1994), to which we have already made reference.

At a comparatively early stage of the Tokyo Trial (August 1946) David Sutton, a member of the International Prosecution Section, read extracts from a summary

---

[3] Harris, *Factories of Death*, 35.
[4] Takao Matsumura (ed.), *Ronso 731 Butai* (A Controversy over Unit 731) (Tokyo, 1994), 12.
[5] Harris, *Factories of Death*, 51.   [6] Ibid. 62.   [7] Ibid. 53–4.

report on the official investigations compiled by the procurator of the Nanking district court and made a short reference to experiments conducted by the 'Tama Detachment' on an unknown number of Chinese civilian captives who were taken away to a medical laboratory 'where the reactions to poisonous serums were tested'. President Webb expressed surprise at this and enquired if there was any further evidence to substantiate such charges. To this Sutton replied no, and an American defence counsel (Captain Alfred Brooks) suggested that this test was nothing more than a series of vaccinations of the people. Another American defence counsel cautioned against the use of a document of this character. Webb decided that this was a mere allegation, unsupported by evidence.

John W. Powell, in his pioneering work on the Harbin atrocities, alleges that one member of the prosecution was involved in promising Lt.-General Ishii and his colleagues immunity from Allied prosecution in exchange for disclosing to the United States the results of their researches on bacteriological warfare.[8] Apparently the chief prosecutor and the US War Crimes Branch in Washington were parties to what appears to have been a genuine conspiracy, together with the chief of General MacArthur's Intelligence Section.

If the Tokyo Trial had meted out victor's justice, it did so not in the retrospective sense suggested by Minear in his book of that title,[9] but in the prospective sense that the victorious United States had already begun preparing for another war.

Unfortunately Unit 731 turned out to be only one connecting link between wartime Japan and the post-war Japan that became entangled in American Cold War strategies. Bureaucracy and heavy and chemical industries were other links. Though the former was temporarily crippled at the top under the occupation reforms and the latter were destroyed and dismantled to a great extent, they all rose again, like a phoenix from the ashes of war debris to which Japan had been reduced in August 1945.

[8] See John W. Powell, in the *Bulletin of Concerted Asian Scholars* (1980) and the *Bulletin of Atomic Scientists* (October 1981), referred to in Harris, *Factories of Death*, 116.

[9] Richard H. Minear, *Victors' Justice: The Tokyo War Crimes Trial* (Princeton, 1971).

Bibliographical Essay

This is not a comprehensive survey of books on modern Japanese history. The output of historical research has been remarkable for the last thirty years, partly because Japan's economic growth made a great stir in academic circles as much as elsewhere, and also because specialization in research has gone deeper and grown more diversified. The following is no more than a survey of the books that are immediately relevant to the topics dealt with in this study.

The publication in 1960 of *A History of Modern Japan* (a Pelican Book) by Richard Storry in its own way marked an epoch in the western historiography on modern Japan. The book is in full sympathy with its subject and reveals a first-hand knowledge of the Japanese mind acquired at a time when the author was an impressionable young teacher in northern Japan in the 1930s—see also his *The Double Patriots* (London, 1967). His Pelican book was reprinted five times with revisions, the last being the 1982 edition. The bibliography (of books in English) was also gradually expanded until the last edition (which was reprinted in 1990 as a Penguin book), contains far more books published after 1960 than those before, the ratio being roughly 3 to 1.

Japanese historiography on modern Japanese history and its western counterpart have by and large been separated from each other. It is true that western historiography took great pains to digest Japanese sources and works (often critically), but the Japanese in comparison have remained more or less isolated and self-contained, though tendencies of this kind are being overcome by the growing international exchange of historians and their views.

Japanese historians for a long time suffered from the political circumstances of their country and even from direct political intervention. Studies of Japanese history in pre-war Japan were greatly handicapped by the prevailing ideology of emperor worship and excessive nationalism. The imperial theory of national history incorporating the mythical origins of the imperial family in recorded history and blurring the boundary between legend and history had long been accepted as legitimate. The prosecution of Tsuda Sokichi, Professor of Waseda University, for his unorthodox views of the era of gods is noted in the text of this book. Such taboos were eliminated from historical studies under the American occupation, but no sooner had Japan regained independence than political pressure was brought to bear on history writing, though mainly limited to school textbooks. In 1957 *A History of Japan* by Ienaga Saburo, to be published by Sanseido, was disqualified by the Ministry of Education as a textbook for high-school education because the last chapter, dealing with reforms under the American occupation, the new constitution, the Cold War and the Korean War, and Japanese rearmament, was 'improper in selection of historical facts'. The official in charge of textbook censorship added: Ienaga's manuscript submitted for official approval remained 'distant from the purposes of education in Japanese history, which are to appreciate our ancestors' endeavours through learning, to enhance our national consciousness as Japanese and to foster abundant affection for our race': see *Kentei Fugokaku Nihonshi* (A History of Japan, A Textbook Censored and Disqualified) by Ienaga Saburo (Tokyo, 1974). Thus began a long-drawn-out battle between Ienaga and the legal authorities over the constitutionality of textbook censorship.

This should not give the impression that history writing in Japan always suffered from official intervention. The pre-war literature in history and historical sources found one of its best achievements in *Meiji Bunka Zenshu* (Works of Meiji Civilization) (24 vols., Tokyo, 1927–9), edited by Yoshino Sakuzo and others, including one volume devoted to *Jiyu Minken* (Liberty and People's Right). Kume Kunitake (compiler), *Tokumei Zenken Taishi Beio Kairan Jikki* (Iwakwa Embassy, A Record of its Tours of Observation in America and Europe) (1978); modern edn. edited by Akira Tanaka, 5 vols. (Tokyo, 1978), can be regarded as a basic work that provides important clues for an understanding of Japan's modernization. Hideo Ono, *Nihon Shinbun Hattatsu Shi* (History of the Development of Newspapers in Japan) (Osaka and Tokyo, 1922) traces the evolution of newspapers from their modest beginnings as translations or transcriptions of foreign journals, the appearance of the first daily in Yokohama, the struggle for freedom of the press, the era of newspapers as party organs, the role of the press in the Taisho political changes, and almost inevitably ends with an account of the right-wing attack on newspapers at the time of the Russian Revolution and the Rice Riots. Taisuke Itagaki (ed.), *Jiyutoshi* (History of the Liberal Party) (2 vols., Tokyo, 1911; repr. 3 vols., Tokyo, 1957–8) is a semi-official history of the earliest viable political party in Japan. Some of the biographical studies of Meiji leaders could be regarded as works of political history: Ito Hirobumi Denki Hensan Iinkai (Committee to Edit the Life of Ito Hirobumi), *Ito Hirobumi Den* (The Life of Ito Hirobumi) (3 vols. Tokyo, 1940); Iichiro (Soho)Tokutomi, *Koshaku Yamagata Aritomo Den* (The Life of Marquis Yamagata Aritomo) (3 vols. Tokyo, 1933). To these could be added Eiichi Shibusawa (ed.), *Tokugwa Yoshinobu Ko Den* (The Life of Tokugawa Yoshinobu) (8 vols., Tokyo, 1917), Yoshinobu being the last shogun.

The early 1930s witnessed the publication of Marxist literature dealing especially with the history of Japanese capitalism, some focusing on the Meiji Restoration, such as Eitaro Noro, *Nihon Shihonshugi Hattatsu Shi* (History of the Development of Japanese Capitalism) (Tokyo, 1933) and Moritaro Yamada, *Nihon Shihonshugi Bunseki* (Analysis of Japanese Capitalism) (Tokyo, 1929). The world depression and the rise of fascism would at least partly explain the force of the argument presented by Marxist writers. They were, however, ruthlessly suppressed, and some paid for their academic and political conscience with their life. They were rehabilitated when Japanese military fascism collapsed, but Marxism, as we shall see, became a bone of contention again in post-war historiography. There is a very good summary in English of the Marxist analyses of Japanese capitalism: Germaine A. Hoston, *Marxism and the Crisis of Development in Prewar Japan* (Princeton, 1986).

In Richard Storry's aforementioned book, enriched as it is with episodes and anecdotes, political and diplomatic history predominate, pushing aside economic and social history and squeezing the history of opposition almost out of recognition. This is true of his otherwise admirable book *Japan and the Decline of the West in Asia 1894–1943* (London, 1979) which, though, ends on the hopeful note that Japan's hegemonic nationalism, obsessed with her national ranking in the world order, is giving way to a more realistic view of her own strength, her potentialities and limitations.

Before Richard Storry we have two outstanding historians of modern Japan in the West: George Sansom and E. H. Norman. Sansom's *Japan: A Short Cultural History*, first published in 1931, revised in 1946 (London: the Cresset Press), reprinted by Tuttle in 1973 and several times thereafter, begins with an account of the mixed origins of the Japanese race in prehistoric times, examines myths and chronicles, cult and religions, arts and letters, and surveys the rule of the samurai which ended with the downfall of feudalism. His insight into Japanese culture and society, and his command of historical detail are admirable, but the book touches upon modern Japan only in its last few pages. His next work, *Japan in World History*, originally published in 1951 by the Institute of Pacific Relations and reissued by Tuttle in 1977, though slight in size, is penetrated by a deep insight into Japanese history, though it is an attempt to look at it 'from outside'. Sansom's *The Western World and Japan* (London, 1956) deals squarely with the central issues of modern Japan, how Japan took up the western challenge, born of the industrial revolution and the French Revolution, with vigour, and carries his dissection of Japanese society down to the end of the nineteenth century. He emphasizes that there was no sudden break with the past in 1868 but only 'a gathering of speed' owing to western pressure on the one hand and to growth of domestic elements tractable or favourable to a modern state on the other. His massive study of Japanese history came out in three volumes, all published by the Cresset Press: *A History of Japan to 1334* (1958); *1334–1615* (1961); and *1615–1867* (1964), covering mainly the declining period of the Tokugawa Bakufu.

E. H. Norman, in his major work *Japan's Emergence as a Modern State* (New York, 1940), considered the Meiji Restoration to be a revolution from above, as the work of 'enlightened absolutism', while liberal institutions still remained 'luxuries' to the Japanese who had to hurry up in introducing reform so as not to sink into the position of a colony. His emphasis on 'semi-feudal' relationships that remained within Japanese capitalism may link his studies with Marxism, especially with the 1932 Comintern thesis on Japan, while his study *Ando Shoeki and the Anatomy of Japanese Feudalism*, first appearing in *Transactions of the Asiatic Society of Japan*, 3:2 (Dec. 1949), and reprinted by University Publications of America, 1979, showed the author to be more concerned with critics of feudalism. In translation *Ando Shoeki* exerted a profound influence on post-war Japanese intellectuals, though it was largely ignored in the West (with the exception of George Sansom and later John W. Dower).

Equally prominent among Storry's predecessors were Hugh Borton of Columbia University and Edwin Reischauer of Harvard University. Hugh Borton's *Japan*

Since 1931 originally published in 1940 by the Institute of Pacific Relations (reprinted in 1973 by Greenwood Press) is a survey of Japanese politics in the 1930s as it headed towards 'a centralized corporate state' and 'military fascism'. *Japan's Modern Century* by the same author (New York, 1955), though more substantial in terms of the period covered and the range of topics, seems marred by the Cold War ideology. The collapse of the Tokugawa 'dictatorship', the emergence of a centralized monarchy, the building of the empire, and the defeat in a total war: all these were compensated by post-war affluence, and he added: 'Japan's economic problems are interrelated with the larger political problem of stopping communism in Asia.'

Edwin O. Reischauer's *Japan: Past and Present* (originally published in 1946; London, 1947; 3rd revised edn. 1964) is concerned with the problem of Japan's modernization which was facilitated by a strong national consciousness as well as by studies of European science in the Tokugawa era. The development of 'a full-fledged commercial economy' in this era provided the necessary background for modernization. Rapid modernization, which amounted to a revolution in Japanese society and government, was carefully planned at the top and enforced upon the people. The education system that emerged made use of the modern totalitarian technique of utilizing education for political indoctrination, and in this Japan was decades ahead of Germany. Reischauer, however, saw in post-war Japan 'a champion of world peace and international trade'. At the same time he declared that the greatest failure of the American occupation authorities was their inability to contain Marxist influences in the press and universities, while the course of post-war Japanese politics was viewed largely as the continuation of pre-war tendencies such as the predominance of efficient civil bureaucracy. Reischauer's *Japan, the Story of a Nation* (New York, 1970; revised edn. 1974) is a more balanced work, drawing inspiration from Sansom's *History of Japan*. The book is divided into three equal parts: traditional Japan; modernization, which ends with the Second World War; and post-war Japan, the future role of which remains unpredictable.

There is some truth in John Dower's allegation in his 'E. H. Norman, Japan and the Use of History', an introduction to *Selected Writings of E. H. Norman* (New York, 1975), that the 'modernization theory' was produced by Reischauer as a new ideology with which to discredit Marxism, then still influential in Japanese historiography—a distant echo of the more virulent form of Cold War strategy called McCarthyism, to which E. H. Norman fell victim. (See Roger Bowen, *Innocence Is Not Enough: The Life and Death of Herbert Norman* (New York, 1986).

Continuity was given a new emphasis by Reischauer in his studies of modern Japanese history: Japan's past was presented as continuous economic expansion led by business interests working through the Diet, and its reversal by the military and even the war itself were depicted as mere deviations. The year 1960 was a crucial one in post-war Japanese historiography. As Reischauer himself writes in his autobiography, *My Life Between Japan and America* (New York, 1986), the 1960 Hakone Conference of American and Japanese historians, organized by John Hall, Marius Jansen, Don Shively, and others, led to a 'modernization controversy' that marked the beginning of a setback for Marxism in the Japanese historiography, while producing volumes of well-researched articles especially by the Americans. See Marius Jansen (ed.), *Changing Attitudes Toward Modernization* (Princeton, 1965); William W. Lockwood (ed.), *The State and Economic Enterprise in Japan* (Princeton, 1965); R. P. Dore (ed.), *Aspects of Social Change in Modern Japan* (Princeton, 1968); John W. Hall and Marius Jansen (eds.), *Studies in the Institutional History of Early Modern Japan* (Princeton, 1968); Donald H. Shively (ed.), *Tradition and Modernization in Japanese Culture* (Princeton, 1971). The Japanese participants in the Hakone talks tended to associate the process of modernization with the march of democracy and socialism, while Reischauer himself sought to dissociate modernization from value judgements about such matters as democracy or human rights, though the term implied an acceptance of the concept of progress, scientific methods, industrialization, urbanization, and centralization, themselves a set of values.

The last two volumes of the *Cambridge History of Japan* deal respectively with the nineteenth and the twentieth centuries of modern Japanese history. The volume for the nineteenth century (first published in 1989), edited by Marius Jansen, consists of twelve essays, each on a specific topic. The volume for the twentieth century (first published in 1988), edited by Peter Duus, contains fourteen essays. From the introductory essays for each volume it is possible to discern the views of the editors in assembling the essays by specialist historians in their respective fields. Marius Jansen, the author of *Sakamoto Ryoma and the Meiji Restoration* (Princeton, 1961; Stanford, 1971), an excellent study of that great political change written as a political biography of one of its most dedicated and versatile champions, now took up a definitely anti-Marxist stance: he held up the Bolshevik Revolution in Russia as one source which vitiated Marxist interpretations of the Meiji Restoration by Japanese historians, as they argued over whether it was the foreign capitalist threat to Japan or the development of modern capitalism in Japan that brought about the political change, of whether the Restoration was the product of an emperor-centred absolutism or a bourgeois revolution. Jansen, too, was of the view that the Hakone Conferences deserved special attention as they put an end to these 'sterile' Marxist arguments which had 'bedevilled' all political and economic discussions among Japanese intellectuals up to the 1950s. He also believed that modernization was a neutral term, although it entailed bureaucratization, the spread of education, more industrialization, and an acceptance of a world order based on a free-market economy. The rise of an expansionist empire was 'unforseen' and 'unfortunate'. The works of 'value-free analysis', however, failed to explain the negative aspects of the progress made, above all the rise of military fascism and the war itself. Jansen's smaller work, based on his lectures, *Japan and its World: Two Centuries of Change* (Princeton, 1980), perhaps is more valuable, as it faces the changes squarely and takes the side of peace, democracy, and the environment.

Peter Duus, the author of a book on Taisho democracy, *Party Rivalry and Political Change in Taisho Japan* (Cambridge, Mass., 1968) joins with the school of continuity against that of discontinuity, for he believes that the dividing-line of 1945 that separates 'Japan Incorporated' from the old imperial Japan had become blurred as time went on. Thus, modern Japanese history moves from the anticipation for autonomy to the assertion of 'complete autonomy' or 'anti-imperialist imperialism', then to dependence (under the American occupation), and from dependence again to an autonomy free from US tutelage and aspiring for international recognition. Military fascism in both Japan and Hitler's Germany is seen as the catalyst of the post-war new world order. As for post-war changes, 'many structural features once labeled as "backward" came to be regarded as the foundation of the ongoing "economic miracle"'. Value-free historians were apt to regard the 'economic miracle' as the final word on Japan and as something everlasting.

As for Japanese historiography, histories of Japan consisting of a dozen, sometimes over two-dozen volumes, involving nearly 100 authors, have begun to appear. *Iwanami Koza Nihon Rekishi* (Iwanami Lectures on History of Japan) (1st series, 23 vols., 1962–4; 2nd series, 26 vols., 1975–7) was matched or even superseded in popular appeal by a series published by Chuokoron, *Nihon no Rekishi* (History of Japan) (26 vols, 1973–4, a single author for each volume), followed by other series published by Yamakawa, Shogakkan, Tokyo University Press, and others. One of the latest series was twenty-five volumes of *Nihon Tsushi* (Complete History of Japan) (Tokyo, 1993–6) with a special emphasis on culture and society, again it is a collection of individual essays by numerous authors. The editors of *Nihon Tsushi* are more or less agreed on the decisive impact of 'Social History' on Japanese historiography, as an approach which broke Marxist historiography ('a theory of single linear development by stages', according to one of them) to pieces and drew attention away from the state and closer to the common people and to a nostalgia for their ancient roots. This change in Japanese historiography 'away from modernity' and from Marxism apparently took place in the 1970s when Japan, already a world economic power, grew content with its political and social setup (a conservative and predominantly middle-class society), which seemed to guarantee economic success for ever.

Apart from these collective efforts, which somewhat resemble durable consumer goods both in size and price, we have several outstanding works by single authors. One is Shuichi Kato, *A History of Japanese Literature* (3 vols., London, 1979), an intellectual history of Japan, the third volume of which, *The Modern Years*, is relevant to our purposes. Takafusa Nakamura, *Showashi* (A History of Showa) (Tokyo, 1993) is another valuable study.

The following are bibliographical notes on works in English on the history of modern Japan. For general and introductory works, apart from several already mentioned, the following are interesting and stimulating: John Whitney Hall, *Japan From Prehistory to Modern Times*, originallly published in German in 1968 (English edn., New York, 1970); Jean-Pierre Lehmann, *The Image of Japan From Feudal Isolation to World Power, 1850–1905* (London, 1978); and *The Roots of Modern Japan* (London, 1982); Mikiso Hane, *Modern Japan: A Historical Survey* (Boulder, 1986; 2nd edn., 1992); Janet E. Hunter, *The Emergence of Modern Japan: An Introductory History Since 1853* (London, 1989); W. G. Beasley, *The Rise of Modern Japan: Political, Economic and Social Change Since*

1850 (London, 1990; 2nd edn., 1995); Sir Sidney Giffard, *Japan Among the Powers 1890–1990* (New Haven, 1994); Ann Waswo, *Modern Japanese Society 1868–1994* (Oxford, 1996).

For Part I of this book the following works are to be recommended: Ryusaku Tsunoda, W. Theodore de Bary, and Donald Keene (eds.), *Sources of Japanese Tradition* (New York, 1958; 2 vol. edn., 1964) is most useful for most of the topics dealt with in this study. The main theme of the present work has been well discussed in Bob Tadashi Wakabayashi, *Anti-Foreignism and Western Learning in Early-Modern Japan: The New Theses of 1825* (Cambridge, Mass., 1986). This can be supplemented by J. Victor Koschmann, *The Mito Ideology: Discourse, Reform, and Insurrection in Late Tokugawa Japan 1790–1864* (Berkeley, 1987). The following list of books on the earlier history may be of use: G. R. Boxer, *The Christian Century in Japan* (Berkeley, 1951); Michael Cooper (ed.), *They Came to Japan: An Anthology of European Reports on Japan, 1543–1640* (Berkeley, 1965); George Alexander Lensen, *The Russian Push Toward Japan: Russo-Japanese Relations, 1697–1875* (Princeton, 1959); Charles David Sheldon, *The Rise of the Merchant Class in Tokugawa Japan, 1600–1868* (Locust Valley, New York, 1958); Herbert Bix, *Peasant Protest in Japan 1590–1884* (New Haven, 1986); Stephen Vlastos, *Peasant Protests and Uprisings in Tokugawa Japan* (Berkeley, 1986); Anne Walthall, *Social Protest and Popular Culture in Eighteenth-Century Japan* (Tucson, 1986); Anne Walthall (ed. and trans.), *Peasant Uprisings in Japan* (Chicago, 1991); Robert Bellah, *Tokugawa Religion, The Cultural Roots of Modern Japan* (New York, 1957; pbk. edn. 1985); Masao Maruyama, *Studies in the Intellectual History of Tokugawa Japan*, trans. Mikiso Hane (Tokyo, 1974); Kojiro Yoshikawa, *Jinsai, Sorai, Norinaga: Three Classical Philosophies of Mid-Tokugawa Japan* (Tokyo, 1983); Tetsuo Najita, *Visions of Virtue in Tokugawa Japan: The Kaitokudo or Merchant Academy of Osaka* (Chicago, 1987); Donald Keene, *The Japanese Discovery of Europe: Honda Toshiaki and Other Discoverers, 1720–1798* (London, 1952); Grant K. Goodman, *Japan: The Dutch Experience* (London, 1986); R. P. Dore, *Education in Tokugawa Japan* (London, 1965; pbk. edn., 1992); Conrad Totman, *Politics in the Tokugawa Bakufu 1600–1843* (Cambridge, Mass., 1967; pbk. edn., Berkeley, 1988); Conrad Totman, *Japan Before Perry, A Short History* (Berkeley, 1981).

For bakumatsu (end of Bakufu) Japan, Conrad Totman, *The Collapse of the Tokugawa Bakufu, 1862–1868* (Honolulu, 1980), Albert M. Craig, *Choshu in the Meiji Restoration* (Cambridge, Mass., 1961; 3rd printing, 1978), and H. D. Harootunian, *Toward Restoration: the Growth of Political Consciousness in Tokugawa Japan* (Berkeley, 1970) are perhaps essential. For international relations in the same period there is an interesting study: Grace Fox, *Britain and Japan, 1858–1883* (Oxford, 1969). W. G. Beasley's two works, new and old, are also to be consulted: *Great Britain and the Opening of Japan, 1834–1858* (London, 1951) and *Japan Encounters the Barbarian: Japanese Travellers in America and Europe* (New Haven, 1995). Between these two works appeared his major work: W. G. Beasley, *The Meiji Restoration* (Stanford, 1971). Equally valuable is Andrew Cobbing, *The Japanese Discovery of Victorian Britain* (London, 1998).

Various aspects of the restoration-reform were dealt with in a collection of essays: Marius B. Jansen and Gilbert Rosman (eds.), *Japan in Transition from Tokugawa to Meiji* (Princeton, 1986). There is a biography of Thomas Glover who assisted the Satsuma–Choshu forces prior to their successful *coup d'état*: Alexander McKay, *Scottish Samurai, Thomas Blake Glover 1838–1911* (Edinburgh, 1993). Sir Ernest Satow's memoirs, *A Diplomat in Japan*, originally published in 1921, republished with an introduction by Gordon Daniels (Oxford, 1968), gives a valuable insight into the restoration movement. We have an excellent concise economic history, G. C. Allen, *A Short Economic History of Modern Japan* (4th edn., London, 1981) and a specialist work, John G. Roberts, *Mitsui: Three Centuries of Japanese Business* (2nd edn., New York, 1989): each in its own way reveals economic and financial aspects of the restoration and a lot more in the longer period each deals with. Daikichi Irokawa, *The Culture of the Meiji Period*, trans. ed. by Marius B. Jansen (Princeton, 1985), examines Meiji culture in its many layers and ends with 'The Emperor System as a Spiritual Structure'. Among the Meiji men of enlightenment, Fukuzawa Yukichi wrote *An Outline of a Theory of Civilization* (orig. publ. 1875), trans. by Dilworth and Hurst (Sophia University Press, 1981); *The Autobiography of Fukuzawa Yukichi* (orig. publ. 1899), trans. by E. Kiyooka (Tokyo, 1981), and Carmen Blacker published a study of Fukuzawa under the title *The Japanese Enlightenment* (Cambridge, 1969). Chomin Nakae, *A Discourse of Three Drunkards on Government*, trans. by Nobuko Tsukui (New York, 1984), is entertaining as well as enlightening. There are other studies: Joseph Pittau, *Political Thought in Early Meiji Japan 1868–1889*, (Cambridge, Mass., 1967); Thomas Havens, *Nishi Amane and Modern Japanese Thought* (Princeton, 1970); *Meiroku Zasshi, Journal of the Japanese Enlightenment*, trans. with an introduction by William Reynolds Braisted (Tokyo, 1976). Tokutomi Soho, whose publishing office Minyusha (Friends of the People) was called Kanyusha (Friends of the Government Officials) by the opposition press at the time of the Hibiya riot of 1905, has attracted much attention: his early work *The Future Japan* was translated and edited by Vinh Sinh (Alberta, 1989); see also John D. Pierson, *Tokutomi Soho 1863–1957, A Journalist for Modern Japan* (Princeton, 1980). Uchimura Kanzo wrote his own autobiography in English: *How I Became a Christian* (1895; Kokubunkan edn., 1971), and there is a study of Uchimura's 'independent Christianity', Carlo Caldarola, *Christianity: The Japanese Way* (Leiden, 1979). For the radicalization of the Liberty and People's Right movement, see Roger Bowen, *Rebellion and Democracy in Meiji Japan* (Berkeley, 1980). The rise of nationalism in the mid-Meiji period is dealt with in Kenneth B. Pyle, *The New Generation in Meiji Japan, Problems of Cultural Identity, 1885–1895* (Stanford, 1969).

For the Meiji political leaders the following works are to be consulted: Kengi Hamada, *Prince Ito* [Hirobumi] (Tokyo, 1936; University Publications of America reprint, 1979); Roger F. Hackett, *Yamagata Aritomo in the Rise of Modern Japan, 1838–1922*, (Cambridge, Mass., 1971); Ivan Parker Hall, *Mori Arinori* (Cambridge, Mass., 1973). Okuma Shigenobu is perhaps best served by subsequent studies: Junesay Iddittie, *The Life of Marquis Shigenobu Okuma: A Biographical Study in the Rise of Democratic Japan* (Tokyo, 1956); Joyce C. Lebra, *Okuma Shigenobu, Statesman of Meiji Japan* (Canberra, 1973); and

Okuma himself compiled a collection of essays, a record of progress in Meiji, some written by former prime ministers and cabinet ministers: Count Shigenobu Okuma (ed.), *Fifty Years of New Japan*, English version ed. by Marcus B. Huish (London, 1910; Kraus reprint, New York, 1970). For the Meiji Constitution, see Hirobumi Ito, *Commentaries on the Constitution of the Empire of Japan*, trans. by Ito Miyoji (2nd edn. Tokyo, 1906), George M. Beckmann, *The Making of the Meiji Constitution: The Oligarchs and the Constitutional Development of Japan, 1868–1891* (Lawrence, Ka., 1957), and Carol Gluck, *Japan's Modern Myths: Ideology in the Late Meiji Period* (Princeton, 1985). For 'constitutional politics' in this period, see Junji Banno, *The Establishment of the Japanese Constitutional System*, trans. by J. A. A. Stockwin (London, 1992), and Andrew Fraser, R. H. P. Mason, and Philip Mitchell, *Japan's Early Parliaments, 1890–1905* (London, 1995).

There is a useful study of the Sino-Japanese War: Stewart Lone, *Japan's First Modern War: Army and Society in the Conflict with China, 1894–95* (London, 1994). The foreign minister Mutsu's memoirs are most valuable: Munemitsu Mutsu, *Kenkenroku: A Diplomatic Record of the Sino-Japanese War, 1894–95*, ed. and trans. Gordon Mark Berger (Tokyo, 1982). M. Frederick Nelson, *Korea and the Old Orders in Eastern Asia* (originally published by Louisiana State University Press, 1945, and reissued New York, 1967) is relevant to the central issue of the war. So is a more recent study, Hilary Conroy, *The Japanese Seizure of Korea, 1868–1910* (Philadelphia, 1960). See also C. I. Eugene Kim and Han-kyo Kim, *Korea and the Politics of Imperialism 1976–1910* (Berkeley, 1967) and Peter Duus, *The Abacus and the Sword: The Japanese Penetration of Korea*, (Berkeley, 1995).

For Meiji industrialization and its critics, see Richard J. Samuels, *The Business of the Japanese State* (Ithaca, NY, 1987); Stephen E. Marsland, *The Birth of the Japanese Labour Movement* (Honolulu, 1989); Hyman Kublin, *Asian Revolutionary: The Life of Sen Katayama* (Princeton, 1964); F. G. Notehelfer, *Kotoku Shusui, Portrait of a Japanese Radical* (Cambridge, 1971); E. Patricia Tsurumi, *Factory Girls: Women in the Tread Mills of Meiji Japan* (Princeton, 1990); Kenneth Strong, *Ox Against the Storm: A Biography of Tanaka Shozo, Japan's Conservationist Pioneer* (Tenterden, Kent, 1977). Kenneth Strong translated into English some of the Meiji-Taisho novels dealing with social issues such as Naoe Kinoshita, *Pillar of Fire* (London, 1972) and Toson Shimazaki, *The Broken Commandment* (Tokyo, 1974).

Part II of this study begins with the Russo-Japanese War, the background of which can be studied in Ian Nish, *The Origins of the Russo-Japanese War* (London, 1985) and *The Anglo-Japanese Alliance: The Diplomacy of Two Island Empires 1894–1903* (London, 1966); Shunpei Okamoto, *The Japanese Oligarchy and the Russo-Japanese War* (New York, 1970); James William Morley (ed.), *Japan's Foreign Policy 1686–1941: A Research Guide* (New York, 1974). As for Taisho politics and democracy, apart from Peter Duus's book cited above, the following works are to be consulted: Robert Scalapino, *Democracy and the Party Movement in Pre-war Japan: The Failure of the First Attempt* (Berkeley, 1953); Henry Dewitt Smith II, *Japan's First Student Radicals* (Cambridge, Mass., 1972); Stephen S.

Large, *The Rise of Labour In Japan: The Yuaikai, 1912–1919* (Tokyo, 1973); Michael Lewis, *Rioters and Citizens: Mass Protest in Imperial Japan* (Berkeley, 1990); Tetsuo Najita and J. Victor Koschmann (eds.), *Conflict in Modern Japanese History, The Neglected Tradition* (Princeton, 1982); Sharon H. Nolte, *Liberalism in Modern Japan: Ishibashi Tanzan and his Teachers, 1905–1960* (Berkeley, 1987). Mikiso Hane, *Peasants, Rebels, and Outcasts: The Underside of Modern Japan* (New York, 1982), a study of the underprivileged, covers a longer period. For Japan's military role in the First World War and after, see Charles B. Burdick, *The Japanese Siege of Tsingtau: World War I in Asia* (Hamden, Conn., 1976), and James William Morley, *The Japanese Thrust into Siberia 1918* (New York, 1954). Yoshitake Oka wrote two compact but outstanding political biographies: *Five Political Leaders of Modern Japan* (Tokyo, 1986), dealing with five prime ministers, Ito, Okuma, Hara, Inukai and Saionji, and *Konoe Fumimaro: A Political Biography* (Tokyo, 1983). Saionji, the last *genro*, has a full-size biography for himself: Leslie Connors, *The Emperor's Adviser: Saionji Kinmochi and Pre-war Japanese Politics* (London, 1987). For social thought and movements, see Saron L. Sievers, *Flower in Salt: The Beginnings of Feminist Consciousness in Modern Japan* (Stanford, 1983); Dorothy Robins-Mowry, *The Hidden Sun: Women of Modern Japan* (Boulder, Col., 1983); Thomas A. Stanley, *Osugi Sakae: Anarchist in Taisho Japan* (Cambridge, Mass., 1982); Gail Lee Bernstein, *Japanese Marxist: A Portrait of Kawakami Hajime, 1879–1946* (Cambridge, Mass., 1876); Robert Schildgen, *Toyohiko Kagawa, Apostle of Love and Social Justice* (Berkeley, 1988); Geroge B. Bikle, *The New Jerusalem: Aspects of Utopianism in the Thought of Kagawa Toyohiko* (Tuscon, 1976); Stephen S. Large, *Organized Workers and Socialist Politics in Interwar Japan* (Cambridge, 1981); George M. Beckmann and Okubo Genji, *The Japanese Communist Party, 1922–1945* (Stanford, 1969); G. O. Totten, *The Social-Democratic Movement in Prewar Japan* (New Haven, 1966); John Crump, *The Origins of Socialist Thought in Japan* (London, 1983); two books by Sheldon Caron, *The State and Labor in Modern Japan* (Berkeley, 1987), and *Molding Japanese Minds: The State in Everyday Life* (Princeton, 1997). For Nitobe Inazo, a scholar-diplomat, there is a collection of essays: John F. Howes (ed.), *Nitobe Inazo: Japan's Bridge Across the Pacific* (Boulder, Col., 1995); this ought to be supplemented by a critical study: Eiiichiro Uchikawa, *Nitobe Inazo: The Twilight Years*, trans. Michael Newton (Tokyo, 1985).

For the pre-war economic history Takafusa Nakamura, *Economic Growth in Prewar Japan* (New Haven, 1971), is useful. Chalmers Johnson, *MITI and the Japanese Miracle: The Growth of Industrial Policy, 1925–1975* (Stanford, 1982; Tuttle edn. 1986, 1992), emphasizes the pre-war economic bureaucracy. See also Mikio Sumiya and Koji Taira (eds.), *An Outline of Japanese Economic History 1603–1940* (Tokyo, 1979), and Koji Taira, *Economic Development and the Labor Market in Japan* (New York, 1970). Japanese imperialism assumed a growing importance and has been the theme of many analytical as well as descriptive studies. The following are some of the important contributions: W. G. Beasley, *Japanese Imperialism 1894–1945* (Oxford, 1987); Akira Iriye, *After Imperialism: The Search for a New Order in the Far East 1921–1931*, (Cambridge, Mass., 1965); Ian Nish, *Japan's Struggle with Internationalism: Japan, China and the*

League of Nations, 1931–3 (London, 1993). Marius B. Jansen, *The Japanese and Sun Yat-Sen* (Cambridge, Mass., 1954), provides an interesting side-view. John Dower, *Empire and Aftermath: Yoshida Shigeru and the Japanese Experiences, 1879–1954* (Cambridge, Mass., 1988), is an excellent study of a hawkish diplomat and post-war liberal prime minister. Peter Duus, Ramon H. Myers, and Mark R. Peattie (eds.), *The Japanese Informal Empire in China, 1895–1937* (Princeton, 1989), contains thirteen essays by different authors. Harumi Goto-Shibata, *Japan and Britain in Shanghai, 1925–31* (London, 1995), presents excellent results of hard research. The rise of the military has been studied by Richard J. Smethurst, *A Social Basis for Prewar Japanese Militarism: The Army and the Rural Community* (Berkeley, 1974), and William Fitch Morton, *Tanaka Giichi and Japan's China Policy* (Folkestone, Kent, 1980); Ivan Morris (ed.), *Japan 1831–1945: Militarism, Fascism, Japanism?* (Lexington, Mass., 1963); O. Tanin and E. Yohan, *Militarism and Fascism in Japan*, with an introduction by Karl Radek (London, 1934; Greenwood reprint, 1973); Ben-Ami Shillony, *Revolt in Japan: The Young Officers and the February 26, 1936 Incident* (Princeton, 1973); Mark R. Peattie, *Ishiwara Kanji and Japan's Confrontation with the West* (Princeton, 1975); Robert Butow, *Tojo and the Coming of the War* (Princeton, 1961).

For the study of Japanese fascism, in addition to Richard Storry's *Double Patriots* already cited, the following books are useful: Thomas R. H. Havens, *Farm and Nation in Modern Japan: Agrarian Nationalism, 1870–1940* (Princeton, 1974); George M. Wilson, *Radical Nationalist in Japan: Kitta Ikki* (Cambridge, Mass., 1869); Masao Maruyama, *Thought and Behaviour in Modern Japanese Politics*, ed. Ivan Morris (Oxford, 1963; expanded edn. 1969).

One Japanese publication is almost essential to a study of modern Japanese history. Misuzu-shobo, a Tokyo publisher, undertook the publication of *Gendaishi Shiryo* (Sources of Modern History), 45 vols., (1962–76), dealing with the Richard Sorge Spy Affair (vols. 1–3, 24), the Nationalist movement (vols. 4–5, 23), the Kanto Earthquake and the Koreans (vol. 6), the Manchurian Incident (vols. 6, 11), Japan's war against China (vols. 8–10, 12–13), the Socialist movement (vols. 14–20), Taiwan (vols. 21–2), Korea (vols. 25–30), the Manchurian Railway (vols. 31–3), the Pacific War (vols. 34–6, 38–9), the General Headquarters (vol. 37), thought control (vol. 42), media control (vols. 40–1), national mobilization (vols. 43–4), and The Public Order Preservation Act (vol. 45).

'The Confessions of the Emperor Showa', *Bungei-Shunju* 68:13 (Dec. 1990) will be a useful source, if used critically.

For more details about Emperor Hirohito, see Stephen S. Large, *Emperor Hirohito and Showa Japan: A Political Biography* (London, 1992); Edward Behr, *Hirohito Behind the Myth* (New York, 1989); Kiyoko Takeda, *The Emperor System in Modern Japan*, The Richard Storry Memorial Lecture No. 3 (Oxford: St Antony's College, 1989); Carol Gluck and Stephen R. Graubard (eds.), *Showa: The Japan of Hirohito* (New York, 1992); David Anson Titus, *Palace and Politics in Prewar Japan* (New York, 1974).

Ian Nish, *Japanese Foreign Policy 1869–1942: Kasumigaseki to Miyakezaka*

(London, 1977), covers the whole period from Meiji to Showa. For thirteen years preceding Pearl Harbor there are five volumes of edited translations by James William Morley of a seven-volume study of *Taiheiyo Senso eno Michi* (The Road to the Pacific War), edited by the Japanese Association on International Relations and published by the Asahishinbun (1962–3). These, all published by the Columbia University Press, are *Japan Erupts: The London Naval Conference and the Manchurian Incident, 1928–1932* (1984); *The China Quagmire: Japan's Expansion on the Asian Continent, 1933–1941* (1983); *Deterrent Diplomacy: Japan, Germany, and the U.S.S.R., 1935–1940* (1976); *The Fateful Choice: Japan's Advance into Southeast Asia, 1939–1941* (1976); *The Final Confrontation: Japan's Negotiations with the United States, 1941* (1994). Joseph C. Grew (US ambassador to Japan, 1932–42), *Ten Years in Japan* (New York, 1944) is useful.

For the Asia-Pacific War or the Pacific War itself, the following can be consulted: Saburo Ienaga, *Japan's Last War: World War II and the Japanese, 1931–1945* (Oxford, 1979); Akira Iriye, *Power and Culture: The Japanese–American War 1941–1945* (Cambridge, Mass., 1981); Merion and Susie Harries, *Soldiers of the Sun: The Rise and Fall of the Imperial Japanese Army* (New York, 1991); Arthur J. Marder, Mark Jacobsen, and John Horsfield, *Old Friends New Enemies: The Royal Navy and the Imperial Japanese Navy* (Oxford, 1990); John Costello, *The Pacific War* (New York, 1981). The following are some of the studies of particular battles and campaigns: Alvin Coox, *Nomonhan: Japan against Russia, 1939* (Stanford, 1985; pbk edn. 1990); Eric Hammel, *Guadalcanal: Starvation Island* (New York, 1987); Louis Allen, *Burma: The Longest War 1941–45* (London, 1984); Simon Foster, *Okinawa 1945: Final Assault on the Empire* (London, 1994); Sheldon H. Harris, *Factories of Death: Japanese Biological Warfare, 1932–45, and the American Cover-up* (London, 1994). See also General Douglas MacArthur, *Reminiscences* (New York, 1964; Da Capo pbk., 1964).

Part III of this study deals with 'Reconstruction and Reorganization' in the post-war years. Japan had to settle accounts with her war responsibilities. For the Tokyo War Crimes Trial, see: Richard H. Minear, *Victors' Justice: The Tokyo War Crimes Trial* (Princeton, 1971; Tuttle pbk. edn. 1972); John Pritchard, *An Overview of the Historical Importance of the Tokyo War Trial* (Oxford, 1987); Philip R. Piccigallo, *The Japanese on Trial* (Austin, Tex., 1979); Chihiro Hosoya *et al.* (eds.), *The Tokyo War Crimes Trial: An International Symposium* (Tokyo, 1986); B. V. A. Rölling and Antonio Cassese, *The Tokyo Trial and Beyond* (Cambridge, 1993).

Yet Japan's post-war itself has become a subject of historical study. *Vide* Paul J. Bailey, *Postwar Japan, 1945 to the Present* (Oxford, 1996); John W. Dower, *Japan in War and Peace* (New York, 1993); Andrew Gordon (ed.), *Postwar Japan as History* (Berkeley, 1993); Mikiso Hane, *Eastern Phoenix: Japan Since 1945* (Boulder, Col., 1996). For post-war economic history, see Takafusa Nakamura, *The Postwar Japanese Economy: Its Development and Structure, 1937–1994* (2nd edn., Tokyo, 1995), and Shigeto Tsuru, *Japan's Capitalism: Creative Defeat and Beyond* (Cambridge, 1993; pbk. edn. 1994).

For an understanding of the changing nature of the American occupation of Japan, Theodore Cohen, *Remaking Japan: The American Occupation as New*

Deal, ed. Herbert Passin (New York, 1987), is a valuable contribution. Equally useful are Robert A. Fearey, *The Occupation of Japan: Second Phase, 1948–50* (New York, 1950); Mark Gayn, *Japan Diary* (New York, 1948; Tuttle edn., 1981); Grant K. Goodman, *The American Occupation of Japan: A Retrospective View* (Lawrence, Ka., 1968); Howard B. Schonberger, *Aftermath of War: Americans and the Remaking of Japan, 1945–1952* (Kent, Ohio, 1989); Robert E. Ward and Yoshikazu Sakamoto (eds.), *Democratizing Japan: The Allied Occupation* (Honolulu, 1987); Ian Nish (ed.), *The Occupation of Japan 1945–1952* (London, 1991); Justin Williams, *Japan's Political Revolution Under MacArthur* (Tokyo, 1979); Michael Schaller, *The American Occupation of Japan: The Origins of the Cold War in Asia* (Oxford, 1985). R. P. Dore, *Land Reform in Japan* (Oxford, 1959), is an almost classic study. Eleanor M. Hadley, *Antitrust in Japan* (Princeton, 1970) and Michael D. Stephens, *Japan and Education* (London, 1991) are also useful.

From a sociological and cultural viewpoint the following are useful: Ruth Benedict, *The Chrysanthemum and the Sword: Patterns of Japanese Culture* (1946; Tuttle edn., 1954); Chie Nakane, *Japanese Society* (Harmondsworth, 1973); and Tadashi Fukutake, *The Japanese Social Structure: Its Evolution in the Modern Century*, trans. Ronald P. Dore (Tokyo, 1982; 2nd edn., 1989); these help explain the peculiarities of Japanese society. These peculiarities, presented as 'unique' to Japan as an economic power, were critically examined by Peter N. Dale, *The Myth of Japanese Uniqueness* (London, 1986).

For other topics of post-war history, see Gordon Daniels and Reinhard Drifte (eds.), *Europe and Japan: Changing Relationship Since 1945* (Ashford, 1986); Ronald Dore, *Flexible Rigidities: Industrial Policy and Structural Adjustment in the Japanese Economy, 1970–80* (London, 1986); Rokuro Hidaka (ed.), *The Price of Affluence: Dilemma of Contemporary Japan* (Tokyo, 1984); J. Victor Koschmann (ed.), *Authority and the Individual in Japan: Citizen Protest in Historical Perspective* (Tokyo, 1978); James H. Buck (ed.), *The Modern Japanese Military System* (Sage Publications, 1975); George R. Packard, *Protest in Tokyo: The Security Treaty Crisis of 1960* (Princeton, 1966); John Jonathan, *Mishima: A Biography* (Tokyo, 1974); Robert A. Scalapino and Junnosuke Masumi, *Parties and Politics in Contemporary Japan* (Berkeley, 1971); Haruo Shimada, *Japan's 'Guest Workers'* (Tokyo, 1989); Arthur Stockwin, *The Japanese Socialist Party and Neutralism* (Melbourne, 1968) and *Japan: Divided Politics in a Growth Economy* (2nd edn., London, 1982); Nathaniel Thayer, *How the Conservatives Rule?* (Princeton, 1969); Frank K. Upham, *Law and Social Change in Postwar Japan* (Cambridge, Mass., 1987); Osamu Watanabe, *Nakasone Yasuhiro and Post-war Conservative Politics: An Historical Interpretation* (Oxford: Nissan Occasional Paper, no. 18, 1993); Karel van Wolfren, *The Enigma of Japanese Power* (London, 1989); Kosaku Yoshino, *Cultural Nationalism in Contemporary Japan* (London, 1992).

Among books dealing with current social issues the following deserve special attention: David E. Kaplan and Allec Dubro, *Yakuza: The Explosive Account of Japan's Criminal Underworld* (Reading, Mass., 1986) and David E. Kaplan and Andrew Marshall, *The Cult of the End of the World: The Incredible Story of Aum* (London, 1996).

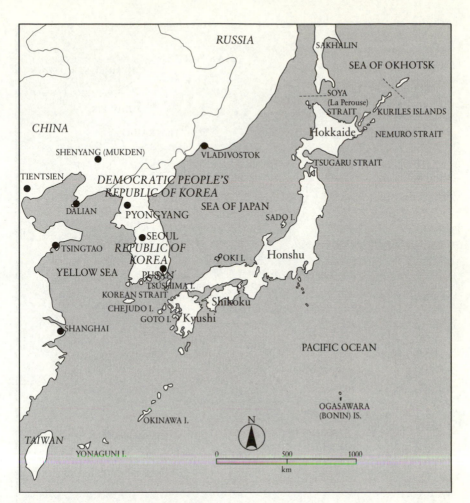

RUSSIA

SAKHALIN

SEA OF OKHOTSK

CHINA

SHENYANG (MUKDEN)

VLADIVOSTOK

SOYA
(La Perouse)
STRAIT

KURILES ISLANDS

Hokkaide

NEMURO STRAIT

TIENTSIEN

DEMOCRATIC PEOPLE'S
REPUBLIC OF KOREA

SEA OF JAPAN

TSUGARU STRAIT

DALIAN

PYONGYANG

SADO I.

TSINGTAO

SEOUL

REPUBLIC OF
KOREA

OKI I.

Honshu

YELLOW SEA

PUSAN

TSUSHIMA I.

KOREAN STRAIT

Shikoku

CHEJUDO I.

GOTO I.

Kyushi

SHANGHAI

PACIFIC OCEAN

OKINAWA I.

OGASAWARA
(BONIN) IS.

N

TAIWAN

YONAGUNI I.

0   500   1000

km

MAP 1. Japan and her Neighbours

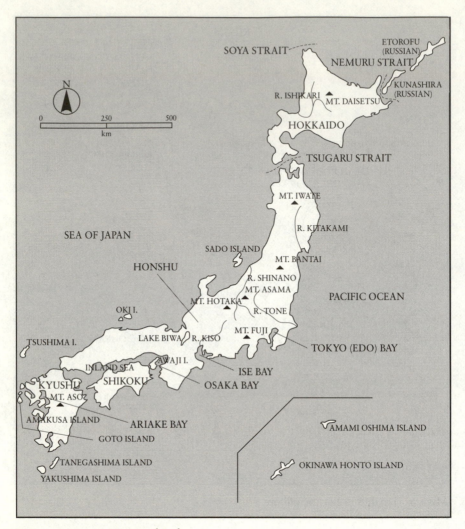

MAP 2. Japan—Geographical

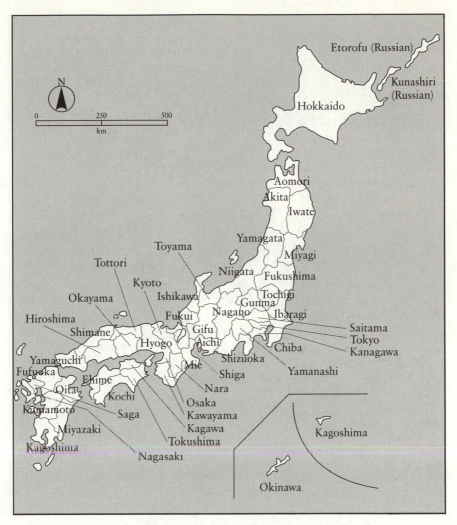

MAP 3. Japan—Prefectual

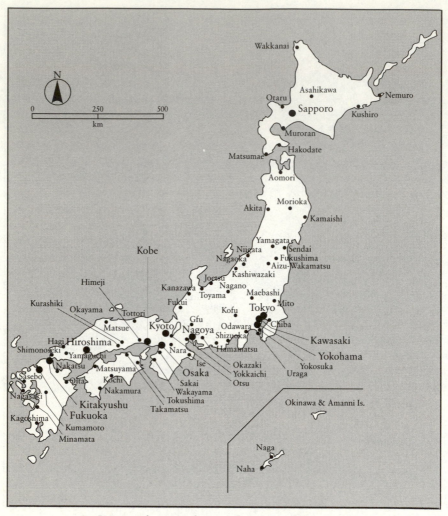

● Cities with a population of over 1 million in 1995

MAP 4. Japan—Urban

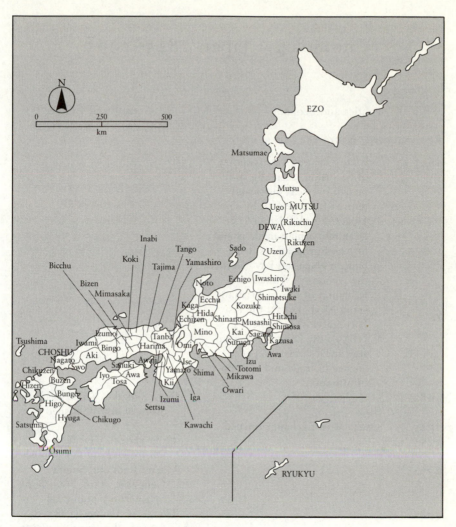

MAP 5. Pre-Meiji Provinces (Kuni or Han)

Chronology: Japan 1825–1995

Politics and Economy	Society and Culture

Relevant events before 1825

1635–41   *Sakoku* (closure of the country or Seclusion) formally completed: overseas visits and returns from abroad by the Japanese forbidden (1635); Deshima, a man-made island for the European residents built in Nagasaki Bay (1636); the Amakusa–Shimabara Rebellion of local Christians suppressed (1637); the last Portuguese ships expelled (1639); the Dutch allowed to stay at Deshima (1641) to engage in trade and to supply information

1682   Ihara Saikaku, *Japan's Family Store-House* published

1725   Osaka Rice Exchange opened

1755   Ando Shoeki, *The Way of Nature and Labour* published

1774   Maeno Ryotaku, Sugita Genpaku, *et al., New Book of Anatomy* published

1783   The great Tenmei (1781–8) famine: the eruption of Mt Asama (1783) causes a famine accompanied by rural uprisings and urban unrest

1792   A Russian expeditionary ship led by Adam Laxman comes to Ezo (Hokkaido), bringing back Daikokuya Kodayu, a Japanese castaway

1798   Honda Toshiaki, *Tales of the West* published

1806–7	Russian attacks on Japanese settlements in Sakhalin and Etorofu
1808	A British ship *Paeton* enters Nagasaki Bay in an operation against Dutch ships
1823	
1824	British crew of a whaling ship found on the coast near Mito asking for food and water: 300 fishermen arrested for trading with the British

1823 — Sato Nobuhiro, *Secret Policy of Intermixing*

From Seclusion to Expansion, 1825–1900

1825	Edict to Expel Foreign Ships 'without second thought' issued by the Bakufu

1825 — Aizawa Seishisai in support of the edict writes *New Thesis*, 'a bible' to the activists in the movement to 'revere the emperor and expel the barbarians'

1828–9	Franz von Siebold, physician to the Dutch Factory, arrested and expelled for obtaining a map of Japan, Ezo, and Sakhalin

1829 — Katsushika Hokusai, *36 scenes of Mt. Fuji* completed

1837	Unsuccessful attempts made by the American ship *Morrison* to deliver Japanese castaways near Edo and Kagoshima

1838 — Takano Choei writes *A Dream Tale*, Watanabe Kazan *Cautious Arguments*, both criticizing Bakufu policy of affronting western powers

1839	Takano and Watanabe arrested
1839–42	The Anglo-Chinese Opium War: its outbreak reported by a Dutch ship to the Nagasaki magistrate (1840)

1842 The 1825 Edict to Expel Foreign Ships withdrawn

1844 Dutch government urges 'the King of Japan' to open the country so as to avoid another Opium War

1845–52 American, French, British, and Russian warships and other vessels actively engaged in Japanese waters

1853 Arrival at Edo Bay of US East India Squadron under Commodore Perry with President Filmer's letter requesting 'friendly commercial intercourse' with Japan; Perry chooses to withdraw his fleet; President's letter hotly discussed among Japan's feudal lords

 12th Tokugawa shogun Ieyoshi dies; his son Iesada becomes 13th shogun

1854 Perry returns with a stronger fleet to Edo Bay; treaty for peace and amity concluded (Kanagawa Treaty); similar treaties concluded with Britain and Russia

      Yoshida Shoin, Choshu samurai, fails in an attempt to stow away on Perry's ship

1855 Bakufu receives from the Dutch king a steamship later named *Kankomaru* and opens a naval college at Nagasaki

1856 Arrival at Shimoda of Townsend Harris, first US consul

1858 Ii Naosuke becomes Great Councillor of Bakufu; believing national security to be more important than emperor's wishes, he signs Treaty of Amity and Commerce with USA; followed by similar treaties with Holland,

Russia, Britain, and France
acknowledging regulative
tariff and extraterritorial
rights for the foreigners
(unequal treaties)

Ii's handling of shogunal
succession by choosing a
young heir of a collateral
Tokugawa family as 14th
shogun Iemochi increases his
unpopularity

Fukuzawa Yukichi opens a han
school for Dutch studies in
Edo (origins of Keio
University)

1858–9 'Ansei purge' involves imprisonment and execution of Ii's
critics

1860 Ii assassinated by Mito and
Satsuma samurai

First mission sent to America,
one party to San Francisco on
board a Japanese ship
manned by Japanese crew, the
other to Washington to ratify
the treaty

At three open ports, Kanagawa,
Nagasaki, and Hakodate, free
trade is permitted with five
treaty powers

Emperor Komei allows his
daughter to marry shogun
Iemochi on condition that
Bakufu should repudiate the
treaties (the marriage takes
place in 1862)

1861–2 Attacks on foreigners rampant;
an English merchant slain by
Satsuma samurai at
Namamugi near Yokohama
(Namamugi Affair, 1862)

1862 Bakufu students, Nishi Amane,
Tsuda Mamichi, Enomoto
Takeaki, sent to Europe

1863 Bakufu obliged to comply with
the court's wishes by naming

the day of expulsion of
foreigners
Choshu forts at Shimonoseki
attack American, French, and
Dutch ships and are quelled
by US and French warships
and French marine
British fleet shells Kagoshima as
an act of retribution for the
Namamugi Affair
Kobu-gattai (union of court and
Bakufu) advocates temporarily placed in power in the
court

Five Choshu students including
Ito Hirobumi and Inoue
Kaoru sent to England to
study

1864   Choshu troops repulsed in
Kyoto (*Kinmon no Hen*)
First Choshu Expedition
launched by Bakufu with an
imperial order
Combined fleet of Britain, USA,
Holland, and France attack
and destroy Choshu forts at
Shimonoseki; peace treaty
concluded puts an end to *joi*
in Choshu

1865   Choshu prepares for war with
Bakufu
Commercial treaties approved
by the emperor

Fifteen Satsuma samurai,
including Mori Arinori, sent
to England to study

1866   Anti-Bakufu alliance formed
between Choshu and Satsuma
Second Choshu Expedition
resulting in defeat for Bakufu
forces
Death of Shogun Iemochi;
Tokugawa Keiki (Yoshinobu)
becomes 15th shogun

Fukuzawa Yukichi, *Conditions
of the West*

1867	Death of Emperor Komei; succeeded by his son Mutsuhito	
	Keiki proposes to return Bakufu's power to the throne	
	War against the Bakufu secretly prepared by the court, Satsuma, and Choshu	
	Hyogo (Kobe) and Osaka opened (7/12 lunar calendar, 1 Jan. 1868)	
	Imperial Restoration proclaimed (9/12 lunar calendar, 3 Jan. 1868)	
	The first western-style spinning-mill established at Kagoshima	
1868–9	Boshin Civil War; Bakufu forces defeated at the Battle of Toba-Fushimi (January 1868), Keiki's retirement to Mito putting an end to Tokugawa Bakufu (April 1868), 33 han in north-east Japan resisting the imperial army, Enomoto Takeaki's 'Ezo Republic' surrenders (May 1869)	
1868	Charter Oath announced (March)	
	Edo renamed Tokyo; Edo Castle becomes Imperial Palace; Meiji adopted as era name	
		The new government, committed to Shintoism, harasses Buddhist temples
1869	Emperor moves to Tokyo (March)	
		A Shintoist shrine opened in Tokyo to enshrine those killed on the government side in the Boshin War (renamed Yasukuni Shrine in 1879)
		Over 3,000 Nagasaki Christians deported
1870		Kato Hiroyuki writes *General Principles of True Politics*, a Lockian treatise

1871   Han domains abolished and
        replaced by 'Ken' (pre-
        fectures) in new local govern-
        ment system
        Sino-Japanese Friendship Treaty
        signed
        Iwakura Embassy sent to
        America and Europe to
        negotiate treaty revision and
        to study western civilization
        on the spot (returns in 1873)
        New Currency Act adopted with
        one yen for one ryo

                                    Old social statuses replaced by
                                    new system: titled aristo-
                                    crats, old samurai, commoners,
                                    and new commoners (old
                                    underprivileged and dis-
                                    criminated people)

1872   Promulgation of Education Act
        aiming at establishment of
        universal national education
        Railway service started between
        Shinbashi and Yokohama
        Government's model silk spin-
        ning-mill opened at Tomioka
        An imperial edict turns the
        kingdom of Ryukyu into
        Okinawa Han which becomes
        Okinawa Ken in 1875
        An edict for national conscrip-
        tion issued
        Gregorian calendar adopted:
        3rd day of 12th month
        becomes 1 January 1873 (6th
        year of Meiji)

                                    Publication of Fukuzawa,
                                    Encouragement of Learning
                                    begins
                                    Tokyo *Nichi Nichi Shinbun*
                                    founded

1873   Land tax reform: private land-
        ownership created, tenancy
        system left untouched
        Council of State decides to send
        Saigo Takamori on a mission

to Korea to break Korean
insistence on seclusion; the
decision rescinded when
Iwakura embassy returns;
Saigo and his allies (including
Itagaki Taisuke) resign from
government (*Seikanron*
defeated)

1874 Itagaki and others form the
Party of Patriots and present
the Memorial for Popular
Assembly (beginning of *Jiyu
Minken* movement)
Risshisha set up in Kochi by
Itagaki
Punitive expedition carried out
against Formosa on the pre-
text of Ryukyu fishermen
having been murdered by
Taiwan tribesmen
Mitsubishi Trading Company,
entrusted with government
transport ships for Formosan
expedition, becomes
Mitsubishi Shipping Com-
pany (1875)

Mori Arinori and others found
Meiroku (Meiji 6th Year)
Society and start *Meiroku
Journal*, first liberal political
forum

1875 Treaty concluded with Russia
for exchange of Sakhalin (to
Russia) with Kuriles (to
Japan)
Three Japanese warships bom-
bard Korean shore battery on
Kanghwa Island

Fukuzawa, *Outline of Civilization*

1876 Japan's gunboat diplomacy
resulting in Kanghwa Treaty
with three Korean ports
opened
Mitsui Bank and Mitsui Trading
Company founded

1877	Seinan Civil War: Saigo's forces, discontented former samurai, defeated by the government army of conscripts	
		Tokyo University established
1878	Takehashi Incident, a mutiny in the imperial guard at Takehashi, Tokyo	
		College of Technology opened
1879		*Asahi Shinbun* founded in Osaka
1878–80	Ueki Emori and others revitalize the Party of Patriots which develops into the Alliance to Promote a National Diet (1880)	
1881	Altogether 39 private draft constitutions published this year	
	Okuma Shigenobu's memorandum for British system of constitutional government results in his forced retirement from government	
	Government announces its decision to open a national assembly in 1890 and to prepare a constitution in the meantime	
	Jiyuto (Liberal Party) formed with Itagaki as president	
	Mitsubishi acquires Takashima coal mine once owned by government	
		Toyo Jiyu Shinbun (Oriental Free Press) founded with Nakae Chomin as editor
		Genyosha (Korean Strait Society) formed by Toyama Mitsuru
1882	Rescript to Soldiers and Sailors (*Gunjin Chokuyu*) issued	
	Departure of Ito Hirobumi for Europe to study constitutional principles and practices	
	Rikken Kaishinto formed with	

Okuma Shigenobu as
president
Fukushima Incident: Aizu
liberals attack a local police
station
Bank of Japan established

Chomin translates Rousseau's
Social Contract

1883   Ito returns from Europe, having
studied under Rudolf von
Gneist and Lorenz von Stein

Baba Tatsui writes *Tenpu
Jinken Ron* (Rights of Man)

1884   Peers Decree issued, creating
prince, marquis, count,
viscount, and baron
Chichibu Incident or peasant
war involving over 10,000
local people, some organized
in Konminto (Party of
Sufferers)

Rokumeikan bazaars and dance
parties started

1884–5   Failure of Seoul uprising of
progressive Koreans, some
trained in Japan; tension rises
between Japanese and
Chinese troops stationed in
Seoul; Tientsin Treaty signed
(1885) to avoid possible
military confrontation

1885   Osaka Incident: arrest at Osaka
of Oi Kentaro and other
Minken activists for amassing
weapons to help Korean
progressives
Nihon Yusen Kaisha (NYK)
(Japan Mailship Company)
formed by Mitsubishi Shipping Company and one other
Cabinet system introduced with
Ito Hirobumi as prime minister

Fukuzawa Yukichi writes
'Datsua-ron' (Exit Asia, Enter
Europe) in his journal
Jiji-shinpo

1886	Educational reform introduced under Mori Arinori, minister of education with 'imperial university' (former Tokyo University), schools for primary and secondary education, and normal schools	
		Tokutomi Soho publishes *The Future Japan*
1887	Government-owned shares of NYK transferred to Imperial Household	
	Osaka Boseki, first steam-powered cotton-spinning mill, founded	
	Minken democrats present Three Great Propositions, including freedom of speech	
	570 'undesirable' people expelled from Tokyo under the Public Order Preservation Ordinance	
		Nakae Chomin writes *Discourse by Three Drunkards on Government*
1888	Privy Council created, with Ito as president, and examines draft constitution	
	State-owned Miike coalmines sold to Mitsui Coal Mining Company	
		Nipponjin (fortnightly) founded by Shiga Shigetaka, Miyake Setsurei, and Kuga Katsunan
		Tokyo Asahi Shinbun founded
		Osaka Mainichi Shinbun started
1889	The Constitution of Empire of Great Japan promulgated (11 February)	
	Mori Arinori assassinated (11 February)	

Okuma, foreign minister,
attacked and seriously
wounded by a member of
Genyosha for his handling of
treaty revision (October)

Kuga Katsunan founds daily
Nippon

1890   At the first general election
Jiyuto and *Kaishinto* win a
majority (July)
Imperial Rescript on Education
issued (October)
Adoption of Civil Code
postponed

1891

Tanaka Shozo brings to the
notice of the Diet the pollution caused by Ashio copper
mine
Uchimura Kanzo forced to
resign from the First High
School for insufficient
courtesy shown during the
reading of the Imperial
Rescript on Education (*Lèse
Majestè* Incident)

1892   Violent intervention in the
second general election
directed by home minister
Shinagawa Yajiro
Oi Kentaro forms *Toyo Jiyuto*
(Oriental Liberal Party)

1894   Trade and Navigation Treaty
signed with Britain abolishing
extraterritorial rights and
rearranging custom duties;
similar treaties signed with
USA, Italy, Russia, Germany,
and France by 1897; revised
treaties enforced in 1899;
tariff autonomy attained in
1911
Tonghak rebellion in Korea
occasions the dispatch of
Chinese troops and the issue
of Korean reform gives excuse
for Japan to send troops to

Korea and declare war on
China in August

Pyongyang occupied and
China's North Sea fleet vir-
tually destroyed (September);
Port Arthur captured
(November)

Emperor moves to Hiroshima
for duration of war followed
by Diet

1895   Shimonoseki Peace Treaty concluded with Chinese stipulating recognition of Korean
independence, cession to
Japan part of Liaotung
peninsula and Taiwan, a
liberal war indemnity, and so
on (17 April)

Japan accepts German, Russian,
and French demand for
Liaotung peninsula to be
given up (4 May)

War to subdue Taiwan begins
and lasts till 1902

Japanese minister to Korea and
his subordinates carry out the
murder of pro-Russian Queen
Min (October)

Toyo Keizai Shinpo (Oriental
Economist) founded

Foreign minister, Mutsu
Munemitsu finishes writing
Ken Ken Roku (Record of
Worries and Endeavours)

1896   Yamagata–Lobanov protocol
permitting Russia and Japan
to keep equal numbers of
troops in Korea

1897   Gold Standard adopted on the
strength of war indemnity
from China

Katayama Sen becomes director
of Kingsley Hall, Tokyo

Takano Fusataro, *Summons to
Workers*

Takano forms Association for
Promoting Trade Unions
Katayama helps Tekko Kumiai
(Iron Workers Union)
Shakaiseisaku Gakkai (Social
Policy Association) founded
Kyoto Imperial University
founded

1898   *Jiyuto* and *Shinpoto* (former
        Kaishinto) merge and form
        Keinseito (Constitutional
        Politics Party)
        Ito, *genro*, converted to party
        politics, allows *Kenseito* to
        form government with
        Okuma as prime minister
        Germany secures lease of
        Kiaochow and Russia that of
        Port Arthur and Tailenwan
        Nishi-Rosen agreement fails to
        satisfy Japanese formula of
        Mankan-kokan (exchange of
        Manchuria with Korea)
        Civil Code along German lines
        enacted

Toa Dobunkai (East Asia
Common Letter Society)
founded by Konoe Atsumaro
Shakaishugi Kenkyukai (Society
for Study of Socialism)
formed by Christian social-
ists, including Katayama
Yokoyama Gennosuke, *The
Low Strata of Society in
Japan*

1899

Road to Catastrophe, 1900–1945

1900   Japan sends largest contingent
        of troops to protect foreign
        legations during Boxer
        Rebellion
        Association to Promote Univer-
        sal Suffrage submits petition
        to the Diet
        Public Order Police Act enforced
        Industrial Union Act

adopted to protect small
landowners-farmers

Ito Hirobumi sets up *Rikken
Seiyukai* (Friends of Consti-
tutional Politics), absorbing
Jiyuto

Ito forms first *Seiyukai* government

1901　Government's Yawata Steel Mill
starts operation

Kokuryukai (Amur River
Society) formed by Uchida
Ryohei

Social Democratic Party formed
but at once suppressed

Aikokufujinkai (Patriotic
Women's Association)
started

1902　Anglo-Japanese Alliance signed
in London (January)

Kotoku Shusui publishes
*Imperialism: Monster of the
20th Century*

1903　Ito succeeded by Saionji
Kinmochi as president of
Seiyukai

Russia fails to keep her promise
to China to withdraw troops
from Manchuria

Seven pro-war professors urge
strong policy against Russia

Ministry of Agriculture and
Commerce (Section for
Commerce and Manufacture)
compiles *Conditions of
Mechanics*

Weekly *Heimin Shinbun*
(People's Newspaper) started
by Kotoku and others

1904　Japan declares war on Russia
(February): army advances
into southern Manchuria;
Port Arthur captured with
great sacrifice (Russians surrender in January 1905)

Anti-war campaign pursued by
Heimin Shinbun

1905   Seoul–Pusan railway opened
(January)
Japanese win Battle of Mukden
(March); in naval battle in
Tsushima Strait Russian
Baltic Fleet annihilated (May)
Peace treaty concluded at
Portsmouth, New Hampshire
(August), gives Japan south-
ern Sakhalin, Port Arthur,
Tailen and railway in south-
ern Manchuria but no
indemnities
Riot at Hibiya Park, Tokyo,
against terms of peace
(September) develops into a
nationwide movement
Anglo-Japanese Alliance
extended as a defensive and
offensive agreement empha-
sizing Japan's 'paramount'
interest in Korea and
mentioning Britain's general
interest in East Asia and India
(September)
Treaty to turn Korea into
Japanese protectorate by
depriving her of diplomatic
right imposed on protesting
Koreans (November)

1906   Ito Hirobumi arrives in Seoul as
first resident-general
South Manchurian Railway
Company set up

Kita Ikki, *National Polity and
Pure Socialism*
Japan Socialist Party formed
(suppressed in 1907)

1907   Korean domestic administration
transferred to resident-
general; Korean army
dissolved
Russo-Japanese rapprochement
with secret convention

recognizing Japanese interest
in Korea and Russian in
Outer Mongolia

Korean attempt to send representatives to Hague World
Peace Conference fails to gain
support

1909   Ito Hirobumi resigns from
Regency-General (October);
shot dead at Harbin by a
Korean An Ju Kon

1910   Terauchi Masakata, army
minister, appointed resident-
general of Korea; 'reign of
terror' in Korea; Annexation
of Korea enforced with
Terauchi as first governor-
general (August)

Imperial Reservist Association
founded by Tanaka Giichi

Shirakaba, literary journal,
founded by Mushanokoji
Saneatsu

1911   Factory Act adopted (enforcement delayed till 1916)

Kotoku Shusui and 23 other
anarchists sentenced to
death: 12, including Kotoku,
executed (January)

Hiratsuka Raicho and others
start *Seito* (Blue Stocking),
journal for 'new women'

1912   Death of Emperor Meiji (30
July) and succession by his
son Yoshihito; era name
Taisho adopted

Army minister and *genro*
Yamagata between them force
Saionji government to resign

Katsura Taro, Yamagata's
protégé, forms his third
government

Movement to defend constitutional politics launched

Yuaikai (Friendly Society)
organized by Suzuki Bunji

Minobe Tatsukichi develops
organ theory of the emperor
in his *Kenpo Kowa* (Dis-
course on the Constitution)

1913   'Conversion of Katsura':
premier announces plan to
start new political party
Popular protests continue;
Katsura resigns (*Taisho
Seihen*, Political Change)
After Katsura's death by cancer
his party *Rikken Doshikai*
(later *Kenseikai*, yet later
Minseito, rival to *Seiyukai*)
launched

Daisan Teikoku (Third
Empire), liberal journal,
started by Kayahara
Kazan

1914   Prompted partly by Britain,
Japan declares war against
Germany (23 August)
German islands in the Pacific
occupied by Japanese navy
(October)
Germans in Tsintao surrender
after two months' siege
(November)

Shimamura Hogetsu and
Matsui Sumako present
dramatization of *Resurrec-
ion* by Tolstoy
Natsume Soseki writes
'Kokoro' (Heart) in *Asahi
Shinbun*

1915   Japan's '21 Demands' against
China presented to Yuan Shi-
kai, Chinese president

1916

Yoshino Sakuzo writes 'On the
Fundamental Principles of
Constitutional Politics' in
Chuo Koron, advocating
Minponshugi (people-ism)
Kawakami Hajime writes *Tales
of Poverty* in *Asahi Shinbun*

1917   Industrial Club of Japan
       founded by leaders of modern
       industries

1918   Siberian intervention intended
       by Japanese military as an
       attempt to build a buffer state
       against Bolsheviks begins as
       Allied operation partly to
       rescue the trapped Czech
       troops
       Hara Takashi, *Seiyukai* presi-
       dent, forms his government

       Rice riots starting with fisher-
       men's wives spread to large
       towns and coalmines
       Radicalization of students
       illustrated by formation of
       Shinjinkai (New Men's
       Society)

1919   Siberian expedition: other Allied
       troops being evacuated by
       early 1919, Japanese alone
       fight on
       Kwantung Army (*Kantogun*)
       created (April)
       Saionji and Makino lead
       Japanese delegation at Paris
       Peace Conference: Japan's
       demand for former German
       interests in Shantung Province
       resulting in anti-Japanese
       demonstrations in China and
       among Chinese students in
       Tokyo; Japan's claims for
       former German Pacific islands
       north of equator approved
       Declaration of Korean Indepen-
       dence by Koreans in Tokyo
       and Seoul: 1 March indepen-
       dence movement forcibly
       suppressed

1920   Nikolaevsk disaster: Japanese
       residents and garrison perish
       in armed conflict with parti-
       san troops
       Economic crisis: silk industry
       hard hit and 21 banks closed

Yawata Steel strike involving
3,000 workers
First May Day observed by
syndicalist unions of printers
and newspapermen
Kobe Co-operatives formed

1921   Washington Conference to limit
naval strength of major
powers held (November till
February 1922); Four-Power
Agreement (USA, Britain,
France, and Japan) to respect
each other's territories in the
Pacific; Anglo-Japanese Alliance allowed to lapse
(December)
Prime minister Hara assassinated, allegedly for his weak
diplomacy

Yuaikai develops into *Nihon
Rodo Sodomei* (General
Alliance of Trade Unions in
Japan)
Great strike of shipyard workers
in Kobe
Japan Peasant Union formed
Kita Ikki, *Unauthorized History
of Chinese Revolution*

1922   Nine-Power Agreement
(February) to respect Chinese
territorial integrity and to
maintain open-door policy in
China; German interests in
Shantung province to be
returned to China
Evacuation of troops from
Siberia completed (October)
except for northern Sakhalin
(occupation of which ends in
1925)

(Clandestine) Japanese Communist Party formed
Suiheisha (Society of Levellers)
formed at a conference of
3,000 buraku delegates
Kita Ikki, *Outline of Measures
for Reconstruction of Japan*

1923		Kanto earthquake (1 September): the number of the dead reaching over 140,000
		Osugi Sakae, anarchist leader, murdered by military police
1924	Kato Takaaki, *Kenseikai* leader, forms *Goken* (to defend constitution) coalition government	
		Communist Party dissolves itself preferring tactic of united front
1925	Universal Manhood Suffrage Act adopted: all male adults over 25 enfranchised	
	Public Order Preservation Act passed against 'dangerous thought' inimical to the imperial throne and private property	
	Diplomaic relations with Soviet Union established	
		Hosoi Wakiji writes *Jokoaishi* (Sad Story of Female Textile Workers)
1926	Death of Taisho Emperor (December); succession by his son Hirohito; new era, Showa, begins	
		Revived Communist Party seriously handicapped by doctrinal disputes
1927	Financial crisis: Suzuki Shoten and 25 banks go bankrupt	
	Japan's first expedition to Shantung Province intended to restrain Chiang kai-shek's northern expedition	
1928	Second Shantung expedition results in armed clash with Chinese troops in Tsinan (May); continued Japanese presence encourages anti-Japanese boycott movements	
	Chang Tsho-lin, Manchurian warlord, murdered by	

Kwantung Army staff officer
and co-plotters (June)
Maximum penalty of death
introduced in amendment to
Public Order Preservation Act
(June, approved by Diet in
March 1929)

Mass arrest of communists
(March)

1929 Emperor Showa's displeasure
with handling of culprits of
Chang's murder causes prime
minister Tanaka Giichi to
resign

Judgement given on students
indicted for upholding revo-
lutionary ideas (*Gakuren
jiken*), first application of
Public Order Preservation
Act
Yamamoto Senji murdered by
right-wing terrorist (March)
Kobayashi Takiji, *Factory
Ship*
Shimazaki Toson, *Yoakemae
(Before the Dawn)* (1929–35)

1930 Return to gold standard with
old parity aggravates
depression
London Naval Disarmament
Conference at which Japan
accepts inferior ratio for
auxiliary vessels displeases
navy's 'fleet faction'
Military operation carried out
against native Taiwanese at
Musha who are protesting
and rising against policy of
social control by police
Prime minister Hamaguchi (of
Minseito) shot and seriously
wounded (November) (dies
April 1931)

1931 Gold standard suspended when
Inukai's *Seiyukai* government
is formed

Tachibana Kozaburo sets up
Aikyojuku, a school for
patriotic rebels and insurgents

Civilian and military activists plan a *coup d'état* (March 1931 Incident)

Clash between Korean and Chinese peasants in Manchuria developing into a skirmish between Japanese and Chinese troops (Manposan Incident) (July)

Officers and men in the Railway Guards of Kwantung Army, by blowing up the railway-line near Mukden and blaming the Chinese for this, provide an excuse to attack Chinese troops (Manchurian Incident, September): fighting spreads

1932   Japanese attack on Shanghai factory, stronghold for anti-Japanese boycott, develops into full-scale war (January): cease-fire with British–American intervention

Manchukuo puppet state established with Pu-yi, last Chinese emperor, as emperor (March)

Inoue Junnosuke (February) and Dan Takuma of Mitsui (March) shot dead by members of the Blood Pact League

Prime minister Inukai Tsuyoshi shot dead (May) by a group of navy officers

Shakai Taishuto (Social Mass Party) formed

Lytton report on Manchuria submitted to Japan (October)

Noro Eitaro and others start publishing *Nihon Shihonshugi Hattatsushi Koza* (Lectures on the History of the Development of Japanese Capitalism)

Institute for Study of National Spirit and Culture set up under education minister Hatoyama Ichiro

Kawakami Hajime translates Comintern thesis on Japan for JCP; another round-up of communists

Kokubo fujinkai (National
Defence Women's Associa-
tion) set up

1933   League of Nations disapproves
of Japan's control of
Manchuria: Japanese delegation led by Matsuoka Yosuke
walks out and Japan with-
draws from the League
(March)
Tenko (mass conversion) of
convicted communists begins

Kawakami and Otsuka
Kinnosuke arrested (March)
and tried under the Public
Order Preservation Act
Professor Takigawa of Kyoto
University suspended for his
liberal ideas on criminal law
(April)
Tenko (conversion) statement
by two communist leaders
Sano and Nabeyama (June),
followed by similar *tenko* by
many others

1934   Noro Eitaro, *kozaha* academic,
tortured to death at police
station (February)
Essence of National Defence
issued by army newspaper
unit (October)

1935   Professor Minobe attacked by a
peer for his organ theory of
emperor; Diet resolves to
reject his theory; his books
suppressed, and he himself
later assaulted
East Hopei Autonomous Anti-
Communist Council, puppet
provincial government, set up
1936   Konoe's statement not to deal
with Nationalist China
Anti-Cominern Pact signed with
Germany (Italy and Spain
added later)

26 February Incident: attempt at *coup d'état* by young officers and men of the first division by killing cabinet ministers and chief army inspector; disowned by emperor, they surrender

1937   Clash between Japanese and Chinese troops at Marco Polo Bridge (Lukouch'iao) (July) develops into full-scale war
Konoe declares 'New Order' in East Asia
American gunboat *Panay* sunk by Japanese bombing (December)
Nanking Massacre (December–January 1938)

1938   National Mobilization Bill for state control of industries passed (April)
Sanpo or *Sangyo Hokokokurenmei* (Industrial Patriotic Association) formed (August)
Japanese troops occupy Canton and Wuhan cities (October)

Ishikawa Tatsuzo, *Ikiteiru Heitai* (Living Soldiers) (*Chuo Koron*, March), heavily censored
Hino Ashihei, *Mugi to Heitai* (Wheat and Soldiers) (*Kaizo*, August) describes the hardship suffered by common soldiers in the Xozhou campaign
Books on social policy and ideas by Kawai Eijiro suppressed and Kawai obliged to retire from his university

1939   Nomonhan Incident (battle) (May–August): forces of Kwantung Army defeated
Second World War begins in Europe (September)

1940   Wang Ching-wei, defected
        nationalist leader, sets up his
        govenment in Nanking
        (March)
        Establishment of *Hakko Ichiu*,
        stated to be Japan's basic
        goal, and that of Great East
        Asia Co-Prosperity Sphere as
        her immediate aim (July)
        Britain, under Japanese pres-
        sure, temporarily closes the
        Burma Road supply route to
        Chungking, China's new
        capital
        Vichy regime permits Japanese
        forces to station in northern
        Indochina (September)
        Tripartite Alliance concluded
        with Germany and Italy
        (September)
        Association to Assist Emperor's
        Rule set up (October)

                                        2,600th year of the legendary
                                            imperial calendar celebrated
                                        Tsuda Sokichi of Waseda
                                            University indicted and tried
                                            for his unorthodox view on
                                            the age of the gods (trial
                                            1941–2)

1941   Japanese–Soviet Neutrality Pact   Rationing of rice introduced
        concluded by foreign minister
        Matsuoka in Moscow (April)
        Germans start invasion of
        Russia (June)
        Southern Indochina occupied by
        Japanese forces (July)
        US oil embargo imposed on
        Japan (August)
        Tojo Hideki becomes prime
        minister (October)
        Hull Note delivered: America's
        negative reply to Japanese
        programme of withdrawing
        troops from China in 25
        years (November)

	Carrier-based Japanese planes attack and destroy the bulk of US Pacific Fleet anchored at Pearl Harbor: (7 December): declaration of war follows Initial victories: two British capital ships destroyed off Malaya (December); Hong Kong occupied (December)	
1942	Sumatra oil-fields seized (February); British forces at Singapore surrender (February) followed by capitulation of Dutch East India Forces (March); Rangoon occupied (March); American and Philippino resistance at Batan and Coregidor end (March) First US air raid on Japanese cities (April) Naval Battle of Coral Sea (May) marks turning of tide; Japanese attack on Midway Island (June) proves a costly disaster; Battle over Guadalcanal lost (July–February 1943)	Students' enlistment in munition industry begins Dainihon Fujinkai (Great Japan Women's Association) set up Patriotic Writers' Association formed with Tokutomi Soho as chairman
1943	Japanese troops at Attu (in the Aleutians) fight to the death (May); Japanese losing war in mid-Pacific islands	Serialization in *Chuo Koron* of *Sasameyuki* (Makioka Sisters) by Tanizaki Junichiro banned
1944	Burma campaign begins (March); Japanese attempt to reach Impahl frustrated; general retreat ordered (July) Mortal blow dealt to Japanese navy in naval battle off Mariana Islands (June) Fall of Saipan makes US bombing of Japanese mainland possible Tojo replaced as prime minister by Koiso Kuniaki (July) Naval battle and land battle at Leyte (October–December)	*Chuo Koron* and *Kaizo* suppressed

lost: suicide *kamikaze* planes
first introduced

1945   Air-raid on Tokyo (10 March)
as disastrous in its effect as
atomic bombing

Battle of Okinawa (April–June):
more civilians perish than
military personel

420 Chinese workers killed by
troops at Hanaoka copper
mine for their protest against
bad working conditions
(July)

Potsdam Declaration stating
terms of peace announced on
26 July but ignored by prime
minister Suzuki Kantaro

Atomic bomb dropped at
Hiroshima (6 August)

Declaration of war by Soviet
Union against Japan (8
August)

Second atomic bomb dropped at
Nagasaki (9 August)

Emperor Hirohito announces
acceptance of Potsdam
Declaration by radio broadcast (15 August)

Reconstruction and Reorganization, 1945–1995

1945   Higashikuninomiya Naruhiko
forms his government (17
August)

General MacArthur, Supreme
Commander of Allied Forces
arrives at Atsugi (30 August)

Document for Japan's surrender
signed on USS *Missouri* in
Tokyo Bay (2 September)

MacArthur appointed Supreme
Commander of Allied Powers

GHQ directive to allow free
discussion on emperor's
status, release political prisoners, and abolish thought
police (4 October)

Higashikuni government resigns (5 October); Shidehara Kijuro forms his government (9 October)

MacArthur urges Shidehara to carry out Five Great Reforms (11 October)

Japan Socialist Party founded with Katayama Tetsu as secretary (November)

Nippon Jiyuto (Japan Liberal Party) with Hatoyama Ichiro as president started by his faction in old *Seiyukai* (November)

Nippon Shinpoto (Japan Progressive Party) formed by Diet members formerly of *Minseito* and *Yokusan Seijikai* (November)

Communist Party of Japan revived (December)

Yomiuri newspaper democratization strike (October)

1946 Emperor's rescript on himself being human (January)

Purge of militarists and extreme nationalists (January)

First general election under new electoral law (*Jiyuto 141, Shinpoto 94, Shakaito* or Socialists 93, among others): 39 women elected (April)

Holding Company Liquidation Committee set up to carry out dissolution of *zaibatsu* (edict in April)

Keizai Doyukai (Economic Fellowship Association) set up (April)

Yoshida Shigeru succeeding purged Hatoyama forms his first *Jiyuto* government (May)

Sodomei or *Rodokumiai Sodomei* (General Federation of Trade Unions) formed (August)

Sanbetsu or *Sangyobesu*

Rodokumiai Kaigi (National
Congress of Industrial
Organization) formed
(August)

Keidanren (Federation of
Economic Organizations) set
up (August)

Economic Stabilization Bureau
set up (September)

Labour Relations Adjustment
Law enacted: labour disputes
to be treated as economic
issues (September)

Amended Land Reform Act
adopted; owners-farmers to
become predominant in agriculture (October)

New (peace) Constitution promulgated (November)

Ruth Benedict, *Chrysanthemum
and Sword*

1947   SCAP injunction against a
planned general strike of 1
February

Minshuto (Democratic Party)
led by Ashida Hitoshi
replaces the *Shinpoto*
(March)

Basic Education Law enforced
(March)

Labour Standard Act adopted
(April)

Socialists emerge as leading
party at general election
(April); Katayama forms
Socialist-led coalition government (May)

Japan Teachers' Association
formed (June)

Draper Report on economic
recovery of Japan marking the
beginning of 'reverse course'
(October)

Decentralized police system
created by Police Law
(December)

National control of coal mines
introduced for three years to
promote priority production
(December)

Amended Civil Code adopted:
traditional family system legally put an end to (December)

Home Ministry dissolved
(December)

1948   *Nikkeiren* (Japan Federation of
Employers) set up (April)

Imperial Rescript on Education
declared no longer valid
(May)

25 class A war criminals found
guilty at International Military Tribunal for Far East
(November); 7 including Tojo
executed (December)

Zengakuren (All-Japan General
Federation of Student
Unions) launched
(September)

1949   New education system
modelled after American
system introduced (April)

'Dodge Line' of tight money and
budget announced (March);
exchange rate of 360 yen for
one dollar introduced (April)

Ministry of International Trade
and Industry (MITI) established (May)

Administration Personnel Act
(May) enables drastic reduction of number of public
employees

Discharge of 126,000 national
railway workers (July)

Shimoyama Incident (July)

Mitaka Incident (July)

Matsukawa Incident (August)

1950   Purge of JCP leaders (May)

Korean War breaks out (June)

Police Reserve Forces created
(July)

Sohyo (General Council of
Trade Unions) established
(July)

Red Purge from businesses and
journalism launched (July)
De-purge of war collaborators
and former army and navy
officers (October–November)

Tanro (Japan Coalminers'
Union) organized (April)

1951 Japanese economy restored to
its pre-war level
San Francisco Peace Treaty and
Japan–US Security Treaty
concluded (September)

1952

Prevention of Subversive
Activities Act (drafted
March, enacted July) causes
strikes and protests culminating in violent demonstration in Palace Square on 1
May

Socialist split between left and
right over San Francisco
settlements (October)

Rashomon, a film produced by
Kurosawa Akira, wins international recognition

1953

First victims of Minamata pollution disease identified
(December)

1954 Board of Defence and Self-
Defence Forces started (July)

US nuclear test at Bikini Atoll
contaminates Japanese fishing boat and its crew (March)

1955

First concerted (spring) wage
offensive (*Shunto*) led by
Sohyo (January)

Japan admitted to GATT (June)
Two socialist parties, left and
right, merge into Japan
Socialist Party (October)
Two conservaive parties, *Jiyuto*
and *Nihon Minshuto*

(formerly *Minshuto*) merge
into *Jiyu Minshuto* (Liberal
Democratic Party, LDP)
(November)

GNP surpasses pre-war peak

Campaign against extension of
US military airbase at Sunaga
launched (May)

1956   Japan admitted to UN
(December)

1957   Kishi, de-purged in 1952,
becomes prime minister of
LDP government (February)

1958   Police Duties Law Amendment
Bill, Kishi's measure to
strengthen police power,
frustrated owing to strong
opposition from socialists
and *Sohyo* (October–
November)

1959

Great Miike Miners' Struggle
begins (October) and lasts till
November 1960

1960   Nishio faction breaks away from
JSP and forms Democratic
Socialist Party (January)

Ministry of Local Government
created (July)

Massive demonstration against
Security Treaty takes place
around Diet building (26
April)

Security Treaty adopted by the
Diet of LDP members alone
(19 May)

Death of a girl student in a
police counter-attack (15
June) helps calm government
and opposition

Kishi announces his decision to
resign (23 June)

New prime minister Ikeda
Hayato announces National
Income Doubling Plan
(December)

JSP chairman Asanuma stabbed
to death (October)

1964   Sato Eisaku succeeds Ikeda as
prime minister (November)
Komeito (Clean Politics Party)
allied with a Buddhist organization formed (November)

Shin–Tokaido bullet train
service begins (October)

1965   *Beheiren* (Citizens' Federation
for Peace in Vietnam) goes
into action (April)
Japan–Korea Basic Treaty (or
Normalization Treaty) concluded (June)

1967   Day to Commemorate the
Founding of State introduced
(November)

1968   Anti-war riot at Shinjuku
Station, Tokyo (October)

1969   Student power rages: 110
universities in serious trouble
(August)

1970   New US–Japan Security Treaty
stipulates political and
economic co-operation in
East and Souh-East Asia as
well as automatic extension
(June)
Environmental Pollution Prevention Act adopted (July)

World Exposition opened at
Senri, Osaka (March till
September)
Red Army faction of students
hijack JAL plane to Pyonyang
(April)
Mishima Yukio commits
seppuku suicide at SDF
headquarters (November)
Nakane Chie, *Japanese Society*

1971   Agreement for Restitution of
Okinawa signed (June)
Board of Environment set up
(July)

Emperor Hirohito visits Europe
(September–October)

1972   'Kaku–Fuku(da) War' for LDP
presidency won by Tanaka
Kakuei (July)
Tanaka forms his government
(July)
Tanaka visits Beijing; recogni-
tion of People's Republic as
government of whole China
(September)
Land and share price specula-
tion encouraged by Tanaka's
reconstruction plan

Tanaka Kakuei, *On Recon-
struction of Japanese
Archipelago* published (June)

1973   Floating exchange rate system
introduced (February)
First oil crisis causing 'crazed
prices' inflation obliges
Tanaka to suspend his plan
(October)
After 1973 Japanese economy
enters a period of slow
growth

Sato Eisaku receives Nobel
Peace Prize (October)

1974   Tanaka meets hostile reception
in Bangkok and Jakarta
(January)
Tanaka resigns and Miki forms
his government (December)

Tanaka's 'money politics'
criticized in *Bungei Shunju*
(November)

1975   Emperor Hirohito's visit to
USA (October)
National strike of public
employees defeated, marking
end of orthodox trade
unionism (November)

1976   Lockheed Scandal involving
Tanaka disclosed (February)
1978   Fukuda government decides era
name to be continued by law
(October)

Second oil crisis (December)

1980   Japan becomes top export
country in automobiles and
steel, surpassing USA

Premier Ohira's attempt to
introduce general consumer
tax proves unpopular

Ohira's government pulled
down by non-cooperation of
hostile LDP factions (May)

Ohira dies of heart attack in the
midst of ensuing general
election (June)

1981   Privatization of nationalized
industries creates NTT and
JT (April)

1983   Prime minister Nakasone
describes Japan as an
unsinkable aircraft-carrier
(January)

1986   Doi Takako elected JSP chair-
person, first female party
leader in Japan (September)

Nakasone makes a racist speech
regarding American intellectual level (September)

1987   Beginnings of bubble economy
helped by 'abnormal' monetary relaxation

National Railway divided into 6
regional JRs (April)

Nakasone embarks upon educational reform to produce 'a
good Japanese'

Rengo (All-Japan Trade Union
General Federation) created
(November)

1988   Recruit Scandal disclosed,
involving Nakasone and other
LDP politicians (July)

Takeshita LDP government
forces through Diet 6 tax
reform bills including one for
introduction of 3% consumer
tax (November)

1989   Emperor Hirohito dies
(7 January)

In House of Councillors election
LDP defeated by JSP and its
allies (July)

Rengo absorbs *Sohyo*
(November)

1990

Mayor of Nagasaki stabbed and
seriously wounded for his
criticism of Emperor Showa
(January)

State funeral for Emperor Showa
takes place (February)

Bubble economy begins to
collapse: estate loan restriction imposed (March)

1991 Kaifu's LDP government decides
to contribute $9 billion in
support of American-led
multinational forces in Gulf
War (January)

1992 Miyazawa, Kaifu's successor,
forces through Diet a UN
Peace Keeping Co-operation
Bill (June)

SDF units sent to Cambodia for
PKO (September)

1993 Hosokawa Morihiro, former
governor of Kumamoto,
forms new party *Nihon
Shinto* (Japan New Party)
(May)

Miyazawa government defeated
on the issue of electoral
reform (June): LDP splits

Former LDP members form new
parties: Takemura Masayoshi
Sakigake (Pioneers Party),
Hata Tsutomu and Ozawa
Ichiro *Shinseito* (New Life
Party) (June)

General election shows LDP
losing majority, JSP suffering
'historic set-back', signifying
practical end of '1955
system' (July)

Hosokawa forms non-LDP coalition government (July)

1994   Electoral reform results in a
            compound system of small
            constituencies and propor-
            tional representation
            (January)
            Hosokawa, implicated in a
            political scandal, resigns
            (April)
            Hata of *Shinseito* forms minor-
            ity coalition government
            (without JSP) which lasts two
            months (April–June)
            Murayama Tomiichi, JSP chair-
            man, succeeds Hata and
            forms LDP–JSP–*Sakigake*
            coalition government (June)
            Opposition parties form
            Shinshinto (New Frontier
            Party) (December)

1995   Kobe earthquake, with the
                                                number of the dead reaching
                                                6,308 (17 January)
                                                Sarin attack by Aum Shinrikyo
                                                cultists on Tokyo underground
                                                trains kills 12 people (March)

            Yen appreciates: 80 yen for one
            dollar, the highest on record
            (April)
            Murayama visits Beijing to
            express 'deep regret' over
            Japan's aggressive war (May)
            Diet adopts 50th post-war year
            resolution from which 'no
            war' has been rescinded
            (June)
            Murayama 'apologizes' for
            Japan's colonial rule and
            aggression in his discourse on
            15 August
            Rape of a schoolgirl by US
            servicemen in Okinawa leads
            to Governor Ota taking
            strong (but difficult) action
            against US bases (September)

Final settlement reached on the compensations of Minamata pollution victims (October)

Government decides to allocate 685 billion yen to enable *jusen* to dispose of bad credit (December)

Relevant events after 1995

1996   Murayama resigns and Hasihmoto Ryutaro (LDP) forms his own government (January)

JSP changes its name to Social Democratic Party (January)

Kan Naoto (*Sakigake*), new minister of health and welfare, discloses collusion between ministry, pharmaceutical company (Midori Juji or Green Cross), and specialist doctors as regards HIV infection among haemophiliacs and offers apologies (February)

Kan and Hatoyama Yukio set up *Minshuto* (Democratic Party) (September)

1997   Nomura Securities's close relations with *Sokaiya* disclosed (March)

Yamaichi Securities shown to be engaged in illegal deals for *Sokaiya* (July)

Final verdict given to Ienaga textbook lawsuit: Supreme Court rules against education ministry's claims on some points but decides in favour of the textbook screening system as such (August)

Hokkaido Development Bank closes business (November)

Yamaichi Securities decides to 'terminate itself' (November)

Shinshinto dissolved
(December)

1998   In election of House of
Councillors LDP suffers 'dis-
astrous' defeat: LDP loses 16,
Minshuto gains 9, *Kyosanto*
(Communists) gain 9, SDP
loses 7 (July)

Hashimoto resigns and Obuchi
Keizo of the largest LDP fac-
tion forms his government
(July)

Sound Finance Bill adopted
(October)

Sakigake wound up (October)

Japan Long-term Credit Bank,
practically bankrupt,
temporarily nationalized
(October)

Glossary

Aikoku Fujinkai Patriotic Women's Association founded in 1901 by upper-class women, having all the women of the imperial family as honorary members.

Aikoku Koto Party of Patriots, formed by Itagaki Taisuke, Eto Shinpei, and others in 1874 with a manifesto for a popular elective assembly.

Aikokusha Society of Patriots, founded in 1875; the first national political party in Japan; the Society developed into the Alliance to Promote a National Diet in 1880.

Anpo Japan–US Security Treaty signed in 1951; *Anpo Toso* means the national campaigns and demonstrations against the Security Treaty in 1960.

Ansei era name of the period which corresponds to 1854–8; associated with the great purge of loyalists by Ii Naosuke.

Bakufu the term literally means the tented headquarters of a military campaign; applied to a military government headed by a shogun (generalissimo) appoined as such by an emperor.

Bakuhan system Tokugawa political system based on a balance beween the Bakufu and the 260 odd han of various types.

Bakumatsu the closing period of the Tokugawa bakufu.

Bansei-ikkei eternal succession of one imperial line, referring to the imperial rule under the Meiji Constitution.

Bansha no Goku the term means 'Scholars of Western Studies in Prison', referring to Watanabe Kazan, Takano Choei, and others, arrested, imprisoned, or otherwise confined in 1839.

Buraku simplified term for *Hisabetsuburaku* (a village or hamlet discriminated against on social grounds). Its origins can be traced to the Ritsuryo system of the seventh century under which the notion of the mean and lowly and the unclean in terms of types of occupation emerged. Land inspection of the seventeenth century drove some of the landless people into degrading jobs, thus creating the lowest social status and obliging them to live in buraku, segregated hamlets and urban ghettos. The decree of their 'emancipation' of 1871 did not alter the nature of discrimination against them in selecting one's occupation or spouse. In 1975 there were 4,374 buraku across Japan and their population exceeded 1 million, about half of whom lived in Kansai area.

Chozenshugi transcendentalism or aloofness from party politics, distrusting political parties, an attitude and policy pursued by Yamagata Aritomo and his followers.

Daimyo title applied in the Edo period to the lord who has obligations to serve the Bakufu and whose domain produced more than 10,000 koku of rice.

Dai Nippon Kokusuikai Great Japan National Essence Society founded by Tokonami Takejiro (home minister) as a result of his intervention in industrial disputes of 1919.

Dai Toa Kyoeiken or Great East Asia Co-Prosperity Sphere, regarded as the aim of Japan's war in Asia and the Pacific; the term used by foreign minister Matsuoka Yosuke in his discouse in August 1940.

Datsua-ron 'Exit Asia, Enter Europe', the title of Fukuzawa Yukichi's article published in March 1885.

Domei *Zen Nihon Rodo Sodomei* (All-Japan General Federation of Labour), right-wing trade union federation formed in 1964, an heir to *Sodomei* (founded in 1946); led by textile and seamen's unions opposed to *Sohyo*.

Fudai daimyo Tokugawa's hereditary vassals since before the Battle of Sekigahara of 1600.

Fukoku kyohei 'enrich the nation and strengthen arms', a Meiji political slogan widely shared.

Genro elderly statesmen, an appellation given to top leaders of the Meiji Restoration and Meiji politics who exerted great informal influence, assisting the emperor in the selection of prime ministers and other important matters of the state.

Genroin the senate, a deliberative institution which existed from 1875 to 1890.

Genroku era name of the period corresponding to 1688–98, associated with the rule of the fifth shogun Tokugawa Tsunayoshi.

Genyosha Korean Strait Society, a nationalist and expansionist body founded by Toyama Mitsuru and Hiraoka Kotaro in 1881.

Goken undo Defence of the Constitution movement; the first movement, 1912–13; the second 1923.

Goshi gentry, upper strata of farmers, often former samurai or farmers given some samurai privileges.

Gyokusai a fight to the death, as at Saipan or Attu during the Pacific War.

Hakko ichiu 'making the whole world one house', a wartime slogan proclaimed in Konoe's statement on 1 August 1940.

Han originally meaning hedge or fence, used in the Edo period as the term applied to the territories and administrative structure and personnel of a daimyo enjoying a revenue of more than 10,000 koku. First used in 1702; replaced by ken in 1871. There were 266 han in 1865.

Hanbatsu Seifu Hanbatsu government, *Hanbatsu* refers to the clan clique dominated by former samurai from Satsuma and Choshu.

HCLC Holding Company Liquidation Commission set up in 1946 as a major step to dissolve *zaibatsu*.

Heisei era name chosen after Showa and after a controversy over whether an era name corresponding to an emperor's reign should be legally enforced or not (1989–).

Hinomaru a flag with red disk, enforced on all Japanese ships in 1854; adopted by the Meiji government as a national flag in 1870; antipathy to 'Hinomaru' lingers on because of its association with the Asia-Pacific War and war atrocities and sufferings.

Honne usually hidden, real intentions or realities.

Hyakusho ikki peasant uprisings against extortionist officials, merchants, and moneylenders rampant in the latter half of the Tokugawa period.

Ie system or **kazoku seido** the patriarchical family system, formally established by the Meiji Civil Code in 1898 and formally abolished by the new Civil Code in 1948.

IMTFE International Military Tribunal for the Far East, which opened in May 1946 and gave its verdict in November 1948.

Jinshin Koseki household registers completed for the whole country in 1872, providing an administrative basis for conscription, taxation, and education; Jinshin in the old calendar corresponds to the fifth year of Meiji or 1872.

Jitsugaku commonly used as the term implying practical, useful branches of learning; first applied by neo-Confucian scholars in the early Edo period to describe studies of real, moral life as against speculative studies of the afterlife; in the late Edo period, an emphasis placed on studies useful to national and local politics and economy, natural, experimental sciences; the term applied by Fukuzawa Yukichi to studies conducive to national and individual independence, from the abacus to philosophy.

Jiyu Minken Liberty and People's Right, a popular slogan and movement for democracy persued in the 1870s and early 1880s.

Jiyuto (1) Liberal Party, formed in 1881 with Itagaki Taisuke as president and Ueki Emori and Baba Tatsui among its prominent propagandists; dissolved in 1884; revived in 1891; merged into *Kenseito* in 1898 and finally into *Seiyukai*. (2) Liberal Party, formed in 1950, succeeding its predecessors *Nihon Jiyuto* (Liberal Party of Japan) and *Minshu Jiyuto* (Democratic Liberal Party), led by Yoshida Shigeru for many years; merged into LDP in 1955.

Joi 'Expel the barbarians', a slogan denoting the overwhelming reaction of the Japanese, the court, the Bakufu, and the great han (up to a point), to the western demand for opening the country in the 1850s and 1860s.

Kaikoku 'Opening the country', a catchphrase commonly used in the Bakumatsu period.

Kanmin chowa 'Harmony of the government and the people', a phrase used by Fukuzawa Yukichi and others in the 1880s.

Keiretsu Post-war business conglomerations shaped around a *keiretsu* bank, which took the place of a holding company for *zaibatsu* after the latter's dissolution.

Kenri right or rights.

Kenseikai Constitutional Politics Association formed in 1916 with Kato Takaaki as president; the party strove for and obtained universal suffrage in 1925; it developed into *Rikken Minseito*.

Kenseito Consitutional Politics Party, formed in 1898 from the merger of *Jiyuto* and *Shinpoto*; it managed to form the first Okuma government but soon split between *Kenseito* (former *Jiyuto*) and *Kenseihonto* (former *Shinpoto*); the former merged into *Rikken Seiyukai* in 1900, while the latter into *Rikken Kokuminto* in 1910.

Kiheitai Choshu's peasant army (though over 40 per cent of its members were samurai) formed in 1863 by Takasugi Shinsaku.

Kobu-gattai 'Union of the Imperial Court and the Shogunate', a compromise measure proposed during the Bakumatsu period.

Kodoha Imperial Way Faction, an army faction headed by General Mazaki Jintaro and General Araki Sadao; concerned with the solution of the rural problems which affected many young officers; it lost power after the failure of the 26 Februry (1936) uprising.

Koenkai support clubs, usually for a member or an aspiring member of the Diet; for instance, *Etsuzankai* for Tanaka Kakuei, Blue Cloud School for Nakasone Yasuhiro.

Kokkai Kisei Doumei Alliance to Promote a National Diet, formed in 1880, which played a central role in the Liberty and People's Right movement.

Koku About 5 bushels, used as the unit to measure the wealth, especially of han, in terms of taxable rice produced in the domain. The koku was also used in measuring the size of a ship, 1 koku being about 10 cubic feet for ships.

Kokubo Fujinkai National Defence Women's Association, founded in 1932 with the support of the Ministry of War.

Kokuryukai Amur River Sociey, an aggressively expansionist body founded in 1901 by Uchida Ryohei.

Kokutai form of a state defined by the nature of its sovereignity; in Japanese history *kokutai* meant the mythical, familial state with the emperor, the descendant of the Sun Goddess, as the supreme ruler.

Konminto Party of Sufferers; they formed the core of the Chichibu peasant army of 1884.

Komeito Clean Politics Party, formed in 1964 by Soka Gakkai, a lay Buddhist mass organization, a new religious sect derived from the Nichiren sect.

Koseisho a new ministry formed in 1938 out of the two sections in the Ministry of Home Affairs dealing respectively with social security and public health; served military needs during the war and developed close links with pharmaceutical companies that did not always promote the best interest of medical services.

Kozaha the name derives from *Nihon Shihonshugi Hattatsushi Koza* (Lectures on the Development of Capitalism in Japan, 1932–3) edited by Noro Eitaro, Hirano Yoshitaro, Yamada Moritaro, Otsuka Kinnosuke. *Kozaha* Marxists argued that the semi-feudal relationship of production and exploitation remained within the modern framework of capitalism, and advocated democratic reorganization, including a peasant revolution to be followed by a socialist revolution.

Kwantung Army or **Kantogun** a Japanese army in Manchuria created in 1919 at the time of the Siberia intervention by uniting the Manchuria Independent Guard to patrol the South Manchurian Railway territories and the Port Arthur Fortress Headquarters; the Manchurian Incident of 1931 was engineered by its officers; defeated by the Russians in border skirmishes, especially at Nomonhan and finally by the invading Russians in August 1945.

LDP Liberal Democraic Party (*Jiyu Minshuto*) formed in 1955 through the merger of the Liberal Party and the Japan Democratic Party.

Mangyo Manchurian Heavy Industries Development Company, established in 1937 by transferring Nissan, the new *zaibatsu*, to Manchuria and by giving it privileges as a semi-state industry in Manchukuo.

Mankan Kokan a strategic and diplomatic idea to exchange Manchuria with Korea (*Kankoku*); partly realized in the Nishi–Rosen agreement of 1898 and ended with the signing of the Anglo-Japanese alliance in 1902.

Manmo 'Manchuria and Mongolia', a term used when these areas were regarded by the military and nationalists as Japan's vital sphere of influence in the 1930s.

Mantetsu South Manchurian Railway Company, established in 1906 to administer the railways, mines, and steel-mills in southern Manchuria obtained as a result of the Russo-Japanese War; after the Manchurian Incident it developed into a gigantic combine (it had 80 subsidiaries) the bulk of which was transferred to *Mangyo* in 1937.

Meiji era name of the period corresponding to 1868–1912.

Meiji Ishin the Meiji Restoration or imperial restoration of 1868, achieved as a result of a power struggle between Satsuma, Choshu, the court, and their allies on the one hand and the Bakufu and the han loyal to it on the other.

Meirokusha the earliest academic society of modern studies, founded in 1874 by Mori Arinori and supported by Fukuzawa Yukichi, Nishi Amane, Tsuda Mamihi, Kato Hirouki, and others.

Minponshugi 'people-ism', a definition of democracy compatible with the monarchical Meiji Constitution, advocated by Yoshino Sakuzo and others.

MITI Ministry of International Trade and Industry, formed in 1949, sometimes regarded as the core institution of 'Japan Incorporated'.

Naiyu Gaikan 'Worries within, trouble without'; a Chinese phrase given wide currency by Fujita Yukoku, the Mito scholar.

Nipponshugi Japanism, a modern nationalism advocated by Shiga Shigetaka and Kuga Katsunan in the 1890s.

Osei fukko restoration of the Imperial rule.

Rangaku Western studies (*Yogaku*) spread through the Dutch and their interpreters in Nagasaki during the Tokugawa period; medicine, astronomy, and gunnery were among the subjects eagerly studied.

Rengo All-Japan Trade Union General Federation created in 1989; by absorbing *Sohyo* it became the largest and most representative trade union federation.

Rikken Doshikai Constitutional Society of the Like-Minded, founded with Kato Takaaki as president in December 1913 after the death of Katsura Taro who had planned and promoted it; merged into *Kenseikai* in 1916.

Rikken Kaishinto or **Kaishinto** Constitutional Progressive Party founded in 1882 by Okuma Shienobu and others; merged into *Shinpoto* in 1896.

Rikken Kokuminto or **Kokuminto** formed in 1910 and led by Inukai Tsuyoshi; the party took the initiative in the Defence of Constitution Movement, 1912–13; it promoted the cause of universal suffrage; dissolved in 1922.

Rikken Minseito or **Minseito** formed in 1927 by the merger of *Keiseikai* and *Seiyuhonto* (of Tokonami); more liberal, urban and bourgeois than its rival, the landlord-oriented *Seiyukai*; supported naval disarmament in 1930.

Rikken Seiyukai or **Seiyukai** founded by Ito Hirobumi in 1900 by absorbing *Kenseito*; it established an electoral basis in the provinces by controlling farm societies and promoting the construction of roads, railways, and schools, while permeating the House of Peers and Home Ministry bureaucrats; after Ito, party leadership was taken up in turn by Saionji, Katsura, Hara Takashi, Takahashi Korekiyo, Tanak Giichi, Inukai Tsuyoshi, and Suzuki Kisaburo; the party became increasingly rightist and expansionist.

Risshisha Society of the Ambitious, founded in Kochi in 1874; the society played a central role in the Liberty and People's Right movement.

Rodokumiai Kiseikai Association for Promoting Trade Unions formed in 1897 by Takano Fusataro and Kataya Sen.

Rodo Nominto Labour Farmer Party, established in 1926 as a parliamentary reform party; it soon became leftist with Oyama Ikuo as chairman; engaged in a Hands Off China movement and contested the first general election under universal suffrage; ordered to dissolve in 1928.

Ronin masterless samurai, often found among the loyalist activists; sometimes used to describe unattached adventurers such as *Tairiku ronin* (continental or China adventurers).

Ronoha a Marxist group opposed to *Kozaha* and JCP; Sakai Toshihiko, Yamakawa Hitoshi, Arahata Kanson, Inomata Tsunao, and others sought to bring socialism into *Sodomei* and started in 1927 a new organ *Rono* (Labour and Farmer) from which derived the name *Ronoha*; they believed Japan to be ripe for a socialist revolution, preferring to adopt a united front tactic; suppressed in 1937 under the pretext that Ronoha socialists were preparing a Popular Front.

Sakoku Tokugawa policy of seclusion of the country introduced in the 1640s and enforced till the 1850s.

Sankin Kotai a system of alternate (every other year) attendance by Daimyo at Edo Castle introduced in 1635 as a measure for ensuring the security of the Bakufu; strict conditions attached to the system were mitigated in 1862 as han became more independent.

Sat-Cho Satsuma and Choshu, usually referred to as the *Sat-Cho* alliance of 1868 or as the *Sat-Cho Hanbatsu Seifu* (Clan-Clique Government), the Meiji autocratic government led by former samurai from Satsuma and Choshu.

SCAP Supreme Commander of the Allied Powers, i. e. General Douglas MacArthur.

SDF Self-Defence Force, created in 1954 together with the Board of Defence.

Seii Taishogun 'Generalissimo to Conquer the Barbarians' appointed in the eighth century to subdue the Emishi (the northern barbarians); prototype of 'Shogun'.

Seikanron 'Punishing Korea Policy', a policy to deal forcibly with Korea, which was reluctant to recognize the new Meiji government; the defeat of its advocates, Saigo Takamori most prominent among them, led to the Seinan Civil War.

Shakai Minshyuto Social Popular Party, formed in 1926 by right-wing socialists who split from *Rodo Nominto* as the latter became leftist; with Abe Isoo and Yoshino Sakuzo among its promoters and Katayama Tetsu as general secretary; it supported the Manchurian Incident but appeared not nationalistic enough to national socialists like Akamatsu Katsumaro who split away; the party merged in the Socialist Mass Party in 1932.

Shakaishugi Kenkyukai Society for the Study of Socialism, the first organization in Japan devoted to socialist studies, founded in 1898 by Christian socialists like Abe Isoo, Katayama Sen, and others (including Kotoku Shusui).

Shakai Taishuto Socialist Mass Party, formed in 1932 with Abe Isoo as chairman; the party initially upheld an anti-communist and anti-fascist cause; the party secretary Aso Hisashi strengthened ties with the military and declared support for 'the sacred war' when war against China broke out in 1937; the party committed itself so strongly to the war effort that it expelled Abe Isoo, Katayama Tetsu, Nishio Suehiro, and Mizutani Chozaburo; it dissolved itself before any other party in 1940 in order to merge into Konoe's new totalitarian party.

Shinpoto Progressive Party, formed in 1896 by *Kaishinto* and others with Okuma as party leader; merged into *Kenseito* in 1898.

Shishi men of high purpose, usually indicating patriotic samurai devoted to the imperial cause, very active towards the end of the Tokugawa period.

Shizoku a new status given to former samurai in Meiji Japan.

Shogun See also *Seii Taishogun*; Minamoto Yoritomo was the first shogun and Tokugawa Yoshinobu the last.

Showa era name given to the period 1926–89.

Shunto concerted wage offensive in the spring resorted to by *Sohyo* with much effect; the first *Shunto* occurred in January 1955.

Sodomei or **Nihon Rodokumiai Sodomei** General Federation of Trade Unions in Japan, founded in August 1946; though originally anti-communist, the left-wing of *Sodomei*, led by Takano Minoru, took the initiative to start *Sohyo* in 1950; the right wing split away from *Sohyo* and formed its own trade union federation, which was later called *Domei* (see the entry).

Sohyo or **Nihon Rodokumiai Sohyogikai** General Council of Trade Unions in Japan, founded in 1950 as a moderate trade union federation worthy of support from GHQ and the Japanese government; under the leadership of Takano Minoru (general secretary in 1951) *Sohyo* became a militant trade union centre, allied with the left-wing socialist party; with Ota Kaoru, successor to Takano, industrial struggle added to *Sohyo* weapons; privatization of public utilities deprived Sohyo of much of its strength derived from unions of public employees; absorbed in *Rengo* in 1989.

Sokaiya 'General Meeting-mongers'; some of the *yakuza* groups who threatened to disrupt general meetings of shareholders and obtained hush money from the companies concerned for promising good behaviour.

Sonno 'revere the emperor', the loyalist slogan most persistent before and during the Meiji Restoration.

Taisei Yokusankai Association to Assist the Emperor's Rule set up in October 1940, 'a new poitical system' of a totalitarian nature formed on the ruins of all the political parties that had voluntarily dissolved themselves.

Taisho era name for the period corresponding to 1912–26.

Taisho democracy democratic tendencies and movements in the Taisho period, some liberal, some socialistic, and some even expansionist.

Tatemae formal structure, appearance, or pretence.

Tenmei era name of the period corresponding to 1781–8, known for the massive eruption of a volcano, a great famine, and a succession of peasant uprisings.

Tennosei the emperor system born of the Meiji Restoration and strengthened by the Meiji constitution and the Imperial Rescript on Education.

Tobaku 'overthrow the Bakufu', a political slogan and tactic adopted mainly by Choshu and Satsuma before the Meiji Restoration.

Tokko or **Tokko Keisatsu** special higher police, set up in 1911 after the Treason Trial and strengthened by the Public Order Preservation Act of 1925; engaged in suppression of speeches, publications, and meetings supposedly inimical to the foundation of the state and society.

Tokkotai special attack units known for *kamikaze* suicide planes; first used in the Battle of Leyte, October 1944, and also in the Battle of Okinawa in April–June 1945; over 3,000 young men died in such units.

Tonghak Rebellion a peasant war in south-western Korea, led by the party of Tonghak (eastern studies); this provided an occasion for China and Japan to send troops to Korea and led to the Sino-Japanese war.

Toseiha Control Faction in the army; it sought to extend internal control of the army, rejected idealistic tendencies shown by *Kodoha* officers, was eager to strengthen ties with new bureaucrats so as to prepare for a general mobilization of men and resources; after the defeat of *Kodoha* in the 26 February Incident it ceased to be a faction.

Tozama daimyo outer daimyo; those who opposed Tokugawa in 1600 but were allowed to continue in the outer regions of the country (Choshu and Satsuma are the most obvious examples).

Yakuza the name derived from 8, 9, 3 (*ya*, *ku*, *san*), three bad numbers in traditional betting; hence 'bad people' engaged in gambling as an occupation; they value traditional human relations, and are ready to use violence; sometimes called *boryokudan* (violent groups).

Yuaikai Friendly Society, first viable trade union in Japan, founded by Suzuki Bunji in 1912.

Yushi Sensei Seifu government of autocracy by officials; early Meiji governments were criticized by their opponents because men of Satsuma and Choshu practically monopolized government offices.

Zaibatsu literally means 'money clique'; family-dominated industrial, commercial, and financial conglomerations; Mitsui, Mitsubishi, Sumitomo, and Yasuda usually referred to as the four great *zaibatsu*.

Zengakuren All-Japan General Federation of Student Unions, founded in 1948, prominent in the *Anpo* struggle, later split into many warring sects.

Index